All About Law

Fifth Edition

Exploring the Canadian Legal System

Author Team

Dwight L. Gibson
Terry G. Murphy
Frederick E. Jarman
Derek Grant

**Consultant &
Contributing Author**

Kathleen Elliott

THOMSON

NELSON

Australia   Canada   Mexico   Singapore   Spain   United Kingdom   United States

THOMSON

NELSON

All About Law: Exploring the Canadian Legal System

Fifth Edition

Dwight L. Gibson, Terry G. Murphy,
Frederick E. Jarman, Derek Grant

Director of Publishing
David Steele

Publisher
Mark Cressman

Senior Managing Editor
Nicola Balfour

Consultant & Contributing Author
Kathleen Elliott

Program Manager
Leah-Ann Lymer

Developmental Editors
Jessica Pegis
Dayne Ogilvie

Senior Production Editor
Carol Martin

Proofreader
Laura Edlund

Indexer
Noeline Bridge

Art Director
Ken Phipps

Interior Designer & Compositor
Allan Moon

Cover Design
Peter Papayanakis

Production Coordinator
Sharon Latta Patterson

Permissions
Karen Becker, Vicki Gould

Printer
Transcontinental Printing Inc.

Reviewers
Karen Andrews
Rexdale Community Legal Clinic
Toronto, ON

Neil Boyd
Simon Fraser University
Vancouver, BC

Gillian Demeyere
University of Toronto
Toronto, ON

Linda Draper
London, ON

Madam Justice Gloria Epstein
Ontario Superior Court of Justice

R. Kim L. Evans
Moncton, NB

John Joseph Kelly
Mississauga, ON

Stan Kopciuch
Regina, SK

M. Kaye Joachim
University of Toronto
Toronto, ON

Rocky Landon
Kingston, ON

Mary Anne MacArthur
Mississauga, ON

Kimberley Smith Maynard
Barrister and Solicitor
Trenton, ON

Sylvia Parris
Halifax, NS

Allan Phillips
Elkford, BC

Lynne Thompson
North Battleford, SK

Anthony Viola, Jr.
Hamilton, ON

Mike Whittingham
Richmond, BC

Toni Williams
Osgoode Hall Law School of York
University
Toronto, ON

National Library of Canada Cataloguing in Publication Data

Main entry under title:

All about law: exploring the Canadian legal system

5th ed.
Includes index.
For use in secondary schools.
ISBN 0-17-620148-3

1. Law—Canada. I. Gibson, Dwight L., 1944–
KE444.G62 2002   349.71
C2002-900881-6

Table of Contents

Law is an essential part of Canada's culture. Without law, we cannot function effectively in our daily lives. A broad knowledge and understanding of law is not only a vital part of your education, but is also an important factor in the operation of a democratic and orderly society.

The authors are pleased to present the fifth edition of *All About Law*, which has been thoroughly revised for the 21st century. Unit 1 explores the purpose, history, and types of Canadian law. This unit includes information about the *Anti-Terrorism Act* and its impact on Canadian law, as well as a new section on international law and its role in resolving conflict. Laws that protect civil and human rights are covered in Chapter 2. Chapter 3 examines groups that have experienced discrimination and looks at the legal initiatives proposed to remedy the injustices.

In Unit 2, you will be introduced to criminal law and the major legislative amendments made recently to the *Criminal Code*, particularly the *Youth Criminal Justice Act* and the *Controlled Drugs and Substances Act*.

Various aspects of tort law, family law, and contract law will likely affect you throughout your life. Units 3, 4, and 5 provide in-depth coverage of these types of law.

Features of the Fifth Edition

- ☑ Each chapter opens with a timely photo that invites discussion of a major theme in the chapter. The **Chapter at a Glance** previews the main topics of the chapter, and the **Focus Questions** outline the key questions.

- ☑ **Agents of Change** profiles a person or event that has helped to bring about change in Canadian law.

- ☑ **The Law** provides excerpts from legislation or legal documents and accompanying questions to help you interpret them.

- ☑ **Issue** explores a "hot topic" related to the chapter content. Both sides of challenging issues are presented, followed by thought-provoking questions.

- ☑ **Looking Back** provides a historical perspective on specific aspects of Canadian law.

- ☑ **You Be the Judge** presents a brief legal scenario or quotation and invites you to interpret it and consider a course of action.

- ☑ **E-activity** connects you to **www.law.nelson.com,** where you will find related Web activities and links.

- ☑ **Did You Know?** offers relevant and interesting facts that correspond to the main text.

- ☑ **Review Your Understanding** follows each major section within a chapter. These questions will help you to check your knowledge and understanding of the material you have just covered.

- ☑ **Careers** explores the career opportunities within a particular area of law, such as human rights commissioner, correctional services officer, or Small Claims Court clerk. Each Careers feature includes a Web activity and an additional career exploration activity.

- ☑ **Case** features provide an extensive collection of relevant case studies from across Canada. We have used as many recent cases as possible. Precedent-setting and historically valuable cases are also included.

    Each case ends with questions covering points of law and giving you the opportunity to clarify and analyze reasons for judgments. In answering these questions, you will consider the information you have learned in the chapter, along with the details presented in the case itself. You will soon recognize that concepts covered in other chapters are interrelated.

Each case has been identified with a complete citation so that you are aware of the date of the case and the court in which it was heard. Abbreviations used in case citations are explained in **Citation References** in Appendix B on page 604.

For a complete list of cases in this book, see the **Table of Cases** in Appendix C on page 605.

☑ Each chapter concludes with a **Chapter Review,** consisting of:

Chapter Highlights, summarizing the main points of the chapter—a useful study aid

Review Key Terms, testing your comprehension of the most important legal terms used in the chapter

Check Your Knowledge, containing knowledge and understanding questions and emphasizing the skills of summarizing, identifying, and comparing

Apply Your Learning, providing additional case studies for analysis

Communicate Your Understanding, offering further opportunities for presenting arguments in oral or written form, justifying opinions, and debating ideas

Develop Your Thinking, presenting opportunities for more in-depth research projects, role-plays, and simulations

☑ As a handy reference, the *Canadian Charter of Rights and Freedoms* is provided in Appendix A on page 600. You will be asked to refer to it throughout your study of law.

☑ Difficult legal terms and concepts are boldfaced throughout. Their definitions are located in the **Glossary** on page 609.

☑ A comprehensive **Index** is located on page 623.

Learning Outcomes

Learning to reason logically and make informed decisions are important goals of education. The study of law is a major step to achieving this goal. The questions and activities throughout the book will give you opportunities to develop legal knowledge and understanding, as well as skills in thinking and inquiry. You will also improve your communication skills and apply what you have learned to your academic, personal, and professional life.

Acknowledgments

To my wife, Louise Pauzé Lord, and my children, Michael and Corrie, for their support—*DLG*

To my wife, Katherine (Kit); Jamie and Laura; Karen, Russell, and our first granddaughter, Macy; to my mother, Louise; and to Madam Justice Gloria Epstein for her invaluable assistance in the family law unit—*TGM*

To my dear friend, Norman Walker—*FEJ*

To my wife, Georgette, and in memory of Yvette Stainton—*DG*

> Whatever our goals—peace, an end to discrimination, a better environment, a greater prosperity for the citizens of the world—the law is an essential tool for achieving them.
>
> Beverley McLachlin
> Chief Justice, Supreme Court of Canada

An Introduction to Law

Law: Its Purpose and History

Focus Questions

- What is law? Why do societies have laws?
- What are the historical roots of Canadian law?
- Who is responsible for law making in Canada?
- How are Canadian laws interpreted, applied, and enforced?

Chapter at a Glance

Figure 1-1

Infinity and beyond? International treaties prevent any one nation from claiming space. But as more space stations are built, the "law of space" will become an important issue. Speculate as to who will make space law.

1.1 Introduction

Society is fascinated with the law. Laws are every-where and control much of what you do and how you behave. If a sensational trial or legal case happens to be in the news, most people will be talking about it. Law is also a popular theme in books, television, and films.

Most people have had direct experience with the law or know someone who has. Because laws and legal issues affect everyone, it is important to know your rights and responsibilities under the law. It is also important to understand why Canada has so many laws and what some of them are. Every country has a history and culture that have shaped its laws and punishments. What is legal in one country is not necessarily legal in another. Studying a nation's legal system is very much like studying its language. Law tells a great deal about its past. It also reveals current values and beliefs.

Canada is a **democracy,** which means that its citizens elect law makers who make laws that suit the majority of Canadians. The law is constantly changing to reflect changing values and beliefs. By voting, Canadians choose politi-cians to make laws that best suit their needs and opinions at that time. These elected officials control the law-making process and its interpretation and enforcement.

In this chapter, you will begin to learn the language and history of law, how laws are made, and how they are interpreted and enforced.

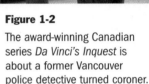

Figure 1-2

The award-winning Canadian series *Da Vinci's Inquest* is about a former Vancouver police detective turned coroner.

1.2 What Is Law and Why Do We Have It?

What would happen if a game such as hockey were played without rules? Some players might use violence because there would be no penalty for injuring another player. They would take advantage of other players during the game. Referees would be useless because they could not keep order without rules. The game would deteriorate into a series of fights and injuries, and the spec-tators would probably leave. In the end, violence rather than skill would win games. In fact, sports mirror real life: Without rules to govern relations between people, disorder and conflict would arise.

Similarly, clubs and organizations need rules to run meetings, to encourage open and honest debate among members, and to reach agreement (by voting or a show of hands) on important decisions.

Whenever people form groups, they need to make some rules. Rules and laws are necessary to keep peace and order because people do not agree with each other all the time. Without clearly defined rules, the only law might be the survival of the strongest.

Figure 1-3

Donald Brashear and Marty McSorley fight during a hockey game in Vancouver. What would happen if hockey were played without rules? (See Issue, page 312.)

Rules or Laws?

Rules of a game or an organization apply only to participants in the game or members of the organization. A **law,** on the other hand, applies to all members of society at all times.

It is important to understand the difference between a rule and a law. If you want to become a member of a group, you have to follow its rules. For example, some schools have rules about wearing uniforms. Those rules apply only to those students who attend the school. A law is a legal rule made by the government. It must be obeyed by everyone who chooses to live in that society. If a member of society breaks the law, he or she is punished. Therefore, as an individual, you are free to do what you want, with one exception: You must not do those things the law forbids, or prohibits.

Although most people willingly accept laws that set speed limits on highways, restrict the use of certain drugs, and control pollution, some people do not. If Canadians do not agree with a law in this country, they can join pressure groups and **lobby** the government to change the law. Lobby groups try to raise public awareness about certain laws and pressure the government to change the law to reflect their opinions and needs. Lobby groups may also challenge laws by going through the courts or by organizing peaceful demonstrations. Canada is a free country, so people can oppose laws in a number of ways, but only up to a certain point. If protesters break the law, they can be arrested for their actions.

Why Do We Have Laws?

Janelle lived by herself on an island and did whatever seemed right to her. She did not need any laws. But Stacie was shipwrecked during a storm and landed on Janelle's island. Now Janelle had to adjust her needs, desires, and actions to accommodate Stacie. Janelle and Stacie had a discussion and developed some rules. These rules became laws when the two agreed that certain rules would always control their actions. For example, the agreement, "We will always share all our food, so that each of us gets an equal portion" is a law. So is "Neither of us will make noise after the other has gone to sleep." Laws usually create clear understandings about expected behaviour. They are necessary for people to live together peacefully in society.

Suppose more people are shipwrecked on the island. If the number of people increases, so will the need for laws. There might even be a need to write down the laws, so that they are available to everyone. Then, if people break the law, they cannot say that they did not know about it. Of course, as the number of laws increase, people will have less freedom to do what they want as individuals.

As a society grows, it needs more laws to control and limit the behaviour of its citizens. For example, taking someone else's property or life is against the law in most societies. So is cheating in business or speeding on a highway. To enforce these laws, a society introduces punishments for breaking the law. The harshness of these penalties will depend on the values and customs of each society. Stealing in Canadian society might result in a suspended sentence, a jail sentence, or some form of alternative justice, such as a healing circle. In other societies, the convicted person might have a hand amputated or might even be executed.

The Functions of Law: What Laws Do for Us

One important function of law is to settle disputes, or disagreements. If a dispute arises between two opposing teams during a sports event, it is usually resolved by consulting the rules of the game. Similarly, laws help to resolve disputes through discussion or negotiation, or through the courts. Laws help to create order and ensure that disagreements are solved peacefully and fairly.

Establishing Rules of Conduct

You live in fairly close contact with your neighbour—that is a part of living in society. Under such conditions, conflicts naturally arise. Laws exist to reduce or eliminate these conflicts and to create a safer place to live. For example, the provincial and territorial Highway Traffic Acts set minimum driving ages, speed limits, and competency tests for drivers' licences. Other traffic laws describe proper procedures for signalling, passing, and the use of safety restraints. If there were no such laws, the streets would be much less safe than they are.

Protecting Rights and Freedoms

Laws serve no purpose if they cannot be enforced. To enforce laws, we have the police and the courts. The Royal Canadian Mounted Police (RCMP), provincial police, and local police forces have the right to charge people who have broken the law. People who are charged with criminal offences must answer for their actions to the courts.

Criminal law is a branch of law that deals with illegal actions and their penalties. These laws are designed to discourage people from harming others. But law makers are not free to make any law they wish in order to control society. Both law makers and law enforcement agencies are limited by constitutional law, described on page 8. The *Canadian Charter of Rights and Freedoms* is part of Canada's Constitution. It ensures that limitations of individual rights are not taken too far.

Case

While on an environmental studies field trip, Jamie, Kirk, and Greg, three students from Crestview Secondary School, became trapped in a cave by a landslide. The three began to examine their situation. They noticed a trickle of water on the wall of the cave. Greg said he had learned in a science class that as long as there was water, they could live without food for about 30 days. They all noted that there was no animal or vegetable matter in the cave. However, Greg mentioned that if two of them reached a state

continued ▶

of desperation and killed the third and ate his flesh, they could survive for nearly another two weeks. As Jamie had a calendar watch with a luminous dial, keeping track of time was no problem.

On the 27th day, Kirk suggested that they draw lots to determine who would be killed for the benefit of the other two. When lots were drawn later that day, Kirk lost. He pleaded with Jamie and Greg to reconsider, but they pointed out that he had suggested the draw and that they had all agreed to it. Just as they were about to strangle Kirk, a rescue team broke through to save them.

For Discussion

1. **Did the boys pass a law? Explain your reasoning.**
2. **If Jamie and Greg had strangled Kirk, what could they have been charged with? What might have been their defence?**
3. **Suppose Jamie and Greg were found guilty of killing Kirk, and their lawyer pleaded for mercy. If you were the judge, what factors would you consider in allowing a plea for mercy?**

Protecting People

Criminal activity is not the only reason we have laws. Laws also protect people in many other situations. For example, a business might be tempted to ask you to forget about school and work 18 hours a day during the holiday rush. However, labour laws usually limit the number of hours the employer can legally ask an employee to work. They also require the employer to pay a minimum wage and provide safe and clean working conditions. Contract law protects people in situations where they are asked to sign agreements that provide little or no benefit to them. The divisions of Canadian law that deal with each of these issues are discussed in greater detail in Section 1.3 of this chapter.

Review Your Understanding (Pages 3 to 6)

1. **Explain why a knowledge of law is important.**
2. **Justify the importance of voting in a democracy.**
3. **Justify why laws and rules are necessary in society.**
4. **Distinguish between a rule and a law.**
5. **Identify factors that might cause laws to change.**
6. **Justify, with concrete examples, the importance of law enforcement in our society.**
7. **Describe how laws specifically protect individuals. In what ways do they protect society as a whole?**

1.3 The Divisions of Law

Law can be divided into two basic types: substantive law and procedural law. Substantive law (the substance of the law) consists of all laws that list the rights and obligations (duties) of each person in society.

For example, one type of substantive law is property law. This law allows Canadians to own property and enjoy certain rights. Property owners have the right to
- expel trespassers
- sell the property

- use their property in any way they wish as long as it does not interfere with others
- sue those who damage or interfere with the enjoyment and use of the property

At the same time, property owners have the obligation, or duty, to

- maintain the property
- make sure it is safe for others to enter
- pay property tax

What happens when legal rights are not respected or legal duties are not performed? Procedural law (the process of law) outlines the steps involved in protecting the rights given under substantive law. For example, what if the owner of a woodlot finds that a local snowmobile rental business is providing rides on her land and damaging her newly planted trees? Substantive law gives her the right to do something about it. Procedural law outlines the steps she can take to stop the problem and get compensation for the damage.

Figure 1-4

Students protest university policies by occupying the vice president's office. What law has been broken here?

Substantive Law

Substantive law is divided into public and private law. Each is discussed in this section.

Public Law

Public law controls the relationships between governments and the people who live in society. It represents laws that apply to all individuals. The main types of public law are criminal, constitutional, and administrative law.

Criminal Law Canada's criminal law is a set of rules passed by Parliament. These rules define acts called "crimes" that are considered to be offences against society. Crimes include murder, kidnapping, sexual assault, break and enter, and theft. The rules also set penalties for those who break the law. Most of Canada's criminal law is found in the *Criminal Code,* where many criminal acts and their punishments are described. The *Controlled Drugs and Substances Act* and the *Youth Criminal Justice Act* are other examples of criminal law. The main purposes of criminal law are to punish offenders and to protect society and its members. You may come in contact with criminal law as a victim, a witness, a juror, or as an accused person.

When a crime has been committed against society, both the accused and society are represented by lawyers. Society is represented by a **Crown attorney,** who tries to prove the charges against the accused person (the **defendant**) beyond a reasonable doubt. The court must determine whether the person is "guilty" or "not guilty" of the crime of which he or she is accused. Criminal law is examined in greater detail in Unit 2.

▮ The Divisions of Canadian Law

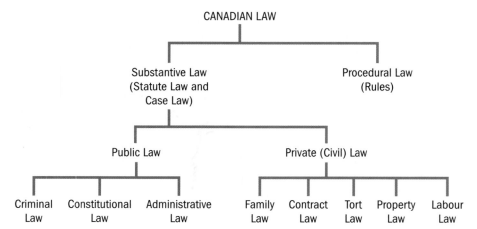

Figure 1-5

Which type(s) of law has affected you personally?

ⓔ activity

Visit **www.law.nelson.com** and follow the links to learn how different administrative boards govern the relationship between citizens and government.

Constitutional Law Government in Canada does not have unlimited power. The powers it does have are divided among several levels of government. The laws that set out the structure of the federal, provincial, and territorial governments and the division of powers among them is called constitutional law. Canada's Constitution, which outlines our most basic laws, is the *Constitution Act, 1982.* The Constitution will be discussed in more detail later in this chapter.

Administrative Law The area of law that controls the relationships between citizens and government agencies is administrative law. For example, liquor control boards manage the sale and consumption of alcoholic beverages and grant licences to serve them. The Canadian Radio-television and Telecommunications Commission (CRTC) controls broadcasting licences, cable television service, and telephone rates. The decisions of these government agencies have a major influence on our lives.

Private (Civil) Law

Private law outlines the legal relationships between private citizens, and between citizens and organizations (e.g., companies). Another name for private law is civil law. Its main purpose is to manage the behaviour of persons and organizations in conflict with each other and to pay damages to those who have been wronged.

There is no Crown attorney involved in civil actions or cases. Each person in a civil case is usually represented by a lawyer. The person who starts the case (the action or lawsuit) is called the **plaintiff.** The person whom the plaintiff is suing is called the defendant. The plaintiff sues because he or she believes that the defendant has caused him or her harm, loss, or injury.

There is a difference between the level of proof required in criminal law and civil law. In criminal law, the Crown attorney must prove the charges against the accused beyond a reasonable doubt. But in civil cases, the plaintiff has to prove that the defendant is at fault and caused damage. The defendant will try to produce evidence against this argument. The judge has to decide which story contains more truth and is believable (the balance of probabilities) and make a judgment. Civil law is covered in more detail in Units 3 to 5.

It is possible for the same incident to result in both a criminal and a civil action. Suppose Alex, a private pilot, does not maintain his aircraft as recommended and the plane is forced down, injuring his passengers. Breath samples taken by police after the crash also show that Alex was intoxicated at the time of the accident. As a result of the crash, Alex could be charged by the police with a crime (operating an aircraft while impaired) and sued by his passengers in a civil action for negligence (because he did not keep the plane in proper repair). There is no particular order in which these two cases would be tried. Usually, whichever case is ready first will be tried first.

Private (civil) law can be further subdivided into family, contract, tort, property, and labour law.

Family Law Family law deals with the relationships between individuals living together as spouses or partners, and between parents and children. This area of law is constantly changing. Many recent issues deal with the increasing numbers of common-law and same-sex relationships. Other issues include unpaid support payments to spouses and children, separation and divorce, division of property, and child custody. Family law is discussed in greater detail in Unit 4.

Contract Law Contract law outlines the requirements for legally binding agreements. Such agreements impose rights and responsibilities on the parties involved. A contract may be something as simple as buying a CD (you offer to pay for it, and the store accepts your money), or as complicated as an agreement between a company and the government to build new aircraft for hundreds of millions of dollars. If someone does not fulfill the terms of a contract, there is a breach of contract and the legal agreement is broken. The injured party can take legal action in the courts and sue for damages. Contract law is discussed in greater detail in Unit 5.

Tort Law Tort law deals with wrongs, other than a breach of contract, that one person commits against another person. For example, a patient can sue a surgeon for malpractice or negligence (carelessness) that occurred during an operation. Negligence is the major cause of action in tort law. Tort law is discussed in greater detail in Unit 3.

Property Law Property is anything that has a cash value. Property law is a set of legal rules that controls the use, enjoyment, and rental of property. Many of the laws affecting property were established by the English courts hundreds of years ago. Property law is discussed in Chapter 18.

Labour Law Labour law governs the relationships between employers and employees. It is often called employment law. It deals with issues such as minimum wage, pay equity (equal pay for equal work), proper dismissal, working conditions, and workers' compensation. Labour law is discussed in greater detail in Chapter 19.

Review Your Understanding (Pages 6 to 9)

1. **Distinguish between substantive and procedural law. Create examples to illustrate the distinction.**
2. **Distinguish between the parties in a criminal trial and the parties in a civil trial. To what extent are they similar or different?**
3. **You have been hired to present a summary of the divisions within Canadian law. Briefly describe the categories of public and private law and provide an example to illustrate each type of law.**

1.4   The Early History of Law

The laws of ancient civilizations have had a great influence on the development of Canadian law. In early societies, local customs and beliefs were the law. Customs were traditionally accepted and were usually based on common sense. It was not necessary to write them down because everyone was aware of them and passed them on by word of mouth to future generations. As societies grew, the laws became more complex. It became too difficult for many citizens to know and understand these laws. Yet, for justice to be served, people had to be aware of them. It finally became necessary for existing laws to be written down in a permanent form.

ⓔ activity

Visit **www.law.nelson.com** and follow the links to learn about the Code of Hammurabi.

The Code of Hammurabi

Hammurabi was a famous king who ruled Babylonia (now Iraq) about 3800 years ago. He decided to take nearly 300 laws and record them in a way that could be understood by his citizens. This set of laws, known as the Code of

---

The Law   The Code of Hammurabi

Excerpts from the Code of Hammurabi (1750 B.C.E.)

3. If a man has borne false witness in a trial, or has not established the statement that he has made, if that case be a capital [very serious] trial, that man shall be put to death.

46. If a man neglects to strengthen his dike, and a break is made in his dike, and he lets water carry away farmland, the man in whose dike the break has been made shall restore grain that he has damaged.

195. If a man has struck his father, his hands shall be cut off.

196. If a man destroy the eye of another man, they shall destroy his eye.

218. If a surgeon has operated with the bronze lancet on a patrician [aristocrat] for a serious injury, and has caused his death, or has removed a cataract for a patrician with a bronze lancet, and has made him lose his eye, his hands shall be cut off.

For Discussion

1. **Express your immediate response to the punishments listed.**
2. **Identify the beliefs and values that are reflected in these laws.**
3. **Compare the values reflected in the Code of Hammurabi with our current values reflected in Canadian laws.**

Hammurabi, is one of the most important and earliest records we have of written laws. Hammurabi had these laws carved in columns of stone, one of which was unearthed by an archaeologist in Susa, Iran, in 1901, and is now displayed in the Louvre Museum in Paris, France.

A code is simply a written collection of a country's laws, arranged so that they can be used and understood. This process of preparing a code is called **codification.** The Code of Hammurabi was organized under headings such as family, criminal, labour, property, trade, and business. Babylonian judges could match a person's offence and punishment by looking at the written law rather than deciding for themselves what punishment to pass. Crimes punishable by death required a trial by a panel of judges. The Code followed the principle that the strong should not injure the weak. **Retribution** was important because it was believed that for every crime there should be a deserved punishment: "An eye for an eye, a tooth for a tooth."

Moses and Mosaic Law

Centuries after Hammurabi died, Moses gave laws to the Hebrew people. Many of these laws were similar to those listed in the Code of Hammurabi. This Mosaic law is set out in the first five books of the Old Testament. The Bible tells the story of Moses climbing Mount Sinai to receive from God the Ten Commandments engraved on two stone tablets. The Ten Commandments, which forbid such acts as killing, adultery, and bearing false witness, continue to hold a central position in the teachings of both the Jewish and Christian faiths. The punishments of Mosaic law were severe—for example, the punishment for adultery was execution by stoning (pelting a person to death with stones).

FRANK & ERNEST® by Bob Thaves

Figure 1-6

Why do you think that 10 commandments are not enough?

The Law   **Mosaic Law**

Excerpts from Exodus (1240 B.C.E.)

21:15 Whoever strikes his father or his mother shall be put to death.

21:17 Whoever curses his father or his mother shall be put to death.

21:29 When an ox has been accustomed to gore in the past, and its owner has been warned but has not kept it in, and it kills a man or a woman, the ox shall be stoned, and its owner shall also be put to death.

22:1 If a man steals an ox or a sheep, and kills it or sells it, he shall pay five oxen for an ox, and four sheep for a sheep. He shall make restitution; if he has nothing, he shall be sold for his theft.

23:1 You shall not utter a false report. You shall not join hands with a wicked man to be a malicious witness.

For Discussion

1. **Compare Mosaic law with the Code of Hammurabi. Identify the similarities and differences that exist.**

2. **Interpret from the excerpt the important beliefs of the ancient Hebrew people.**

3. **How have these beliefs contributed to Canadian law?**

In our society, a person is usually punished for theft by paying a fine or serving a jail term. Mosaic law, on the other hand, required the offender to repay the victim for goods stolen. In recent years, some form of **restitution** has become a more common punishment and is discussed further in Chapter 9.

Roman Law

Roman law, the legal system that began in early Rome, became the basis of law for Western Europe, except England. As the Roman Empire grew, the number of laws increased and they became more complex. The Romans created a profession devoted to the study of legal matters. This marked the beginning of law as we know it today, and the role of lawyers.

By the year 100 C.E., the Roman Empire had spread over much of Europe, and it remained intact until the 5th century. As a result, Roman laws influenced most European countries. However, the emperor Constantine transferred the capital of the Empire to Byzantium, in what is now Turkey, in 324 C.E. The Byzantine emperor Justinian (527–564 C.E.) codified 1000 years of Roman laws and produced what is known as the Justinian Code. The Code was a collection of past laws, opinions from leading Roman legal experts, and new laws enacted by Justinian. These laws emphasized **equity:** the idea that law should be fair and just, and that all people are equal under the law, regardless of their wealth and power.

In 1804, after the French Revolution, Emperor Napoleon Bonaparte revised French law, which had been based on Roman law and the Justinian Code. This new set of civil laws was called the Napoleonic Code, or the French *Civil Code.* It also emphasized equity and justice for all. Because Napoleon conquered much of Europe in the early 1800s, this new set of laws became a model for many European countries. Today, it is the basis of law in many modern democratic countries. In Quebec, civil law is still based on the Napoleonic Code.

Review Your Understanding (Pages 10 to 12)

1. **Explain the significance of the Code of Hammurabi.**
2. **Compare the concepts of retribution and restitution. Which concept is more likely to be considered in the area of criminal law?**
3. **What is the Justinian Code?**
4. **Explain the significance of the French *Civil Code* to the development of Canadian law.**

activity

Visit **www.law.nelson.com** and follow the links to learn about the Quebec *Civil Code.*

You Be the JUDGE

"It is better that ten guilty persons escape than one innocent suffer."

— Sir William Blackstone, *Commentaries on the Laws of England,* 1756

- How does William Blackstone's notion of justice compare with our notion of justice today? Explain your opinion.

1.5 The Development of Canadian Law

Canadian law is based upon the laws of France and England, the countries that colonized Canada. However, there are important differences between the legal systems of the two countries. Early on, French law was codified and written down. English law, on the other hand, was not codified or written down until quite late in England's history. Over hundreds of years, the English Parliament has passed laws codifying many of its court decisions and customs. However, much of English law has still not been written down.

Feudalism and Common Law

In 1066, William, Duke of Normandy (in what is now France), invaded England and conquered it. As the king of England, William introduced a system of government from Europe called **feudalism.** The king owned all the land and divided much of it among his lords and nobles. In return, the lords became the king's vassals (servants) and promised him loyalty and military service. In turn, these lords had vassals of their own who farmed the lands and gave

Looking Back   A Verdict by God?

In medieval Europe and England, people were very religious. Everyone assumed that God would protect people from harm. So, when a legal case was hard to decide, the judge would sometimes order a new trial to be "decided" by God.

In a trial by fire, the accused had to hold a red-hot iron. The hand was then wrapped in cloth and uncovered after three days. If the burn had healed cleanly, the accused was judged innocent. But if the hand was infected, the accused was judged guilty. In a trial by water, the accused might be thrown into a pond or lake with his or her hands bound. If the accused sank, the verdict was innocent, but the accused often drowned before being rescued. An accused person who floated on the water was pronounced guilty because water was considered a symbol of purity that had rejected the accused.

Trial by combat was another method used to render a verdict or settle disputes. Nobles often fought this type of "trial" in the form of a duel. It was believed that God would help determine who was in the right. In a criminal case, if the accused was killed, the verdict was guilty. Even if the accused was only wounded but lost the duel, he would be hanged immediately if that was the punishment for the offence.

Another custom used to establish guilt or innocence was compurgation. Eleven persons would swear for the accused that he or she was innocent. These persons were called "compurgators," from an old word that means to swear an oath together before God. If the court was satisfied with the 11 compurgators, the accused would be released. However, if the accuser produced 11 witnesses of higher rank than those of the accused, the verdict would be guilty.

Trial by fire and trial by combat disappeared from the legal system centuries ago. But the idea behind compurgation survives in the 12-member jury that decides the guilt or innocence of some accused persons. At many trials today, the accused also presents character witnesses who testify that the accused is a person of good character (and therefore should be believed).

For Discussion

1. Identify the values and beliefs that underlie the trials described in this Looking Back. Comment on their fairness from your point of view.

2. Generally, the wealthy and powerful settled cases through trial by combat. Explain why they would be more likely to use this trial method.

3. How do the beliefs of Canadians compare to those of medieval Europeans?

4. Compare the medieval system of compurgation with our jury system today.

Figure 1-7

This medieval painting depicts a trial by combat.

part of their produce to the lords and the Church. Some of them also served in the armies of the lords. The feudal system in England formed the basis for our modern property laws.

A lord's land was called his manor, or estate, and he ran it as he saw fit. For example, a lord acted as the judge in any trial of a vassal accused of breaking the law. Injustice often resulted. One lord might find a vassal guilty of theft and order repayment, plus compensation for trouble to the victim. Another might sentence the vassal to death for the same crime. In response to this unfairness, the king appointed a number of judges who travelled throughout England and held hearings and trials called assizes on controversial or disputed cases. These judges met regularly in London to discuss cases and share experiences. By the 13th century, the laws and punishments were more similar for both criminal and civil cases.

As judges developed regular punishments for specific crimes, these legal decisions became the basis of English common law, so called because it was common to the whole of England. Because the legal system had become more just, it earned new respect. This common-law system was introduced to North America by the colonists who first travelled here.

Precedent

Common law is based upon an important principle known as the rule of **precedent.** A "precedent" is something that has been done that can later serve as an example or rule for how other things should be done. The rule of precedent came about when a case and its decision became common knowledge in the English legal community. As a result, all judges who heard cases with similar facts would give similar decisions. By treating similar cases alike, English judges established the same standard of judging offences throughout the country. At first, these case decisions existed only in the judges' memories and were known as "unwritten law." But this system was considered to be an improvement over the right of a lord to judge cases however he chose. People who were dissatisfied with court decisions could appeal to the monarch, who had the authority to overrule judges' decisions.

Today, lawyers and judges still refer to earlier decisions on cases that are identical or similar to the one they are dealing with as precedents. These earlier cases are considered examples that should be followed. They influence and guide judges when they reach a verdict and pass sentence.

The rule of precedent introduces a degree of certainty into the law. It means that everyone, including the accused, can examine previous similar cases and the arguments that were used and expect a somewhat similar result. Trial lawyers spend much time presenting earlier cases in the hopes of persuading the judge to reach a similar decision. Many older cases in this text are landmark judgments that set precedents that are still followed by the courts when reaching decisions in new cases.

Following precedent too closely can cause a problem if the precedent is not recent. For example, the traffic rules for horse-drawn buggies are not suitable for cars speeding along a modern expressway. Henry VIII of England issued a law that cats should be allowed to roam at will (because of the huge numbers of rodents in England at the time). This law would not be a suitable precedent for the rules of a modern apartment complex.

Case Law

As the number of judges and cases increased, recording decisions became necessary. Many cases decided in court are recorded and published in paper and electronic form. Thus, common law is often called case law. You can retrieve these cases at law libraries by consulting such reporters as *Canadian Criminal Cases* (C.C.C.), *Reports of Family Law* (R.F.L.), or *Supreme Court Reports* (S.C.R.), or by searching with these key words on the Internet.

Each recorded case is given a title, or **citation.** The citation lists basic information: who is involved in the case, whether the case is public or private (civil) law, and the year the court decision was reached. It also identifies which court heard the case and the name of the law reporter in which the court decision appears. If the volumes of the law reporter are organized by year, that year may be different from the year of decision and will be added to the citation, placed within square brackets. This information makes it easy to locate the case in a law library.

▋ Elements of a Citation

Criminal Citation

R.	v.	Bates	(2000),	35	C.R.	(5th)	327	(Ont. C.A.)
Regina or *Rex* (Latin for "queen" and "king") represents society	*versus* (Latin for "against")	defendant (accused)	year of decision	volume number	name of reporter where case is reported (e.g., *Criminal Reports*)	series	page number	jurisdiction (federal, province, or territory) and court (e.g., Ontario Court of Appeal)

Civil Citation

Langille et al.	v.	McGrath	(2000),	233	N.B.R.	(2d)	29	(N.B.Q.B.)
plaintiff and others (Latin *et alia* for "and others")	*versus* (Latin for "against")	defendant (accused)	year of decision	volume number	name of reporter where case is reported (e.g., *New Brunswick Reports*)	series	page number	jurisdiction (federal, province, or territory) and court (e.g., New Brunswick Court of Queen's Bench)

Figure 1-8

These charts show the elements of a citation for a criminal case and for a civil case. See Appendix C: Table of Cases, page 608, for how to cite cases found on the Internet.

Case

R. v. Davis

(1995) 30 Alta. L.R. (3d) 361
Alberta Provincial Court

One Friday evening the accused, Marlene Davis, and four female friends were partying at Eddy's Lounge in Edmonton, Alberta. They arrived about 10:30 P.M. and shared pitchers of beer until 2:00 A.M., by which time the accused and some of her friends were well under the influence of alcohol.

About this time, Davis left her table with a mug of beer in hand, and walked toward the bar where she became involved in an argument with Darrin Huculak, a former boyfriend of one of her friends. In an attempt to temper this argument, a third person, Wayne Grant, stepped between the accused and Huculak at the bartender's request. Davis spat at Huculak over Grant's shoulder and then threw the contents of her beer mug at Huculak. However,

the mug slipped and hit Grant in the mouth, causing him serious cuts and injuries.

The accused was charged with assault with a weapon, but was found guilty of the lesser charge of common assault.

For Discussion

1. What type of law is involved in this case?
2. Explain each component of the citation for the case.
3. Interpret from the case study what actions would constitute an assault.
4. Why was Davis charged with assault with a weapon?
5. Evaluate whether there was an intent to injure.
6. What factors do you think the judge took into consideration in convicting Davis on the lesser charge of common assault?

Case

Gauthier v. Beaumont

[1998] 2 S.C.R. 3
Supreme Court of Canada

Gauthier was suspected of theft and was taken to a police station in a Quebec town. Here he was beaten and threatened with death by two police officers. He later spent a few days in hospital, but he did not give the real cause of his injuries. He feared for his life and left Quebec to live in Western Canada. Later he was contacted by a member of the Quebec Police Commission who asked him to testify against the officers. He testified before the commission under police protection. He was also a witness at the trial of the officers. Both officers were convicted and sent to prison.

More than six years after the beatings, Gauthier sought damages against both former police officers and the town that employed them. He stated that his rights, guaranteed under the Quebec *Charter of Human Rights and Freedoms*, had been trespassed upon and broken. At the trial, the judge asked why he had taken so long to sue for damages. He said

that he had been so damaged by the beatings he had been unable psychologically to do so. Two psychiatrists supported his statement. The trial judge disagreed. He said Gauthier had waited too long to take legal action. Since he had testified before the police commission and the trials of the ex-police officers, he should have taken legal action at that time. The case was over the six-year legal limit, and so the judge dismissed it. Gauthier appealed his case to the Supreme Court of Canada, which ruled in his favour. He was entitled to damages.

For Discussion

1. Why did the trial judge dismiss Gauthier's case? Was he right to do so?
2. What factors do you think the Supreme Court took into consideration in reversing the trial judge's decision?
3. A Statute of Limitations is set up to prevent legal action after a certain time period. Identify arguments in favour of and against a six-year limitation period in a civil action.

In summary, the most significant meaning of the term "common law" is that it is the law based on judges' trial decisions, precedent, and reported case law. It is distinct from the statute law made by governments, and it serves as a major part of Canadian law today.

The Rule of Law

During the reign of England's King John (1199–1216), an important development in the history of English law occurred. The king considered himself above the law and abused the power of his position. Eventually, the most powerful groups in the land (the nobility, the clergy, and freemen) forced King John to sign the Magna Carta, the "Great Charter," in 1215. This famous document recognized the principle of the **rule of law.**

As a result, King John and all rulers after him had to obey the law. The idea of equality became important for the first time. In addition, no ruler could restrict the freedoms of the people without reason, and the people's legal rights could not be changed without their consent. The Magna Carta also guaranteed the right of *habeas corpus,* which means that any person who was imprisoned without an explanation was entitled to appear before the courts within a reasonable time. The accused could then be released if held unlawfully, or tried by peers (equals) if charged with an offence.

Canadians are governed by the rule of law. This means that every dispute must be settled by peaceful means, either by discussion and negotiation or by due process in the courts. Canadians, as well as citizens of other democracies, are not allowed to settle disputes through violence. Nor are its government officials allowed to make up or change the rules without consulting anyone else. The rule of law exists because our society believes that the concept of "might" is not right. Resolving disputes by peaceful means is better, not only for the individuals involved, but also for society itself. The rule of law brings order to people's lives by preventing the use of violence and the abuse of human rights.

Figure 1-9

King John receives the Magna Carta.

Parliament and Statute Law

Although King John and his successors had to obey the law, they still struggled for power with the English nobles. Around 1265, a group of nobles revolted against King Henry III to make him reform the English legal process. These nobles wanted to reduce the king's power and acquire more power for themselves. As a result, representatives were called together from all parts of England, forming the first Parliament. The job of Parliament was to help make laws for the country. Over the next four centuries, Parliament struggled for power with the monarchs of Britain.

Figure 1-10

William III holds the *Bill of Rights* in his hand.

Parliament Replaces the King

A crisis arose in 1688 when King James II tried to gain more power at the expense of Parliament. He was trying to make England a more Catholic country, but most English people were strongly opposed to that. Both the nobles and the bishops of the Church of England revolted against him and forced him to flee. They made his daughter, Mary, and her husband, William, the queen and king of Britain. In 1689, Parliament passed the *Bill of Rights* guaranteeing free speech, free elections, and freedom of assembly.

This event came to be known as the "Glorious Revolution" because it was achieved with very little violence. Parliament had triumphed, and no future monarch could simply ignore Parliament's wishes. Over the next three centuries, Parliament was increasingly seen as the institution that represented the people and their wishes. This was an important step in the development of democracy.

Statute Law

One of the most important functions of Parliament is to pass laws, or **statutes.** As British society changed, common law and case law could not provide answers to every legal situation. Parliament began to fill the gap and make new laws to deal with new situations. In addition, many common-law decisions made by the courts were codified by Parliament and became statute law. One important outcome was that members of the public could now read the laws and know what they said.

In making a decision in any case, courts must consider both the common law and the statute law. Canada's substantive law represents common-law decisions and statute laws passed by government.

Review Your Understanding (Pages 12 to 18)

1. What is feudalism and how did it work?
2. Why were the king's courts or assizes preferred to the manor courts of the feudal lords?
3. How is the rule of precedent used in today's system of law?
4. Express an argument for the continued use of precedent in our legal system today. Counter this argument by examining a disadvantage of the precedent system.
5. How is a citation useful in law?
6. What is common law?
7. Explain the significance of statute law as a source of law.

1.6 The Development of Canada's Constitution

In Canada, the powers of government to make law, and the levels of government responsible for making law, are described in the Constitution. The British Parliament passed our first constitution, the *British North America Act* (BNA Act). It came into effect on July 1, 1867. A new country called the Dominion of Canada was born. At that time, it consisted of the provinces of Ontario, Quebec, New Brunswick, and Nova Scotia. But Canada was not a fully independent country because Britain still controlled Canada's foreign affairs. For example, Canada could not make its own treaties with other countries. When Britain declared war, Canada was also automatically at war. In addition, the Judicial Committee of the Privy Council of Britain was Canada's highest court. It could overrule decisions made by the Canadian courts.

Figure 1-11

The Queen signed the *Constitution Act, 1982,* in Ottawa.

Gradually, Canada assumed more control over its own affairs. In 1931, the *Statute of Westminster,* passed by the British Parliament, gave Canada control over its foreign affairs. In 1949, the Supreme Court of Canada became Canada's highest court of appeal. But there was still one link to Britain that prevented Canada from being a truly independent country. Because the BNA Act was a British statute, it could only be changed or amended by the British Parliament. Canada had to ask Britain about any changes it wanted to make. For example, in 1940, when the Canadian federal government wanted to include unemployment insurance in the BNA Act as one of its powers, the British Parliament had to pass the amendment.

During the 20th century, Britain was more than willing to give Canada its own constitution and allow it to be a truly independent country. But for many decades, the federal and provincial governments were suspicious of each other and unwilling to risk losing any powers. Therefore, they could not agree on a formula to amend (change) the constitution, if change became necessary.

But in 1981, after many years of negotiation, Canada finally came up with a method of changing its constitution. The formula for change, called the **amending formula,** requires the consent of (1) the Canadian Parliament, and (2) two-thirds of the provinces with 50 percent of the population to approve any change. The constitution document was transferred to Canada from Britain on April 17, 1982, and Canada finally became an independent country.

The BNA Act was renamed the *Constitution Act, 1867.* Although the *Constitution Act, 1867,* is still the main part of the *Constitution Act, 1982,* key elements of the *Constitution Act, 1982,* include the amending formula and a new *Canadian Charter of Rights and Freedoms.*

The Division of Powers

The *Constitution Act, 1867*, lists the powers of the federal, provincial, and territorial governments. It outlines which government has **jurisdiction,** or authority, to make laws in specific areas. The federal government's powers are outlined in section 91, while those of the provincial governments are outlined in section 92. Section 93 gives the provinces control over education.

Although the division of powers in the Constitution is spelled out clearly, many current issues create disputes between governments. For example, providing health care is a provincial responsibility. But the federal government tries to set Canada-wide legal standards to guarantee equal access for all Canadians. However, some provinces argue that if the federal government wishes to set legal standards, it should provide more money than it does to operate the provincial systems. Sometimes, these disputes between levels of governments end up in court.

Cities and Townships: A Third Level of Government

Although the *Constitution Act, 1867*, established only two levels of government, the provinces have given some of their powers to a third level, the local municipality. Municipalities include cities, towns, townships, villages, and counties. Most of the bylaws that govern the activities of a local community are passed by a municipality. These bylaws govern, for example, garbage collection, emergency services, building permits, water services, night-time noise, and even regulations about stray dogs and cats.

▌ Constitution Act, 1867—Division of Power

Federal Government Powers (Section 91)	Provincial Government Powers (Section 92)
• peace, order, and good government • criminal law • unemployment insurance • banking, currency, and coinage • federal penitentiaries • marriage and divorce • postal services • Aboriginal peoples and their lands	• property and civil rights • marriage ceremonies • police forces and provincial courts • highways and roads • provincial jails • hospitals

Figure 1-12

Federal and provincial government powers as set forth in the *Constitution Act, 1867*

Review Your Understanding (Pages 19 to 20)

1. How did the *British North America Act* lay down the structure for the Canadian Constitution?

2. Discuss the importance of the *Statute of Westminster*.

3. Why did it take so long for Canada to get control of its own constitution?

4. Distinguish between the *Constitution Act, 1867*, and the *Constitution Act, 1982*.

5. Distinguish between sections 91 and 92 of the *Constitution Act, 1867*, by discussing the constitutional division of powers.

6. What is the third level of government in Canada? What type of laws does it pass?

1.7 How Laws Are Made in Canada

When Canadian governments want to make or change laws, they must consider what effect that might have. An unpopular law might cause a member of Parliament (MP) to be defeated in the next election. Before a law is changed or a new law is created, governments spend time and money researching the effects the law is likely to have. A law that the government has proposed is called a **bill.** Once it is passed, it becomes an act, or statute law.

How Federal Laws Are Passed

Parliament makes our federal laws. It is located in Ottawa, Canada's capital city. It consists of three parts: the House of Commons, the Senate, and the governor general, who represents Canada's Queen, Elizabeth II. The House of Commons is the part of Parliament that has the most important role in making laws. Its representatives are elected by the citizens of Canada.

Each member of Parliament is an elected representative of a riding. Canada is divided into ridings, each with approximately the same number of voters so that every geographical area is represented by an MP. The political party that has the largest number of members elected to the House of Commons forms the government. The other parties in the House are called opposition parties. There are 301 MPs in the House of Commons.

The leader of the party that has the largest number of elected members is the prime minister. He or she appoints elected members (MPs) of his or her party to the Cabinet. Cabinet ministers are the heads of government departments that employ thousands of civil servants. They see that federal

Did You Know?

In 2004, the number of MPs will increase to 308 because of population growth in British Columbia, Alberta, and Ontario.

▌ Passage of a Bill into Law at the Federal Level

Who	Stage
House of Commons	**First Reading** Bill introduced by a Cabinet minister or private member First vote taken **Second Reading** Bill introduced again and debated in general Second vote taken **Committee Stage** Bill usually sent to select committee, standing committee, or committee of the whole House Bill studied in detail, and changes (amendments) often made; each section may be voted on separately **Third Reading** Bill briefly debated Third vote taken
Senate	Bill goes through three readings and committees, as in the House of Commons
Governor General	Signs bill to become a law

Did You Know?

Members of the Senate and the governor general are not elected. They are appointed to their positions by the prime minister.

Figure 1-13

Should bills be read once only? Why or why not?

Figure 1-14

The Right Honourable Adrienne Clarkson, Governor General

laws are carried out (refer to Figure 1-12 for the list of federal powers).

When a government wants to introduce a new law in Canada, a Cabinet minister introduces a bill into the House of Commons. If the prime minister's party has a majority government (more than half the elected MPs), there is usually no difficulty getting the bill passed. Once approved, it is sent to the Senate. If approved there, it is sent to the governor general, who signs it into law. When a bill becomes law, all Canadians have to obey it or face the consequences.

How Provincial Laws Are Passed

A provincial legislature passes a bill in much the same way as Parliament. However, provincial and territorial governments do not have a Senate. Once a bill passes through three readings in the provincial legislative assembly, it goes to the lieutenant-governor (the Queen's provincial representative) for his or her signature.

How Municipal Bylaws Are Passed

In general, an elected council led by a mayor or reeve votes on municipal bylaws. The details of the procedure vary from one municipality to another.

Review Your Understanding (Pages 21 to 22)

1. Why is the House of Commons the most powerful part of Parliament?
2. What are the responsibilities of Cabinet ministers?
3. Compare the passage of federal legislation with that of provincial legislation. How are they similar? How are they different?
4. Think of a change you would like to see in the law. Describe the process by which this idea could become a reality. Clearly identify the steps needed to pass a bill into a law.

1.8   Canada and International Law

In recent times, we have been hearing a great deal about globalization. Globalization is the transformation of the world into a global community. It has occurred because of many events, including the end of the Cold War (1945–1990) between the West and East, the creation of new trading alliances among the nations, and the electronic revolution. Globalization has had legal consequences as well as social and economic ones. As interactions among nations have become more complex, more disagreements have arisen.

International law governs relationships between states. States must follow the rules of international law when they form relationships with each other. In international law, the term "state" refers to a group of people that (1) is recognized as an independent country, and (2) has territory ruled by a sovereign (independent) government that can enter into relations with other states. Canada is one of 191 sovereign states in the world today.

International law is based on three types of law: customary law, treaty law, and resolutions.

Customary Law

Over time, states establish practices that they follow consistently and which they assume are obligatory (required). Customary law is formed from these practices. It is not written down in formal codes, but is found in the written judgments in international court cases and in the writings of legal experts. Customary law recognizes the following basic principles, which are based on the idea that states have certain rights and obligations:

Figure 1-15

If Quebec were to separate from Canada, it would have to be recognized by other nations as a sovereign state.

- **Sovereignty**

  A nation's absolute right to govern itself is called **sovereignty.** There is no sovereign world government. Authority to govern rests in each of the 191 independent states that make up the world. Sovereignty implies a state's control over its territory to the exclusion of other states, and the authority to govern that territory and apply the laws there. Under international law, sovereign states have equal status, regardless of their military or economic power, how much land they occupy, or the size of their population.

- **Recognition**

  New states gain recognition as sovereign nations by being recognized by other countries. However, such recognition is not guaranteed. For example, if Quebec or another part of Canada were to separate from Canada, it would have to convince other countries that it should be granted the status of a sovereign state. Other nations might not support this idea, especially if people in the breakaway territory didn't truly support independence.

- **Consent**

  States are bound by new international laws only after they freely give their consent. If a nation signed an agreement because it was being threatened with invasion by another state, the international community would not recognize the agreement.

- **Good Faith**

  States are expected to conduct their affairs with reasonableness and common sense. They must show good faith in the way they interpret and use international laws.

- **Freedom of the Seas**
  States cannot claim ownership of any portion of the high seas. States are expected to use the high seas, the airspace above the high seas, and the seabed with due regard for the interests of other states. During wartime, states may interfere with each other's shipping routes as a form of retaliation.
- **International Responsibility**
  A state that does not meet an international obligation has committed a wrongful act. It may face criminal penalties and/or the duty to compensate the wronged party. Examples of wrongful acts include unfair aggression against another state or causing an environmental catastrophe inside another state's borders.
- **Self-Defence**
  The *Charter of the United Nations* declares that the threat or use of force against other states is unlawful. However, international law recognizes that states have the right to defend themselves against the hostile acts of other states.
- **Humanitarianism**
  Humanitarianism is respect for the interests of humankind. Examples of humanitarianism include providing famine relief to developing countries or disaster relief to countries that have experienced a natural disaster.

Treaty Law

International treaties are another part of international law. These are binding written agreements, freely entered into by states, that spell out their rights and obligations to each other. Bilateral treaties are treaties made between two states. Multilateral treaties involve three or more states.

▌ Five Steps in the Treaty-Making Process

1. Negotiate the precise content and wording of the treaty.
2. Formally sign the treaty. This means that the state leaders who sign the treaty support it completely.
3. Ratify (approve) the treaty. This step commits all the states to follow the treaty.
4. Let the treaty "come into force." This happens when a specified number of states ratifies the treaty.
5. Implement and enforce the treaty. These measures ensure that everyone complies with the terms of the treaty.

Figure 1-16

What is the difference between this negotiation process and the negotiation process you use in your home or school life?

Special classes of international treaties include
- charters (treaties that establish international organizations)
- conventions (treaties that are negotiated by many countries, to which all countries of the world may become partners)
- protocols (treaties that add to earlier treaties on the same topic)

In 2001, representatives from 178 states, including Canada, formally adopted the 1997 Kyoto Protocol on global warming. The Kyoto Protocol called for industrialized nations to reduce emissions of "greenhouse gases" linked to global warming to 5 percent below 1990 levels. The Kyoto agreement will come into force once 55 countries, including those nations responsible for most of the greenhouse emissions, have ratified the agreement.

The United States refused to endorse the Kyoto Protocol. The United States, which produces one-quarter of all greenhouse gases, claimed that the Kyoto Protocol was seriously flawed and would harm the U.S. economy. China and India also chose not to sign the agreement. In Canada, the Alberta government indicated that it would move to block Canada's ratification of the protocol. Alberta is Canada's main producer of oil and natural gas.

The Kyoto Protocol highlights the promise and limitations of international law. Success will depend on the willingness of the international community to cooperate. Such cooperation can be threatened when sovereign states put their national interests ahead of global interests.

Treaties are the main method for addressing international problems and conflicts. They deal with a wide range of matters, including the following:

- **Territory**
  The state has a fundamental interest in the rules that govern its right to define its territory and its international borders, including territorial limits off seacoasts. Although almost all the world's land mass is now owned by individual states, international treaties ban further seizure of territory in three areas: the world's oceans, Antarctica, and outer space.

- **Diplomatic Law and Immunity**
  States carry on their relations through diplomats and envoys. These representatives have certain privileges and immunities—in other words, they have more leeway in their behaviour than average citizens and may not suffer the same penalties for breaking the law. These privileges and immunities are now codified in the 1961 *Vienna Convention on Diplomatic Relations*.

- **The Protection of Nationals Abroad**
  Foreign nationals (people travelling to other nations) are entitled to the protection of life, liberty, and property. However, international law recognizes the right of states to seize or nationalize private property in the national interest, provided the state offers prompt compensation.

- **Extradition and Asylum**
  States have made **extradition** treaties with each other. These treaties let nations bring home people who are trying to escape justice. To extradite someone is to return that person to his or her country to face the penalties there. In the absence of a treaty to the contrary, a state may grant asylum, or a safe place, in its own territory to any individual.

- **International Trade**
  Globalization has encouraged states to create several new international trade agreements, including the *North American Free Trade Agreement* (NAFTA). Canada, the United States, and Mexico formed this agreement in 1994 with the goal of gradually eliminating tariffs on goods and services traded among the three countries.

You Be the JUDGE

Canada and the United States have an extradition treaty. However, in February 2001, the Supreme Court of Canada ruled that Canada's Constitution forbids the extradition of Canadian citizens and foreigners to the United States if they face a possible death penalty there.

- Do you think that the Supreme Court ruling could encourage American fugitives facing the death penalty to seek haven in Canada? Explain.

You Be the JUDGE

In January 2001, a Russian diplomat in Ottawa, Andrei Knyazev, killed a woman with his car. He refused a breath test, saying he had diplomatic immunity. He was expelled from Canada and returned to Moscow. International law bans the detention of diplomats and protects them from prosecution. Canadian courts have ruled that a breath test is detention.

- Should diplomats have the right to refuse the breath test? Explain.

- Research the final outcome of the Knyazev case and revise your explanation.

December 1948
Adopts the *Universal Declaration of Human Rights*

July 1951
Adopts the *Convention Relating to the Status of Refugees*

June 1968
Approves the *Treaty on the Non-Proliferation of Nuclear Weapons* and calls for its ratification

December 1979
Adopts the *Convention on the Elimination of All Forms of Discrimination Against Women*

November 1981
Adopts the *Declaration on the Elimination of All Forms of Intolerance and Discrimination Based on Religious Belief*

December 1982
117 countries sign the *United Nations Convention on the Law of the Sea*

December 1984
Adopts the *Convention Against Torture and Other Cruel, Inhumane, or Degrading Treatment or Punishment*

September 1990
Adopts the *Convention on the Rights of the Child*

September 1996
Adopts the *Comprehensive Nuclear Test-Ban Treaty*

- **Arms Control**

  During the Cold War, fear of global catastrophe prompted states to create treaties aimed at preventing nuclear war. Some of these treaties banned the testing of nuclear weapons in the atmosphere, prevented the spread of nuclear weapons, and reduced the number of nuclear warheads and missiles held by the major nuclear powers.

In the case of both customary laws and treaties, sovereign states can agree among themselves to new international laws or change existing international laws as they see fit.

Resolutions

In international law, resolutions are considered "soft law" because they do not have the force of customary law or treaties. They are not considered binding on countries, even on those that vote for them. Despite these disadvantages, resolutions serve a purpose. They can be adopted fairly quickly and are often used to focus international attention on an issue or situation that demands quick action. Resolutions can also form the basis for later negotiations on treaties.

The Role of International Organizations

Today, several organizations are involved in developing and applying international laws and in resolving disputes between states.

The United Nations

The United Nations (UN) was established on October 24, 1945, following the end of World War II (1939–1945). Memories of that terrible conflict were still fresh. Fifty-one states signed the United Nations Charter, which committed them to preserving peace through international cooperation and collective security, and to promoting respect for human rights. Since its creation, the United Nations has played an important role in developing international law and in promoting cooperation among nations. Canada has been a major supporter of the United Nations and has contributed to its work in many ways.

The United Nations is not a world government, as some believe. It does not have sovereign authority to make laws. Rather, it passes resolutions. Success in transforming these resolutions into action rests on the willingness of the United Nation's member states (189 at last count) to work together cooperatively.

The UN General Assembly All UN member states are represented in the General Assembly, where each state has one vote. A two-thirds majority makes decisions on major matters such as international peace and security and the admission of new members. The General Assembly cannot demand action by a member state, but its resolutions carry strong moral authority, especially when a vote has been almost unanimous.

Figure 1-17
Identify the world issues addressed in the UN resolutions.

Figure 1-18
The General Assembly of the United Nations

The UN Security Council The Security Council is the body of the United Nations responsible for maintaining international peace and security. Under the UN Charter, member states are obligated to carry out the Council's decisions. The Security Council has 15 members, five of which have the status of "permanent members." These are China, France, Great Britain, the Russian Federation, and the United States. Permanent members have veto power over all decisions of the Council. The veto gives any permanent member the authority to stop the Security Council from taking an action.

In the event of warfare between two or more states, the Security Council will try to arrange a cease-fire. Once this occurs, the Council may send a peacekeeping mission to the area of conflict to help maintain the truce and to keep the opposing forces apart. On very rare occasions, the Security Council has used military action to enforce its decisions. The best example of this is the intervention of UN troops in the Korean War during 1950–1953. Canada contributed military forces to the UN operation.

In 1956, Lester Pearson, then Canada's secretary of state for external affairs, was instrumental in bringing about the United Nation's first major peacekeeping operation. British, French, and Israeli forces had invaded Egypt after Egyptian President Nasser had nationalized the Suez Canal. As Canada's representative at the United Nations, Pearson persuaded the Security Council to approve the sending of a UN Emergency Force to Egypt to supervise the withdrawal of the invading forces. Pearson was awarded the 1957 Nobel Peace Prize in recognition of his efforts. Since 1956, Canada has participated in almost all UN peacekeeping missions.

The UN Charter also permits the Security Council to impose **sanctions** against states threatening or breaking the peace. Sanctions are a kind of penalty and can take a number of forms; for example, breaking of vital importing or exporting relationships with a nation.

In 1990, the UN Security Council imposed economic sanctions against Iraq after it invaded Kuwait and refused to withdraw its forces. Following the Persian Gulf War (1990–1991) and the restoration of Kuwait sovereignty, the Security Council voted to continue sanctions against Iraq. The United Nations had to be satisfied that Iraq had dismantled all weapons of mass destruction—and the facilities to develop them—before it withdrew sanctions.

In 2001, UN sanctions remained in effect, although restrictions had been eased for several years under an "oil for food" provision. This arrangement allowed Iraq to sell certain quantities of oil and oil products so it could buy some essential goods for its people. The Iraqi population has suffered malnutrition and other serious health problems because of the sanctions.

The Law | The Charter of the United Nations

An excerpt from the *Charter of the United Nations*

Chapter VII, Article 41

The Security Council may decide what measures not involving the use of armed force are to be employed to give effect to its decisions, and it may call upon the Members of the United Nations to apply such measures. These may include complete or partial interruption of economic relations and of rail, sea, postal, telegraphic, radio, and other means of communication, and the severance of diplomatic relations.

For Discussion

1. **How might sanctions affect a country's population?**
2. **Should innocent civilians suffer under sanctions for the mistakes of their government?**
3. **What practical problems make enforcing sanctions difficult?**

The International Court of Justice

The International Court of Justice (ICJ), or World Court, is the judicial arm of the United Nations. Based in The Hague, the Netherlands, the ICJ hears only civil cases. Only member states of the United Nations can bring cases before the ICJ.

The International Court of Justice bases its decisions on international law. It has had limited success, hearing only a small number of cases since its creation in 1945. Many countries say they are not willing to submit themselves to the jurisdiction of the ICJ. On occasion, countries involved in a dispute have agreed to submit a dispute to the ICJ on a conditional basis. The effect of this is to make any ICJ decisions not binding.

A Permanent International Criminal Court?

In 1945, when four nations established the International Military Tribunal in Nuremberg, Germany, they were taking the first step toward creating a permanent international criminal court. The Nuremberg Tribunal tried Nazi leaders for crimes punishable under international law. A trial of this nature had never been held before, and it established important new precedents in international law.

The Charter of the Nuremberg Tribunal defined three classes of international crimes:

- crimes against peace (planning or waging a war in violation of treaties or agreements)
- **war crimes** (violations of the customs of war, e.g., murder, slave labour, murder or ill-treatment of prisoners of war, killing of hostages, plunder of public or private property)
- crimes against humanity (murder, extermination, enslavement, deportation, or persecution on political, racial, or religious grounds)

During the 1990s, interest in establishing a permanent international court gained new support. Revelations about the horrors of "ethnic cleansing" in the former Yugoslavia, where widespread killing and mistreatment of civilians took place, and genocide in Rwanda, shocked people around the world.

In 1993, the UN Security Council established the International Criminal Tribunal in The Hague, the Netherlands. This court has the authority to prosecute persons responsible for committing serious criminal violations of international law in the former Yugoslavia and Rwanda. In 1996, Justice Louise Arbour of the Court of Appeal for Ontario was appointed to a four-year term as chief prosecutor for the International Criminal Tribunal.

In 1998, at a conference in Rome, representatives from more than 110 countries signed a treaty to establish a permanent international criminal court. Located in The Hague, the court will hear cases related to war crimes.

Review Your Understanding (Pages 22 to 29)

1. How is sovereignty a key concept in international law?
2. Distinguish between customary law and treaties as sources of international law.
3. What matters do international treaties govern?
4. Outline the process by which international treaties are made.
5. Why is the United Nations such an important international organization? Evaluate the importance of the United Nations in terms of international security.
6. Distinguish between the UN General Assembly and the Security Council.
7. Should individuals, and not just states, be held accountable for wartime actions? Explain.

On September 11, 2001, international terrorists unleashed a series of attacks against the United States. Television images of the destruction were broadcast live to a global audience. Although these attacks were confined to American soil, people around the world expressed disbelief and outrage.

The chain of events began early in the morning, when teams of terrorists hijacked four American passenger jets shortly after takeoff from Boston and New York. At 8:45 A.M., the hijackers of American Airlines Flight 11 deliberately crashed the plane into the north tower of the World Trade Center (WTC) in New York City. At 9:03 A.M., a second hijacked airliner smashed into the WTC's south tower. Although the 110-storey towers withstood the impact initially, they began to melt from the extreme heat of the burning jet fuel. At 10:05 A.M., the south tower collapsed, followed by the north tower at 10:28 A.M.

Meanwhile, at 9:43 A.M., American Airlines Flight 77 crashed into the Pentagon building near Washington, DC. Twenty minutes later, the fourth aircraft plunged into an empty field near Pittsburgh, Pennsylvania, as passengers battled with their hijackers to retake control. The total death toll from these attacks was 19 terrorists and more than 2600 innocent people.

On September 11, Canada responded quickly to the crisis, allowing 242 aircraft bound for the United States to be diverted to Canadian airports. Within weeks after the tragedy, Canada mounted its own defence against escalating global terrorism: a comprehensive and far-reaching anti-terrorism plan.

The stated objectives of Canada's anti-terrorism plan are to protect Canadians from terrorist acts; stop terrorists from entering Canada; arrest and prosecute terrorists; work with American authorities to secure

Figure 1-19
The World Trade Center's twin towers melted and collapsed following the terrorist attacks on September 11, 2001.

the Canada–U.S. border; and cooperate with the international community to bring terrorists to justice. In brief, the anti-terrorism plan is Canada's answer to the question: What must a country do to maintain its security in light of the events of September 11?

To accomplish these objectives, the federal government has taken a number of actions, including:

Border Security: increasing the number of immigration control officers overseas to detect fraudulent documents and identify criminals, terrorists, and others ineligible for entry before they reach Canada; introducing a fraud-resistant "resident card" for new residents; increasing security staff at ports of entry; streamlining deportation orders against those who violate Canada's immigration laws; purchasing new equipment and other technologies to uncover and deter terrorist activities; and joining the United States as a full partner in integrated border enforcement teams.

International Law Enforcement: collaborating with international law enforcement agencies to identify and dismantle terrorist organizations and networks; freezing the assets of organizations in Canada that fund or facilitate international terrorism; and preventing these groups from raising money.

Military Action: sending a Canadian naval task group to the Arabian Sea in late 2001; and sending ground forces to Afghanistan in early 2002. Both initiatives supported U.S. operations against pro-terrorist forces in Afghanistan.

New Laws: introducing sweeping new legislation— such as the *Anti-Terrorism Act* and the *Public Safety Act*—to fight terrorism.

The *Anti-Terrorism Act* received **royal assent** on December 18, 2001. This legislation created ways to deter (prevent), disable, identify, prosecute, convict, and punish terrorist groups and their members operating in Canada. Highlights of the new law include:
- a legal definition of terrorism
- terrorist offences defined and added to the *Criminal Code*
- new investigative tools for law enforcement agencies, including more power to use electronic surveillance
- new powers for police to make preventive arrests of suspected terrorists, without charge. Police may also compel (pressure) individuals with information about a terrorist group or a terrorist

offence to appear before a judge to provide that information
- changes to courtroom proceedings to protect classified information

In November 2001, the federal government proposed the *Public Safety Act,* the other cornerstone of its anti-terrorism legislation. The *Public Safety Act* brought changes to numerous federal statutes, including the *Aeronautics Act,* the *Immigration Act,* and the *National Defence Act.* It also made law the *Biological and Toxin Weapons Conventions Implementation Act.* Provisions of the *Public Safety Act* include the following:
- authority for Cabinet ministers to issue "interim orders" to deal with immediate threats and emergencies
- tighter security over aviation, explosives, pipelines, and transmission lines
- controls over the export and transfer of technologies sensitive to national security
- measures to prevent money laundering by terrorists and the proliferation (spread) of biological weapons
- powers to arrest and detain foreign nationals within Canada who cannot properly identify themselves
- declaration of hoaxes causing public danger or anxiety as criminal offences
- authority for the federal government to establish "military protection zones"

Some commentators have referred to the events of September 11 as the defining moment of the 21st century. Only history will tell if this is true. What is certain is that September 11 was a potent agent of change in Canada, resulting in increased government powers, changes in Canadian law and attitudes toward national security, and closer ties to the United States.

For Discussion

1. **What new measures have been taken by border officials to increase security?**

2. **What new powers do law enforcement officials have under the *Anti-Terrorism Act*? Could these powers violate rights of law-abiding citizens? Explain.**

3. **Under the *Anti-Terrorism Act,* is compelling individuals to provide information a violation of individual rights? Explain.**

4. **Speculate on future developments to Canada's anti-terrorism plan.**

Mediation: Can It Replace the Courts?

Traditionally, courts have handled disputes over legal issues such as property damage, inheritance, or child custody. However, in recent years, overcrowding of the courts has created a backlog of cases. Delays can result in injustice for many; and the expense of court cases can deny justice to people with a low income. Alternatives to using the courts to solve disputes have become more popular.

Several methods of **alternative dispute resolution (ADR)** have been developed to settle legal conflicts outside the courts:

- Negotiation: Two parties communicate with each other until a decision is reached.
- Mediation: A third party (a mediator) listens to the two parties in the dispute and helps them make a decision that both will accept.
- Arbitration: A third party (an arbitrator) listens to the two parties and makes a decision. Often, the arbitrator is a respected expert, and the parties must agree in advance to accept the arbitrator's decision.

The most commonly used method is mediation. Mediators are neutral parties who are trained to help the people involved in the dispute come up with solutions to their problems. The mediator hopes that if the parties find a solution that seems fair to both, they will abide by it.

Mediation is not new. It has long been used successfully to resolve disputes between labour and management. However, ADR programs are now finding their way into other areas of law. The Canadian Bar Association, the professional association of lawyers, has counselled its members to become experts in ADR methods. Its journal has referred to ADR as a "growth industry."

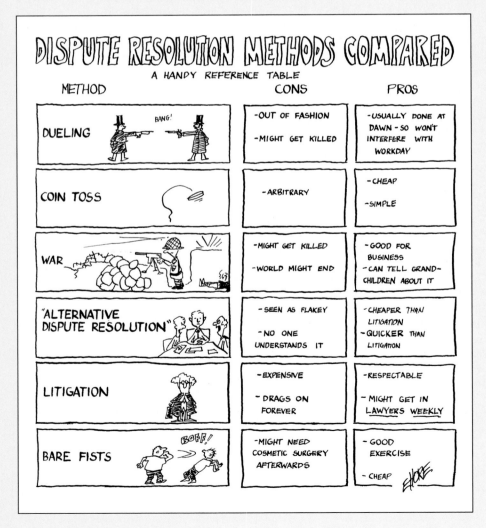

Figure 1-20

From war to ADR, this cartoon summarizes the options.

On One Side

Those who support mediation programs to deal with most conflict situations argue that the court system takes too long, is too expensive, and does not guarantee satisfaction.

They suggest that if people learn how to use ADR, including anger and stress management, they will come to accept and even expect to settle their differences through conflict resolution programs. As far as crime is concerned, they argue that the majority of crimes in Canada are nonviolent. Many of these cases could also be settled through mediation. This would relieve the criminal courts of a tremendous burden.

On the Other Side

Critics of ADR believe that mediation is fine for small disagreements, but not for legal battles. They argue that each party wants to win the case, and probably prefers to gamble on winning the case in court.

They also point out that ADR methods would not necessarily be cheaper because the same lawyers who would represent the disputants (the people involved in the dispute) in court now offer their services as mediators. They believe that ADR will just create another layer of bureaucracy and expense for disputants.

Instead of ADR, critics advocate speeding up the legal system and making it more efficient, by creating more courts and appointing more judges to handle the backlog of cases.

The Bottom Line

A solution for the long delays in Canada's justice system must be found. Greedy landlords and employers, for example, sometimes depend on the fact that their victims cannot afford the long wait for justice from the civil courts. Charges against criminal suspects are sometimes dropped because delays violate the rights of the accused under the *Canadian Charter of Rights and Freedoms* (see *habeas corpus*, page 17). But dropping the charges violates the rights of the victim.

activity

Visit **www.law.nelson.com** and follow the links to learn more about ADR as a mechanism for conflict resolution.

What Do You Think?

1. **Assume that you have been consulted as a legal expert to offer your recommendation for which process is more appropriate to resolve a legal dispute. For each case, give a rationale for selecting either the mediation process or the court process.**
   - **Divorced parents both want sole custody of their child.**
   - **A divorcing couple can't agree on who should get the car.**
   - **A woman accuses a man of stalking her, but he denies it.**
   - **A university student wants to move out of his apartment, but he has signed a lease.**
   - **A woman is charged with killing her spouse.**
   - **A teen is caught shoplifting a pair of jeans.**
   - **A man believes he has been wrongly dismissed from his job.**

2. **Assume that you are involved in a labour dispute over the issue of working conditions. Create an organizer that evaluates the advantages and disadvantages of each alternative dispute resolution method (negotiation, mediation, and arbitration) in resolving the labour dispute. Based on the information in your organizer, recommend one of the three approaches to resolve the dispute. For extended research, interview a labour union representative and report on his or her view of the merits of each method of dispute resolution.**

Chapter Review

Chapter Highlights

- Canada is a democracy. Its citizens elect law makers who make laws that suit the majority of Canadians.
- Rules and laws are necessary to keep peace, order, and fairness.
- Laws tell people what they can and cannot do, and settle disagreements.
- The *Canadian Charter of Rights and Freedoms* helps to protect the rights of Canadians.
- Public law controls the relationship between the government and the people.
- Criminal law defines offences against society.
- Constitutional law outlines the structure of the federal and provincial governments and their respective powers.
- Private (civil) law outlines the rights and responsibilities of private citizens and organizations.
- Old laws are often the basis of modern laws. Some important sources of modern law are the Code of Hammurabi, Mosaic law, Roman law, and the Napoleonic Code.
- Lawyers and judges refer to earlier court decisions called precedents.
- A law passed by Parliament is called a statute.
- Canada's first constitution was called the *British North America Act*.
- The name of Canada's Constitution today is the *Constitution Act, 1982*.
- The House of Commons is the most powerful branch of Parliament because it passes most laws.
- International law regulates the conduct of states and is based on customary laws, and international treaties and resolutions.
- The United Nations is the most prominent international organization in the world today.
- The International Court of Justice rules on civil disputes between states.

Review Key Terms

Name the key terms that are described below.

a) a state's authority to govern itself
b) the legal right of a person who is imprisoned without explanation to appear in court within a reasonable time
c) agreement between states to return fugitives from justice to their home countries
d) lists basic facts in a legal case and makes it easy to locate the case in a law library
e) a political, social, and economic system that existed in Europe between the 9th and 15th centuries that was based on the relationship of lord and vassal
f) a person who is sued in a civil action or charged with a criminal offence
g) the basic rule that neither individuals nor the government is above the law
h) to seek to influence the government to make certain laws
i) a prosecutor in criminal matters who works on behalf of society
j) a court decision used to decide a similar case
k) penalties or restrictions imposed on a country
l) the procedure to change Canada's Constitution
m) criminal acts that violate the customs of war
n) the authority or power to make laws
o) the person who sues in a civil action
p) a proposed law

Check Your Knowledge

1. Explain the importance of the common-law system of precedent to the development of our contemporary legal system.

2. How does the rule of law ensure a just and fair system of law today?

3. Differentiate between criminal law and civil law.

4. Identify one of the most important functions of Parliament.

Apply Your Learning

5. After a big argument over a family matter, a teenage son strikes his father, causing serious injury.
   a) Under Babylonian law, has the son committed an offence? If so, what would have been the punishment?

b) Under Mosaic law, what penalty would the son have received?

c) Under current Canadian law, what penalty might the son receive?

6. Your community institutes a voluntary "blue box" recycling program. In a television interview, Gina states that she does not intend to recycle because she does not have time to rinse her metal cans and plastic containers.

a) Why would Gina *not* be breaking the law?

b) How could the recycling program receive the status of a law?

7. *R. v. Dudley and Stephens* (1884), 14 Q.B.D. 273 (England)

The accused, Dudley and Stephens, along with Brooks and a 17-year-old boy, Parker, were shipwrecked some 2500 km from the Cape of Good Hope in an open boat. They had only two tins of turnip and no water. On the fourth day, they caught a turtle. After that, they had no more food. They managed to catch some rainwater in their oilskin caps.

On the 18th day, Dudley and Stephens spoke to Brooks about what should be done if no more food was obtained. They suggested that Parker, who was suffering the most and had no family, should be sacrificed to save the rest. Brooks disagreed.

On the 20th day, while Parker was asleep, Dudley made signs to Stephens and Brooks indicating the youth should be killed. Stephens agreed; Brooks dissented. Dudley offered a prayer and killed Parker. The three men then fed on the remains of the youth for four days, at which time a passing vessel picked them up. They were returned to England, where Dudley and Stephens were put on trial for murder.

The accused were found guilty of the charge, because there was no legal justification for their killing of Parker. However, Queen Victoria granted them royal mercy and commuted (changed) their death sentence to one of life imprisonment because of public sentiment and concern. The legal authorities then took further action and released Dudley and Stephens after six months' imprisonment.

a) Why wasn't Brooks charged with murder? Do you agree? Why or why not?

b) Should Dudley and Stephens have been charged with murder? Why or why not?

c) As the Crown attorney, outline your case against the accused.

d) Five judges tried this case. The argument presented by the defence dealt mainly with the necessity of the actions of the accused for their survival. Should necessity be a valid argument or defence? Explain.

8. In August 2001, the International Criminal Tribunal at The Hague convicted Radislav Krstic of genocide. Krstic is a former Bosnian Serb general. International law defines genocide as "acts committed with intent to destroy, in whole or in part, a national, ethnical, racial, or religious group."

Krstic was sentenced to 46 years in prison for his role in the massacre of more than 7000 unarmed Muslim men and boys in Srebrenica in July 1995. During the trial, prosecutors presented evidence of the crime, including accounts of survivors, documents from the Bosnian military, and photos of mass graves. The three presiding judges concluded that while Krstic did not order the assault on Srebrenica, he played a key role in the executions and deportations that followed.

a) Under what class of international crimes does genocide fall?

b) What evidence did prosecutors use to prove the case against Krstic?

c) Decide whether or not the sentence that Krstic received was fair. Justify your answer.

Communicate Your Understanding

9. The Magna Carta is now recognized as one of the most important documents in the development of democracy. Here are three of its clauses:

"No freeman shall be taken, imprisoned except by the lawful judgment of his peers [equals], or by the law of the land."

"To no one will we sell, to none will we deny or delay, right or justice."

"No scutage [tax] shall be imposed except by the consent of the common council."

Using your own words, interpret the meaning of each clause. Explain why each clause is important in a free society.

10. In pairs, select one of the topics below. One student will prepare an argument in favour of the statement and the other student will prepare a counterargument against the statement. Support your position with examples.
    a) People are basically bad. They need laws and punishments to control them.
    b) The crime rates in Canada are high because the punishments are too weak.
    c) Canadian law makers should bring in punishments similar to those in the Code of Hammurabi and Mosaic law.

Develop Your Thinking

11. You have been asked to create a brief legal history lesson for students in an introductory history course at your high school. Create an organizer chart that identifies the various historical legal systems that have contributed to contemporary Canadian law. In your chart, identify the system, briefly summarize its main beliefs and values, and identify the influence on our current laws.

12. How have laws and rules affected your daily activities today? Develop your answer by clearly indicating examples where rules have influenced your actions and areas where laws have regulated your conduct.

13. Why are international laws important in the global society? Identify major obstacles to achieving international agreements and cooperation. Extend your research by providing examples from current print media or from news on the Internet.

The Rights and Freedoms of Canadians

Focus Questions

- How has the concept of human rights developed over the years?
- What rights exist in the *Canadian Charter of Rights and Freedoms* to protect Canadians?
- How do Canadian courts interpret the *Charter*?
- Has the *Charter* given the courts too much power?
- What rights do provincial Human Rights Codes and the *Canadian Human Rights Act* protect, and how are they enforced?

Chapter at a Glance

Figure 2-1

Police and activists clash at the Quebec City Summit of the Americas in April 2001. Should police be allowed to use force during demonstrations? How do you respect both the rights of trade delegates and the rights of protesters during trade talks?

2.1 ___Introduction___

Canada is often considered to be one of the best countries in the world in which to live. One reason for this is that Canada places a high value on **civil rights** and freedoms and on human rights. It is important to understand that civil rights and freedoms limit the power that a government has over its citizens. **Human rights** protect people from being unfairly discriminated against by other individuals. Compared to people in many other countries, Canadians can feel secure in almost all areas of their lives. Canadians are free because laws are passed and enforced to protect their rights and freedoms. In fact, many other countries look toward Canada as an example of what a free society can be.

Wealth, gender, race, age, beliefs, family status, and so on are not supposed to determine how you are treated in Canada. Today, everyone is considered equal under the law. This belief is a foundation of Canadian society and Canadian law. As a result, Canadians expect their laws to be fair and just for everyone. This situation is quite new. In Chapter 3 you will learn that Canada has not always treated different groups of people as if they were equal.

Being equal under the law is a very recent legal concept in human history. If you were born a slave in ancient Babylon in 1700 B.C.E., you had few legal rights—unless you married someone of a higher class. If you were born a peasant in 16th-century France, you would probably die a peasant. For thousands of years, the vast majority of people had few, or no, rights. People had little opportunity to improve their lives. It took many hundreds of years for the concept of human rights and freedoms to take root and spread. Many wars and revolutions had to be fought. In the next section, a few major events in that struggle will be examined.

2.2 ___The Development of Human Rights and Freedoms___

As you learned in Chapter 1, the earliest legal codes imposed laws and punishments that most Canadians today would consider cruel. These laws were meant to ensure that these societies would survive. Concerns about human rights matters simply were not an issue.

Much later, events in England exposed dramatic changes in beliefs about rights and freedom. In 1215 C.E., King John signed the Magna Carta. This was historic because it limited the monarch's power, which had once been absolute. Only lords and barons received more rights, however, not ordinary people. More than 400 years later, Queen Mary II and her husband William III had to sign the English *Bill of Rights* in 1689 in order to rule from the throne. All future monarchs had to promise to obey the laws of Parliament and to allow free elections. But again, only nobles and wealthy landowners could vote and control Parliament.

These and other events showed that beliefs about rights could lead to changes in the way people were governed. By the end of the 17th century

Did You Know?

It was 1832 before middle-class men got the **franchise** (right to vote) in England. Working-class men had to wait until 1885. English women didn't get the franchise at all until 1918, and then they had to be over the age of 30.

in the West, human beings were thought by many legal and moral thinkers to have **natural rights,** such as the rights to life, liberty, and security. Such rights were thought to exist independently of any rights or duties created by ruler, government, Church, or society. Those in power were very threatened by these ideas, which spread quickly in Europe and North America.

Rights and Revolutions

In 1775, the American Revolution broke out when people in the Thirteen Colonies fought for their independence from Great Britain. Anger had grown as the Parliament in London passed laws that suited Great Britain, not its colonies. Americans were outraged. They had no elected representatives in the British Parliament. The British ignored American demands and imposed new taxes. Parliament also passed laws that restricted the territory into which the American colonies could expand. Protests became violent, and such slogans as "no taxation without representation" stirred up resentment against the British.

On July 4, 1776, the American Congress issued the *Declaration of Independence.* Written by Thomas Jefferson, it proclaimed the existence of a new country—the United States of America. Great Britain, the most powerful nation in the world at the time, sent in more troops and ships to fight the revolutionary forces. The war raged on until 1783, when the Americans drove out the last British forces at New York. The *Treaty of Paris* was signed, and the United States of America was born.

It took several years for the Constitution of the United States to be written and agreed upon. It became law in 1788. The group of generally wealthy, educated men who created it did not include a bill of rights. Like many thinkers of the time, they feared that giving rights to common people might lead to "mob rule." In other words, most people couldn't be trusted to govern themselves. Critics attacked the Constitution saying the new government would abuse the civil rights of Americans—just as the British government had. In

The Law   The American Declaration of Independence

Excerpts from the American *Declaration of Independence* (1776)

We hold these truths to be self-evident, that all Men are created equal, that they are endowed by their Creator with certain unalienable Rights ... these are Life, Liberty, and the pursuit of Happiness.

- That to secure these rights, Governments are instituted among Men, deriving their just powers from the consent of the governed.
- That whenever any Form of Government becomes destructive of these ends, it is the Right of the People to alter or to abolish it.

For Discussion

1. In your own words, write down the major understandings contained in these excerpts.

2. Why was this document so revolutionary?

3. As Canadians, do we accept these ideas today? If so, in what ways?

Figure 2-2

King Louis XVI was beheaded during the French Revolution.

1791, 10 **amendments** (changes) were made to the Constitution. These became the U.S. *Bill of Rights*, and they are still the basis of freedom and civil rights for Americans.

The American Revolution (1775–1783) inspired people in many parts of the world, including what is now Canada. The revolution itself was influenced by new ideas that had been sweeping through England, France, and other parts of the West. In the 17th and 18th centuries, scientific breakthroughs led philosophers to believe that human societies must be improved. They questioned the powers of the Church and rulers. Perhaps the most revolutionary idea was that the rules governing people must be changed if they failed to protect the "natural rights" of citizens.

In the 18th century (1700s), a group of French thinkers known as the *philosophes* wrote books and pamphlets attacking the power of the French king, nobles, and the Church. They wanted an end to the feudal system and more freedom for the French people. These ideas helped start the American Revolution. France also sent ships and troops to help the Americans. Returning soldiers brought back stories of the successful American Revolution and the ideas of liberty and equality. This fed the growing demands for change in France.

In 1789, the year after the U.S. Constitution became law, the French people rose up to overthrow their rulers. Thousands and thousands of people died. The kings and nobles of Europe attacked the new nation, but were fought back. Never before had the common people of a country in Europe successfully overthrown their monarch, nobles, and Church. Feudalism and the privileges of rulers and Church were abolished. A National Assembly (similar to the House of Commons) was set up, and its members were elected by the people. The Western idea of a "nation–state," as we understand it today, came out of these revolutions. Previously, people had owed their loyalty to lords, monarchs, and the Church.

On August 26, 1789, the National Assembly passed the *Declaration of the Rights of Man and of the Citizen*. It guaranteed all French citizens their basic freedoms and became the basis of future modern democracies.

The Law The Declaration of the Rights of Man and of the Citizen

Excerpts from the *Declaration of the Rights of Man and of the Citizen*

The representatives of the French people, organized in National Assembly ... set forth in a solemn declaration the natural, inalienable, and sacred rights of man.

Article 1. Men are born and remain free and equal in rights.

Article 2. The aim of every political association is the preservation of the natural ... rights of man. These rights are Liberty, Property, Security, and Resistance to Oppression.

Article 3. The source of all sovereignty [independence and the power to make laws] lies essentially in the Nation.

continued ▶

Article 4. Liberty consists of the power to do whatever is not injurious to others.

Article 7. No man may be accused, arrested, or detained except in cases determined by the Law.

Article 9. [E]very man is presumed innocent until declared guilty.

Article 11. Free communication of ideas and opinions is one of the most precious of the rights of man. Consequently, every citizen may speak, write and publish freely.

Article 17. Since the right to Property is ... sacred, no one may be deprived thereof unless a legally established public necessity obviously requires it.

For Discussion

1. What groups of people in French society would oppose the *Declaration of the Rights of Man and of the Citizen*? Which ones would approve? Explain why.

2. What is so revolutionary about this document?

3. According to this law passed by the National Assembly, where does all power lie?

4. Explain what is meant by the word "nation" in this document.

5. Compare the excerpts from the American *Declaration of Independence* (1776) with the *Declaration of the Rights of Man and of the Citizen* (1789). What similarities exist?

The Abolition of Slavery

Many groups of people did not gain rights during the revolutions of the 18th century. Slaves continued to be legally defined as "property," not as "humans" or "citizens." Over a 300-year period, 15 million people had been captured in Africa to be traded as slaves in Europe and North America. They and their children were seen only as a source of labour. During the 19th century, most Western countries came to see the injustice in this system and abolished slavery.

Some countries fought wars over slavery. In North America, the Southern states separated from the United States after Abraham Lincoln became president in 1861 on a platform of opposing the spread of slavery. The bloody American Civil War (1861–1865) broke out, and more than 600 000 people were killed before it ended. The Northern, or Union, forces fought to abolish slavery. The Southern, or Confederate, forces fought to keep slavery legal. In 1865, the Northern forces won, and the 13th amendment to the U.S. Constitution abolished slavery forever.

The Universal Declaration of Human Rights

World War II was the most destructive war in history and one that truly spanned the globe. Millions of people were killed, most of them defenceless civilians. Before World War II began,

Figure 2-3

The atomic bomb was used for the first and only time against human beings at the end of World War II. How did this affect public awareness of human rights?

e activity

The United Nations plays a key role in the fight for human rights. Visit **www.law.nelson.com** and follow the links to learn more about how the United Nations works globally against injustice.

e activity

Visit **www.law.nelson.com** and follow the links to learn about the work of the Canadian Human Rights Foundation and its role in human rights education in Canada and around the world.

the German government targeted groups of people to be rounded up and sent to prison camps. These included Jews, the Roma (gypsies), gays and lesbians, people with mental disabilities, and members of certain religious faiths and political parties. Many of the prison camps later became extermination camps, where millions of prisoners were killed. People around the world were horrified when the camps were opened up after the war. More than 6 million Jewish men, women, and children had been slaughtered.

In 1945, world leaders formed a new international organization: the United Nations. Its stated purpose was "to save succeeding generations from the scourge of war." One of the first steps the United Nations took was to try to guarantee all people certain rights and freedoms. These are what we understand today to be "human rights." Unlike "natural rights," human rights are quite detailed in order to include all groups of people. To achieve this goal, the UN Human Rights Commission was set up to produce a list of human rights and freedoms for all people throughout the world.

The *Universal Declaration of Human Rights* was adopted by the United Nations on December 10, 1948. It was the first time nations from around the world had signed a formal agreement on specific rights and freedoms for all human beings. The Declaration listed these rights in detail and has been used to raise awareness of their importance ever since. It is, however, only a vision of the world as it could be. For billions of people, perhaps the majority of people, its guarantees are unfulfilled. More than 50 years after it was passed, the Declaration remains a standard that many countries have tried to live up to and to put into effect.

The Law · The Universal Declaration of Human Rights

Excerpts from the *Universal Declaration of Human Rights*

Article 1
All human beings are born free and equal in dignity and rights.

Article 2
Everyone is entitled to all the rights set forth in this Declaration, without distinction of any kind, such as race, colour, sex, language, religion, political or other opinion, national or social origin, property, birth or other status.

Article 3
Everyone has the right to life, liberty and security of person.

Article 4
No one shall be held in slavery or servitude.

Article 5
No one shall be subjected to torture or to cruel, inhuman or degrading treatment or punishment.

Article 7
All are equal before the law and are entitled without any discrimination to equal protection of the law.

Article 9
No one shall be subjected to arbitrary arrest, detention or exile.

Article 11
1) Everyone charged with a penal offense has the right to be presumed innocent until proved guilty according to law in a public trial.

Article 13
1) Everyone has the right to freedom of movement.

Article 18
Everyone has the right to freedom of thought, conscience and religion.

Article 19
Everyone has the right to freedom of opinion and expression.

continued ▶

Article 20

1) Everyone has the right to freedom of peaceful assembly and association.

Article 23

2) Everyone, without any discrimination, has the right to equal pay for equal work.

For Discussion

1. Summarize or paraphrase each section in these excerpts. Share your interpretation with other class members.

2. Compare the clauses of the *Universal Declaration of Human Rights* to other, earlier documents that you have studied.

Which new clauses have been added in this document?

3. Justify the importance of documents like the *Universal Declaration of Human Rights* to the international community.

4. Which countries do you know of that do not live up to the human rights listed in this document? Give specific examples.

5. What action can be taken by the international community to enforce human rights in countries where they are ignored?

6. Explain why the *Universal Declaration of Human Rights* has been called the "Magna Carta of humanity."

Agents of Change   John Humphrey

It is 1998, in Ottawa. The occasion is the 50th anniversary of the *Universal Declaration of Human Rights*. Nelson Mandela, president of South Africa, is unveiling a memorial to a great Canadian: John Humphrey. Most Canadians have never heard of Humphrey, but to Mandela he is a human rights pioneer. John Humphrey is the person who wrote the first draft of the *Universal Declaration of Human Rights*, a document that changed the world.

Humphrey was born to a prosperous family in New Brunswick in 1905, but his childhood was not exactly easy. His father died when Humphrey was a baby. Then, at the age of seven, Humphrey had to have one arm amputated. Children at school taunted him. Humphrey fought back many times, only to be physically punished at school. These early experiences shaped Humphrey. He learned that fighting solved nothing and that individual rights had to be protected against authorities, including governments. He went on to study law at McGill University in Montreal during the Great Depression (1929–1939), and the suffering he witnessed had a great impact on him.

Humphrey came to believe that people must have economic, cultural, and social rights. And if these human rights were to have any legal power, they would have to be tied to civil and political rights. Without such legally recognized human rights, people would continue to suffer and be exploited.

These convictions led Humphrey to the United Nations just after World War II. As the first director of the United Nations' human rights division, he put his beliefs into his drafts for the *Universal Declaration of Human Rights*. John Humphrey retired from the United Nations in 1966 to teach law at McGill University. He also helped to establish Amnesty International Canada and the Canadian Human Rights Foundation. In 1994, at the age of 89, he stopped teaching at McGill. He died the following year. His achievements have only recently begun to be recognized.

Figure 2-4
John Humphrey

For Discussion

1. Why is John Humphrey considered a human rights pioneer?

2. How did John Humphrey's early experiences shape his interest in rights protection?

3. Why is it important that human rights be tied to civil and political rights?

The U.S. Constitution became law in 1788 without a bill of rights. That took another three years. The *British North America Act* created Canada in 1867, without a bill of rights. That took another 93 years.

- Would this mean that people enjoyed fewer rights in Canada than in the United States? Explain.

Review Your Understanding (Pages 38 to 43)

1. Why is Canada considered to be one of the best countries in which to live?
2. Explain the meaning of the term "natural rights."
3. Briefly describe the factors that led to the American Revolution.
4. What impact did the U.S. *Bill of Rights* have on the development of laws?
5. What factors contributed to the French Revolution? What effect did the revolution have on the system of government in France?
6. The abolition of slavery is considered to be an important and necessary step in the advancement of human rights. Justify why this is so.
7. Explain the significance of the *Universal Declaration of Human Rights*.

2.3 Human Rights in Canada after World War II

As you learned in Chapter 1, much of Canadian law is based on English common law. Common law is unwritten and based on customs and earlier court decisions. As a result, for many years Canadians had legal rights that were not written down but simply understood to exist. One example of this was the right to be charged and tried in a court of law if accused of a crime. After the rights abuses of World War II, many Canadians came to believe that legal rights had to be written down.

In 1945, John Diefenbaker, a young member of Parliament, led a movement to have these rights made into law. He was defeated by MPs who thought that Canada's tradition of common law was good enough. Diefenbaker later became leader of the Progressive Conservative party. In federal election campaigns in 1957 and 1958, he promised a bill of rights for all Canadians.

As prime minister, Diefenbaker kept his promise. Parliament passed the *Canadian Bill of Rights* on August 10, 1960. This federal legislation was not revolutionary. It merely set down in legislation the civil rights and freedoms that Canadians had already enjoyed under common law. It also reminded Canadians of the importance of individual rights.

Figure 2-5

This photograph of Prime Minister John Diefenbaker was taken in 1958, the year in which he promised Canadians their own bill of rights.

Constitutional Protection of Civil Rights

The *Canadian Bill of Rights* did not stop demands for stronger rights protections and was criticized for several reasons. As a federal statute (law), it applied only to federally controlled matters, and Parliament could change it at any time. Not only that, it did little to protect equality rights.

The Law — The Canadian Bill of Rights

The *Canadian Bill of Rights* gave Canadians, "without discrimination by reason of race, national origin, colour, religion or sex, the following human rights and fundamental freedoms":

- the right to life, liberty, and security of the person and enjoyment of property, and the right not to be deprived thereof except by due process of law
- the right to equality before the law and its protection
- freedom of religion, speech, assembly and association, and the press
- the right not to be arbitrarily detained, imprisoned, or exiled
- the right not to receive cruel and unusual treatment or punishment
- the right to be informed promptly of the reason for arrest
- the right to retain and instruct counsel without delay
- the right to obtain a writ of *habeas corpus* to determine the validity of detention
- the right not to give evidence if denied counsel, and protection against self-incrimination
- the right to a fair hearing
- the right to be presumed innocent until proven guilty
- the right to reasonable bail
- the right to an interpreter in any legal proceedings

For Discussion

1. Justify the importance of these rights for a democracy.
2. Why was the *Canadian Bill of Rights* an important step in the development of civil liberties in Canada?
3. A fundamental principle identified in the *Canadian Bill of Rights* is "the right to be presumed innocent until proven guilty." Evaluate the importance of this principle to our justice system.

In the mid-1960s, a new politician entered federal politics. As leader of the Liberal party, Pierre Elliott Trudeau captured the imagination of Canadians. He spoke of a "just society," and he promised greater social justice and stronger guarantees of individual rights. Trudeau remained prime minister for almost 15 years and radically changed law in Canada. Trudeau set up intense negotiations among the federal and provincial governments and was largely responsible for the *Constitution Act, 1982.* This gave Canada its own constitution for the first time.

Many Canadians consider the *Canadian Charter of Rights and Freedoms* to be the most important part of the *Constitution Act, 1982.* It not only lists the civil rights and freedoms of all Canadians, it guarantees them at every level of government: municipal, provincial, territorial, and federal. The *Charter* is not ordinary statute law, but constitutional law. For any amendment to be made, the federal government and at least two-thirds of the provinces with 50 percent of the population must agree. The rights and freedoms listed in the *Charter* are **entrenched,** or part of the Constitution. The entire *Charter* is located in Appendix A, page 600.

Section 24 of the *Charter* details the "enforcement of guaranteed rights and freedoms." It states that anyone whose *Charter* rights have been **infringed** (violated), may "apply to a court ... to obtain such remedy as the court considers appropriate and just." It also dictates that any evidence presented to a court must be gathered in a manner that respects *Charter* rights and freedoms. Otherwise, it will be excluded.

Charter rights and freedoms, however, are not unlimited. Section 1, the **reasonable limits clause,** makes it clear that laws can set limits on your rights and freedoms as long as these "can be demonstrably justified in a free and democratic society." For example, if you are accused of committing a crime, you have the right to trial by jury. Parliament has limited this right, however. For the least serious offences, only a provincial court judge hears cases. It would be too time-consuming and expensive to have all cases heard by judge and jury. You also have freedom of speech, but you do not have the right to spread lies or malicious statements that might injure another person. Libel laws are in place to stop you from doing this.

Section 52 of the Constitution clearly states that "the Constitution of Canada is the supreme [most powerful] law of Canada, and any law that is inconsistent with the provisions of the Constitution is, to the extent of the inconsistency, of no force or effect." This gives Canadian courts much greater powers than they had before the *Constitution Act, 1982*.

Did You Know?

The right to "enjoyment of property" was included in the *Canadian Bill of Rights* but not in the *Canadian Charter of Rights and Freedoms.*

The purpose of the *Charter* is to limit the power of government. One of the ways it does this is to define the protections of rights and freedoms only in general terms. This allows the courts to decide how these protections are to be adapted and used. As a result, Canada's highest court, the Supreme Court, now plays an even more important role in interpreting Canadian values and beliefs.

With its increased importance, the Supreme Court has also become more controversial. The nine Supreme Court justices (judges) have an enormous responsibility. They must balance individual rights with the needs of the community. Some people support this role for the Court, while others fear the Supreme Court has far too much power. Critics point out that Supreme Court justices are appointed by the prime minister, not elected. This, they say, is undemocratic and Canadians must have the power to elect the justices.

Matters Governed by the Charter

When a case concerning a section of the *Charter* comes before a court, the first thing the court must do is decide whether to hear the case. Section 32 makes it clear what the *Charter* does and does not cover.

The *Charter* does protect individual rights from being trespassed upon by the federal, provincial, and territorial governments. As a result of these legal considerations, *Charter* cases often determine what matters are ***ultra vires*** (outside the authority of the government to legislate) and ***intra vires*** (within the authority of the government to legislate).

How to Analyze a Charter Case

- ☑ **1.** Does the *Charter* apply?
- ☑ **2.** Has a *Charter* right or freedom been infringed?
- ☑ **3.** Does the reasonable limits clause justify the infringement?
- ☑ **4.** If not, is there a remedy provided under section 24?

Figure 2-6

When considering a legal case that involves the *Canadian Charter of Rights and Freedoms*, ask these four questions in sequence.

The *Charter* does not cover private legal matters. For example, if you sued a business because you felt it had discriminated against you, the case would fall under common law or other human rights legislation.

The Notwithstanding Clause

Negotiations for the Constitution were very tense. Several provinces, including Quebec and Alberta, feared that the Constitution would give the federal government too much control over provincial matters. There was also concern that the *Charter* would allow courts to change provincial legislation. At the last minute, the federal government and the provinces agreed to include the famous **notwithstanding clause,** section 33 of the *Charter*. This clause lets provincial and territorial governments enact legislation in spite of the fact, or "notwithstanding," that it may violate the *Charter*. It applies to section 2 and sections 7–15 of the *Charter*.

The notwithstanding clause has rarely been used. Perhaps the most famous case is *Ford v. Quebec (Attorney General)* (1988). In 1988, the Supreme Court of Canada ruled that Quebec's Bill 101 violated the *Canadian Charter of Rights and Freedoms*. Bill 101 stated that all public signs in Quebec must be in French only. The Quebec government argued that the law was needed to ensure the survival of the French language. Using the notwithstanding clause, the Quebec government then passed Bill C-178. This allowed Quebec's French-only law on public signs to stay in effect.

Any legislation that is passed using the notwithstanding clause can stay in effect for five years at most. The clause can then, however, be reenacted. Certain rights cannot be overruled using the notwithstanding clause. These include the right to vote, minority language education rights, and mobility rights.

Figure 2-7

Quebec Premier René Lévesque (right) shrugs his shoulders and walks away from Prime Minister Pierre Trudeau (left) after a chat during the Constitution Conference in September 1980.

Did You Know?

Section 30 in the *Charter* says that when it refers to "provinces," it is also referring to Canada's territories.

Review Your Understanding (Pages 44 to 49)

1. Why were the rights of Canadians not written down for many years?
2. What is the basic difference between the *Canadian Bill of Rights* and the *Canadian Charter of Rights and Freedoms*?
3. The *Constitution Act, 1982,* is considered the most important law in Canada. Present an argument in support of that statement.
4. What role does the Supreme Court of Canada play in shaping Canadian law? (See Issue, page 48.)
5. What criticisms have been made of the Supreme Court of Canada?
6. How does the notwithstanding clause limit the power of the Supreme Court of Canada?

The Supreme Court of Canada and the Charter: Democratic or Anti-Democratic?

When it became law in 1982, the *Canadian Charter of Rights and Freedoms* gave courts broad new powers. It meant that if a court finds that any provincial, territorial, or federal law trespasses on rights protected in the *Charter*, it can **strike down** the law or rule that the law is no longer in effect. This has made the Supreme Court very powerful.

Some Supreme Court decisions have been extremely controversial. For example, in *R. v. Morgentaler* (1988), the Supreme Court struck down Canada's abortion law on the grounds that it violated a woman's right to control her own body. In *R. v. Daviault* (1994), it ruled that extreme drunkenness may be a defence in rape. According to that decision, convicting someone who does not know what he or she was doing is a violation of his or her *Charter* rights.

Here are some other cases in which Supreme Court decisions have bewildered many Canadians.

- In *R. v. Silveira* (1995), the Court upheld a conviction for cocaine trafficking, even though the police unfairly searched the accused and abused his constitutional rights. The Court argued that because cocaine use has a devastating effect on society, an illegal search would not offend the Canadian public. In the same year, in *R. v. Collins; R. v. Pelfrey* (1995), the Court dismissed murder charges against two men saying that they had been unfairly denied their *Charter* right to a speedy trial.

- In *R. v. Monney* (1999), the Court decided that it was legal for customs officers to hold a man suspected of smuggling heroin in plastic bags that he had swallowed. The law states that such suspects must be supervised by medical authorities, not customs officials. The Court ruled that it was in the public interest to hold the man and that his *Charter* rights had not been violated.

Figure 2-8

Justice is one of two statues at the entrance of the Supreme Court of Canada in Ottawa. The other is Truth.

- In *R. v. Oickle* (2000), the Court ruled as admissible a confession made by a man who had set seven fires. Police had extracted the confession through threats, promises, and trickery during hours of interrogation, contrary to the *Charter*. The Court decided that the threat the suspect posed to public safety justified this kind of police action.

As you can see, sometimes the Court protects individual rights guaranteed in the *Charter*, and sometimes it does not.

On One Side

Many Canadians believe that the Supreme Court of Canada has become too powerful and that it is time to reexamine the role that the justices play. They oppose the idea that nine appointed judges can overrule laws made by elected representatives. If laws need to be updated and changed, they say, elected law makers should do this. This is the very heart of democracy.

Other people believe that the Supreme Court is protecting individual rights at the expense of the needs of society. According to them, the *Charter* threatens the welfare and safety of Canadians because it guarantees too many individual rights. It does more to protect criminals than it does to guarantee the rights and freedoms of law-abiding Canadians.

On the Other Side

Many Canadians who support the *Charter* point out that it protects their rights and freedoms from government interference. They believe that the courts can respond to changing social attitudes and beliefs much more quickly than elected governments. Because they want to be reelected, politicians often avoid passing controversial legislation. Supreme Court judges may resent being forced to change laws, but they often feel obligated to do so. Their ability to use the *Charter* to overrule certain laws ensures greater fairness and justice.

The Bottom Line

The *Charter* has changed life and law in Canada. It has often placed judges and their decisions in the media spotlight. Supreme Court decisions are especially important because they affect all Canadians. Recently, the Supreme Court has become more conservative in its decisions. This means that its decisions have tended to support governments and laws that protect society rather than individual rights. Perhaps a balance is being reached between the needs of society and the rights guaranteed in the *Charter*.

What Do You Think?

1. Examine the cases mentioned and evaluate whether the court decisions are in favour of individual rights or the needs of society.
2. When are the courts more likely to suspend individual rights in favour of societal rights?
3. In groups, discuss whether or not Supreme Court decisions are having a negative or positive effect on Canadian society. Share your conclusions.
4. Why do some judges resent being forced to change laws through their decisions?
5. Should the needs of society be more important than individual rights, or should individual rights be protected at all costs?

The Canadian Charter of Rights and Freedoms

If a court decides that a legal case does involve the *Charter*, it must then hear evidence to determine if a guaranteed right has been infringed upon. As noted earlier, section 1 of the *Charter*, the reasonable limits clause, allows your rights and freedoms to be limited if there is a justifiable reason to do so.

While reading the following pages, refer to the text of the *Charter* in Appendix A, page 600.

Section 2: Fundamental Freedoms

Section 2 of the *Charter* lists the basic rights and freedoms of all people in Canada. These are called the "Fundamental Freedoms," and the *Charter* divides them into four areas: freedom of conscience and religion; freedom of thought, belief, opinion, and expression; freedom of peaceful assembly; and freedom of association.

Freedom of Conscience and Religion

Freedom of conscience (the personal sense of right and wrong) and religion means that people are free to practise or not practise religion in Canada, without fear of reprisal or attack. This freedom has led to legal disputes. For example, cases have come before the courts involving people who object to being forced to work on religious holidays or to say religious prayers in public schools. The courts have ruled that governments can impose limits on freedom of religion, as long as those limits do not break fundamental beliefs of the religion. Because Canada is a nation of many faiths, legal conflicts also arise when the beliefs of organized religions conflict with other rights and freedoms that are guaranteed in the *Charter*.

Freedom of Thought, Belief, Opinion, and Expression

This *Charter* clause includes all forms of communication and expression, including the mass media, writing, painting, sculpture, and film. Again, there are limits to this freedom. For example, the *Criminal Code* outlaws inciting hatred toward identifiable groups, which are sometimes targeted because of race, colour, religion, and so on. As well, to guarantee a fair trial, sometimes courts will impose a ban on the media publishing or broadcasting the names of accused persons or victims.

Governments also use **censorship laws,** which ban or limit the availability of materials that are found to be obscene. For example, movies are rated according to the violence, crude language, and sex they contain. This limits who can view these films. These laws are passed to protect the community's moral standards (sense of right and wrong). They are also an effort to protect people who might be vulnerable and harmed by these materials.

Case

Aubry v. Éditions Vice-Versa Inc.

[1998] 1 S.C.R. 591
Supreme Court of Canada

Pascal Claude Aubry took civil action against a photographer and the magazine that employed him. The photographer had taken a photograph of Aubry sitting on the steps of a building when she was 17 years old. The magazine then published it without her permission. Aubry claimed that her right to privacy had been invaded and that her image had been used illegally to help sell the magazine.

The defendants argued that because the photograph had been taken in a public place, Aubry could not reasonably expect privacy. Section 2(b) of the *Charter*, they argued, guarantees freedom of expression. Taking the photo was merely using this right artistically. The trial judge ruled in favour of Aubry and ordered the defendants to pay her $2000 in damages. The Supreme Court of Canada upheld that decision.

For Discussion

1. Identify the issues involved in this case.
2. Why did the trial judge and the Supreme Court of Canada rule in favour of Aubry?
3. What precedent has been set here?
4. What conflicting rights and freedoms are being balanced in this case?

Case

R. v. Keegstra

(1990) 117 N.R. 1
Supreme Court of Canada

James Keegstra taught high school in Eckville, Alberta, from the early 1970s until he was dismissed in 1982. In his history classes, Keegstra taught that the Holocaust, in which 6 million Jews died during World War II, had never happened. He described Jews to students as "treacherous," "sadistic," and "power hungry." He taught that they were responsible for economic depressions, chaos, wars, and revolutions. According to Keegstra's lessons, the Holocaust was a fabrication, part of a Jewish conspiracy to rule the world. Keegstra expected his students to repeat these teachings in class and on exams. If they failed to do so, their marks suffered.

In 1984, Keegstra was charged under section 319(2) [then section 281(2)] of the *Criminal Code* with promoting hatred. This section states: "Everyone who, by communicating statements in any public place, incites hatred against any identifiable group where such incitement is likely to lead to a breach of the peace is guilty of (a) an **indictable** [severe criminal] **offence** and is liable to imprisonment for a term not exceeding two years; or (b) an offence punishable on **summary conviction** [can be tried without jury]."

After the longest trial in Alberta history, Keegstra was convicted by a judge and jury in the Alberta Court of Queen's Bench and fined $5000. Keegstra appealed this to the Alberta Court of Appeal. In June 1988, that court unanimously accepted his argument. It held that the *Criminal Code* provision violated his *Charter* right to freedom of expression, and that the *Criminal Code* section was too broad and not a reasonable limit prescribed by law under section 1 of the *Charter*.

The Crown appealed to the Supreme Court of Canada, where the appeal was heard in December 1989. In a 4 to 3 judgment, the Supreme Court upheld the Crown's appeal. All seven judges agreed that the hate law violated the *Charter*'s section 2(b) guarantee of freedom of expression. But four of them—the majority—believed the violation could be justified under section 1 of the *Charter* because it would help protect victims of hate propaganda. The remaining three judges could not justify the law under section 1.

continued ▶

For Discussion

1. What was Keegstra's main defence for his actions?
2. Did Keegstra abuse the public trust he enjoyed as a teacher?
3. In 1988, Ontario Justice Samuel Grange wrote: "Freedom of speech has never been absolute." Which section of the *Charter* supports this view?
4. After the Court's decision, Jim Keegstra said: "If we all have to think the same way, well, then we're just robots.... We were taught in university that you can be skeptical and no, you'll never be taken to court. Well, you see that's not true anymore." Do you agree with Keegstra's opinion? What section of the *Charter* supports his view?
5. Lorne Shipman, of the League of Human Rights of B'Nai Brith, Canada, said: "This decision serves, as all laws do, as a boundary of reasonable societal behaviour and as a deterrent to those whose intent is to cause hatred and upset our fragile dream of equality for all." Defend or refute this statement, referring to the Keegstra decision.

Freedom of Peaceful Assembly and Freedom of Association

Freedom of peaceful assembly is usually associated with the right to hold or attend a public demonstration. It also includes the right of striking workers to picket outside their place of work. The word "peaceful" is important to understand. It allows the state to impose order if it decides a demonstration or picket is out of control.

The *Criminal Code* prohibits **unlawful assembly.** This occurs when three or more persons who share the same purpose create a disturbance that creates fear in others. If a demonstration or strike turns violent—if property is destroyed, people are hurt, or looting takes place—it may be defined as a **riot.** Under the *Criminal Code*, this means that at least 12 people are assembled and "riotously" disturbing the peace. Police can then read the *Riot Act.* If people refuse to leave, they will be arrested and charged. You may want to look again at the photograph that opens this chapter and define exactly what is happening according to these rights and freedoms.

The Law   The Riot Act

An excerpt from the *Riot Act*

Her Majesty the Queen charges and commands all persons being assembled immediately to disperse and peaceably to depart to their habitations or to their lawful business on the pain of being guilty of an offence for which, on conviction, they may be sentenced to imprisonment for life. GOD SAVE THE QUEEN.

For Discussion

1. Why is the Queen mentioned in this law?
2. The maximum sentence for this crime is life imprisonment. In your opinion, is this too harsh? Justify your answer.

Sections 3, 4, and 5: Democratic Rights

Before 1982, the franchise (right to vote) was not guaranteed in law in Canada. Various election acts defined the right, but these ordinary statutes could be changed at any time by Parliament or provincial legislatures. Today, sections 3, 4, and 5 of the *Charter* guarantee the democratic rights of Canadians. Voting rights, which are covered in section 3, are not unlimited. They can be restricted on such grounds as age, residency, and citizenship, as long as these restrictions can be justified.

Section 6: Mobility Rights

You may take it for granted that you can move freely inside and outside Canada. Although section 6 of the *Charter* guarantees these rights, they are not absolute. Section 6(1) restricts this right to Canadian citizens. Section 6(2) extends the right to move freely within Canada to Canadian citizens and permanent residents.

Sections 6(3) and 6(4) recognize the right of provinces to impose restrictions on mobility. Under section 6(3), provinces can restrict the number of newcomers for economic reasons. For example, newcomers may have to reside in a province for a period of time before they can collect welfare. Under section 6(4), provinces can prevent citizens of other provinces from entering if they are looking for work. A province can only pass such a restriction if its employment rate (percentage of those employed) is less than that in the rest of the country. This would protect the province's citizens who are looking for work.

Sections 7–14: Legal Rights

The legal rights that are guaranteed in the *Charter* will be discussed in detail in Unit 2: Criminal Law.

Sections 15 and 28: Equality Rights

Section 15 was probably the most controversial of all *Charter* clauses. During *Charter* negotiations, lawyers, leaders, and groups debated what exactly "equality" meant. Because phrasing was revised again and again, you should carefully analyze the wording in this clause. The *Charter* and Canadian law go to great lengths to make sure that equality is interpreted as equality.

Subsection (1) of section 15 of the *Charter* guarantees that "every individual" has the right to equal treatment by the law. They are entitled to be treated, "in particular, without discrimination based on race, national or ethnic origin, colour, religion, sex, age or mental or physical disability." It is important to understand the phrase "in particular." It means that the list does not cover every basis of discrimination. You could also claim discrimination on something that is unlisted, such as sexual orientation.

Did You Know?

Equality is understood to have four meanings:

1. equal before the law
2. equal under the law
3. equal benefit
4. equal protection

Section 15, the equality section of the *Charter*, applies only to the "individual," not to businesses or corporations.

- As a lawyer for a large corporation, how could you argue that equality rights should also apply to your client?

Equality rights can be restricted if it is believed the controls are fair in a free and democratic society. For example, you can only vote, get a driver's licence, and sign contracts at a certain age.

Section 15(2) allows for affirmative action programs. These are meant to improve conditions for individuals or groups that are "disadvantaged because of race, national or ethnic origin, colour, religion, sex, age or mental or physical disability." Without this subsection, these programs would be constantly challenged in court as discriminatory.

At the time the Constitution was negotiated, it was believed section 15 would have a great impact on legislation across Canada and on the courts. For that reason, section 15 did not come into effect until three years after the *Charter*. This was done so that governments could change legislation to agree with the equality requirements.

Section 28 was added to the *Charter* so that equality of the sexes would be in the Constitution. Unlike section 15, the notwithstanding clause (section 33) does not apply to section 28.

Case

Little Sisters Book and Art Emporium v. Canada (Minister of Justice)

[2000] 2 S.C.R. 1120
Supreme Court of Canada

Little Sisters, a Vancouver bookstore, sells gay and lesbian literature, travel information, and erotica (sexual drawings, pictures, and literature). Eighty percent of the store's erotica is imported from the United States and must pass through customs at the border. The store owners took legal action against the government, claiming that many of the imported materials were being unfairly seized by customs officials, who judged them obscene. According to the *Criminal Code* and earlier court rulings, materials are "obscene" if they show sex with violence. It is up to the importer whose materials have been seized to prove they are not obscene.

The trial judge ruled in favour of the store and found that the largely untrained customs officials were targeting the store because it imported lesbian and gay erotica. In many cases, they were judging the sexual orientation itself to be obscene. The store owners were being discriminated against because their materials contained gay and lesbian content. The section of the *Customs Act* that permitted officials to confiscate and destroy "obscene" materials was illegal because it trespassed upon sections 2(b) and 15(1) of the *Charter*.

The federal government appealed to the Supreme Court, whose decision was mixed. It found that Canada Customs had harassed Little Sisters and had shown "excessive and unnecessary prejudice" toward the lesbian and gay community. The Court also ruled that the government did have the right to seize obscene materials, but customs officials must prove that they were "obscene" and offensive to the community within 30 days. The burden of proof, in other words, was on Canada Customs, not the importer. Customs officials kept the right to seize materials they considered obscene. The Supreme Court ruled that this does not violate individual rights contained in the *Charter*, and that such seizures are in the best interests of the community.

For Discussion

1. Why is the Supreme Court decision considered "mixed"? Why was this a limited victory for Little Sisters bookstore?

2. How was the issue of burden of proof resolved?

3. Present arguments to support the claim that the seizure of materials by the customs officials violated sections 2(b) and 15(1) of the *Canadian Charter of Rights and Freedoms*. Share your arguments with your classmates.

Sections 16–22: Official Languages of Canada

These *Charter* sections outline the status of English and French as Canada's two official languages. They state that both languages have equal importance in Parliament and in all Canada's institutions. The laws of Canada must be printed in English and French, and either language can be used in courts that are federally established. Canadians also have the right to use either language when dealing with federal government offices where there is sufficient demand for bilingual services.

Section 23: Minority Language Educational Rights

Some of the most violent events in Canadian history have resulted from language disputes. In section 23, the *Charter* is very careful to set out rights for minority language education. These rights apply only to Canada's two official languages (French and English), however, and only to Canadian citizens. Because education is a provincial matter, each province decides whether to provide education in a minority language other than French or English.

Figure 2-9

These signs appear throughout New Brunswick, the only officially bilingual province in Canada. What equality rights sections in the *Charter* recognize this fact?

Case

Arsenault-Cameron v. Prince Edward Island

[2000] 1 S.C.R 3
Supreme Court of Canada

A group of parents in Summerside, Prince Edward Island, wanted their children to be educated in French. They applied to the French Language Board to establish a French school for grades 1–6 in Summerside. The Minister of Education agreed that the children were entitled to an education in French and that there were enough of them to set up a school using public funds. He refused to do so, however. Instead, he offered to maintain bussing to an existing French school. The trip took 57 minutes each way.

The parents took legal action against the provincial government, arguing that they had the right to have their children educated in French under section 23 of the *Charter*. The P.E.I. Supreme Court (Trial Division) agreed and ordered the government to provide such a school. On appeal, the P.E.I. Supreme Court (Appeal Division) overruled this decision. The Supreme Court of Canada then ruled that the original decision was the right one and ordered the government to provide such a school.

For Discussion

1. Summarize the meaning of section 23 of the *Canadian Charter of Rights and Freedoms*. (Refer to the *Charter* in Appendix A.)

2. Outline the factors you think the P.E.I. Supreme Court (Trial Division) took into consideration in reaching its conclusion.

3. What factors do you think the P.E.I. Supreme Court (Appeal Division) took into consideration in refusing to set up a school?

4. Prepare an argument in support of the Supreme Court of Canada decision.

Section 23 lays out three criteria for deciding the right of a Canadian citizen to be educated in either French or English, but only one has to be met. There is also a numbers test. A province will provide education in the minority language only where there is a "sufficient" number of people who want it. Each province sets the number at which it calculates the expense of public funding is justified. If a Canadian feels that this right has been unfairly denied, he or she can appeal to the courts. (See Case, page 55.)

Section 25: Aboriginal Rights and Freedoms

Section 25 deals specifically with the **Aboriginal peoples** of Canada. It states that *Charter* rights and freedoms cannot interfere with the treaty rights of the Aboriginal peoples of Canada or with any land claims. Section 35 of the *Constitution Act, 1982*, indicates that "Indians, Inuit, and Métis" make up Canada's Aboriginal peoples. It also guarantees the "existing rights" of Aboriginal peoples. These rights, however, are not mentioned or listed in detail because Canadian politicians and Aboriginal leaders could not agree.

Section 35 of the *Constitution Act, 1982*, promises that "representatives of the aboriginal peoples of Canada" will be involved in a constitutional conference to amend section 25 of the *Charter*. This conference was held in 1983, but Aboriginal leaders and Canadian politicians made little progress. They did agree that Aboriginal and treaty rights would apply to both genders, but talks about self-government and land claims had little success. Since that date, some major land-claim agreements have been reached, and several Aboriginal groups have taken steps toward self-government. Chapter 3 deals with Aboriginal legal issues in greater detail.

Section 27: Multicultural and Heritage Rights

This section of the *Charter* directs governments and courts to consider Canada's multicultural background and peoples when making and interpreting laws. This acknowledges Canadians come from many ethnic backgrounds and have specific identities and needs.

Review Your Understanding (Pages 50 to 56)

1. Why is religion considered a private matter?
2. Identify the restrictions that exist on freedom of expression and communication.
3. How could it be argued that the right of governments to censor what audiences see, hear, or read is for the public good?
4. Under what circumstances can a province prevent citizens of other provinces from entering? How is this justified?
5. How have equality rights been explicitly protected in the *Charter*? Justify the importance of equality in a democracy.
6. How does the *Charter* deal with Canada's official languages? How does it deal with other minority languages?
7. Why have specific Aboriginal rights and freedoms not been defined in either the *Charter* or the Constitution?

2.5 Resolving Infringements of the Charter

If a court decides that a case comes under the *Charter* and that a guaranteed right or freedom has been infringed (trespassed upon), it must then decide if the restriction is "reasonable." As you have learned, section 1 of the *Charter* states that individual rights and freedoms can be restricted for the good of the group. If the court decides the restriction is reasonable, and that it is "demonstrably justifiable in a free and democratic society," then it will remain in place. Usually, it is the government that tries to prove a limit is justifiable. For instance, you have already learned that governments can and do pass laws that limit freedom of expression. For example, freedom of expression is restricted by the law that prohibits promotion of hatred against identifiable groups.

If the court decides that the restriction is unreasonable, however, then the party that was prohibited from carrying on an activity will be able to resume the activity. Imagine, for example, that you have written a petition and you distribute it over the Internet. Someone complains about your petition to police and you are charged with distributing offensive material on the Internet. The court, however, decides that your petition did not violate what is considered "reasonable in a free and democratic society." In this case, you could continue distributing your petition.

In the case *R. v. Oakes* (1986), the Supreme Court of Canada decided that a law that limits a *Charter* right or freedom is "reasonable" if (1) it enforces an important government objective; (2) the restriction on individual rights or freedoms is minimal; and (3) the law is clear and sets exact standards (e.g., precise guidelines on materials that are considered obscene).

To be "justified," both the objective and the means must be defensible in terms of the values of a free and democratic society.

Case

Irwin Toy Limited v. Quebec (Attorney General)

(1989) 58 D.L.R. (4th) 577
Supreme Court of Canada

Irwin Toy Limited sought a declaration that the *Consumer Protection Act* of Quebec, which places limits on commercial advertising "directed at persons under 13 years of age," was *ultra vires* the Quebec legislature, and that it infringed the *Quebec Charter of Human Rights and Freedoms* and the *Canadian Charter of Rights and Freedoms*.

The *Consumer Protection Act* stated that to determine if an advertisement was aimed at persons under 13, presentation and context had to be considered. It was also important to take particular account of the nature and intended purpose of the goods advertised. The way the advertisement was presented, as well as the time and place it was shown, also had to be considered. The Act's regulations listed occasions when advertisements could be aimed at children, for example, to announce a new show. They also listed what could not be contained in advertisements aimed at children. Before being shown, an advertisement could be submitted for evaluation to determine if it was acceptable.

The case was heard in the Superior Court of the District of Montreal, then the Quebec Court of Appeal. Evidence was presented that children under the age of 13 are susceptible to media manipulation. The evidence also suggested people under the age of 13 cannot differentiate clearly between reality

continued ▶

and fiction, or grasp the persuasive intention behind the message. On final appeal, the Supreme Court of Canada ruled that the law did not infringe unreasonably on Irwin's right to freedom of expression.

For Discussion

1. What do you think is the main objective of Quebec's *Consumer Protection Act* in banning advertisements directed at young children?

2. Does discrimination result because Quebec's law can be applied to television programs that originate in Quebec, but not to signals coming from outside the province?

3. Does advertising aimed at children fall within the scope of the provision on freedom of expression?

4. Identify how each of the three "reasonable" conditions set by the Supreme Court in *R. v. Oakes* (see page 57) was met in this case.

5. a) What two things had to be proven in this case to limit freedom of expression under section 1 of the *Charter*?
   b) Which party had to prove that the restriction was justified?

6. Do you agree or disagree with the Supreme Court decision in this case? Explain.

Solutions, or Remedies, under the Charter

There are two ways of enforcing the rights and freedoms guaranteed by the *Charter*. As you read earlier, section 52 of the *Constitution Act, 1982*, allows courts to strike down a law if it breaches (breaks) the *Charter*. Courts can also **read down** the law, which means that the law remains generally acceptable, but not in this particular case.

The second method of enforcing *Charter* rights is for someone to apply to the courts directly, stating that one or more of his or her rights and freedoms under the *Charter* has been violated (see section 24).

Review Your Understanding (Pages 57 to 58)

1. Under what circumstance will the courts decide that a law restricting a *Charter* right or freedom is "reasonable"?

2. Which section of the *Constitution Act, 1982*, lays out how the courts can make laws comply with the *Charter*?

3. Describe the difference between "strike down" and "read down." Which has more legal impact?

4. What remedy does section 24 of the *Charter* provide to an individual whose rights have been infringed upon?

2.6 Human Rights

Civil rights involve relationships between individuals and government. The *Canadian Charter of Rights and Freedoms* lists and protects your civil rights. As you read in the introduction to this chapter, human rights are different. They involve relationships between private individuals. Different levels of government have passed laws that make it illegal for people to discriminate against one another. This is done to ensure that individuals are treated equally and fairly as human beings, regardless of the group(s) to which they belong.

You probably already know about **prejudice** and **stereotyping.** But did you know that only discrimination breaks human rights laws?

Prejudice and Stereotyping

Prejudice involves making a judgment about a person who belongs to a certain group. A prejudiced person pre-judges another individual based on the fact that he or she belongs to a group, not on actual character, skill, or personality. Prejudiced opinions are based on ignorance, not fact, and are usually negative.

Prejudiced beliefs about a group will often influence the way a person deals with all members of the group. For instance, Fred refuses to play baseball with some friends because they have chosen Chantal to be the pitcher. Fred believes that women cannot play baseball. He is demonstrating prejudice because he is applying that belief about a group (women) to an individual member of that group (Chantal).

Stereotyping involves judging one member of a group and applying that judgment to the entire group. Stereotypes are the labels that prejudiced people apply to members of certain groups, regardless of their individuality. Examples include saying that all women are dangerous drivers, that all Asian people are superior at mathematics, and that all teenagers are always negative. Many people deny they are prejudiced, yet they will tell jokes about minority groups and use stereotypes to ridicule their members. These jokes are not harmless—they feed on prejudice and help it spread.

Discrimination

Prejudice and stereotyping are not illegal, but they are part of a belief system that leads to discrimination, and it is discrimination that human rights legislation prohibits. Discrimination occurs when people act on a prejudice or stereotype and treat others unfairly. Two types of discrimination are referred to in law: intentional and unintentional.

Intentional discrimination (sometimes called "differential treatment") occurs when a person or organization knowingly commits a discriminatory act. In other words, the discrimination is on purpose. For example, a man refuses to hire the most fully qualified candidate for an engineering position because she is a woman and he believes that women do not make good engineers. Human rights laws would consider that person guilty of the offence of discrimination. Human rights laws make it illegal for individuals and organizations to discriminate against others.

Unintentional discrimination occurs when people or organizations treat others unfairly but are not aware that their actions are discriminatory. For example, people applying to be law enforcement officers may have to be taller than a certain height. Although this requirement does not discriminate intentionally, it effectively eliminates people who are otherwise qualified for the job.

You Be the JUDGE

In 1990, the Supreme Court of Canada ruled that the federal government can practise age discrimination and force people 65 and over to retire. In 2001, the Ontario *Human Rights Code* also did not protect those who wish to work after the age of 65.

- As a young person entering the work force in a few years, would you fight to have the mandatory retirement age banned? Justify your answer.

Review Your Understanding (Pages 58 to 59)

1. **Distinguish between prejudice, stereotyping, and discrimination.**
2. **Describe incidents of prejudice, stereotyping, and discrimination that you have witnessed.**
3. **What are prejudices often based on?**
4. **How does discrimination affect its victims?**
5. **Distinguish between intentional and unintentional discrimination.**

Did You Know?

Some areas affected by human rights laws are

- provision of goods, services, facilities
- employment
- public accommodation
- job/accommodation ads
- public signs
- employer associations
- contracts
- trade unions

2.7 Human Rights Legislation

Federal, provincial, and territorial governments have passed legislation to protect human rights in matters involving private individuals. In 1977, the federal *Canadian Human Rights Act* came into effect. It guarantees that all Canadians will receive fair and equal treatment in all matters under federal control. For example, federally licensed companies and their employees are covered by this Act.

The provinces and territories have human rights legislation that covers situations that are under their authority. British Columbia's *Human Rights Code,* Quebec's *Charter of Human Rights and Freedoms*, and Alberta's *Human Rights, Citizenship and Multiculturalism Act* are a few examples. Both British Columbia's and Ontario's Human Rights Codes, for example, prohibit discrimination in employment and renting an apartment. They also protect employees from sexual harassment in the workplace.

The Law — The Ontario Human Rights Code

Excerpts from the Ontario *Human Rights Code*

Part 1. Freedom from Discrimination

Services

1. Every person has a right to equal treatment ... without discrimination because of race, ancestry, place of origin, colour, ethnic origin, citizenship, creed, sex, sexual orientation, age, marital status, same-sex partnership status, family status or handicap.

Accommodation of person under eighteen

4. (1) Every sixteen or seventeen year old who has withdrawn from parental control has a right to equal treatment with respect to occupancy of and contracting for accommodation without discrimination because the person is less than eighteen years old.

   (2) A contract for accommodation entered into by a sixteen or seventeen year old person who has withdrawn from parental control is enforceable against that person as if the person were eighteen years old.

Harassment because of sex in workplaces

7. (2) Every person who is an employee has a right to freedom from harassment in the workplace because of sex by his or her employer ... or by another employee.

For Discussion

1. **Explain what is meant by the term "creed" in section 1.**
2. **When can a contract for accommodation be held enforceable against a 16-year-old?**
3. **Explain what is meant by the term "harassment" in section 7(2).**

All provincial and territorial Human Rights Codes are based on the *Universal Declaration of Human Rights*. Within each province and territory, the human rights laws can overrule any other provincial or territorial law. These human rights laws are constantly updated, expanded, and adapted to reflect changing social attitudes and awareness. The Ontario *Human Rights Code* provides a good example of the general areas covered in current Canadian human rights legislation.

Enforcing Human Rights Laws

If you believe your human rights have been violated, you can file a complaint with a human rights commission. No fees are involved. A human rights officer will interview you to get the facts, but the complaint must be made within six months of the date the incident occurred. As the person making the complaint, you are the "complainant." The person you are complaining about is the "respondent." If the commission decides you have a valid complaint that falls under its authority, there will be an investigation.

If your complaint involves an employer, you will sign a formal statement and a copy will be forwarded to the respondent. During the investigation, the commission may examine the respondent's business records for evidence. The respondent cannot hinder the investigation. The human rights officer will interview the complainant, the respondent, and any witnesses for information. If the investigating officer cannot arrive at a solution, **conciliation** takes place. This is an attempt to have both parties agree on a solution, such as an apology, a payment, or rehiring of the complainant. Most cases end here, after both parties examine the evidence.

 activity

Canada protects the human rights of its citizens. Visit **www.law.nelson.com** and follow the links to learn how complaints are resolved under the Canadian Human Rights Commission.

Case

Canadian Union of Public Employees (Airline Division) and Canadian Human Rights Commission v. Canadian Airlines International and Air Canada

(1998) 34 C.H.R.R. D/442
Canadian Human Rights Tribunal

This case involved **pay equity** (equal pay for work of equal value). The union representing flight attendants, most of whom are women, complained that its members were being discriminated against. Their wages were not comparable to pilots and technicians, most of whom are men, for work of equal value. Section 11 of the *Canadian Human Rights Act* clearly states that it is discriminatory to have differences in wages in the same establishment for workers who are performing work of equal value.

Attendants, pilots, and technicians have separate unions and collective agreements concerning wages and benefits, even though they work for the same companies. The Canadian Human Rights Tribunal ruled against the flight attendants. It stated that because of the different unions and collective agreements, they were not working in the same establishment. Therefore, there was no discrimination.

For Discussion

1. **Identify the issue in this case.**
2. **Why did the tribunal rule against the flight attendants?**
3. **If they had been working within the same establishment and had belonged to the same union, how would the flight attendants have argued their case in support of pay equity?**

Visit **www.law.nelson.com** and follow the links to learn about the human rights body in your province or territory.

e activity

If conciliation fails, the government will appoint a board of inquiry or a tribunal. It then hears the facts of the case and has the power to impose a resolution. The purpose of human rights laws is not to punish the respondent, but rather to compensate the victim of discrimination and to prevent similar incidents in the future. But if a respondent refuses to obey an order from a board of inquiry or a tribunal, he or she will face criminal charges and a heavy fine. Either party can appeal the board's or tribunal's decision to the courts as a civil case.

Review Your Understanding (Pages 60 to 62)

1. Distinguish between the scope of the *Canadian Human Rights Act* and the *Canadian Charter of Rights and Freedoms*.
2. Present examples of how human rights laws protect Canadians.
3. Justify the importance of human rights.
4. Why is human rights legislation constantly changing?
5. Assume that you are being discriminated against because of your ethnic origin. Briefly summarize the process for taking a complaint to a human rights commission.

Looking Back   National Security versus Rights and Freedoms

Can democratic states protect themselves in times of crisis without sacrificing the rights and freedoms of their citizens? Canada's own crises have included war, civil unrest, and disasters. Parliament has passed laws allowing the federal government to resolve such emergencies.

The *War Measures Act* was enacted in 1914, following the outbreak of World War I. It could be invoked during war, invasion, or insurrection (uprising) and gave the government vast powers over its citizens; for example, to arrest without charge, to detain without trial, to seize and dispose of private property, and to control the economy. This authority was exercised through Cabinet orders that did not require the approval of Parliament.

During both world wars, Canada invoked the *War Measures Act* to legally intern (detain) thousands of Canadians who were regarded as a threat to national security (see pages 85–86). Then, in October 1970, Prime Minister Trudeau invoked the *War Measures Act* to root out the Front de Libération du Québec (FLQ), a revolutionary separatist group planning to overthrow the Quebec government. FLQ members had just kidnapped James Cross, the British Trade Commissioner, and Pierre Laporte, the Quebec Minister of Employment, whom they later murdered. The federal government jailed over 450 people without charge, alleging that they were security risks. Twenty people were later convicted of an offence.

Figure 2-10

Prime Minister Trudeau was unapologetic for invoking the *War Measures Act* in 1970, but many Quebecers thought it was extreme.

continued ▶

Figure 2-11

Troops swarmed Montreal, Quebec, after Trudeau invoked the *War Measures Act* in 1970.

The *Emergencies Act* replaced the *War Measures Act* in 1988. Many civil rights activists welcomed it as an improvement over the *War Measures Act*. Now, the use of emergency powers could be confined to a specific geographic area, instead of applying automatically to all of Canada. Also, any temporary laws made under the *Emergencies Act* would be subject to the *Canadian Charter of Rights and Freedoms,* and any declaration of an emergency by the federal government would have to be approved by Parliament.

Anti-terrorist legislation was introduced following terrorist attacks on the United States on September 11, 2001. These attacks raised serious concerns about Canada's ability to guard against similar violence. Within two months, the federal government had introduced sweeping new anti-terrorism legislation: the *Anti-Terrorism Act* and the *Public Safety Act*. (See Agents of Change, page 30.)

Civil rights activists criticized the *Anti-Terrorism Act* for undermining the historic rights of Canadians. They argued that the Act's definition of terrorism was too broad and could lead to the arrest of legitimate protesters. They urged that sections of the Act, such as those dealing with "preventive arrests," expire after a fixed time period. Representatives of Canada's Islamic community expressed fear that Muslims would be subjected to "racial profiling." Police might detain individuals as security risks simply because of their Muslim faith, or because they or their family had come from an Islamic country. Canada's Justice Minister answered these concerns by imposing a five-year

sunset clause on powers of preventive arrest, and by clarifying the definition of terrorism.

The *Public Safety Act* was criticized for the enormous powers it gave to individual Cabinet ministers. Critics noted that it allowed the government to declare certain areas "military protection zones." Some wondered if this were a ploy to discourage protests during free-trade talks. Others believed that the legislation did not go far enough. The Canadian Alliance Party argued that the *Public Safety Act* should have made armed "sky marshals" mandatory for passenger aircraft. In the years to follow, there will be no shortage of debate about Canada's top priority. Is it safety and security, or liberty?

For Discussion

1. Compare the powers of the *War Measures Act* with those of the *Emergencies Act,* the *Anti-Terrorism Act,* and the *Public Safety Act.*

2. Do you agree with the federal government's decision to introduce strong anti-terrorism legislation in late 2001? Why or why not?

3. Do you see any of the provisions of the *Anti-Terrorism Act* and the *Public Safety Act* posing a serious threat to the civil liberties of Canadians? Explain your answer.

ⓔ activity

Visit **www.law.nelson.com** and follow the links to learn more about Canada's anti-terrorism laws.

Chapter Highlights

- Only in recent years have the majority of people in Canada been guaranteed equality rights.
- There are two types of freedoms: civil rights and human rights. Civil rights outline the power that government has over its citizens. Human rights protect us from being discriminated against by private individuals, businesses, and institutions.
- The *Canadian Charter of Rights and Freedoms* guarantees the civil rights of Canadians.
- The *Charter* is part of the *Constitution Act, 1982*.
- The *Constitution Act, 1982*, is the most important law in Canada.
- The *Canadian Charter of Rights and Freedoms* states that the welfare (good) of Canadian society is more important than individual rights.
- The Supreme Court of Canada interprets the civil rights listed in the *Charter*.
- Canadians can believe whatever they want as long as their actions do not violate the rights of others.
- Prejudice and stereotyping are hurtful and damaging and lead to discrimination, which is illegal.
- The *Canadian Human Rights Act* (1977) protects human rights at the federal level of government.
- The provinces and territories have Human Rights Codes that address areas under their control.
- People who believe that they have been discriminated against can file a complaint with their human rights commission.

Review Key Terms

Name the key terms that are described below.

a) allows certain limits to be set on rights and freedoms

b) rights that protect one from being discriminated against by other individuals

c) an offence that can be tried without a jury

d) a court decision that indicates a law is generally acceptable, but unacceptable in the case before the court

e) applying characteristics assumed to belong to one member of a group to all members of that group

f) the power of a court to rule that a law is no longer in effect

g) occurs when three or more people create a disturbance that instills fear in others

h) changes made to the Constitution

i) beyond the authority of a government to pass a law

j) allows a provincial or territorial law to be valid even though it contradicts the *Charter*

k) rights that have been violated

l) rights that limit the power of government over its citizens

m) a preconceived opinion about a person who belongs to a particular group

n) the right to vote

Check Your Knowledge

1. Distinguish between civil rights and human rights.

2. How do Canadian courts interpret the *Charter*?

3. Explain how the reasonable limits clause and the notwithstanding clause allow for rights and freedoms to be limited under the *Charter*.

4. Identify the main purpose of human rights legislation.

Apply Your Learning

5. Imagine that you had lived in a society where gender roles were rigid, laws and punishments were strict, police had unlimited powers, and ordinary people had few rights and little freedom. The government has now been overthrown and a new progressive society is to be established. You have been asked to develop a Code of Rights for your society that reflects a new, enlightened vision of what rights should be protected. Make sure you specifically include in your Code of Rights sections dealing with gender roles, the strictness of laws and punishments, powers of police, and the rights and freedoms of your citizens. Refer specifically to legal documents such as the *Canadian Charter of Rights and Freedoms*, the *Canadian Human Rights Act*, and the Human Rights Code of your province for assistance in drafting up your new Code of Rights.

6. As a Canadian high school student well-versed in the *Canadian Charter of Rights and Freedoms*, you have been asked to make recommendations as to what law makers should do in each of the following real-life situations.

a) Some police forces want laws passed that would stop motorists from using cell phones while driving. Police and their supporters argue that people who talk on cell phones while driving are dangerous to themselves and others. They point to a 1997 survey that showed drivers in Canada were four times more likely to have an accident while talking on a cell phone.

   i) Identify and analyze the issues raised.

   ii) Identify which section(s) of the *Charter* could be used to protect individual rights against the proposed law.

   iii) Justify your recommendation as to which direction the law should take.

b) In October 2000, the Canadian media were obsessed with U.S. rapper Eminem. The issue was whether or not he should be allowed to enter Canada and give concerts. Eminem's **misogynist** (showing hatred against women) lyrics describe violent acts against women. Ontario's attorney general asked the federal government to stop Eminem at the border, but federal immigration officials refused. Eminem had never been convicted of any crime, including a hate crime. He could not be denied entry into Canada. As police detective Rob Cooper stated, "although [the lyrics] can be viewed as offensive, certainly to women, they don't constitute hate propaganda under the *Criminal Code*." At the time, the definition of hate crimes included race, ethnic origin, religion, and sexual orientation, but not gender. Eminem performed his concerts in Canada.

   i) Identify and analyze the issues raised.

   ii) Identify which section(s) of the *Charter* could be used to argue that the existing law should be changed.

   iii) Justify your recommendation as to which direction the law should take.

Communicate Your Understanding

7. In pairs, select one of the topics below. One student will prepare an argument in favour of the statement and the other student will prepare a counterargument against the statement. Support your position with examples. Share your opinions with your partner.

a) Canadian society is going to break down and the court system will become ineffective because Canadians have too many civil and human rights, and far too many minority groups are protected under the law.

b) Teenagers are victims of prejudice, stereotyping, and discrimination. Their rights should be expanded to include cheaper car insurance rates and the right to vote and buy alcohol and cigarettes at age 16.

c) The retirement age should be raised to 70 because people are living longer. It is too expensive to pay pensions and benefits to people when they reach the age of 65.

d) In *Singh v. Canada (Minister of Employment and Immigration)* (1985), the Supreme Court of Canada gave illegal immigrants in Canada the same *Charter* rights and protections as Canadians. This is wrong. Once found, illegal immigrants should be deported immediately.

e) Because they have so much power, Supreme Court of Canada judges should be elected.

8. Assume that you have been hired to educate your fellow classmates on human rights protections that apply to high school students in your province or territory. Investigate your own provincial or territorial Human Rights Code, and prepare a brief report to highlight the rights that are protected and how they are enforced. What problems might you anticipate in enforcing rights protection?

Develop Your Thinking

9. Assume that you have been asked to create a human rights time line for a new version of this book. In your time line, highlight the development of human rights from earliest times to today. Summarize, in point form, the significance of each development.

10. In November 2000, Michael Ignatieff gave the CBC's Massey Lecture. "The rights revolution," he said, "which includes children's rights, gay rights, aboriginal rights, language rights, and so on—has changed the way we think of ourselves as citizens, men and women, parents. Enhancing [increasing] equality while safeguarding [protecting] differences is what the rights revolution in Canada is all about. We are closer to Europe because we are less suspicious of government power [than the U.S.].... We believe citizens have a right to free health care, unemployment insurance, and government pensions.... And we are one of the few countries who have thought of how to dissolve the whole experiment [Canadian Confederation] without risking the horror of a civil war."

Develop an argument in favour of the following statement: "Enhancing equality while safeguarding differences is what the rights revolution in Canada is all about." Use examples from the quotation, the text, and from extended research to support this view. Ultimately, how are individual differences safeguarded?

Barriers to Achieving Equality

Focus Questions

- Which groups of Canadians have experienced discrimination?
- Who are some of the people who have worked to make Canada a more just and equal society?
- What forms of discrimination still exist in Canada? What is being done to eliminate them?

Chapter at a Glance

Figure 3-1

Barriers come in all shapes and sizes. In this chapter, you will learn about different types of barriers to achieving equality. What barrier is evident here? How can we ensure better access to facilities for disabled individuals?

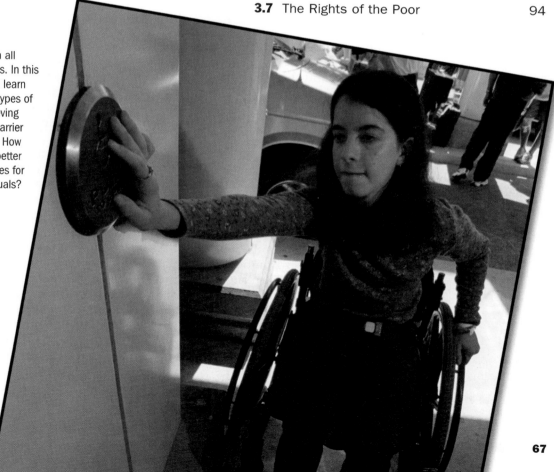

3.1 Introduction

In Chapter 2, you learned that Canada has passed laws to protect the rights and freedoms of its citizens. Although all Canadians are supposed to be equal under the law, equality has not been won without a fight, especially for some groups.

A barrier to achieving equality is anything that prevents someone from participating fully in society. For example, today most people take for granted the right to vote, but for years women were denied this basic right and therefore could not participate fully in the democracy of Canada. Similarly, most Canadians know that it is illegal to discriminate on the basis of race. Yet, in the past, the government of Canada had an immigration policy that was not open to everyone. It took steps to limit immigration from certain countries and barred some races from entering certain professions.

In this chapter, you will read about several groups that have faced discrimination in Canada: women, Native peoples, immigrants, gay men and lesbians, people with disabilities, and people living in poverty. You will examine how these groups addressed the barriers to equality, as well as the reforms they have yet to win.

3.2 Women's Rights

One hundred and fifty years ago, women had few rights and were viewed as possessions by society. They were excluded from universities and professional schools, and they could not vote or run for political office. Working-class women often worked beside their husbands in factories, but most middle-class women stayed at home to take care of their husbands and children. Outside of nursing and teaching, there were few career opportunities for middle-class women.

Toward the end of the 19th century (the 1800s), attitudes toward women slowly began to change. Small groups of women in Canada, the United States, and Europe joined together to fight to obtain **suffrage**—the right to vote. They were known as suffragettes. At first, they were regarded as radicals, or extremists. Almost everyone, including other women, disapproved of them because they challenged old laws and customs.

In 1876, Dr. Emily Stowe established the first suffrage organization in Canada—the Toronto Women's Literary Club. She was a **feminist,** who believed that women should have the same rights as men. She and others worked hard to convince Canadians that women should have the right to vote. However, it would take time to persuade most people that adult women should be able to vote and hold positions held by men.

In 1912, Nellie McClung, a teacher and author, helped to establish the Winnipeg Political Equality League. It became one of the most effective suffrage organizations in Canada. When the league appealed to the Manitoba premier to give women the vote, he replied that "nice women" didn't want to vote. The league responded by staging a mock Parliament at a Winnipeg theatre. A packed audience roared as McClung shot back at the men: "Nice men do not want the vote ... [I]f men start to vote they will vote too much. Politics unsettles men." In 1916, Manitoba became the first province to give women the right to vote. Other Western provinces quickly followed Manitoba's example.

▮ Political Equality for Women

Province/Territory	Suffrage as of	Right to hold office as of
Manitoba	January 28, 1916	January 28, 1916
Saskatchewan	March 14, 1916	March 14, 1916
Alberta	April 19, 1916	April 19, 1916
British Columbia	April 5, 1917	April 5, 1917
Ontario	April 12, 1917	April 24, 1919
Nova Scotia	April 26, 1918	April 26, 1919
New Brunswick	April 17, 1919	March 9, 1934
Yukon Territory	May 20, 1919	May 20, 1919
Prince Edward Island	May 3, 1922	May 3, 1922
Newfoundland & Labrador (not yet part of Canada)	April 13, 1925	April 13, 1925
Quebec	April 25, 1940	April 25, 1940
Northwest Territories	June 12, 1951	June 12, 1951
Nunavut	April 1, 1999*	April 1, 1999

* Date Nunavut was created

Figure 3-2

This chart shows when women in different Canadian provinces and territories won the right to vote and the right to hold office.

Between the Wars

World War I (1914–1918) was another turning point for women. While the men were fighting in Europe, thousands of Canadian women took up their jobs on farms and in factories. These efforts helped to win the war and earned women new respect. By the end of the war, Canadian women, except for Native women, had won the right to vote.

When World War I ended, Canadian men came home and reclaimed their jobs, and most Canadian women returned to their traditional role as homemakers. In 1921, the federal government passed a regulation preventing married women from holding jobs in the government unless they had no other income. Female civil servants had to quit their jobs when they married. The only exception to this rule occurred if no man was available to fill the job. It seemed to many women that they had rights and freedoms only when their country needed them.

That same year, Agnes Macphail became the first woman to be elected to the House of Commons. She believed in women's rights and worked hard to improve them. But women did not rush into politics to try to get elected. They were educated to believe that politics was a "man's occupation" and that their responsibilities lay elsewhere. By 1973, only 22 women had ever been elected to the House of Commons, including Agnes Macphail.

Did You Know?

In 2000, during the federal election, 1808 candidates ran for office. Of these, 375 were women—20.7 percent of all the candidates. Fifty-six women were elected to the House of Commons.

Chapter 3 Barriers to Achieving Equality **69**

France requires that
50 percent of all political
candidates be women,
whether they are running
at a local or federal
level. This **quota system**
was introduced because
for years, only 20 per-
cent of municipal politi-
cians and 10 percent of
National Assembly mem-
bers were women. Political
parties that do not follow
these requirements are
fined.

• Is the quota system in
France fair or does it
discriminate against
men? Explain.

e activity

Discover the Famous Five.
Visit **www.law.nelson.com**
and follow the links to
learn more about the
landmark Persons Case.

▌ **Women Elected to the House of Commons**

Year	Number of Women Elected
1979	10
1980	14
1984	27
1988	39
1993	53
1997	62
2000	56

Figure 3-3

Speculate as to the issues that
might be introduced and debated
in Parliament if more than half of
the elected MPs were women.

The Persons Case

In 1927, five Alberta feminists (the Famous Five) asked Parliament to define
the term "person" as it was used in the *British North America Act*, Canada's
first constitution. They wanted to know if "persons" who qualified for appointment to the Senate included women. No women had been appointed to the
Senate up until this time. In 1928, the Supreme Court of Canada decided
that the word "person" meant male persons only—women were not legal persons and could not hold any appointed office. Canadian law, as interpreted,
was actually preventing women from achieving equality.

This famous case came to be known as the Persons Case. Five determined
women appealed this decision to the Judicial Committee of the Privy Council
in Britain. Canada was still not completely independent of Britain, and this
British court could overrule any decision made by the Supreme Court of
Canada. In 1929, the British court overruled the Supreme Court of Canada's
decision and said that women were indeed legal "persons" who qualified
for appointment to the Senate. In 1930, Carine Wilson became the first
woman to be appointed to the Senate. By 2001, 34 of the 105 Canadian senators were female.

▌ **The Famous Five**

Nellie McClung	Influential politician who fought for "equal pay for equal work." Author of 16 books.
Emily Murphy	First female judge to be appointed in Canada (1916). Writer, politi- cian, and advocate for women's rights.
Irene Parlby	Elected to the Alberta Legislative Assembly in 1921 and appointed to the Cabinet. Canada's representative to the League of Nations in 1930.
Henrietta Edwards	Expert on the legal status of women and children in Canada. Fought for Mothers' Allowance (government money to help families raise children).
Louise McKinney	In 1917, the first woman to be elected to a provincial legislature (Alberta). Suffragette and strong supporter of the temperance movement (dedicated to ending the consumption of alcohol).

Figure 3-4

Identify some of the issues
that were important to the
Famous Five.

After World War II

During World War II, 45 000 Canadian women joined the army. Their jobs included nurses, drivers, firefighters, and radio technicians. They wore uniforms and had military training, but they were not allowed to fight the enemy in combat. In addition, they were paid 20 percent less than men who held the same rank.

Back home, more than 1 million women entered the workforce and encountered the same old attitudes as the war drew to a close. A 1944 Gallup opinion poll showed that 68 percent of Canadian women and 75 percent of men believed that returning soldiers should be hired over women. It wasn't until 1955 that legislation favouring the hiring of men was abolished.

In 1960, Prime Minister John Diefenbaker's government passed the *Canadian Bill of Rights*, the first human rights legislation in Canada. Before this time, the only mention of the rights of Canadian citizens was in the *British North America Act*—legislation that was controlled by the British Parliament. The *Canadian Bill of Rights* was not the last word on human rights, but it did state that it was illegal to discriminate against people because of their sex, race, religion, or colour. Within its first year of passage, it was successfully used in almost a dozen cases of discrimination before the courts.

The *Canadian Bill of Rights* also helped to pave the way for the *Canadian Charter of Rights and Freedoms*. In 1982, protection of women's rights was set forth in section 28 of the *Charter*, which guaranteed rights and freedoms "equally to male and female persons."

Figure 3-5

Irene Parlby was one of the five women behind the Persons Case. How has Canada progressed in its views toward women?

The Law   The Canadian Bill of Rights, Part 1

Excerpts from the *Canadian Bill of Rights*

1. It is hereby recognized and declared that in Canada there have existed and shall continue to exist without discrimination by reason of race, national origin, colour, religion or sex, the following human rights and fundamental freedoms, namely,
    (a) the right of the individual to life, liberty, security of the person and enjoyment of property, and the right not to be deprived thereof except by due process of law;
    (b) the right of the individual to equality before the law and the protection of the law;
    (c) freedom of religion;
    (d) freedom of speech;
    (e) freedom of assembly and association; and
    (f) freedom of the press.

For Discussion

1. Compare the categories of discrimination identified in section 1 of the *Canadian Bill of Rights* with a current sample of provincial human rights legislation (see page 60). What areas of discrimination are now covered in provincial human rights legislation that were not previously addressed in the *Canadian Bill of Rights*?

Women's Issues Today

Today, the women's movement in Canada is still working to resolve a number of equality issues. One organization at the forefront of legal reform is LEAF (Legal Education and Action Fund), which describes itself as "a national, non-profit organization working to promote equality for women and girls in Canada." LEAF uses the equality provisions from the *Canadian Charter of Rights and Freedoms* to safeguard women's rights. It also intervenes in legal cases where women's rights are an issue, such as employment and pay equity, sexual harassment, and discrimination against pregnant women. Many people are surprised to hear that some of these basic issues are not yet resolved.

Pay Equity

Pay equity is the principle of equal payment for work of equal value. Pay equity is the law. In fact, section 11 of the *Canadian Human Rights Act* (1985) guarantees pay equity. Yet inequalities persist, mostly because of lingering traditional attitudes. In 1983, a civil servants' union complained that women were not being paid the same as men. In 1998, the Canadian Human Rights Tribunal ruled that these female employees had been discriminated against over the years and ordered the federal government to pay billions of dollars in back wages. In 1999, the federal government agreed to pay $3.5 billion to 230 000 current and retired workers.

Case

Lesiuk v. Canada (Employment Insurance Commission)

(March 22, 2001) C.U.B. 51142
Canadian Unemployment Board

Lesiuk was the mother of two young children and worked part-time from 1993 to 1998. A person has to work 52 weeks (700 hours) to qualify for employment insurance (sections 6(1) and 7(2) of the *Employment Insurance Act, 1996*). During Lesiuk's 52-week qualifying period, she had worked only 667 hours. Because she was short 33 hours, she was denied employment insurance benefits.

Lesiuk argued that it was wrong to base eligibility requirements on hours worked. Instead, it should be based on the number of weeks worked. The present rules discriminated against women who often have to take only part-time work to be able to raise their children. As a result of these responsibilities, they have fewer hours to work outside the home. Lesiuk appealed the decision to the umpire (arbitrator), who decided in her favour.

The ruling stated that sections 6(1) and 7(2) of the *Employment Insurance Act* were unconstitutional because they trespassed upon section 15 of the *Canadian Charter of Rights and Freedoms*. Sections 6(1) and 7(2) were not covered by section 1 of the *Charter*. The 700-hour requirement discriminated against mothers who work part-time and who, as a group, do two-thirds of all unpaid work in Canadian homes. The limit violates their human dignity. They have fewer hours to devote to work outside the home and this should be recognized in the *Employment Insurance Act*.

For Discussion

1. **Summarize the arguments made by Lesiuk in her appeal.**

2. **Why were sections 6(1) and 7(2) of the *Employment Insurance Act* declared unconstitutional?**

3. **Refer to section 15 of the *Canadian Charter of Rights and Freedoms* and briefly summarize the equality rights provisions. Present an argument, using section 15, that supports the claim that sections 6(1) and 7(2) of the *Employment Insurance Act* are unconstitutional.**

Women working at Bell Canada have fought a similar battle since the mid-1990s. In 1992, Bell Canada and a union representing Bell employees reviewed the value of jobs by "scoring" them, based on their physical and mental demands. Jobs with equal scores were to be considered "work of equal value" and paid accordingly. After a two-year study, it was found that women at Bell Canada had been paid $2 to $5.30 an hour less than men for doing equally valuable work. The union decided it wanted $150 million in pay equity for its members. In 2000, Bell Canada and the union came to a tentative agreement whereby Bell would pay $60 million in back wages. However, the employees rejected the agreement and held out for the larger settlement. This case is still being fought.

Such highly publicized cases are making it more difficult for employers to discriminate against women in the workplace. Though progress has been made in reducing the wage gap between men and women, pay equity is still not guaranteed.

Employment Equity

Employment equity is the principle of equal treatment of all employees based on their abilities. In 1995, the federal government passed the *Employment Equity Act* to correct discrimination experienced by certain groups. In particular, the Act aims to protect women, Native peoples, people with disabilities, and members of visible minorities. This law applies to companies regulated by the federal government that employ 100 or more people. It also applies to the federal government itself and its employees.

This law also requires employers to identify barriers to equality in the workplace, to remedy situations in which barriers exist, and to actively hire and promote minority groups. Failure to obey the law results in a fine of up to $10 000 for a first offence and up to $50 000 for repeated violations. The federal government is dedicated to eliminating all forms of discrimination in the workplace.

The Canadian military is an example of one government organization that has not accepted women easily. Today, women make up 11.4 percent of Canada's armed forces. Only 3.5 percent of female officers and 1.4 percent of female noncommissioned soldiers are in combat positions. Women were first allowed to work in combat jobs in infantry, artillery, and armoured divisions in 1987. Two years later, a Canadian Human Rights Tribunal ordered the military to permit women to serve in all combat jobs, though not on submarines.

Despite these advances, some women in the armed forces have reported harassment. In a 1992 survey, more than a quarter of the women in the armed forces reported that they had been subjected to sexual harassment the previous year. By 2001, a Ministry of Defence report found that the military had failed to integrate women and visible minorities into the armed forces, and that the attitudes of males in the military were often marked by "insensitivity, ignorance and biases." That same year, the military announced it was lifting its ban on women serving in submarines.

More women and visible minorities are being integrated into the armed forces, but it is a slow process. At the moment, more women are leaving Canada's military than are being recruited. Only 2 percent of Canada's armed forces are members of visible minorities and 1.5 percent are Native.

 activity

Visit **www.law.nelson.com** and follow the links to learn more about pay equity and employment equity.

You Be the JUDGE

In 1989, a Human Rights Tribunal said that women should not be allowed to serve in combat positions on a submarine, though they could fight almost anywhere else. The government noted that quarters on a submarine were too confined to allow men and women to mix easily.

- Argue in favour of or against this decision. Justify your position.

Did You Know?

The military has set a target quota for the representation of certain groups:

• Women—28%

• Visible minorities—9%

• Native peoples—3%

Review Your Understanding (Pages 68 to 73)

1. Identify some historic barriers to achieving women's equality.
2. Identify the social attitudes that have created barriers to achieving equality.
3. How did working conditions create barriers to achieving equality?
4. What is suffrage? How did most people view the suffragettes?
5. How have Emily Stowe, Nellie McClung, and Agnes Macphail individually contributed to women's equality in Canada?
6. What effect did World War I have on women in the Canadian workforce? What happened to women's employment after the war?
7. Why was the Persons Case so important for Canadian women?
8. Distinguish between pay equity and employment equity.

Did You Know?

Donald Marshall Jr. was wrongfully convicted of homicide in 1972 and spent 11 years in prison before being acquitted of a crime he did not commit. A subsequent inquiry showed that the Sydney, Nova Scotia, police department that laid the charge was both incompetent and racist.

3.3 Native Peoples

Donald Marshall Jr. is a Nova Scotia Mi'kmaq who fishes for a living. In 1996, he was convicted of fishing off-season without a licence. Marshall appealed this conviction. He argued that he had the right to fish because of a treaty signed in 1760 between the Mi'kmaq and George II of Great Britain. This treaty gave Marshall the right to catch and sell fish without government interference. The Supreme Court agreed with Marshall (see Case, page 75).

The Marshall case highlights the Native peoples' approach to human rights. When they talk about achieving equality, they are usually not referring to individual rights and freedoms. They are referring to their **collective rights**— rights that come from having occupied Canada for thousands of years as distinct nations. These rights focus on land and the right to self-government.

Figure 3-6

Donald Marshall Jr. (centre) walks through Sydney, Nova Scotia, in a peaceful protest over Native fishing rights.

R. v. Marshall

[1999] 3 S.C.R. 456
Supreme Court of Canada

Donald Marshall Jr., a Mi'kmaq, was charged with breaking federal fishing regulations. He was charged with selling 220 kg of eels without a licence, fishing out of season, and using illegal nets. He admitted that he had done all these things but argued that, as a Native person, he had treaty rights that permitted him to catch and sell fish out of season. Marshall argued that a treaty made in 1760 between the Mi'kmaq and the British Crown gave him this right. Therefore, he did not have to obey federal fishing rules. The Nova Scotia trial judge disagreed and found him guilty on all three charges.

Marshall appealed this decision, but the Court of Appeal for Nova Scotia upheld the guilty verdict.

The case was appealed to the Supreme Court of Canada, which reversed the earlier court decisions and ordered that Marshall be acquitted. It argued that the 239-year-old treaty gave the East Coast Native peoples a right to earn a living from commercial fishing, even if it was done out of season.

For Discussion

1. Explain the precedent that was set by this decision of the Supreme Court of Canada.

2. In 2001, a Nova Scotia provincial court judge convicted 35 Native loggers of illegally cutting down trees on Crown land. Why would the Supreme Court not use the Marshall case in defence of the logging?

Historic Barriers

When the Europeans began arriving in North America in the 1600s, the Native peoples were spread across Canada in seven distinct cultural areas. Cooperative relationships soon emerged. In Quebec and the Maritimes, the French and British formed military alliances and partnerships with a number of **First Nations.** The European powers depended on their Native allies to maintain the lucrative fur trade. The Europeans also needed their support during military conflicts such as the Seven Years' War (1756–1763), which ended French rule in what is now Canada.

Canada's present system of Native treaties has its roots in the Royal Proclamation of 1763, which made Britain the only agent for land transfers between Native peoples and settlers. The Proclamation declared that Native lands could be surrendered only to the Crown's representatives at public meetings. This meant that individuals or groups could not buy land privately from Native peoples. In short, the Royal Proclamation of 1763 established a legal framework for treaty making in British North America.

The Royal Proclamation remains an important legal document. It has been described as a kind of Native "Magna Carta" that recognizes Native peoples as nations. Although not everyone agrees with this interpretation, section 25(a) of Canada's Constitution does guarantee "any rights or freedoms that have been recognized by the Royal Proclamation of October 7, 1763."

In 1867, at the time of Confederation, relations between Native peoples and the newcomers were changing dramatically. As waves of European immigrants arrived in search of cheap farmland, Native peoples came to be viewed as a barrier to settlement. Many settlers held racist attitudes.

Between 1871 and 1921, the government of Canada concluded a series of land agreements with Native peoples living on the vast plains and woodlands of Western Canada. The purpose of these treaties was to force the peaceful removal of Native peoples from their traditional lands to make way for European settlement. In exchange, Native peoples were granted reserve lands. This period marked the start of Canada's official policy toward Native peoples. Native peoples were to be "protected" on reserves, "civilized" through being educated in European ways and beliefs, and eventually fully **assimilated** (absorbed) into European Canadian society.

The *Indian Act*, first passed by the federal government in 1868, legalized assimilation. The Act defined who was **"Indian"** and who was not, declaring that Native men who married non-Native women kept their Indian status, while Native women who married non-Native men lost theirs. The Act banned traditional cultural practices such as the potlatch (a ceremonial feast and giving of gifts) of Pacific Coast Native peoples and the sun dance ceremony of the Plains peoples. It also replaced traditional systems of Native self-government with a system of elected band councils, and rejected Native ways of justice.

Until the 1960s, the federal government also gave money to Christian churches to operate residential schools for Native children. The purpose of the schools was to immerse Native children in European Christian culture. The children were taken from their families by government agents and boarded at the schools. There, a child faced punishment for speaking his or her own language. Many of the children were physically and sexually abused by those responsible for them. This abuse left the children with deep emotional scars.

Native Leaders and Lobby Groups

Since the 1950s, Native peoples have fought to reverse the policy of assimilation and be recognized as distinct nations within Canada. In 1951, Native leaders formed the Native Indian Brotherhood to lobby the federal government on Native rights and to press for the settlement of **land claims.**

The movement for Native justice was set back in 1969 when the Trudeau government released its White Paper. This document reflected Prime Minister Trudeau's personal emphasis on individual rights over collective rights. It said that Native peoples had no special status and called for the repeal (withdrawal) of the *Indian Act* and existing treaties. It proposed to "enable the Indian people to be free—free to develop Indian culture in an environment of legal, social, and economic equality with other Canadians." The White Paper only made Native peoples more determined to fight for their rights.

In 1982, Native leaders replaced the Native Indian Brotherhood with the Assembly of First Nations (AFN), a move to better reflect the diversity of Native peoples. The AFN functions as a national lobby organization and represents over 630 First Nations communities across Canada. The AFN presents Native views on such matters as Native and treaty rights, economic development, health, housing, justice, and social development.

activity

Visit **www.law.nelson.com** and follow the links to learn about the Assembly of First Nations.

In July 2000, Matthew Coon Come was elected Grand Chief of the Assembly of First Nations. The leader of Quebec's Crees was known for his outspokenness and had even criticized the Assembly itself, saying it was too much a "service provider" for the Canadian government instead of a strong voice for Native interests.

Matthew Coon Come was born in a hut along a trapline worked by his parents in Northern Quebec. He attended residential schools and later studied law, political science, economics, and Native studies at Trent and McGill universities.

In the 1980s, Coon Come gained attention during his fight against the massive James Bay hydroelectric project, which threatened to flood Cree lands. He drew media focus to the Cree cause by organizing a canoe trip of Cree elders from James Bay to New York City, a potential customer of Hydro Quebec. As a result, the Crees won the right to negotiate how the hydroelectric project was to be developed.

In 1995, Coon Come led a Cree boycott against the Quebec referendum on sovereignty. When the Crees held their own referendum, 95 percent voted against Native peoples and lands being separated from Canada. Later, while speaking at Harvard University, Coon Come publicly rejected the notion that the "secessionist government in Quebec … can forcibly include my people and our traditional land into a sovereign Quebec … with or without their consent."

As the national chief of the Assembly of First Nations, Matthew Coon Come has committed himself to representing the interests of Native peoples—to protect their traditional ways of life and redress their grievances.

For Discussion

1. **What legal and political conflict did Coon Come outline in his speech at Harvard University?**
2. **What Native interests is he trying to protect?**

Figure 3-7

Matthew Coon Come

Landmark Decisions

The Nisga'a

In 1973, the Supreme Court of Canada handed down a decision that would have far-reaching effects. In *Calder v. British Columbia (Attorney General)* (1973), the Nisga'a people of Northwestern British Columbia claimed in court that they had always held legal title to their ancestral lands—in other words, that ownership of their land had never been taken away. After the British Columbia Supreme Court and the British Columbia Court of Appeal ruled against them, the Nisga'a appealed their case to the Supreme Court. Seven judges heard the appeal.

While the Supreme Court dismissed the Nisga'a appeal on a technicality, this case was significant for Native rights in another respect. Six judges agreed that the concept of "Native title" was a valid one, but were split evenly on whether Nisga'a Native title still existed. The three judges who sided with the Nisga'a claim said that, where title had not been extinguished, it might exist wherever land had been occupied and used by Native peoples. They wrote in their judgment: "The Nisga'a tribe has persevered for almost a century in asserting an interest in their lands which their ancestors occupied since time immemorial. The Nisga'a were never conquered nor did they ever enter into a treaty or deed of surrender."

The Trudeau government recognized the significance of the Calder decision, and reversed the stand it had taken in the White Paper (see page 76). It introduced a process for negotiating land claims settlements. Since 1973, several comprehensive land claims settlements have been achieved.

Case

Guerin v. R.

(1984) 13 D.L.R. (4th) 321
Supreme Court of Canada

In 1957, the Indian Affairs branch officer for the Musqueam band in Vancouver negotiated a long-term lease of band land to a local golf club. The *Indian Act* required that leases or sales of Native land to non-Natives must have the approval of the Indian Affairs Department.

In 1975, the Musqueam band sued the federal government, claiming that the branch officer had violated his position of trust. They argued that the lease omitted the terms that had been orally conveyed to him at a special meeting. Specifically, the band had wanted an initial annual rent of $2900 for 15 years. This was to be followed by 10-year renewal periods with rents to be determined at the time of renewal. The lease that the branch officer actually signed provided for renewal periods of 15 years, with increases limited to 15 percent of the previous rental.

The Supreme Court of Canada ruled unanimously in favour of the Musqueam band. It noted that Native peoples had no choice in their land dealings but to work through officials of the Indian Affairs Department, and they relied on these officials to represent their interests. By altering the terms of the Musqueam offer without the band's knowledge or approval, the branch officer had failed in his fundamental duties to the Musqueam band. Moreover, there had been a breach of trust by the federal government.

For Discussion

1. Does the *Indian Act* give Native groups an unrestricted right to sell or lease reserve land? Explain.

2. Why was the Musqueam band dissatisfied with the agreement the branch officer had negotiated?

3. Why did the Supreme Court of Canada rule in favour of the Musqueam band?

4. How might the decision in this case be used by other Native groups to prove that they have received unjust treatment?

Did You Know?

The Nunavut agreement called for the division of the Northwest Territories to create Nunavut. On April 1, 1999, Nunavut became Canada's third territory, with the first Inuit-led government in Canadian history.

The Wet'suwet'en and Gitxsan

In 1997, the Supreme Court of Canada handed down another important decision on Native rights and treaty rights. The case of *Delgamuukw v. British Columbia* (1977) represented a tremendous victory for First Nations. The case was launched in 1984, when 51 Wet'suwet'en and Gitxsan hereditary chiefs took Canada and British Columbia to court to gain ownership of their ancestral lands. After a lengthy court battle, the case finally went to the Supreme Court. The Court did not determine whether the Wet'suwet'en and Gitxsan had actually established title in any of the territories they claimed, and sent that issue back to trial.

However, the Court did something very important. It defined the meaning of Native title, described a test to prove Native title, and showed how Canada's

Constitution protects that title. According to the test, a Native group has title if it can show it had exclusive occupation of the land before Britain declared sovereignty over that land. The Court described the role for negotiations between government and holders of Native title. The Court also held that Native oral histories were acceptable as evidence in a court of law.

The Court noted that Native title and rights are not absolute. Governments may interfere with these rights, but must justify this interference and show that their action meets a strict test. The Delgamuukw decision was very important to Native peoples because it outlined what they could demand in treaty negotiations once they had established Native title.

Developments in the Nisga'a Case

In British Columbia, there are more unsettled land claims than in the rest of the country, mostly because the provincial government steadfastly refused to acknowledge the existence of Native land claims. In 1990, British Columbia finally agreed to engage in treaty talks. In 1993, a treaty commission was established to oversee and facilitate treaty negotiations.

In August 1998, the Nisga'a of the Nass River Valley in Northwestern British Columbia reached a final agreement with the province of British Columbia and the federal government. This agreement was the first treaty ever signed between a Native group and the British Columbia government.

Under the terms of the final agreement, the Nisga'a received the following:
- ownership of approximately 2000 km² of land
- the right to establish a Nisga'a government—the Nisga'a Tribal Council—with jurisdiction similar to that of other local governments
- ownership of surface and subsurface resources on their lands, a share of the Nass River salmon catch, and the Nass-area wildlife harvests
- a Nisga'a-only commercial fishery
- $190 million, payable over 15 years

The final agreement also declared that personal income-tax exemptions for the Nisga'a would be phased out over 12 years. In addition, the *Criminal Code*, the *Canadian Charter of Rights and Freedoms*, and other federal and provincial laws would apply to the Nisga'a as they do to every Canadian.

While many Native peoples celebrated the finalization of the Nisga'a treaty, some criticized it. Neil Skerrik, a Gitxsan leader, declared that the Nisga'a had claimed more territory than they were entitled to, gaining rights and benefits over Native territory rightfully belonging to neighbouring First Nations.

Non-Natives complained that the treaty-making process had excluded local non-Natives and that the negotiations had not been conducted openly. They were angry that local non-Natives would be affected by decisions of the Nisga'a Tribal Council, yet would not be able to vote for Tribal Council members. They argued that the treaty conferred "special status" on the Nisga'a, violating the principle of individual equality.

Figure 3-8

A member of the Gitxsan band celebrates the Supreme Court's Delgamuukw decision.

Did You Know?

Since 1991, the federal government has transferred taxation authority to almost 30 percent of British Columbia's Native bands. This has created a situation where thousands of non-Natives residing on reserve lands are paying taxes to people for whom they cannot vote.

Chapter 3 Barriers to Achieving Equality

In June 2001, the newly elected Liberal government of British Columbia promised to hold a province-wide referendum to determine a set of principles for treaty negotiations. Premier Gordon Campbell declared that the referendum would help build trust by making the treaty process more open. Others argued that the opposite would occur. People would become more rigid in their views, and open confrontation might result as people's ill feelings were aroused.

Native Rights and Canada's Constitution

Canada's Constitution addresses the issue of Native rights in section 25 of the *Charter* and section 35 of the *Constitution Act, 1982* (see The Law, below). In 1987, Prime Minister Brian Mulroney and the 10 provincial premiers agreed on a plan to reform Canada's Constitution. Known as the Meech Lake Accord, the agreement had to be ratified by Parliament and the provincial legislatures before becoming law.

In 1990, the ratification process came to an abrupt end when Elijah Harper, a Cree, and a member of the Manitoba legislature, blocked debate of the Accord by using the parliamentary process. This meant that there would be no vote on ratification in the legislature. Harper strongly opposed the Accord because it did not recognize the First Nations as equal founding partners of Canada. He faced heavy criticism across Canada for his stand, but he was seen by many Native peoples as a champion of their rights.

The Law   The Constitution Act, 1982

Excerpts from the Constitution Act, 1982

Part I. *Canadian Charter of Rights and Freedoms*

25. The guarantee in this Charter of certain rights and freedoms shall not be construed so as to abrogate or derogate from any aboriginal, treaty or other rights or freedoms that pertain to the aboriginal peoples of Canada including

   (a) any rights or freedoms that have been recognized by the Royal Proclamation of October 7, 1763; and

   (b) any rights or freedoms that now exist by way of land claims agreements or may be so acquired.

Part II. Rights of the Aboriginal Peoples of Canada

35. (1) The existing aboriginal and treaty rights of the aboriginal peoples of Canada are hereby recognized and affirmed.

   (2) In this Act, "aboriginal peoples of Canada" includes the Indian, Inuit and Métis peoples of Canada.

   (3) For greater certainty, in subsection (1) "treaty rights" includes rights that now exist by way of land claims agreements or may be so acquired.

   (4) Notwithstanding any other provision of this Act, the aboriginal and treaty rights referred to in subsection (1) are guaranteed equally to male and female persons.

For Discussion

1. What groups does the Constitution identify as "the aboriginal peoples of Canada"?

2. What does the Constitution have to say about the equality of the sexes?

3. Section 25 of the *Charter* and section 35 of the *Constitution Act, 1982,* entrench Aboriginal rights and treaty rights in the Canadian Constitution, but they do not explain what "existing rights" mean. How has this affected the role of the courts in defining Aboriginal rights?

Into the 21st Century

Despite their success in winning recognition of Native and treaty rights, Native peoples still face major barriers to equality. Poverty is widespread, educational achievement is generally low, and serious health and social problems afflict many. In recent years, a number of local Native leaders have declared their communities to be in a state of crisis, citing drug and alcohol abuse, high rates of youth suicide, low employment, and deplorable housing conditions as major causes for concern. In addition, racism directed at Native peoples continues to be a problem.

Although Canadians do not argue against the seriousness of these problems, how they can be solved is the subject of impassioned debate. As you have learned, most Native peoples believe they will achieve their rightful place in Canadian society by having their rights as distinct peoples recognized in law and incorporated into treaties. Prosperity will come with the attainment of Native self-government.

The opposing view is that Native peoples have the same individual rights as other Canadians, and no others. They must give up their demands for self-government and recognition of other special rights. And they must assimilate themselves into the larger Canadian society if they are to have any chance of achieving prosperity and true equality.

Agents of Change — Helen Betty Osborne

Helen Betty Osborne was only 19 when she was abducted and murdered near The Pas, Manitoba, on November 13, 1971. The Native high school student lived on the Norway House Indian Reserve and had dreams of being a schoolteacher. After a prolonged assault by four non-Native men, Osborne was stabbed to death with a screwdriver. The men returned to The Pas and remained free for 16 years. Many people in the community knew what they had done but kept silent.

In 1972, someone tipped off the RCMP about the men. However, the suspects refused to talk, and the RCMP could not gather sufficient evidence to support a murder charge.

Finally, in 1985, the RCMP requested the public's help in solving the case. Several people came forward to say they had heard some of the men talking about the murder. As a result, murder charges were laid against three of the four suspects. One suspect was granted immunity from prosecution in return for his testimony, one was acquitted, and one eventually received a sentence of life imprisonment.

It took over a decade for Osborne's family to receive justice, a fact that was directly attributable to the racism in The Pas at the time of her murder. In the 1970s, Native and non-Native people were segregated in restaurants, bars, and washrooms, and Native women were often harassed in public. Osborne's death and its aftermath changed people's attitudes toward this racist behaviour.

The government of Manitoba eventually apologized to the Osborne family for this great delay in justice. It also passed the *Helen Betty Osborne Memorial Foundation Act*, which established a scholarship fund for Native students pursuing post-secondary education.

Figure 3-9
Helen Betty Osborne

For Discussion

1. **Systemic racism is a form of racism that exists throughout institutions such as the legal system or the education system. Comment on how systemic racism could have played a role in the delay of justice for Helen Betty Osborne or the wrongful conviction of Donald Marshall Jr. (see Did You Know?, page 74).**

Should Native Peoples Have Their Own System of Justice?

Native peoples make up about 3.6 percent of Canada's population, yet they account for 12 percent of male and 17 percent of female convicts serving sentences of two years or more. This is an issue of grave concern to Native leaders such as Matthew Coon Come.

In recent years, several countries, including Canada, have been considering giving Native peoples their own system of justice. Canada has been experimenting with Native justice. In some communities, Native police officers have replaced local police authorities. These officers have a better understanding of Native offenders and their lives, and they can deal with situations more effectively.

Experiments have also included penitentiary ceremonies to help Native inmates. The Stony Mountain Penitentiary in Manitoba has four sweat lodges at the far end of the exercise yard. In these round, tentlike structures, Native prisoners gather once a week to participate in the spiritual program of sweat-lodge ceremonies. According to the prison's warden,

Figure 3-10

A sentencing circle for a 20-year-old shoplifter in Winnipeg in September 1998. It was the first sentence handed down by a sentencing circle under a new provincial program for Native offenders.

the healing process works. He has seen prisoners who have participated in the program completely changed.

Since fines and imprisonment have not been an effective deterrent to Native offenders, Native peoples in some Canadian communities have used their own traditions to deal with lawbreakers. Native justice emphasizes treatment and healing through sentencing circles and healing circles, instead of imprisonment.

In a sentencing circle, the offender is brought before victims and their families, friends, family members, band elders, witnesses, lawyers, and the judge to discuss sentencing. Everyone has an equal say in the sentencing. Although the setting is more relaxed than a courtroom, the encounter between victim and victimizer can be especially intense. The sentence could range from doing community work to banishment to the woods for a set period of time. There the offender must live off the land as his or her ancestors did to be spiritually cleansed and rehabilitated.

In *R. v. Cheekinew* (1993), Justice Grotsky noted that to qualify for a sentencing circle, the accused had to be

- eligible for a suspended sentence, an intermittent sentence, or a short term of imprisonment, coupled with a probation order
- genuinely contrite
- supported in the request for a sentencing circle by the community in which he or she lives
- honestly interested in turning his or her life around

A healing circle is an alternative to traditional punishment. If an offender pleads guilty and agrees to participate in a healing circle, the sentence is usually suspended. The offenders must meet with the victims, their families, and other offenders, and work with them to share their experiences and finally to seek forgiveness for the wrongdoings. The guilty parties must also take courses in anger management.

Defence counsel Gord Coffin in Whitehorse stated: "It is very much harder for a lot of people to bare their soul in front of people who know them. It is easy to stand up in front of a judge and blame the system—it's harder to do that in the community you have harmed."

One Manitoba community reports that in nine years, of the 52 offenders there have been only two repeat offenders. The apparent success of the healing circle has encouraged other communities to experiment with similar programs.

On One Side

Some Canadians oppose the concept of a separate Native justice system. They believe that all Canadians should be treated in the same manner under the criminal justice system. Since the *Canadian Charter of Rights and Freedoms* guarantees equal treatment to all Canadians, there should be no problem. Members of Native communities should not be treated differently. As Canadians, they must obey the laws of the land.

Others argue that a separate justice system for Native peoples will lead to lobbying by other ethnic groups for their own separate justice systems. Denying these factions could lead to resentment, but agreeing to them could lead to chaos in the Canadian justice system.

There is an additional complication: there are legal distinctions among Native peoples themselves. Status Indians and treaty Indians have more rights than non-status and non-treaty Indians. The Métis and the Inuit have also won recognition of certain rights.

These legal distinctions give rise to a difficult question. Should the distinctions be preserved, or do they stand in the way of the achievement of true equality? For some Native spokespersons, such as Ghislain Picard of the Assembly of First Nations, the answer lies in gaining recognition of the sovereign rights of the First Nations, including the right to decide rules of "citizenship."

On the Other Side

Reports from a Manitoba inquiry and from the Law Commission of Canada support the idea of a separate Native justice system. Canada's criminal justice system has not solved the problems encountered in Native communities. Rates of suicide, alcoholism, crime, and imprisonment have never been higher among Native peoples.

Those who support Native justice claim that many Natives turned to alcohol and drugs to block out painful memories of degradation and sexual abuse. Criminal activity followed, taking them in and out of jail. Instead of incarceration, these offenders need to reconnect with themselves and their people through a healing process.

Associate Chief Provincial Court Judge Murray Sinclair agrees. In the 1991 Native Justice Inquiry report, he advocates the use of healing circles. Judge Sinclair calls Canada's treatment of Native peoples by the justice system "an international disgrace" and has called for a separate Native justice system, stating: "They have paid the price of high rates of alcoholism, crime, and family abuse."

The Bottom Line

Native self-government and a separate justice system seem to be compatible objectives. Native peoples have unique needs and concerns. They are striving to meet these needs in a way that reflects their history and culture as well as the demands of the 21st century.

What Do You Think?

1. Explain how sweat-lodge ceremonies and healing and sentencing circles work to achieve Native justice.

2. Outline the pros and cons of a Native justice system in Canada.

3. Explain the link between Native self-government and Native justice. Do you think that one is possible without the other?

4. Should healing circles and sentencing circles be considered for non-Native offenders? Explain.

Review Your Understanding (Pages 74 to 83)

1. Distinguish between collective rights and individual rights.
2. Identify three historic barriers to equality for Native peoples.
3. Distinguish between Native rights and treaty rights.
4. Explain the significance of the Royal Proclamation of 1763.
5. What constitutional guarantees do Native peoples have?
6. What was the significance of the 1969 White Paper released by the Trudeau government?
7. Identify two major criticisms made about the final agreement made with the Nisga'a Treaty in 1998.
8. British Columbia announced that it is planning to hold a referendum on treaty making. What is seen as the benefit of holding a referendum? What concerns have been raised against this proposal?
9. Why is the Delgamuukw case considered to be a landmark decision?

3.4 Immigrants: A Case of Legal Discrimination?

Canada is a nation of newcomers. In the 20th century, more than 10 million immigrants came to Canada from all over the world. They have had a profound effect in shaping Canadian society and culture. In 1971, Prime Minister

▌Immigrant Population in Canada

Place of Birth	Percentage of Canada's Population				
	Before 1961	1961–1970	1971–1980	1981–1990	1991–1996
United States	4.3	6.4	7.4	4.2	2.8
Central & South America	0.6	2.2	6.8	9.7	7.3
Caribbean & Bermuda	0.8	5.7	9.6	6.6	5.5
United Kingdom	25.2	21.3	13.3	5.8	2.4
Other Northern & Western Europe	26.9	11.5	6.0	4.4	3.1
Eastern Europe	16.6	5.2	3.2	10.2	8.5
Southern Europe	21.6	31.0	13.2	5.3	5.0
Africa	0.5	3.3	5.8	5.9	7.3
West-central Asia & the Middle East	0.5	1.9	3.1	7.1	7.9
Eastern Asia	1.9	4.9	10.5	15.8	24.3
South-east Asia	0.2	1.8	11.2	14.9	11.4
Southern Asia	0.4	3.7	8.1	9.1	13.5
Oceania & Other	0.4	1.2	1.5	0.9	1.0

Figure 3-11

What does this table reveal about changes in Canada's immigrant population over time? Based on the trends you see here, predict what the percentages were for 1997 to 2001.

Trudeau proclaimed "a policy of multiculturalism within a bilingual framework." This policy was intended to support the efforts of Canada's ethnic groups in preserving their cultural heritage. Today, Canadians point with pride to the cultural diversity of their country.

Canada has not always embraced the idea of a multicultural society. Until the 1960s, Canadian immigration laws were not truly open, and Canada used its legal powers to keep certain groups of people from entering this country and from achieving equality.

Selective Immigration

In the early 1880s, the Canadian Pacific Railway (CPR) started to build Canada's first transcontinental railroad. More than 10 000 workers came from China to help build the railway. They earned $1 a day, while other workers earned almost twice as much money for performing the same job. By 1885, the railroad was complete and the Chinese workers were no longer welcome in Canada. That year, Parliament imposed a $50 head tax on every Chinese person entering Canada. The tax was designed to discourage them from entering the country. In 1903, the tax was increased to $500.

In 1923, the Canadian government passed the *Chinese Exclusion Act*. It abolished the head tax but made it almost impossible for Chinese citizens to move to Canada. Between 1931 and 1941, the Chinese population in Canada dropped from 46 519 to 34 627 people.

Anti-Asian sentiment in Canada was not limited to the Chinese. In the early 1900s, the British Columbia government discouraged most Asian immigration by barring Asians from the professions and denying them the right to vote. In 1908, Wilfrid Laurier's government introduced a regulation requiring all immigrants to travel to Canada by "direct continuous passage" from their country of origin. This regulation was passed to stop immigration from India, since there was no direct travel between the two countries at the time.

In 1910, the federal Parliament passed a new *Immigration Act* that gave the Canadian government sweeping powers to reject "immigrants belonging to any race deemed unsuitable to the climate or requirements of Canada." In 1917, the newly created Department for Immigration and Colonization devised a list of "preferred" and "non-preferred" countries, which continued legal discrimination against immigrants from Asia.

Wartime Discrimination

During World War I, Ukrainian Canadians were branded as "enemy aliens" because many had come to Canada from Austria–Hungary (Britain's enemy during the war). Thousands of Ukrainian Canadians were **interned** under the *War Measures Act* of 1914. This Act had been passed by Robert Borden's government shortly after the war broke out. It gave the government extraordinary powers; for example, to arrest people without charging them with any offence and to detain them indefinitely (see Looking Back, page 62). About 5000 Ukrainians were imprisoned under the *War Measures Act* and another 80 000 were classified as enemy aliens. They had to wear special identification badges and report to the police regularly.

Did You Know?

Between 1885 and 1923, 81 000 Chinese immigrants paid $23 million in head tax, worth more than $1 billion in today's currency. There are fewer than 1000 citizens still alive today who were forced to pay head tax.

You Be the JUDGE

In 2000, the Chinese Canadian National Council announced that it was planning to sue the federal government for $1.2 billion in damages. The council said it would drop the lawsuit if the federal government compensated anyone who had paid head tax and if it publicly apologized to the Chinese people.

- Should the federal government today have to pay for the wrongs of previous administrations? Explain.

Japanese Canadians were similarly targeted during World War II. Before the war, they had endured anti-Asian discrimination. When the Japanese attacked Pearl Harbor, however, this resentment gave way to near-hysteria in the United States and Canada. Despite RCMP reports that Japanese Canadians posed no threat to Canadian security, the Canadian government began rounding them up in March of 1942. Men, women, and children were placed in internment camps in the interior of British Columbia, where they remained until the end of the war. In the camps, men were forced to work for the government for 25 cents per day. The Canadian government also confiscated their property and sold it at government auctions. After the war, many Japanese families had no homes or possessions and were forcibly resettled in the Prairies and Ontario. Approximately 4300 individuals were deported to Japan, despite the fact that they were English speaking and had no ties to the country.

Canada also refused entry to thousands of Jewish refugees escaping persecution in Nazi Germany on the eve of World War II. It did so on the grounds that their presence would upset Canada's ethnic balance. Anti-Semitism and anti-immigrant feelings were strong in Canada at the time. The refugees were forced to return to Europe where many later perished during the Holocaust.

Immigration Following World War II

In 1947, Prime Minister Mackenzie King announced a new immigration policy designed to attract new immigrants. Its purpose was to foster population growth and expand the Canadian economy. A careful selection process would ensure that the number of new immigrants would not exceed the "absorptive capacity" of the country. King bluntly declared that it was not a "fundamental right" of all foreigners to immigrate to Canada. Only persons whom the government regarded as "desirable future citizens" would be admitted. King considered immigration of non-Europeans undesirable as it would "make a fundamental alteration in the character of our population."

King's new immigration policy brought about a new wave of immigration from Europe. Between 1947 and 1962, Canada admitted nearly 250 000 persons seeking escape from the dreadful conditions that were the result of World War II. In 1956 and 1957, Canada accepted 37 500 Hungarian refugees fleeing a failed uprising against Communist rule in their country.

Beginning in the 1960s, Canada's immigration policy underwent a major change. By 1967, the federal government had eliminated race, religion, and national origin as a basis for selecting immigrants. The termination of this discriminatory practice spelled the dismantling of a major barrier to equality in Canada.

A **points system** was introduced for assessing independent applicants on the basis of education, skills, personal qualities such as resourcefulness and motivation, and occupational demand. Canada remained highly selective in whom it would accept as immigrants, but now selection was based on the ability of immigrants to contribute to the economy.

Large numbers of immigrants from Asia, Africa, the Caribbean, and Latin America began arriving in Canada for the first time as a result of the new regulations. The long-term effect has been a dramatic change in Canada's cultural and social fabric and the emergence of a multicultural society.

Building on the new policy, the *Immigration Act, 1976*, established the basic legal framework for immigration to Canada that exists to this day. Section 3 of the Act spelled out the fundamental objectives of Canada's immigration policy. The *Immigration Act, 1976*, divides persons entering Canada into four categories: visitors, family class immigrants, independent class immigrants, and refugees.

▌ Categories of Persons Entering Canada, *Immigration Act, 1976*

Category	Description
Visitors	Visitors are persons lawfully in Canada for temporary purposes (e.g., tourists, students, temporary workers, and business travellers).
Family Class Immigrants	Canadian citizens or permanent residents can sponsor the immigration of close family relatives if they are willing and able to provide for their housing, food, clothing, medical care, and other expenses.
Independent Class Immigrants	Independent class immigrants are individuals seeking better economic opportunities (e.g., workers, entrepreneurs, and self-employed professionals).
Refugees	Refugees must establish that they have a "well-founded" fear of being persecuted in the country of their nationality for reasons of race, religion, nationality, membership of a particular social group, or political opinion. Once a claim has been approved, a refugee can apply to become a permanent resident of Canada.

Figure 3-12

Name the identifying feature of each category of people entering Canada.

Case

Pushpanathan v. Canada (Minister of Employment and Immigration)

[1998] 1 S.C.R. 982
Supreme Court of Canada

In 1985, Pushpanathan claimed refugee status in Canada under the United Nations *Convention Relating to the Status of Refugees*. Later he was arrested and charged with conspiracy to traffic in heroin with a street value of $10 million. He pleaded guilty to the charge and was sentenced to eight years in prison. In 1991, while on parole, Pushpanathan applied for a renewal of his refugee claim. Immigration Canada refused and tried to have him deported from the country. It argued that the UN Convention states that refugee status should not be granted if the person "has been guilty of acts contrary to the ... principles of the United Nations."

The Federal Court of Canada dismissed Pushpanathan's application for a renewal of his refugee status. The case was appealed to the Supreme Court of Canada, which overruled the Federal Court's decision. In its opinion, Pushpanathan was not a threat to Canadian society and had paid the penalty for his earlier offence.

For Discussion

1. **Which court decision do you agree with and why?**

2. **Should refugees and immigrants who commit a crime in Canada be deported?**

activity

Visit **www.law.nelson.com** and follow the links to learn more about the United Nations *Convention Relating to the Status of Refugees*.

The Act also sets out who may not enter Canada. Inadmissible persons (those who cannot be admitted) include immigrant applicants who are suffering from illnesses that pose a public danger or may place an undue financial burden on health services; persons who lack the funds to support themselves; and convicted criminals or those who pose a risk of committing serious crimes (see Case, page 87). Potential or known terrorists and persons who have been convicted of war crimes are also inadmissible.

To determine whether a prospective immigrant should be prevented from entering the country, immigration officials conduct security checks with police authorities in the applicant's home country. While still outside Canada, an applicant will also have to undergo a complete medical exam that meets Canadian standards.

A New Immigration Act

On November 1, 2001, the *Immigration and Refugee Protection Act, 2001,* replaced the *Immigration Act, 1976.* Highlights of the new Act, which builds on the *Immigration Act, 1976,* include measures to curb abuse of the immigration and refugee system; strengthen sponsorship obligations; streamline the refugee determination process; and facilitate family reunification. The Act also has new selection criteria to attract more highly skilled and adaptable independent immigrants, and provides "front-end" screening measures to better identify and deal with suspected criminals and terrorists and any others who present security risks. Persons involved in smuggling illegal migrants face fines of up to $1 million and life in prison.

Figure 3-13

This man hid in a car seat in an attempt to gain entry to the United States from Mexico. What should Canada do to punish people involved in smuggling illegal migrants?

Canada's immigration laws allow Canada to control its borders. The Canadian government responded to the terrorist attacks in the United States on September 11, 2001, by increasing security along the Canada–United States border and at border crossings and airports. (See Agents of Change, page 30.)

In the face of globalization, Canada may be forced to change certain rules. The governments of Canada, the United States, and Mexico are moving toward a closer economic union. The continued lowering of trade barriers will likely be accompanied by the easing of restrictions on the movement of workers and trade goods across international borders. Such a process is well under way in Europe.

Figure 3-14

Former Canadian Foreign Affairs Minister John Manley and U.S. Secretary of State Colin Powell. Canada increased security along its border with the United States after the terrorist attacks in New York and Washington, DC, in September 2001.

Review Your Understanding (Pages 84 to 89)

1. **Identify how Ukrainian Canadians and Japanese Canadians were the victims of wartime discrimination in Canada.**

2. **Why was Prime Minister Mackenzie King reluctant to allow the immigration of non-Europeans to Canada?**

3. **When did Canada officially end its discriminatory immigration practices?**

4. **Distinguish between family class immigrants and independent class immigrants.**

5. **Distinguish between immigrants and refugees.**

6. **Why don't illegal immigrants apply to enter Canada through established immigration channels?**

7. **Identify three major changes that were introduced in the new *Immigration and Refugee Protection Act, 2001*.**

3.5 Gay Men and Lesbians

The late 20th century marked a turning point in the attitudes toward **homosexuality** and the legal rights of gay men and lesbians. In the past, homosexuality was seen as a crime, and punishments included fines, imprisonment, torture, and even death. In Britain, until 1861, any man convicted of having sex with another man could receive the death penalty. That year, the law was amended so that the punishment could range from 10 years to life imprisonment. Today, some nations retain similar punishments for homosexuality. Up until 1967, Canada regarded homosexuality as a criminal offence and dealt with it in the *Criminal Code*.

Changing Attitudes and Legal Rights

A number of events set the stage for changing views toward homosexuality and for the beginnings of the gay rights movement—a movement for legal rights as well as social acceptance. One of the factors was timing. In the 1960s, young people rebelled against the values and traditions of the previous generation. There was a growing interest in human rights, including women's rights and civil rights for Black Americans and Canadians. In Canada, when Pierre Trudeau became Justice Minister in 1967, he liberalized Canada's divorce laws and rewrote the laws that dealt with abortion and prostitution. He also decriminalized homosexuality, which meant that it was no longer a crime to have a homosexual relationship.

South of the border, another important event occurred. In 1969, police raided the Stonewall Inn, a gay bar in New York City. (Homosexual bars in Canada and the United States were often raided in the 1950s and 1960s.) A riot ensued, involving an estimated 400 people. Four police officers were injured and 13 rioters were arrested. This was the first time that a group of homosexual people had resisted arrest and fought back. This event is widely acknowledged as the start of the gay rights movement in North America. It was only a matter of time before organizations would form to press for rights in the legal arena.

In 1996, the federal government added "sexual orientation" to the *Canadian Human Rights Act*. This meant that homosexuals were now protected from discrimination when it came to matters involving the federal government. However, sexual orientation was not included in the *Canadian Charter of Rights and Freedoms*. In *Moore v. Canada (Treasury Board)* (1996), the Canadian Human Rights Tribunal ordered the federal government to extend employment benefits, such as medical and dental benefits, to partners of same-sex couples. In 1997, the federal government obeyed the order and offered same-sex benefits to its gay and lesbian employees. Many companies, such as IBM, the Royal Bank of Canada, and Bell Canada now offer same-sex benefits to their gay and lesbian employees.

In the case of *M. v. H.* (1999), the Supreme Court of Canada ruled that same-sex couples have the same legal rights and responsibilities as heterosexual couples. (See Case, page 477.) M. and

Figure 3-15

The Canadian music station MuchMusic makes an appearance at Pride Day in Toronto.

H. were lesbians who had lived together as a couple since 1982. M. moved into the home owned by H. Over the years, they started a business together and acquired other properties. By 1992, the relationship ended and M. sought part ownership of H.'s original home in addition to support payments, since she had no money of her own. M. asked the courts to strike down a section of Ontario's *Family Law Act*, which stated that only married and common-law heterosexual partners could claim support payments.

In a 9 to 0 decision, the Supreme Court of Canada concluded that Ontario's *Family Law Act* was unconstitutional because its definition of "spouse" excluded same-sex relationships. H. was ordered to make support payments to M. Several provinces, including the government of Ontario, acted promptly to change dozens of laws, giving same-sex couples equal standing with unmarried heterosexual couples. However, no government has changed the definition of "spouse," which still refers exclusively to a male husband and female wife.

As with feminism, the gay rights movement has depended on people and effective organizing to press for legal equality. One of the most effective organizations in Canada is EGALE (Equality for Gays and Lesbians Everywhere), which has been fighting since 1986, mostly at the federal level. EGALE pressed the federal government to honour its commitment to add "sexual orientation" to the *Canadian Human Rights Act*. It also intervened before the Supreme Court of Canada in support of legal recognition for same-sex relationships.

Case

Trinity Western University v. College of Teachers (British Columbia)

(2001) 82 C.R.R. (2d) 189
Supreme Court of Canada

Trinity Western University is a private Christian institution. All teachers and students must sign a contract in which they agree not to disobey the teachings of the Bible. Unacceptable practices include adultery, the viewing of pornography, gay sex, drunkenness, swearing, abortion, lying, and involvement in the occult. Breaking this contract results in expulsion from the university.

Trinity established a five-year teacher-training program. In 1996, it applied to the British Columbia College of Teachers to assume full control of the program. The British Columbia College of Teachers refused because the program appeared to discriminate against groups of people, including gay men and lesbians. The Supreme Court of Canada ruled that the British Columbia College of Teachers was wrong to deny Trinity full control over its teacher-training program. The Court said the institution and its teachers and students were entitled to their beliefs. Moreover, there was nothing to indicate that teachers graduating from Trinity would discriminate against homosexual people. The college had authority to act only against those who showed discrimination in the classroom. People can believe what they want as long as they do not act on these beliefs. The Supreme Court of Canada also awarded $1 million to Trinity for its legal costs.

For Discussion

1. Identify the main issue in this case.
2. What is your opinion of this ruling by the Supreme Court of Canada?

Review Your Understanding (Pages 89 to 91)

1. **What are the attitudes and social conditions that have created barriers to achieving equality for gay men and lesbians? How are attitudes connected to laws?**

2. **Why is "Stonewall" an important event in the gay rights movements?**

3. **What legal changes have been made in Canada with respect to homosexuality since 1967?**

4. **What are the legal consequences of *Moore v. Canada (Treasury Board)*?**

5. **What are the legal implications of *M. v. H.*?**

3.6 People with Disabilities

There are 600 million people around the world who have mental and physical disabilities. Most of these people still experience barriers to achieving equality, both in the social and legal sense. Such barriers include unequal access to schools, services, and employment, and barriers to mobility—for example, a lack of suitable transportation or poor access to certain buildings. Only recently has attention been focused on the rights of disabled people and the barriers they face in achieving equality.

Today, in many countries of the world, children who are born with disabilities are often abandoned and left to die. Their parents simply have no resources to raise them. Unfortunately, rejection has marked the treatment of people with disabilities throughout history. Even in the 20th century, children born with disabilities were often placed in government-run institutions for disabled people. By the end of World War II, however, parents of disabled children were more interested in having their children fit into society. In addition, disabled adults wanted a say in planning their own futures.

When the United Nations proclaimed 1981 the International Year of the Disabled, the spotlight was thrown on the legal rights of people with disabilities. In the 1980s, across Canada, there was a major movement to close institutions for people with disabilities, including men and women with mental illness. The goal was to allow every member of Canadian society to live in a dignified manner in the community, with the proper supports. Increasingly, Canadians started asking their government to help meet these needs.

People with Disabilities Today

People with disabilities still face many barriers in the 21st century. For example, children with disabilities are guaranteed an education by the *Canadian Charter of Rights and Freedoms*, yet many schools cannot meet their needs on a full-time basis. In 2001, an Ottawa father went to court to force one of the local public schools to accept his nine-year-old son, Zachary, as a full-time student. The school argued that it didn't have the funds to assist Zachary for more than two days per week. Zachary has a seizure disorder and almost no speech. Zachary's father was arrested for mischief for taking Zachary to school on the other three days. Later, the charges against him were dropped.

Did You Know?

In the year 2000, there were 1614 complaints received by the Canadian Human Rights Commission:

- 36% based on disability
- 27% based on race, colour, and national or ethnic origin
- 19% based on sexual discrimination

In 2001, approximately 2000 families of severely disabled children joined together to sue the government of Ontario for $500 million. It was the largest legal action ever started on behalf of disabled children. The families claimed that the government was legally obligated under the *Child and Family Services Act* to provide services for children with severe disabilities. The government said it would help—but that its new funding policy meant the institutions would receive funding, not the parents. As a result, many parents felt they had to give up custody of their children to get care for them. Many of these cases have been settled, and some parents have already received the funds to look after their children.

Today in Canada, businesses and government are still not required to provide complete access for people with disabilities. For example, there is no law stating that there must be wheelchair ramps to enter buildings. It is left up to the company or organization to provide this service. Disabled persons can complain to their provincial human rights commission, but these cases are heard individually. In countries such as Australia and the United States, strict laws make it compulsory to remove barriers for disabled people. In 1990, the U.S. government passed a tough civil law called the *Americans with Disabilities Act*, which ensures equal services for people with disabilities. Under this law, they are also guaranteed equal employment opportunities. Penalties for breaking the law range from $55 000 for a first offence to $110 000 for a second offence. Canada and its provinces and territories have no such guarantees.

Figure 3-16

Ann Larcade and her disabled son, Alexandre. Larcade took part in the class action suit filed by Ontario parents.

Case

Miele v. Famous Players Inc.

(2000) 37 C.H.R.R. D/1
British Columbia Human Rights Tribunal

Vince Miele uses a wheelchair because of a spinal cord injury. He goes to the movies on a regular basis. Miele complained to the British Columbia Human Rights Tribunal that he could not enter a certain movie theatre through the main entrance because of a physical barrier. He had to ask staff to unlock a special door and use an elevator, which was time-consuming and embarrassing. He felt that he should have the same type of easy access provided to other movie patrons.

The British Columbia Human Rights Tribunal agreed that Miele's human rights had been violated—the theatre had discriminated against him because of his physical disability. It ordered the theatre to pay him $4000 in damages for injuries done to his dignity, independence, and self-respect. It also ordered the theatre to provide a door, to be staffed on a permanent basis, for use by disabled persons. This would allow all customers to enter the theatre in a similar manner.

For Discussion

1. Summarize the decision of the British Columbia Human Rights Tribunal.
2. How do damages provide compensation?
3. What precedent has been set here?

Did You Know?

One in six persons is disabled, and yet only one in ten is represented in the workforce.

Figure 3-17

Should some conditions be added, or omitted? Explain.

Provincial human rights commissions listen to complaints from people who believe they have suffered discrimination, including discrimination because of disability. However, these commissions deal only with situations where discrimination has already taken place. Figure 3-17 lists the conditions that the Ontario Human Rights Commission defines as legal disabilities.

▮ Legal Disabilities in Ontario

• Brain injury	• Mental illness	• Physical disability	• Blindness
• Deafness	• Mental retardation	• Substance abuse	• Obesity
• Epilepsy	• Behaviour problems	• Learning problems	

Review Your Understanding (Pages 92 to 94)

1. What is "access"?
2. Why is access a major focus of attention when arguing for the rights of the disabled?
3. Why did families of disabled children sue the Ontario government in 2001?
4. What is the major difference between U.S. and Canadian legislation when it comes to people with disabilities?

3.7 The Rights of the Poor

Although poverty has always existed, only recently has poverty been viewed as a barrier to achieving equality. Traditionally, people who are poor have been blamed for their situation and have been stereotyped as lazy or even criminal. Poverty exists in Canada, despite the fact that it is a wealthy country with a high standard of living.

During the 20th century, the Canadian government introduced many programs to address poverty. In 1927, it introduced old age pensions: $20 a month for needy persons over the age of 70. In 1970, the age qualification dropped to 65 and all Canadians became eligible to receive an old age pension. In 1966, the Canada Assistance Plan was introduced. It was aimed at other groups of needy Canadians. Medicare (free, government-subsidized health care) was introduced in 1968. This plan helped thousands of poor Canadians by giving every citizen in Canada the right to free health care. These initiatives have provided partial solutions to poverty in Canada.

Poverty Today

Today, an estimated 5 million people in Canada are poor, a group that includes 1.3 million children. A family is considered to be poor if it spends more than 55 percent of its income on basic necessities such as food, shelter, and clothing. The National Council on Welfare says that a family of four living in a major Canadian city with an income of less than $32 706 per year is poor, or low income. In rural Canada, the figure is $22 264. These baseline figures are called the poverty line. According to Statistics Canada, 54 percent of women who are single parents live in poverty—that's 314 000 women with 546 000 children. Anyone who depends on social assistance is also considered to live below the poverty line.

Poverty is an important barrier to equal opportunity. Without proper rest or nutrition, for example, children cannot develop normally or learn easily. If they experience failure at school from an early age, they may experience more serious problems later in life. A 2001 study by the University of British Columbia found that each year of education increases a person's average wage by 8.3 percent ($2 490). Poverty is directly related to early school leaving and to a higher rate of unemployment. This is just one example of how the cycle of poverty can continue into adulthood and be so difficult to break. In 1997, Canada's provincial governments developed a strategy called the National Children's Agenda to improve the well-being of children. It recognized that the environment in which children are raised affects them in later life. It noted that governments, as well as parents, are responsible for Canada's children.

Did You Know?

Although Canada's House of Commons voted unanimously in 1989 "to achieve the goal of eliminating poverty among Canadian children by the year 2000," child poverty continued to increase. By 2000, it had increased by 45 percent.

Eliminating Barriers to Opportunity

Some people think that one way to eliminate poverty would be to give all Canadians a **guaranteed annual income (GAI).** A guaranteed income is a set amount of money that all Canadian adults would receive. It would ensure that everyone had enough money to pay for necessities: food, clothing, and shelter. People who support the GAI say that if every Canadian had a guaranteed income, there would be no need for employment insurance, social assistance, or food banks. Since World War II, the government has provided more money for elderly persons who have no other income. Their quality of life has greatly improved. Why can't the government do the same for millions of other poor Canadians? At one time or another, the New Democratic Party (NDP), and the Liberal and Green parties have seriously debated the GAI, but it has never been proposed as law.

Other people say that everyone has the right to decent housing. At one time, in the 1970s and 1980s, the federal government funded the construction of **social housing**—inexpensive housing for low-income Canadians. Today, it does not. In addition, a number of provincial governments have decided that all housing should be the responsibility of private business. People who work

Figure 3-18

Homelessness is an extreme form of poverty. Without a home, people may find that they have even fewer rights. (See Issue, page 558.)

on behalf of poor Canadians say that the shortage of social housing means that low-income households must spend a greater proportion of their income on rent. As a result, they have less money left over for food, transportation, and other necessities.

Not everyone agrees that people who are poor should be provided with income or housing. In some provinces, social assistance has been reduced dramatically or is being tied to other demands. In 1993, Alberta began reducing social benefits and tightened eligibility requirements for welfare. The Ontario government has replaced welfare with "workfare," which requires people to participate in job-search training, community service, and job placement. If people do not spend a required number of hours per week on these activities, their welfare benefits are cancelled. The Ontario government might also introduce literacy testing and drug testing for welfare recipients, on the grounds that illiteracy and drug addiction are barriers to employment. The government would then provide follow-up treatment programs to people who need help with one or both problems. If welfare recipients refused to enter these programs, their welfare benefits would be cut off. Some groups, such as the Campaign Against Child Poverty, believe that such testing would be an infringement of human rights and human decency.

Review Your Understanding (Pages 94 to 96)

1. Why is poverty considered a barrier to achieving equality?
2. When is a family considered poor?
3. What has Canada done to help those who live in poverty?
4. Explain the following statements:
   - Increased education lessens a person's chance of living in poverty.
   - Governments as well as parents are responsible for Canada's children.
5. Should a guaranteed annual income (GAI) be introduced in Canada? Explain.
6. Should governments provide affordable housing for people with low incomes? Justify your opinion.
7. What strategies have the Alberta and Ontario governments used to deal with poverty? Evaluate these strategies.

In Human Rights

There are a surprising number of careers in the human rights field. These include careers in the public service or with agencies charged with protecting the public interest, careers in the field of human resource management, and careers with private organizations advocating for human rights

 Visit www.law.nelson.com and follow the links to learn about the Human Rights Job Board page.

Figure 3-19
Physicians for Human Rights

In Focus

Human Rights Commissioner

Human rights commissioners serve on the federal Canadian Human Rights Commission or on provincial human rights commissions. Most are appointed and work on a part-time basis while working at other jobs. Their duty is to ensure equality of opportunity and freedom from discrimination. Human rights commissioners hear individual complaints from the public, although sometimes they conduct general inquiries. For example, in June 2001, the British Columbia Human Rights Commission announced its intention to investigate Native education. Through recommendations, the commission intends to help eliminate barriers to success that Native students experience.

Employment Equity Officer

Employment equity specialists work in the human resources divisions of companies and public organizations. They help develop and advise on policies and programs to ensure that their employers comply with Human Rights Codes and standards. They also assist in investigating complaints by employees of discrimination and harassment.

Advocacy Group Staff Member/Volunteer

Human rights advocacy groups operate at the local, national, and international levels. They include the Canadian Civil Liberties Association, the Human Rights Institute of Canada, Amnesty International, Human Rights Watch, the International Campaign to Ban Land Mines, and Physicians for Human Rights. These groups fight for human rights by mounting campaigns against instances of human rights abuses. These organizations often operate with small staffs and rely heavily on volunteers. Becoming an advocacy group volunteer could lead to a career in the human rights field.

Career Exploration Activity

As a class, explore the career opportunities in the human rights field. The information you compile can be used to profile various law-related careers for a guidance bulletin-board display, or you may choose to run a law-related career fair.

1. Use the Internet or your nearest employment information centre to conduct research into careers related to human rights.

2. Outline the roles and responsibilities of a human rights commissioner and an employment equity officer and place the information on an index card.

Chapter Review

Chapter Highlights

- Manitoba was the first province to give women the right to vote—in 1916.
- The Persons Case of 1929 established that women were legal persons and could be appointed to political office.
- Women continue to fight for pay equity and employment equity.
- Native peoples are fighting for their collective rights as distinct nations within Canada.
- The courts have played a major role in defining Aboriginal rights.
- Self-government is the goal of many First Nations leaders.
- Several major land claims settlements have been reached in Canada.
- Immigration laws restrict who may enter the country.
- Canada's early immigration laws were often discriminatory against certain groups.
- The *Immigration and Refugee Protection Act, 2001,* replaced the *Immigration Act, 1976.*
- Refugee claimants must establish that they have a "well-founded" fear of being persecuted in their country of origin.
- Immigration has transformed Canada into a multicultural society.
- Traditionally, homosexuality has been treated as a crime.
- The Supreme Court ruled in the *M. v. H.* case that under Canada's Constitution, same-sex couples must be treated the same as married couples.
- Canada has not forced private businesses or government to provide equal access to disabled persons.
- An estimated 5 million Canadians live in poverty.
- The guaranteed annual income has been proposed as a solution to poverty.

Review Key Terms

Name the key terms that are described below.

a) principle of equal treatment of all employees, based on their abilities

b) housing that is subsidized by the government, resulting in lower rents for occupants

c) the term used to recognize the sovereign rights of Canada's first inhabitants.

d) a claim to ancestral land fought in court

e) absorbed into

f) someone who fights for the extension of the rights of women, especially in social and political life

g) right to vote

h) the awarding of points to immigrants based on their education, skills, and personal qualities

i) system that sets aside a share of the total (places, seats, and so on) for a specific group

j) an amount of money given by the government to all citizens of a country to pay for the basic necessities—food, clothing, and shelter

k) confined as enemy aliens or prisoners of war

l) rights as a group or nation

Check Your Knowledge

1. Identify the scope of the *Canadian Bill of Rights* with respect to equality rights. How has the *Canadian Charter of Rights and Freedoms* improved on equality rights?

2. Summarize the opposing views in the debate over collective rights versus individual rights with respect to Native issues.

3. Identify and describe examples of racial discrimination found in Canada's past immigration laws and policy.

4. Five million Canadians live in poverty. In what ways is society addressing issues of poverty in Canada?

Apply Your Learning

5. *Brillinger v. Brockie (No.3)*(2000), 37 C.H.R.R. D/15 (Ontario Board of Inquiry)

   Ray Brillinger, the complainant, placed an order for printing materials (envelopes and business cards) with the respondent, Scott Brockie, President of Imaging Excellence Inc. Brockie refused to take the order on the grounds of his religious beliefs. He believes that homosexuality is contrary to the teachings of the Bible. He argued that his right to freedom of religion under section 2(a) of the *Canadian Charter of Rights and Freedoms* gave him the right to refuse the order. Brillinger argued that section 1 of the Ontario *Human Rights Code*, which guarantees "equal treatment," had been broken and that discrimination existed.

a) Do you think companies have the right to do business with whomever they choose? Explain.

b) Outline arguments for both sides of the case. In whose favour do you think the case will be resolved?

6. *Chartrand v. Vanderwell Constructors (1971) Ltd.* (2001), (Alberta Human Rights & Citizenship Commission)

Jean Chartrand, the complainant, had been employed by the respondent, Vanderwell Constructors, for three years. She quit her job because she believed that she was a victim of sexual harassment. She claimed her shift supervisor had touched her inappropriately and had made sexually offensive remarks. The respondent denied the accusations.

a) What type of evidence would have to be presented for Chartrand to succeed in her claim of sexual harassment?

b) How important is it to be protected from sexual harassment? Do you think that this is a basic human right? Explain.

7. In 2001, immigration officials turned down an application for landed immigrant status from a family from South Africa on the grounds that one of the children, a 14-year-old boy, has Down syndrome and therefore would create an "excessive demand" on Canada's health-care system. The father, a businessman, had been transferred to Canada by his employer in 1996.

The family appealed the decision. Following a review of the case, the Minister of Immigration accepted the appeal and issued a temporary permit allowing the family to remain in Canada. The family will have the opportunity to reapply for landed immigrant status in five years.

a) On what basis do you think the Minister of Immigration accepted the appeal?

b) Should Canada bar applicants who have health problems that pose a potential burden to Canada's health-care system? Justify your position.

Communicate Your Understanding

8. "Societies progress more rapidly if they adopt specific measures to narrow gender gaps." "Societies which restrict women by denying them an education and basic freedoms hurt themselves both economically and socially."
—World Bank Report, 2001

Summarize the meaning of the World Bank Report statements. What do you think can be done to eliminate barriers to achieving equality for women in Canada and in other countries? For extended research, use the library or Internet to identify examples of countries where women are denied an education. Take your research further to determine how one such country is progressing economically. To what extent are the statements by the World Bank true?

9. Do you favour more autonomy for Native peoples, or do you favour their assimilation into Canadian society? Express your opinion and justify your answer with examples.

10. "The state has no place in the bedrooms of the nation." This statement was made by Pierre Elliott Trudeau in December 1967. At the time, he was Justice Minister responding to the criticism that he was making divorce too easy.

a) Evaluate the significance of this quotation? Do you agree with it? Why or why not?

b) Trudeau's remark can be applied to a number of issues today. Identify these issues and comment on the extent to which you think this statement should hold true.

Develop Your Thinking

11. As part of a forum for International Women's Day, you have been asked to develop and present a time line highlighting significant achievements in the rights of women over the last 100 years. Where possible, include the names of the individuals and organizations and evaluate their contributions in developing increased awareness of the rights of women in Canadian society.

12. Civil disobedience (deliberately breaking the law to draw attention to an unfair situation) has been used by many groups. In the early 1900s in Britain, suffragettes chained themselves to buildings, fought with police, went on hunger strikes, and were imprisoned and force-fed.

    a) Research individuals and groups in Canada today that practise civil disobedience as a means of protest.

        Not all civil disobedience is violent. In general, how do law enforcement officials deal with protesters who practise nonviolent civil disobedience? To what extent should the police have the power to limit peaceful civil disobedience? What special training should police have to effectively deal with individuals who are practising civil disobedience?

    b) Does breaking the law sometimes advance the cause of justice or does it always act contrary to justice? Provide specific examples. (Think of the civil rights demonstrations against racial prejudice in the United States.)

13. Assume that you have become a rights activist for disabled persons and you wish to make recommendations to the school board or to your local town council regarding the elimination of barriers to achieving equality. First choose a disability that you wish to investigate and then imagine that you suffer from that disability. What barriers to equality do you experience in your everyday life in the school setting and within the community at large? How could your needs be accommodated? Are there high costs involved? Write a report to your school board or local council, including recommendations.

Ignorantia legis neminem excusat
Ignorance of the law, which everyone is bound to know, excuses no one.
Legal Maxim

Unit 2

Criminal Law

Chapter
4
Criminal Law and Criminal Offences

Focus Questions

- What is a crime?
- What is the difference between summary and indictable offences?
- What elements or conditions must exist for an action to be considered a crime?
- What criminal courts exist to interpret and apply the law?
- How are crimes handled in the courts?

Chapter at a Glance

Figure 4-1

This Vancouver house was the scene of a home invasion. A home invasion involves several people who determine that the residents are home and devise a plan to confront, attack, and subdue them. Robbery is the goal. What kind of evidence might officers be looking for at this crime scene to determine if a home invasion occurred?

The law exists to protect society and individuals and to keep order. **Criminal law** deals with offences committed against society. **Civil law** deals with offences committed against individuals.

The distinction between criminal law and civil law is obvious in the following example. Suppose Ron decides to break into Kathy's house to steal her electronic equipment. He breaks the door lock with a crowbar and enters the house when no one is home. He leaves with a laptop computer, a stereo-CD player, a DVD player, and a digital camera. The *Criminal Code* describes Ron's offence as **"break and enter"** and sets a penalty for committing the offence (see The Law, below).

For breaking and entering, Ron would be charged under criminal law because he has done something that society considers unacceptable. People have the right to live safely in their own homes and to keep their own possessions. If Ron is found guilty, he may have to pay a fine, do community work, and/or be imprisoned. All these penalties will result in a cost to him—either paying money and/or being deprived of his time and freedom. However, none of these penalties compensates Kathy for her personal property losses. For this, she must sue Ron for damages under civil law. This case would be heard at a different time and in civil court. (For information on the civil courts, see Chapter 11.)

Figure 4-2

Ron escapes with Kathy's stereo-CD player. Breaking and entering is a criminal offence, a crime against society.

The Need for Criminal Law

Criminal law helps to keep order in society. Penalties for crimes help to deter (prevent) people from committing crimes. Criminal law emphasizes prevention and penalties. It does not place much emphasis on compensating victims for the losses suffered because of a crime. It is difficult, if not impossible, to compensate victims for certain crimes. The victim of a murder can never be brought back. The victim of a penniless thief will not be repaid.

The Law   The Criminal Code

Excerpts from the *Criminal Code*
348.

(1) Every one who

    (a) breaks and enters a place with intent to commit an indictable offence therein ...

  is guilty

    (d) if the offence is committed in relation to a dwelling-house, of an indictable offence and liable to imprisonment for life, and

    (e) if the offence is committed in relation to a place other than a dwelling-house, of

an indictable offence and liable to imprisonment for a term not exceeding ten years or of an offence punishable on summary conviction.

For Discussion

1. **Why do you think that the punishment for breaking into a dwelling-house (private residence) is more severe than for breaking into a business or store?**

Most people believe that criminal law should protect people and property. Some want harsh penalties to discourage potential offenders or to punish people for wrongdoing. Others want the criminal justice system to rehabilitate, or help, those who have already harmed society. Some think that criminal law should have all these functions.

4.2 The Nature of Criminal Law

Figure 4-3

Former federal Health Minister Allan Rock is shown with the government's legal marijuana crop. Canada's new medicinal marijuana policy came into effect in August 2001. It allows people who require marijuana for medical reasons to be exempt from narcotics laws. They can grow marijuana, or have someone grow it for them, and use it without fear of prosecution.

Parliament decides what is a crime and regularly passes laws to change the *Criminal Code*. At any given time, the *Criminal Code* reflects the values of society by declaring certain actions to be criminal. Reform of the *Criminal Code* usually reflects a shift in these values and may occur because of public pressure. For example, in Canada, there has been some public pressure to decriminalize the use of marijuana, which means that smoking marijuana would no longer be a crime. However, not everyone agrees with this proposed change, and the issue is the subject of heated debate.

Criminal Actions

Because different people have different values and beliefs, they may disagree on which actions are criminal. Law makers, lobbyists, and members of the general public often debate such topics as euthanasia (mercy killing), gun control, abortion, and pornography. In a healthy, democratic society, such debates can help to determine what changes are needed in the law. In general, Parliament will reexamine laws if the public is overwhelmingly in favour of reform, if an issue does not "go away," or if an interest group that opposes an existing law has gained enough support to force a parliamentary debate.

The Law Commission of Canada has suggested that certain conditions must exist for an act to be subject to criminal penalties. These are as follows:

- The action must harm other people.
- The action must violate the basic values of society.
- Using the law to deal with the action must not violate the basic values of society.
- Criminal law can make a significant contribution to resolving the problem.

Any reforms to the *Criminal Code* must take these conditions into consideration.

Agents of Change | Svend Robinson

Svend Robinson is the NDP representative of British Columbia's Burnaby–Douglas constituency. First elected to the House of Commons in 1979 at 26, Robinson began his political career as the youngest member of the NDP caucus. He has been reelected six times.

Robinson is no stranger to controversy. He has engaged in civil disobedience and has taken legal risks to advance the causes he believes in. He supported Sue Rodriguez, a British Columbia woman suffering from Lou Gehrig's disease, in her attempt to convince the Supreme Court of Canada to legalize doctor-assisted suicide. Though Rodriguez's efforts to change the *Criminal Code* failed, she did die in 1994 with the help of an unidentified physician. Robinson was at her bedside and witnessed her death.

Following her death, a special Senate Committee on Euthanasia and Assisted Suicide was appointed on February 23, 1994. It undertook "to examine and report on the legal, social and ethical issues relating to euthanasia and assisted suicide." In 1995, the Senate committee voted 4 to 3 against legalization. It was split on whether the current laws should be rewritten.

In November 1997, Robinson tried to change the law with a private bill. His move, like most bills not sponsored by government, failed. Recent polls indicate there is growing support among Canadians for people being able to take control of their own dying process, but there is no clear consensus about what kind of rules are needed. Despite differences of opinion within its membership, the Canadian Medical Association continues to state that members should not participate in euthanasia and assisted suicide.

See Issue on page 134 for more on euthanasia.

For Discussion

1. Identify information from this profile that suggests Canadian attitudes about euthanasia and assisted suicide are changing.
2. What is the position of the Canadian Medical Association?
3. Should courts decide on issues of euthanasia or assisted suicide or should legislators decide? Explain.

Figure 4-4
Svend Robinson

Review Your Understanding (Pages 103 to 105)

1. Explain the main purpose of criminal law.
2. Describe three functions of criminal law and provide brief examples to support your understanding.
3. When does Parliament decide to make certain actions criminal?
4. Why is it important to have a free and open debate about possible changes in the law?
5. According to the Law Commission of Canada, what conditions must exist for an action to be considered a crime? Express your opinion on whether you think each condition set out by the Law Commission is valid. Provide examples to support your opinion.

 activity

Visit **www.law.nelson.com** and follow the links to learn about law reform and the work of the Law Commission of Canada.

4.3   The Power to Make Criminal Law

In 1867, when Canada became a country, the provinces gave jurisdiction (authority) over criminal law to the federal Parliament. This meant that Parliament had the authority to decide which actions were crimes and to set punishments for crimes (section 91 of the *British North America Act*). Today, this means that if you were to commit a criminal offence in any of the provinces and territories, you would receive the same treatment whether you committed the offence in British Columbia or in Nova Scotia.

Quasi-Criminal Law

Following Confederation, the provinces still had the right to pass some laws. Technically, laws passed by the provinces, territories, or municipalities are not considered part of criminal law. They are referred to as quasi-criminal law because they resemble criminal law but do not deal with actual crimes. Traffic offences that fall under the *Highway Traffic Act* of each province and bylaws passed by municipalities are examples of quasi-criminal law. Breaking these laws usually results in a fine.

The Criminal Code

The *Criminal Code* is the main source of criminal law in Canada. It describes offences that are considered crimes, as well as punishments for crimes. Other criminal offences are listed in statutes passed by Parliament, such as the *Controlled Drugs and Substances Act* (formerly the *Narcotic Control Act*). You will read about these statutes in later chapters.

Parliament is always reforming the *Criminal Code* to meet the needs of Canadian society and to reflect its values. The judiciary (the judges and courts) interpret the criminal laws and apply them to individual cases. Judges have the power to determine if a law trespasses upon a citizen's rights as outlined in the *Canadian Charter of Rights and Freedoms*. If this occurs, the law is ruled to be unconstitutional and no longer in effect. When judges make decisions on important cases, these decisions may become precedents and may be followed by other judges making decisions in similar cases. In this manner, the judiciary helps to influence criminal law in Canada. These precedents are often referred to in the *Criminal Code*.

Review Your Understanding (Page 106)

1. Why was the federal government given jurisdiction over criminal law?
2. Compare quasi-criminal law to criminal law and provide an example of each.
3. Identify the purpose of the *Criminal Code* of Canada.
4. When might a law be ruled unconstitutional?
5. How does the judiciary influence our criminal law?

Did You Know?

The *Criminal Code* does not allow accused persons to defend themselves on the grounds that they did not know they were committing an offence. Section 19 of the Code states that "ignorance of the law by a person who commits an offence is not an excuse for committing that offence."

Did You Know?

In 1993, the *Criminal Code* was changed to make harassment a crime in the wake of some well-publicized cases of stalking and harassment. Criminal harassment includes repeatedly following someone, repeatedly watching someone's house or place of work, and making threats of violence.

Types of Criminal Offences

If you attend a session at a Canadian court, you will hear people being charged with **summary conviction offences** or **indictable offences.** Some offences can be either summary or indictable, depending on the circumstances of the cases. These are called **hybrid offences** because they could belong to either category of offence.

Summary Conviction Offences

Summary conviction offences are minor criminal offences. People accused of these offences can be arrested and summoned to court without delay. The maximum penalty for most summary convictions under the *Criminal Code* is $2000 and/or six months in jail. In other statutes, more severe penalties for summary offences are given. For example, the *Controlled Drugs and Substances Act* specifies a maximum penalty of a fine of $2000 and/or imprisonment for one year for possession of a narcotic.

Indictable Offences

Indictable offences are serious crimes that carry more severe penalties than summary conviction offences. The *Criminal Code* sets a maximum penalty for each offence—up to life imprisonment for some offences, such as homicide. It is up to the trial judge to decide the actual penalty. Some indictable offences have a minimum penalty that judges are forced to impose. For example, impaired driving carries a minimum penalty that can range from a $600 fine to five years imprisonment, depending upon the number of times the accused has committed the offence.

Figure 4-5

This car crashed into a Kingston, Ontario, home. The driver was charged with impaired driving. A passenger and someone in the house were killed. Would this be a summary or an indictable offence?

Hybrid Offences

Hybrid offences are those for which the Crown attorney has the right to proceed summarily, and impose a less severe punishment, or to proceed by indictment. Theft is an example of a hybrid offence, as section 334 of the *Criminal Code* makes clear (see The Law, page 108).

Review Your Understanding (Pages 107 to 108)

1. **Distinguish between a summary and indictable offence.**
2. **Compare the maximum penalty for summary and indictable offences.**
3. **What choices does a Crown attorney have in dealing with a hybrid offence?**

Excerpts from the *Criminal Code*

334.

... everyone who commits theft

(a) is guilty of an indictable offence and liable to imprisonment for a term not exceeding ten years, where ... the value of what is stolen exceeds five thousand dollars; or

(b) is guilty

   (i) of an indictable offence and is liable to imprisonment for a term not exceeding two years, or

   (ii) of an offence punishable on summary conviction,

      where the value of what is stolen does not exceed five thousand dollars.

For Discussion

1. **Under what circumstances would a person be charged by summary conviction?**

2. **Under what circumstances would a person be charged by indictment?**

4.5   The Elements of a Crime

Two conditions must exist for an act to be a criminal offence: ***actus reus*** and ***mens rea***. In Latin, *actus reus* means "a wrongful deed." In other words, it must be shown that the person committed an act prohibited by law. *Mens rea* means "a guilty mind." Therefore, it must also be shown that the accused intended to commit the offence. These two conditions must exist at the same time.

The *Canadian Charter of Rights and Freedoms* states in section 11(d) that a person is "to be presumed innocent until proven guilty according to law." This means that the Crown attorney has the responsibility to prove that *actus reus* and *mens rea* existed at the time the crime was committed. In addition, these conditions must be proven beyond a reasonable doubt. If there is a reasonable doubt in the mind of the judge or jury that the accused committed the crime, the accused will be acquitted and set free.

Actus Reus

The *Criminal Code* usually explains what must occur for an act to be considered a crime. For example, section 348 clearly states that two actions must occur during a break and enter for a wrongful deed (*actus reus*) to have occurred. The first is the break-in itself; the second is the entry.

As you read earlier, Ron committed break and enter. You will recall that he broke the door lock with a crowbar and entered Kathy's house. What if he had only broken a kitchen window? In this case, the break-in would have occurred, but not the entry. However, if Ron reaches an arm through the window to climb in but someone scares him off, he has still entered because a part of his body was in the house.

Actus reus can also describe a failure to do something. For example, it is a crime for parents to withhold the necessities of life from their children.

Figure 4-6

Ron has "entered" Kathy's house by putting his arm through the kitchen window.

Mens Rea

Mens rea is the second condition that must exist for an act to be considered a crime. *Mens rea* exists if the offence is committed with (1) intent or knowledge, or (2) recklessness.

Intent or Knowledge

Intent is really the true purpose of an act. It is based on the facts and on what a reasonable person would be thinking under the circumstances. Ron wants to break into Kathy's house to steal her electronic equipment. He has the intent to rob Kathy. That is the true purpose of his act, even if he denies it.

Intent can be either general or specific. A **general intent** to perform an action means that the intent is limited to the act itself and the person has no other criminal purpose in mind. In the case of assault, for example, the Crown need only prove the intent to apply force. Intent can be inferred from the fact that the accused *did* apply force. Similarly, for a charge of trespassing at night, once the Crown has proven that the accused *was* on someone else's property at night, the intent to be there is inferred. There is no need to prove any other *mens rea* to prove that a crime was committed.

Specific intent exists when the person committing the offence has a further criminal purpose in mind. For example, you can infer specific intent from Ron's offence of break and enter because it involves (1) an intentional illegal action (breaking and entering a place) that is committed with the intent to commit (2) a further illegal action (robbery, an indictable offence).

You Be the JUDGE

In the case of *R. v. Daviault* (1994), the Supreme Court of Canada ruled that "extreme drunkenness" was an appropriate defence for certain crimes, for example, sexual assault. It argued that the intoxication of the defendant was so extreme that the situation was unlikely to happen again.

- What element of a crime is missing in a situation of extreme drunkenness? Should self-induced intoxication be a defence to drunkenness? Explain.

Case

R. v. Molodowic

[2000] 1 S.C.R. 420
Supreme Court of Canada

The accused suffered from a severe mental disorder known as paranoid schizophrenia. After shooting and killing his grandfather, he drove to a friend's house and reported what had happened. He asked the friend to call the police. After the police informed the accused of his rights, he gave them a statement.

The accused was charged with second-degree murder and was tried by a judge and jury. In his defence, two psychiatrists testified that the accused had a mental disorder and honestly believed that he had to kill his grandfather to end his mental torment. They said that the accused did not have the ability to appreciate that his action was morally wrong at the time of the killing. The accused was convicted of second-degree murder; he appealed

the verdict and the appeal was dismissed. The issue in the appeal was whether the verdict was unreasonable given the impact of the mental illness on criminal responsibility.

The Supreme Court ruled that the appeal should be allowed. A verdict of not criminally responsible by reason of mental disorder was entered.

For Discussion

1. Were *actus reus* and *mens rea* present at the time this crime was committed? Explain.

2. Why do you think the Supreme Court allowed the appeal?

3. Should mental illness be used as a reason to nullify criminal responsibility? Explain your opinion.

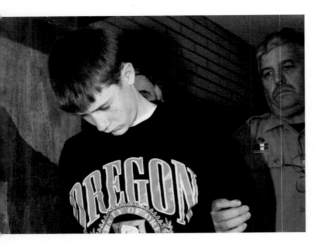

Figure 4-7

Some U.S. states allow minors to be tried as adults for some murder cases and for sex crimes if the defendant is at least 14 years old. Kip Kinkel, shown here, murdered his parents before attacking his classmates, killing two and injuring 25. He was sentenced to life imprisonment.

The law considers some people to be incapable of forming the intent necessary to commit a crime. Examples include people suffering from some forms of mental illness, minors (children), or people who are so drunk or "high" that they do not understand what they are doing (see Case, page 109). These persons will be considered in Chapters 8 and 10.

Knowledge

The **knowledge** of certain facts can also provide the necessary *mens rea*. For example, section 342(1)(d) of the *Criminal Code* says: "Every person who uses a credit card knowing that it has been revoked or cancelled is guilty" of an indictable offence. Here, it is only necessary to prove that the person used the credit card, knowing that it had been cancelled. It is not necessary to prove that there was an intent to defraud.

Motive

The reason for committing an offence is called the **motive.** Motive is not the same as intent, and it does not establish the guilt of the accused. The fact that Ron wanted to steal Kathy's electronic equipment in order to pawn it for cash is not relevant to his guilt. In addition, a person can have a motive and not commit an offence. Suppose that a suspicious fire kills a man whose wife is having a serious affair with another man. The wife may have had a motive to kill, but unless it can be shown that she acted to cause the fire, or failed to act, she has not committed an offence. Motive may be used as circumstantial evidence—indirect evidence that would lead you to conclude that someone is guilty. However, the elements of the offence must be proven to obtain a conviction. The judge may also refer to the motive for an offence during sentencing.

Recklessness

Recklessness is the careless disregard for the possible results of an action. When people commit acts with recklessness, they may not intend to hurt anyone. However, they understand the risks of their actions and proceed to act anyway. Driving over the speed limit and cutting people off in traffic could result in criminal charges if injury occurs as a result of these actions. *Mens rea* would exist if such recklessness were proven.

Offences without a Mens Rea

Some offences are less serious than those found in the *Criminal Code.* To prove that these offences occurred, it is not necessary to prove *mens rea*. These offences are usually violations of federal or provincial regulations passed to protect the public. Speeding, "short-weighting" a package of food, and polluting the environment are all examples of regulatory offences. Regulatory offences also carry lesser penalties. As a result, they do not carry the stigma associated with a criminal conviction.

Case

R. v. Wilson

[2001] B.C.W.L.D. 561
British Columbia Court of Appeal

Marven Wilson was convicted of dangerous driving causing death and received a sentence of four years. The same judge also acquitted him of impaired driving causing death. Wilson decided to appeal his sentence.

In 1996, Wilson had tried to overtake a pickup truck driven by his friend Todd McComber. Both had been drinking alcohol. Wilson hit McComber's truck, which caused it to roll over several times. Rocky Cameron, a passenger, was thrown from the truck and died of his injuries. Neither man was wearing a seat belt. Police arrested Wilson for being intoxicated in a public place, but did not take breath samples. Wilson had several previous convictions for drinking and driving, not wearing a seat belt, and speeding.

In his appeal, Wilson argued that the sentence was too harsh. He said that the trial judge had made a mistake—the judge had convicted him of dangerous driving causing death while under the influence of alcohol but had acquitted him of the impaired driving charge. This was a contradiction. The three Court of Appeal judges agreed with Wilson and reduced his sentence to three years' imprisonment.

For Discussion

1. **Is there intent or recklessness in this case? Explain.**
2. **What contradiction is the Court of Appeal referring to in the trial decision?**
3. **What mistake did the arresting police make and how did it influence the decision of the case at trial?**
4. **Which verdict do you support? Justify your opinion by using the facts from the case to support your view.**

Case

R. v. Memarzadeh

(2001) 142. O.A.C. 281
Ontario Court of Appeal

On June 29, 1997, Said Memarzadeh was released from a police station with a written promise to appear in court on a certain date. Later that day, a citizen complained that a number of items had been stolen from a home near the police station. Although there was no evidence that a break-in had occurred, Memarzadeh's written notice to appear in court was found in the home.

Memarzadeh was arrested and convicted of break and enter. He received a 30-day sentence. At his trial, he said he could not remember being at the police station on the day of the break and enter. It also emerged that he had spent eight years in an Iranian jail as a political prisoner and had undergone three brain operations following some severe beatings.

Memarzadeh successfully appealed his conviction for break and enter. The appeal court decision said there was no evidence that the home had been broken into, or that the accused had been on the premises. The fact that Memarzadeh's document—the promise to appear in court—was found in the home did not prove he had been there.

For Discussion

1. **Identify the *actus reus* in this case.**
2. **Did *mens rea* exist here? Explain.**
3. **With which decision do you agree, the trial court decision or the appeal court decision? Explain your answer.**

There are two types of regulatory offences: **strict liability offences** and **absolute liability offences.** To prove a strict liability offence, it is only necessary to prove that the offence was committed. The accused can put forward the defence of **due diligence,** which means that the accused took reasonable care not to commit the offence or honestly believed in a mistaken set of facts.

Absolute liability offences are similar to strict liability offences in that the Crown does not have to prove *mens rea.* However, absolute liability offences have no possible defence—due diligence is not accepted as a defence for committing such offences. If the person committed the *actus reus,* he or she is guilty, no matter what precautions were taken to avoid committing the offence.

Canadian law does not specify which regulatory offences are strict liability or absolute liability. It is left to the courts to decide what the government intended. Because absolute liability offences provide little opportunity for a successful defence, the Supreme Court of Canada ruled in *Re B.C. Motor Vehicle Act* (1985) that a prison term for an absolute liability offence was unconstitutional.

Figure 4-8

Ron is checking Kathy's windows to see how secure they are. He has gone beyond the preparation stage and is making an attempt to break and enter Kathy's house.

Attempt

A person who intends to commit a crime but fails to complete the act may still be guilty of a criminal offence. In Ron's case, a police officer could have observed him walking around the house at night with a flashlight, trying the doors to see if they were locked. Ron would be found guilty of an **attempt** to break and enter under section 24(1) of the *Criminal Code.*

As with any crime, proving attempt means proving that there was intent to commit the offence. The *actus reus* for an attempt begins when the person takes the first step toward committing the crime. It is the judge who decides—even in trial by jury—when the preparation stage has ended and the attempt stage has begun. For example, Ron prepared for his crime by buying housebreaking tools and noting when Kathy entered and left the house. However, it was only when he took his first step toward the actual break-in that he attempted the crime.

During a trial, if the Crown is unable to prove that the offence was committed but only that an attempt was made, the accused may be convicted of the attempt. If the accused was originally charged with the attempt, but the evidence indicates that the offence was actually committed, the judge may order the accused to be tried for the offence itself.

Conspiracy

A **conspiracy** is an agreement between two or more people to commit a crime or to achieve something legal by doing something illegal. For example, if Ron and Hank discuss their plans to break into Kathy's house to steal her

R. v. Bernier

2001 BCCA 394
British Columbia Court of Appeal

A trial judge convicted Bernier of robbery while using a firearm; assault while using a weapon; breaking and entering a residence and committing theft; and possession of stolen property of a value less than $5000. Bernier appealed the first two conviction charges but not the other convictions.

Bernier was a member of a home-invasion gang in 1997. The gang broke down the door of Dean Eve's basement apartment while one member yelled: "Police, on your hands and knees!" They handcuffed Eve, who testified that one of the gang members had a gun. The gang members told him they were looking for money and drugs. They took $300 and then hit Eve on the head with the butt of the gun, causing injury. When the homeowner returned, he found that his upstairs apartment had been ransacked and several items were missing. When the gang members were arrested, some of the stolen items were found in their possession.

Bernier's trial judge ruled that he had intent to aid others to commit an offence. Bernier claimed that he did not know that a gun would be used during the home invasion. He felt that he should be found not guilty of the weapons offences. On appeal, the three judges could find no evidence that Bernier knew of a weapon or ought to have known that it would be used at the scene of the crime. They substituted the more serious weapons charges with the less serious charges of robbery and assault.

For Discussion

1. What is a "home invasion"? What crimes are associated with it?

2. Why do you think "robbery while using a firearm" and "assault while using a weapon" are more serious than "robbery" and "assault"?

3. Why do you think the appeal court substituted the less serious charges of robbery and assault?

---

credit cards, they have conspired to commit a crime. Even if they do not carry out the plan, they have agreed to a conspiracy to commit the crime.

In a conspiracy, all the people involved must be serious in their intention to commit the crime. Jokes or threats are not considered conspiracy.

Review Your Understanding (Pages 108 to 113)

1. Identify the two elements that must exist for a crime to be committed.

2. *Actus reus* does not always require an action to be committed. Give an example of such a circumstance.

3. Distinguish among the different categories of *mens rea* and provide an example for each.

4. Distinguish between general and specific intent.

5. How is motive used in a criminal trial?

6. For which offence is the defence of due diligence available? Explain how it would be used.

7. Identify the element of a crime that must be proven in an absolute liability offence. Why do such regulatory offences exist?

8. When does an attempt begin? Provide an example of a situation where a criminal charge of attempt could be made.

9. When could individuals be charged with conspiracy?

Parties to an Offence

A person who commits an offence, aids a person to commit an offence, or abets a person in committing an offence is defined as a party to a crime under section 21 of the *Criminal Code*.

Aiding or Abetting

Aiding means to help someone commit a crime. **Abetting** means to encourage someone to commit a crime. Two things must be proven before an accused can be convicted of aiding or abetting. First, the accused had knowledge that the other person intended to commit the offence. Second, the accused actually helped or encouraged the person to commit the offence. Mere presence at the scene of the crime does not provide conclusive evidence of aiding or abetting. Under section 21(2) of the *Criminal Code*, a person who plans an offence is just as guilty as a person who actually commits it.

To counsel (suggest) or incite (urge) someone to commit a crime is also an offence. If Ron urges a friend to take an unlocked car with the keys in it for a joy ride, he is inciting another to commit an offence. Even if the offence is not carried out, the person who incites the offence—Ron—can receive the same penalty as the person who attempts it.

Accessory after the Fact

An **accessory after the fact** is someone who helps a criminal escape detention or capture. Helping someone escape capture includes providing food, clothing, or shelter to the offender. One exception to this law is the favoured relationship between a legally married couple. A man or a woman cannot be held responsible for assisting in the escape of a spouse and someone escaping with the spouse.

Did You Know?

Husbands and wives are exempt from being charged as accessories to each other because of traditional attitudes. Many of our current laws were inherited from the common law, where the wife was considered to be one with her husband. It has been suggested that these laws do not reflect current values in our society.

Case

R. v. Goodine

(1993) 141 N.B.R. (2d) 99
New Brunswick Court of Appeal

One summer afternoon in 1992, Todd Johnston went for a ride with his girlfriend and two friends, Jason Boyd and Cory Goodine. After driving on some country roads near Arthurette, New Brunswick, Johnston stopped the truck. Without warning, he shot Boyd in the head with a revolver. He then removed Boyd's body from the truck and dragged it a short distance.

Still holding the revolver, Johnston ordered Goodine to "get off the truck and help me because you're in on this, too." Goodine obeyed Johnston's orders to drag the body into the woods. When the victim moaned, Johnston shot Boyd again in the back of the head. Medical evidence at trial indicated that either shot would have caused Boyd's death.

A few days later, Goodine told two of his friends about the murder and led them to Boyd's body. The next day, the friends reported the incident to the police, who arrested Goodine and charged him with being an accessory after the fact to murder. The accused was acquitted following a trial by jury. The Crown appealed to the Court of Appeal, but the appeal was dismissed.

continued ▶

For Discussion

1. Why did the Crown appeal the accused's acquittal?
2. What is the *actus reus* of accessory after the fact?
3. Why was Goodine not charged with aiding and abetting?
4. What defence would be open to Goodine to explain his actions?
5. On what basis do you think the jury acquitted Goodine? Explain.

Review Your Understanding (Pages 114 to 115)

1. According to section 21 of the *Criminal Code*, who may be a party to an offence?
2. Distinguish between "aid" and "abet."
3. What is the significance of section 21(2) of the *Criminal Code*?
4. Identify who may be considered an accessory after the fact.

4.7 Our Criminal Court System

Thousands of cases go to trial each year. The cost of operating the criminal justice system, which is paid for by the taxpayer, is very high. As a result, the structure and procedures of Canadian courts are constantly changing to provide greater efficiency.

Jurisdiction over the court system is divided between the federal and provincial governments. The *Constitution Act, 1867*, gave the provincial governments jurisdiction over the administration of justice in their provinces. The provinces organize and maintain their provincial courts by, for example, providing courthouses and court staff. The federal government controls criminal law and establishes procedures to be followed in criminal matters.

The *Constitution Act, 1867*, also gave the federal government the authority to set up two other courts. One of these is the Court of Appeal for Canada, known as the Supreme Court of Canada. The other court is the Federal Court, which reviews decisions of federal boards and commissions, among other activities. It does not, however, deal with criminal law.

▌ The Criminal Court System in Canada

Supreme Court of Canada

- is the highest appeal court in Canada
- has unlimited jurisdiction in criminal matters
- hears appeals from provincial appeal courts
- hears cases of national importance; for example, interprets the *Charter* or clarifies a criminal law matter
- generally grants leave (permission) before the appeal will be heard
- sets national precedent; decisions must be followed by all judges in all courts of Canada

continued ▶

Did You Know?

The *Anti-Terrorism Act* states that someone who knowingly takes in a terrorist, takes part in terrorism, or is an accomplice commits an indictable offence and could receive up to 10 years' imprisonment. Facilitating a terrorist act could get up to 14 years. Convicted leaders of terrorist acts can receive up to life imprisonment.

ⓔ activity

Visit **www.law.nelson.com** and follow the links to learn about the Federal Court of Canada.

▊ The Criminal Court System in Canada (continued)

Provincial Supreme Court of Appeal (names vary)

- hears appeals from the Trial Division of Provincial Supreme Courts
- sets province's precedent; decisions must be followed by all judges in that province

Provincial Supreme Court—Trial Division (names vary)

- tries the more severe crimes such as manslaughter and sexual assault, and most severe indictable offences such as murder and treason
- hears criminal appeals in summary conviction cases
- sets province's precedent; decisions must be followed by Provincial Court judges in that province

Provincial Courts—Criminal Division

- arraigns (reads the charge and enters the plea) all criminal cases
- holds preliminary hearings in most severe indictable offences, but the accused can elect to have the case tried in higher court
- hears and tries criminal summary conviction cases and the least serious indictable offences such as theft under $5000

Figure 4-9

Distinguish between the "highest" and "lowest" courts in Canada. Identify the jurisdiction for each level of court.

Case

Reference Re Milgaard

[1992] 1 S.C.R. 866
Supreme Court of Canada

David Milgaard was found guilty of the rape and murder of Gail Miller in a trial by judge and jury in 1970. He was sentenced to life in prison at the age of 17. The Saskatchewan Court of Appeal affirmed his conviction, and his request to appeal to the Supreme Court of Canada was dismissed. Milgaard went to prison.

In 1992, the Supreme Court of Canada reviewed the case because of fresh evidence. One of the key witnesses at the original trial admitted he had lied about Milgaard's involvement in the crime. The Supreme Court ruled that the continued conviction of Milgaard was a miscarriage of justice. However, it was not satisfied beyond a reasonable doubt that Milgaard was innocent. It recommended that the conviction be quashed and a new trial ordered.

Figure 4-10

David Milgaard and his mother, Joyce, walk through the Winnipeg Airport the day after DNA evidence cleared him of the 1969 rape and murder of Gail Miller.

continued ▶

It also noted that the attorney general for the province of Saskatchewan did not have to pursue a new trial. Milgaard was released after serving 22 years in jail.

In 1997, a new forensic tool—DNA testing—proved that Milgaard was innocent of the crime, and his name was cleared forever. In 1999, Larry Fisher, a serial rapist who had seven rape convictions, was convicted of the original crime. The Canadian and Saskatchewan governments awarded David Milgaard and his family $10 million in damages and apologized for the injustice that had been done to him. It was the largest settlement in Canadian history.

When asked about his wrongful conviction, Milgaard replied, "The question shouldn't be, how do I feel about this? The question should be, how did this happen?"

For Discussion

1. **Should a 17-year-old be imprisoned with hardened criminals? Explain.**
2. **Summarize the ruling of the Supreme Court of Canada in this case.**
3. **Did Milgaard and his family receive adequate compensation for his 22 years spent in jail. Explain.**

Criminal Offences and Procedures

As noted earlier, summary offences and more serious indictable offences have different trial procedures. These will be examined in more detail in the following chapters.

▌ Examples of Categories of Indictable Offences

Least Serious Trial procedure similar to summary offences	More Serious Accused selects one of three trial procedures	Most Serious Trial usually before judge and jury
theft (under $5000)	manslaughter	murder
mischief (under $5000)	assault	treason
fraud (under $5000)	sexual assault	piracy
driving while disqualified	weapon offences	bribing a judicial official

Summary and Minor Indictable Offences Procedures

There is a six-month limitation period for the laying of a charge for a summary offence. This means that a person must be charged within six months of committing an offence. The provincial court judge hears the evidence and gives the verdict for summary and minor indictable offences.

For some quasi-criminal offences under provincial jurisdiction, such as traffic offences, a court appearance is not usually necessary. However, entering a plea of "not guilty" in such a situation requires a court appearance. Merely signing the "guilty" plea on the ticket citation or order is sufficient. Of course, the fine must also be paid.

⊜ activity

Visit **www.law.nelson.com** and follow the links to learn more about the David Milgaard case.

Figure 4-11

Why do you think there are different trial procedures for different types of offences?

Case

R. v. Wust

[2000] 1 S.C.R. 455
Supreme Court of Canada

The accused pleaded guilty to a charge of robbery with a firearm. When he was sentenced, he had been in custody for seven and a half months. The judge sentenced him to four and a half years' imprisonment less one year for time already served.

The Crown appealed the sentence, arguing that it was far too light. It wanted a sentence of seven to eight years with no time off for time served. It argued that the three-and-a-half-year sentence was less than the four-year mandatory sentence required for using a gun while committing a crime. In its opinion, the judge had made an error when deciding the sentence.

The Supreme Court of Canada disagreed. It ruled that the goal of sentencing is to provide a fair sentence and the best person to do this is the judge who passes sentence. Judges give credit for time already served when deciding the sentence and this is what happened here. The Supreme Court ruled that the original sentence must stand.

For Discussion

1. How would you classify the offence of robbery?
2. What is the mandatory sentence required for using a gun while committing a crime?
3. Do you think the Supreme Court is setting a precedent in this case? Explain.

Did You Know?

In 1998, 76 percent of violent crimes in Canada were assaults. Of these, 90 percent did not involve a weapon or result in serious injury. The next largest category of violent crimes was robbery. Less than 1 percent of violent crimes involved homicide or attempted homicide. Violent crimes accounted for 12 percent of all crimes committed.

Indictable Offences Procedures

If an offence is indictable, there is no time limit for the laying of a charge after the offence has been committed. Minor indictable offences are treated very much like summary offences. For more serious indictable offences, the accused is allowed to choose the trial procedure: by a provincial court judge, a higher court judge, or a judge and jury. Most indictable offences are classified as serious. They include such offences as sexual assault and weapons offences. The most serious indictable offences are tried by a judge and jury. These include murder and treason.

Review Your Understanding (Pages 115 to 118)

1. What types of cases does the Supreme Court of Canada handle?
2. What is the legal effect when a decision is made by the Supreme Court of Canada?
3. What types of cases are handled by the Federal Court of Canada?
4. What functions do the provincial Supreme Courts perform?
5. How are summary, minor indictable, and quasi-criminal offences handled?

In Criminal Law

Careers in police work or correctional services are well suited to people who are self-confident and assertive and who can remain calm in hazardous situations. Being a keen observer of people and having an ability to work independently, as well as part of a team, are other desirable qualities for this line of work.

ⓔ Visit www.law.nelson.com and follow the links to research the different programs in criminology offered by Canadian colleges and universities.

Figure 4-12
Police officers

Figure 4-13
Correctional services officer

In Focus

Police Officer

Police officers are responsible for maintaining public safety and order and enforcing laws and regulations. Police assigned to criminal investigations gather evidence from crime scenes, interview witnesses, make arrests, and testify in court. Officers assigned to traffic patrol enforce traffic laws, provide emergency assistance, and investigate traffic accidents. Police officers visit classrooms or community centres to talk about crime prevention and safety.

Probation Officer

Probation officers interview offenders to determine if they can safely rejoin the community. They help

to plan rehabilitation programs and set limits on the conduct of offenders. Clients must meet with their probation officers on a regular basis to evaluate progress and to determine if probation orders are being followed.

Correctional Services Officer

Correctional services officers watch over prisoners and maintain order in correctional facilities. They supervise prisoners during work periods, mealtimes, and recreational breaks. They also guard prisoners moving between correctional facilities and monitor any potential prison disturbances and escape attempts. Officers work outdoors in all kinds of weather conditions. Indoors, conditions for these officers can be noisy and overcrowded.

Career Exploration Activity

As a class, explore the career opportunities in police work and correctional services. The information you compile can be used to profile various law-related careers for a guidance bulletin-board display, or you may choose to run a law-related career fair.

1. Use the Internet, your local employment information centre, or contact the local authorities to conduct research into these careers.

2. Briefly summarize the education and training requirements, wage rates, working conditions, and future job prospects for police, probation, and correctional officers. Record the information on index cards.

Will Stricter Gun Control Make Canada a Safer Place?

Figure 4-14

This pro-gun rally was held in Ottawa in September 1998 to protest the *Firearms Act*. What do some of the signs say about protesters' views?

In 1995, Parliament passed the *Firearms Act*. This law required any Canadian who had a gun to obtain a licence for it by January 1, 2001. A licence allows a person to own or buy guns and ammunition. Gun owners who fail to obtain a licence can be imprisoned for up to five years or have their guns seized. Canadians who applied for a gun licence in time paid $10 for a licence. Those who did not make the deadline have to pay $60 and attend a firearms course costing up to $60.

About 1.8 million gun owners applied for licences and met the deadline, but there are still an estimated 400 000 owners who have not. According to the Fire Arms Centre, 2238 licences have been refused. Anyone who does not have a licence will have his or her firearms seized by the police and can receive up to five years in prison.

By January 1, 2003, gun owners must also register each gun that they own with the government. Anyone "knowingly neglecting to register a firearm" can be imprisoned for up to 10 years.

The licensing and registration of firearms gives authorities a computerized record of all gun owners and the weapons in their possession.

The *Firearms Act* also sets a compulsory minimum four-year prison term for anyone convicted of using a gun in a serious crime such as murder, robbery, or sexual assault.

On One Side

Opponents of the *Firearms Act* view it as a threat to gun ownership in Canada. Hunters, target shooters, and gun collectors say they should be allowed to pursue their hobbies without being regulated. The National Firearms Association, with 100 000 members, argues that the new law will make it more difficult for Canadians to defend themselves and their property. It claims that the new law puts unfair restrictions on law-abiding citizens.

Others view gun ownership as a democratic right that government has no right to limit. This group points out that since firearms are used in only 6 percent of adult crimes, restricting the rights of all Canadians is unfair. They say gun registration is the first step toward banning guns altogether.

On the Other Side

Supporters of the *Firearms Act* include police, victims' groups, women's groups, experts in suicide prevention, and emergency room physicians. This side believes that stricter gun controls are making Canada a safer place. Firearms are responsible for 1400 deaths in Canada each year. Of these, 75 percent are suicides and 15 percent are homicides. Firearms are also a leading cause of death among teens. Tougher gun laws could make it more difficult to own guns and could reduce impulsive suicides in this age group.

Some supporters of gun controls want the government to go further. They want to make it illegal to own or use any kind of gun. They say that if this step were taken, there would be a dramatic drop in gun-related crimes. They point to the high rate of crime and violence in the United States, where citizens own an estimated 212 million firearms.

The Bottom Line

In 1997, the Alberta government challenged the legality of the *Firearms Act* in court. It argued that guns were property and that property falls under the jurisdiction of the provincial governments.

In 2000, the Supreme Court of Canada ruled that the *Firearms Act* was legal. The federal government has control over criminal law and guns are linked to crime, not property. By requiring gun owners to get licences and register their weapons, the government is keeping guns out of the hands of criminals. Investigating the backgrounds of those who apply for licences ensures that only those who are law-abiding citizens will receive one.

What Do You Think?

1. Briefly outline the requirements for gun ownership under the *Firearms Act*.
2. Distinguish between a licence and a registration.
3. Under what circumstances do you think a licence application would be refused?
4. Identify the arguments that are presented for and against the *Firearms Act*.
5. Why did the Alberta government challenge the *Firearms Act*? How did the Supreme Court rule on this issue?

ⓔ activity

Visit **www.law.nelson.com** and follow the links to learn more about gun control in Canada.

Agents of Change   Suzanne Laplante-Edward

On December 6, 1989, a gunman entered Montreal's École Polytechnique. He killed 14 female engineering students and injured 13 others before killing himself. This event, known as the Montreal Massacre, was the worst mass murder in Canada's history.

The Montreal Massacre was a major impetus for gun control legislation in Canada. Parents of the slain victims became some of the most effective lobbyists for Bill C-68 (the *Firearms Act*). Suzanne Laplante-Edward is the mother of Anne-Marie Edward, one of the victims. She describes Canada's gun control legislation "as our daughter's legacy."

In recent years, Laplante-Edward has openly criticized opponents of the *Firearms Act*. "Now that the law is passed and being implemented, we resent having to continually defend it against the gun lobby's relentless attempts to undermine it," she said recently. "Opponents argue that the law 'punishes' law-abiding gun owners. I ask you: how does registration and licensing compare to the loss of a child? What sane person could make such an argument?"

Chief Brian Ford, of the Ottawa–Carleton Regional Police and Secretary–Treasurer for the Canadian Association of Chiefs of Police (CACP), said that the parents of the Montreal Massacre victims had a huge impact on the system: "In many ways, December 6, 1989 ... highlighted the flaws in Canada's old gun laws." Ford pointed out that without information about gun ownership, police "cannot control the illegal gun trade or enforce safe storage requirements. Police chiefs across Canada remain committed to the new gun control legislation."

For Discussion

1. How did the Montreal Massacre affect gun control legislation in Canada?
2. Some people argue that the Montreal Massacre was not a typical crime and that the push for gun control legislation in its wake was based on emotion rather than true need. Argue for or against this statement.

Figure 4-15
Suzanne Laplante-Edward

Chapter Review

Chapter Highlights

- Criminal law deals with offences against society.
- Civil law deals with offences against individuals.
- Through penalties, criminal law deters people from committing offences.
- Civil law emphasizes compensation for damages.
- Criminal law is the responsibility of the federal government.
- Quasi-criminal law deals with offences such as traffic violations.
- Summary offences are minor criminal offences.
- Indictable offences are more serious criminal offences.
- The Crown must prove its case beyond a reasonable doubt.
- *Actus reus* and *mens rea* must exist to prove someone guilty.
- Ignorance of the law is no excuse.
- Aiding and abetting a criminal is a crime.
- Supreme Court of Canada decisions must be followed by lower courts.
- Each province has a Trial Division and an Appeal Division for important criminal cases.
- All criminal cases start in provincial court, Criminal Division.
- Provincial court judges try summary and minor indictable offences.
- An accused has a choice of trial procedures for more serious indictable offences.
- The most serious indictable offences are tried by judge and jury.

Review Key Terms

Name the key terms that are described below.

a) a person who helps an offender escape detention

b) cause or reason to commit a criminal act

c) failing to pay attention to the possible injuries that might result from an action

d) planning and acting together for an unlawful purpose

e) law that deals with offences against society

f) taking reasonable care not to commit an offence

g) Latin phrase meaning "a wrongful action"

h) Latin phrase meaning "a guilty mind"

i) knowing certain facts, which provides the necessary *mens rea* for an offence

j) the first step toward committing the crime

k) minor criminal offences that are tried immediately

l) serious crimes that carry more severe penalties than summary conviction offences

m) offences that are punishable as indictable or summary offences

n) criminal liability based on the commission of an offence

o) criminal liability in which intent is assumed to be present but need not be proven

p) encouraging another person to commit a crime

Check Your Knowledge

1. What is a crime and how is it dealt with in Canadian society?

2. Explain the types of criminal offences and provide an example of each.

3. Distinguish between the *actus reus* and *mens rea* in a criminal offence and provide an example for each.

4. Summarize the structure of the criminal court system and identify the types of cases heard in each court.

Apply Your Learning

5. In groups, examine the Law Commission's four conditions that must exist in order for something to be considered a crime. Apply them to child pornography. What are your conclusions regarding each of the four conditions as they relate to this offence?

6. *R. v. Oommen*, [1994] 2 S.C.R. 507 (Supreme Court of Canada)

   In the early morning hours, Oommen killed Beaton as she lay sleeping on a mattress in his apartment. He fired nine to 13 shots at her from a semi-automatic repeating rifle. The evidence disclosed no rational motive for the killing.

At the time of the killing, Oommen believed that the members of a local union were conspiring to destroy him. He became fixated with the idea that his "assailants and enemies" had commissioned Beaton to kill him.

At the trial, Oommen relied on the defence of mental disorder. Psychiatrists testified that he possessed the general capacity to distinguish right from wrong and knew it was wrong to kill a person. But they also said that on the night of the murder, his delusion deprived him of that capacity. The trial judge rejected the defence of mental disorder. Oommen knew right from wrong and he was not relieved from criminal responsibility. He was convicted of second-degree murder and sentenced to life imprisonment without eligibility of parole for 10 years.

a) What is the *mens rea* requirement of second-degree murder? Did Oommen possess this *mens rea?*

b) Did either his motive or his delusion have any effect on the decision? Explain.

7. *R. v. Kirkness*, [1990] 3 S.C.R. 74 (Supreme Court of Canada)

Kirkness had been drinking with his friend Snowbird when they agreed to break into a house at Snowbird's suggestion. Kirkness used the handle of a garden tool to open a window of the house of an 83-year old woman. Snowbird proceeded to sexually assault the woman. While this was happening, Kirkness stole various things in the house. Snowbird dragged the unconscious woman into the hallway and began to choke her. Kirkness asked him "not to do that because he was going to kill her." Snowbird then suffocated the victim.

Is Kirkness a party to the murder? Why or why not?

8. *R. v. Wilkins* (1964), 44 C.R. 375 (Ontario Court of Appeal)

A police officer parked his motorcycle, but left it running while he went to write a ticket. Wilkins drove the motorcycle a short distance to play a joke on the officer. He was charged with the theft of the motorcycle. Theft requires the intent to convert an object to one's own use.

What was Wilkins' motive? Can he be found guilty of theft? Explain.

9. *R. v. Jackson* (1977), 35 C.C.C. (2d) 331 (Ontario Court of Appeal)

Deralis was a trafficker in narcotics. Jackson, a friend, agreed to store 3 kg of marijuana in his apartment. Jackson did it because he knew that Deralis had a record, whereas he did not, and because it would help Deralis escape detection. The police found the marijuana. Jackson was found guilty of possession. The Crown appealed to obtain the more serious conviction of trafficking. It argued that Jackson had aided and abetted Deralis in his trafficking.

Should Jackson be found guilty of trafficking for aiding and abetting Deralis? Explain.

Communicate Your Understanding

10. The maximum penalty for break and enter is life imprisonment. First offenders sometimes get a suspended sentence. In 1997, 25 percent of those who were convicted did not receive a prison sentence and for those who did, the average sentence was four months. No one received more than three years. Develop arguments to either support or criticize the sentencing here.

11. "The law exists to protect society and individuals and keep order." Based on the following statistics from Statistics Canada (1999), develop arguments that would support the above statement.

- 91 percent of Canadians stated they were satisfied with their personal safety, compared to 86 percent in 1993.
- 25 percent reported they had been a victim of a crime, compared to 23 percent in 1993
- 37 percent of these crime victims did not report the incidents to police, compared to 42 percent in 1993.
- 54 percent believed that crime levels in their neighbourhoods had remained the same in the past 5 years, compared to 43 percent in 1993.
- 29 percent believed that crime rates had increased, compared to 46 percent in 1993.

12. From a newspaper or the Internet, collect five criminal law articles on cases that have not yet gone to trial. Write a brief summary of the facts of each case. Consult the *Criminal Code* and comment on the following:
   a) For each case, indicate the offence committed, the *actus reus,* the *mens rea,* and the maximum penalty for the offence.
   b) Summarize the evidence that you think the Crown and defence might present.
   c) Indicate whether you think the accused will be found guilty or not guilty at trial. Give reasons for your decision.

Develop Your Thinking

13. Consider the following facts as reported by GPC Research in 2000:
   - 17 percent of Canadian households have at least one firearm.
   - 10 years ago 24 percent of households had guns.
   - 13 percent of urban homes and 30 percent of rural homes have guns.
   - 87 percent of firearms owners are male.
   - 98 percent of firearms owners were aware that they had to purchase a licence by January 1, 2001.
   a) What has been the trend in gun ownership in Canada?
   b) Why do you think there is a difference in the percentages of gun owners in urban and rural Canada?
   c) Despite being aware of the law, 400 000 Canadians still have not applied for their licences. Why do you think this is the case?

14. In groups, brainstorm and list some of the causes of crime. Develop a second list of suggestions about how these causes could be eliminated. How realistic are these suggestions? What limitations exist? Share your conclusions.

The Criminal Code

Focus Questions

- What are crimes of violence?
- What changes have been made to the *Criminal Code* that reflect the changing views of society?
- What actions are considered to have a high social impact and are debated by society and in Parliament?
- What acts are considered property crimes?
- What laws in the *Criminal Code* protect children?

Chapter at a Glance

Figure 5-1

Two power company employees work to disconnect power to a telephone booth in Edmonton on July 2, 2001. The booth was one of several damaged during a post-Canada Day celebration. What penalties would you impose on people who commit the offence of mischief?

5.1 Introduction

The Canadian *Criminal Code* is a federal statute that reflects the social values of Canadians. In Chapter 4 you learned that the Code is often amended to reflect these changing values. While some actions are removed from the Code, others are added if society considers them criminal. For example, using the Internet to distribute child pornography has recently been declared a criminal activity. Currently, bills are before Parliament to establish sex offender registries, to make it illegal for anyone to use the Internet to prey on children, and to increase the penalties for people who maltreat animals. These bills reflect some social concerns of the early 2000s.

The *Criminal Code* is the main body of criminal law and identifies hundreds of acts that are considered criminal. About 80 percent of all criminal offences committed in a given year are *Criminal Code* offences. Because criminal law is federal law, the offences are treated identically across Canada. Many of these offences, along with their penalties, are listed on pages 155 to 157.

As you become more familiar with the *Criminal Code*, you will notice that the offences listed are described precisely. Careful wording is necessary to ensure that citizens are not arrested on a criminal charge if they are involved in a non-criminal matter, or that they are not set free on a technicality. The elements required for the Crown to obtain a conviction must be specified clearly. Despite the precise wording, many cases are appealed on a point of law because lawyers and judges may interpret the law in different ways.

Although it is impossible to cover all the offences in the *Criminal Code* in this text, you will examine the most common crimes and those that involve significant social issues.

▌Criminal Code Incidents, 2000

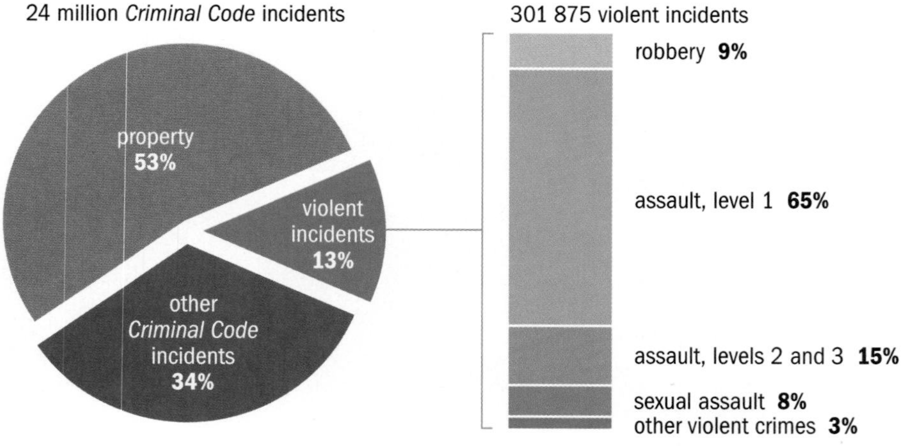

24 million *Criminal Code* incidents

property 53%

violent incidents 13%

other *Criminal Code* incidents 34%

301 875 violent incidents

robbery 9%

assault, level 1 65%

assault, levels 2 and 3 15%

sexual assault 8%

other violent crimes 3%

Figure 5-2

In 2000, 13 percent of *Criminal Code* incidents included crimes of violence. Why do you think that assault, level 1 (see Assault, page 133) makes up the largest percentage of violent incidents?

Violent crimes are offences that harm the human body in some way. The severe penalties cited in the Code of Hammurabi (see page 10) show that protection of one's person has always been considered important. Approximately 13 percent of all *Criminal Code* offences committed are of a violent nature (see Figure 5-2). In this section, you will examine the following violent crimes: homicide, assault, sexual offences, abduction, and robbery.

Homicide

Killing another human being, directly or indirectly, is **homicide.** Homicide is a criminal offence if it is "culpable"—in other words, deserving of blame. **Murder, manslaughter,** and **infanticide** are **culpable homicide. Non-culpable homicide** is not criminal and occurs when death is caused by complete accident or in self-defence.

activity

Visit **www.law.nelson.com** and follow the links to find more recent statistics on homicide in Canada.

Did You Know?

In 2000 there were 542 homicides in Canada. The number of homicides has gradually decreased, from a high of 635 in 1996.

▌ Homicide Rates for the Provinces and Territories, 2000

Province/Territory	Rate per 100 000 people	Province/Territory	Rate per 100 000 people
Alberta	1.9	Nunavut	10.8
British Columbia	2.1	Ontario	1.3
Manitoba	2.6	Prince Edward Island	2.2
New Brunswick	1.3	Quebec	2.0
Newfoundland & Labrador	1.1	Saskatchewan	2.5
Northwest Territories	2.4	Yukon Territory	6.5
Nova Scotia	1.6		

Figure 5-3

Prepare a bar graph to illustrate these statistics.

▌ Types of Homicide

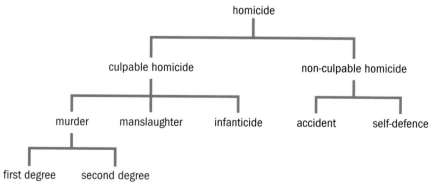

Figure 5-4

What do you already know about these types of homicide?

Murder

The most serious violent crime that one person can commit against another is murder—intentional killing. In this situation, the accused may be found guilty even if he or she did not have the intent to kill. Section 229 of the *Criminal Code* specifies the circumstances under which a person may be found guilty of murder, even if there was no intent to commit murder.

The Law   ## The Criminal Code

Excerpts from the *Criminal Code*
229.

Culpable homicide is murder

(a) where the person who causes the death of a human being
   (i) means to cause his death, or
   (ii) means to cause him bodily harm that he knows is likely to cause his death, and is reckless whether death ensues or not;

(b) where a person, meaning to cause death to a human being or meaning to cause him bodily harm that he knows is likely to cause his death, and being reckless whether death ensues or not, by accident or mistake causes death to another human being, notwithstanding that he does not mean to cause death or bodily harm to that human being; or

(c) where a person, for an unlawful object, does anything that he knows or ought to know is likely to cause death, and thereby causes death to a human being, notwithstanding that he desires to effect his object without causing death or bodily harm to any human being.

For Discussion

1. In your own words, describe when culpable homicide is murder.

2. For each subsection of section 229, give an example of a scenario that would fall within the description.

Suppose Anya fires at Harry with intent to kill, but her shot kills Martin instead. Anya is still guilty of murder although she did not intend to kill Martin. Similarly, if Dom seeks revenge against Elliot by committing arson, and the resulting fire causes the death of Freeman, who is in the building, Dom will be charged with murder, even though there was no intent to harm Freeman.

Canada recognizes two classes of murder: **first-degree murder** and **second-degree murder.** These crimes are described in section 231 of the *Criminal Code*. According to the Supreme Court of Canada, this section is "designed to impose the longest possible term of imprisonment without eligibility for parole upon those who commit the most grievous murders."

First-degree murder occurs if any one of the following situations exists:

- The murder is planned and deliberate, for example, murder for hire. "Planned" and "deliberate" are not the same. Planned refers to a "scheme or design" that has been thought out carefully. In addition, the person must have carefully "considered and weighed" the consequences of his or her actions. Deliberate means "considered" and "not impulsive."
- The victim is a law enforcement agent, such as police officer or someone working in a prison.
- The death occurs while another offensive crime is being committed. These crimes include hijacking an aircraft, sexual assault, aggravated sexual

assault, sexual assault with a weapon, threats or causing bodily harm to a third party, kidnapping and forcible confinement, and hostage taking.

- The murder was caused while committing or attempting to commit an offence related to criminal harassment.
- The murder is committed while using explosives to commit an offence in association with a criminal organization.
- The murder was committed while committing, or attempting to commit, an indictable offence that could also be considered a terrorist activity.

Murder that does not fit into any of the above categories, but is still caused intentionally, is classified as second-degree. The minimum sentence for both first- and second-degree murder is life imprisonment.

The cause of death is known as **causation** and is usually an issue in murder trials. For example, if Tina is struck by Glen and falls into a river and drowns, the trial will consider whether Glen's striking or the drowning caused her death. In many cases, evidence given by an expert can help to pinpoint causation. It is necessary to prove causation in order to convict a person of first-degree murder. The Crown must prove that the accused "participated in the murder in such a manner that he was a substantial cause of the death of the victim."

Case

R. v. Martineau

[1990] 2 S.C.R. 633
Supreme Court of Canada

Tremblay and Martineau set out with a pellet pistol and rifle to commit a crime. Although armed, Martineau thought that it would only be a break and enter. They entered the McLeans' house and robbed the couple. Then Tremblay shot and killed them. After Martineau heard the shot that killed the first victim, he allegedly said, "Lady, say your prayers."

Martineau asked Tremblay why he killed the couple, and Tremblay replied that the couple had seen their faces. Martineau responded that they couldn't have seen his because he was wearing a mask.

The Supreme Court of Canada held that section 213(a) [now section 230] of the *Criminal Code* was inconsistent with sections 7 and 11(d) of the *Charter*. Furthermore, the sections could not be justified by section 1 of the *Charter*.

The *Criminal Code* states: "Culpable homicide is murder where a person causes the death of a human being while committing or attempting to commit ... breaking and entering ... whether or not he knows

that death is likely to be caused to any human being, if (a) he means to cause bodily harm for the purpose of ... (ii) facilitating his flight after committing or attempting to commit the offence, and the death ensues from the bodily harm."

For Discussion

1. The Supreme Court of Canada stated: "in a free and democratic society that values the autonomy and free will of the individual, the stigma and punishment attached to murder should be reserved for those who choose intentionally to cause death or who choose to inflict bodily harm knowing that it is likely to cause death." What is the *mens rea* of murder? How could it be argued that Martineau did not have the required *mens rea* for murder?

2. The Court ruled that for a conviction of murder to be sustained, subjective foresight of death must be proven beyond a reasonable doubt. Interpret what you think is meant by the term "subjective foresight."

R. v. Charemski

[1998] 1 S.C.R. 679
Supreme Court of Canada

Charemski was charged with the murder of his estranged wife. She was found in the bathtub in her apartment on Christmas Day, her head at the tap end, with hot water burns on the skin. Charemski had travelled from Vancouver, British Columbia, to London, Ontario, to see his wife. The evidence implicating him in the murder was as follows:

- Charemski was present at his wife's apartment building on the night that she died, and he phoned her from the foyer.
- In early conversations with the police, Charemski said his wife complained about forgetting things and about falling asleep in the bathtub, sometimes for an hour or two, and that she had almost drowned on a couple of occasions.
- He could not account for the time between his arrival at his wife's apartment building on Christmas Eve and the time he was picked up by a taxi and left for Toronto, during which time the victim died.
- He told police that his wife had taken lovers in the past and was always "making problems" for him.
- He received social assistance and held a life insurance policy on the deceased in the amount of $50 000.
- The deceased's key to her apartment could not be found.

- The deceased told her doctor that when she had lived with Charemski she had been afraid of him and had wanted to move away from him.

The Crown presented no evidence that Charemski was in his wife's apartment on the given night. There was no evidence of fingerprints or of foul play in the apartment. The Crown could not prove that he actually knew how his wife died until police told him. Forensic evidence was inconclusive on the manner of death, whether from natural causes, accident, suicide, or homicide.

The trial judge directed a verdict of acquittal because he believed that no reasonable jury could return a verdict of guilty because of the lack of evidence as to the cause of death. The Ontario Court of Appeal set the verdict aside and ordered a new trial. Charemski appealed to the Supreme Court of Canada, which upheld the Court of Appeal decision.

For Discussion

1. **Discuss the importance of causation as it relates to a criminal trial.**

2. **What must the Crown prove in order for the charge of murder to be made out?**

3. **The evidence against Charemski was mostly circumstantial (indirect) evidence. How do you think this evidence would have been used in the Charemski case?**

4. **What factors do you think the Supreme Court of Canada took into consideration in ordering a new trial?**

Manslaughter

Manslaughter is causing the death of a human, directly or indirectly, by means of an unlawful act. Manslaughter is not murder and requires only general intent. For example, if Marina loses control of her car while speeding and kills a pedestrian, she could be charged with manslaughter, not murder. The *mens rea* for manslaughter is that a reasonable person would recognize that the unlawful act could physically harm or kill the victim.

Sometimes, people charged with murder are convicted of manslaughter. This can happen if the accused successfully uses one of two defences: provocation or intoxication. For a provocation defence, it must be shown that the accused caused another's death "in the heat of passion caused by sudden provocation." Further, the provocation must be a wrongful act or insult, and must be something that would cause an ordinary person to lose self-control (excepting drugs or alcohol). Finally, the killing must take place during the loss of self-control. If, after being provoked, the accused has time to plan the killing of the other person, the charge will be murder, not manslaughter.

The issue of intoxication is often significant in murder cases because being drunk or "high" can affect a person's ability to predict the consequences of his or her actions. The Crown must prove both the killing and the necessary intent if the accused uses the intoxication defence. If there is doubt as to the ability to form the necessary intent because the accused ingested alcohol or drugs, the accused must be found guilty of manslaughter, not murder.

Case

R. v. Parent

[2001] 1 S.C.R. 761
Supreme Court of Canada

Parent was charged with first-degree murder. He shot his estranged wife of 24 years in a fit of rage after she threatened to "wipe him out completely" during a divorce dispute. Parent and his wife Bédard had equal shares in a convenience store. A dispute over division of their assets followed their 1992 separation. The dispute led to a significant reduction of their wealth.

In 1996, the day Bédard was to buy her husband's share of the business after it had been seized by the bank, Parent showed up at the sheriff's office where the sale was to take place. An argument followed, and Bédard issued her threat. Parent, a former police officer, pulled out his revolver and fired six bullets at her. He then quietly walked away, but turned himself in later that night.

Parent testified that he never intended to kill his wife, but that he overreacted to her insults. At his murder trial, the judge instructed the jury that Parent could be found guilty of the lesser offence of manslaughter because he killed during a "fit of rage." The jury found him guilty of manslaughter, and he was sentenced to 16 years in prison. The Crown appealed to the Quebec Superior Court, which upheld the original jury decision. The Crown then appealed to the Supreme Court of Canada, which ordered a new trial on second-degree murder charges. (Intense anger alone is insufficient grounds to reduce murder to manslaughter.)

R. v. Thibert

[1996] 1 S.C.R. 37
Supreme Court of Canada

Thibert was charged with the first-degree murder of his wife's lover, Sherren. Two months before the murder, his wife told him that she was having an affair. The next morning, he met his wife in an attempt to persuade her to return home. She was accompanied by Sherren. Thibert was unsuccessful and later called her at work to arrange a meeting to again discuss her return. He had been successful in convincing her to stay once before.

Thibert placed a rifle in his car before leaving to meet her, thinking that he might have to kill Sherren. He testified that while driving, he abandoned that thought and decided to use the gun as a bluff to get his wife to go with him. Thibert met his wife and followed her into the parking lot of her workplace. Sherren came out of the building and began to lead her back into the office. Thibert removed the rifle from his car, whereupon his wife told Sherren that the rifle was not loaded. Sherren walked toward Thibert, taunting him by saying, "Come on big fellow, shoot me? You want to shoot me? Go ahead and shoot me." He kept moving toward Thibert, ignoring instructions to stay back. Thibert testified that his eyes were closed as he tried to retreat and the gun discharged.

The trial judge allowed the jury to consider the defence of provocation. However, the judge did not instruct the jury that the Crown had to disprove

continued ▶

provocation beyond a reasonable doubt. Thibert was found guilty of second-degree murder. In a majority decision, the Alberta Court of Appeal dismissed Thibert's appeal. His appeal to the Supreme Court of Canada was allowed, and a new trial on the charge of second-degree murder was ordered.

For Discussion

1. **Identify the elements that must be present for provocation to be a valid defence.**

2. **Prepare an organizer to match the evidence in each case with the elements that must be present for provocation to be a valid defence.**

3. **Compare the verdicts at trial level for each case. Why do you think they were different?**

4. **Did Parent demonstrate the elements necessary for his defence of provocation? Explain your position with evidence from the case.**

5. **Did Thibert demonstrate the elements necessary for his defence of provocation? Explain your position with evidence from the case.**

6. **In Thibert's case, the majority decision of the Supreme Court of Canada indicated that the second "element requires that the accused act upon that insult on the sudden and before there was time for his passion to cool. To be sudden provocation, the wrongful act or insult must strike upon a mind unprepared for it, and it must make an unexpected impact that takes the understanding by surprise and sets the passions aflame." Compare the Parent and Thibert cases. Did that second element exist in these cases? Justify your opinion by providing supporting evidence from each of the cases.**

Figure 5-5

Until 1972, it was a criminal offence to attempt suicide. Today, it is recognized that people who attempt suicide benefit from counselling and other forms of treatment, not punishment.

Infanticide

Infanticide is the killing of a newborn by his or her mother. An infanticide charge means that the accused has not yet recovered from the effects of childbirth and is suffering from depression or mental disturbance. The maximum punishment is imprisonment for five years. Infanticide is a charge seldom seen before the courts.

Suicide and Euthanasia

It is an offence to counsel anyone to commit suicide, or to help anyone accomplish the deed. Until 1972, it was also an offence to attempt to commit suicide.

Assisted suicide is a controversial issue. Some chronically ill Canadians have argued that they have the right to assistance when they wish to commit suicide. Disability rights groups often oppose legalizing assisted suicide because they believe that people who have disabilities may be pressured to end their lives.

A related issue is **euthanasia,** sometimes called mercy killing. This means that one person acts to end another person's life. There are different levels of consent to euthanasia. For example, if Judith, a patient with terminal cancer, has expressed a wish to die, ending her life under these circumstances would be called "voluntary euthanasia." On the other hand, Dieter, another patient with terminal cancer, has not expressed a wish to die. Perhaps he cannot express such a wish (e.g., because he is in a coma), or perhaps he does not wish to die. Ending his life under these circumstances would be called involuntary euthanasia (see Issue, page 134).

Assisting a suicide, voluntary euthanasia, and involuntary euthanasia are treated as homicide under the *Criminal Code*. However, cases involving elderly, disabled spouses are often dealt with compassionately by the courts.

Under Canadian law, patients who are considered to be of sound mind have the right to refuse treatment for an illness, even if lack of treatment results in death, more severe illness, or greater pain. A more difficult situation arises in the case of a person whose judgment is considered questionable. Some provinces deal with this situation by encouraging residents to sign personal care directives while they are of sound mind. A personal care directive answers questions regarding life support. This helps a future legal guardian to assess what the person would really want, if it becomes impossible to communicate. In the absence of a directive, legal guardians or physicians make decisions that seem appropriate to them, within the guidelines of medical ethics and human rights legislation.

⊖ activity

Visit **www.law.nelson.com** and follow the links to learn more about euthanasia.

Assault

Three levels of **assault** are listed in the *Criminal Code*. They are classified according to their severity, with increasing penalties. Intent is a key element in all three. If the action is the result of carelessness or reflex, rather than intent, there is no assault. A threat can be an assault if there is an ability to carry it out at the time it is made.

The first level of assault consists of any of the following actions:
- applying intentional force to another person, either directly or indirectly, without that person's consent
- attempting or threatening, by an act or a gesture, to apply force
- approaching or blocking the way of another person, or begging, while openly wearing or carrying a weapon or an imitation of a weapon

Harmful words do not equal an assault—the words must be accompanied by gestures. For example, if Rodney tells Adnan, "I am going to belt you," it is not an assault unless Rodney also waves a fist. On the other hand, an assault can occur even if the victim is unaware of it. If someone shoots a gun at someone and misses, there may be an assault. In addition, consent is not necessarily given just because the victim participates in an activity that poses some risk. For example, in Olympic boxing, both fighters consent to being struck with gloved fists on the head and on the body above the belt, but they do not consent to being bitten, or kicked, or struck in any way below the belt.

You Be the JUDGE

An Angus Reid Group survey recently noted that 16 percent of Canadians thought it should be a criminal offence for a parent to spank a child. Men and women equally opposed making spanking a criminal offence.

- Should it be a criminal offence for a parent to spank a child? Explain your position.

▌ Levels of Assault According to Severity

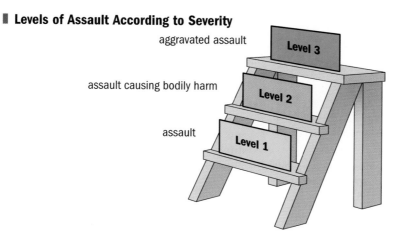

aggravated assault — Level 3

assault causing bodily harm — Level 2

assault — Level 1

Figure 5-6

Level 3 is the most severe form of assault and so carries the heaviest penalties.

Should Euthanasia Be Legalized?

In 2001, the Netherlands (Holland) became the first Western country to legalize euthanasia (mercy killing). The Dutch law created a new debate in Canada over whether or not Canada should follow the Dutch example. Euthanasia has been hotly debated in Canada for many years.

The sensitive nature of euthanasia emerged in 1993 when Robert Latimer killed his 12-year-old daughter, Tracy, with carbon monoxide in the cab of his truck. Tracy suffered from severe cerebral palsy and could not talk, walk, or take care of herself. At his trial, her father maintained that he had ended his daughter's life out of compassion. In other words, he made the decision to end Tracy's life for what he considered to be good reasons. Despite Latimer's defence that he killed out of "compassion," the Saskatchewan Court of Queen's Bench in *R. v. Latimer* (1997) found him guilty of second-degree murder and made him ineligible for parole for 10 years. In 2001, the Supreme Court of Canada unanimously upheld this decision in *R. v. Latimer* (2001).

The Latimer decision divided Canadians. Some thought that Latimer had received a just punishment because Tracy Latimer had not consented to euthanasia. Others thought the punishment was too severe. In an Ipsos-Reid opinion poll, 26 percent of Canadians believed that the sentence was deserved, while 71 percent thought it should be reduced and 2 percent had no opinion.

On One Side

In an age of medical technology, machine-supported life can be carried on for months, even years. Some believe that those who are terminally ill or suffering from severe mental and/or physical damage should be allowed to die instead of being kept alive by machines. Some also believe that people should be allowed to make decisions for others who are suffering and cannot express their own wishes. In general, supporters of euthanasia believe that life should be free of pain and that human dignity should be preserved.

The organization Dying with Dignity wants the *Criminal Code* changed to make hastening death legal in certain situations. This group wants some form of euthanasia to be clearly defined in the *Criminal Code* and legalized.

See Agents of Change on page 105 to learn about one politician's attempts to legalize euthanasia.

Figure 5-7

Robert Latimer at his Saskatchewan farm following the 2001 Supreme Court decision that upheld his second-degree murder conviction

On the Other Side

Opponents of euthanasia argue that legalizing it could cause harm. They question why euthanasia is necessary, saying that doctors are not obligated to treat an illness unless they expect to achieve a benefit for the patient. If better pain management is required, then it should be available, even if it does nothing to prolong life.

Some people, including certain people with disabilities, fear that legal euthanasia compromises their rights. They believe that human beings should not be allowed to decide who should live or die Moreover, the law should protect people who cannot consent to euthanasia.

The Bottom Line

Euthanasia raises some important legal, medical, and moral questions:
- Should a person be forced to face an agonizing death without dignity?
- Should doctors and family members be legally permitted to decide the fate of a patient who has no hope of recovery?
- Should the courts decide whether a human being will live or die?
- Should the law regarding euthanasia be changed?

What Do You Think?

1. Dutch law requires the following when euthanizing people:
   - The patient must be suffering unbearable pain.
   - All other medical options have been exhausted.
   - Voluntary and informed consent must be obtained.
   - A second opinion must be obtained from another doctor.
   - The act of euthanasia must be carefully carried out.

   Express your opinion on this law by commenting on each of the specific requirements identified above.

2. How does the issue of euthanasia relate to the Robert Latimer case?

3. Express your opinion on the euthanasia debate. Use the questions raised in The Bottom Line to guide your response. Provide examples to support your opinion. Share your opinion with a classmate.

Figure 5-8

Traci Walters leans on her scooter at the Supreme Court building in June 2000. She and other members of groups advocating the rights of disabled people were attending the Latimer trial.

The second level of assault is **assault causing bodily harm.** It is committed by anyone who, while committing assault, carries, uses, or threatens to use a weapon or an imitation of a weapon, or causes bodily harm. "Bodily harm" is defined as anything that interferes with the victim's health or comfort in more than a fleeting, trifling way.

The third level of assault is **aggravated assault.** This is the most severe form of assault. It is committed if a person wounds, maims, disfigures, or endangers the life of the victim. The *mens rea* required is only to commit bodily harm, and not necessarily to wound, maim, disfigure, or endanger the life. The defence of consent may not be accepted in some circumstances for this level of assault.

Case

R. v. Godin

(1994) 89 C.C.C. (3d) 574
Supreme Court of Canada

Godin was taking care of his girlfriend's baby. The baby was cranky and vomited his milk. Godin called an ambulance. At the hospital, the baby was diagnosed as having suffered a major head trauma. X-rays revealed a fracture of the skull. Internal bleeding had caused the baby to be critically ill. There was also bruising on the top of the baby's mouth. The doctor expressed an opinion that it would take a "violent impact" to cause such an injury.

Godin told the ambulance attendants that the baby had choked on his medication. When confronted with the skull fracture, he explained that he had slipped down the stairs while carrying the child, and the child had struck the door frame.

Godin was charged with assault causing bodily harm. At trial, he testified that while administering medication to the baby, the baby choked. Godin said he panicked and slapped the baby on the back, and

the baby struck his head on the table. The trial judge noted that Godin never sincerely endeavoured to provide a totally candid account of what took place that night. The judge noted that "in the face of such strong inculpatory facts, the accused, in my view, had to offer some explanation which might reasonably be true or otherwise ... he runs the risk of being convicted."

Godin was convicted, but the New Brunswick Court of Appeal upheld his appeal and ordered a new trial. The Crown appealed to the Supreme Court of Canada, which reinstated the trial decision.

For Discussion

1. On what basis would Godin have appealed to the New Brunswick Court of Appeal?

2. What factors do you think the trial court took into consideration in deciding that Godin had the necessary *mens rea* for assault causing bodily harm?

3. Why did the Supreme Court reinstate the trial decision?

Sexual Assault

The offences of rape and indecent assault were rewritten in the 1980s to emphasize the violent, rather than sexual, nature of these crimes. How can it be determined if the conduct of the accused was sexual in nature? A number of factors are relevant: the part of the body touched; the nature of the contact; the situation in which it occurred; the words and gestures accompanying the act; and all other circumstances surrounding the conduct, including threats, which may or may not have been accompanied by force.

There are three levels of **sexual assault,** which parallel the three levels of assault described on page 133. The definition of the first level of sexual assault is the same as assault, except that it occurs in relation to sexual conduct.

The second level is defined in section 272(1) as follows: "Every person ... who, in committing a sexual assault, (a) carries, uses or threatens to use a weapon or an imitation of a weapon; (b) threatens to cause bodily harm to a person other than the complainant; (c) causes bodily harm to the complainant; or (d) is a party to the offence with any other person, is guilty of an indictable offence and liable ... to imprisonment for a term not exceeding fourteen years." Note that the wording does not include the words "knowingly" or "with intent," so this is a general intent offence.

Aggravated sexual assault, the most severe form of sexual assault, is defined in section 273: "(1) Every one commits an aggravated sexual assault who, in committing a sexual assault, wounds, maims, disfigures or endangers the life of the complainant. (2) Every person who commits an aggravated sexual assault is guilty of an indictable offence and liable ... to imprisonment for life."

The *actus reus* of sexual assault is the sexual touching to which the victim does not consent. The *mens rea* of sexual assault can rest on knowledge that the victim gave no consent; recklessness; or willful blindness (the perpetrator avoids asking the victim if consent is being given). Consent is frequently an

You Be the JUDGE

In Texas, some sex offenders have been ordered to post signs declaring their whereabouts, such as "Danger: Registered Sex Offender Lives Here." Texas law also requires the publication of sex offenders' pictures and addresses. In Canada, police sometimes warn the public that a sexual offender has moved into an area.

• Does announcing the presence of a sexual offender violate his or her rights under the *Canadian Charter of Rights and Freedoms*? Explain.

▌ Where Sexual Assaults by Strangers Occur

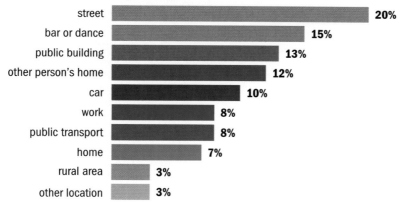

Location	Percentage
street	20%
bar or dance	15%
public building	13%
other person's home	12%
car	10%
work	8%
public transport	8%
home	7%
rural area	3%
other location	3%

Figure 5-9

The majority of sexual assaults by strangers occur outside the home.

The Law   The Criminal Code

Excerpts from the *Criminal Code*
273.1

(2) No consent is obtained, for the purposes of sections 271, 272 and 273, where

   (a) the agreement is expressed by the words or conduct of a person other than the complainant;

   (b) the complainant is incapable of consenting to the activity;

   (c) the accused induces the complainant to engage in the activity by abusing a position of trust, power or authority;

   (d) the complainant expresses, by words or conduct, a lack of agreement to engage in the activity; or

   (e) the complainant, having consented to engage in sexual activity, expresses, by words or conduct, a lack of agreement to continue to engage in the activity.

For Discussion

1. Interpret, in your own words, the meaning of "no consent."

issue in sexual assault trials, especially since there are usually few witnesses to sexual assault. The situations in which consent is not deemed to have been given in sexual assault cases is outlined in section 273.1(2) of the *Criminal Code* (see The Law, page 137).

Case

R. v. Cuerrier

[1998] 2 S.C.R. 371
Supreme Court of Canada

In 1992, Cuerrier tested positive for HIV. A public health nurse instructed him to wear a condom every time he had intercourse. He was also supposed to tell any future sexual partner that he was HIV-positive. Cuerrier angrily rejected this advice, complaining that he would never have a sex life if he told anyone about his HIV status. He soon began an 18-month relationship with the complainant, K.M. They had sex more than 100 times, most of it unprotected. Cuerrier assured her that he had tested negative for HIV eight or nine months earlier. K.M. developed hepatitis. She was informed that her HIV test was negative, but that Cuerrier had tested positive. She was advised to be tested further to determine if she had developed the virus.

On hearing that the relationship had ended, a public health nurse delivered letters to Cuerrier ordering him to inform his future partners that he was HIV-positive and to use condoms. Cuerrier then began a sexual relationship with B.H. They had mostly unprotected sex about 10 times. B.H. then learned that Cuerrier had HIV. He apologized for lying, but B.H. complained to authorities and Cuerrier was charged with two counts of aggravated assault. At the time of the trial, neither complainant had tested positive for the HIV virus.

The Crown's position was that Cuerrier had committed fraud when he lied and that the women had therefore not consented to sexual intercourse, but were instead assaulted. The trial judge entered a **directed verdict** acquitting the respondent. The British Columbia Court of Appeal refused to set aside the acquittals. The Crown appealed to the Supreme Court of Canada. The appeal was allowed and a new trial ordered.

For Discussion

1. **Identify the elements that must be proven for the accused to be found guilty of aggravated assault.**

2. **The *Criminal Code* provides that no consent is obtained where the complainant submits or does not resist by reason of fraud. This fraud or dishonest actions or behaviour must relate to the obtaining of consent. Explain how fraud could be a factor in the Cuerrier case.**

3. **The majority decision of the Supreme Court of Canada stated: "The consent cannot simply be to have sexual intercourse. Rather, it must be consent to have intercourse with a partner who is HIV-positive." How did the Supreme Court further clarify the issue of consent?**

4. **How did the actions of Cuerrier endanger the life of the complainant?**

Consent is not a defence where the victim is under 14 years of age, unless the accused is less than three years older than the victim. In *R. v. M. (M.L.)* (1994), a 16-year-old girl had been sexually assaulted by her step-father. The Supreme Court of Canada ruled that it is not necessary for the victim to physically or verbally resist an attacker to establish lack of consent. The girl had said that she was too frightened to resist.

Self-induced intoxication is not a defence if the accused "departed markedly from the standard of reasonable care." In other words, if the accused drank so much that loss of self-control was bound to occur, intoxication cannot be used as a defence. The law was clarified following a sensational case, *R. v. Daviault* (1994), where the court held that self-induced intoxication can be a defence in a sexual assault case if there is reasonable doubt that the accused could form an intent. The accused had been drunk during an attack on a 65-year-old partially paralyzed woman. Many Canadians were outraged by this judgment, and the *Criminal Code* was later amended to clarify the issue of criminal fault by reason of intoxication.

The *Criminal Code* permits one spouse to charge the other spouse for any level of sexual assault, whether or not they are living together.

Is the past conduct or lifestyle of the complainant relevant in a sexual assault trial? These factors may influence a jury to decide whether or not consent was given or whether the accused could honestly have believed that it was. The *Criminal Code* now prohibits evidence of sexual reputation from being raised in court in order to challenge or support the credibility of the complainant. However, evidence about the sexual activity of the complainant can be introduced after a judge has determined its value to the fairness of the trial. In section 276, the Code explains what the judge must consider in determining whether to admit the evidence, and in what situations the information should be made public.

In 1997, the *Criminal Code* was amended to allow personal records of the victim to be entered as evidence at trial (see The Law, below). Among the records that are included are medical, psychiatric, therapeutic, counselling, education, employment, child welfare, adoption, and social services records, as well as personal journals and diaries. The *Criminal Code* also specifies when personal records should be admitted as evidence, how this decision should be made, and whether the evidence should be published.

You Be the JUDGE

"On appeal, the idea also surfaced that if a woman is not modestly dressed, she is deemed to consent. Such stereotypical assumptions find their roots in many cultures, including our own. They no longer, however, find a place in Canadian law."
—Chief Justice Beverley McLachlin, Supreme Court of Canada

- Discuss the meaning of Chief Justice McLachlin's comment with respect to the issue of consent.

The Law   The Criminal Code

Excerpts from the *Criminal Code*

276.

(3) In determining whether evidence is admissible under subsection (2), the judge, provincial court judge or justice shall take into account

  (a) the interests of justice, including the right of the accused to make a full answer and defence;

  (b) society's interest in encouraging the reporting of sexual assault offences;

  (c) whether there is a reasonable prospect that the evidence will assist in arriving at a just determination in the case;

  (d) the need to remove from the fact-finding process any discriminatory belief or bias;

  (e) the risk that the evidence may unduly arouse sentiments of prejudice, sympathy or hostility in the jury;

  (f) the potential prejudice to the complainant's personal dignity and right of privacy;

  (g) the right of the complainant and of every individual to personal security and to the full protection and benefit of the law; and

  (h) any other factor that the judge, provincial court judge or justice considers relevant.

For Discussion

1. Summarize the factors that must be weighed by a judge in determining the admissibility of evidence of a complainant's sexual activity.

Other Sexual Offences

The law protects young people from being pressured into sexual relationships with older people. The *Criminal Code* states that it is an offence for a person to touch, for sexual purposes, a part of the body of a person under the age of 14, or to invite, counsel, or incite that person to touch, for sexual purposes, a part of the body of any person. Whether or not the victim consented is irrelevant unless the accused is less than three years older than the victim.

A similar offence exists if the person is in a position of trust or authority toward a person 14 years of age or more but under the age of 18, or the victim is in a relationship of dependency with the accused. The accused cannot offer a defence by saying that he or she did not know the age of the victim; that is, the accused must have taken all reasonable steps to determine the age of the complainant in order to mount this defence. It is irrelevant to the defence if the victim consented. Generally, a person who is aged 12 or 13 cannot be tried for these offences.

Figure 5-10

These Toronto residents were unhappy that a convicted child molester was being released into their neighbourhood. Was it appropriate for police to notify them that the offender had a history of reoffending?

Other sexual offences are as follows. It is an offence to
- commit bestiality, or compel (force) another to commit bestiality, or to commit bestiality in the presence of a person under the age of 14, or to incite a person under 14 to commit bestiality
- **procure** a person under the age of 18 for the purpose of engaging in any sexual activity prohibited by the *Criminal Code*
- as owner, occupier, or manager of premises, knowingly permit a person under the age of 18 to resort to, or to be in or on the premises for the purpose of, engaging in any sexual activity prohibited by the *Criminal Code*
- in the home of a person under 18, participate in adultery or sexual immorality or indulge in habitual drunkenness or any other form of vice, and thereby endanger the morals of the child or render the home an unfit place for the child to be in
- commit an indecent act in a public place, or be nude in a public place, or be nude on private property and exposed to public view
- commit **incest** (have sexual intercourse with a blood relative)
- exploit sexually a person with a mental or physical disability

A related addition to the Code allows a judge to prohibit sex offenders from frequenting places where children gather and from being employed in positions of trust over children.

ⓔ activity

Visit **www.law.nelson.com** and follow the links to learn more about organizations that are concerned with missing children.

Abduction

Because the number of separated and divorced families in Canada is rising, so is the number of abductions. **Abduction** is the forcible removal of an unmarried person under the age of 16 from the care of a parent, guardian, or any other person who has lawful care of the child. Foster parents are considered guardians, as is a child welfare agency that has custody of the child.

A separate offence is the unlawful taking, enticing, concealing, detaining, receiving, or harbouring of a person under the age of 14 by anyone other than the parent or guardian.

Disputes over custody may result in one parent enticing a child away from the custodial parent. The offence of enticing was created to cover such situations. **Enticing** occurs when a custodial parent refuses to give access to a child according to the terms of an agreement, or a non-custodial parent detains or runs away with the child during a time of access.

One defence against enticing is that the other parent consented to the action. Another is that it was necessary to protect the child from imminent harm. Accommodating a child who prefers to live with the non-custodial parent is not a defence.

Figure 5-11

These Canadian children were reunited with their father, Craig Merkley, in January 2001. They had been abducted by their mother, Merkley's former wife. Few child abduction cases involve strangers.

Robbery

Robbery is theft involving violence, the threat of violence, assault, or the use of offensive weapons. When the Crown is basing its case on the threat of violence, it must prove that the victim felt threatened and that there were reasonable and probable grounds for the fear. For example, phrases such as "Empty your till!" or "This is a holdup!" have been accepted as threats of violence. These phrases imply that violence will result if the command is not obeyed. Similarly, using a finger or fist to simulate a weapon has been accepted in court as a threat of violence. Holding an imitation weapon is classified as using an offensive weapon. The severe punishment for robbery—life imprisonment—reflects society's revulsion for criminals who steal using violence.

It is also an offence to mask or colour one's face with the intent to commit an indictable offence.

Review Your Understanding (Pages 127 to 141)

1. What constitutes a violent crime?
2. Distinguish between culpable and non-culpable homicide.
3. Identify the *mens rea* and *actus reus* of murder.
4. Distinguish between first- and second-degree murder, and describe the penalties for each.
5. Identify the *mens rea* and *actus reus* of manslaughter.
6. Under what circumstances could a charge of murder be reduced to manslaughter?
7. Identify the factors that must be present for a culpable homicide to be considered infanticide.

Did You Know?

In 1999, of the 410 children abducted in Canada, only 52 were kidnapped by strangers. The remaining 358 were abducted by a parent.

8. **Distinguish among the three levels of assault.**
9. **Distinguish among the three levels of sexual assault.**
10. **In what situations is consent not a defence to sexual assault?**
11. **Distinguish between abduction and enticing.**
12. **Describe four separate offences that pertain to sexual intercourse involving persons under the age of 18.**
13. **Describe the elements of robbery.**

5.3 Actions with High Social Impact

Certain actions have a high social impact and are often debated by the public and the media, as well as in Parliament. This section examines some of these actions and the issues raised by them.

Abortion

Abortion was removed from the *Criminal Code* in 1989. However, Nova Scotia tried to continue regulating abortion by passing the *Medical Services Act*. It tried to stop abortions from being performed in private clinics and charged Dr. Henry Morgentaler with 14 counts of performing unauthorized abortions in a private clinic. The trial judge dismissed the charges, as did the Nova Scotia Court of Appeal on a Crown appeal. Both courts ruled that the Nova Scotia legislature did not have the power to pass the *Medical Services Act* because it was a criminal law and outside the jurisdiction of the province.

The abortion debate often turns on whether a fetus should be considered a human being. (The legal definition of a fetus is "an unborn product of conception after the embryo stage.") The *Criminal Code* defines the matter in section 223. The Supreme Court of Canada has not ruled on when a fetus becomes a human being. In one case it gave no ruling on the issue, stating that it was up to Parliament to legislate on such an important matter. A similar decision was made in *R. v. Sullivan*.

Did You Know?

In a recent survey of Torontonians, only about one in three people knew that Canada has no laws limiting the availability of abortion.

The Law   The Criminal Code

Excerpts from the *Criminal Code*
223.

(1) A child becomes a human being within the meaning of this Act when it has completely proceeded, in a living state, from the body of its mother whether or not

  (a) it has breathed,

  (b) it has an independent circulation, or

  (c) the navel string is severed.

(2) A person commits homicide when he causes injury to a child before or during its birth as a result of which the child dies after becoming a human being.

For Discussion

1. **Summarize the *Criminal Code* definition of when a child becomes a human being.**

R. v. Sullivan

(1991) 63 C.C.C. (3d) 97
Supreme Court of Canada

Jewel Voth hired two midwives, Mary Sullivan and Gloria Lemay, to deliver her baby. The two women had no formal medical training, but had some experience with home births and had done some background reading. Voth began a difficult labour on May 7, 1985. After several hours, the baby's head emerged. Despite repeated attempts, the midwives could not extract the baby from the birth canal. The midwives called an ambulance, and Voth was taken to a hospital emergency department where the baby was delivered within two minutes of arrival, using standard obstetrical techniques. By that time, the baby had suffocated from lack of oxygen. Attempts to revive the child failed.

Sullivan and Lemay were charged with one count of criminal negligence causing death to the child and a second count of criminal negligence causing bodily harm to the mother (see page 153 for more on criminal negligence). At trial in Vancouver's County Court in October 1986, they were convicted on the first charge but acquitted on the second charge. The two women were given suspended sentences and placed on three years' probation.

The women appealed their conviction to the British Columbia Court of Appeal. In July 1988, that court dismissed the charge of criminal negligence causing death and substituted a conviction on the second count of criminal negligence causing bodily

harm. The court did so even though the Crown had not appealed the acquittal by the trial judge on that charge. The court's decision was based on the fact that an injury to the unborn child equalled an injury to the mother. In its judgment, the court stated: "As a matter of law, a child remains part of the mother when it is in the birth canal."

Sullivan and Lemay appealed their substituted conviction to the Supreme Court of Canada. In the meantime, the Crown appealed the overturning of the trial conviction on the first count. The appeals were heard in late October 1990. In a unanimous decision released on March 21, 1991, the Supreme Court upheld the acquittal of the two Vancouver midwives.

For Discussion

1. Read the section on criminal negligence on page 153. Express your opinion as to whether you think Sullivan and Lemay were guilty of criminal negligence. Use facts from the case to support your opinion.

2. Prepare an organizer to summarize the main arguments that would be presented by the Crown and by the defence.

3. Why would the British Columbia Court of Appeal dismiss the conviction of the charge of criminal negligence causing death and substitute a conviction for criminal negligence causing bodily harm?

4. What is the significance of the Supreme Court of Canada decision?

Canada's Abortion Law

The Canadian Parliament banned abortion completely in 1869, shortly after Confederation. The penalty for performing an abortion was life imprisonment. Pressure to liberalize Canada's abortion law began in the 1960s and came primarily from medical and legal associations, but also from various women's and social justice groups.

In 1967, Justice Minister Pierre Trudeau presented a bill to liberalize Canada's abortion law. The bill became law in 1969, exactly 100 years after abortion was first made illegal in Canada.

Abortion remained in the *Criminal Code*, but would be permitted under certain circumstances. A woman could get a legal abortion if she had the permission of a therapeutic abortion committee: three doctors at an accredited hospital. The committee would approve the abortion if it was determined that continuation of the pregnancy would endanger or would likely endanger the woman's life or health.

This law specified that it was an offence for any person, including the woman herself, to procure a miscarriage without the permission of the abortion

continued

committee. Even if an attempt to abort met with failure, all concerned with the abortion were liable to prosecution.

In 1988, the Supreme Court of Canada ruled that the 1969 amendments to the *Criminal Code* on abortion were unconstitutional.

Figure 5-12

Nurses rallying against abortion. Abortion is a highly sensitive issue. In the late 1960s, Pierre Trudeau liberalized Canada's abortion law.

In 1989, after the Supreme Court decision, a bill on abortion legislation was introduced into Parliament. It would have permitted abortions only when a doctor considered a woman's physical, mental, or psychological health to be threatened. The House of Commons passed the legislation, but it was subsequently defeated in the Senate. Justice Minister Kim Campbell announced that the government would not introduce new legislation. Thus, Canada does not have a law that prohibits abortion.

Despite the fact that there are no restrictions on the availability of abortion in Canada, the majority of abortions are performed during the first 12 weeks of pregnancy. Most physicians will not perform an abortion past 20 or 21 weeks unless there are health or genetic reasons.

For Discussion

1. **Outline Canada's abortion law from 1969 to 1988. Indicate under what circumstances abortion would have been considered a crime during this period.**

2. **Explain Canada's current legal status on abortion.**

Weapons

The *Criminal Code* defines a weapon as anything used or intended for use
- in causing death or injury to a person
- in threatening or intimidating any person

The object in question need not have been designed as a weapon.

Prohibited weapons include gun silencers, switchblade knives, automatic firearms, rifles and shotguns that are sawed off or otherwise modified, and any other weapon that has been declared prohibited. **Restricted weapons** include firearms that can be fired with one hand; semi-automatic weapons having a barrel length from the muzzle end of the barrel, up to and including the chamber, of less than 470 mm; firearms that can be folded or telescoped; firearms that can fire bullets in rapid succession; and any other weapon that has been declared restricted.

The federal government now requires that all owners and users of firearms—an estimated 3 million Canadians—obtain a Possession and Acquisition Licence (PAL) and register their firearms, whether restricted or not. Any restricted or prohibited firearm registered under the previous system must be re-registered by December 31, 2003 (see Issue, page 120).

The PAL is valid for five years. To apply, a person must be 18 years of age and complete an application form. Young people aged 12 to 17 can obtain a PAL with parental permission, but their parents must agree to supervise the use of the firearm. A PAL is not issued until a safety check is run on the applicant. Applicants must pass the Canadian Firearms Safety Course to qualify for a PAL.

Canadians with a PAL may own and use firearms, borrow firearms in the same class as their own, and obtain ammunition. The PAL specifies what class(es) of firearms the person can own: non-restricted, restricted, or prohibited.

To discourage people from keeping weapons illegally, the government sometimes offers "amnesty periods" during which weapons can be registered or turned into police with no questions asked. Police donate the weapons to institutions, use them for safety education training, or destroy them.

Canadian society is alarmed by the use of weapons during the commission of serious crimes. The *Criminal Code* provides a one-year minimum sentence for using a firearm while committing an indictable offence. In serious cases, that sentence can be increased up to 14 years. For some offences, such as attempted murder, manslaughter, robbery, sexual assault with a weapon, and kidnapping, the minimum penalty is increased to four years. The sentence must follow any other punishment for the indictable offence. Thus, a person sentenced to 10 years for the indictable offence and one year for the use of the firearm while committing the offence would have a sentence of 11 years. If the person has a previous firearms conviction, the minimum sentence is increased to three years, and if there is more than one weapons offence, each sentence must be served consecutively (i.e., follow the other).

Other firearm offences listed in the *Criminal Code* include

- pointing a firearm at another person without lawful excuse, whether the firearm is loaded or unloaded
- carrying or possessing a weapon, an imitation of a weapon, a prohibited device, or any ammunition or prohibited ammunition for a purpose dangerous to the public peace, or for the purpose of committing an offence
- carrying a concealed weapon, prohibited device, or any prohibited ammunition
- not reporting to a peace officer the finding of a prohibited weapon or firearm
- not reporting misplacing or losing, or having had stolen from one's possession, a restricted weapon for which a registration certificate has been issued
- altering, defacing, or removing the serial number on a firearm
- possessing a firearm that has an altered, defaced, or removed serial number
- using, carrying, shipping, or storing a firearm, prohibited weapon, restricted weapon, prohibited device, or any ammunition or prohibited ammunition in a careless manner or without reasonable precautions for the safety of other persons

Figure 5-13

Owners and users of firearms must have a licence.

You Be the JUDGE

Young people aged 12 to 17 can also obtain a Minor's Possession Licence (MPL) that lets them use a non-restricted firearm for target practice, hunting, instruction in the use of firearms, and taking part in organized shooting competitions, and that lets them buy ammunition. The MPL does not allow people to buy a firearm.

- Should persons between the ages of 12 and 17 be allowed to use firearms? Justify your opinion.

Opinions About Prostitution in Toronto

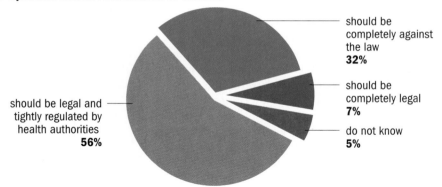

should be
completely against
the law
32%

should be
completely legal
7%

do not know
5%

should be legal and
tightly regulated by
health authorities
56%

Figure 5-14

What can you infer from these statistics? Identify some reasons for keeping prostitution illegal.

Offences Relating to Prostitution

Prostitution is legal in Canada. However, some activities related to prostitution, such as **soliciting** and keeping a common bawdyhouse (a place of prostitution), are illegal. Soliciting is communicating for the purpose of prostitution. According to the Supreme Court of Canada, such communication must be "pressing or persistent" to be an offence.

Procuring involves directing customers to the services of a prostitute or living off the earnings of a prostitute, even on a part-time basis. The penalty for procuring is much more substantial than the penalties for soliciting or keeping a common bawdyhouse.

Soliciting can be considered a "crime without a victim," but many would argue that prostitutes are victims of procuring. Nonetheless, some Canadians believe that the government should not interfere with the morals of its citizens by legislating such matters. However, legislators are concerned about the issues that surround prostitution: its frequent occurrence in crime areas, its connections with the drug trade, exploitation of prostitutes by pimps, and the impact of prostitution on neighbourhoods.

Some provinces have moved to protect underage prostitutes. Alberta's *Protection of Children Involved in Prostitution Act* allows authorities to pick up suspected prostitutes under 18 years of age. They are taken to a safe house and can be held for up to 72 hours without being charged. The safe house provides an opportunity for the youths to be free of their pimps and to receive counselling.

Obscenity

Obscenity, described in section 163 of the *Criminal Code*, continues to be controversial. The Supreme Court of Canada generally follows the "community standards test." It notes that "the courts must determine as best they can what the community would tolerate others being exposed to on the basis of the degree of harm that may flow from such exposure." Sex acts must be "degrading or dehumanizing" to be deemed obscene. The courts are frequently put in the position of determining whether something is obscene or a work of art.

R. v. Butler

(1992) 70 C.C.C. (3d) 129
Supreme Court of Canada

Butler opened the Avenue Video Boutique in Winnipeg in 1987. His shop sold and rented "hard-core" videotapes and magazines as well as sexual paraphernalia. During the first month of operation, police entered the store with a search warrant and seized the inventory. Butler was charged with selling obscene material, possessing obscene material for the purpose of distribution, possessing obscene material for the purpose of sale, and exposing obscene material to public view.

Butler reopened the store and again was charged. At trial, he was convicted of eight counts relating to eight videotapes and fined $1000 per offence. Acquittals were entered on the remaining 242 charges. The Crown appealed the 242 acquittals and Butler cross-appealed the eight convictions. The majority of the Manitoba Court of Appeal allowed the appeal of the Crown and entered convictions for Butler with respect to all the counts. Butler appealed to the Supreme Court of Canada.

In its decision, the Supreme Court of Canada divided pornography into three categories:

- *Explicit sex with violence,* which would almost always constitute undue **sexual exploitation.**
- *Explicit sex without violence that subjects people to degrading or dehumanizing treatment,* which may be undue (excessive) if the risk of harm is substantial. Whether the exploitation is undue would depend on
  - a determination of what the community would tolerate others being exposed to on the basis of the harm that may flow from such exposure. Harm can be presumed if the material predisposes a person to act in an antisocial manner.
  - whether the materials place women (and sometimes men) in positions of subordination and therefore infringe the principle of equality.
- *Explicit sex without violence that is neither degrading nor dehumanizing,* which would be tolerated. The onus is on the government to prove that the exploitation is undue. Any doubt will be resolved in favour of freedom of expression.

The Court ruled that section 163 of the *Criminal Code* violates the guarantee to freedom of expression in section 2(b) of the *Charter,* but that it is a reasonable limit prescribed by law and is therefore constitutional. Butler's case was sent back to trial to be decided on the basis of the new rules.

For Discussion

1. Explain the differences between the categories of pornography established by the Supreme Court of Canada.

2. Which category would always be classified as obscene?

3. What two factors would be used to determine if the exploitation of sex was undue (excessive)?

4. How did the Supreme Court rationalize keeping section 163 in the *Criminal Code* if it violated section 2(b) of the *Charter*?

5. What criteria should be used to determine whether material is degrading? For example, should the criteria be based on what you think other people should not view or what you think you should not view?

Section 163(8) states: "For the purposes of this Act, any publication a dominant characteristic of which is the undue exploitation of sex, or of sex and any one or more of the following subjects, namely, crime, horror, cruelty and violence, shall be deemed to be obscene." The expressions "dominant characteristic" and "undue exploitation" are the bases on which many defences are founded.

A variety of offences relate to obscenity: making, printing, circulating, mailing, or distributing obscene material; and presenting or taking part in an immoral theatrical performance. Police can obtain a warrant to seize any materials that they consider to be obscene and lay charges. Customs officers also have the right to seize materials considered obscene and forbid their entry into Canada.

Concern about the exploitation of children in pornography has resulted in amendments to the *Criminal Code*. Child pornography is defined as "a photographic, film, video or other visual representation, whether or not it was made by electronic or mechanical means, (i) that shows a person who is or is depicted as being under the age of eighteen years and is engaged in or is depicted as engaged in explicit sexual activity." Any person in possession of, producing, or distributing and selling any child pornography is guilty of an offence.

Corruption and Abandonment of Children

Parents or guardians of children may not procure them for prostitution or for any sexual activity prohibited by the *Criminal Code*. As well, it is an offence to own, occupy, or manage a place that children are using for sexual activity prohibited by the Code. It is also an offence to abandon or expose a child under the age of 10 if endangering the child's life or permanently harming his or her health is likely.

To protect the public from high-risk sexual offenders, Parliament is considering a national sex offender registry system. Similar registries now exist in Ontario. Information would be kept at the Canadian Police Information Centre, which is maintained by the RCMP. The information would then be available to police forces across Canada. Convicted offenders would be required to register their current addresses with the police.

Parliament may also establish the offence of cyberstalking (luring through the Internet). The aim is to protect children from predators who strike up acquaintances with lonely or naive boys and girls. In recent years, there have been cases of children leaving home to meet or live with a cyber acquaintance in another city or country. The offence would make it illegal to communicate for sexual purposes with someone believed to be a child.

Figure 5-15

What can young people do to avoid being "stalked" on the Internet?

Review Your Understanding (Pages 142 to 148)

1. Identify the significance of the 1988 Supreme Court of Canada decision regarding abortion.
2. Distinguish between prohibited and restricted weapons.
3. What must a citizen in Canada do in order to legally possess or use a gun?
4. Describe five offences pertaining to weapons, other than those that deal with prohibited and restricted weapons.
5. a) Distinguish between procuring and soliciting.
   b) What elements must exist for a conviction on soliciting?
6. Discuss four issues related to prostitution that are of concern to legislators.
7. How does the *Criminal Code* define obscenity?

5.4 Property Crimes

At one time, protection of property was one of the most important functions of criminal law. Until the 18th century, death was a common penalty for theft. Property such as livestock and horses was so important to owners that society demanded this extreme punishment. The *Criminal Code* continues to provide major penalties for offences against property. In fact, property offences make up approximately two-thirds of all offences listed in the *Criminal Code*. The major property crimes are arson, theft over $5000, theft under $5000, motor-vehicle theft, break and enter, possession of stolen goods, and fraud.

Arson

Owing to an increase in intentional fires and explosions, the *Criminal Code* was amended in 1990 to include more acts under the definition of **arson.**

The Code defines arson as the intentional or reckless causing of damage by fire or explosion to property, whether or not the arsonist owns the property. If the arsonist is aware that someone occupies the property, or is reckless in that regard, or if the fire or explosion causes bodily harm to another person, the maximum penalty is life imprisonment. Where there is no danger to life, the maximum penalty for arson is 14 years in prison.

Committing arson with intent to defraud—for example, to collect on an insurance policy—carries a maximum penalty of 10 years. Possessing any explosive material or device, such as a bomb, for the purpose of committing arson is illegal. Finally, to set off a false fire alarm is a hybrid offence: the maximum penalty is two years if the Crown proceeds by indictment.

Theft

Theft has a number of elements. Each element must be proven for a successful conviction.

- The act must be fraudulent, which means that the person who is stealing must have intended to do something wrong.
- The person taking the item must not have any **colour of right** to it. "Colour of right" means that the person has a legal right to the item.
- The accused must have an intent to deprive the owner of the item or convert it to his or her own use.

If the value of the goods is below $5000, the offence is generally known as theft under $5000. If the value is over $5000, the offence is known as theft over $5000. The penalties are substantially different. Theft under $5000 is a hybrid offence with a maximum penalty of two years. Theft over $5000 has a maximum penalty of 10 years.

A person can also be charged with theft based on the principle of recent possession. When arrested, a person who has possession of items that were recently stolen must be able to explain at trial how he or she came to possess them. If the accused provides an explanation, the onus is on the Crown to disprove it. If the Crown fails to do so, the accused must be acquitted.

In 2000, there were
293 416 break-ins—a
9 percent decrease from
the previous year and
the lowest rate since
1978. Sixty percent of
the break-ins occurred
in homes. At the same
time, a survey of 26 000
people showed that fewer
people are reporting
break-ins to police. Why
would people decide not
to report them?

Break and Enter

The law considers break and enter, commonly called burglary, a serious offence. The terms "break" and "enter" are defined in sections 321 and 350 of the *Criminal Code*. Section 321 states: "In this Part, 'break' means (a) to break any part, internal or external, or (b) to open any thing that is used or intended to be used to close or to cover an internal or external opening." Section 350(a) states: "A person enters as soon as any part of his body or any part of an instrument that he uses is within any thing that is being entered." Due to an increase in home invasions in larger cities, amendments to the *Criminal Code* proposed in 2001 would permit tougher penalties for break-and-enter crimes involving a home.

The offence of break and enter is described in section 348 of the *Criminal Code* (see The Law, page 103).

When someone illegally enters a residence by some other means (not by break and enter) to commit an indictable offence, there is a separate offence—being unlawfully in a dwelling-house (residence). The penalty for this offence is less severe than it is for break and enter. It is also an offence to possess housebreaking, vault-breaking, or safe-breaking tools if circumstances indicate that the owner possessed such tools for the purpose of breaking in. No break-in need actually occur.

Case

R. v. Holmes

(1988) 64 C.R. (3d) 97
Supreme Court of Canada

Holmes was charged with possession of housebreaking tools, under section 309(1) [now 351(1)] of the *Criminal Code*. The tools were a pair of pliers and a pair of locking pliers. If such tools give rise to a reasonable inference that they could be used for housebreaking, the section requires an owner to prove that the tools have no illegal purpose.

Holmes argued that this requirement violated the presumption of innocence guaranteed by section 11(d) of the *Canadian Charter of Rights and Freedoms*. It reversed the burden of proof by making him prove that he was innocent. Before entering his plea, Holmes moved to have the indictment quashed (suppressed). The trial judge granted the motion. The Crown appealed, and the Ontario Court of Appeal set aside the order. Holmes appealed to the Supreme Court of Canada.

The Supreme Court of Canada ruled that the words "reasonable inference" do not permit a finding of guilt unless something is proved beyond a reasonable doubt. Therefore, the Crown had to prove that there was possession, and that the tools were obtained for the purpose of committing a crime. The words "without lawful excuse, the proof of which lies upon him" were included in the Code to make available the defence of innocent purpose. Hence, the section did not require the accused to prove that the tools were not for an illegal purpose and therefore did not violate section 11(d).

For Discussion

1. **Identify the three elements that must be proved for the Crown to obtain a conviction on possession of housebreaking tools.**

2. **Interpret the meaning of section 11(d) of the *Charter* and explain how it relates to the burden of proof on the prosecution.**

3. **Reverse onus means the accused has to prove he or she is innocent. How does a reverse onus limit the right protected under section 11(d)?**

4. **On what basis did the Supreme Court of Canada rule that the offence was not one of reverse onus?**

5. **Explain the defence of innocent purpose.**

Possession of Stolen Goods

It is an offence for someone to possess anything that he or she knows was obtained during the commission of an indictable offence. In addition, owning a car with a licence plate whose serial numbers are removed or destroyed will lead to the presumption that the car was obtained during the commission of an indictable offence.

Fraud

Making false statements to obtain credit or a loan is a crime. For example, if Connie applies for a loan on the Internet and lies about her salary and her assets, she could be charged with obtaining credit by **false pretences** under section 361(1) of the *Criminal Code*: "A false pretence is a representation of a matter of fact either present or past, made by words or otherwise, that is known by the person who makes it to be false and that is made with a fraudulent intent to induce the person to whom it is made to act on it."

Credit is a form of money. In fact, the amount of "money" that can be spent using stolen credit cards can sometimes exceed the amount that one thief can carry away from the bank. Section 342 of the *Criminal Code* describes the offence of credit card fraud.

The *Criminal Code* also states that anyone who writes a cheque for which insufficient funds are available when the cheque is cashed is guilty of an offence. It is a defence if the person can prove that, when the cheque was issued, there was every reason to believe that the funds were available.

The Law　　　The Criminal Code

Excerpts from the *Criminal Code*

342.

(1) Every person who

　(a) steals a credit card,

　(b) forges or falsifies a credit card,

　(c) possesses, uses or traffics in a credit card or a forged or falsified credit card, knowing that it was obtained, made or altered
　　(i) by the commission in Canada of an offence, or
　　(ii) by an act or omission anywhere that, if it had occurred in Canada, would have constituted an offence, or

　(d) uses a credit card knowing that it has been revoked or cancelled,

is guilty of

　(e) an indictable offence and is liable to imprisonment for a term not exceeding ten years, or

　(f) an offence punishable on summary conviction.

For Discussion

1. Why do you think the number of offences related to credit card fraud is increasing?

2. In your opinion, would use of more personal identification, such as fingerprints on a scanner, be better identification for credit? What shortcomings are there to using such techniques?

Review Your Understanding (Pages 149 to 151)

1. Explain the elements necessary for a theft conviction.
2. Interpret the legal meaning of the terms "break" and "enter."
3. Explain the concept of reverse onus as it applies to the possession of housebreaking instruments and the possession of stolen goods.
4. Discuss three examples of fraud.

5.5 Other Crimes

The following offences are significant because they occur frequently, are recent additions to the Code, or are of general interest.

Terrorism and Terrorist Acts

activity

Visit **www.law.nelson.com** and follow the links to learn more about UN conventions and protocols related to terrorism.

The terrorist events of September 11, 2001, resulted in several changes and additions to the Canadian *Criminal Code* (see Agents of Change, page 30). Canada also signed 14 United Nations conventions related to terrorism, including the *Suppression of Terrorist Financing Convention* and the *Suppression of Terrorist Bombings Convention.*

The Canadian government defines "terrorist activity" as "an action that takes place either within or outside of Canada that is an offence under one of the UN anti-terrorism conventions and protocols; or is an action taken for political, religious or ideological purposes and intimidates the public concerning its security, or compels a government to do something, by intentionally killing, seriously harming or endangering a person, causing substantial property damage that is likely to seriously harm people or by seriously interfering with or disrupting an essential service, facility or system." The activity does not have to take place in Canada—it can be against a Canadian citizen or government facility located outside Canada.

You Be the JUDGE

Does the definition of "terrorist activity" cover events such as those in the United States on September 11, 2001? Explain.

The *Criminal Code* now allows the government to publish the names of groups, referred to as "entities," that are acting as, or on behalf of, a terrorist group.

Canada, along with many other countries, took action to cut off the sources of funds that terrorists use to carry out their activities. It is now an offence to knowingly collect or provide funds, either directly or indirectly, to carry out terrorist crimes. The government also has the right to freeze any property that is being used in any way to assist a terrorist group. To further control use of property by terrorists, financial institutions must report to the government any assets in their possession that belong to a listed entity. Legislation was also enacted to make it a criminal offence to commit any indictable offence under *any* Act of Parliament for the benefit of, under orders of, or in association with a terrorist group.

The cause of most terrorist activities is hatred of a particular group. The *Criminal Code* amendments give a judge the right to order the deletion of hate propaganda contained on Internet sites. The damaging of a religious property motivated by bias, prejudice, or hate was also added as an offence.

Criminal Harassment

The offence of criminal harassment (stalking) was added to the *Criminal Code* in 1993. It prohibits anyone from repeatedly communicating with or following another person, any member of the other person's family, or anyone known to that person, where in all the circumstances, they reasonably fear for their safety.

ⓔ activity

Visit **www.law.nelson.com** and follow the links to learn more about criminal harassment.

▮ **Criminal Harassment: Relationship of Accused to Victim, 1999**

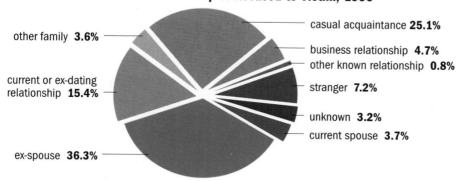

- other family **3.6%**
- current or ex-dating relationship **15.4%**
- ex-spouse **36.3%**
- casual acquaintance **25.1%**
- business relationship **4.7%**
- other known relationship **0.8%**
- stranger **7.2%**
- unknown **3.2%**
- current spouse **3.7%**

Figure 5-16

Women were victims in 75 percent of the incidents. Why do you think it is most likely for an ex-spouse to be engaged in criminal harassment? Draw another conclusion from the data.

Criminal Negligence

The definition of **criminal negligence** is found under section 219 of the *Criminal Code*.

Criminal negligence comprises three categories: criminal negligence in the operation of a motor vehicle (examined in Chapter 6); criminal negligence causing bodily harm (see *R. v. Sullivan,* page 143); and criminal negligence causing death. Intent is not necessary. Indifference as to what the reasonable person would do under the circumstances may result in a conviction. Thus, a person who drives in a manner very different from that of the reasonable person and who is inconsiderate of the safety of others is criminally negligent. See Chapter 12 for more on negligence.

The Law — The Criminal Code

Excerpts from the *Criminal Code*

219.

(1) Every one is criminally negligent who

   (a) in doing anything, or

   (b) in omitting to do anything that it is his duty to do,

shows wanton or reckless disregard for the lives or safety of other persons.

(2) For the purposes of this section, "duty" means a duty imposed by law.

For Discussion

1. Give examples of wanton or reckless disregard for the lives or safety of other persons that could result from the operation of a motor vehicle.

Mischief

The offence of **mischief** can relate to a variety of circumstances involving the deliberate destruction or damaging of property. Today, some of the most valuable property is electronic information (data). Because of the possibility that data may be deliberately destroyed, for example, by a computer virus, the definition of mischief includes harm to data. These offences are defined in sections 430(1) and 430(2) of the *Criminal Code*.

The Law   The Criminal Code

Excerpts from the *Criminal Code*

430.

(1) Every one commits mischief who wilfully

   (a) destroys or damages property;

   (b) renders property dangerous, useless, inoperative or ineffective;

   (c) obstructs, interrupts or interferes with the lawful use, enjoyment or operation of property; or

   (d) obstructs, interrupts or interferes with any person in the lawful use, enjoyment or operation of property.

(1.1) Every one commits mischief who wilfully

   (a) destroys or alters data;

   (b) renders data meaningless, useless or ineffective;

   (c) obstructs, interrupts or interferes with the lawful use of data; or

   (d) obstructs, interrupts or interferes with any person in the lawful use of data or denies access to data to any person who is entitled to access thereto.

For Discussion

1. Why is section 430(1.1) significant in our society today?

2. Assume you were having a loud party at your house. Under what circumstances could you be charged with the offence of mischief?

Review Your Understanding (Pages 152 to 154)

1. Name some offences considered to be terrorist activities according to the *Criminal Code*.

2. What elements must be proven to obtain a conviction on a charge of criminal negligence?

3. How does the *Criminal Code* define mischief relating to data?

5.6 Offences and Penalties

The following is a list of the offences and penalties found in the *Criminal Code*.

Indictable Offence—Life Imprisonment

Accessory after fact to murder
Aircraft, endangering safety
Arson, disregard for life

Break and enter, dwelling-house
Criminal negligence causing death
Explosives, intent to cause harm, death
Explosives, used against a public building, with intent to cause death

Extortion
Hijacking
Hostage taking
Kidnapping
Killing unborn child in act of birth
Mail, stopping with intent to rob
Manslaughter
Mischief (if dangerous to life)

Murder
Murder, attempted
Murder, conspiracy to commit
Riot Act, hindering reading of
Robbery
Sexual assault, aggravated
Terrorism, any indictable offence at the direction
    of or in association with a terrorist group

Indictable Offence—14 years

Administering noxious thing endangering life
Aircraft, taking explosives or weapons on
Aggravated assault
Arson, damage to other's property
Bribery of judicial officers, peace officers
Causing bodily harm by criminal negligence
Causing bodily harm with intent
Contradictory evidence by witness
Counterfeit money, making, possessing, or
    uttering

Criminal organization, participating in
Fabricating evidence
Facilitating a terrorist activity
Firearm, use of during offence
Impeding attempt to save life
Incest
Passport, forging or using forged [passport]
Perjury
Piracy
Sexual assault, using weapon,
    or causing bodily harm
Suicide, counselling, aiding

Indictable Offence—10 years

Abduction of person under 14
Assault causing bodily harm
Cattle theft
Credit, obtained by false pretense
Criminal negligence causing bodily harm
Disguise with intent to commit indictable offence
Face masked or coloured
False pretence, property obtained by (over $5000)
Housebreaking instruments—possession

Mail theft
Prison breach
Procuring
Sexual intercourse, administering drug, liquor
    for illicit
Terrorism, participating in a terrorist group,
    concealing a terrorist
Terrorist activities, financing, providing property
Theft, or possession of property obtained by
    crime, if over $5000

Indictable Offence—5 years

Abduction of person under 16
Bigamy
Childbirth, failing to obtain assistance in
Explosive, illegal possession
Fire, setting by negligence
Fraud upon the government
Genocide, advocating

Indignity to dead body
Infanticide
Marriage, procuring feigned
Municipal corruption
Polygamy
Sexual activity, parent procuring (under 14)
Traps likely to cause bodily harm
Unlawful drilling

Indictable Offence—2 years

Abandoning child
Administering noxious things to annoy
Automobile master key, selling
Cheating at play
Coin device, possession of instrument for breaking
Common bawdyhouse, keeping
Common nuisance
Corrupting children
Disobeying order of court
Disposing of body of child to conceal birth
Duelling

Eavesdropping equipment, illegal possession of
Escape, permitting or assisting
False message
Gaming-house, keeping
Gaming- or betting-house, found-in
Intercepted information, illegal disclosure of
Lotteries, illegal
Mail, using to defraud
Misconduct of officers executing process
Procuring own miscarriage
Riot, taking part
Sexual activity, parent procuring (under 18)
Spreading false news

Hybrid Offence

The number in parentheses indicates the maximum penalty in years if the offence is tried by indictment. If two numbers are shown, the first is the maximum penalty in months for the summary offence if other than the usual six months.

Abduction in contravention of custody order (10)
Abduction where no custody order (10)
Assault, assaulting a peace officer (5)
Assault, causing bodily harm (10)
Bodily harm, unlawfully causing (10)
Break and enter, non-dwelling-house (10)
Buggery, bestiality (10)
Computer, unauthorized use (10)
Credit card, theft; forgery (10)
Dwelling-house, unlawfully in (10)
Escape, unlawfully at large (2)
Failing to appear at court (2)
False alarm of fire (2)
Firearm, pointing (5)
Forcible entry (2)
Forgery (10)
Harassment, criminal (5)
Hatred, incite or promote (2)
Mailing obscene matter (2)

Mischief motivated by bias, prejudice, or hate (18, 10)
Mischief, over $5000 (10), under $5000 (2)
Morals, corrupting (2)
Necessaries, failing to provide (2)
Obstructing, resisting an officer (2)
Pornography, making child (10)
Pornography, possession of child (5)
Probation order, failure to obey (2)
Public mischief (5)
Recognizance, breach of (2)
Sexual assault (10)
Sexual exploitation, 14 to 18 (5)
Sexual exploitation of person with disability (18 m) (2)
Sexual interference, under 14 (10)
Sexual purposes, removal of child from Canada for (5)
Sexual touching, invitation to, under 14 (10)
Theft, or possession of property obtained by crime, if under $5000 (2)
Threat, to harm or cause death (18 m) (2)
Threat, uttering (18 m) (5)
Weapon, unauthorized possession of prohibited, restricted (5)
Weapon, concealed or in motor vehicle (5)

Summary Offence—6 months

Advertising reward and immunity
Animals, injuring or endangering
Assembly, participating in unlawful
Causing a disturbance
Coin, defacing
Gaming- or betting-house, found-in
Impersonating a peace officer
Impersonating at an examination
Indecent act, telephone call
Loitering
Motor vehicle theft
Nudity
Slug, having or making
Soliciting
Trespassing at night
Water-skiing, failure to watch, or at night
Weapon, at a public meeting

Minimum Penalties

Betting, illegal (1st offence: 2 years; 2nd: 14 days to 2 years; 3rd: 3 months to 2 years)
Criminal negligence causing death, using a firearm (4 years to life)
Firearm, imitation, using to commit an offence (1st offence: 1 to 14 years; 2nd: 3 to 14 years)
Firearm, using to commit an offence (1st offence: 1 year; 2nd: 3 years)
Hostage taking, using firearm (4 years to life)
Kidnapping, using firearm (4 years to life)
Manslaughter, using firearm (4 years to life)
Murder, attempted, using firearm (4 years to life)
Robbery, using firearm (4 years to life)
Sexual assault, aggravated, using firearm (4 years to life)
Sexual assault, using firearm (4 to 14 years)

Chapter Review

Chapter Highlights

- The charge for a homicide depends upon the person killed and the intent.
- Assault charges can be one of three charges, depending upon the severity of the assault.
- Sexual assault charges can be one of three charges, depending upon the severity of the assault.
- Consent is frequently an issue in a sexual assault trial.
- There is legislation designed to protect children.
- Weapons are classified as prohibited and restricted weapons.
- Soliciting, keeping a common bawdyhouse, and procuring are illegal.
- The community standards test is followed by courts in determining obscenity.
- Property crimes make up approximately two-thirds of *Criminal Code* offences.
- Arson is the intentional or reckless causing of damage by fire or explosion.
- The penalties for theft under $5000 and over $5000 are significantly different.
- It is an offence to be in the possession of property while knowing that it was obtained by the commission of an indictable offence.
- The offence of "obtaining by false pretences" requires that the person knows that the facts presented are false.
- The offence of mischief refers to the deliberate damaging of property.

Review Key Terms

Name the key terms that are described below.

a) the cause of death, usually an issue in murder trials

b) forcible removal of a child

c) anything that serves to indicate a person has true ownership of something

d) any weapon that has been declared prohibited

e) painlessly putting to death as an act of mercy a person suffering from an incurable and disabling disease

f) communicating for the purposes of prostitution

g) theft involving violence, threat of violence, assault, or the use of offensive weapons

h) killing of an infant shortly after birth, by its mother who has become mentally disturbed from the effects of giving birth

i) the deliberate destruction or damage of property

j) planned and deliberate killing

k) to live off the earnings of a prostitute

l) intent to wound, maim, or disfigure

m) intentional damage by fire

n) blamable killing

o) the act of fraudulently taking something

p) a representation known to be false

Check Your Knowledge

1. Indicate, by providing examples, what would be considered crimes of violence.

2. Outline actions that are considered to have a high social impact and are debated by society and in Parliament.

3. Identify the actions that are considered property crimes. Provide examples.

4. Provide examples of laws in the *Criminal Code* that are specifically designed to protect children.

Apply Your Learning

5. For each of the following incidents, indicate the offence that will be charged, the elements that must be proven for a successful conviction, and the maximum penalty.
   a) The accused killed her child shortly after childbirth.
   b) The accused wrote obscenities on the side of a building.
   c) The accused entered a home and stole a television.
   d) The accused quickly spent money that he found deposited mistakenly in his bank account.
   e) The accused set fire to his friend's car.
   f) The accused pushed his friend down the stairs. The friend died.

6. *R. v. Creighton*, [1993] 3 S.C.R. 3 (Supreme Court of Canada)

Creighton, Caddedu, and Martin shared a large quantity of alcohol and cocaine at Martin's apartment over an 18-hour period. All the parties involved were experienced cocaine users. Creighton injected cocaine into Martin's forearm with her consent. She immediately began to convulse violently and appeared to cease breathing. The other two could not resuscitate her. Caddedu wanted to call 911 but was dissuaded by Creighton, who placed Martin on the bed, cleaned the apartment of any possible fingerprints, and left with Caddedu. Seven hours later, Caddedu returned and called for emergency assistance. Martin was pronounced dead. As a result of the injection, she had experienced a cardiac arrest and later asphyxiated on the contents of her stomach. The defence conceded that trafficking had taken place. The Crown argued that Creighton was guilty of manslaughter as the death was the direct consequence of an unlawful act.

What factors could the Crown consider in their argument for manslaughter?

7. *R. v. Thornton* (1993), 82 C.C.C. (3d) 530 (Supreme Court of Canada)

Thornton was well-informed about HIV and its means of transmission. He knew that he was a member of a group that was highly at risk of contracting AIDS. Moreover, he knew that he had twice tested positive for HIV antibodies and that he was therefore infectious. Thornton nevertheless donated blood to the Red Cross in 1987.

Thornton was charged with committing a common nuisance, which is defined as doing an unlawful act or failing to discharge a legal duty and thereby endangering the life, safety, health, property, or comfort of the public. The *Criminal Code* provides in section 216 that "every one who undertakes to administer surgical or medical treatment to another person or to do any other lawful act that may endanger the life of another person is, except in cases of necessity, under a legal duty to have and to use reasonable knowledge, skill and care in so doing."

How could it be argued that Thornton was guilty of the crime of common nuisance?

8. Examine the following statistics related to homicides in Canada in 1999, as reported by Statistics Canada in October 2000.
- Canada's homicide rate was its lowest since 1967.
- Canada's homicide rate was one-third less than the American rate, but higher than most European rates.
- Almost 90 percent of accused persons were male, as were two-thirds of homicide victims.
- About 8 percent of homicide incidents were murder–suicides.
- Thirty-one percent of homicides involved firearms.
- Handguns were used in 55 percent of all firearm homicides.
- The majority of firearms-related deaths were a result of suicide.
- Four out of five victims of spousal homicide were female.
- Fifty-one percent of female homicide victims were killed by someone with whom they had an intimate relationship, compared with 6 percent of male victims.
- Of the children under 12 who were killed, 80 percent were killed by a parent.
- Sixty-four percent of people accused of homicide had a previous criminal record.

What conclusions can be drawn about homicide offences and weapons-related offences in Canada?

Communicate Your Understanding

9. Assume that the next session of Parliament is considering opening debate on the *Criminal Code* in relation to the following topics:
   - censorship
   - euthanasia
   - weapons

   Select one topic and write a letter to your local member of Parliament, outlining your position on how to balance individual and societal interests. Extend your research by providing examples from the news.

10. Investigate current issues in criminal law by selecting three news articles from print or online sources that deal with criminal law matters. For each article, complete the following:
    a) Briefly summarize the article.
    b) Outline at least two main criminal issues discussed.
    c) Where possible, identify the opinion of the author.
    d) Express your opinion on this criminal matter, and justify your view by providing examples to support it.

Develop Your Thinking

11. How have changes in attitudes and societal values brought about changes in criminal law? Support your answer by providing examples of recent changes to criminal law in Canada by researching from the text, current print media, or the Internet.

12. The *Criminal Code* specifies a number of offences that are often referred to as "crimes without victims." They include communicating for the purpose of prostitution, obscenity, and keeping a bawdyhouse (brothel). Should the police control such activities, or should people be allowed to decide for themselves whether or not to engage in them? Explain. How could it be argued that there are victims in these crimes?

Drug Use, Drinking, and Driving

Focus Questions

- What basic drug offences are found in the *Controlled Drugs and Substances Act*?

- What rights do police have for the search and seizure of controlled drugs?

- Which offences are connected with impaired driving?

- What changes in the law have been made to reduce the occurrence of drinking and driving?

- What are the costs to Canadian society of illegal use of drugs and impaired driving?

Chapter at a Glance

Figure 6-1

A customs agent holds a brick of hashish concealed in food packages. This drug bust in Montreal yielded 10 000 kg of hashish. It takes millions of dollars to fight the illegal drug trade. Do you think this money is well spent?

6.1 Introduction

Did You Know?

Some authorities recently told the United Nations: "We believe that the global war on drugs is now causing more harm than drug abuse itself." How might this be possible?

Driving under the influence of alcohol and using illegal drugs are serious crimes that trouble Canadians. These crimes are costly to Canadian society, resulting in more tax spending on health care and legal aid, and soaring insurance rates. Federal and provincial governments have tried to solve these problems by introducing stiffer penalties and other **deterrents,** and by giving the police greater powers. Still, there is a widespread belief that neither drug traffickers nor impaired drivers are penalized severely enough. In this chapter, you will examine these crimes in more detail as well as the legislation designed to protect Canadian society.

The Cost of Illegal Drugs

Worldwide, governments spend millions monitoring drug traffic and arresting people involved in the drug trade. It is also expensive to prosecute crime related to illegal drugs; for example, murder, property damage, assaults, theft, and robbery. The illegal drug trade feeds large fortunes to criminal organizations. Do such costs justify the "war on drugs," or should governments just legalize the possession and use of certain drugs? Revenue generated by the world's illicit drug industry is estimated to be $600 billion. Annual production of marijuana in British Columbia is valued at $6 billion, which would make it the largest industry in the province.

6.2 The Controlled Drugs and Substances Act

A **drug** has been defined as "any substance that by its chemical nature alters structure or function in a living organism." Of course, not all chemicals with these effects are classified as illegal drugs. Otherwise, tea, beer, cola, and aspirin would be classed with heroin and cocaine. Drugs are classified as criminal because using or possessing them is restricted by law. Thus, the fact that marijuana is not a narcotic has been ruled by the courts to be irrelevant; marijuana is still on the list of substances defined as a controlled drug by Parliament. The rel-

Figure 6-2

Controlled substances are used legitimately by some Canadians to manage pain. How can prescription medication be kept away from addicts?

evant statute relating to the use of drugs—the *Controlled Drugs and Substances Act*—was enacted in 1997. It is a combination of the old *Narcotic Control Act* and sections of the *Food and Drugs Act*.

The *Controlled Drugs and Substances Act* criminalizes possession of, and trafficking in, a variety of illegal and controlled drugs. The Act has four basic schedules, or lists:

- Schedule I lists the most dangerous drugs, including narcotics such as heroin and cocaine.
- Schedule II lists cannabis (marijuana) and its derivatives.
- Schedule III lists many of the more dangerous drugs previously found in the *Food and Drugs Act,* such as lysergic acid diethylamide (LSD).
- Schedule IV lists drugs that must be controlled but that have therapeutic use, such as barbiturates.

Two other schedules that will be referred to below are Schedules VII and VIII. Schedule VII refers to cannabis resin and cannabis in amounts up to 3 kg; Schedule VIII refers to cannabis resins in amounts up to 1 g and to cannabis in amounts up to 30 g. The Act defines a **controlled substance** as being any substance included in Schedules I to IV.

Possession

It is an offence to possess any drug listed in Schedules I to III. Canadians are allowed to possess drugs found in Schedule IV, which are for therapeutic use. Figure 6-3 summarizes the penalties for possessing drugs found in Schedules I, II, VIII, and III.

▌ Penalties for Possession

Schedule and Substance	Offence	Penalty (maximums)
Schedule I Dangerous drugs	If a first offence and tried as a summary offence	$1000 and/or 6 months
	If a subsequent offence	$2000 fine and/or 1 year
	If tried as an indictable offence	7 years
Schedule II Cannabis (marijuana) and its derivatives	If a first offence and tried as a summary offence	$1000 and/or 6 months
	If a subsequent offence	$2000 and/or 1 year
	If tried as an indictable offence	5 years less a day
Schedule VIII Cannabis resin up to 1 g and cannabis up to 30 g	If charged under Schedule VIII, the offence is always tried as a summary offence.	$1000 and/or 6 months
Schedule III Dangerous drugs formerly listed in the *Food and Drugs Act*	If a first offence and tried as a summary offence	$1000 and/or 6 months
	If a subsequent offence	$2000 and/or 1 year
	If tried as an indictable offence	3 years

e activity

Visit **www.law.nelson.com** and follow the links to learn about drug awareness programs.

Figure 6-3

A person found with one marijuana cigarette will not be treated the same as someone who has a large amount of cannabis. In many locations, possession of a Schedule VIII amount of marijuana is ignored. The Crown can also discriminate between first offenders and those with numerous possession convictions.

Excerpts from the *Criminal Code*

4.

(3) For the purposes of this Act,

(a) a person has anything in possession when he has it in his personal possession or knowingly

  (i) has it in the actual possession or custody of another person, or

  (ii) has it in any place, whether or not that place belongs to or is occupied by him, for the use or benefit of himself or of another person; and

(b) where one of two or more persons, with the knowledge and consent of the rest, has anything in his custody or possession, it shall be deemed to be in the custody and possession of each and all of them.

For Discussion

1. Describe what "possession" means, referring to section 4(3)(a)(i) of the *Criminal Code*. Give examples of how this situation could occur.

2. Why would the law allow a charge of possession even if the person does not actually have the drugs?

3. Kim knows that Cheryl's locker at school is about to be searched for illegal drugs, so she agrees to put the drugs in her own locker. What part of the definition of possession applies to Cheryl?

Even if you possess a small quantity of a drug, you can still be charged with possession. As long as the drug is identifiable, a charge can be laid. In addition, the *Controlled Drugs and Substances Act* adopts the definition of possession given in section 4(3) of the *Criminal Code*. A person is defined as "having possession" even when he or she does not technically own the drug. Having control over a drug can therefore lead to a charge. For example, Deirdre, who gives a controlled substance to Max for safekeeping, is guilty of possession. Taia, who is part of a group using a controlled substance, can also be found in possession. If five people are sharing a marijuana "joint," they could all be convicted of the offence of possession. The owner of the house in which the five are smoking the drug is particularly vulnerable, even if he or she does not use the marijuana, because allowing its use in his or her home implies consent.

When prosecuting a drug case, the Crown must prove possession and show that the drug in question is a controlled substance. In addition, the Crown must show that there was intent to possess; that is, the accused must know that the substance is a drug. The Supreme Court of Canada ruled in *R. v. Beaver* (1957) that *mens rea* is a necessary element of the offence. Beaver had a package he thought contained sugar of milk, a white powder. In fact, it contained a narcotic. Beaver was acquitted.

In 2001, regulations under the *Controlled Drugs and Substances Act* were changed to allow patients with terminal illnesses, chronic conditions, or chronic pain to either grow their own marijuana or designate someone to grow it for them. The federal health department is paying a Saskatchewan company to grow the marijuana for eligible patients. The legal users of marijuana under this legislation must carry an identification card.

Did You Know?

A 2000 *National Post*/COMPAS poll showed that 53 percent of Canadians opposed buying or using marijuana for personal use. Sixty-nine percent thought that marijuana possession could be punishable by a fine instead of imprisonment.

R. v. Hamon

(1993) 85 C.C.C. (3d) 490
Quebec Court of Appeal

Hamon was found guilty of growing and possessing marijuana. He challenged the constitutionality of the relevant sections of the *Narcotic Control Act*, now known as the *Controlled Drugs and Substances Act*. He argued that the provisions violated section 7 of the *Canadian Charter of Rights and Freedoms*. Hamon based his challenge on the following points:

- "Liberty" as used in section 7 includes the right to make fundamental personal decisions without state interference.
- There are benefits to the non-abusive use of marijuana.
- If the objective is to protect people with whom he associates, a complete ban on cultivation and possession is unnecessary.
- The prohibition is not entirely rational since the government has not prohibited alcohol or tobacco use.
- Marijuana is not a narcotic and is not similar to narcotics.
- The prohibition could be achieved by regulating the use of marijuana.
- It is unnecessary to prohibit marijuana given its actual effects.

The Quebec Court of Appeal dismissed Hamon's appeal of his conviction.

R. v. Parker

(2000) 188 D.L.R. (4th) 385
Ontario Court of Appeal

The accused, Terrance Parker, had suffered from epileptic seizures for almost 40 years. He tried to control the seizures through surgery, which failed, and conventional medicine, which was moderately successful. Smoking marijuana reduced the number of seizures substantially. He had no legal source of marijuana, so he grew his own. His home was searched twice, and he was charged. He brought forward the defence that the legislation infringes his rights as guaranteed by section 7 of the *Charter.* The trial judge stayed the cultivation and possession charges against Parker. To protect Parker and others like him

Figure 6-4
What does Parker's message say to you?

who need to use marijuana as medicine, the trial judge read into the legislation an exemption for persons possessing or cultivating marijuana for their "personal medically approved use." The Crown appealed that decision.

The Ontario Court of Appeal agreed with the trial judge that Parker should have the right to grow marijuana for his medicinal use. However, the appeal court did not agree with the trial judge's unilateral decision to amend the legislation. The court declared the prohibition on the possession of marijuana in the Act to be of "no force and effect" for a period of one year, to allow Parliament to amend the legislation.

For Discussion

1. What does section 7 of the *Charter* guarantee? Discuss the guarantee as it applies to Hamon's and Parker's defences.

2. Present a counterargument for each of Hamon's arguments.

3. What does it mean to "stay" the charges against Parker?

4. The trial judge "read into the legislation" an exemption. What does that mean? Why did the appeal court overrule this decision of the trial judge?

5. The court declared the prohibition on the possession of marijuana for medical purposes to be of "no force and effect." What does that mean?

Prescription Shopping or Double Doctoring

Some people need controlled drugs for medical reasons, for example, for a severe chronic condition or for relief from cancer pain. Other people are addicted to certain controlled substances. Such people may engage in **prescription shopping** or **double doctoring;** that is, they try to obtain the same prescription from a number of doctors. It is an offence to seek or obtain a narcotic or prescription from a doctor without disclosing all other controlled drugs or prescriptions for controlled drugs received within the previous 30 days. If tried as a summary offence, a first offence carries a penalty of $1000 and/or six months in prison. If the person has committed the offence before, he or she may be fined $2000 and/or sent to prison for one year. If tried as an indictable offence, the penalties range from 18 months to 7 years, depending on the substance.

Offences Related to Trafficking

According to the *Controlled Drugs and Substances Act,* to **traffic** is to "to sell, administer, give, transfer, transport, send or deliver the substance." Section 5 of the Act states that no person shall traffic in, or possess for the purpose of trafficking, any substance included in Schedules I, II, III, or IV or any substance believed to be that substance. The penalties for trafficking vary and are listed in Figure 6-5.

Because trafficking has such a broad definition—merely to give drugs to another person constitutes trafficking—no profit motive is necessary. How much assistance must someone give a drug buyer before the law views it as trafficking? This issue was addressed in *R. v. Greyeyes.*

▌ Penalties for Trafficking

Schedule and Substance	Offence	Penalty (maximums)
Schedule I Dangerous drugs	If tried as an indictable offence	Life
Schedule II Cannabis (marijuana) and its derivatives	If tried as an indictable offence	Life
	If amount trafficked not more than amount specified in Schedule VII (3 kg)	5 years less a day
Schedule III Dangerous drugs formerly listed in the *Food and Drugs Act*	If tried as a summary offence	18 months
	If tried as an indictable offence	10 years
Schedule IV Controlled drugs with therapeutic use	If tried as a summary offence	1 year
	If tried as an indictable offence	3 years

Figure 6-5

The maximum penalties for trafficking vary with the type of controlled substance. Trafficking in what substances could result in a penalty of life imprisonment?

R. v. Greyeyes

[1997] 2 S.C.R. 825
Supreme Court of Canada

Ernest Greyeyes sold five joints of marijuana to Constable Morgan, an undercover RCMP officer. The next day, Morgan asked Greyeyes if he knew where he could get some cocaine. Greyeyes said that if Morgan would drive him, he would take him to an apartment building to get some. The sellers were not at home, so Morgan and Greyeyes returned in the evening and entered the building together. Greyeyes talked to the occupants through the closed door and negotiated a deal. The purchase price was to be $40 for the cocaine, and the items were exchanged under the door. Morgan drove Greyeyes home and gave him $10 for helping to obtain the cocaine.

At trial, Greyeyes was acquitted of trafficking in cocaine but the Saskatchewan Court of Appeal overturned the acquittal and entered a conviction. Greyeyes's appeal to the Supreme Court of Canada was dismissed.

For Discussion

1. Examine the wording of what constitutes the offence of trafficking. Is possession an included element of the offence?

2. Review the elements necessary to be found guilty of aiding and abetting an offence, as discussed in Chapter 4, page 114. What are those elements?

3. Compare the sentences for possession and trafficking of a Schedule I drug to a Schedule III drug. In a case with facts similar to *R. v. Greyeyes,* would it be fair that a buyer could possibly receive a possession penalty whereas a person who assists in finding drugs could possibly receive a trafficking penalty? Support your opinion.

4. In your opinion, should Greyeyes be found guilty of possession, possession for the purpose of trafficking, aiding or abetting for the purpose of possession, trafficking, or aiding and abetting in trafficking? Support your opinion.

5. Having police officers pose as drug dealers to entrap offenders of illegal-drug laws has been criticized as being unethical. Do you agree or disagree? Why?

The amount of controlled drug seized may determine whether a charge of trafficking is laid. Before 1986, if the accused was found guilty of possession, the onus was on that person to prove that he or she did *not* have the controlled drug for the purpose of trafficking. In *R. v. Oakes* (1986), the Supreme Court of Canada ruled that this "reverse onus" violated the presumption of innocence contained in section 11(d) of the *Canadian Charter of Rights and Freedoms*. Since then, the onus has been on the Crown to prove that the person possessed the controlled drug for the purpose of trafficking. The Crown may be aided in proving trafficking if drug paraphernalia (equipment) is found, such as scales or pipes. Large amounts of cash may also be used as evidence that trafficking has occurred.

Police often act as undercover agents in stopping the drug trade, and the procedures they use to obtain evidence may open the door to an offender's appeal. Some of these practices, such as having police officers pose as drug dealers to **entrap** drug offenders, seem to undermine the integrity of the justice system by allowing the police too many powers. Several court rulings have sent a message to police that they may not entrap individuals or use

You Be the JUDGE

"[T]he offence of trafficking is taken extremely seriously by both the courts and the public.... It goes without saying that someone branded as a 'trafficker' is held in extremely low regard by the public."
—Supreme Court Justice Claire L'Heureux-Dubé

• Do you agree with this statement? Support your opinion.

physical violence to obtain evidence. Nor may police undertake **random virtue testing,** which is the practice of investigating an individual for drug offences without having reasonable and probable grounds for so doing.

Importing and Exporting

Section 6 of the *Controlled Drugs and Substances Act* makes it an offence to import or export any substance listed in Schedules I to IV. The accused need not bring the goods into the country; simply arranging for their importation can result in a conviction. The penalties for importing and exporting a controlled substance are listed in Figure 6-6.

▌ Penalties for Importing and Exporting Controlled Substances

Schedule and Substance	Offence	Penalty (maximums)
Schedule I Dangerous drugs	If tried as an indictable offence	Life
Schedule II Cannabis (marijuana) and its derivatives	If tried as an indictable offence	Life
Schedule III Dangerous drugs formerly listed in the *Food and* *Drugs Act*	If tried as a summary offence	18 months
	If tried as an indictable offence	10 years
Schedule IV Controlled drugs with therapeutic use	If tried as a summary offence	1 year
	If tried as an indictable offence	3 years

Figure 6-6

The maximum penalties for importing and exporting controlled substances vary from one year to life imprisonment depending on the type of substance.

Producing a Controlled Substance

The amount of marijuana being grown in Canada has increased greatly. Growing marijuana is illegal, unless permitted by the federal health department. It is also illegal to produce any other drug specified in Schedules I to IV. The penalties for producing a controlled substance are listed in Figure 6-8.

Figure 6-7

These imported fake duck eggs were filled with heroin and were seized by customs agents in Toronto and Vancouver.

▌Penalties for Producing a Controlled Substance

Schedule and Substance	Offence	Penalty (maximums)
Schedule I Dangerous drugs	If tried as an indictable offence	Life
Schedule II Cannabis (marijuana) and its derivatives	If tried as an indictable offence	7 years
Schedule III Dangerous drugs formerly listed in the *Food and Drugs Act*	If tried as a summary offence	18 months
	If tried as an indictable offence	10 years
Schedule IV Controlled drugs with therapeutic use	If tried as a summary offence	1 year
	If tried as an indictable offence	3 years

Figure 6-8

It is illegal to produce a controlled substance unless authorized to do so. The production of dangerous drugs and narcotics may result in a penalty of life imprisonment.

Possession of Property Obtained by Certain Offences

It is also an offence to possess any property you know was obtained through the commission of a crime. Similarly, it is an offence to possess the cash obtained from selling the property. This section of the *Criminal Code* is used to charge those who do not take part directly in offences such as trafficking, but who share in the proceeds of illegal drug sales. Therefore, if Sam accepts gifts from Clara knowing the gifts were obtained from trafficking, Sam can be charged. If the value of the property exceeds $1000, the penalty for an indictable offence is up to 10 years in prison. If the value of the property is less than $1000, the penalty ranges from a $2000 fine plus six months in prison for a summary conviction, and if indictable up to two years in prison.

Enterprise Crime and Laundering

Money or property associated with a crime such as trafficking is often "laundered" by criminals to remove the taint of the crime. To **launder** means to use, transfer the possession of, send, transport, transmit, alter, dispose of, or otherwise deal with any property obtained through crime. By making laundering an offence, police are able to reduce the easy movement of property, especially cash, obtained through the drug trade. Because many of the illegal drugs sold in Canada come from foreign sources, it is quite common for the profit from the sale of the drugs to be transferred outside Canada. Since it is believed that profits from the sale of illegal drugs fund terrorism, the federal government has stepped up its surveillance of large amounts of money leaving the country.

Since 2000, certain groups must report cross-border transactions exceeding $10 000, large cash transactions, and "suspicious" transactions. This law applies to lawyers, accountants, real-estate agencies, and financial institutions, including banks. The government has set up an office to investigate each reported transfer. The law calls into question lawyer–client confidentiality, and may one day be challenged in the courts. The penalties are substantial: $2 million dollars and/or five years in jail.

Figure 6-9

In 1996, owners of this company in Vancouver were charged with an international money-laundering scheme and drug operation.

Police Rights of Search and Seizure under the Act

The *Controlled Drugs and Substances Act* grants police the right to search for controlled substances and drugs. Other rights that are incidental to the search, such as arrest, are granted by the *Criminal Code*. Search and arrest are discussed in more detail in Chapter 7.

Section 11 of the *Controlled Drugs and Substances Act* states that a warrant can be issued by a judge for a search if police believe an offence is in progress. An officer may act without a warrant if the situation is urgent and it is impractical to obtain one. For example, an officer would be compelled to force a search if the suspect is obviously flushing evidence down the toilet. The Act provides that the officer can use as much force as is necessary in these circumstances to enter the premises.

Upon entry, the officer can search anyone if there are reasonable grounds to believe that the person possesses a controlled substance. The officer may seize any controlled drugs or substances, or any items reasonably believed to contain or conceal one. Objects that may have been used in the commission of the offence may also be seized.

Case

R. v. Adams

(2001-08-13) ONCA C34243
Ontario Court of Appeal

The police had reasonable and probable grounds to arrest Fritz Adams for trafficking in narcotics. They entered his rooming house by tricking the superintendent into believing they were investigating a noise complaint. They found Adams in the laundry room, and he was arrested after police found narcotics in his pocket. At trial, the Crown argued that the police did not need to obtain a warrant because Adams had no expectation of privacy while in the laundry room. Furthermore, the Crown argued that the superintendent gave informed consent to the officers' entry. Adams was found guilty of drug trafficking by a judge alone.

Adams appealed the decision to the Ontario Court of Appeal, stating that his right to be secure against unreasonable search and seizure under section 8 of the *Charter* was violated. He acknowledged that the police had reasonable and probable grounds to arrest him, but argued that the superintendent only let them enter because he was given false information. Adams also argued that the arrest was illegal because the police failed to obtain a warrant to enter a dwelling-house as required by the *Criminal Code*. Adams was acquitted by the court.

In *R. v. Feeney* (1997), the Supreme Court of Canada outlined the following with respect to police entering a dwelling-house:

- The privacy interest outweighs the interest of the police, and arrests without a warrant in dwelling-houses are prohibited.
- There are exceptions with respect to the unreasonableness of searches without a warrant.
- Privacy issues must give way to the interest of society in ensuring adequate police protection when there is hot pursuit.
- Even if a warrant is obtained, proper announcement must be made before forcibly entering a dwelling-house to make an arrest.

For Discussion

1. Why would Adams prefer to have been tried by a judge alone instead of a judge and jury?

2. If the police had been refused entry by the superintendent, what means could they have used to obtain the legal right to enter?

3. What is "hot pursuit"? Did it exist in this case? Explain.

4. Applying the Feeney decision to the Adams case, do you think that Adams's right to privacy outweighed the desire of the police to make an arrest? Explain.

The *Controlled Drugs and Substances Act* does not give police the power to stop and search a person for drugs in a public place. The *Criminal Code* authorizes this type of search. However, there must be reasonable grounds for believing that the person is in possession of a drug.

Sentencing

In 1999, the *Controlled Drugs and Substances Act* was amended to reflect the occasionally violent nature of illegal drug transactions and the vulnerability of youth. The Act outlines the principles of sentencing in this area, noting that sentencing must contribute to respect for the law and the maintenance of a just, peaceful, and safe society. Sentences must encourage offenders to rehabilitate (reform) themselves, seek treatment in appropriate circumstances, and acknowledge the harm done to victims and to the community.

The amendments also specified circumstances where the offence would be considered especially serious:

- if a weapon was used, carried, or threatened to be used
- if violence was used or threatened
- if the offender trafficked or tried to traffic substances found in Schedules I to IV in or near a school or any public place usually frequented by persons under 18 years of age
- if the offender trafficked or tried to traffic substances found in Schedules I to IV to a person under 18 years of age
- if the offender was previously convicted of a substance offence
- if the offender used the services of a person under the age of 18 years to commit, or be involved in, the commission of a substance offence

Parliament's concern with these factors is so great that if one of these factors exists and the judge does not sentence the offender to prison, he or she must give reasons for that decision.

Agents of Change   The Drug Treatment Court in Toronto

The Toronto Drug Treatment Court—the first of its kind in Canada—was established in 1998 for a six-year trial period. Its purpose is to keep offenders in the criminal justice system receiving both community support and treatment under judicial supervision for 12 to 18 months.

This unique court is based on the principles that treatment for offenders' drug problems will reduce their dependency on drugs, prevent them from reoffending, and provide an alternative to incarceration, thereby saving the system money. The program is directed at nonviolent offenders who are addicted to cocaine or opiates, with a focus on youth, women and men from diverse communities, and street prostitutes.

The Drug Treatment Court is a combined effort of the Centre for Addiction and Mental Health, the criminal justice system in Toronto, the Toronto Police Service, the City of Toronto Public Health and Healthy City Office, and various community-based service agencies.

For Discussion

1. Identify the objective of the Toronto Drug Treatment Court program.
2. How does this program save the criminal justice system money?
3. Why do you think this program is directed at the groups identified?

Should People Who Use Illegal Drugs Be Punished?

Marijuana, cocaine, and heroin are just three of the illegal drugs listed in the *Controlled Drugs and Substances Act*. Twenty-three percent of Canadians admit to using cannabis (marijuana and a related substance, hashish) at least once in their lifetimes. Four percent have admitted to using cocaine at least once.

▌ Drug Use in Canada
(percentage of population)

Substance	1989	1998
Cannabis	6.5	7.5
Cocaine, including crack	1.4	0.7
Heroin	0.4	1.0

Figure 6-10

Why do you think that the use of cannabis has increased rather than cocaine or heroin?

Cannabis generally induces a state of relaxation, heightened sensory awareness, a sensation that time is slowing down, and a rapid heartbeat. Some studies have shown that it may be more damaging to health than ordinary cigarettes. It can cause physical addiction, paranoia, and damage to body organs.

Cocaine is a stimulant extracted from the South American coca bush. Its use can lead to severe physical, psychological, and dependency problems. Regular use can damage nasal passages, cause impotence, and create paranoia or depression. Large doses can cause violent behaviour, convulsions, and even death.

Heroin is a substance derived from the opium poppy. It can produce a "rush" and a feeling of excitement immediately after it is taken. As the body develops a tolerance for the drug, increasing amounts are needed to achieve the same effect. It is highly addictive, and nausea, diarrhea, and pain are symptoms experienced after the drug's effect wears off.

On One Side

Many people think drug abuse is a serious offence. They believe that higher fines and longer jail sentences for drug users and traffickers would reduce drug use. They applaud the fact that in 1999, there were 39 percent more arrests for possession of marijuana than in the previous year; 21 126 people were convicted of a marijuana offence; and 13 percent of this group served time in jail. These Canadians want the police to have greater powers to search for illegal drugs so that the

▌ Drug Incidents, Canada, 2000

65 196 drug offences, an increase of 5.6% over previous year

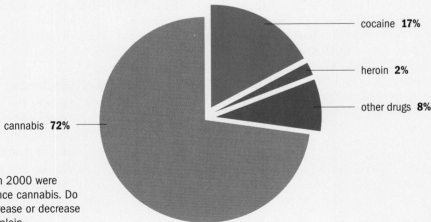

cocaine **17%**

heroin **2%**

other drugs **8%**

cannabis **72%**

Figure 6-11

Most drug incidents in 2000 were related to the substance cannabis. Do you think this will increase or decrease in the near future? Explain.

laws can be more easily enforced. The $100 million a year it costs Canadian taxpayers to enforce Canada's drug laws is money well spent. If tough drug laws are not enforced, society will be weakened and destroyed.

On the Other Side

Other Canadians feel that stiffer penalties will not rehabilitate drug users. Those who use illegal drugs should be treated rather than punished. They applaud a 2000 Ontario Court of Appeal ruling, which stated that the sections on marijuana in the *Controlled Drugs and Substances Act* are unconstitutional because they fail to recognize the drug has medicinal uses (see Case, page 165).

Some people think the millions of dollars spent to arrest and punish drug offenders would be better spent treating drug addicts to cure and rehabilitate them. They note that many important organizations think the government should decriminalize the use and possession of marijuana. The Canadian Medical Association, Canadian Bar Association, Canadian Council of Churches, Association of Police Chiefs, and RCMP all favour decriminalization.

The Bottom Line

As long as particular drugs are identified as illegal, the *Controlled Drugs and Substances Act* must restrict them. But should drug users be considered victims who require treatment rather than offenders? Canada's law makers have been reluctant to deal with the issue. Recently, the British Columbia Court of Appeal in *R. v. Malmo-Levine* (2000) refused to overturn the conviction of possession of marijuana. It argued that it is up to Parliament to change the law, not the courts.

▌ Support for Legalization of Marijuana in Canada

Year	Percentage of Population
2000	47
1995	31
1990	24
1985	30
1980	29
1975	26

Figure 6-12

Why do you think support for the legalization of marijuana has grown steadily since 1975?

⊖ activity

Visit **www.law.nelson.com** and follow the links to learn more about the issue of decriminalizing marijuana.

What Do You Think?

1. Why do people use illegal drugs? What are some problems associated with these drugs?

2. In a group, identify arguments that support stiffer penalties for illegal drugs. Outline arguments that support rehabilitation of users. Present your arguments to the class.

3. Why do recent court decisions on drug use appear contradictory?

4. Why is public opinion so important in determining drug-use laws in Canada? Does there appear to be a trend? Explain.

5. As a class, discuss the idea that all drugs should be decriminalized with no penalties for their use. Identify the advantages and disadvantages for society.

6. Explain the meaning of the following quote from Raymond Kendall, Secretary General of Interpol, and give your opinion: "The prosecution of thousands of otherwise law-abiding citizens every year is both hypocritical and an affront to individual civil and human rights."

Review Your Understanding (Pages 162 to 173)

1. a) What is the definition of a drug?
   b) On what is the criminal classification of drugs based?
2. Describe two situations in which someone may be charged with possession, while not having physical possession.
3. Is intent necessary for possession? Explain.
4. What changes were made to the *Controlled Drugs and Substances Act* in 2001 due to the ruling in *R. v. Parker*?
5. How does the *Controlled Drugs and Substances Act* define trafficking?
6. What two points must the Crown prove to obtain a conviction for trafficking?
7. Who can be charged with the offence of importing and exporting narcotics?
8. What is prescription shopping?
9. Describe a situation in which a warrantless search would be legal. Explain why.
10. Identify the circumstances that are to be considered serious when a judge is sentencing an offender.

Did You Know?

Impaired driving is the main criminal cause of death in Canada. On average, there are four deaths and 125 injuries daily as a result of impaired driving. How does society pay for drinking-and-driving accidents?

6.3 Drinking and Driving

Canadian citizens and legislators continue to worry about drinking and driving. Those who engage in such reckless behaviour are penalized by law and criticized by society. The federal government has increased *Criminal Code* penalties for the offences related to impaired driving. Despite the increase, more than 83 000 impaired driving charges were laid in the year 2000. The provinces and territories, which regulate highways, the licensing of drivers, and alcohol consumption, have introduced measures to deter impaired driving by reducing offenders' access to motor vehicles.

Definition of a Motor Vehicle

As you read, keep in mind that a **motor vehicle** is defined in the *Criminal Code* as "a vehicle that is drawn, propelled, or driven by any means other than by muscular power, but does not include railway equipment." In other words, issues related to driving apply to boats and aircraft in addition to automobiles, trucks, motorcycles, snowmobiles, and other motorized land vehicles.

Figure 6-13

Under the law, snowmobiles are considered motor vehicles.

Dangerous Operation of a Motor Vehicle

It is an offence to operate a motor vehicle in a manner dangerous to the public on a street, road, highway, or other public place. The definition of a "public place" has been examined in case law and has been found to include parking lots at shopping plazas and schools, as well as private roads regularly used by the public.

To obtain a conviction on "dangerous operation of a motor vehicle," the Crown must establish fault. In determining fault, the court must consider the standard of care that a prudent and responsible driver would have exercised. All factors, including the nature, condition, and use of the public place where the offence occurred, and the amount of traffic at the time and in that place, are considered. There does not have to be any "public" present at the time of the offence—only an expectation that someone could have been present. Chapter 12 discusses standard of care in more detail.

Case

R. v. MacGillivray

[1995] 1 S.C.R. 890
Supreme Court of Canada

On a warm, clear summer day, the beach at "the rocks" at Cribbons Point in Nova Scotia was active with swimmers, divers, and sunbathers. Several family members were on board MacGillivray's boat as it bounced in the water and headed toward seven boys. The boys waved their arms and shouted, as did those on the shore, to alert MacGillivray of the dangerous situation. The boat was up at such an angle that MacGillivray did not see the boys, and the propeller struck and killed one of them.

Some witnesses testified that the boat was travelling over the speed limit. The trial judge found that no one was leaning over the side to look out for dangers. MacGillivray was found guilty of dangerous operation of a motor vehicle. His appeals to the Nova Scotia Court of Appeal and the Supreme Court of Canada were dismissed.

R. v. Hundal

[1993] 1 S.C.R. 867
Supreme Court of Canada

The Supreme Court of Canada stated in *R. v. Hundal* that when a judge assesses a situation of dangerous driving, he or she "should be satisfied that the conduct amounted to a marked departure from the standard of care that a reasonable person would observe in the accused's situation." In this case, a trucker was driving in heavy afternoon traffic on a wet, four-lane street in downtown Vancouver. He thought that he could not stop when a light turned amber. He testified that he sounded his horn and proceeded through the intersection. He struck a car going across the intersection, killing the driver. The trial judge found that Hundal's actions represented a gross departure from the standard of care to be expected from a prudent driver.

For Discussion

1. What standard of care should MacGillivray have shown while driving his boat?

2. What facts indicate that Hundal's actions were a gross departure from the standard of care expected from a prudent driver?

3. What penalty would you impose on MacGillivray? What penalty would you impose on Hundal?

Failure to Stop at the Scene of an Accident

If you are involved in an accident, you must stop at the scene. The law requires you to give your name and address to the other party. If the other party has been injured or appears to require assistance, you must offer assistance.

The penalty for failure to stop was increased in 1999 (see Figure 6-17, page 180). Legislators were concerned that impaired drivers were leaving accident scenes to avoid being charged with impaired driving causing death. Occasionally, there is a justifiable excuse for leaving the scene of an accident; for example, leaving to get help. However, there is no justification if the accused knows an accident has occurred, panics, and leaves. Drivers who try to escape the scene while being chased by police are committing the offence of flight.

Impaired Driving

Impaired driving has become the main criminal cause of death in Canada. Yet, offenders have often received sentences that seem trivial compared with the consequences of their actions. Canadians have urged legislators to increase penalties for this offence, as a deterrent. The penalties have increased twice since 1985. Section 253 of the *Criminal Code* describes the offence of impaired driving.

The Law   The Criminal Code

Excerpts from the *Criminal Code*

253.

Every one commits an offence who operates a motor vehicle or vessel or operates or assists in the operation of an aircraft or of railway equipment or has the care or control of a motor vehicle, vessel, aircraft or railway equipment, whether it is in motion or not,

(a) while the person's ability to operate the vehicle, vessel, aircraft or railway equipment is impaired by alcohol or a drug; or

(b) having consumed alcohol in such a quantity that the concentration in the person's blood exceeds eighty milligrams of alcohol in one hundred millilitres of blood.

For Discussion

1. **Identify three ways the offence of impaired driving can be committed, as specified in the first paragraph of section 253.**

2. **Give two examples of how a person can be in care and control of a motor vehicle when it is not in motion.**

3. **Martin takes a sedative drug, knowing that it might impair his ability to drive. He hopes that he will arrive at his destination before it takes effect. He is involved in an automobile accident due to his sedation. Is Martin guilty of impaired driving? Explain.**

Section 253 actually sets out four offences:
- driving while ability is impaired by alcohol or drugs
- having care or control of a motor vehicle when impaired by alcohol or drugs
- driving while the **blood–alcohol level** is over 80 mg in 100 mL of blood
- having care or control of a motor vehicle when the blood–alcohol level is over 80

A person can be charged with the first two offences when the blood–alcohol level is below 80.

For a person to be charged with either of the "care or control" offences, it is not necessary for the vehicle to be in motion, or even running. *Mens rea* exists when there is intent to assume the care or control of the vehicle after consuming alcohol and while impaired. In addition, *mens rea* exists when the blood–alcohol level is over 80. *Actus reus* is the action of assuming care or control. Sitting in the driver's seat implies care or control, unless the driver can establish that he or she did not intend to set the car in motion. In other cases, such as when the driver is lying down in the car, the Crown must prove beyond a reasonable doubt that the accused was in care or control of the vehicle.

The issue of whether a vehicle was in the "care or control" of the accused has been central to many cases. A person who was standing beside his vehicle after having called a tow-truck has been ruled to be in care or control, as has a person who sat in her car for 15 minutes after stopping.

The term "impaired" in section 253(a) is not defined in the *Criminal Code*. The court need not factor in a blood–alcohol level that would establish the person as impaired. Rather, it is up to the court to determine, on the evidence presented, whether the ability to drive was impaired. It also does not matter how the accused was driving. What is important is establishing that the driver's ability to operate a vehicle is impaired. Finally, the word "drug" is interpreted much more broadly than one might think. In one case it was found to include a chemical in plastic model cement.

▌ Criminal Code Traffic Incidents, 2000

117 060 persons charged

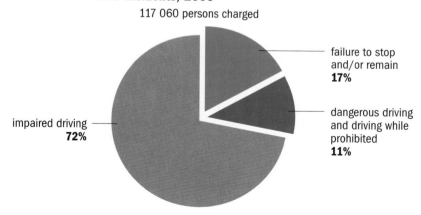

impaired driving
72%

failure to stop and/or remain
17%

dangerous driving and driving while prohibited
11%

Figure 6-14

In 2000, most *Criminal Code* traffic incidents were related to the offence of impaired driving. Do you think the laws against impaired driving need to be strengthened?

Tests for Impaired Driving

Justice Finlayson noted in *R. v. Seo* (1986) that the most effective deterrent to impaired driving is the possibility of detection. The *Criminal Code* outlines many procedures to aid in detection of impaired driving; for example, taking breath samples and doing blood tests. Drivers may also be asked to pass balance and coordination tests any time after being stopped.

Breath Tests

The use of roadside stops has been found constitutional by the Supreme Court of Canada, whether they are part of an organized program or done randomly. Drivers have questioned the right of the police to stop them when they have

Figure 6-15

A roadside screening test

You Be the JUDGE

During holidays, some police forces randomly stop vehicles at checkpoints to establish if drivers have been drinking. The Supreme Court of Canada has ruled that such programs are legal because they are a temporary activity and can proceed without a warrant.

- Some officers want these programs to operate year-round. Would you support this idea? What might stand in the way?

Did You Know?

A national Canada Safety Council survey found that 70 percent of Canadians said they never drive after drinking any amount of alcohol. Do you think that impaired-driving laws keep your peers from drinking and driving? Why?

no reasonable grounds to suspect an offence has been committed. However, the courts have recognized Parliament's intention to reduce the problem of drinking drivers and have ruled that spot checks are a reasonable limit prescribed by law.

When stopped in a roadside spot check, a driver may be asked by the police to undergo a **roadside screening test.** The officer will demand that the driver breathe into an approved testing device. The demand may be made only if the officer has reasonable grounds to suspect that the driver has consumed alcohol. It is an offence to refuse the demand. Approved roadside screening devices are described in the *Criminal Code.* Failing the screening test does not mean one is automatically charged with an offence—the results can only be used to show that the officer had grounds to demand a breath sample.

Several legal principles related to roadside testing have been established. For example, the officer who demands the test must decide upon the adequacy of the results—that decision cannot be made by another officer at the scene. Moreover, the courts have ruled that it is not necessary for the testing officer to show the results of a roadside test to the person tested.

If the roadside test indicates that a breath sample is required, the officer will take the driver to the police station for more breath tests. Because the driver is required to accompany the officer, that person is being **detained,** and arrest or release should soon follow. Under the *Canadian Charter of Rights and Freedoms,* the person must be advised of his or her right to legal counsel without delay and be able to obtain free advice from a legal-aid lawyer. This is not an absolute right. A person is given only a reasonable time to obtain counsel. The *Charter* also guarantees the right to discuss with counsel in private.

Two breath samples must be taken, with an interval of at least 15 minutes between them. The officer must communicate clearly that a breath sample is being demanded, not requested. The demand must be made "forthwith or as soon as practicable." Each case is weighed on its own merits to determine whether this requirement has been met. A number of cases have indicated that the officer must be certain the person has the ability to understand his or her rights. A person would probably be acquitted if he or she refused to take a test and was later found to have a concussion, or to be so drunk as to be incapable of understanding the demand.

Blood Samples

If the person cannot physically give a breath sample, the officer may demand a blood sample. Blood samples are drawn only under the direction of a qualified medical practitioner. The practitioner can refuse if taking a sample would endanger the life or health of the accused. The sample must be taken within four hours of the alleged offence. Two blood samples are actually taken, one of which is made available to the accused for testing. If the accused is not able to give permission for a blood sample, a warrant must be obtained. In *R. v. Colarusso,* however, the Supreme Court of Canada admitted blood samples that were obtained under questionable circumstances. In collisions where there is injury or death, a warrant to take a blood sample from an unconscious driver can be obtained if the officer believes that the driver is impaired.

At the roadside or at the police station, an officer may also require a driver to perform a sobriety test, such as walking a straight line. In such cases, the driver is being detained. Courts have ruled that the demand to perform such tests is valid, as long as the evidence of failing the test is used only to decide whether the person should be asked to submit a breath sample. The Supreme Courts in Alberta, Nova Scotia, and Prince Edward Island have ruled that there is no legislation giving officers the right to demand the test.

Figure 6-16
Providing a breath sample at the police station

Case

R .v. Colarusso

(1994) 87 C.C.C. (3d) 193
Supreme Court of Canada

Colarusso was driving without his lights on. He rear-ended a pickup truck, sending it into a ditch, where it flipped over. The occupants of the truck were seriously injured. An off-duty police officer saw Colarusso stop briefly before he continued southbound in the northbound lane. Colarusso then collided head-on with another car. An occupant of that car was killed. Colarusso was injured.

Colarusso was arrested at the scene by officers who observed signs of impairment. He was charged with a number of offences, including criminal negligence causing death, and advised of his *Charter* rights. Officers demanded a breath sample. Before that could occur, Colarusso was driven by the police to a hospital for treatment of injuries. No breath test was given, nor did the police make a demand for a blood sample.

In hospital, Colarusso agreed to give blood and urine samples for medical purposes. He gave the urine sample in the presence of a police officer. The samples were sent to the hospital lab to be used in tests. The coroner investigated the scene of the second accident, and then went to the hospital to investigate the car occupant's death. He needed samples of Colarusso's blood and urine. The coroner gave the samples to the police, requesting that they be taken to the Centre of Forensic Sciences and stored properly.

The Crown called the forensic toxicologist who had analyzed Colarusso's samples at the request of the coroner. The toxicologist testified that at the time of the accidents, Colarusso's blood–alcohol level was between 144 and 165. Colarusso argued that the evidence of the toxicologist should be excluded because the blood and urine had been seized in violation of his rights under section 8 of the *Charter*. He was convicted at trial, and his appeals to the Ontario Court of Appeal and Supreme Court of Canada were dismissed.

For Discussion

1. **What is a forensic toxicologist?**
2. **What is a coroner?**
3. **Consider the evidence samples:**
   a) **Who obtained the blood and urine samples and for what purpose?**
   b) **How did the police get access to the samples?**
   c) **Did the way the police gained access to the samples bring the administration of justice into disrepute? Explain.**
4. **Should the Crown be able to use the samples obtained by the coroner as part of its case? Why or why not?**
5. **Why do you think the Supreme Court of Canada found that the evidence could be admitted?**

e activity

Visit **www.law.nelson.com** and follow the links to find out about recent impaired driving cases.

Did You Know?

The following provinces and territories can discharge a person from an impaired-driving conviction and impose treatment for alcohol or drug addiction.

- Alberta
- Manitoba
- New Brunswick
- Northwest Territories
- Nova Scotia
- Prince Edward Island
- Saskatchewan
- Yukon Territory

Penalties

The penalties for impaired-driving offences are outlined in Figure 6-17. Note that a second offence does not necessarily mean a second charge on the same offence, but simply two motor vehicle offences related to drinking. In *R. v. Kumar* (1993), the Supreme Court of British Columbia ruled that the penalty for a second offence can be varied if it is found to be cruel and unusual punishment and therefore contravenes section 12 of the *Canadian Charter of Rights and Freedoms*.

In some jurisdictions, a judge may **discharge** an offender who would benefit from treatment for alcohol or drug addiction. This may be done in cases of impaired operation of a motor vehicle and operating a motor vehicle with a blood–alcohol level over 80. Releasing the offender must not be contrary to the public interest, and the offender must go for treatment.

As you read through Figure 6-17, you will see that impaired driving, driving with a blood–alcohol level over 80, and refusing to provide a breath sample result in a driving prohibition. These are prohibitions under the *Criminal Code*. It is an offence to operate a motor vehicle if you have been disqualified from doing so.

Penalties for Driving Offences under the Criminal Code

Offence	Details of Offence	Penalty (maximums unless otherwise noted)
Dangerous driving	Hybrid	5 years
Dangerous driving causing bodily harm	Indictable	10 years
Dangerous driving causing death	Indictable	14 years
Failure to stop	Hybrid	5 years
Failure to stop, bodily harm	Indictable	10 years
Failure to stop, death	Indictable	Life
Flight from a peace officer	Hybrid	5 years
Flight resulting in bodily harm	Indictable	14 years
Flight resulting in death	Indictable	Life
Driving while impaired; driving with over 80 mg of alcohol per 100 mL of blood; refusal to provide a breath or blood sample	First offence	Fine of not less than $600 and 1 to 3 years' driving prohibition*
	Second offence	Minimum 14 days and 2 to 5 years' driving prohibition
	Subsequent offences	Minimum 90 days and minimum 3 years' driving prohibition
	Summary	6 months
	Indictable	5 years
Impaired driving causing bodily harm		10 years
Impaired driving causing death		Life

* If the offender participates in an alcohol ignition antilock program (see page 182) for 1 year, the 1-year minimum can be reduced to 3 months.

Figure 6-17

Fines, driving prohibitions, or jail terms may be the maximum penalty given for specific driving offences under the *Criminal Code*. If the offence involves death, a penalty of life imprisonment may result.

There are additional penalties that can be imposed, depending on the liability of the offender. If the person caused death or bodily harm by criminal negligence, or was charged with manslaughter, dangerous operation of a motor vehicle, fleeing a peace officer in a motor vehicle, failure to stop at the scene, or impaired driving causing bodily harm or death, he or she may be ordered not to drive after release from prison. These orders may remain in effect for several years.

Case

R. v. Thompson

(2001) 141 O.A.C.1
Ontario Court of Appeal

Officer Shields observed Thompson's vehicle hugging the white dotted line between lanes on Arrow Road in Toronto. She directed Thompson to pull over. Because Thompson said he had consumed "one or two beers" and because his eyes were red and bloodshot, she demanded he take a roadside test. On the first try, Shields could not hear the tone that the device was supposed to make, nor could she hear any air passing through the mouthpiece. On the second and third attempts, air did enter the machine but without sufficient pressure to activate the device. She then arrested Thompson for failure to provide a sample.

At trial, Shields could not specifically say that she had checked for obstructions in the mouthpiece before Thompson blew in it. There was nothing in her notes to indicate that she had. She gave evidence that checking was part of her standard practice. Thompson was found guilty. He appealed to the Ontario Court of Appeal, which upheld his conviction.

Thompson appealed for two reasons. First, Shields had not checked the mouthpiece. Second, Thompson said the section in the *Criminal Code* stating that a person has committed an offence if a sample is not provided when demanded violated his rights under sections 7 and 10(b) of the *Canadian Charter of Rights and Freedoms*. He believed that the demand resulted in an illegal **detention,** and denied his right to retain and instruct counsel without delay and to be informed of that right.

For Discussion

1. In your opinion, should the fact that Shields did not specifically know whether she had checked the mouthpiece, nor have any note concerning that procedure, have resulted in an acquittal? Explain.

2. What do sections 7 and 10(b) of the *Canadian Charter of Rights and Freedoms* provide?

3. The results of a roadside test are not used to determine level of impairment, but only to determine if further tests should be given. A person is then given the standard warning concerning the right to remain silent and right to counsel. In this era of cellular phones, should a person be able to obtain counsel before doing a roadside test? Explain.

4. The appeal court referred to the following passage in *R. v. Milne* (1996) regarding the use of roadside tests. "[The] objective ... is to provide the police with the tools needed to remove impaired drivers from the highway immediately and thereby avoid the calamitous results likely to occur if they are allowed to proceed. The objective is not to convict impaired drivers at any cost." In your opinion, is the requirement to do a roadside test an acceptable denial of the right to "life, liberty and security of the person"? Explain your views.

Provincial and Territorial Offences Related to Impaired Driving

Under their authority to regulate motor vehicles, the provinces and territories have been trying to reduce access to vehicles by drunk drivers. Some of these initiatives are discussed below. (See also Agents of Change, page 267.)

Figure 6-18

Dave Wilson, president of MADD (Mothers Against Drunk Driving) Winnipeg, displays an antilock device to deal with repeat drunk drivers. The unit is part of the ignition and prevents the car from starting if alcohol is detected.

Certain laws allow vehicles to be stopped at random. When a police officer stops someone under the authority of a provincial or territorial statute, the smell of alcohol or drugs, or evidence discovered during a safety check, may lead to further investigation under the *Controlled Drugs and Substances Act* or the *Criminal Code.* The officer must have grounds for searching the automobile for the offence in question: he or she cannot undertake a search simply in the hopes of finding illegal items.

The provinces and territories may also suspend the licences of persons convicted under the *Criminal Code* for additional periods. A convicted offender may therefore be subject not only to a fine or imprisonment, but also to a suspension.

The provinces and territories have legislation permitting the short-term (i.e., 12- to 24-hour) suspension of a driver's licence if the driver has consumed alcohol. In Ontario, a driver's licence can be taken away for 12 hours if an approved screening device shows a blood–alcohol level of over 50. Removal of a driver's licence in British Columbia can occur if the reading is over 30. Anyone who drives during this period can, of course, be charged with the additional offence of driving without a licence.

Under provincial or territorial law, the offender may have to install an "antilock" device on the vehicle. The driver must blow into a mouthpiece located on the dashboard. If the reading is over the limit set for the driver, the car will not start. The device also records how many times the driver tried to drive while drunk. Such information can later be used as evidence of driving while intoxicated. Studies have shown that the rearrest rate for offenders with an antilock device is 75 percent lower than those without the device.

Provincial and territorial legislation can also define repeat-offender status and increase penalties for this category. Manitoba, for example, has a mandatory jail term for repeat offenders if convicted twice within five years. Now, the provinces and territories are trying to broaden the definition of "repeat offender." Some believe that offences committed within the last 10 years, and not just the last five years, should be taken into consideration.

Quebec has introduced compulsory assessment and treatment of offenders who have a blood–alcohol level greater than 80. The tests establish when a motorist is a problem drinker. While offenders are receiving treatment, their licences are suspended. After successfully completing the treatment, the offender gets the licence back, but must agree to use an antilock device on the car for a specified time. The new rules impose a blood–alcohol level limit of 0 on all drivers of public vehicles, which includes taxis, buses, and transport trucks.

activity

Visit **www.law.nelson.com** and follow the links to learn about the antilock device for vehicles.

Figure 6-19
Under a graduated licensing program, a driver's licence is awarded in stages. Training may take several years to complete. What are the advantages and disadvantages of such a system?

Finally, graduated licensing programs require new drivers to gain extensive road experience before becoming full-fledged drivers. Where this program is in effect nothing over a 0 blood–alcohol level is tolerated for probationary drivers.

Other Consequences for the Drinking Driver

Impaired driving has other important consequences. A conviction will result in **demerit points,** which could lead to licence suspension. It may also lead to an increase in the offender's automobile insurance rate. An insurer can even refuse to pay any claim on behalf of a person who is at fault in an accident that occurred because of impaired driving or while the person's licence was suspended.

You Be the JUDGE

In *R. v. Seo* (1986) (page 177), the court noted: "Increased penalties have not been an effective deterrent."

- What are some of the advantages and disadvantages of having increased penalties for drinking and driving offences?

Review Your Understanding (Pages 174 to 183)

1. What circumstances are considered in establishing fault for the dangerous operation of a motor vehicle?

2. What is a public place, in relation to the operation of a vehicle?

3. Identify the offences that supplemented the law on negligence in the operation of a motor vehicle. Why were they added?

4. What must a driver do at the scene of an accident in which he or she is involved?

5. What does "care or control" mean with respect to a motor vehicle?

6. Discuss in detail the two offences that relate to impaired driving.

7. What procedures must the police follow when administering a roadside test?

8. When can blood samples be taken as evidence of impaired driving?

9. Summarize the provincial and territorial laws that are aimed at reducing drinking and driving.

10. What consequences other than a fine or imprisonment does a conviction for impaired driving carry?

Chapter Review

Chapter Highlights

- The cost to society of impaired driving and drug use is significant.
- The laws concerning use of drugs are found in the *Controlled Drugs and Substances Act*.
- Controlled substances are those listed in Schedules I to IV of the *Controlled Drugs and Substances Act*.
- "Possession" of an illegal drug does not necessarily mean that it has to be on your body.
- In particular circumstances, individuals can legally use marijuana for medicinal purposes.
- Double doctoring, which is obtaining two prescriptions for a controlled drug, is illegal.
- Police should not engage in entrapment or random virtue testing of citizens.
- Police need a search warrant to enter a premises, unless in "hot pursuit."
- Judges must consider special sentencing provisions for drug offences.
- Impaired driving is the main criminal cause of death in Canada.
- It is an offence to operate a motor vehicle dangerously in a public place.
- The penalty for failure to stop was increased to deter impaired drivers from fleeing.
- It is up to the court to determine, based on the evidence, whether a driver was impaired.
- Police have the right to conduct roadside screening tests.
- A person can be required to perform a sobriety test, such as walking a straight line.
- To keep impaired drivers from using their vehicles, the provinces and territories have instituted penalties that are imposed in addition to the *Criminal Code* penalty.

Review Key Terms

Name the key terms that are described below.

a) to manufacture, sell, or give illegal drugs to another person

b) to transfer money obtained from drug-related or other criminal activities

c) trying to obtain the same narcotic prescription from different doctors

d) without grounds, to try to find out if someone is a drug dealer by encouraging him or her to sell drugs

e) a breath test carried out to determine if further breath samples should be given

f) points that accumulate, resulting in a driver's licence being suspended

g) police investigation of an individual for drug offences without having reasonable and probable grounds for so doing

h) any substance that by its chemical nature alters structure or function in a living organism

i) any substance contained in Schedules I to IV of the *Controlled Drugs and Substances Act*

Check Your Knowledge

1. Distinguish among the various drug-related offences and provide examples for each.

2. Outline the rights police have for the search and seizure of controlled drugs.

3. Summarize the main *Criminal Code* offences associated with a motor vehicle.

4. Identify the types of evidence that can be used in an impaired-driving case and the conditions under which it can be obtained.

Apply Your Learning

5. *R. v. Kuitenen and Ostiguy,* 2001 BCSC 677 (British Columbia Supreme Court)

   Kuitenen and Ostiguy were charged with producing a controlled drug and with possession for the purpose of trafficking in a controlled drug. The RCMP received information from an informant, believed to be reliable, that there was a significant amount of marijuana growing on a property on the Davis Lake Road in British Columbia. The informant explained that the owner of the property was purchasing inordinately large amounts of diesel fuel, which could possibly be evidence of a growing operation. The informant gave the police the licence number of a vehicle, which turned out to belong to Kuitenen.

The police did not believe they had sufficient grounds to obtain a search warrant. The police decided to fly over the property, which included Kuitenen's house, using a helicopter equipped with a "FLIR." The device is capable of measuring heat loss from buildings, which in turn may indicate the presence of marijuana production. They viewed videotape of the fly-over, and concluded that there appeared to be an underground structure on the property. The police made more flyovers, without a warrant, and said: "If we were up high enough we would not be invading anyone's privacy." However, on one of the videos, they could see a person urinating. Believing that a marijuana-cultivation operation was on the property, the officer obtained a search warrant. There is no doubt that the evidence obtained as a result of the helicopter surveillance was crucial in securing the general warrant. The police entered the property and found a large marijuana-cultivation operation.

a) Did Kuitenen have a reasonable expectation of privacy?
b) Did the flyovers together with the use of intrusive technology constitute an unlawful search and seizure? Explain.
c) Would the admission of the evidence bring the administration of justice into disrepute? Explain.

6. *R. v. Lauda* (1999), 121 O.A.C. 365 (Ontario Court of Appeal)

Crime Stoppers received a tip that marijuana was being grown in a cornfield in Bentinck Township in Ontario. A police constable went to the property without a warrant, located the cornfield, and found approximately 100 marijuana plants among the corn. The police returned another day to find Lauda cutting the marijuana. He was arrested and charged with producing marijuana and possession of marijuana.

The police then obtained a search warrant for the cornfield and the adjacent residence and outbuildings. In the basement, behind a false wall, they located $24 950 in cash, various firearms, and over 1100 g of marijuana; in other parts of the house they found cannabis resin, hashish oil, marijuana buds and seeds, and a marijuana plant. In a nearby shed, they located a 22-L can containing isopropyl alcohol, a substance used for making hashish oil.

The property was surrounded by fencing, as was the cornfield where the marijuana was being grown. Entry to the property was barred by a locked gate and "no trespassing" signs were clearly posted. Embedded screws in the lane were to prevent vehicular access to the cornfield. The trial judge indicated that it is unrealistic to assume that these items could be expected to provide privacy in a country setting. Hunters, hikers, and snowmobilers are notorious for disregarding such signs.

In the United States, in *Oliver v. United States* (1984), the "open fields doctrine" was established. It states that the protection against unreasonable searches and seizures does not extend to unoccupied lands, except those immediately surrounding the home where the right to privacy may reasonably be expected.

In Canada, if the fields are considered part of the dwelling, and there is a reasonable expectation of privacy, a search warrant would be needed.

a) In your opinion, was a search warrant required for the police to legally enter the cornfield? Explain.
b) Should the open fields policy be used in Canada to deter the growing of marijuana? Explain.

7. *R. v. St. Pierre*, [1995] 1 S.C.R. 791 (Supreme Court of Canada)

St. Pierre was charged with having the care or control of a motor vehicle while her blood–alcohol level was over 80. She was stopped because a police officer saw her driving erratically. She failed a roadside screening test and was taken to the police station for more breath tests. She had to wait about an hour for her testing session. She went to the washroom three times during that period.

Both of her breath samples produced a reading of 180. St. Pierre showed the officer two empty 50 mL vodka bottles and told him she was an alcoholic and had consumed the contents of the bottles while in the washroom, to calm herself. The officer testified that the bottles contained no residue and did not smell of vodka. The *Criminal Code* provides that the results of the tests are evidence of driving with a blood–alcohol level over 80, unless there is evidence to the contrary.

St. Pierre was acquitted by the trial judge. The summary conviction appeal court upheld the acquittal, but the Ontario Court of Appeal allowed the Crown's appeal. St. Pierre appealed to the Supreme Court of Canada.

a) Was there a way to determine what St. Pierre's blood–alcohol level was at the time of driving? Explain.

b) Along with driving with a blood–alcohol level of over 80, what other charge could have been laid?

c) Based on the facts, what do you think was the ruling of the Supreme Court of Canada?

8. *R. v. Polashek* (1999), 172 D.L.R. (4th) 350 (Ontario Court of Appeal)

Polashek was legally stopped by police. The police officer had a 20- to 30-second conversation with Polashek and detected a strong odour of marijuana coming from the vehicle. The officer did not see any smoke, nor could he tell if the odour was of burned or unburned marijuana. He told Polashek that he smelled marijuana, to which Polashek replied "No, you don't." Based on the smell, Polashek's response, the area of Mississauga where Polashek was stopped, and the time of night, the officer believed that he had grounds for making an arrest for possession of narcotics.

A search of Polashek found a dark tarlike substance, which the officer believed to be marijuana, and $4000. A search of the trunk revealed wrapped bags of marijuana, a scale and rolling tobacco, and a small amount of LSD. Polashek was then arrested for possession of a narcotic for the purpose of trafficking. He was informed of his right to counsel at that time.

Polashek was found guilty at trial. He appealed, based on what is referred to in the United States as the "plain-smell doctrine." He argued that the police officer had no right to search his vehicle based on the smell of marijuana coming from it. He thus argued that his right to be free from unreasonable search and seizure under section 8 of the *Canadian Charter of Rights and Freedoms* was violated.

In referring to the plain-smell doctrine, the court noted that it was decided in a similar United States case that the smell of marijuana lingers. The marijuana could have been smoked five minutes ago or several hours ago by someone else. The accused was acquitted.

a) In your opinion, did the officer have grounds to conduct a search?

b) Should the plain-smell doctrine be followed in Canada? Support your opinion.

Communicate Your Understanding

9. For each of the following incidents, prepare a sentence for the offender. Write each answer as if you were a judge who was going to deliver it in court, giving reasons for the sentence.

a) LeBeau was charged with four counts of criminal negligence causing death, one count of criminal negligence causing bodily harm, four counts of impaired driving causing death, and one count of impaired driving causing bodily harm. The charges arose as a result of a high-speed car crash. Four young occupants were killed, and the other two occupants, including LeBeau, were seriously injured.

b) Taylor was found guilty of impaired driving causing death, impaired driving causing bodily harm, and failure to stop at the scene of an accident. Taylor had driven through a stop sign and hit another vehicle. One person was killed, others were injured, and Taylor fled the scene. He was later apprehended after having consumed more alcohol. Two weeks earlier he had committed the offence of driving while impaired.

c) McIvor, 20, drunk and stoned on marijuana, left a party and drove his girlfriend's car down a gravel road at speeds of up to 150 km/h. He lost control of the vehicle and ploughed into Hansen. She was out on her morning walk. McIvor thought about hiding her body and then setting the car on fire to avoid being caught. Instead he took off, leaving Hansen to die in the ditch.

d) Bozzard sold some marijuana to a young person aged 14. The marijuana also found its way into the hands of others at the buyer's school.

10. Hard-core drinkers and those who engage in heavy drinking sessions are the focus of current drinking-and-driving legislation. These offenders have no regard for the public awareness campaigns on the issue, the denunciation that accompanies the offence, or the threat of harsh punishment. The Canada Safety Council estimates that 80 percent of offenders drive while suspended. Chronic offenders are estimated to be responsible for 30 percent of impaired driving fatalities. In a Statistics Canada survey, binge drinking was defined as "the consumption of five or more alcoholic beverages" per occasion. It was found that 24 percent of youths aged 15 to 19 binge-drank monthly, as did 29 percent of men and 19 percent of women.

Write a short paper indicating
a) what legislation is available to deter hard-core drinkers from reoffending
b) your views on whether such legislation is effective
c) what legislation you think could be enacted to deter binge-drinkers further

11. Obtain current information on either drug use and drug laws or drinking-and-driving laws in Canada and another country. Prepare a one-page report comparing your findings about the two countries, including the laws, penalties, and statistics on occurrences of offences. Create a poster or use graphics software to illustrate your information.

12. From a newspaper, collect five examples of legal cases involving drug offences or drinking-and-driving offences. Prepare a summary of each case, showing the offence committed; the facts in favour of the Crown and the defence, respectively; the maximum penalty for the offence; and the sentence, if possible. Attach the newspaper articles to your summary.

13. Using one of the newspaper articles that you collected in Question 12 as a springboard, prepare a five-minute speech outlining your views on the topic of drug use and drug laws or drinking-and-driving laws.

Develop Your Thinking

14. One of the arguments given in support of legalizing the possession of marijuana in amounts sufficient for one's own use is that less damage is caused by use of marijuana than from use of alcohol. In your opinion, is that argument valid in supporting the legalization of marijuana? Support your opinion.

15. a) What is random virtue testing? Why do the police use it in drug-related cases?
    b) In what way does random virtue testing violate rights protected in the *Charter*?
    c) In your view, does the use of random virtue testing tend to bring the administration of justice into disrepute? Explain.

16. *John v. Flynn* (2001), 201 D.L.R. (4th) 500 (Ontario Court of Appeal)
    Shawn Flynn showed up at his overnight shift after drinking heavily. During the shift, he drank in his truck in the parking lot on his break, and again when his shift ended at 6:30 A.M. He then drove home, had a snack, and headed out to play cards and drink beer at a friend's house. Shortly

thereafter, while driving on the wrong side of a snow-covered highway, he struck Claude John's car, severely injuring him. Evidence at the trial indicated that no one saw Flynn drinking at work that night, nor any signs of impairment. However, evidence did indicate that Flynn's employer, Eaton Yale Ltd., was aware that workers consumed alcohol in the parking lots during their breaks. John sued and was awarded $620 052.88. The employer was found to be 30 percent liable. The decision was appealed. In a previous case, *Jacobsen v. Nike Canada Ltd.* (1996), the employer actually supplied the alcohol to its employees. (See also *Hunt v. Sutton Group Incentive Realty Inc.* (2001), page 352.)

a) In your opinion, what responsibility does the employer have for employees in situations such as this?

b) What is the main difference between the John case and the Jacobsen case?

c) In your opinion, should the employer be found liable in the John case? Why?

17. It has been stated that, regarding drinking and driving, "What people fear most is not the fine but the loss of their vehicle." Express your opinion on this statement. Support your view by researching current laws that may result in the loss of a vehicle for drinking and driving.

18. Invariably, after the sentencing of an impaired driver who has caused death, people react to the sentence by saying it is too low. A Canada Safety Council survey showed that 65 percent of Canadians think that impaired driving laws are not strict enough. (However, only 20 percent actually knew the penalties for impaired drivers.)

In your opinion, should there be a minimum sentence for impaired driving offences? If so, should the minimum be higher? Support your opinion.

19. A proposal by the Vancouver Police Department would have required convicted drunk drivers each to display the letter "D" on their car window. In Ohio, judges are permitted to issue a special licence plate to convicted drunk drivers who need their cars for work. Police then know that the car is only to be used for that purpose.

In your opinion, should sentencing of impaired drivers include identifying them to the general public?

Chapter 7

Bringing the Accused to Trial

Focus Questions

- What is a legal arrest?
- What are the legal rights of the police and the accused?
- What steps can police take when someone is a suspect?
- What legal procedures can take place before a trial?

Chapter at a Glance

Figure 7-1

This man was one of six people arrested after police found 2500 kg of hashish in a sailboat docked at Tangier, Nova Scotia. What do you already know about the steps involved in making an arrest?

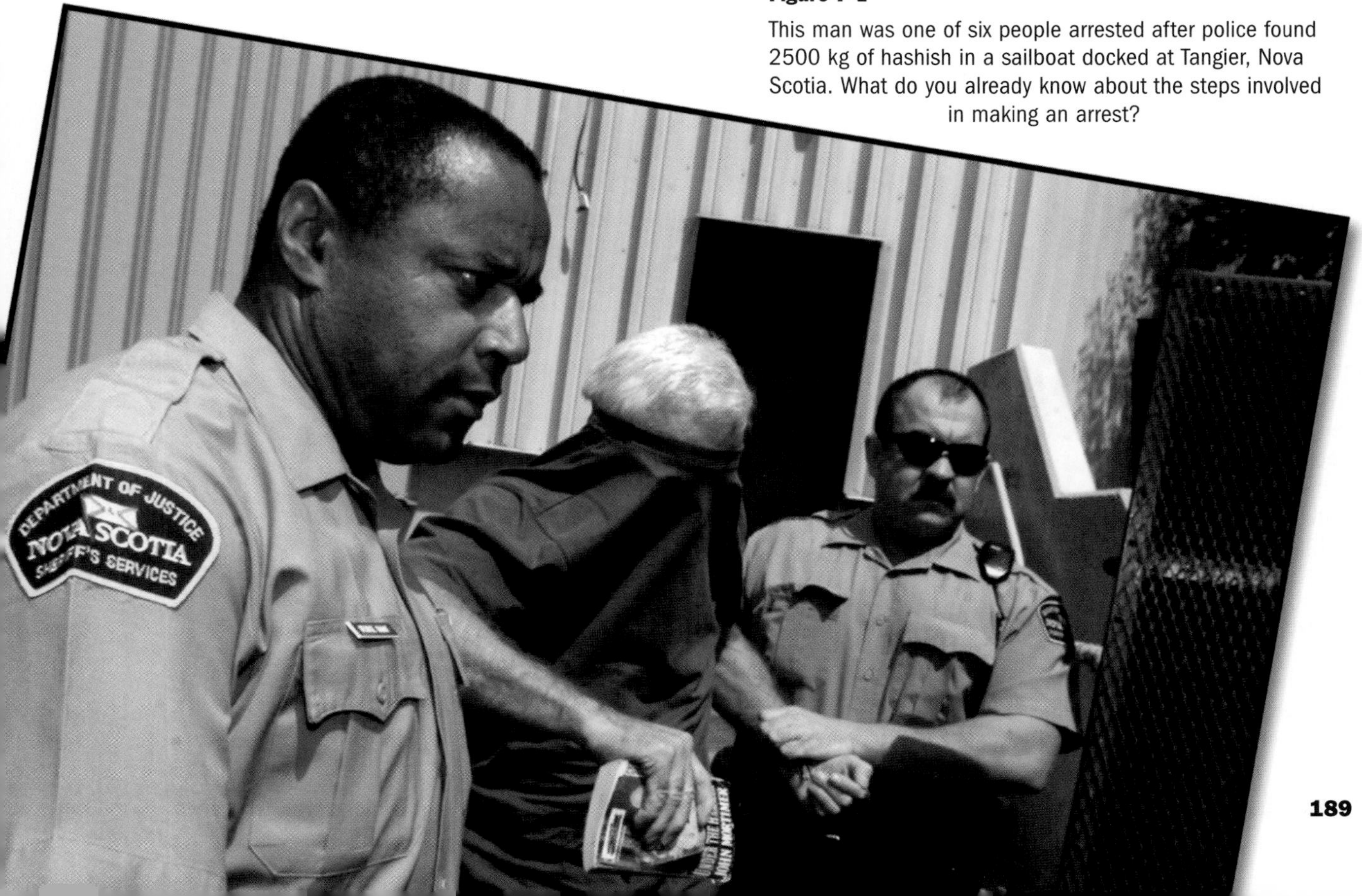

7.1 Introduction

Friction between the public and the police can occur when someone is arrested. This is especially true when the accused is innocent or confused. Although the police may have evidence that an offence has been committed and are authorized to make an arrest, the accused has certain legal rights that he or she may exercise during and after the arrest.

Many Canadians often confuse their rights with those of American citizens. There are important differences. Canada's law tries to protect Canadian society by trying to balance the investigation and arrest rights of the police with individual rights guaranteed in the *Canadian Charter of Rights and Freedoms.* As you read this chapter, be aware of this balance. It will help you understand how laws are designed to protect you in Canadian society.

7.2 Arrest

Merely suspecting that someone did something is insufficient grounds to **arrest** a person. First, police officers must determine that an offence has been committed. Second, they must have reasonable grounds to believe that the suspect committed the offence. When police are ready to apprehend and charge a suspect, they have three choices available to them. They can issue an **appearance notice,** arrest the suspect, or obtain a warrant for arrest.

Appearance Notice

The police may issue an appearance notice for summary conviction offences, hybrid offences, and less serious indictable offences. This document names the offence with which the accused has been charged. It also gives the time and place of the court appearance. The officer must believe that the accused will appear in court on the given date. The accused must also sign the document and receive a copy of the notice. The officer will then swear an **information** before a judge or justice of the peace. This document states that the officer believes on reasonable grounds that the person named in the appearance notice committed the offence.

Arresting the Suspect

For more serious indictable offences, the police will arrest the suspect and take the suspect into **custody.** Arresting officers must
- identify themselves
- advise the accused that he or she is under arrest
- inform the accused of the right to a lawyer (section 10(b) of the *Canadian Charter of Rights and Freedoms*)
- inform the accused of the charges. Section 10(a) of the *Canadian Charter of Rights and Freedoms* states that "everyone has the right on arrest or detention to be informed promptly of the reasons therefor."

The purpose of the arrest is to lay charges, preserve evidence, and prevent the accused from committing further offences. Any officer can arrest without a warrant if there are reasonable grounds to believe that someone has committed an indictable offence, is committing an indictable or a summary offence, or is about to commit an indictable offence. After the arrest, the officer must swear an information before a judge or justice of the peace.

The Law

When arresting a suspect, the police must read the following:

1. Notice on arrest: I am arresting _____ for _____ (briefly describe reasons for arrest).

2. Right to counsel (lawyer): It is my duty to inform you that you have the right to retain and instruct counsel without delay. Do you understand?

3. Caution to charged person: You (are charged, will be charged) with _____. Do you wish to say anything in answer to the charge? You are not obligated to say anything unless you wish to do so, but whatever you say may be given in evidence....

For Discussion

1. Why is it important to read this notice to accused persons upon their arrest?

If the accused resists arrest, the police can use as much force as is necessary to prevent an escape. The police are criminally liable for the use of unnecessary force. In certain circumstances, they can apply force that could cause death or serious injury if it protects others from death or bodily harm. In 1994, Parliament passed a law that gave police and anyone assisting them the power to use deadly force. They can do so in the following situations:
- The behaviour of a suspect might cause serious harm or death to others.
- The suspect flees to escape arrest.
- There is no alternative means to prevent escape.

▌ How an ADVANCED TASER Works

A compressed nitrogen gas capsule disperses two electrified projectiles that are connected to the weapon by insulated wire, up to a range of 4.5 m. The power surge instantly disrupts the central nervous system and results in muscle spasms that cause the person to fall to the ground.

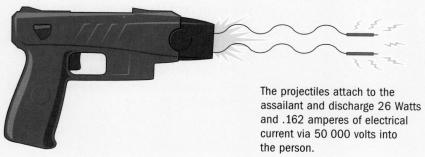

The projectiles attach to the assailant and discharge 26 Watts and .162 amperes of electrical current via 50 000 volts into the person.

Figure 7-2

In several Canadian cities and towns, police are experimenting with TASERs or remote stun guns. These guns discharge 50 000 volts into suspects and stun them. They cost $700 each and are an alternative to the standard handguns issued to police officers.

Warrant for Arrest

If the accused flees the scene of a crime, police can swear an information before a judge or justice of the peace. A document called a **summons** orders the accused to appear in court at a certain time and place. It is delivered to the accused by a **sheriff** or a deputy.

If the police can show the judge that the accused will not appear in court voluntarily, the judge will issue a **warrant for arrest.** It names or describes the accused, lists the offence(s), and orders the arrest of the accused. There must be reasonable grounds to believe that the accused has committed the offence. Otherwise, judges will refuse to issue either a summons or a warrant.

Figure 7-3

A security camera shows a store detective (left) apprehending and arresting a suspect.

Case

R. v. Macooh

[1993] 2 S.C.R. 802
Supreme Court of Canada

An officer saw Macooh drive through a stop sign at 3:45 A.M. in Spirit River, Alberta. (Driving through a stop sign is a summary offence.) The officer turned on his cruiser's emergency signals and followed the suspect. Macooh accelerated and drove through two more stop signs before stopping at an apartment building and running toward the back door. The officer yelled at him to stop, but he entered the building. The officer followed him to an apartment and called out at the door. He identified himself as an RCMP officer. Receiving no answer, he entered the apartment and found Macooh in bed.

The officer advised Macooh that he was under arrest for failing to stop for a police officer. The accused appeared to be impaired and resisted the officer. He was arrested and charged with impaired driving, failing to stop for a peace officer, failing to provide a breath sample, and assaulting a peace officer with intent to resist arrest.

At trial, the provincial court judge ruled that the officer's entry into the dwelling-house while in hot pursuit of Macooh for a provincial offence was unlawful. Therefore, his arrest was also illegal. In addition, since the entry was illegal, all the evidence obtained resulting from the entry was not admitted. Macooh relied on sections 7 and 9 of the *Charter* as part of his defence. He was acquitted on all charges.

The Alberta Court of Appeal and the Supreme Court of Canada both ruled that the right of arrest on private property during immediate or hot pursuit was not limited to indictable offences. Macooh's arrest was therefore lawful. He was convicted on all charges.

For Discussion

1. **What indications are there that the officer was in "hot pursuit"?**

2. **What rights do police who are in hot pursuit have to enter a dwelling?**

3. **What rights does Macooh have under sections 7 and 9 of the *Charter*? How could you argue that the arresting officer limited these *Charter* rights?**

4. **What arguments would support the officer's position that the limitation of sections 7 and 9 was reasonable in this situation?**

5. **What precedent did the Supreme Court set in this decision?**

Arrest by Citizens

Citizens can make an arrest under certain circumstances. This law gives store detectives, private detectives, and other citizens the authority to make arrests.

The Law The Criminal Code

Excerpts from the *Criminal Code*

494.

(1) Any one may arrest without warrant

(a) a person whom he finds committing an indictable offence; or

(b) a person who, on reasonable grounds, he believes

   (i) has committed a criminal offence, and

   (ii) is escaping from and freshly pursued by persons who have lawful authority to arrest that person.

(2) Any one who is

(a) the owner ... of property, or

(b) a person authorized by the owner ... of property, may arrest without warrant a person whom he finds committing a criminal offence on or in relation to that property.

For Discussion

1. Summarize the circumstances under which a citizen can make an arrest.

2. What are the potential problem(s) of making a citizen's arrest? Would you make one? Explain.

Review Your Understanding (Pages 190 to 193)

1. Why is there sometimes conflict between the police and the public when arrests are made?

2. Why is it important to know your legal rights?

3. When does an arrest take place? What is its purpose?

4. Describe in detail the three choices available to police when they believe an offence has been committed.

5. Why must police swear an information before a judge or justice of the peace?

6. a) How much force may police use when making an arrest?

   b) What can happen if police use too much force?

   c) Should police be forbidden to use any kind of force when making an arrest? Explain.

7. Distinguish between a summons for arrest and a warrant for arrest.

7.3 Duties of Police Officers

In Canada, there are three levels of policing: federal, provincial, and municipal. The Royal Canadian Mounted Police (RCMP) is the federal (national) police force. The provincial police forces in Ontario and Quebec are the Ontario Provincial Police (OPP) and the Sûreté du Québec (SQ). In all other provinces, the RCMP also serves as the provincial police force. Municipal police,

e activity

Visit **www.law.nelson.com** and follow the links to learn more about the RCMP.

such as the Moose Jaw Police Department, enforce municipal laws. The RCMP, the OPP in Ontario, and the SQ in Quebec carry out the duties of the municipal police in areas that do not have their own municipal police forces.

Police Conduct

Police officers are responsible for their conduct and behaviour when carrying out their duties. If they break the rules of police conduct, they can be charged under criminal law or sued under civil law. Each province has a board that reviews complaints from citizens concerning police conduct. Police officers often have to make quick decisions to save their own lives and those of others. At all times, officers must follow section 25 of the *Criminal Code*, which requires an officer to act "on reasonable grounds ... and in using as much force as is necessary for that purpose."

The Police Log

Police officers are usually the first persons at a crime scene. They must bring law and order to the situations they encounter. They must also secure the crime scene so that crucial evidence does not get contaminated. Police officers keep an accurate log (written record) of what they see and hear at the scene of the crime. These logs may be an important factor in determining the value of evidence presented in court.

Review Your Understanding (Pages 193 to 194)

1. **Describe the three levels of policing in Canada.**
2. **What can happen to police who abuse their power?**
3. **Why are police logs important?**

7.4   Citizens' Rights

The legal rights of citizens who are detained and/or arrested are outlined in sections 7 to 11 of the *Canadian Charter of Rights and Freedoms* (see Appendix A, page 600). However, the meaning of many of these clauses remains open to court interpretation.

An informed and responsible citizen may want to cooperate with the police. Innocent persons often show their innocence by immediately giving information to the police. This can save time and money. Despite the presumption of innocence, the police tend to form conclusions based on an individual's behaviour when being questioned.

Rights on Being Detained

When an officer stops someone for questioning, that person is being detained. People who are detained do not actually have to answer questions unless they are in a specific situation, such as a police spot check on a busy highway, or being placed under arrest. Detention should lead quickly to arrest—otherwise, the person should be free to go. If a police officer insists on questioning or searching a reluctant individual, that person should immediately demand to see a lawyer and write down the badge number of the officer and the names of any witnesses.

A citizen who is detained illegally may sue the police for false arrest or detention or complain to the police commission. A citizen is allowed to use as much force as necessary to resist an illegal arrest or search. However, the force used must be reasonable.

Rights on Being Arrested

Someone who is charged with committing a crime has the right to be informed promptly of the reason for the arrest and the right to obtain a lawyer without delay (section 10 of the *Charter*). The Supreme Court of Canada has ruled that this includes being advised of the availability of a **duty counsel**—a lawyer on duty at the court. The police must also inform the accused that legal aid is available if that person cannot afford a lawyer.

A request by the accused to contact a lawyer must be honoured immediately. Anyone who has decided to hire a lawyer can refuse to answer any further questions, except those necessary to complete the charge, such as name, address, occupation, and date of birth. One study found that almost 60 percent of defendants gave verbal statements and 70 percent gave written statements to police before contacting a lawyer. Perhaps these people thought it would be better to answer police questions because refusing to talk could create a bad impression. However, any statements volunteered to the police can be used as evidence.

When people are read their rights, they must truly understand them. If the accused are intoxicated, the police must wait until they are sober. If the accused cannot understand English or French, they must be read their rights through an interpreter. Once they decide to contact a lawyer, they must have access to a telephone. They must be allowed to talk privately with their attorneys. They also have the right to give up counsel and answer police questions.

DOUG USES HIS ONE CALL UNWISELY...

Figure 7-4

How would you use your one phone call?

Police Rights

The police have the right to **search** the accused upon arrest to look for evidence related to the charge or for any item that might help the accused to escape or cause harm. The police may take away the possessions of the accused. The police also have the right to take the accused to the police station. Here, a more thorough search is likely to take place. This might involve a strip-search and skin-frisk, or a body cavity search if drugs are involved. Extensive body searches must be conducted by officers of the same sex as the accused, and they cannot be done without sufficient reason. The police may wish to fingerprint and photograph the accused at this time, or later.

The accused does not have to take part in a **line-up,** where several individuals, including the suspect, line up for possible identification by the victims or witnesses. Nor must the suspect take a **polygraph test** (lie detector test), or give blood, urine, or breath samples (except in cases of impaired driving offences). Accused persons should consult with their lawyers about these procedures. Section 487.04 of the *Criminal Code* does allow police to obtain DNA samples from a suspect, but they must have a warrant to do so. It actually might be to the suspect's advantage to permit evidence to be collected. For instance, when murder has been committed under the influence of drugs or alcohol, the extent of the influence might affect the outcome of the trial or even the sentence.

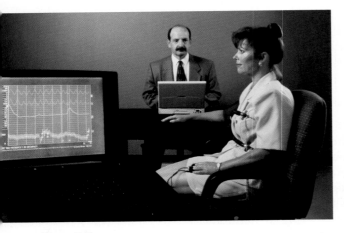

Figure 7-5

A polygraph test in progress

Review Your Understanding (Pages 194 to 196)

1. Refer to sections 7 through 11 of the *Canadian Charter of Rights and Freedoms* (see Appendix A, page 600) and summarize the legal rights of Canadians.

2. Why is it important to cooperate with the police? Under what circumstance might this not be advisable?

3. For each of the rights of the police, state the corresponding right of a citizen:
   a) the right to question before arrest
   b) the right to search a person before arrest
   c) the right to question after arrest
   d) the right to search a person after arrest.

4. What rights do the police have concerning the following: fingerprinting, requesting a line-up, a polygraph test, or a blood sample?

5. Why is it sometimes to a suspect's advantage to let the police collect evidence?

7.5 Search Laws

The police may wish to search the residence of the accused to look for evidence related to the charge. To do so, they must have a **search warrant,** a legal document issued by the court to increase police authority.

Obtaining the Search Warrant

To apply for a search warrant, an officer must swear before a justice of the peace or a judge that an offence has been committed and that there are reasonable grounds to believe that evidence of a crime exists on the property.

If the officer's testimony is accepted, a search warrant is issued. If the information about the evidence being on the property was received from an informer, the officer must outline to the court why the informer is reliable before a warrant will be issued. Section 8 of the *Charter* guarantees citizens the right to be secure against unreasonable search or seizure.

Telewarrants can be obtained by telephone or other telecommunication means, such as by fax or e-mail. This process allows for the warrant to be obtained quickly in the likelihood that evidence may be destroyed.

Using the Search Warrant

A warrant can be used to search a residence only on the date indicated, between 6:00 A.M. and 9:00 P.M. The search can involve only those areas and items outlined in the warrant. Only the items mentioned in the warrant can be seized, unless other illegal items are found during the search. The officers must have reasonable and probable grounds that such items were used when committing a crime or were obtained illegally. The officers cannot go beyond the terms of the warrant in hope of finding something illegal that would justify the laying of a charge. The items seized can be kept for up to three months, or for a longer period if they are needed as evidence at trial.

Search Laws and Rules

Police can demand to enter a property when they are carrying a search warrant. If permission is refused, or if no one is home, the police have the right to break into the premises. However, the police are liable for any excessive force used. Anyone who answers the door can ask the police to show him or her a copy of the search warrant before allowing them entry. If the document is not correct in every detail, entry can be refused. Once inside, the police can only search a person after arrest, unless they believe that the person possesses illegal drugs, liquor, or weapons.

Police do not need a search warrant if individuals agree to be searched. These persons voluntarily give up their constitutional rights. Police may have to prove in court that this consent was voluntary.

Police need a warrant when using electronic surveillance equipment, such as video surveillance, tracking devices, or telephone recorders that intercept private conversations. Judges must be assured that such devices will not interfere with the bodily integrity or property of the people being monitored. The vast majority of warrants issued to police for this purpose involve the illegal-drug trade.

The *Anti-Terrorism Act* permits police to use electronic surveillance on suspected terrorists for up to one year. Usually, such permission is granted by a superior court judge for only 60 days, although this can be renewed.

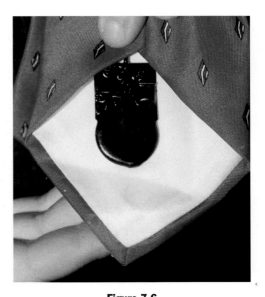

Figure 7-6

This tiny microphone is concealed in a tie and can be used to collect vital evidence about drug trafficking or other crimes.

Case

R. v. Araujo

[2000] 2 S.C.R. 992
Supreme Court of Canada

Several accused persons faced charges of trafficking in cocaine. Much of the evidence against the accused came from wiretapping evidence by the RCMP.

During the trial, the defence argued that the 130-page application for permission to wiretap was flawed. The application had mixed up some of the names of informants, as well as the information they had given to the RCMP. Therefore, the judge who had given permission to do the wiretapping had received false information, and the wiretap was illegal. The trial judge agreed and the wiretap evidence was not introduced into court. The accused were acquitted and released.

The Crown appealed the verdict and the British Columbia Court of Appeal reversed the trial judge's decision and ordered a new trial. The defence appealed to the Supreme Court of Canada. The Supreme Court ruled against the defence, and the appeal was denied. The Court said that when the RCMP applied for permission to wiretap, it convinced the judge that there was no other way of obtaining evidence to convict the accused.

Previously, the RCMP had used surveillance and search warrants, but these methods had produced no evidence. The RCMP had also considered using undercover agents, but concluded that this was too risky. The judge had concluded that the only way to apprehend the higher-ups in this cocaine drug ring was to give permission for the wiretap.

The Supreme Court acknowledged that there were errors in the wiretap application, but noted that the application did not seek to mislead the judge. They were honest mistakes. The police had reasonable and probable grounds to suspect that the accused were members of the drug ring and the wiretap evidence supported this suspicion. It was necessary to use wiretapping to get enough evidence to convict the accused.

For Discussion

1. Why do the police have to get permission from a judge to wiretap?

2. On what basis were the accused acquitted and released at trial?

3. Compare the trial decision to that of the Supreme Court of Canada. Why did the Court allow the wiretap evidence?

Exceptions to Search Laws

There are some important exceptions to the search laws you have just learned about. Under the *Controlled Drugs and Substances Act*, the police may search any place that is not a private residence without a warrant if there is a reasonable belief that it contains illegal drugs. Anyone found inside these premises can also be searched without a warrant. These types of searches usually take place when there is no time to obtain a warrant or because of the need for a surprise entry.

Under provincial liquor laws, police may search a vehicle for illegal alcohol without a warrant. In addition, if police stop a motor vehicle and become suspicious that the driver is hiding something, they can search the vehicle without a warrant if they have reasonable and probable grounds that an offence is being committed or has been committed. The police may also search for illegal weapons without a warrant in any place that is not a private residence (e.g., a car).

Case

R. v. Richardson

(2001) 153 C.C.C. (3d) 449
British Columbia Court of Appeal

Two officers set up a traffic roadblock looking for drivers who might be driving under the influence of alcohol or driving without valid licences or insurance. At 1:30 A.M., the police noticed a car approaching the roadblock. It slowed down and then approached them. The officers detected a strong smell of marijuana and asked Richardson and two other occupants to get out of the vehicle. When confronted about the strong smell, Richardson produced a small metal box that contained small amounts of marijuana and hashish oil. The officers then asked Richardson to open the trunk of the car. In it they found 11 bags of marijuana and $6000 in cash.

Richardson protested against the search, claiming that it was illegal. The officers had no warrant to search the car. The police handcuffed Richardson because he was obstructing a legal search. The officers believed they had a legal right to search the car. They charged Richardson with possession of a narcotic for the purpose of trafficking and possession of cannabis resin.

In court, Richardson argued that the officers had searched the car illegally and that the evidence should not be admitted in court. It was a violation of sections 8 and 10 of the *Charter*. The trial judge ruled that the evidence was admissible under section 24(2) of the *Charter*. The judge convicted Richardson of possession of marijuana for the purpose of trafficking and gave him a six-month suspended sentence. Richardson appealed. The question was whether it was appropriate to exclude the evidence found in the trunk of the car because of the abuse of police powers. The appeal court dismissed Richardson's appeal. It ruled that the circumstances justified the search and the handcuffing. The charge was a serious one, and to exclude the evidence would weaken the public's confidence in the legal system.

For Discussion

1. **The defence and the Crown referred to sections 8, 10, and 24(2) of the *Canadian Charter of Rights and Freedoms*.** Look up these sections and summarize them in your own words.

2. **On what basis could the defence argue that the police abused their powers?**

3. **How did the appeal court justify including the evidence?**

Review Your Understanding (Pages 196 to 199)

1. Describe how a search warrant is obtained and used.

2. What should a person know when police officers arrive with a search warrant?

3. What is a telewarrant and what is its purpose?

4. What restrictions are there on the use of electronic surveillance equipment used under the authority of a warrant?

5. Outline the important exceptions to search laws for illegal-drug and alcohol offences.

6. Under what circumstances can police search motor vehicles? What are they usually looking for?

 activity

Visit **www.law.nelson.com** and follow the links to learn how wiretapping is used to fight telemarketing fraud.

7.6 Release Procedures

Most people accused of crimes are not locked up after being arrested. They may be taken down to the police station where the police record the criminal charges. The officer in charge of the lockup or station may release people charged with summary convictions, hybrid offences, or indictable offences that carry a penalty of five years or less. If there are grounds to believe that further offences will be committed or that the accused will not appear in court, the accused may be confined until a bail hearing takes place.

For indictable offences carrying a penalty of more than five years' imprisonment, accused persons must be brought before a judge within 24 hours, or as soon as possible, for a bail hearing. "Bail" is money or other security paid to the court to ensure the appearance of the accused at a later date. Once bail is paid, the accused is released. The judge decides whether or not bail will be granted. If bail is granted and the accused fails to appear on the court date, the person who posted the bail loses the money.

In 1985, the *Criminal Code* was changed to put less emphasis on the payment of money as a condition of being released. The old bail laws were thought to discriminate against the poor. Now, if a person pleads not guilty, the judge must release the accused on his or her promise to appear. Only if the Crown attorney can show that the accused would likely miss his or her court date or be a threat to the protection and safety of the public can bail be denied.

If the charge is serious, such as a murder charge, the accused must show why he or she should not be kept in custody and should be released until the court date appearance. This is known as **reverse onus.** The responsibility is on the accused to prove that no threat exists to society and that he or she will appear when so ordered. For other criminal offences, it is up to the Crown attorney to prove that the accused should not be released.

Case

R. v. Mapara

(2001) 149 B.C.A.C. 316
British Columbia Court of Appeal

In 2001, Sameer Mapara was convicted of first-degree murder, a crime that carries a minimum penalty of 25 years' imprisonment. His trial lasted five months. He appealed the decision and asked to be released on bail until his appeal was decided. He argued that he had no previous criminal record and posed no threat to anyone. He also promised to turn himself into custody if his appeal was rejected.

The Crown opposed his release on the following grounds:

- There was no guarantee Mapara would surrender himself back into custody.
- He was a flight risk.
- He had originally emigrated from Kenya and could easily go back there, where he had family and friends.

The Crown argued that public confidence in the justice system would be shaken if persons appealing first-degree murder convictions were allowed out on bail.

Mapara is married and has four young children. He has serious financial difficulties. His father-in-law is suing him for $780 574, and the Bank of Montreal has reported that he issued cheques for $107 242.45 without sufficient funds.

The British Columbia Court of Appeal observed that Parliament has not excluded persons who have been convicted of first-degree murder from seeking

continued ▶

release on bail. It wondered what the bail conditions would be for such a serious offence. It concluded that it would consider the matter and make a judgment at a later date.

For Discussion

1. What is reverse onus? How can it be applied to this case?

2. What argument has the Crown used to oppose granting bail?

3. How do Mapara's personal circumstances support his request to be released on bail?

4. Why did the appeal court not immediately reject his request?

5. What judgment would you render on Mapara's request to be released on bail? Explain your answer.

Judicial Release Procedures

If released, the accused is required to sign an **undertaking** and to live up to the conditions set by the court. These conditions might include a curfew, orders not to associate with former friends or go to certain places, and an order to report to a police station once a week. These regulations are designed to help the accused avoid further trouble with the law before the court hearing. The accused might also be required to sign a **recognizance.** This document states that the accused recognizes that he or she is charged with an offence, and that he or she promises to appear in court on a certain date. Depending on the case, the accused may pay money in order to be released.

Release Denied

If the accused is not released by the judge, he or she is entitled to appeal the decision to a higher court. If, for any reason, the accused is kept in prison without being arrested, or is denied a bail hearing, an application for a writ of *habeas corpus* can be made. This writ requires the accused to appear in court, to swear that he or she has been denied these rights, and to ask for release. A judge rules on the application. If the writ is granted, the accused is released.

Fingerprints and Photographs

People who are charged with indictable offences and are released may be fingerprinted and photographed before the release. Of course, this step would be unnecessary if these procedures were done at the time of the arrest.

When people are acquitted of a crime, they do not automatically have the right to insist that fingerprint and photo records be

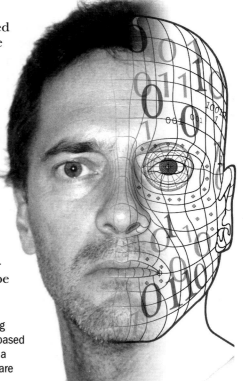

Figure 7-7

Biometrics is a new science that establishes the identity of individuals by measuring their physical features; for example, their nose, eyes, lips, ears, and hairlines. It is based on the idea that the distances between someone's features can be represented by a mathematical pattern. Why do you think gambling casinos and some police forces are using biometrics technology?

removed from police files. There is no law that says this must happen. Each police force decides whether or not to comply with this request. Similarly, if someone is mistakenly arrested and fingerprinted, it is difficult to have the file destroyed.

Protection of Society

Maintaining the balance of rights between citizen and society is a matter of concern to Canadians. Too much emphasis on individual rights can lead to less emphasis on the protection of society, possibly leading to an increase in crime. On the other hand, too much emphasis on the protection of society can result in a police state and the elimination of individual rights. It is up to the public and police to reduce the possibility of conflict. The public can contribute by not exploiting their rights to take advantage of others and the Canadian legal system. The police can contribute by not abusing their powers and by remaining aware of their duty to society.

Review Your Understanding (Pages 200 to 202)

1. After being arrested, which categories of accused persons might be released until their court appearances?
2. Under what circumstances will suspects not be released until their court date appearances?
3. Why were the bail laws revised?
4. How could it be argued that reverse onus breaks the rule that someone is presumed innocent until proven guilty? How could its use be justified in our society?
5. Distinguish between an undertaking and a recognizance, and identify the purpose of each.
6. Why is *habeas corpus* an important legal right in a democracy?
7. What happens to the fingerprints and photographs of people who are acquitted? Do you agree with this procedure?
8. Why is it important to maintain the balance of individual rights and the protection of society as a whole? In your opinion, is this balance being achieved?

7.7 Awaiting Trial

The accused should consult a lawyer and reveal everything that is connected to the case. The lawyer can then prepare the best defence possible. The lawyer will study legal texts and laws related to the offence, interview witnesses, and examine previous court decisions and precedents to gather the necessary background for the case. The accused has the right to make suggestions to the lawyer. If there is a serious disagreement, the accused can change lawyers, or the lawyer can withdraw from the case.

Legal Aid

Section 10(b) of the *Canadian Charter of Rights and Freedoms* states that all Canadians have the "right to retain and instruct counsel without delay" for criminal cases. If the accused cannot afford a lawyer, he or she can apply for "legal aid": a court-appointed lawyer paid for by the government. Legal aid is provided only to those who receive social assistance or those whose family incomes are below social assistance levels. Besides criminal cases, legal aid is also available in civil and family court cases. People who are awarded legal aid can choose which lawyer will represent them.

Disclosure

The Law Commission of Canada says that **disclosure** is one of the most important features of the criminal justice system. Prior to a trial by jury, the Crown attorney and the defence are required to meet and reveal all the evidence that both sides have for the upcoming trial. The Crown must show its evidence so that the accused can fully understand the Crown's case and can prepare a defence. The defence may put forward evidence or arguments that prove to the Crown that it does not have a case. If the defence proves its case, charges will be dropped and no trial will occur.

Disclosure has become more important in recent years and has reduced the number of jury trials. It also reduces the time and cost of trials. It helps to ensure that the accused gets a fair trial because once people know all the evidence that will be used against them, they can prepare a proper defence. In non-jury trials, the accused or the Crown may ask for such a meeting for the same purpose.

Collecting Evidence

Before a criminal trial, both the Crown and the defence may examine exhibits that have been offered to the court as evidence in the trial. Such items might include weapons, clothing, traces of blood or other fluids, or fingerprints. In so doing, they are making use of **forensic science.** Forensic science uses medicine and other sciences to try to solve legal problems. The term is perhaps used most often in connection to an autopsy, an examination to determine the cause of death. Forensic scientists can find clues in samples of blood and other bodily fluids, teeth, bones, hair, fingerprints, handwriting, clothing fibres, and other items. These clues can help to determine the guilt or innocence of the accused.

Recent technology has led to many advances in forensic science. For instance, fingerprinting now involves computers rather than ink and paper. A computer can be used to compare fingerprints to a vast number of other fingerprints on file, reducing to a few hours a task that used to take months. This automated system was established in 1976.

Another new procedure is DNA matching. This technique is based on the fact that every cell of a particular human being contains a unique form of the complex chemical DNA (deoxyribonucleic acid). The unique profile of each person's DNA makes possible the technique of DNA matching.

activity

Visit **www.law.nelson.com** and follow the links to learn more about legal aid.

Did You Know?

There are approximately 1.1 million applications in Canada for legal aid each year, and almost 750 000 of them are approved.

activity

Technology has increased our ability to rely on evidence gathered at the crime scene. Visit **www.law.nelson.com** and follow the links to learn more about DNA.

Forensic scientists can tell a person's sex from a hair root and determine the probable make, model, and year of a hit-and-run vehicle from a speck of paint. The RCMP's forensic crime laboratories handle thousands of cases a year.

This is a powerful tool. It allows the Crown to enter into evidence a DNA match; for example, a hair sample matching that of the accused found on the victim's body at the scene of the crime. The defence can also show that there is no match between the accused and the evidence collected at the scene of the crime.

Because of the importance of DNA matching as evidence, the *Criminal Code* was amended in 1995 to permit police to obtain DNA samples from suspects. A warrant is required. In 2000, the RCMP opened a DNA data bank that stores the genetic profiles of people convicted of serious crimes. The purpose of the data bank is to track criminals and solve crimes. It cost $10.6 million to set up and its operation costs are $5 million a year. (See Issue, page 210.)

Case

R. v. Feeney

(2001) 152 C.C.C. (3d) 390
British Columbia Court of Appeal

Feeney was accused of murdering an 85-year-old man by striking him repeatedly on the head with a crowbar. He was also accused of stealing the man's cash, cigarettes, beer, and truck. The deceased's truck was found later in a ditch with a bloody crowbar beside it. A cigarette butt was found at the victim's mobile home, as were fingerprints.

The police entered Feeney's home and seized a bloody shirt; they did not have a search warrant. At his trial, Feeney's sister testified that she saw him arrive home on the day of the murder and saw bloodstains on his shirt. But she said that she did not know if she was dreaming or could actually remember what she had seen. Feeney was convicted of second-degree murder. On appeal, the Supreme Court of Canada set aside the conviction and ordered a new trial. The police had not obtained a search warrant and the search of Feeney's home was illegal. The bloody shirt could not be used as evidence, even though the blood stains matched the victim's blood type.

During the second trial, the RCMP obtained other evidence to prove Feeney's guilt. The cigarette butt was analyzed to provide DNA material. A warrant was issued under section 487.05 of the *Criminal Code* to obtain a blood sample from Feeney. There was a match: the DNA on the cigarette butt was the same as Feeney's. The RCMP also obtained a set of fingerprints from the Calgary Police Department, which had fingerprinted Feeney the previous year for a break and enter. There was another match: the fingerprints were the same as those found at the scene of the crime. Feeney's sister also changed her testimony and said that she had actually seen Feeney with the bloodstains and that it was not a dream.

Feeney's lawyer argued that the fingerprint evidence should not be considered because it had been obtained after an illegal arrest. Section 487.05 of the *Criminal Code* should not apply because Feeney's rights had been violated under sections 7 and 8 of the *Charter*. He noted that evidence given by Feeney's sister was unreliable and should not be considered. Despite these arguments, the second trial jury found Feeney guilty of second-degree murder. On appeal, the British Columbia Court of Appeal rejected his defence arguments and upheld his conviction.

For Discussion

1. Why do you think the RCMP did not obtain a search warrant before searching Feeney's home?

2. Why did the Supreme Court order a new trial?

3. Why did the RCMP have to obtain new evidence for Feeney's second trial?

4. What new evidence did the RCMP obtain for use in the second trial?

5. Do you agree with the appeal court's decision? Explain.

In the early 1980s, a young British geneticist was experimenting with extracting DNA from human muscle tissue and made an astounding discovery. Alec Jeffreys realized that random segments of human DNA—the protein molecules in cells that determine the genetic characteristics of all living things—are "genetic markers." They are as unique to each individual (with the exception of identical twins) as a fingerprint.

Jeffreys found a way to process these markers, using electricity and radioactive labelling, so that they formed a distinct bar-code-like pattern on X-ray film. Police could then match with great probability the bar codes from DNA evidence at a crime scene with DNA samples taken from suspects. Jeffreys called his technique "DNA fingerprinting."

Jeffreys' technique first came to public attention when it helped to solve the murders of two British women in the mid-1980s. The police arrested a 17-year-old male and sent semen and blood samples to Jeffreys for testing. The results proved that the young man was not the murderer. Jeffreys would later recall that this was "the first man ever proved innocent by molecular genetics, and without the evidence he would have gone to jail for the rest of his life." The police then required that all males in the area between the ages of 13 and 30 give blood samples for DNA testing. There was still no match.

Later, 27-year-old Colin Pitchfork was overheard in a bar boasting to friends that he had persuaded a friend to give a blood sample for him. Police arrested him, and DNA tests showed that he had likely committed both crimes. He was given two life sentences. This was the first time that DNA testing had pointed to a criminal.

For his contribution to forensic science, Jeffreys was knighted by the Queen in 1994.

For Discussion

1. **What discovery did Alec Jeffreys make with respect to DNA?**
2. **Briefly summarize the technique of DNA fingerprinting.**
3. **Explain the significance of the Colin Pitchfork case.**

Figure 7-8

Alec Jeffreys

Court Appearances

When the accused appears in court, the provincial court judge will set a trial date or ask for an **adjournment,** which puts the matter over to a later date. This gives the accused time to obtain legal advice. The judge will also indicate in which court the case will be tried. The three possibilities are determined by the type of offence:

- Offences over which a provincial court has absolute authority include all summary and minor indictable offences, and they are listed in section 553 of the *Criminal Code*. They include theft, fraud, mischief (all under $5000), and keeping a bawdyhouse.
- For more serious indictable offences, the accused can elect to be tried by a provincial court judge without a jury; or tried in a higher court by a judge alone or a judge and jury. These crimes include assault, sexual assault, and weapons offences.

- Offences that can be tried usually by a judge and jury in a supreme court of the province are the most serious indictable offences. These are listed in section 469 of the *Criminal Code* and include treason, murder, and piracy. Only 5 percent of crimes are heard at the superior court level. When the accused appears in provincial court, the judge will set a date for a preliminary hearing.

The Plea

Someone charged with committing a criminal offence enters a plea in provincial court. The person states whether he or she is guilty or not guilty of the charge read in court. About 90 percent of accused Canadians plead guilty at this stage of the process.

If the accused pleads guilty to a summary conviction or minor indictable offence, he or she is sentenced immediately or remanded (sent back) into custody. The **remand** can last up to eight days, or until the judge can review the circumstances of the case and the criminal records of the accused and pass sentence. If the accused pleads not guilty, the provincial court judge will set a trial date. If the accused pleads guilty to a serious indictable offence and wants to be tried by a provincial court judge, the same procedures will apply as for summary convictions and minor indictable offences.

Preliminary Hearing

The **preliminary hearing** lets the provincial court judge decide whether there is sufficient evidence to proceed with a trial in a higher court. It only takes place when the accused pleads not guilty to an indictable offence and chooses to be tried by a higher court judge or a judge and jury. During the preliminary hearing, the judge hears evidence and the testimony of witnesses to determine if a reasonable case can be made against the accused. If the evidence is insufficient, the charges are dropped and the accused is free to go. If there is sufficient evidence, the trial date is set by the judge.

The defence does not need to call evidence at the preliminary hearing, but can cross-examine the Crown witnesses. If evidence is presented, it is recorded and may be brought up at trial to attack the credibility of witnesses who change their story. Such evidence may also be useful if the witnesses later refuse to testify, flee, or die.

Sometimes the defendants will skip the preliminary hearing and go directly to trial. This is done if (1) the accused has decided to plead guilty; (2) the accused wants to have the trial date set as early as possible; or (3) the accused wants to avoid negative publicity that may result from the preliminary inquiry.

Case

R. v. Olubowale

(2001) 142 O.A.C. 279
Ontario Court of Appeal

The accused was arrested and charged with murder. At his preliminary hearing, the Crown presented this evidence: The accused was a bouncer at a tavern. A group of men were asked to leave the tavern and the bouncer followed them outside. The victim made racial comments to Olubowale and a fight ensued.

Olubowale weighed twice as much as the victim and was 30 cm taller. He was also a trained boxer. Witnesses said the accused hit the victim three times with blows described as "precise," "powerful," "full force," and "very strong." Olubowale delivered the last blow after chasing the victim around a car. The victim fell and hit his head on the concrete and died of his injuries. At his preliminary hearing, the accused asked the judge to reduce the charge to manslaughter.

Section 229 of the *Criminal Code* defines murder as follows:

(a) where the person who causes the death of a human being

   (i) means to cause his death, or

   (ii) means to cause him bodily harm that he knows is likely to cause his death, and is reckless whether death ensues or not.

The provincial court judge would not reduce the charge to manslaughter and committed the accused to stand trial for murder. Olubowale appealed this ruling. The Ontario Court of Appeal decided that the accused could not be tried under section 229(a)(i). But it also ruled that Olubowale's actions were reckless because he knew his actions were likely to cause death (section 229(a)(ii)). The appeal was dismissed and the accused was ordered to stand trial for murder.

For Discussion

1. **When is a preliminary hearing held?**
2. **Why were Olubowale's actions considered reckless?**
3. **What would have happened if the appeal court had upheld the appeal?**

Resolution Discussions

Before trial, defence attorneys may encourage the accused to participate in a resolution discussion. The result can be a **plea negotiation,** commonly known as plea bargaining. Plea and sentencing decisions are discussed in these pre-trial resolution meetings. If there is strong evidence against the accused, the defence may encourage the person to plead guilty to a lesser charge in hope of receiving a lighter sentence. A guilty plea to a lesser charge benefits the court. It saves time and money and eliminates jury selection.

Plea negotiations may free up the court system, but they are not formally recognized in the *Criminal Code*. During discussions, the accused may give up the right to a fair public hearing in court, where he or she might receive a "not guilty" verdict. If the plea cannot be negotiated, any evidence that was revealed during the negotiations can be used at trial. This may weaken the position of the accused.

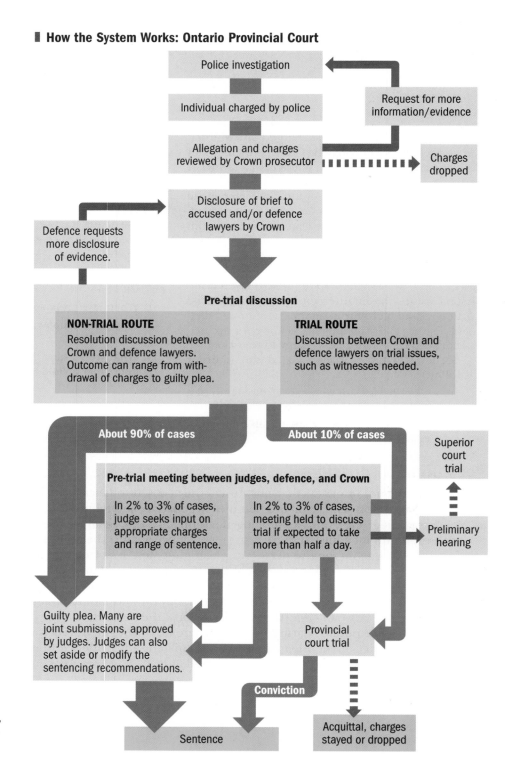

How the System Works: Ontario Provincial Court

Police investigation

Individual charged by police

Request for more information/evidence

Allegation and charges reviewed by Crown prosecutor

Charges dropped

Disclosure of brief to accused and/or defence lawyers by Crown

Defence requests more disclosure of evidence.

Pre-trial discussion

NON-TRIAL ROUTE
Resolution discussion between Crown and defence lawyers. Outcome can range from withdrawal of charges to guilty plea.

TRIAL ROUTE
Discussion between Crown and defence lawyers on trial issues, such as witnesses needed.

About 90% of cases

About 10% of cases

Superior court trial

Pre-trial meeting between judges, defence, and Crown

In 2% to 3% of cases, judge seeks input on appropriate charges and range of sentence.

In 2% to 3% of cases, meeting held to discuss trial if expected to take more than half a day.

Preliminary hearing

Guilty plea. Many are joint submissions, approved by judges. Judges can also set aside or modify the sentencing recommendations.

Provincial court trial

Conviction

Sentence

Acquittal, charges stayed or dropped

Figure 7-9

This diagram shows the process a case goes through, from the initial police investigation to sentencing.

Plea negotiations are often regarded as compromising justice. The 1993 plea bargain that resulted in a 12-year sentence for Karla Homolka led some experts to question its value and legitimacy. Homolka was sentenced before the public became aware of many of the gruesome facts that were revealed during the trial of her ex-husband Paul Bernardo. (The pair had been accused of torturing and killing several young women.) By court order, testimony in her case could not be reported until his trial was complete. Supporters of the Homolka plea bargain point out that Homolka's evidence, made available through plea negotiations, was needed to establish the strongest possible case against Bernardo (*R. v. Bernardo* (1995)).

Without plea negotiations, the court system would be overwhelmed by the number of cases going to trial. Through such negotiations, justice is served. The Crown obtains a conviction and the accused receives a penalty, although not the maximum one. It can save victims or their families a great deal of suffering. They do not have to take the witness stand and relive their ordeals.

Review Your Understanding (Pages 202 to 211)

1. What information does a defence lawyer use to prepare the background for a case?
2. Why is legal aid an important part of the legal system?
3. Why is disclosure an essential part of the criminal justice system?
4. How is forensic science used in the criminal justice process?
5. Explain the purpose of the DNA data bank.
6. What is the purpose of an adjournment?
7. On what basis does the *Criminal Code* establish the court in which a case will be tried?
8. What is a plea? What percentage of accused Canadians plead guilty?
9. (a) Identify the purpose of a preliminary hearing.
   (b) Under what circumstances would the accused skip a preliminary hearing?
10. Explain plea negotiation and outline the advantages and disadvantages of the process.

Should a Suspect Be Forced to Provide Samples for DNA Testing?

Deoxyribonucleic acid (DNA) contains the genetic code of life and is a powerful form of genetic fingerprinting. When a DNA sample is taken from someone, it is turned into an image that is unique to that individual, much like a fingerprint. The chances of any two individuals, except identical twins, having the same DNA image (print) is about one in 10 billion.

Since its discovery in 1984, DNA matching has been used over a thousand times in Canadian courts. Even microscopic traces of blood, bone, hair, saliva, or semen left at the scene of the crime contain DNA.

The importance of DNA testing was seen in the highly publicized case of Guy Paul Morin, who was convicted in 1992 of murdering nine-year-old Christine Jessop, his next-door neighbour (*R. v. Morin* (1993)). Six years earlier, he had been acquitted of the same crime. Following his second trial, he was sentenced

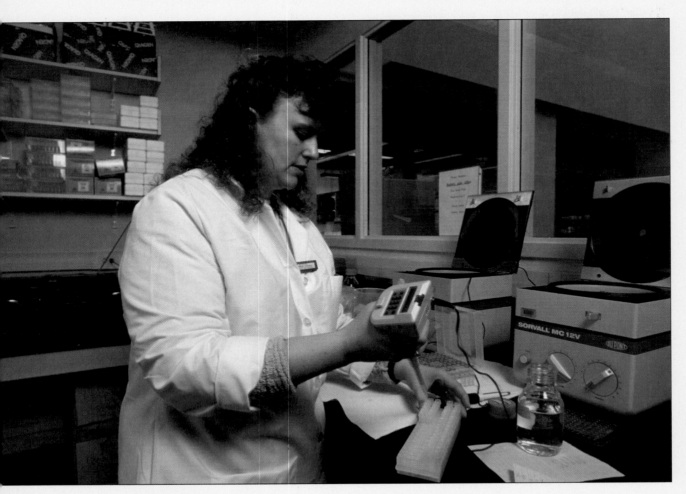

Figure 7-10

This scientist is working with DNA samples, an expensive and delicate operation.

to life imprisonment with no hope of parole for 25 years. In 1995, he was released from prison after DNA testing proved that he had not committed the crime. He received an apology from the Ontario government, and he and his family were awarded $1 250 000 in damages. (See also *Reference Re Milgaard* (1992), page 116.)

Despite its usefulness in solving crimes, DNA testing raises issues about the civil rights of Canadians. In 2000, the *Criminal Code* was changed to require that all persons convicted of serious crimes such as murder and sexual assault provide DNA samples to be kept on file. Crown attorneys can also ask judges for permission to obtain samples from people who have been convicted of lesser crimes. These samples must be given, even if the convicted person refuses to comply.

On One Side

Police consider DNA matching the biggest crime-solving breakthrough of the century. DNA testing can help to solve crimes quickly, and in many cases can eliminate suspects. Canadian police would like to follow the example of the British police force and collect DNA samples from anyone who is charged with a criminal offence. Arrested persons must provide these samples, even though they have not been convicted.

The public also largely supports DNA testing because it seems to increase public safety. Supporters of victims' rights want all suspects of violent crimes to provide DNA samples. A 1995 public opinion poll showed that 88 percent of Canadians support the use of DNA in criminal trials. They believe that since the purpose of DNA evidence is to determine the guilt or innocence of the suspect, there should be no argument about its use.

On the Other Side

Critics argue that compulsory DNA testing infringes upon the *Canadian Charter of Rights and Freedoms*. They feel that the individual's right to protection from unreasonable search and seizure is violated when suspects are forced to provide samples for DNA testing. They maintain compulsory DNA sampling is an invasion of privacy, similar to tapping a telephone or obtaining other evidence without a warrant.

Moreover, controversy surrounds the test itself. Scientists can never say with absolute certainty that two DNA samples are perfectly matched. They can only make a statement of probability. Critics say that more work needs to be done to improve the reliability and accuracy of DNA testing. They fear that juries could be overwhelmed by the scientific evidence of a DNA match. They may overlook other evidence that points to the innocence of accused persons.

The Bottom Line

There is no doubt that DNA tests are a powerful tool in police investigations. Should suspects be forced to provide samples for testing against their wishes? Or should the rights of the individual outweigh those of society?

What Do You Think?

1. What is meant by genetic fingerprinting?
2. Why is the Guy Paul Morin case considered to be so important? What would have happened to him without DNA testing?
3. What civil rights issues are raised by DNA testing?
4. Why do the police and victims' rights groups support compulsory DNA testing?
5. What arguments do the critics of DNA testing present?
6. State and explain your position on DNA testing. Use information from this Issue to support your opinion.

Chapter Review

Chapter Highlights

- Awareness of your legal rights and police powers will protect you.
- When making an arrest, the police must have reasonable grounds that the suspect committed the offence.
- When apprehending a suspect, the police can issue an appearance notice, arrest the suspect, or obtain a warrant.
- Police can use as much force as necessary to prevent an escape.
- Citizens can make an arrest under certain circumstances.
- Police are responsible for their behaviour and conduct when carrying out their duties.
- Police must inform those under arrest of their rights.
- Police must obtain a search warrant to search a private residence.
- Before trial, the accused can apply to be released on bail.
- Some arrested persons can apply for legal aid.
- Prior to a trial by jury, the Crown attorney and the defence meet to review the evidence.
- DNA testing has become an important part of collecting evidence.
- A preliminary hearing enables the provincial court to decide whether there is enough evidence to be tried by a higher court.

Review Key Terms

Name the key terms that are described below.

a) the use of medicine and science to solve legal problems

b) to look for evidence related to a charge

c) a lawyer on duty at the court

d) a document that names the offence with which the accused has been charged

e) a lie detector test

f) setting a trial over for a later date

g) an order to appear in court at a certain time and place

h) a document stating that the accused recognizes that he or she is being charged and promises to appear in court on a certain date

i) to be sent back into custody

j) the process of revealing all evidence to both sides

k) a document giving police the right to search a specific location

l) a written document made under oath by a police officer stating reasonable and probable grounds to believe an offence has been committed

m) the process of encouraging an accused to plead guilty to a lesser charge in hope of receiving a lighter sentence

n) to deprive a person of his or her liberty in order to lay a charge, preserve evidence, or prevent the person from committing another offence

o) a document signed by the accused with conditions to follow

p) a formal document naming the accused, listing the offence, and ordering the arrest

Check Your Knowledge

1. Outline the requirements for a legal arrest.

2. Identify the legal rights of an accused on arrest or detention.

3. Identify the powers of the police with regard to a proper search.

4. Identify the different types of pre-trial release and provide an example of each.

Apply Your Learning

5. Page was a back-seat passenger in a car stopped by police for speeding. When the police noticed several open beer cans near Page, they assumed he was guilty of drinking in public and demanded identification. Page refused to cooperate and became obnoxious and demanded to be let go. The police refused and Page became noisier and began to cause a disturbance. The police then arrested him. A shoving and pushing match then broke out. Page was charged with two counts of assault.

   a) Why was Page charged with assault?

   b) Should Page be found guilty of assault? Explain.

6. *R. v. Van Haarlem* (1991), 64 C.C.C. (3d) 543 (British Columbia Court of Appeal)

Van Haarlem was charged with attempted murder, robbery, and unlawful confinement. As part of his release conditions, he was not to contact any person who had been called as a witness at the preliminary hearing. The following day, by chance, he met an officer whom he had known for many years and who had testified at the preliminary hearing. They agreed not to talk about the case. In the course of their conversation, Van Haarlem made an incriminating remark, indicating that he would have pleaded guilty if not for the fact that an acquaintance had testified against him at the preliminary hearing.

a) For what reason did the accused plead not guilty at the preliminary hearing?

b) Should the incriminating remark evidence be admitted? Why or why not?

7. *R. v. Broyles*, [1991] 3 S.C.R. 595 (Supreme Court of Canada)

Broyles was convicted of second-degree murder. The body of the victim was found under a stairwell seven days after her death. The police arranged for a friend to visit him while he was in custody. They provided the friend with a body-pack recording device. The friend encouraged Broyles to ignore his lawyer's advice to keep silent. The tape recording established that Broyles knew the victim was dead the day that she went missing. On the recording, Broyles admitted, "the cops don't know that I knew she was downstairs." The evidence was admitted to the court and Broyles was convicted. He appealed to the Supreme Court of Canada.

a) On what basis would Broyles appeal his conviction?

b) Were the police justified in their actions in this case? Explain.

c) On the basis of the information provided, why do you think the Supreme Court of Canada allowed the appeal? Explain.

8. *R. v. Smith*, [1991] 1 S.C.R. 714 (Supreme Court of Canada)

Smith, severely beaten in a fight, left the scene but returned with a shotgun and shot the victim in the face and the chest. He surrendered to police. The police read him his rights and Smith indicated he understood them. Before consulting a lawyer, he made a statement in which he admitted the shooting. He said that he was drunk and provoked. After his statement was taken, the police advised Smith that the victim had died. Smith appealed his conviction on the basis that he was not informed on his arrest of the fact that the victim was dead.

a) How would the fact that Smith was drunk and provoked affect the charge laid against him?

b) Did the police proceed properly? Explain.

Communicate Your Understanding

9. In groups, role-play an arrest by outlining the dialogue that should take place between a police officer and a suspect. Select a *Criminal Code* offence that you have previously studied and identify the section number from the Code. Ensure that the requirements of the *Canadian Charter of Rights and Freedoms* are met with your arrest procedure.

10. Adapted from an article in *The Toronto Star*, March 10, 2001, p. A27

A motorist was ordered to pull over by a police officer. He refused and stepped on the gas. A chase took place at twice the speed limit and he went through a red light. Finally, he was cornered by four squad cars. He fell out of the car drunk. His blood–alcohol level was three times above the legal limit. In a plea bargain, the charges of having too much alcohol in his blood and fleeing police were dropped. He pleaded guilty to impaired driving. The *Criminal Code* states that the punishment for impaired driving for a first offender ranges from a $600 fine to a one- to three-year licence suspension. A plea bargain was negotiated, and the Crown and the defence recommended a $600 fine and a one-year suspension in return for a guilty verdict. The judge considered the following factors: the defendant's apology; he had a steady job; he had not hurt anyone; and he was a first-time offender.

The judge suspended his licence for a year and sentenced him to 30 days. He was allowed to serve his time at home.

Outline the position of the Crown and defence in their plea bargain. Outline the position of the judge with respect to the sentence issued. Write a one-paragraph reaction to this case and how the process of plea bargaining is used in the criminal process.

11. In pairs, select one of the topics below. One student will prepare an argument in favour of the statement and the other student will prepare a counterargument against the statement. Support your arguments with examples. Share your opinions.
a) Police should have the right to go on strike.
b) Everyone in Canada should be photographed and fingerprinted to make law enforcement easier.
c) Police should not carry guns except under special circumstances.
d) Anyone with a criminal record should not be released on bail.
e) Police should be forbidden from engaging in high-speed chases.

Develop Your Thinking

12. Assume that you are a member of a civil liberties association that wants to ensure that individual rights are protected at all costs. Outline the legal rights that you feel must be given to an accused person. Now, assume you are the head of a police services board that wants to make sure that society is protected at all costs. Outline the types of actions that you feel police are justified in using to protect society. Use examples from the text or other sources to support each position.

13. A police officer was demoted for failing to meet quotas (fixed numbers) for laying charges. The officer was expected to lay four *Criminal Code* charges, three liquor-licence charges, and five radar-related traffic charges each month. Should police officers have a quota system? Explain.

Chapter 8

Trial Procedures

Focus Questions

- How does the adversarial system work?
- What procedures are followed in selecting a jury?
- What different types of evidence can be used by the Crown and the defence?
- What defences can the accused use?
- What is the significance of the judge's charge to the jury?
- What sections of the *Charter* apply to evidence and the rights of the accused?

Chapter at a Glance

Figure 8-1

The judges of the Supreme Court of Canada are formally called "Justices." They are chosen from the highest courts in the provinces and territories. What do you already know about the role of judges?

8.1   Introduction

Trial procedures in Canada are based on the **adversarial system,** which involves two opposing sides: the Crown (representing society) and the defence (representing the accused). The onus is on the Crown to prove beyond a reasonable doubt that the accused committed the offence. For a conviction, both the *actus reus* ("wrongful deed") and *mens rea* ("guilty mind") elements of the offence must be proven.

As you learned in Chapter 4, the type of offence committed determines the kind of trial available to the accused. This chapter focuses on trial by judge and jury. If the accused is tried in a provincial court for a summary conviction or indictable offence, trial procedures are similar to trial by judge and jury. No jury is chosen, however, and the proceedings are less formal. The judge acts as both judge and jury.

8.2   Courtroom Organization & Beginning Motions

Canadian trial procedures are adapted from English law and are basically the same in each province and territory. The roles of various people involved in these procedures are outlined on the pages that follow.

▎A Typical Canadian Courtroom

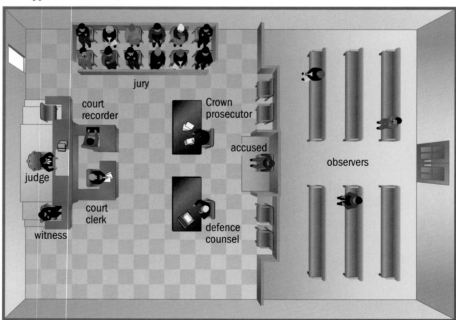

Figure 8-2

This diagram shows the participants in the criminal justice system. Do you know what role each individual plays in the trial process?

Courtroom Organization

The Judge

Judges are often referred to as "the Bench" or "the Court." The federal government appoints all judges except for provincial or territorial court judges, who are appointed by each province and territory. The judges of the Supreme Court of Canada are formally titled "Justices." They are paid by the federal government and are generally chosen from among the highest courts of the provinces and territories or from among lawyers who have had at least 10 years of experience.

Judges have full control of the courtroom during preliminary hearings and trials. They can exclude the public—and even the accused—if they think this is necessary to administer justice and maintain order. Cameras of any sort are generally not permitted in Canadian courtrooms. Broadcasts of Supreme Court of Canada hearings, however, have become quite routine.

The decisions judges make on whether evidence and questioning are admissible can greatly influence the outcome of trials. They can also form the basis for appeals. In non-jury trials, the judge decides the question of guilt and sets the sentence.

Some jurisdictions also appoint justices of the peace, who have less power than judges. Justices of the peace may preside over the court of first appearance, where the charge against the accused (defendant) is first read. They may also issue documents for police, such as search and arrest warrants, and certain documents for judicial matters. In some jurisdictions, justices of the peace may conduct trials for offences against municipal bylaws and provincial laws, such as the *Highway Traffic Act*.

The Crown Prosecutor

Because crime is considered to be an act against society, governments hire lawyers to be Crown prosecutors (Crown attorneys). Prosecutors are responsible to see that justice is done. As you have already learned, the "burden of proof" is on the Crown. This means the Crown prosecutor must prove beyond a reasonable doubt that the accused committed the offence.

Crown prosecutors must present all available evidence, even if it may weaken their case. If necessary, the judge can direct the prosecutor to call witnesses whose **testimony** (declarations sworn under oath) may damage the Crown's case. Prosecutors have great influence. For example, they consult with police on cases and decide whether to lay criminal charges. They can also withdraw charges that have been laid.

The Defence Counsel

The defence counsel represents the accused to ensure that their legal rights are protected. The accused can represent themselves in lower courts, but it is usually wise to hire professional counsel. Because lawyers are trained in procedural and substantive law, they can direct a case through the courts. They will also advise clients on the law involved in the case and how best to proceed. Defence lawyers must represent their clients to the best of their ability, even in cases where the crime is very offensive to the public.

You Be the JUDGE

In June 2001, the Supreme Court of Canada ruled that Quebec judge Richard Therrien should be fired for hiding a criminal conviction of harbouring (giving shelter to) Front de libération du Québec (FLQ) members in 1971, when he was a 19-year-old law student. Therrien had an excellent reputation and the conviction had been pardoned. The Court stated that a "judge is a 'place apart' in our society and must conform to the demands of this exceptional status."

- Was the Supreme Court ruling justified, or did it discriminate against someone based on his past? Explain.

activity

Visit **www.law.nelson.com** to learn about the Justices of the Supreme Court of Canada.

The Court Clerk and Court Recorder

The **court clerk** reads out the charge against the accused, swears in witnesses, tags evidence, and handles much of the paperwork and routine tasks required by the court.

The **court recorder** sits near the witness box to record, word for word, all evidence given and all questions and comments made during a trial. Because the court relies on an accurate record and may request that evidence be read back, this is a very exacting job. These records are kept and transcripts are made available later, if necessary, for appeals.

The Sheriff

The sheriff and his or her deputies carry out much of the court administration and trial preparation. It is their job to make sure the accused appears in court, to find prospective jurors, and to assist the judge. The sheriff also serves summonses and carries out court orders, such as seizing and selling property to settle claims for damages.

Other Court Officials

Probation officers may be present in provincial or territorial courts, and judges may ask them to conduct interviews with convicted offenders. Such information may help judges in setting sentences.

Nonprofit organizations such as the John Howard Society, Elizabeth Fry Society, and Salvation Army may have representatives in court to help defendants. Services to help victims are also more easily available than they were in the past.

ⓔ activity

Visit **www.law.nelson.com** to learn about nonprofit organizations that help people involved in the criminal justice system.

Case

Nelles v. Ontario

[1989] 2 S.C.R. 170
Supreme Court of Canada

In March 1981, nurse Susan Nelles was charged with murdering four infants at Toronto's Hospital for Sick Children. Nelles was held in isolation for five days and released on $50 000 bail given by her mother. At the conclusion of the preliminary inquiry, Justice David Vanek discharged Nelles on all counts. "I fear the rather astonishing fact is that there is simply no case against Susan Nelles at all," he stated.

In 1985, Nelles sued the Ontario attorney general's office and the two Crown prosecutors in charge of her case for malicious prosecution. She claimed financial compensation for the pain, public humiliation, and mental anguish that she had suffered since 1981. Two lower courts had ruled that Nelles could not sue because attorneys general and Crown prosecutors are **immune** (completely protected) from such legal action.

The Supreme Court of Canada judgment, however, stated: "Granting an absolute immunity to prosecutors is akin to granting a licence to subvert individual rights." In other words, Nelles could pursue her lawsuit. The Supreme Court made it clear, however, that there must be proof that the prosecutors had laid charges without reasonable and probable grounds and displayed "malice in the form of deliberate and improper conduct."

In 1991, the Ontario government agreed to pay Nelles $60 000 for the "severe mental anguish" she suffered after being wrongly accused. Nelles received an additional $30 000, and a scholarship

continued ▶

of $20 000 was established in her name at Queen's University School of Nursing. An endowment fund of $10 000 was also set up in memory of her father and brother. Both were doctors and both had died during the decade-long legal battle. Family friends speculated that the stress contributed to their deaths. The province also paid $255 000 in legal fees to Nelles. It was the first time the province of Ontario had paid an individual for personal suffering caused by criminal proceedings that ended in a dismissal.

For Discussion

1. **What significant precedent did the Supreme Court set in this case? Why do you think it is considered a landmark decision?**

2. **In your opinion, should the state be responsible for the acts of the Crown prosecutors, or should Crown prosecutors be personally liable? Explain.**

Motions at the Beginning of a Trial

At the beginning of a trial, the Crown prosecutor and the defence may present motions to the judge. These can relate to any procedure that will be used during the trial. One such motion, a **stay of proceedings,** can stop the trial until further action is taken. In some circumstances, a stay of proceedings can stop the trial from proceeding at all. The case of *R. v. Askov* was very controversial in this regard, and it led to thousands of cases being stayed.

Case

R. v. Askov

[1990] 2 S.C.R. 1199
Supreme Court of Canada

Askov, Melo, Hussey, and Gugliotta were charged with conspiracy to commit extortion against Belmont. Belmont operated a Montreal agency that supplied exotic dancers to licensed premises in Ontario. He wanted to enter the Toronto market, where Melo was the supplier.

Belmont told police Melo had demanded a 50 percent commission to operate in Toronto, and an undercover officer was assigned to act as Belmont's driver and bodyguard. Belmont refused to pay the commission and was threatened with a sawed-off shotgun and knife by Melo and Askov. Two more men were arrested later, and all four spent almost six months in custody before being released on bail.

The Crown prepared to set a preliminary hearing date in December 1983, which was rescheduled to February 1984 at the request of the accused. On that date, all counsel agreed to July 4, 1984, as the new date for the preliminary hearing. Because of courtroom scheduling conflicts, the preliminary hearing could not be completed until September— 10 months after the arrests. The accused were ordered to stand trial. The earliest trial date was October 1985, almost two years after the arrests. In October 1985, the case was again delayed. Other cases had priority. A trial was rescheduled for September 1986.

The trial began nearly three years after the arrests. The defence moved to stay the proceedings on the grounds that the trial had been unreasonably delayed and that this had violated the defendants' rights as guaranteed under section 11(b) of the *Charter*. The judge agreed and stayed the charges.

The Crown appealed to the Ontario Court of Appeal, which ordered the trial to proceed. It found there was no misconduct on the part of the Crown, no indication of any objection by the accused to adjournments, and no evidence of prejudice to the accused. This was appealed to the Supreme Court of Canada, which set aside the appeal court judgment and stayed the proceedings.

continued ▶

The Supreme Court ruled that four factors must be considered in determining whether the delay in bringing the accused to trial had been unreasonable: length of the delay, explanation for the delay, waiver of time period, and prejudice to the accused.

The Court also indicated: "The delay is of such an inordinate length that public confidence in the administration of justice must be shaken.... Justice so delayed is an affront to the individual, to the community, and to the very administration of justice." The Court suggested a guideline of institutional delay of eight to ten months for proceedings in Provincial Court, and six to eight months from the preliminary hearing until trial.

For Discussion

1. What right is guaranteed by section 11(b) of the *Charter*?
2. What was the main cause of the delays in this situation?
3. Indicate how each of the four criteria set by the Supreme Court of Canada was met in the Askov case.
4. Why is it so important to have a trial within a reasonable time for (a) the accused, (b) society, (c) victims, and (d) witnesses?
5. Should the time limits set by the Supreme Court of Canada be applied rigidly? Why or why not?

Review Your Understanding (Pages 216 to 220)

1. a) What system of trial procedures is used in Canada?
   b) Describe the roles of the parties involved and their functions.
2. Who appoints judges to the various levels of courts?
3. For what reason have judges been held to a higher standard of conduct than ordinary people?
4. Which side in a criminal trial bears the burden of proof?
5. Why is the role of court recorder so important to the appeal process?
6. Why might motions be made at the beginning of a trial?
7. Explain the significance of a stay of proceedings.

8.3 Juries and Jury Selection

Although the jury system is not perfect, it usually satisfies the public more than trial by judge. A jury lets the public see conflicts resolved by peers, rather than by a judge alone. A jury also reflects the conscience of the community. Juries are expensive, however, and they are used only for the more serious indictable offences. For certain less severe indictable offences, the accused can choose between trial by judge or trial by judge and jury. A judge alone will try the accused for summary offences. See pages 155 to 157 for a list of summary and indictable offences.

Advantages of Trial by Jury

Trial by jury involves the public in the administration of justice, which also helps to educate the public. The use of juries means that judges do not have to make all court decisions. Juries are composed of people from many different backgrounds, who bring a fresh perspective to the courtroom and

▌ Offences Requiring Trial by Jury

- murder
- treason
- alarming Her Majesty
- intimidating Parliament or a legislature
- bribery by the holder of a judicial office
- seditious (or subversive) offences

- piracy or piratical acts
- inciting to mutiny
- attempting or conspiring to commit any of the above offences
- accessory to murder or treason

Figure 8-3

Should an accused person always be able to choose the form of trial he or she wants? Explain.

who can reject oppressive laws. As well, a jury may base its decision on current social values, rather than strict legal precedent.

Trial by jury also has advantages for the accused. The defence needs to convince only one juror to favour the accused or have reasonable doubt: a jury's decision must be unanimous. Dramatic rhetoric may be more likely to move a juror than a judge, who hears lawyers' arguments routinely. Moreover, a jury may feel empathy for the accused, especially if the charge is one with which they identify.

Advantages of Trial by Judge

Trial by judge also has advantages. Judges may be less prejudiced than some jurors, who may look down on an accused who is poorly dressed, for example. Some jurors may also allow disgust at an offence—such as child abuse or impaired driving—to cloud their judgment. Legal technicalities may also confuse jurors. A jury may be as convinced by the eloquence of a good Crown prosecutor or defence counsel as by actual evidence. A judge is trained to make a decision based on the facts and the law. Finally, a judge presents reasons for the decision—a jury does not. These reasons may help either side to determine grounds for an appeal.

Jury Selection

Empanelling—the process of selecting the 12 jurors—can take many days. First, a list of jurors is created from a list of all people living in the area where the court is located. The list is usually computer-generated according to scientific criteria. A selection committee headed by the sheriff then randomly picks 75 to 100 names from the list. The people selected are summoned to appear at the court by notice from the sheriff. The more controversial the case, the more people are called. A prospective juror who does not appear can be issued a warrant and can even be criminally charged.

At the start of a trial, prospective jurors assemble in the courtroom. Cards bearing each name are placed in a barrel, and each person steps forward after his or her name is drawn. The judge may exempt anyone with a personal interest in the case, a relationship with a trial participant, or a personal hardship. The

Figure 8-4

Gillian Guess (left) was convicted of obstruction of justice in 1998 in Vancouver for having an affair with the accused while serving on the jury hearing his case. She was the first juror in Canada ever to be charged with willfully obstructing justice.

ℯ activity

Visit **www.law.nelson.com** and follow the links to learn more about the selection process and the responsibilities of a juror.

For the trial of Socrates more than 2400 years ago, there were 500 jurors. The guilty decision was by a vote of 280 to 220.

- Are 12 jurors enough people to provide a cross-section of society? Explain your opinion.

Figure 8-5

What other categories of people do you believe should be exempted from jury duty?

judge can also direct a juror to stand aside for any reasonable cause. If a full jury cannot be selected from the remaining prospective jurors, those asked to stand aside will be called again. The defence and the Crown prosecutor can then accept or reject them as jurors.

The judge decides what questions prospective jurors can be asked. In selecting a jury, the Crown and defence must consider the value systems of prospective jurors. For example, how might an older male, a feminist, an older female, or a young bachelor view the accused in a case involving obscenity? Ethnicity, religion, age, financial status, occupation, sexual orientation, intelligence, and gender are only a few characteristics that are considered.

Each province or territory determines who can serve on a jury. Generally, prospective jurors must be Canadian citizens, between the ages of 18 and 69, and speak either English or French. See Figure 8-5 for a list of people who are usually exempted from jury duty.

▌People Usually Exempted from Jury Duty

- MPs, senators, members of provincial legislatures and municipal governments
- judges, justices of the peace, lawyers, law students
- doctors, coroners, veterinarians
- law enforcement officers, special constables, sheriffs, prison wardens and guards, and their spouses
- people who are visually impaired
- people with a mental or physical disability that seriously impairs their ability to complete jury duty
- anyone who has served on a jury within the preceding two or three years
- anyone convicted of an indictable offence that has not been pardoned

The Challenges

The Crown prosecutor and the defence counsel each want a jury responsive to their position. So, they challenge, eliminate, or accept various prospective jurors. The defence has the first right to challenge a prospective juror. After that, the prosecutor and the defence alternate the first right of challenge. Three types of challenges can be used to eliminate prospective jurors.

Challenge of Jury List

Either side can challenge the jury list. Usually, this will only succeed if it can be shown that the sheriff or selection committee was fraudulent or partial, or showed willful misconduct in selecting prospective jurors. For example, the selection committee may have excluded any citizens from a particular ethnic group. However, there is no requirement that there must be a person on the jury who has the same ethnic origin as the accused.

Challenge for Cause

A **challenge for cause** is made on the basis that prospective jurors do not meet the provincial or territorial requirements governing juries. For instance, perhaps they are not on the jury list or are in an exempted category. They may have formed an opinion on the case, or they may not speak and understand English or French.

Any number of challenges for cause can be made, as long as the judge rules the causes are valid. If the defence does challenge for cause, the Crown can try to prove the cause is untrue. The judge will appoint the last two of the jurors who have already been selected, or two other persons, to decide if the challenge should be accepted.

Peremptory Challenge

A **peremptory challenge** allows both the defence and the Crown to eliminate a prospective juror without giving a reason. Each side is allowed a set number of peremptory challenges, based on the charge:
- high treason or first-degree murder—20 challenges
- a charge where the penalty is five years or over—12 challenges
- a charge where the penalty is under five years—4 challenges

If the full jury of 12 cannot be selected because of challenges, more prospective jurors can be called from the jury list. In some circumstances, the judge may order the sheriff to take prospective jurors off the street.

Case

R. v. Find

(2001) 82 C.R.R. (2d) 247
Supreme Court of Canada

Karl Find was tried on 21 charges of sexual assault involving three complainants who were between six and 12 years of age when the alleged offences took place. Prior to jury selection, the defence applied to challenge prospective jurors for cause on the basis that they might be prejudiced against Find. The defence believed that the ages of the alleged victims, the high number of alleged assaults, and the alleged use of violence might make jurors partial to the alleged victims.

Defence counsel proposed to ask prospective jurors these questions:
- Do you have strong feelings about the issue of rape and violence on young children?
- If so, what are those feelings based on?
- Would those strong feelings concerning the rape and violence on young children prevent you from giving Mr. Find a fair trial based solely on the evidence given during the trial of this case?

The trial judge rejected the request, stating that it did not fall within the *Criminal Code*, section

638(1)(b). This section states that a challenge for cause exists if the juror "is not indifferent between the Queen and the accused."

Later, during empanelling, a prospective juror, the father of two children, said: "I just don't think I could separate myself from my feelings towards them and the case." The defence peremptorily challenged the man.

The defence later appealed the trial judge's decision not to allow the challenge for cause to the Supreme Court of Ontario and the Supreme Court of Canada on the grounds that Find's *Charter* rights had been violated. Both courts upheld the trial judge's decision.

In both appeals, Find cited *R. v. Koh* (1998). In this case, the Ontario Court of Appeal ruled in 1998 that a challenge for cause should be permitted if requested by an accused who is a member of a visible minority. A possible question in this situation could be: "Would your ability to judge the evidence in this case without bias, prejudice, or partiality be affected by the fact that the person charged with the offence is of East Asian/Chinese origin?"

The Ontario Court of Appeal drew a distinction between racial prejudice and prejudice against persons charged with sexual assault. Racial prejudice

continued ▶

is a "want of indifference towards the accused." The connection between racial prejudice and a particular accused is direct and logical. Prejudice against persons charged with sexual assault, however "is a want of indifference towards the nature of a crime and will rarely, if ever, translate into partiality in respect of the accused."

In its decision, the Supreme Court of Canada also ruled that Find was not entitled to challenge the prospective jurors for cause. The aim of the jury selection process is to find impartial, not favourable, jurors, the Court said. To allow a challenge for cause under section 638(1)(b), it must be shown that there is widespread bias in the community, and that this bias might influence the decision-making process of the jury.

For Discussion

1. **What is the difference between a peremptory challenge and a challenge for cause?**

2. **What do you think "indifferent between the Queen and the accused" mean?**

3. **On what section of the *Canadian Charter of Rights and Freedoms* did Find's defence rely?**

4. **What is the difference between "racial prejudice" as presented in *R. v. Koh* and "prejudice against persons charged with sexual assault"?**

5. **What is a bias?**

6. **What conditions did the Supreme Court of Canada say must exist if a challenge for cause on the basis of impartiality is to succeed?**

7. **If you were a juror in *R. v. Find*, would the nature of the alleged offences influence your partiality? Explain.**

Jury Duty

After being selected, each juror is sworn in and then sits in the jury box. Prospective jurors who were not selected can leave, but they may have to return for later trials held during that session of the court. Selected jurors may also be required to return for later trials. The judge may waive this requirement, particularly if a trial is lengthy.

At the start of a trial, the judge informs jurors of their duties. They may or may not take notes, depending on the judge and jurisdiction. In all trials, however, jurors must not

- discuss the case with anyone other than other jurors
- follow media reports about the case
- disclose any information from jury discussions that is not revealed in open court

During most trials, jurors go home at the end of each day. The judge may, however, **sequester** the jury for the entire trial. This means the jury is housed and fed away from home until they reach their formal decision—the **verdict.** Jurors are isolated from families, friends, and work and can communicate only with one another and the court officer appointed to look after their needs. Sequestering is used to prevent jurors from being influenced by outside information or by anyone with an interest in the case. Thus, the verdict should be based solely on evidence presented in court. In all trials, jurors are sequestered when they retire to reach a verdict.

A juror can be discharged during a trial if he or she is unable to continue for a valid reason. If the jury falls below 10 jurors, however, a new trial must be ordered. Jurors may be entitled to a token payment for their services, which increases if the trial is lengthy.

You Be the JUDGE

In past centuries, jurors were instructed that they must agree on a verdict and would not be discharged until they did so. The jury was sequestered in the jury room without food, drink—or heat— until it reached a verdict.

- Should jurors ever be sequestered? Discuss.

1. Identify the advantages and the disadvantages to the accused of a trial by jury?
2. How does the use of juries benefit the legal system?
3. Describe the steps followed in jury selection.
4. Identify eight categories of people who are excluded from jury duty, and give one reason why you think each category is ineligible.
5. In a table, summarize the jury challenges available to the Crown and to the defence.
6. Describe three grounds on which a prospective juror may be challenged for cause.
7. Explain sequestering and identify the circumstances under which juries are sequestered today.

8.4 Presentation of Evidence

After the judge has instructed the jury, the actual trial begins.

Arraignment

The first step in the trial proper is the **arraignment,** or the reading of the charge to the accused. This must be the charge contained in the indictment or an acquittal may result. The accused then enters a plea of guilty or not guilty. If the accused refuses to plead, a not-guilty plea is entered on his or her behalf. The accused is usually arraigned in his or her first court appearance, and rearraigned for trials in higher courts.

Crown Evidence

Section 11(d) of the *Charter* guarantees that any accused person is "presumed innocent until proven guilty." After the arraignment, the onus is on the Crown to rebut—to counter or disprove—this presumption of innocence.

The Crown first presents an opening statement, which summarizes its case against the accused. It then calls evidence in the form of witness testimony and exhibits. All evidence that is relevant, reliable, and fair is admissible. The Supreme Court of Canada has ruled that it is not necessary for the Crown to call obvious witnesses, even the victim, if the relevant evidence that person might give can be presented in other ways.

Direct evidence is usually obtained in the testimony of witnesses who actually saw the offence being committed. In many instances, however, there may be no such witnesses. Direct evidence is the most common kind of evidence, but it is not the most reliable. Eyewitness accounts may be contradictory, and witnesses may not recall what they saw with complete accuracy. Their memories may change over time.

Figure 8-6

In 1959, 14-year-old Steven Truscott was convicted of raping and murdering a 12-year-old girl on purely circumstantial evidence. He was sentenced to hang, but was released after spending 10 years in prison.

ⓔ activity

Visit **www.law.nelson.com** and follow the links to learn more about the Steven Truscott case.

Circumstantial evidence is indirect evidence. It can indicate that it is highly probable the accused is the only one who could have committed the criminal offence. Generally, however, circumstantial evidence alone is not enough to convict. In *R. v. Truscott* (1967), however, the Supreme Court of Canada stated that circumstantial evidence alone was enough to convict "if the evidence presented to the jury points conclusively to the accused as the perpetrator of the crime and excludes any reasonable hypothesis of innocence."

Evidence must be proven as it is presented. If a glove was found at the scene of the crime, it must be proven that the glove being entered as an exhibit is that same glove. If counsel is claiming that a certain person owned the glove, it must also prove that fact. Some evidence is easily proven. Fingerprints may connect a gun to its owner, or DNA tests may link the accused to the scene of a crime. Once evidence has been presented and proven, the jury, or the judge in a non-jury trial, must decide which facts they believe.

The **examination-in-chief** is the first questioning of a witness. Because the Crown interviews its witnesses during preparation, it knows what answers to expect. Therefore, it can ask no **leading questions** during an examination-in-chief. Leading questions indicate the answer, generally a "yes" or "no" response. "Did you see the accused driving a yellow car through the red light at 1:45 A.M.?" is a leading question, as opposed to, "What happened at the intersection at 1:45 A.M.?"

After the Crown is finished, the defence cross-examines the witness and may use leading questions. The judge and jury then weigh the evidence to decide what evidence is the most convincing. Here the witness's **credibility** (reliability) is a key factor. The Crown may reexamine the witness in relation to points brought up by the defence. If the judge permits, the defence may then recross-examine. Either side will often ask questions that have little to do with the case, but that may reveal the character of the witness.

The purpose of a trial is to find the truth. The process of a trial is to test the truth of evidence. This allows each side to get more information from the other side's witnesses and to uncover any conflicts or contradictions with evidence they may have given previously. Because the jury must decide the question of guilt solely on the basis of evidence, both sides will try to cast doubt on the other side's evidence. Once the Crown has called all its witnesses, it rests its case. It can reopen its case only if the judge decides that it would serve justice to do so.

Defence Evidence

Before it calls any evidence, the defence can make a motion for a **directed verdict.** The defence will do this only if it believes the Crown has not proven its case. If the judge agrees that the essential elements of an offence (*actus reus* and *mens rea*) have not been proven, he or she will instruct the jury to give a directed verdict of "not guilty."

If the judge rejects the defence motion for a directed verdict, the case continues. The defence then presents its case. Again, to win its case, the defence only needs to establish a reasonable doubt about whether the accused committed the offence. It does not have to prove that the accused is innocent.

The defence usually summarizes what it hopes to show and then presents evidence in the form of witnesses. Now it is the defence side that cannot ask leading questions. As the Crown cross-examines witnesses to rebut defence evidence, it may use leading questions. The Crown may also give evidence in reply if the defence raises a new matter that the Crown had no opportunity to deal with during its examination-in-chief. The defence then has the right to present **surrebuttal** (evidence to counter the Crown's rebuttal evidence).

▋ Steps in Presenting Evidence

1. Crown starts with examination-in-chief of witness.
2. Defence may cross-examine witness.
3. Crown may reexamine witness.
4. Defence may recross-examine with judge's permission.
5. Defence presents evidence.
6. Crown may cross-examine witness.
7. Defence may reexamine witness.
8. Crown may make rebuttal.
9. Defence may make surrebuttal.

Figure 8-7

What is the goal of the Crown and the defence in presenting evidence to a jury? Should the Crown have to call the victim as a witness so that the defence has an opportunity to cross-examine? Explain.

Witnesses

Before the trial, the Crown gives the defence a list of Crown witnesses. Either the Crown or the defence may pay witnesses, but only if they are expert witnesses whose special knowledge can help the court. Although witnesses usually appear voluntarily, they may be served a **subpoena,** a court document that orders them to appear. A witness who refuses to appear can be served with an arrest warrant and detained for 30 days. If a judge finds it is justified, the witness may be detained for up to 90 days. Any witness who fails to attend a trial to give evidence may be found guilty of **contempt of court** and fined or imprisoned for 90 days.

Once the trial begins, the defence can ask to have witnesses who have not yet testified removed from the courtroom. This is done to keep witnesses from changing their testimony. As each witness takes the stand, he or she must take an **oath** (swear to tell the truth) on the Bible or make an **affirmation** (a solemn and formal declaration) to tell the truth.

A witness who knowingly gives false evidence with intent to mislead commits the criminal offence of **perjury.** It is also an offence for a witness to give contradictory evidence. The maximum penalty for both offences is 14 years' imprisonment.

Anyone who can understand the nature of the oath or the affirmation and the questions asked by the various parties can be called as a witness. If a witness is found not to be mentally competent, his or her evidence can be declared inadmissible. A child who does not understand the nature of an oath or affirmation can give unsworn evidence, providing the child understands the need to tell the truth. In the charge to the jury, the judge should indicate the admissibility of such evidence. Because children may be frightened, the judge may allow them to give evidence from behind a screen and, for certain sexual offences, on videotape.

An **adverse witness** is hostile to a particular position and may be called by both the defence and the Crown. The side that calls an adverse witness cannot bring forward evidence of the witness's bad character. It can, however, contradict the adverse witness by offering other evidence. With the court's permission, it can also present previous statements the witness made that conflict with his or her present testimony.

The accused does not have to take the witness stand. If the accused exhibits a poor attitude or appearance, it may be in his or her best interest not to take the stand. This may also be true if the Crown's cross-examination asks the accused questions that could lead to conviction. The fact that the accused does not take the stand should not be a factor in determining whether the Crown has proved its case. Regardless, a jury, or the judge in a non-jury trial, may view it as an indication of guilt.

The most important aspect of witness testimony is its credibility. Witnesses are often asked repeatedly to recall things that they heard or saw. This is done to see if their answers are the same as in earlier accounts. Each side hopes to discredit the other's witnesses. Evidence will often be contradictory, but that does not mean that witnesses are lying. People see things differently. Besides credibility, the weight that should be given to evidence is also significant. It is up to the jury, or the judge in a non-jury trial, to decide on the credibility of a witness and the weight his or her evidence deserves.

▌Questions a Judge or Juror Should Ask of Evidence

☑ Does the witness have an interest in the outcome of the case?

☑ Has the witness been influenced about the case since the offence occurred?

☑ Do other witnesses support this witness's evidence?

☑ Does the witness's testimony conflict with evidence he or she has given earlier?

Figure 8-8

What is the judge or juror trying to find out about evidence by asking these questions? What questions could you add to this list?

Rules of Evidence

Rules of evidence have developed over many years and are very complex. Most are contained in common law, but there are also provisions in statute law, such as the *Canada Evidence Act*. If the admissibility of evidence is questioned during a trial, the judge will order a *voir dire*. This is a trial within a trial to see if evidence can be shown to the jury. After the jury has left the courtroom, the Crown and defence present their positions to the judge. Even the accused may have to take the stand. The judge considers the presentations and the rules of evidence and then decides whether all, none, or part of the evidence is admissible. The jury then returns, and the trial continues.

Self-Incrimination

Section 13 of the *Canadian Charter of Rights and Freedoms* protects witnesses from **self-incrimination,** which is behaviour or evidence that indicates one's guilt. It clearly states that evidence a witness gives in a court must not be used later to "incriminate that witness in any other proceeding." This encourages witnesses to answer all questions.

The *Canada Evidence Act* states that a witness can object to questions on the grounds of self-incrimination. As with the *Charter,* evidence that a witness has given in one court cannot be used against him or her in another criminal court case. The only exception is in a case of perjury. Police can also use evidence a witness has given in court to gain more evidence to lay a charge against that witness. For example, Kyla testifies that she shot the prison guard, not Gunnar, who is charged with the murder. The Crown cannot use Kyla's testimony as a basis for charging her with the murder of the guard. Her admission may, however, lead police to investigate. If they find enough new evidence to indicate that Kyla did indeed commit the offence, they can lay a charge of murder against her based on that evidence—and that evidence alone.

Case

R. v. White

[1999] 2 S.C.R. 417
Supreme Court of Canada

Lawrence O'Brien was struck by a vehicle while changing a tire near Fernie, British Columbia, and died a few hours later. The next morning, Joann White telephoned the RCMP and advised them that while driving the night before, she had swerved to miss a deer and had hit a man. She panicked and left the scene. White gave the same information to an officer who visited her home and was then read her rights. She then contacted a lawyer, who told her not to give any statement to the police.

The officer then asked White if it was true she had swerved to miss a deer. "Actually there were two," she replied. The officer told White that under the *Motor Vehicle Act,* she had to provide a statement if requested to do so by police. The officer told White that this statement could not be used against her in court. The officer, however, did not expressly request a statement under the *Motor Vehicle Act.*

White was charged under section 252(1)(a) of the *Criminal Code* with failing to stop at the scene of an accident. The defence argued that White's various statements to police were involuntary and that they were obtained in violation of section 10(b) of the *Charter.* Furthermore, admitting them into evidence would violate the principles of fundamental justice under section 7 of the *Charter* because one must not be compelled to incriminate oneself. A *voir dire* was held on these issues.

White stated that she knew when the accident happened that she had a duty to report it. She continued to feel obligated to speak to the police officer even after she had spoken to a lawyer. At the close of the Crown's case, defence counsel brought a motion to dismiss the charge against White because the Crown had no evidence to identify the person driving the truck that had struck and killed O'Brien. The motion was granted and the respondent was acquitted. Crown appeals to the Court of Appeal for British Columbia and to the Supreme Court of Canada were dismissed.

For Discussion

1. **What protections do sections 7 and 10(b) of the *Charter* provide?**

continued ▶

2. What significance is there to the fact that White believed she had to give a report of the accident?

3. The *Motor Vehicle Act* states that information given as part of a motor vehicle report cannot be used in a criminal proceeding. Why would this provision not apply to charges brought under the *Criminal Code*?

4. If you were White, what would you have done when the police arrived? Explain.

5. Should White's statements be disregarded because of self-incrimination? Explain your opinion.

Types of Evidence

Privileged Communications

You Be the JUDGE

The goal of a trial is to present all the evidence related to the case in order to establish the truth.

- If this is so, why should spouses not be required to give evidence?

Privileged communications are any communications that cannot be required to be presented in court as evidence. Communication between spouses, for example, is said to be privileged. This means the Crown cannot compel the spouse of an accused person to give evidence *against* the accused for any communication that took place during the marriage or spousal relationship.

Of course, the accused's spouse may give evidence for the defence. Some exceptions apply—for example, in crimes of violence against the spouse, certain crimes related to sex, and some offences committed against **minors.** In *R. v. Salituro* (1991), the Supreme Court of Canada ruled that irreconcilably separated spouses could give testimony against their spouse.

Other privileged communications include conversations between parishioners and clergy, patients and doctors, and so on. Privileged communication can be nullified (have no force) in court, however, if the **dominant party** (the person in the position of power who receives the communication) presents the evidence. If the privilege is nullified, the information can be brought forward. Even a client's admissions to his or her lawyer can be brought forward as evidence, but only if the client agrees.

Types of Evidence

- privileged communications
- similar fact evidence
- hearsay evidence
- opinion evidence
- character evidence
- photographs
- intercepted and video evidence
- polygraph evidence
- confessions

Similar Fact Evidence

Similar fact evidence is evidence that shows the accused has committed similar offences in the past. The Crown generally uses this kind of evidence to imply that the accused has committed the offence again, or to refute defence claims that the offence was a mistake or accident. Because similar fact evidence discredits the accused's past, it must be relevant to the case. Such evidence can be extremely damaging to the accused's case if the jury gives it too much weight. Generally, the judge will hold a *voir dire* to determine whether to admit similar fact evidence.

Figure 8-9

Which type of evidence must be treated as a "last resort"?

Hearsay Evidence

Hearsay evidence is something that someone other than the witness has said or written. For example, Georgina says she heard Silas say he had seen Anton—the accused in a murder trial—stab and kill Gavin. This is hearsay, and usually it would not be admitted as evidence. Hearsay is admissible, however, in some circumstances. An out-of-court statement may be admitted as evidence, but only as proof that the statement was made, not for its content. Hearsay evidence is also admissible if the witness is quoting a person who was dying, as long as the evidence would have been admitted if the person had lived.

To be admitted, hearsay evidence must be necessary and reliable. In *R. v. Kahn* (1990), for example, the Supreme Court of Canada ruled that a statement made by a three-and-a-half-year-old to her mother 15 minutes after the girl had allegedly been sexually assaulted, was found to be "necessary and reliable" and was admitted as evidence. The original trial judge would not let the girl testify at the time of trial. The Supreme Court of Canada ruled that the girl's statement to her mother was "admissible as a spontaneous declaration made under the stress or pressure of a dramatic or startling event."

Opinion Evidence

Opinion evidence is what an expert witness thinks about certain facts in a case. Unless the expert is qualified, however, his or her opinion is generally inadmissible. To be admitted, opinion evidence must be relevant and necessary to

Case

R. v. R. (D.)

[1996] 2 S.C.R. 291
Supreme Court of Canada

D.R. and H.R. are the birth father and mother of three children. D.W. is the boyfriend of H.R., who divorced D.R. All three are hearing impaired. Only D.W. can speak. The children accused all three adults jointly with several counts of sexual assault and gross indecency, and one count of assault. D.R. and H.R. were charged with incest and several additional counts of assault causing bodily harm. The alleged incidents took place when the children ranged in age from one to 10.

Because of the parents' marriage breakdown and lack of child-rearing skills, the children were placed in foster care with the K. family. Unsupervised visits with D.R. were frequent, and supervised visits with H.R. and D.W. infrequent.

The children made multiple allegations of sexual abuse against their parents, D.W., the K. family, and many K. family relatives. One of the girls described to a doctor events that allegedly had taken place in D.R.'s home, which she could not remember in court. The children were described as being hyperactive, with aggressive sexual behaviour. They described many bizarre events that allegedly occurred while they were in the care of their birth parents. There was also evidence that the children tended to lie to cover up the sexual activity that took place between them.

The defence called Dr. Elterman, an expert in childhood development and characteristics of child abuse, to give evidence. The trial judge, however, prevented Elterman from testifying about his conclusions on the reliability of the children's memories of specific events. To do so, the judge stated, would take away the court's role in making findings of credibility.

The accused were found guilty of some of the charges, but not guilty of the incest and gross indecency charges. The Saskatchewan Court of Appeal upheld the decision, but the Supreme Court of Canada ruled that H.R. and D.W. must be retried, and it acquitted D.W. of sexual assault.

For Discussion

1. Why do you think credibility was so important in this case? Whom might you have trouble believing?

2. What example of hearsay evidence can you find in this case? Should it be included or excluded as evidence? Defend your position.

3. Did Dr. Elterman give opinion evidence? Should this evidence have been admitted? Explain.

4. Why were the evidence of the one girl to the doctor and the evidence of Dr. Elterman so important in this case?

Many trials demand that highly technical evidence and legal interpretations must be understood.

• Should trials make less use of juries and rely more on the expertise of judges? Explain your opinion.

help the judge or jury reach a decision. Expert evidence can have a major impact because a judge or jury may see the expert as being infallible (incapable of making a mistake). For that reason, a judge will only allow the evidence if it is on a topic that is outside the "experience and knowledge of a judge or jury."

Character Evidence

The Crown often wants to introduce evidence of any negative character traits and previous convictions of the accused. This kind of character evidence is prejudicial (intended to influence the jury to convict). Therefore, the Crown is restricted in its use. For example, the Crown may not use a series of questions to indicate that the accused has a criminal character or nature. The jury must decide the question of guilt from the facts of the case, not from prior history.

The defence, however, is allowed to introduce character evidence to support the accused's credibility. If convincing enough, this kind of evidence may lead to acquittal. There is a cost, however. If the defence introduces evidence of good character, the Crown is free to introduce evidence of previous convictions. The *Canada Evidence Act* states that witnesses may be questioned about any previous criminal convictions as a way to verify their credibility. This also applies to an accused person who chooses to testify. Questioning must not attack the credibility of the accused, however, unless such cross-examination is relevant to the fact that the accused is falsifying his or her evidence.

Photographs

Photographs may be entered as evidence if they can be identified to be an accurate portrait of the crime scene. Often, the photographer and film processor must take the stand to describe how the photographs were taken and processed. A judge has the right to not admit photographs that are meant merely to inflame the jury.

Electronic Devices and Video Surveillance

Evidence obtained through electronic interception devices or video surveillance will be admitted in court only if *Criminal Code* procedures have been strictly followed. The Code states that electromagnetic, mechanical, or other devices must not be used to intercept private conversations unless this is authorized by a court order or one of the parties involved in the conversation has consented. Court rulings have stated, however, that electronic surveillance must be "treated as a last resort."

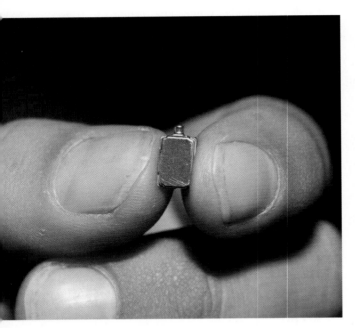

Figure 8-10

This sophisticated chip is not only a microphone; it is also a high-powered transmitter.

The *Criminal Code* also permits police to intercept private conversations without authorization in certain circumstances. The police officer must believe the situation is an emergency, that interception is needed immediately to prevent an unlawful act that would cause serious harm to any person or to property, and that one of the parties under surveillance is either performing that act or is its intended victim. As well, a person who fears bodily harm can authorize police to intercept his or her private conversations without obtaining judicial permission. This right can be critically important in cases of spousal abuse and stalking.

Video surveillance evidence can be admitted in court. Search warrants are not needed for video surveillance in public places, but are required if video, interception, and listening devices are used with respect to a person or a person's property. The judge must set terms and conditions in the warrant that will ensure privacy is respected in those areas in which a person has reasonable expectation of privacy.

Polygraph Evidence

The Supreme Court of Canada ruled in *R. v. Phillion* (1978) that polygraph (lie detector) tests are hearsay and therefore inadmissible as evidence. The Court stated that all the polygraph operator could do in presenting evidence was state what the accused had said. Furthermore, because the accused did not have to take the stand, only the way in which the machine was used could be cross-examined, not the responses of the person tested. The Court doubted the ability of the operator to analyze the test. It also expressed concern that the jury would accept the polygraph test as being infallible and convict the accused based on test results, not the credibility of evidence presented in the case.

Confessions

A **confession** is an accused person's acknowledgment that the charge, or some essential part of it, is true. The *Charter* states that anyone who is detained or arrested must be promptly informed that she or he has a right to legal counsel before making any statement. Any statement that is taken from an accused person who has not been told of his or her *Charter* right can later be excluded as evidence. A statement can be either **inculpatory,** which is an admission, or **exculpatory,** a denial.

How a confession is obtained also affects its admissibility. If there is reason to believe the confession was not voluntary—that police promised leniency, for example, or subjected the accused to lengthy questioning—the judge may reject it as evidence. Even if such a confession is admitted as evidence, the jury may reject it or give it little weight in reaching its decision.

Case

R. v. Oickle

[2000] 2 S.C.R. 3
Supreme Court of Canada

Eight fires involving four buildings and two motor vehicles had occurred in and around Waterville, Nova Scotia. The fires appeared to have been deliberately set. Oickle, a member of the volunteer fire brigade, responded to each fire and was one of eight people asked to take a polygraph test.

Before taking the test, Oickle was told of his rights to silence, to counsel, and to leave at any time. He was also told that although polygraph results were not admissible, anything he said was. Oickle was told he had failed the polygraph test, which was an "infallible determiner of truth." He was again reminded of his rights and then questioned for an hour. After 40 minutes of further questioning, Oickle confessed to setting fire to his fiancée's car and gave a statement. He was arrested and again informed of his rights.

Oickle's police interview was videotaped. It showed that at 8:30 P.M., he told police he was tired. They informed him he could call a lawyer. A third officer then interrogated Oickle for more than an hour, and he confessed to setting seven of the eight fires. Oickle was placed in a cell to sleep at 2:45 A.M. At 6:00 A.M., an officer noticed that Oickle was awake and crying, and he asked if he would agree to a reenactment. The videotape showed Oickle being told that he could stop the reenactment at any time. Oickle was driven to the various fire scenes, where he described how he had set each fire. He was charged with seven counts of arson.

Oickle was fully informed of his rights at all times and never subjected to harsh or overbearing interrogation. He was not deprived of sleep, food, or drink, and he was never offered any inducements that might undermine the reliability of his confessions. The police did offer psychiatric help, but not in exchange for a confession.

The trial judge held a *voir dire* and ruled that Oickle's statements, including those on the video, were voluntary and admissible, and convicted him. The Nova Scotia Court of Appeal excluded the confessions and entered an acquittal. The Supreme Court of Canada reversed that decision and reinstated the conviction.

For Discussion

1. What is a *voir dire* and why did the trial judge hold one in this case?
2. Why would police videotape the interviews?
3. Why would the polygraph results not be admissible? Is a polygraph infallible?
4. What type of confession did Oickle give to police?
5. Summarize the evidence that could be used to support the view that Oickle's confession was voluntary. Counter this by summarizing the evidence that supports the view that the confession was involuntary. Which view of the evidence do you support? Why?
6. If you were his lawyer, would you have Oickle take the stand to cast doubt on the polygraph test results? Why or why not?

Illegally Obtained Evidence

The admission of illegally obtained evidence has been debated ever since the *Canadian Charter of Rights and Freedoms* (see section 24) was passed. In each trial, it must be decided if admitting the evidence in question would bring the "administration of justice into disrepute." This relies on whether "the reasonable person," fully informed of the facts, would be shocked if a judge allowed the evidence to be admitted. The severity of the offence, how it was committed, and how the evidence was obtained must all be considered.

Review Your Understanding (Pages 225 to 234)

1. Summarize the order in which evidence is presented and state the purpose of each stage of the examination.
2. What is a leading question? Provide an example of this type of question.
3. Why is a leading question not asked in an examination-in-chief? When would it be appropriate to ask a leading question? Why?
4. When would the defence ask the judge for a directed verdict?
5. What are the characteristics of admissible evidence?
6. Compare direct evidence and circumstantial evidence.
7. Explain the consequences of not attending court when issued a subpoena. When would an order for contempt of court be issued?
8. Who may be called as a witness?
9. Distinguish between credibility of witnesses and the weight given to evidence.
10. Who determines credibility of witnesses?
11. Describe the concept of privileged communications, and indicate under what circumstances the court can nullify them.
12. Briefly describe each of the following kinds of evidence: character, hearsay, opinion, and similar fact. Provide an example for each.
13. Under what circumstances is a confession inadmissible in court?
14. Describe the present status of the use of each of the following in Canadian courts: photographs, videotape recordings, interception devices, and polygraph evidence.

"Oh-oh, we're in trouble!"

Figure 8-11

Why would a smoking gun be considered damning evidence?

8.5 Defences

Various defences are used to prove that the accused is not guilty of the offence charged or guilty of a lesser offence. The best possible defence is an acceptable **alibi,** a defence that places the accused somewhere else at the time the offence occurred. It is important that the accused disclose any alibi to the Crown at the earliest opportunity. Failing to do so may erode the credibility of both the accused and the alibi.

Self-Defence

The *Criminal Code* permits you to defend yourself, those under your protection, your movable property, and your dwelling and real property. However, you can only use force that is "necessary" and "reasonable," according to the circumstances.

Section 38 of the *Criminal Code* allows you to stop a thief from taking your personal property, or to take it back, as long as you do not strike the thief or cause bodily harm. You can do more to defend your dwelling. Under section 40, you are "justified in using as much force as is necessary to prevent any person from forcibly breaking into or forcibly entering the [your] dwelling-house without lawful authority."

Excerpts from the *Criminal Code*

34.

(1) Every one who is unlawfully assaulted without having provoked the assault is justified in repelling force by force if the force he uses is not intended to cause death or grievous bodily harm and is no more than is necessary to enable him to defend himself.

(2) Every one who is unlawfully assaulted and who causes death or grievous bodily harm in repelling the assault is justified if

　(a) he causes it under reasonable apprehension of death or grievous bodily harm from the violence with which the assault was originally made or with which the assailant pursues his purposes; and

　(b) he believes, on reasonable grounds, that he cannot otherwise preserve himself from death or grievous bodily harm.

35.

Every one who has without justification assaulted another but did not commence the assault with intent to cause death or grievous bodily harm, or has without justification provoked an assault on himself by another, may justify the use of force subsequent to the assault if

　(a) he uses the force

　　(i) under reasonable apprehension of death or grievous bodily harm from the violence of the person whom he has assaulted or provoked, and

　　(ii) in the belief, on reasonable grounds, that it is necessary in order to preserve himself from death or grievous bodily harm;

　(b) he did not, at any time before the necessity of preserving himself from death or grievous bodily harm arose, endeavour to cause death or grievous bodily harm; and

　(c) he declined further conflict and quitted or retreated from it as far as it was feasible to do so before the necessity of preserving himself from death or grievous bodily harm arose.

For Discussion

1. Summarize the self-defence sections of the *Criminal Code*.

2. If you are physically threatened, what amount of force can you use to defend yourself? What other conditions must be satisfied if your action is to be legally justified as self-defence?

3. If you were physically threatened with death, how much force could you use to repel that threat?

Case

R. v. Charlebois

[2000] 2 S.C.R. 674
Supreme Court of Canada

Patrick Charlebois was charged with first-degree murder for shooting his best friend, Éric Jetté. Charlebois claimed that he had an overwhelming fear of Jetté. Evidence indicated that Jetté had a history of violence and had dominated and exploited Charlebois. On the night of the shooting, Jetté had arrived at Charlebois's apartment. He flicked a knife at Charlebois, saying, "Yeah, we're going to have some fun tonight, you and me." Charlebois became more concerned after Jetté saw a firearm that he had refused to sell Jetté, pretending he had lost it. Charlebois tried to sleep in his bedroom, but was overwhelmed by panic. He took his rifle and shot Jetté, asleep on the couch, in the back of the head. The defence relied on the self-defence provisions of section 34(2) of the *Criminal Code*.

The trial judge outlined the three elements of self-defence for the jury: (1) the existence of an unlawful assault; (2) a reasonable apprehension of a risk of death or grievous bodily harm; and (3) a

continued ▶

reasonable belief that it is not possible to preserve oneself from harm except by killing. If the jury found that Charlebois believed all three elements to be true, then it must determine whether "a reasonable person" in Charlebois's situation "would have had the same perceptions."

Charlebois called a psychiatrist in his defence, who offered an opinion that Charlebois was suffering from acute anxiety at the time of the shooting. Evidence was also presented that Charlebois was not a violent person.

Charlebois was found guilty of second-degree murder. His appeals to both the Quebec Court of Appeal and the Supreme Court of Canada were dismissed.

For Discussion

1. **Why was Charlebois found guilty of murder in the second degree, not the first degree?**

2. **What type of evidence did the psychiatrist give? As a juror, what weight would you give it?**

3. **What three key elements must exist for self-defence to succeed as a defence? Did they exist in the Charlebois case?**

4. **Jurors had to determine if Charlebois acted as "a reasonable person" would in the same situation. What is a "reasonable person"? Did Charlebois behave as a "reasonable person" in this case? Explain your opinion.**

Legal Duty

Legal duty allows certain people to commit acts that would otherwise be offences. For example, a police officer can drive above the speed limit when chasing a suspected criminal. In recent years, however, several innocent bystanders have been killed in police chases. An officer may also use as much force as necessary to make an arrest. Section 43 of the *Criminal Code* is very controversial because it allows a parent, schoolteacher, or person standing in the place of a parent, to use "reasonable force" to correct a child (see Issue, page 442).

Excusable Conduct

As discussed in Chapter 5, provocation may be used as a partial defence for a charge of murder. Excusable conduct also includes **duress,** which is the threat or use of violence. In *R. v. Morgentaler* (1988), the Supreme Court of Canada stated that the defence would be successful only in "urgent situations of clear and imminent peril when compliance with the law is demonstrably impossible." Provisions for this defence are also found in section 17 of the *Criminal Code*.

Honest mistake may also be accepted as a defence under excusable conduct. It means the offender truthfully did not know he or she had committed a crime. This defence is most commonly used by people who are found in possession of unpaid items while shopping. The onus is on the Crown to prove that the person accused of shoplifting did it intentionally. The accused's credibility will largely determine whether this defence succeeds.

You Be the JUDGE

The Children's Aid Society can legally remove children from homes where they believe abuse is occurring—even if force has to be used to take children from their parents.

- Should the Society have to prove before a court that abuse exists before removing the children? Explain.

The Law   The Criminal Code

Excerpts from the *Criminal Code*

17.

A person who commits an offence under compulsion by threats of immediate death or bodily harm

from a person who is present when the offence is committed is excused for committing the offence if the person believes that the threats will be carried out and if the person is not a party to a conspiracy

continued ▶

or association whereby the person is subject to compulsion, but this section does not apply where the offence that is committed is high treason or treason, murder, piracy, attempted murder, sexual assault, sexual assault with a weapon, threats to a third party or causing bodily harm, aggravated sexual assault, forcible abduction, hostage taking, robbery, assault with a weapon or causing bodily harm, aggravated assault, unlawfully causing bodily harm, arson or an offence under sections 280 to 283 (abduction and detention of young persons).

For Discussion

1. Under what circumstances can section 17 be used as a defence if a person commits an offence under compulsion by threats?

2. Why do you think the section 17 defence is not available for the list of "does not apply" offences?

3. In some cases, such as spousal assault, the threat may not be "immediate." How much weight should be given to the "threat of immediate death or bodily harm" requirement in such cases?

Case

R. v. Ruzic

(2001) 153 C.C.C. (3d) 1
Supreme Court of Canada

Ruzic arrived at Pearson International Airport with 2 kg of heroin strapped to her body and readily admitted to possession of heroin and use of a false passport. Ruzic testified that a man named Mirkovic had approached her in Belgrade. She described him as a "warrior," a member of a mafia-like criminal group. An expert witness testified that such groups did exist in Belgrade and that people living in Belgrade at the time did not feel safe or believe that police could be trusted.

Ruzic alleged that over the course of two months, Mirkovic became threatening and physically violent. He ordered her to meet him at a hotel, where he strapped the heroin to her body and instructed her to take it to a restaurant in Toronto. If she did not deliver the packages, he would harm her mother. Ruzic said fear for her mother's safety prevented her from reporting Mirkovic to police or government officials.

Ruzic challenged the constitutionality of section 17 of the *Criminal Code* because it requires that threats must be "of immediate death or bodily harm from a person who is present when the offence is committed." Her position was that such a requirement restricted her rights under section 7 of the *Charter*. The common-law defence of duress only required that the situation must deprive the accused of any safe avenue of escape.

The jury acquitted Ruzic. The Crown's appeals to both the Ontario Court of Appeal and the Supreme Court of Canada were dismissed.

For Discussion

1. What do section 7 of the *Charter* and, in general terms, section 17 of the *Criminal Code* provide?

2. What is a common-law defence? In what way is the common law defence of duress different from the statute law in section 17 of the *Criminal Code*?

3. The Supreme Court of Canada stated: "[B]y the strictness of its conditions, section 17 breaches section 7 of the *Charter* because it allows individuals who acted involuntarily to be declared criminally liable." Explain what this means in relation to this case.

4. In declaring section 17 of the *Criminal Code* to be in violation of section 7 of the *Charter*, the Supreme Court of Canada stated that the principles of fundamental justice "are to be found in the basic tenets [beliefs] of our legal system." In your opinion, was fundamental justice applied in this case? Explain.

5. What effect does the Supreme Court of Canada's ruling have on the future use of section 17 of the *Criminal Code*?

Mental Disorder

The use of mental disorder as a defence has been debated among members of the legal profession for many years. The terms "mental disorder" and "unfit to stand trial" are defined in section 2 of the *Criminal Code*.

The Law   The Criminal Code

Excerpts from the *Criminal Code*

2.
In this Act ... "mental disorder" means a disease of the mind; ... "unfit to stand trial" means unable on account of mental disorder to conduct a defence at any stage of the proceedings before a verdict is rendered or to instruct counsel to do so, and, in particular, unable on account of mental disorder to

(a) understand the nature ... of the proceedings,

(b) understand the possible consequences of the proceedings, or

(c) communicate with counsel.

For Discussion

1. **In your own words, outline the meaning of "unfit to stand trial" according to section 2.**

Mental Fitness to Stand Trial

An accused can be remanded for up to 60 days to evaluate his or her fitness to stand trial. This may include an assessment of his or her mental status at the time of the offence. A provincial or territorial review board determines if the accused is fit to stand trial; the accused is then sent back to court. If he or she is fit to stand trial, the case is heard. Usually, evidence given during a court-ordered psychiatric assessment is not admitted without the accused's consent.

If the accused is unfit, the court can order treatment to make him or her fit to stand trial. An inquiry is held every two years, until the accused is tried, to make sure that there is still enough evidence to bring him or her to trial.

Mental Fitness at the Time of the Offence

There is a presumption of sanity, just as there is a presumption of innocence. In *R. v. Swain* (1991), the Supreme Court of Canada ruled that the Crown could not introduce evidence of mental disorder unless it had already proved *actus reus* and *mens rea*. The defence can independently decide whether to introduce the defence of mental disorder.

If an accused is found not guilty because of insanity, the verdict must state that "the accused committed the act or omission but is not criminally responsible on account of mental disorder." The court then holds a hearing to determine what to do with the accused, or the review board determines the future of the offender.

The court and the review board must protect the public. They consider "the mental condition of the accused, the reintegration of the accused into society, and the other needs of the accused." The mental state of the accused at the time of the hearing, not at the time of the offence, is the main concern. If considered not to be a threat, the accused may be discharged absolutely. Otherwise, the discharge will have conditions, or the accused will be held in custody in a hospital. Treatment, however, must not be a condition of release.

You Be the JUDGE

In 1984, a man was found to be not fit to stand trial, because of insanity, for a murder committed in 1982. In 2001, a review board declared that the man was now fit to stand trial. In a similar case, a review board decided to send a person to trial for an offence committed 22 years earlier. An appeal court overturned that decision.

- Should a time limit be set for bringing a person before a court to answer to charges?

- What section(s) of the *Charter* might the appeal court refer to in order to overturn the review board decision?

Should Prolonged Abuse Be a Defence for Killing?

The Supreme Court of Canada first recognized prolonged abuse as a defence in *R. v. Lavallee* (1990), when it upheld a jury's acquittal of Angelique Lyn Lavallee. Lavallee had shot her partner in the back of the head as he left a room one evening because she was afraid he would kill her later that night. He had physically abused her for many years. The Court found that it was "reasonable" for Lavallee to believe she had no other choice than to use lethal force to defend herself.

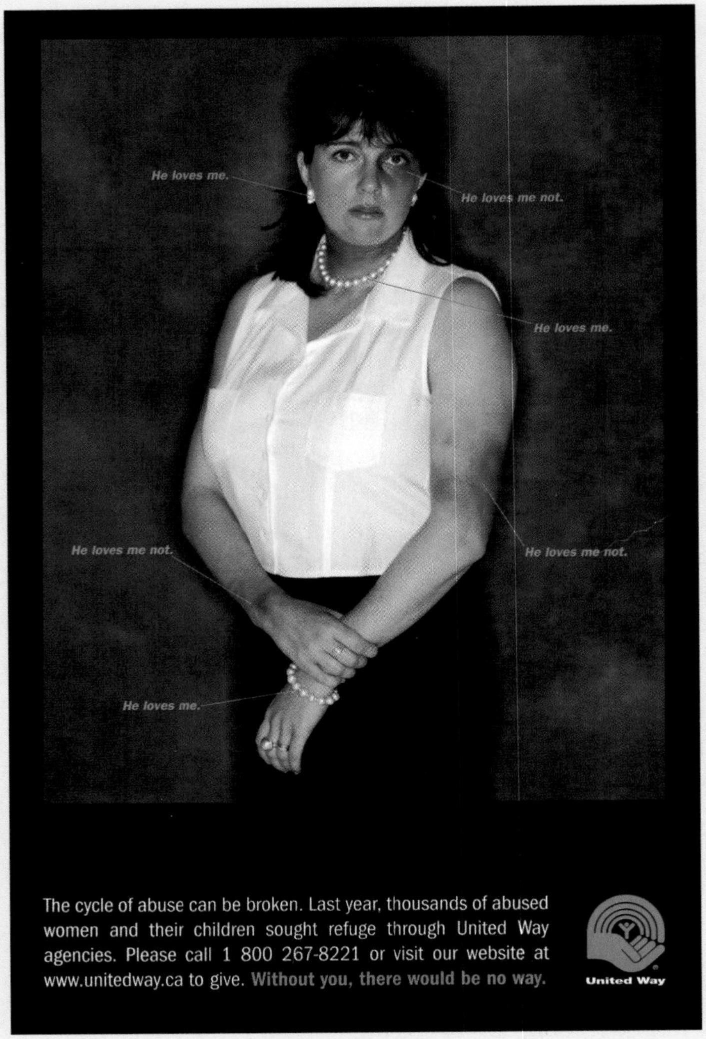

This groundbreaking decision set a legal precedent and "battered-woman syndrome" became a legal defence. Today, judges refer to it when giving legal reasons for their verdicts in cases involving similar circumstances.

In *R. v. Malott* (1998), for example, the Supreme Court of Canada upheld the conviction of Margaret Ann Malott. Malott had shot and killed her spouse of 19 years, but she also shot and stabbed his girlfriend, who recovered. Malott's spouse had mentally and physically abused her throughout their relationship. On several occasions, the abuse was so severe she reported him to police.

Because of the battered-woman defence, the jury found Malott guilty of the lesser charge of second-degree murder and recommended the minimum penalty. The judge agreed. Malott appealed the verdict, but lost her appeal. Without the defence of battered-woman syndrome, the charge might have been murder in the first degree, with the minimum penalty of 25 years' imprisonment.

On One Side

In the past, the legal system failed battered women. The majority of abused women did not report the abuse. Those who did often found police officers did not like to get involved. Statistics reveal that women are far more likely to be victims of spousal murder. Between 1974 and 1990 in Ontario—the year of the Lavallee decision—417 women were killed by their spouses, as compared to 141 men.

Often victims would not lay charges, even when the abuse led to hospitalization or involved weapons. If they did lay charges, victims would often drop them later because of fear, shame, and self-blame. It was only a matter of time before the effects of repeated and prolonged spousal abuse would be recognized as a legal defence in spousal killings.

He loves me.

He loves me not.

He loves me.

He loves me not.

He loves me not.

He loves me.

The cycle of abuse can be broken. Last year, thousands of abused women and their children sought refuge through United Way agencies. Please call 1 800 267-8221 or visit our website at www.unitedway.ca to give. Without you, there would be no way.

United Way

Figure 8-12

This United Way poster is one of many efforts to raise public awareness of a serious issue.

Today, the courts recognize battered-woman syndrome as a legal defence. Law makers, however, must do more. They must change the *Criminal Code* to clearly define this and other forms of self-defence. The law is still unfair to those who kill others after years of abuse and who fear for their lives. If justice is to be done, the law must give more consideration to the mental states of the victims of prolonged abuse when they kill in self-defence.

On the Other Side

Critics oppose battered-woman syndrome as a defence for a number of reasons. By recognizing victimization as a defence, some say, courts have tried to make a right out of two wrongs. It is the court's job to make existing laws work, not to give approval for breaking them.

Other critics say the Lavallee decision reinforces a sexist stereotype that women are weak and must be treated differently. They state that abused women should act responsibly to remove themselves from their abusers and end their abusive relationships long before killing is necessary. Such critics want governments to raise public awareness about abuse and its destructive effects. They suggest that women need to be educated about what they can do in abusive situations. If these steps are taken, women will not tolerate abusive relationships and will know how to deal with them before it is too late.

The Bottom Line

During the 1990s, the legal system recognized spousal abuse as a serious and widespread problem. Police now have clear charging practices to respond to abusive spouses. In some communities, police officers themselves will charge the abuser if the abused spouse will not do so. This ensures that charges are laid and then followed up in court. In 1993, anti-stalking laws were also passed (see Chapter 5, page 153). In 2001, the federal government considered changes to the *Criminal Code* to clarify definitions of self-defence.

What Do You Think?

1. Define "battered-woman syndrome" in your own words.

2. How has battered-woman syndrome been used in criminal court cases in recent years?

3. Compare the Lavallee and Malott cases. How are they similar and how are they different?

4. Why do you think many abused women drop the charges against their abusive partners?

5. Create a three-column organizer. In the first two columns, list arguments for and against battered-woman syndrome as a legal defence. In the third column, write your opinions of these arguments.

6. Men are also abused by their spouses. Do you think the courts would accept a battered-man syndrome defence if a man killed his spouse? Why or why not?

Intoxication

The Chapter 4 discussion of specific and general intent offences is important if you are to understand the intoxication defence. To review: a general intent offence is one in which the intent relates solely to committing the act. For example, Janik strikes Fred, but only out of anger. Janik has committed assault, a general intent offence. Compare this with the person who strikes another with the intent (purpose) to kill. This is aggravated assault, and it is a specific intent offence.

Any intoxicated person who was unable to form intent before striking someone cannot be found guilty of aggravated assault. He or she can, however, be found guilty of assault, a general intent offence. All that needs to be proved is that the intoxicated person did strike someone. Similarly, a person charged with murder can use the defence of intoxication. If successful, this will lower the conviction from murder (a specific intent offence) to manslaughter (a general intent offence).

The relationship of intoxication to assault and sexual assault was discussed in Chapter 5. As that discussion made clear, there are situations in which self-induced intoxication is not a defence to a criminal act.

Automatism

Automatism has been described as "unconscious, involuntary behaviour—the state of a person who, though capable of action, is not conscious of what he is doing." Sleepwalking, convulsions, and behaviour caused by psychological stress are some examples. To be acquitted on this defence, the accused must prove that he or she was in a state of automatism when committing the offence.

Automatism caused by a disease of the mind is called "insane automatism." Here the source of the malfunction is rooted in the psychological or emotional makeup of the person. If this state is proved, the accused is entitled to a verdict of "not criminally responsible on account of a mental disorder." The offender would then be subject to the procedures outlined under mental disorder.

Case

R. v. Stone

[1999] 2 S.C.R. 290
Supreme Court of Canada

Bert Stone was charged with murdering his wife. He claimed that while driving, his wife's verbal insults forced him to pull off the road. From there, he said, he remembered only a "whoosh" sensation washing over him. When his eyes refocused, Stone said, he found his wife's body slumped over the seat. In his hands was a hunting knife with which he had stabbed her 47 times. Stone said he had no memory of stabbing his wife.

Stone then disposed of the body, checked into a hotel, collected a debt, sold a car, and flew to Mexico. While in Mexico, he said, while recalling a dream, he remembered stabbing his wife twice before experiencing a "whooshing" sensation. He returned to Canada, spoke to a lawyer, and surrendered himself to police. Later, the defence psychiatrist described the wife's "verbal abuse" as "exceptionally cruel, psychologically sadistic, and profoundly rejecting."

In his defence, Stone claimed insane automatism, non-insane automatism, lack of intent, and alternatively, provocation. The judge ruled that as the only

continued

possible cause of Stone's state was anxiety—which is an internal factor—he must have been suffering from a disease of the mind in the legal sense. Thus, the jury should consider only insane automatism.

The jury decided that Stone's defence of insane automatism was not proven; that he was criminally responsible, but not guilty of second-degree murder. He was found guilty of manslaughter and sentenced to seven years in prison. The British Columbia Court of Appeal upheld the conviction and dismissed the Crown's appeal of the sentence. The Supreme Court of Canada dismissed Stone's appeal of his conviction and the Crown's appeal of the sentence.

For Discussion

1. Distinguish between insane and non-insane automatism.
2. What evidence is there that Stone was in a state of insane automatism?
3. Why would Stone prefer to have his defence of non-insane automatism be successful rather than his defences of insane automatism and provocation?
4. Why was Stone found guilty of manslaughter and not second-degree murder?

Consent

Consent can be used as a valid defence, but only if the party injured by the accused could and did consent to the action. For example, many hockey and football players have been charged with assaulting opponents during a game. The defence is usually that by playing the game, the injured party consented, or agreed, to the game's rough physical contact.

The defence of consent can never be used in cases involving firearms, murder, or for various sexual offences committed against persons under the age of 14. Consent in relation to sexual assault is discussed in Chapter 5.

Entrapment

Entrapment is a police action that encourages or aids a person to commit an offence. It is not recognized as a defence, but rather as an abuse by the police. A judge who finds that entrapment has occurred should stay the proceedings.

Mistake of Fact

Ignorance of the law is generally not accepted as a defence. Ignorance of the facts, however, will be accepted as a defence, but only under two conditions:

1. The mistake was genuine and not the result of the accused neglecting to find out the facts.
2. The law accepts ignorance of the facts as a defence.

Figure 8-13

In *R. v. McSorley* (2000), National Hockey League player Marty McSorley was found guilty of assault with a weapon for hitting another player during a game. McSorley did not have to spend time in jail and will have no criminal record. (See Issue, page 312.)

For example, you receive counterfeit money while shopping. When you try to pay a bill with it, you are arrested. You cannot be considered negligent for not finding out that the money was counterfeit—people do not usually check every bill they receive. In another example, you buy a used bicycle that was advertised in a bulletin board notice. Later, you are arrested under the *Criminal Code*, which states that it is an offence to "knowingly" possess stolen goods. If you can prove that you did not know the goods were stolen, then your mistake-of-fact defence will succeed.

Double Jeopardy

Double jeopardy means to be tried twice for the same offence. Under section 11 of the *Charter*, it is prohibited: "Any person charged with an offence has the right ... if finally acquitted of the offence, not to be tried for it again and, if finally found guilty and punished for the offence, not to be tried or punished for it again."

In a case of double jeopardy, a pre-trial motion can be made using one of two pleas:

- In a plea of *autrefois acquit*, the accused states that he or she has already been acquitted of the charge.
- In a plea of *autrefois convict*, the accused states that he or she has already been convicted on the charge.

The judge then investigates the matter and rules on whether the current charge is based on the same facts as the previous charge that was tried. If so, the judge will dismiss the case.

You Be the JUDGE

Twenty years ago, a person was tried and found not guilty of committing a series of gruesome murders. New DNA evidence, however, proves beyond a doubt that the person did commit at least one of the murders.

- Could this person be brought back before the courts to answer new charges? Explain.

Review Your Understanding (Pages 235 to 244)

1. Describe a situation in which an alibi could successfully be used as a defence.

2. How much force can you legally use to defend yourself or your property?

3. Define "legal duty" and give two examples of its use as a defence.

4. Name two categories described as excusable conduct, and give an example of each.

5. In your own words, outline what is meant by "unfit to stand trial" according to section 2 of the *Criminal Code*.

6. a) Why is the defence of mental disorder used only for the most serious offences?

   b) Summarize the steps that occur before the trial of a person with a mental disorder.

   c) Who decides on the future of a person deemed not criminally responsible?

7. a) Why would an accused invoke the defence of intoxication if charged with an offence requiring specific intent?

   b) In what situations would the defence of intoxication fail?

8. Identify three examples of automatism.

9. Against what offences can the defence of consent not be used?

10. **Is entrapment recognized as a defence? Explain.**

11. **Describe the two conditions that must exist for mistake of fact to be used as a defence.**

12. **a) What is double jeopardy?**

    b) Describe the difference between *autrefois acquit* and *autrefois convict*.

8.6 Reaching a Verdict

The verdict—the decision as to whether the accused is guilty—is the culmination of the trial process.

The Summation

After all witnesses have been called, each side presents its **summation** (a summary of all its key arguments and evidence) to the court. If the defence presented evidence on behalf of the accused, it makes its summation first. Otherwise, the Crown closes first. No new evidence can be introduced at this time.

The Charge to the Jury

Once summations have been presented, the judge makes the **charge to the jury.** This review of the facts defines and explains the law applying to the case for the jury. For example, the judge might point out that intent must be proven for a guilty verdict, or that if the evidence does not establish beyond a reasonable doubt that an offence was committed, the jury might bring a conviction for an attempt. The judge may also indicate how the evidence should be weighed.

Once the judge has finished the charge, either side can challenge it for legal errors. The jury, however, is excluded from the courtroom while the two sides outline any reasons for such a challenge. When the jurors return, the judge may present a recharge. Many appeals result from the judge's charge to the jury.

Jury Deliberation

To deliberate its decision, the jury leaves the courtroom in the custody of the sheriff. One of the jurors is selected to be the foreperson. Unless note taking was allowed, jurors must rely only on their memory to decide what facts they believe or disbelieve. Because a verdict must be unanimous, the jury may return to the courtroom and ask for certain evidence or laws to be reviewed.

The jury's role is to determine the facts of the case; the judge's role is to determine the law. Jurors should follow a two-step process in applying the facts to the law. First, they should discard any evidence that they do not believe. Second, they should determine the weight that they are going to give the remainder of the evidence.

Did You Know?

In 2001, the Canadian Judicial Council announced plans to distribute templates (guides) to help judges make their charges to the jury. The templates include hundreds of standardized charges written in plain, understandable language. The Supreme Court of Canada's Chief Justice Beverley McLachlin described this as "one of the most far-reaching law reform projects ever completed in this country." How might these templates benefit the court system in Canada?

Adam® by Brian Basset

Figure 8-14

What is the judge doing in this cartoon?

You Be the JUDGE

Not all people agree that a jury's decision needs to be unanimous. Some legal minds have suggested that a majority decision, or a majority decision of 10 jurors, or a majority decision after the jury has deliberated for a specified length of time should be valid.

- Is there merit in any of these suggestions?

The set of facts that the jury believes will determine which law applies to the case, and thus what decision the jury makes. In a murder case, the jury may believe the facts presented by the Crown that indicate a hunter intentionally killed the deceased. The hunter would then be convicted of murder. Alternatively, the jurors may believe the facts presented by the defence, which show that the accused did not intend to kill the deceased. The jury might then find the hunter guilty of manslaughter.

Finally, the jury must apply the concept of reasonable doubt. If the jury believes the defence's evidence or cannot decide whom to believe, it must acquit. If the jurors have a reasonable doubt, they must acquit the accused, even if they do not believe him or her. In other words, the jury must give the accused the benefit of a doubt.

If the jury cannot reach a verdict, it presents this fact to the judge. The judge may review the evidence and ask the jurors to deliberate further. If the jury still cannot reach a unanimous decision—and the judge is satisfied that further deliberation will not help them do so—the jury may be dismissed. This is called a **hung jury.** The accused may then be tried by a new jury. The decision of the judge to declare a hung jury cannot be appealed.

When the jury does reach a verdict, the foreperson presents it to the court. Both the defence and prosecution can ask that jurors be polled individually. Each juror must then stand and state "guilty" or "not guilty." Then, after being instructed never to disclose anything that occurred in the jury room, the jurors are discharged from their duties.

A defendant who is acquitted by the jury is permitted to leave. A defendant who has been found guilty will either be sentenced then or at a later date. The jury usually has no influence in deciding the penalty, except when an accused is found guilty of second-degree murder. Although not required to do so, the jury may make a recommendation to the judge regarding the number of years that the offender should serve before being eligible for parole. Appeals and sentencing are examined in Chapter 9.

R. v. G. (R.M.)

[1996] 3 S.C.R. 362
Supreme Court of Canada

R.M. was charged with sexually assaulting his step-daughter when she was 12 years of age. A doctor indicated that there were signs of sexual intercourse. Testimony also indicated that the complainant believed she was unduly confined in an overly strict environment and that she wished to live with her natural father. R.M.'s defence was that the step-daughter either fabricated or imagined the incidents so that she could move out. An alibi suggested R.M. was not present when some of the alleged incidents took place.

The trial judge's charge to the jury indicated that the sexual assault had been established and that the only issue for the jury was whether R.M. was the perpetrator. The defence objected to the judge's charge to the jury. The judge then recharged the jury, instructing them that they had to determine whether a sexual assault had occurred.

After deliberating from 2:20 P.M. until 9:15 P.M., and again the next morning, the jury notified the judge they could not reach a verdict. The judge recalled the jury, urging them to consider the public expense and inconvenience of a new trial. The judge also told the jury that a new trial would cause hardship for the accused and the complainant, and that the minority might want to consider what the majority was saying. The judge indicated that the jurors should "not betray their oath" and that they did not have to agree. Fifteen minutes later, the jury returned a verdict of guilty. The British Columbia Court of Appeal dismissed R.M.'s appeal, but the Supreme Court of Canada ordered a new trial in a 6 to 3 decision.

For Discussion

1. Why did the judge have to recharge the jury?

2. The task of a jury is to reach a verdict based solely on evidence presented in court. What directions in the judge's recharge might have changed the focus of the jury from that task?

3. Should the judge's direction to the jury to "not betray their oath" be enough to counter the other statements that implied the jury had to come to a decision? Explain.

Review Your Understanding (Pages 245 to 247)

1. What determines which side presents its summation first?
2. What is the role of the judge in a trial by jury?
3. What is the purpose of the charge to the jury?
4. What happens in a trial in which there is a hung jury?

Chapter Review

Chapter Highlights

- The adversarial system is used in trials.
- Judges must make many significant decisions during a trial.
- The Crown prosecutor represents society in showing why the accused is guilty.
- The rules governing the empanelling of a jury are very specific.
- During jury selection, both the Crown and defence can reject prospective jurors.
- The jury must base its verdict on evidence presented in court.
- Both the Crown and the defence have the opportunity to present evidence and question the other's witnesses.
- A witness's credibility may determine the weight that should be given to his or her evidence.
- A *voir dire* is held to determine the admissibility of evidence.
- The judge determines the admissibility of evidence.
- The *Criminal Code* specifies the criteria for establishing whether an accused is fit to stand trial.
- If intoxication or automatism is a successful defence, the accused could not form the necessary intent.
- A mistake of fact requires that the accused used due diligence in trying to find the facts.
- An accused cannot be tried twice for the same offence.
- In her or his charge to the jury, the judge reviews the facts and explains the law applying to the case.
- The jury should apply the facts of the case to the law in making its decision.

Review Key Terms

Name the key terms that are described below.

a) to be tried twice for the same offence
b) to isolate a jury until members reach a decision
c) stopping a trial until further action is taken
d) evidence that shows that the accused had previously committed a similar offence
e) a jury that cannot reach a unanimous decision
f) a document ordering a person to appear in court as a witness

g) the process of selecting 12 jurors
h) indirect evidence
i) a trial within a trial to decide upon the admissibility of evidence
j) knowingly giving false evidence with intent to mislead
k) the challenge of a juror without giving a reason
l) the challenge of a juror because the juror has particular knowledge about the case
m) the accused has already been acquitted of the charge
n) a type of statement in which the accused denies the truth of a charge
o) committing a crime under the threat of death or immediate bodily harm
p) a promise to tell the truth

Check Your Knowledge

1. Identify the individuals involved in the criminal trial process and describe their roles.

2. Outline the process of jury selection.

3. Outline the steps in the criminal trial process, and briefly explain the function of each part.

4. Explain the legal defences to criminal charges, and provide an example for each defence.

Apply Your Learning

5. From a newspaper or the Internet, collect five articles concerning criminal law cases. For each case, comment on the following:
   a) the offence committed
   b) the statute or legal source of the offence
   c) the evidence that the Crown and the defence could present
   d) any possible defence available to the accused
   e) the judge's decision, if available

6. Prepare an organizer to compare the advantages and disadvantages of trial by jury.

7. *R. v. Leipert*, [1997] 1 S.C.R. 281 (Supreme Court of Canada)

Police received a tip from a Crime Stoppers informant that Leipert was growing marijuana in his basement. A police officer walked a sniffer dog by the house on several occasions, and each time the dog indicated there was marijuana in the house. The officer then obtained a search warrant. After the house was searched, the officer charged Leipert with cultivation of marijuana and possession of marijuana for the purpose of trafficking.

At trial, Leipert stated that the *Charter* entitled the defence to see the Crime Stoppers report on the tip. The Crown refused to disclose, on the grounds of informer privilege. The judge edited out all references to the identity of the informer and ordered disclosure. The Crown then asked to rely on the warrant only without referring to the tip. The trial judge refused, the Crown stopped presenting evidence, and the defence decided to call "no evidence." The judge rendered an acquittal. The Crown appealed to the Supreme Court of British Columbia.

Prepare a decision on behalf of the Supreme Court of British Columbia, justifying your decision as to whether the Crime Stopper tip should be admitted as evidence.

8. With a partner, create a list of interview questions to ask a Crown prosecutor and a defence counsel. Your questions should refer to specifics about their jobs and their roles in the criminal justice system, and relate to what they see as strengths and weaknesses in the adversarial system. Share your questions with the class in order to generate a class list of questions. Invite a Crown prosecutor and defence counsel to come to your class. During the presentation, make notes on their answers to your questions. Distinguish among opinion, fact, and bias in their presentation.

9. The number of Canadians who successfully used the defence of "not being criminally responsible" by reason of mental disorder increased from 149 in 1991 (the year the current law was introduced) to 615 in 1998. Before the current law, an accused who pleaded the defence of "criminally insane" could be placed indefinitely in a mental institution. In a 1999 decision, the Supreme Court of Canada warned provincial and territorial review boards that offenders deemed not criminally responsible should be institutionalized only if they pose a significant threat to the public. A review of the 1991 legislation was required in 1996, but still had not been done by 2001. Should offenders found not guilty because of a mental disorder be required to be institutionalized for a period of time? Justify your opinion.

Communicate Your Understanding

10. Research any of the following organizations that help people involved in the criminal justice system. Your summary should include the name of the organization, where it can be accessed, its goals, and a brief account of the services it provides.
    a) John Howard Society
    b) Elizabeth Fry Society
    c) Salvation Army
    d) Aboriginal Justice Learning Network
    e) Association in Defence of the Wrongly Convicted

11. Clayton Ruby is one of Canada's most famous defence counsels, and he regularly writes and speaks on the justice system. The following excerpts from a story in the *Ottawa Citizen*, June 24, 2001, outline Ruby's views on the relationship between the Crown and the defence.

> The Canadian justice system will never learn the lessons of the wrongly convicted so long as police and prosecutors approach criminal trials as a war with defence lawyers, says Toronto lawyer Clayton Ruby.
>
> Two principal causes of miscarriages of justice—the failure of the Crown to disclose vital information to

the defence and the prosecution's use of jailhouse informants—result from this mindset, says Mr. Ruby....

"The way we think about crime produces miscarriages of justice," Mr. Ruby says. "It is not a war. There is no enemy. It's just all of us trying to deal with a social problem. The trial is an exercise in producing a just result, not a victory, but a just result."

a) Summarize Clayton Ruby's view on the relationship between the Crown and the defence.

b) Identify whether each of the statements is opinion, fact, or argument.

c) Ruby refers to the "wrongly convicted." Research information on one of the following cases that deal with wrongful conviction: *R. v. Michaud, R. v. Stinchcombe, R. v. Truscott, R. v. Morin, R. v. Sophonow,* and *R. v. Marshall.* Present a summary of the case to your class. Include the basic facts of the case and what may have led to the wrongful conviction.

12. In the summer of 2000, British Columbia Supreme Court Justice Ron McKinnon allowed television cameras and radio microphones into the Victoria courtroom to record final submissions. The trial involved Chinese migrants who had been smuggled by boat into British Columbia. "Courtrooms are among our most public spaces, where fundamental decisions are made affecting all of us," Justice McKinnon told the media. "If we believe that justice must be seen to be done, this is a logical step." Explain Justice McKinnon's position in your own words. Prepare an argument in support of Justice McKinnon's statement or a counterargument that refutes his claim.

Develop Your Thinking

13. As a defence counsel, outline what you would do in the following situations. Your client
    a) brings you evidence that would obviously incriminate her
    b) admits to committing the offence—an offence you abhor
    c) tells you that he is going to have the main witness killed before the trial begins
    d) tells you that she did not commit the crime, but knows who did
    e) has no respect for the legal process and becomes disruptive during the trial
    f) has secretly instructed his friend to burn evidence before police find it

14. The adversarial system is not the only system of trial procedures. In the inquisitorial system, the judge also finds evidence and examines witnesses, not just the defence and the prosecution. Research the inquisitorial system, and prepare an organizer to show how it differs from the adversarial system.

From Sentencing to Release

Focus Questions

- What are the traditional objectives of sentencing?
- What are the goals of sentencing as specified in the *Criminal Code*?
- What sentencing options are available to a judge?
- What rights does a victim have in the criminal law process?
- What appeal processes are available to the offender and the Crown?
- What is the objective of release?
- What are the various types of release that apply to inmates?

Chapter at a Glance

Figure 9-1

Rachel Savage travelled to Cowansville Institution near Montreal to attend the parole hearing of her attacker, William Imming. In recent years, victims have played a more active role in the criminal justice system. Why would a victim want to attend an offender's parole hearing? Would you exercise this option if you could?

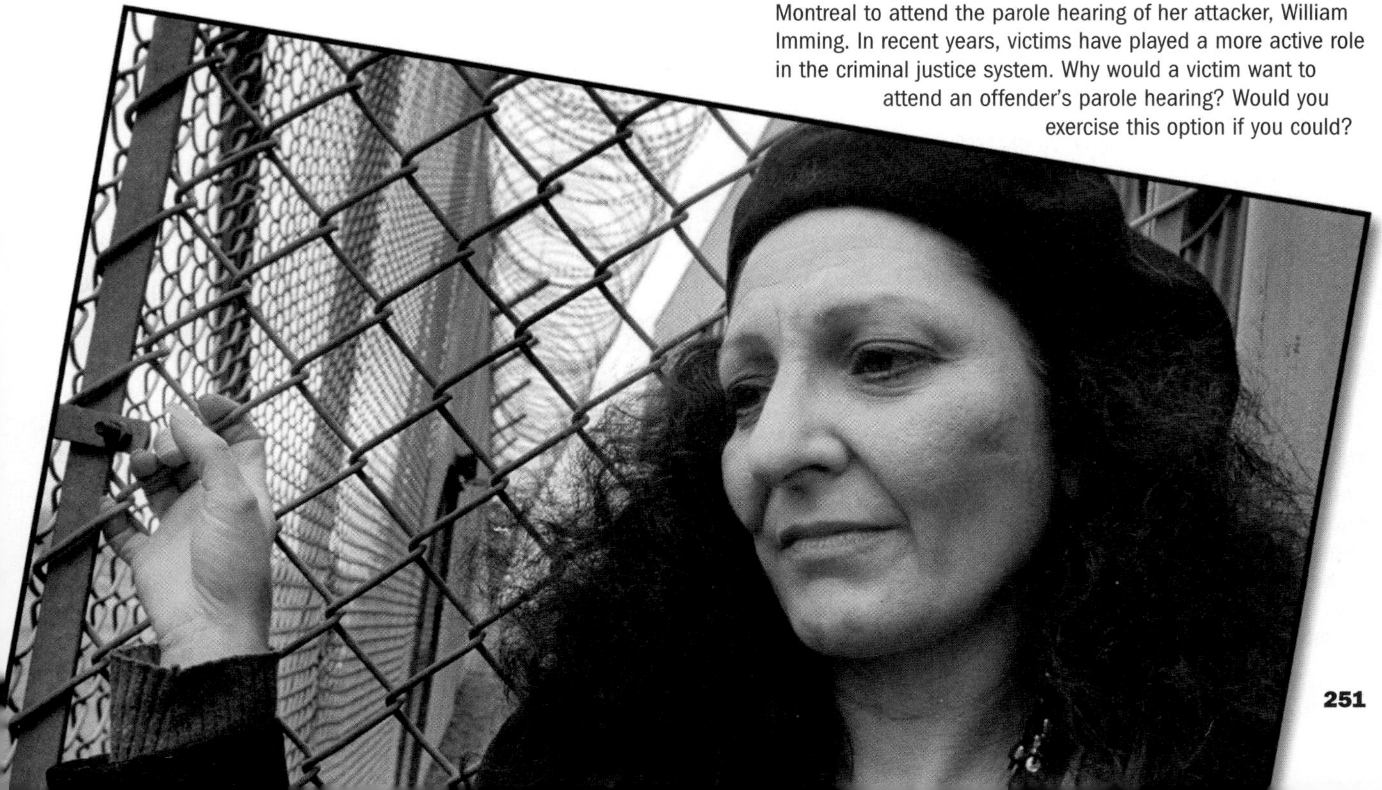

9.1 Introduction

Imposing a sentence is one of the most difficult tasks faced by judges. Once a sentence has been imposed, both the accused and society may appeal to a higher court. Eventually, the offender may enter a correctional facility. In Canada, this may involve time in a federal or provincial facility, depending on the nature and severity of the crime.

In this chapter, you will examine the sentencing and release of offenders. These areas of the law are controversial. Those who seek to punish offenders want to keep them in prison as long as possible. Other people believe that employment, education, and social programs can help the offender return to the community. In all cases, these theories must be balanced with the concern for public safety.

Most offenders are eventually released back into society. The system of conditional release allows the offender to serve the remainder of the sentence in the community while under supervision. Although the law provides for conditional release, not all inmates qualify for it, but those who do are usually successful in completing their sentences in the community.

9.2 The Process and Goals of Sentencing

Sentencing reflects social values. Some people believe that Canadian prisons are too "soft" on inmates and provide too many privileges. Others believe that prisons have many problems; for example, they are expensive to run and fail to reform certain criminals. Some people think that nonviolent offenders should pay their debt to society in other ways.

▌ Factors a Judge Must Consider

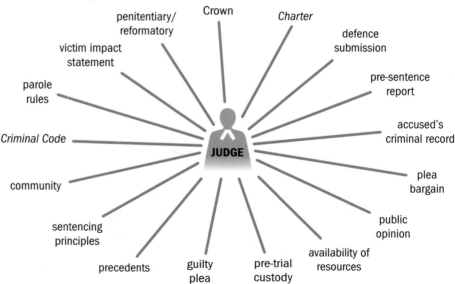

Figure 9-2

Judges must consider these factors when determining an appropriate sentence. Try rank-ordering these factors from most important to least important.

Sentencing may occur immediately after the accused has been found guilty or many weeks later. A judge may order a probation officer to prepare a **pre-sentence report,** which describes the offender's situation. The report will include interviews with the offender and others who are familiar with the person's history and potential. The judge will consider the report when passing sentence. Pre-sentence reports are usually not made for minor offences.

The defence and the Crown have the right to respond to sentencing and to call witnesses to testify about the offender's background. The Crown may raise any previous criminal record at this time. The convicted person may also make a statement. If the Crown and the offender disagree on the evidence at the time of sentencing, the judge can listen to sworn evidence.

When passing sentence, the judge must refer to the *Criminal Code*, which specifies the penalties available. The judge must also consider that Canadians have the right not to be subjected to "cruel and unusual punishment" according to the *Canadian Charter of Rights and Freedoms.*

Imposing a Sentence

Unlike judges in other countries, Canadian judges have considerable freedom in imposing sentences. For example, an offender found guilty of an indictable offence that carries a maximum penalty of 14 years can receive any term up to the maximum. To determine the correct penalty, judges often refer to precedents—previous similar cases. If a certain offence usually results in a certain sentence, the judge can take advantage of that pattern of sentencing. However, judges are not required to follow sentences imposed in similar cases.

When sentencing, a judge may also consider the time spent in custody awaiting trial and/or sentencing, the circumstances of the convicted person, and the potential for rehabilitation. The victim may also be considered. The judge may ask for a **victim impact statement.** This is a statement made in court by the victim and others affected by the offence. It describes the impact of the offence on their lives. Victim impact statements are especially significant for offences such as assault causing bodily harm, sexual assault, and murder, which may result in lasting psychological and financial damage to the victim or the victim's family.

Finally, the judge must consider the will of Parliament. In recent years, Parliament has toughened its stance toward people who have committed offences of harassment or sexual assault, or who have been involved in organized crime. In such instances, penalties have been increased or judges have been given more leeway to prescribe an appropriate sentence. Parliament has also noted that fewer offenders should be imprisoned, and it has introduced the **conditional sentence** and the label **long-term offender.**

Purpose and Principles of Sentencing

In 1995, Parliament added a statement about sentencing to the *Criminal Code*. This statement is found in section 718 (see The Law, page 255) and gives judges some direction in sentencing. It is based on the idea that appropriate sentencing promotes respect for law and the maintenance of a just, peaceful, and safe society.

Case

R. v. Goltz

[1991] 3 S.C.R. 485
Supreme Court of Canada

Goltz had his driver's licence suspended after accumulating numerous penalty points. He was stopped while speeding, and the officer noted that his licence had been suspended. He was found guilty of driving while prohibited under the British Columbia *Motor Vehicle Act*. The minimum penalty of seven days' imprisonment was imposed, along with a $300 fine. The Provincial Court found that imposing a minimum sentence of imprisonment did not infringe on the guarantee against cruel and unusual punishment in section 12 of the *Canadian Charter of Rights and Freedoms*.

Goltz appealed to the County Court, which ruled that the sentencing provision violated section 12 of the *Charter* and could not be justified under section 1. The Crown appealed to the British Columbia Court of Appeal, which agreed with the County Court findings. The Crown appealed to the Supreme Court of Canada.

In a 6 to 3 decision, the Supreme Court said that for a punishment to be "cruel and unusual," it must be "grossly disproportionate" to the crime, that is, not fit the crime. The seriousness of the offence, the personal characteristics of the offender, and the circumstances of the case must be considered. Other factors to be considered include whether the punishment

- is necessary to achieve the goals of the corrections system
- is founded on recognized sentencing principles
- has valid alternatives
- is not similar to punishments imposed for similar crimes in the same jurisdiction

The Supreme Court did not find the sentence "grossly disproportionate" to the crime. It viewed the offence as serious, noting that Goltz "knowingly and contemptuously" violated his driving restrictions, which are designed to protect public safety. The justices who voted against this ruling said that the sentence would, in some cases, be disproportionate to the crime. Therefore, it would violate the guarantee against cruel and unusual punishment.

For Discussion

1. Outline the factors to be considered in determining whether a punishment is grossly disproportionate to the crime.

2. Give reasons why most of the Supreme Court justices did not believe that the seven-day minimum sentence was cruel and unusual punishment.

3. In your opinion, would a minimum sentence of seven days' mandatory imprisonment plus a fine for driving while prohibited "be clearly disproportionate and shocking to the Canadian conscience, and hence violate the guarantee against cruel and unusual punishment"? Explain.

Historically, there have been four main goals when punishing offenders: **deterrence, rehabilitation, retribution,** and **segregation.** There is much debate about whether any of these goals are being met within the current prison system. These goals are outlined on the pages that follow.

Deterrence

Section 718 says that sentencing should deter people from breaking the law and should reflect society's intolerance of lawbreaking. It states that sentencing should deter an offender from committing a criminal offence in the future (specific deterrence). In addition, all members of society should be deterred from committing a similar crime (general deterrence).

Excerpts from the *Criminal Code*

718.

The fundamental purpose of sentencing is to contribute, along with crime prevention initiatives, to respect for the law and the maintenance of a just, peaceful and safe society by imposing just sanctions that have one or more of the following objectives:

(a) to denounce unlawful conduct;

(b) to deter the offender and other persons from committing offences;

(c) to separate offenders from society, where necessary;

(d) to assist in rehabilitating offenders;

(e) to provide reparations for harm done to victims or to the community; and

(f) to promote a sense of responsibility in offenders, and acknowledgment of the harm done to victims and to the community.

For Discussion

1. In your view, what are the three most important objectives of sentencing? Explain your choices.

Rehabilitation

The *Criminal Code* also says that sentencing should rehabilitate offenders. Over the years, society has come to view rehabilitation—sometimes called resocialization—as an important goal of sentencing. Today, for example, inmates are provided with job counselling and training. Supervised parole helps offenders to prepare for a return to society. Such assistance is intended to support former inmates when they return to society and reduce **recidivism** (return to prison upon being convicted of new offences).

Retribution

Retribution is not a sentencing objective, according to Canada's *Criminal Code*. However, the sentence imposed on an offender is a form of retribution. In *R. v. M (C.A.)* (see Case, page 263), the Supreme Court of Canada defined retribution as "an objective ... that properly reflects the moral culpability of the offender, ... the intentional risk-taking of the offender, the consequential harm caused by the offender, and the normative character of the offender's conduct."

Figure 9-3

Many Canadians view rehabilitation as an important goal of sentencing. Here, an inmate is involved in community service.

Segregation

The *Criminal Code* does state that one purpose of sentencing is to segregate offenders from society. Although Canada's **incarceration** (imprisonment) rate is not as high as that of the United States, it does have one of the highest rates in the world (see Figure 9-4, page 257). In recent years, the Canadian government has moved to reduce the number of offenders who are imprisoned. However, imprisonment is usually a given for a serious crime such as murder.

Other Goals of Sentencing

Section 718 includes additional sentencing objectives. It directs judges to consider reparations (repayment) for harm done to victims and the community, and it provides sentencing alternatives for this option. The *Criminal Code* also states that sentences should reflect the harm done to victims and to the community. Judges should consider whether the offender has shown any remorse for his or her conduct.

You Be the JUDGE

"Society, through the courts, must show its abhorrence of particular types of crime, and the only way in which the courts can show this is by the sentences they pass."

—Justice Lawton in *R. v. Sargeant* (1975)

- In your opinion, should judges be reacting to public opinion when sentencing? Explain.

Proportionality in Sentencing

The *Criminal Code* states that a sentence must be proportional. That means that the severity of the punishment must reflect the harm committed. For this reason, the most severe sentences are handed down for offences that are most offensive to society.

The *Criminal Code* also directs judges to increase or reduce a sentence under certain conditions. If there are **mitigating circumstances** (circumstances of the crime that lessen the responsibility of the offender), the penalty may be reduced. If there are **aggravating circumstances** (circumstances of the crime that increase the responsibility of the offender), the penalty may be increased.

Parliament defines aggravating circumstances as an offender's bias or hatred toward the victim; evidence that the offender abused a spouse or child, abused a position of trust or authority in relation to the victim, or committed the crime in association with a criminal organization.

Lastly, in section 718.2, the *Criminal Code* directs judges to
- give similar sentences for similar offenders committing similar offences in similar circumstances
- not impose consecutive sentences that are unduly long or harsh
- not deprive offenders of their liberty if less restrictive options are available
- consider all options other than imprisonment that are reasonable, especially for Aboriginal offenders

Case

R. v. Gladue

[1999] 1 S.C.R. 688
Supreme Court of Canada

Gladue was charged with second-degree murder and pleaded guilty to manslaughter after jury selection. At age 19, she suspected her fiancé was having an affair with her sister. She stabbed him with a knife after being provoked. She had a blood–alcohol content of between 155 and 165 at the time. Gladue was pregnant with her second child at the time of the murder. She had been raised by her father from age 11, after her mother left the home.

At the sentencing hearing, the judge considered a number of factors about Gladue. She was a young mother, and her only offence was an impaired driving conviction. At the time of the offence, she had a hyperthyroid condition, which caused her to overreact to emotional situations. She had showed signs of remorse and had entered a guilty plea. Her family had supported her, and she had attended alcohol abuse counselling and upgraded her education while on bail. She was pregnant with her third child at the time of sentencing.

The sentencing judge also considered a number of factors concerning the incident. She had stabbed

continued ▶

her fiancé twice, the second time while he was fleeing. The remarks that she made before and immediately after the stabbing left no doubt that she intended harm. She was the aggressor. During the time she was on bail, Gladue pleaded guilty to having breached her bail on one occasion by consuming alcohol.

Gladue was sentenced to three years' imprisonment and a 10-year weapons prohibition because the judge considered it to be a very serious offence. Her appeals to both the British Columbia Court of Appeal and the Supreme Court of Canada were dismissed.

For Discussion

1. What circumstances concerning Gladue and this incident would you consider mitigating if you were the sentencing judge?
2. What circumstances concerning Gladue and this incident would you consider aggravating if you were the sentencing judge?
3. If you were sentencing Gladue, what objectives of sentencing would you consider? Explain your choices.
4. What sentence would you have imposed on Gladue? Explain.

Review Your Understanding (Pages 252 to 257)

1. What is the purpose of a pre-sentence report? What might such a report contain?
2. What factors must a judge consider when deciding upon a sentence?
3. What is a victim impact statement and what is its purpose?
4. Briefly explain the four objectives of sentencing and provide an example for each.
5. Explain the term "recidivism."
6. Describe the concept of proportionality as it relates to sentencing.
7. Distinguish between aggravating and mitigating circumstances.
8. Describe two aggravating circumstances specified in the *Criminal Code* that should be considered when sentencing.

9.3 Sentencing an Offender

For most people, the word "sentencing" means imprisonment. However, society's views toward appropriate sentencing have been changing. Because of the high cost of maintaining the prison system, **diversion programs**—sentences that keep offenders out of the prison system—are increasing. Diversion programs are less costly than prison; they prevent the accused from socializing with other convicts; and they allow the accused to repay society in a more meaningful way.

Figure 9-4

Why do you think the rates of incarceration differ substantially in different countries?

▌ Rates of Incarceration, 2000

Country	Rate for every 100 000 citizens
United States	699
New Zealand	149
Britain & Wales	124
Canada	118
Germany	97
France	89
Denmark	61
Finland	57

Did You Know?

In the last century, at least once each decade since 1914, Canada has launched at least one commission of inquiry into the use of imprisonment. What does this suggest about Canada's concern for the sentencing process?

Absolute or Conditional Discharge

If a sentence is less than 14 years and the crime carries no minimum sentence, the offender may receive an **absolute discharge** or a **conditional discharge.** In either case, no conviction is recorded against the offender. Generally, a discharge is granted when it is the offender's first offence, or when the publicity attached to the case is so negative it becomes a kind of penalty. In *R. v. Fallofield* (1973), the British Columbia Supreme Court said that a discharge must be in the best interests of the accused and that it must not be contrary to the public interest.

An absolute discharge is effective immediately with no conditions attached. A conditional discharge means that the accused can avoid a record of conviction provided he or she follows certain conditions laid out by the judge in a **probation order** at the time of sentencing. Probation orders are discussed below.

Suspended Sentence and Probation

A judge may also give a **suspended sentence** after considering the age and character of the accused and the nature of, and the circumstances surrounding, the offence. When a sentence is suspended, it is delayed. If the offender meets certain conditions, it will never be served. The offender still has a record of conviction and could be placed on **probation** for up to three years. Probation orders can be used in addition to fines and in addition to sentences of less than two years. A suspended sentence cannot be given when there is a minimum sentence required by the *Criminal Code.*

A probation order requires that the accused keep the peace, be of good behaviour, appear before the court when required to do so, and do anything else the judge orders. For example, the offender usually reports to a probation officer and agrees not to carry a weapon. An offender who ignores the probation order may have to return to court.

Conditional Sentence

If a sentence is less than two years and the crime carries no minimum sentence, the judge may impose a conditional sentence. The judge sentences the offender to a term of less than two years in prison, but allows the offender to serve the time in the community. The judge must be satisfied that the offender will not endanger the safety of the community. A conditional order is issued, requiring the offender to keep the peace, be of good behaviour, and appear before the court when asked. There may be additional orders to abstain from drugs or alcohol and not carry a weapon.

Allowing offenders to serve their sentence in the community has been hotly debated in Canada. Since most prison sentences are less than two years, and few offences provide a minimum sentence, most offenders are eligible for a conditional sentence. The result is that people who have committed some serious crimes—sexual assault, assault with a weapon, theft, trafficking, and other violent offences—can serve their sentences in the community.

Did You Know?

In a 12-month period ending in 2000, there were 15 800 conditional sentences. This was up 11 percent from the previous period.

▌ How Courts Apply Conditional and Suspended Sentences

Conditional Sentence	Suspended Sentence
Sentence of imprisonment is imposed, but offender is released on a conditional order.	Sentence is not imposed, but offender is released on a probation order.
Offender *must* remain within the territorial jurisdiction of the court.	Offender *may* be ordered to stay within the territorial jurisdiction of the court.
Offender *may* be ordered to attend a treatment program.	Offender *may* be ordered to attend a treatment program, but only if offender agrees.
Offender *may* immediately be imprisoned to serve original sentence if conditional order is breached.	Offender *may* be sent back to trial judge to be sentenced for original offence if probation is breached. Offender can also be tried for breach of probation.

Figure 9-5

In what ways do conditional and suspended sentences appear to be the same?

Conditional sentences are intended to be heavier than suspended sentences. In reality, however, there is not much difference in their application by the courts.

Suspension of a Privilege

Many offences call for the **suspension** of a social privilege, such as a driver's licence or a licence to serve liquor in a restaurant. A person whose driver's licence has been suspended will usually have to surrender it before leaving the courtroom. In many jurisdictions, authorities can refuse to issue or renew a licence if a fine has not been paid. This measure has been introduced to reduce the tremendous backlog of unpaid fines and to encourage respect for the decisions of the court.

Peace Bond

A **peace bond** is a court order requiring a person to keep the peace and be of good behaviour for up to 12 months. A peace bond is often used in minor assault cases. Under the *Criminal Code*, someone who reasonably believes that another person will injure him or her, harm family members, or damage property can apply to have that person enter a peace bond. Once the accused has entered a peace bond, charges may be withdrawn, but other conditions are imposed. Usually the accused has to avoid the person who asked that the bond be imposed and agree not to own any weapons.

Parliament has amended the *Criminal Code* so that certain parties may be required to enter into a peace bond on the complaint of a citizen. For example, if a citizen swears that someone may commit a sexual offence against someone under the age of 14, the judge may order that person to refrain from having contact with persons under 14 years of age, or from being at a public swimming area or public park where persons under the age of 14 are present.

Restitution or Compensation

Restitution, also called **compensation,** is a relatively new penalty that requires the offender to repay the victim. The purpose is to reduce the impact of the offence on the victim and compensate the victim.

A victim may ask for restitution at the time of sentencing. The courts must now consider restitution in all cases involving harm to property or expenses arising from bodily harm. In granting restitution, the judge may consider a victim impact statement along with the offender's ability to provide restitution. If cash compensation is ordered, payments can be made over time. Restitution can also take the form of work. The victim can still sue the offender to obtain anything to which he or she feels entitled. The penalty for ignoring a court order granting restitution is imprisonment.

Some communities have programs that bring together the offender and victim and let them work out the compensation. Supporters of this idea believe that it has a more positive effect on the offender than would a prison sentence. The meeting also lets the victim communicate the impact of the crime directly to the offender.

Community Service Orders

A judge may sentence an offender to work a certain number of hours for a local organization or on a government project. This is known as a **community service order.** In requiring offenders to make a useful social contribution, community service orders may enhance their self-worth. In addition, community service allows the offender to associate with people in the community, instead of with criminals in institutions. Finally, community service occupies much of the offender's free time. For these reasons, community service may prevent the offender from committing other offences. Community service orders that will benefit the community are frequently part of a sentence for high-profile individuals. For example, a recording artist may be sentenced to perform a concert for a specific charity.

Deportation

Anyone who is not a Canadian citizen and who commits a serious offence within Canada can be **deported** to his or her country of origin or to any other country. Usually, the federal government applies to the courts for such a deportation order. Under the *Extradition Act*, Canadian residents who commit serious offences in other countries can be returned to those countries to stand trial or receive punishment.

Fines

For summary offences committed by individuals, the *Criminal Code* generally sets the maximum fine at $2000. Under other statutes, the maximum can be higher. To show society's concern about violent offences, the penalty for assault when the Crown proceeds summarily is $5000. For corporations, the maximum fine for summary offences is $25 000. No maximum fine is provided for indictable offences. If the penalty for an offence is five years or less, the offender may pay a fine instead of going to prison. Where the maximum penalty is more than five years, a fine may be imposed but only in addition to imprisonment. The judge establishes the amount of the fine.

An offender may ask to have at least 14 days to pay the fine. A **fine option program** is also available for both provincial and federal offences. Instead of paying a fine, an offender can earn credits for doing work similar to community service. The fine option program is not available in some provinces, such as Ontario.

Imprisonment

Canadians can go to prison for up to six months for most summary conviction offences. Some offences, such as uttering threats, assault with a weapon, sexual assault, and failure to comply with a probation order carry a penalty of up to 18 months. The maximum imprisonment for indictable offences can be two years to life imprisonment, depending on the seriousness of the crime. For offences such as driving while impaired and failure to give a breath sample, there is a minimum penalty. The offender may pay a fine instead of serving a sentence of less than five years; this option is not available if the sentence is over five years. Also, fines cannot be substituted if the stated penalty defines a minimum jail term. For a fuller list of offences and their penalties, see Chapter 5, pages 154 to 157.

A judge decides if the amount of time an offender has been kept in custody before trial will count toward a sentence. The standard rule is that pre-trial custody is equal to twice the time when considering a penalty. Thus, a person who has been in custody three months awaiting trial will have "served" six months of the sentence imposed. The reason for doubling the time is that there is no parole taken from the time, and there are usually no rehabilitation or recreational facilities available. It is considered to be dead time.

Figure 9-6

The forms of custodial sentences available are often subject to public criticism.

If the prison sentence is 30 days or less, the offender is usually kept at the local detention centre. If the sentence is more than 30 days but less than two years, the offender is placed in a provincial prison or reformatory. If the sentence is two years or more, the offender is sent to a federal institution (penitentiary).

People convicted of two or more offences may serve the sentence either concurrently or consecutively, at the judge's discretion. Offenders receive a **concurrent sentence** when they are convicted of two or more crimes and serve both penalties at the same time. Concurrent sentencing is used when the

WIZARD OF ID   BY BRANT PARKER & JOHNNY HART

Dated 9-23-1985. By permission of Johnny Hart and Creators Syndicate, Inc.

Figure 9-7

What is the difference between a consecutive sentence and a concurrent sentence?

You Be the JUDGE

Four offenders from Quebec received concurrent 45-month sentences for drug-related crimes. They got an additional 45 months, to be served consecutively, for belonging to a gang. The offenders could not apply for parole until they had served half of their prison terms.

• What objectives of sentencing do you think were being served by this sentence? Explain.

Did You Know?

Approximately half of the offenders admitted to federal institutions used alcohol and/or drugs on the day they committed the offence.

offences are similar or were committed at the same time. Offenders receive a **consecutive sentence** when they are convicted of two or more crimes, and they serve the penalties one after the other.

Because Parliament wants to curb the activities of criminal organizations, it has amended the *Criminal Code* to let judges impose a sentence of up to 14 years on offenders taking part in organized crime. This sentence is always served consecutively—in other words, it adds up to 14 years to any other sentence imposed. A sentence for an offence related to a terrorist activity must also be served consecutively to any other sentence given.

At the discretion of the judge, an offender may receive an **intermittent sentence,** serving it on weekends or even at night while maintaining a job. An intermittent sentence can be imposed only if the original sentence is less than 90 days. The court would also issue a probation order, outlining the conditions for the offender when not in prison.

The **principle of totality** guides sentencing. This means that someone who is convicted of several violations of the same offence, or of committing an offence while on probation for a similar offence, usually does not receive an overlong prison term. For instance, for someone found guilty of 24 charges of passing forged cheques, a year's sentence for each violation would be severe. A more reasonable total penalty would be two years. However, the penalties should not be so lenient that people are encouraged to commit multiple crimes.

Sentencing Dangerous and Long-Term Offenders

Someone who commits a serious personal injury offence may be declared a **dangerous offender** or a long-term offender. These offenders have little hope of being rehabilitated, or they pose a threat to society. A serious personal injury offence is an indictable offence (other than treason or first- or second-degree murder) involving violence or attempted violence, or conduct that endangers the life, safety, or psychological makeup of the victim. It also includes sexual assault.

For someone to be declared a dangerous offender, one of the following conditions must exist. The offender

• has a pattern of aggressive behaviour that is unlikely to change
• is indifferent to the consequences of his or her behaviour
• committed such a brutal offence that future behaviour is likely to be abnormal
• has sexual impulses that will likely cause injury or pain to others

The declaration is made at a hearing following a psychiatric assessment of the offender. Prospects for treatment or a cure are irrelevant. The offender is not sentenced on the original offence but receives an **indeterminate sentence.** In other words, the offender stays in an institution until it can be shown that he or she is able to return to society and display normal behaviour. The National Parole Board reviews the situation of dangerous offenders regularly.

To protect society from sexual offenders, a new sentencing category—long-term offender—was added to the *Criminal Code* in 1997. Sometimes, the Crown applies for this designation if it cannot prove the offender is dangerous. A long-term offender is someone who
- repeatedly displays behaviour that could cause death, injury, or psychological harm
- would likely reoffend following a sexual offence

The offender is sentenced for the original offence and receives an additional sentence of up to 10 years of community supervision.

Figure 9-8

Marlene Moore was the first woman to be declared a dangerous offender in Canada. Some experts believe that she should never have been labelled a dangerous offender. Moore never committed a homicide. She was prone to slashing herself and eventually committed suicide in her cell at the Kingston Penitentiary for Women.

Case

R. v. M. (C.A.)

[1996] 1 S.C.R. 500
Supreme Court of Canada

M. pleaded guilty to numerous counts of sexual assault, incest, and assault with a weapon, in addition to other lesser offences. M. had displayed a pattern of sexual, physical, and emotional abuse toward his children over several years. During his third marriage, M. fathered nine children. An officer sent to M.'s residence said it was the worst situation he had ever seen and that the children needed to be taken into care. The trial judge said the offences were "as egregious [shocking] as any offences that I have ever had the occasion to deal with." He hoped that the sentence that he imposed "will give the parole system an opportunity to function appropriately. I think they [the children] require a significant period of rehabilitation, of counselling."

None of the offences committed by M. carried a penalty of life imprisonment. One offence had a maximum term of imprisonment of 14 years, six offences had maximum terms of imprisonment of 10 years, and the remaining lesser offences carried maximum sentences of five years. The Crown requested a consecutive sentence of more than 20 years, given the seriousness of M.'s crimes. Psychological and psychiatric reports indicated that M. had little hope of rehabilitation. The children provided victim impact statements, which indicated that the physical, sexual, and emotional abuse would have devastating long-term consequences.

Defence replied that the Crown's request was excessive and that a sentence of 10 to 14 years was sufficient to meet the sentencing goals of deterrence. M., who was 52 years of age when sentenced, had personal experiences with abuse as a minor, was willing to forgo a trial wherein his children

continued ▶

would have had to give painful evidence, and expressed remorse for his crimes. M. also suffered from the trauma of two near-death experiences.

M. was sentenced to 25 years by the trial judge. The British Columbia Court of Appeal reduced the sentence to 18 years and 8 months, which included time prior to sentencing. The original sentence was reinstated by the Supreme Court of Canada.

The following points were made in the deliberations of the various courts:

- The results of studies have questioned the deterrent effect of penalties.
- As a general rule, any sentence over 20 years should carry a fixed parole eligibility date of seven years.
- Protection of society increases with sentences of 20 years or more.
- Canadian courts, possibly under the "totality principle," have been reluctant to impose a sentence of more than 20 years.

For Discussion

1. In a chart, compare the mitigating and aggravating factors that the judge should consider when imposing a sentence for this case.

2. In your opinion, would a sentence of more than 20 years provide specific deterrence or general deterrence? Explain.

3. Given that M. was 52 years of age when sentenced, would society be better protected by a sentence over 20 years? Should his age be relevant when considering a sentence? Explain.

4. What is the totality principle? In your opinion, is this a just case for ignoring it? Explain.

5. What sentencing option is available to keep an offender in prison for a lengthy period of time?

Capital Punishment

The issue of **capital punishment** (the death penalty) has been debated in Parliament and in the media. In 1962, the law on capital punishment was amended to distinguish between two categories of murder: capital and non-capital. Capital murder (murder requiring the death penalty) included planned and deliberate murder, murder committed during a violent crime, murder committed under contract, and the murder of a police officer or prison guard while on duty. All other types of murder were non-capital (punishable by life imprisonment).

Before 1962, a person convicted of a capital murder was sentenced to death by hanging, but the sentence could be commuted (changed to a lesser penalty) by the federal Cabinet. After 1962, all death sentences were commuted to life imprisonment by the federal Cabinet. Because so many sentences were commuted, capital punishment was debated in Parliament. In 1967, capital punishment was suspended for five years, except for convicted murderers of police officers and prison guards. In 1972, the suspension was extended for another five years. In 1976, by a six-vote margin, Parliament abolished the death penalty for *Criminal Code* offences. The issue was debated again in 1984, and capital punishment was not returned. Capital punishment remains a controversial issue.

Review Your Understanding (Pages 257 to 264)

1. What is a diversion program? What are the benefits of diverting people from prison?

2. a) What is probation, and what might a probation order involve?
   b) Discuss breach of probation.

3. a) Distinguish between an absolute and a conditional discharge.
   b) Distinguish between a conditional discharge and a suspended sentence.
4. a) What is the objective of a conditional sentence?
   b) What factors must be present for a judge to consider a conditional sentence?
5. Give two examples of the suspension of a social privilege.
6. What is a peace bond, and what is its purpose?
7. a) When must a judge consider ordering restitution to a victim?
   b) What developments are occurring in the area of compensation?
8. Why are community service orders used?
9. a) In what situations can a fine be imposed instead of imprisonment?
   b) What is a fine option program?
10. Distinguish among the following types of sentences: consecutive, concurrent, intermittent, and indeterminate.
11. Distinguish between a dangerous offender and a long-term offender.

9.4 Restorative Justice and Victims of Crime

Did You Know?

The Supreme Court has stated that the purpose of section 718.2(e) is to combat the problem of too many Aboriginal people in prisons and to encourage a restorative approach to sentencing.

Restorative justice focuses on healing relationships. Rather than focusing on dealing with the crime, it tries to deal with those who have suffered because of the crime: the offender, the victim, and the community. Until quite recently, criminal law did not consider or provide for the suffering of victims of crime. The victim usually did not come into contact with the offender after the criminal incident. Under restorative justice, the offender and the victim play major roles in resolving the conflict. For more information on restorative justice, see Issue, page 268.

Sentencing, Healing, and Releasing Circles

In Chapter 3, you learned that circles are often used by Aboriginal communities to resolve disputes. **Sentencing circles** bring together the offender, the victim, family and community members, a judge, lawyers, and the police to recommend the sentence for the offender. The victim and the community are able to express their views concerning the offence. They may even take part in developing the offender's sentence.

Healing circles are held to resolve the conflict between offender and victim. They allow each to voice his or her feelings and to indicate that they have undergone a personal healing.

Releasing circles are held in Aboriginal communities at the end of a sentence. Members of the National Parole Board, the community, and the offender meet. The purpose is to prepare a plan for the successful return of the offender to the community.

Case

R. v. Pena (sub nom. R. v. Ignace)

(1998) 156 D.L.R. (4th) 713
British Columbia Court of Appeal

In the "Gustafsen Lake standoff," where the incident occurred, the 18 accused claimed that the property was sovereign Native territory over which the police and the courts had no jurisdiction. The accused occupied the property and refused to vacate it. They used weapons in a way that endangered lives. A lengthy standoff involving hundreds of police resulted.

After the defendants were convicted at trial for mischief to private property of a value exceeding $5000, four of the accused—Pena, Deneault, Rosette, and Bronson—applied for an order requiring their sentencing to include a sentencing circle. Bronson was the only non-Native of the four. She was convicted of owning a weapon for the purpose of endangering the public peace and mischief causing actual danger to life.

To determine if a sentencing circle should be recommended, the court referred to the following criteria established in *R. v. Morin* (1995) by the Saskatchewan Court of Appeal:

- The accused must agree to be referred to the sentencing circle.
- The accused must have deep roots in the community in which the circle is held and from which the participants are drawn.
- There are elders or respected non-political community leaders willing to participate.
- The victim is willing to participate and has not been subjected to coercion or pressure in so agreeing.
- In family assault cases, the court should try to determine if the victim is subject to battered-spouse syndrome.

- Disputed facts have been resolved in advance.
- The case is one in which a court would be willing to take a calculated risk and depart from the usual range of sentencing.

The court stated that this case was not an appropriate one for a sentencing circle for the following reasons:

- The convictions arose out of a social protest.
- The offences occurred in a remote and isolated area on ranch land in the Cariboo. The offences did not arise out of community social conditions, so no "community" would be in a position to work with the offenders or monitor their behaviour.
- The initiative for this application did not come from any community, but from the applicants. Not all the applicants were from the area where the offences took place.
- There was no indication the applicants were sorry for what they had done or prepared to consider abandoning the tactics that led to their involvement in the offences.

For Discussion

1. In what ways does a sentencing circle meet the objectives of restorative justice?

2. Why is it important that a sense of community be present for a sentencing circle to be effective?

3. Outline reasons why a sentencing circle would not be a good option in this case.

4. In your opinion, will sentencing circles ever become a widely used sentencing option? Explain.

Victims of Crime

The Crown prosecutes a criminal matter on behalf of society, not the victim. The Crown decides on the charge to be laid, introduces the evidence, and asks for a penalty. Although victims help to solve crimes, they often feel left out of the process. New research has shown that when victims participate in the criminal process, they may heal more quickly from the event. As a result, changes have been introduced to give the victim a larger role. In 1985, the United Nations General Assembly approved a *Charter of Victims' Rights*. It provides the basis for similar documents in some provinces and territories.

In most provinces, victims can obtain some support services at the time of the offence. Some services are offence-specific, such as a sexual assault crisis centre. Others provide assistance to all victims of crime. Twenty-four-hour crisis and support lines are frequently available. In some jurisdictions, victim/witness assistance programs provide information about the prosecution process and emotional support during the trial and sentencing. Crown attorneys are directed to keep the victims informed of the charges, plea, and sentencing.

Support staff may also assist with the preparation of a victim impact statement. This statement can only outline the harm done to, or loss suffered by, the victim and/or his or her family members. It can be presented to the judge before sentencing. The statement cannot include any other commentary, including a suggested sentence. The victim may also ask to read the statement in court. The victim can also be called as a witness at a sentencing hearing.

 activity

Visit **www.law.nelson.com** and follow the links to learn more about MADD.

Agents of Change MADD Canada

MADD Canada (Mothers Against Drunk Driving) is one of Canada's first victims' rights groups. Founded in 1990, MADD is a volunteer organization that assists the victims of drunk drivers and their families. It also works to reform laws against impaired driving and helps to prevent underage drinking. Its Designated Driver Program for safe, sober transportation has been adopted across Canada.

Drunk driving is a serious problem in Canada. Impaired drivers kill an average of 4.5 Canadians every 24 hours. Drunk drivers kill twice the number of those murdered every year, yet it is estimated that only 1 in 445 impaired trips results in the drunk driver being caught.

In 1999, the federal government passed tougher drinking and driving laws. These reforms were largely the result of MADD Canada's work. The minimum federal fine for impaired driving was increased from $300 to $600. The penalty for someone convicted of impaired driving whose licence had already been suspended was increased from two years in prison to five years. Judges may now require convicted drunk drivers to enter rehabilitation programs as part of their sentence. Victims of drunk drivers can now read their impact statements in court.

Despite these victories, MADD Canada wants even tougher laws. It wants mandatory life sentences for drunk drivers who kill another human being. It wants the government to lower the blood–alcohol concentration from 80 to 50, as other countries have done. It also wants the government to create a Victims' Bill of Rights, which would outline the human rights of victims of crime. MADD argues that such a bill would focus more attention on the rights of the victim in court.

For Discussion

1. **Should drunk drivers who kill someone receive a mandatory life sentence? Explain.**
2. **What rights should a victim have in court?**

Figure 9-9

Andrew Murie, National Executive Director of MADD

Are Restorative Justice Programs Good for Victims?

It costs Canadian taxpayers an estimated $10 billion a year to pay for policing, the court system, and corrections. If the personal costs of victims were included in this figure—for example, pain and suffering or lost days of work—the total annual cost of crime would be $46 billion.

Victims' rights have received much more attention in recent years than previously. Canada has passed federal, provincial, and territorial laws to protect the rights of victims and to involve them in what happens to those who caused them damage.

On One Side

Some Canadians believe that victims should play a major role in restorative justice programs (see page 265). These programs bring together victims, offenders, and community members following the commission of a crime. Through mediation and discussion, program participants seek ways to fix the damage caused by a crime.

Restoration programs emphasize healing, forgiveness, and community involvement. They reach out to victims, their families, and offenders. In an effort to prevent future crime, they try to explore why the offender committed the crime. The process helps victims describe how the crime affected them and their family members. It also permits offenders to explain their actions, express their remorse, and compensate the victim.

Figure 9-10

Allowing victims to meet offenders in a non-threatening setting is the goal of restorative justice programs. Still, many victims decline to participate.

The federal government changed the *Criminal Code* in 1996 to support these programs. The government states that "all available sanctions other than imprisonment that are reasonable in the circumstances should be considered for all offenders, with particular attention to the circumstance of aboriginal offenders." Canada has approximately 200 restorative justice programs, and they appear to be working. Both Aboriginal and non-Aboriginal offenders may participate. An RCMP study reported that 85 percent of offenders lived up to the conditions of their restorative justice programs. These programs also seem to be meeting the needs of victims and the community.

On the Other Side

Many victims are afraid to meet their offenders and feel threatened when they do. Some victims say that the crimes committed against them are so terrible that they could never meet the offenders or work with them to find solutions. They also do not want to be inconvenienced by taking time off work to attend these meetings.

Victims' rights groups say that restorative justice programs pay too much attention to offenders. They believe that victims are pressured to get involved with such programs. Governments should take some of the money spent on restorative justice programs to increase compensation for victims of crime.

Some of these critics applaud other changes made by the government, however. For example, amendments to the *Criminal Code* in 1999 allow victims to read a victim impact statement in court. Judges can also order offenders to pay damages to victims. If an offender does not pay, the victim has the right to go to civil court and seize the assets and wages of the offender.

The Bottom Line

Restorative justice programs are useful to victims, and they also benefit governments. They are designed to keep offenders out of prison, thereby reducing the number of cases before the courts and saving the system money. Although many victims support these programs, they also want laws that punish offenders and prevent crime. The most important purpose of the legal system is to protect society, not rehabilitate offenders. Supporters of restorative justice programs think that people who commit less serious offences can benefit from these programs. They say that such offenders will only be hardened in prison, and that an emphasis on support and treatment programs can help these people rejoin society instead of turning to a life of crime.

What Do You Think?

1. Explain the term "restorative." What are the purposes of restorative justice programs?
2. What roles do crime victims play in these programs? How can they benefit?
3. What criticisms have been made of these programs?
4. What evidence is there that victims' groups have achieved more protection for crime victims in recent years?
5. How do restorative justice programs seem to be in conflict with victims' groups?
6. Outline your opinions of restorative justice programs and victims' groups. Discuss with a classmate.

The *Criminal Code* lets the Crown request restitution for the victim. The judge can also consider restitution, without the formal application of the victim. Restitution can be given for

- damage
- loss or destruction of property
- bodily harm, including loss of income or support and psychological services
- costs incurred by spouses who have been forced from their home because of bodily harm or the threat of bodily harm

Restitution can even be ordered for "indirect" victims. If a stolen car is sold to someone in good faith, and the car is later seized as part of a criminal proceeding, restitution can be ordered for the purchaser to cover losses.

Parliament takes restitution seriously. It has given judges the power to insist that the restitution order be paid before any fine that is imposed. This may help to ensure that the victim is compensated even when the offender has few resources.

Under the *Corrections and Conditional Release Act* (formerly the *Parole Act*), the victim has the right to know the offence for which the offender was convicted, the length of the sentence, and the penitentiary where the sentence is being served. The Act permits victims to provide information about the crime when the inmate is applying for parole. The victim may attend parole sessions and provide a statement to help officials assess whether an offender's release might pose a risk to society. The victim can also be told the date of the offender's release, his or her destination, and any conditions that were attached to the release. Any other person who can show the parole board that he or she has been harmed "as a result of an act of the offender" may receive this information as well. In some provinces, a victim can register to receive prompt information related to the movement of provincially sentenced inmates within the prison system, as well as inmate leaves or escapes. Victims may also contact the supervision probation officer dealing with community supervision.

ⓔ activity

Visit **www.law.nelson.com** and follow the links to learn more about organizations that support victims of crime.

Criminal Injuries Compensation Fund

The Criminal Injuries Compensation Fund has existed since 1973. Financed by the federal and provincial governments, this fund uses public money to compensate a person who is injured in some way when a crime is committed, or when he or she assists an officer making an arrest, makes a citizen's arrest, or tries to prevent a crime. Victims sometimes turn to the fund because the criminal has no money or has not yet been caught.

The award is intended to cover specific situations, such as lost pay, pain and suffering from injuries, support of a child born as the result of rape, medical bills and prescriptions, loss of income by dependants if the victim dies, funeral expenses, or anything else that the board feels is reasonable. Each situation must be verified, and the victim must return the money if he or she successfully sues the offender for compensation.

Victim Assistance Fund

The Victim Assistance Fund was established to set up education, counselling, and other programs for victims of crime. Part of the fund's financing is provided by convicted offenders, who must pay a surcharge on their fines. This can be up to 15 percent of the fine, or an amount not greater than $10 000 where no fine is imposed.

Review Your Understanding (Pages 265 to 271)

1. What are the purposes of sentencing circles, healing circles, and releasing circles?
2. Summarize the programs available to victims
   a) at the time of the offence
   b) during the trial and sentencing
   c) after the offender has been convicted
3. Outline the right of a victim to receive restitution.
4. a) What is the purpose of the Criminal Injuries Compensation Fund?
   b) Name five types of losses that are covered by the fund.
5. What is the purpose of the surcharge on fines paid by convicted offenders?

9.5 Appeals

The right to request an appeal of a court decision is an important part of criminal procedure. Both the accused and the Crown have rights of appeal, as outlined below. The party that makes the appeal request is called the **appellant** and the other party is called the **respondent.** If the appeal is requested for a reason that is not set out in law, the request will be dismissed. Appeal courts are discussed in Chapter 4.

Generally, a period of 30 days is allowed to apply for an appeal. The accused may apply to be released during the appeal time. If the court agrees to a release, conditions may be imposed.

For appeals of summary offences, the court examines the transcript of the trial. Sometimes, it examines a statement of facts agreed on by the defence and the Crown. For appeals of indictable offences held in the higher courts, the appellant and the respondent present their arguments. New evidence, referred to as fresh evidence, is admitted only if it is relevant, credible, and would have affected the results of the trial.

The defence can appeal a conviction, a verdict, a sentence, or rulings on fitness to stand trial for a summary conviction offence. The appeal can be based on a question of law and/or fact. An appeal on the basis of law may question a judge's interpretation of the law. An appeal on the basis of fact is usually based on whether evidence was relevant or credible. The Crown can also appeal a summary offence decision.

The defence can appeal a conviction for an indictable offence on the following grounds:
- a question of law
- a question of law and fact, or fact alone, if the court gives its permission
- any other reason that the appeal court believes is worthy

The Crown can appeal a decision of not guilty for an indictable offence on the following grounds:
- a question of law
- the sentence, if the court gives its permission
- a trial judge orders that an indictment is invalid, or the judges stay the proceedings

The Court of Appeal collects the necessary information to consider the appeal: a transcript of the evidence taken at trial, charges to the jury, reasons for the trial judge's decision, and possibly a report from the trial judge. The appeal court votes on the final decision. The reason for the majority decision is disclosed, and any dissenting judges may state why they disagreed. The court can also rule on which party will pay the costs of the appeal.

The defence may be successful if the evidence does not support the guilty decision, if an error of law was made, or there has been a miscarriage of justice. The accused is then released. The appeal court may also change the verdict of the original court, change the sentence, or order a new trial. Based on the rule of precedent, the lower courts must follow the decisions of a higher court.

Review Your Understanding (Pages 271 to 272)

1. **On what basis can the accused appeal a summary offence decision?**
2. **Distinguish between a question of law and a question of fact.**
3. **On what basis can the Crown appeal an indictable offence decision?**
4. **On what information does the appeal court base its decision?**
5. **Identify the options the appeal court has in making its decision.**

9.6 Prison

Canadians differ widely in their opinion of how prisons should operate and how offenders should be treated. Some people believe that offenders should remain in prison for as long as possible—the maximum allowed by law. Others believe that since offenders are partially shaped by society, it should work to rehabilitate them.

Entering the Prison System

The rules governing **conditional release** are outlined in the *Corrections and Conditional Release Act*. An offender who goes to prison comes under the jurisdiction of provincial or federal **correctional services**. Each province has its own correctional services regulations and is responsible for offenders in provincial prisons. Offenders in these institutions have been sentenced to prison terms of less than two years. Correctional services are responsible for

- incarcerating all offenders
- processing parole applications
- supervising offenders who are granted any type of early release
- supervising offenders released from institutions before the end of their sentence
- running probation services

Inmates in provincial institutions serve time in closed custody, open custody, or community correctional centres. **Closed custody** is reserved for offenders who are dangerous, likely to escape, or are hard to manage. **Open custody** institutions provide an opportunity for the inmate to work, usually in forest management and maintenance, or farming. Inmates in **community correctional facilities** are allowed to work or go to school on a daily basis, returning to the correctional facility at night. Many of the residents are inmates on day parole.

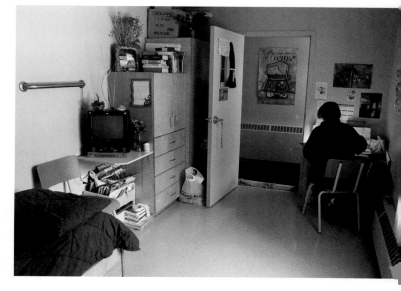

Federal correctional facilities have different levels of security: maximum, medium, and minimum. Community correctional centres offer less security than minimum-security prisons.

How are offenders assigned to institutions? After sentencing, they are assessed to determine their level of risk and their need for rehabilitation. Next, an institution is selected, based on the type of offence committed, the risk of escape, the availability of rehabilitation programs, and the location of the offender's family members. Attempts are also made to place offenders where they will have contact with their own culture and language. Those convicted of first-degree and second-degree murders have to serve a minimum of two years in maximum-security prisons before being permitted to apply to move to lower-security ones.

In prison, an inmate is assigned to a case management team that helps the inmate with rehabilitation and encourages him or her to broaden social contacts. Institutions offer a broad range of programs, including life skills and literacy programs, and treatment programs for substance abuse, sex offences, and family violence. Inmates are also encouraged to enroll in educational programs. They are paid a daily allowance, which can be used at the canteen.

While in prison, inmates are subject to the discipline procedures in the *Corrections and Conditional Release Act*. The Act governs the day-to-day management of inmates, including their placement and transfer, general living conditions, discipline, searches, and health care.

Figure 9-11

An inmate reads in her room at the women's prison in Joliette, Quebec in February 2001. This is a medium-security facility.

Review Your Understanding (Pages 272 to 273)

1. **List the responsibilities of correctional services.**
2. **Distinguish between open and closed custody.**
3. **What is a community correctional facility and what level of security is provided?**
4. **Identify the factors considered when assigning an offender to a correctional institution.**
5. **What determines the location in which an offender spends a prison term?**
6. **What is the purpose of a case management team?**

9.7 Conditional Release

The goal of conditional release is to allow an offender to return to society under supervision in preparation for an unsupervised release. The National Parole Board, appointed by the federal government, has jurisdiction over parole for all of Canada, with the exception of the provincial prisons in Quebec, Ontario, and British Columbia. These provinces have their own parole boards. The primary consideration for determining whether an inmate should be released is public safety. Conditional release programs are described in detail in this section.

▌ Release Programs for Federal Prison Inmates

Type of Release	When Granted	Duration
Escorted absences	Any time	5–15 days
Unescorted absences	After one-sixth of sentence is served, or six years, whichever is greater	2 days if in medium security 3 days if in minimum security
Day parole	Before full parole	Daily; return to halfway house
Full parole	After one-third of sentence is served, or seven years, whichever is less	Until completion of sentence if conditions are followed
Statutory release	After two-thirds of sentence is served	Until completion of sentence if conditions are followed

Figure 9-12

While a variety of release programs are available to offenders, they will not always be granted. What main factor do you think is taken into consideration in deciding on the form of release?

Temporary Absence

Escorted and unescorted absences may be granted to allow offenders to participate in rehabilitation programs, obtain medical treatment, or attend significant family events. All offenders are eligible for absences based on medical or humanitarian grounds. For other types of absences, only those classified as medium or minimum security are eligible.

During escorted absences, offenders are accompanied by correctional services staff or citizen volunteers. All offenders are eligible for escorted absences from the time they enter prison. Unescorted absences are not given to maximum-security offenders. Inmates eligible for an unescorted absence are also eligible for work release. Those who committed a violent offence, a sexual offence involving children, or a drug-related offence may be eligible for unescorted temporary absences with the permission of the National Parole Board.

Escorted and Unescorted Absences, Year Ending in 2000

Absences	Escorted	Unescorted
Number granted	40 392	7307
Completed successfully	99.92%	99.44%

Figure 9-13

Both escorted and unescorted absences have high success rates. Why do you think this is so?

Day Parole To parole an offender is to release him or her after a portion of the sentence has been served. Under **day parole,** an offender is released during the day but must return to the institution or a halfway house each night. Day parole allows offenders to go to work or school to prepare for full parole or **statutory release.** An inmate serving a life sentence is eligible for day parole three years before full parole eligibility.

Full Parole At the start of an offender's incarceration, a date is automatically set for a review for **full parole.** Any judge imposing a penalty of two or more years has the right to increase the minimum time that must be served before parole eligibility. It can be increased up to one-half of the sentence, or 10 years, whichever is less.

During the parole review, a great deal of information is compiled:

- What efforts has the offender made in prison?
- What are the results of a personality assessment?
- Has the offender received and benefited from treatment?
- Does the offender understand the nature and seriousness of the offence?
- Does the offender have a place to live following release?
- Does he or she have any job prospects?

After this information is compiled, a parole hearing is set. The offender and anyone over 18 years of age may attend the hearing as an observer, with the board's permission. The board reviews the information before it. As you learned earlier, it may also include a submission from a victim or parties who have been harmed by the offender.

The parole board is empowered to set a date for parole, reserve its decision until further investigation, defer parole, or deny parole. If parole is denied, the board generally must review the case every two years. If parole is granted,

Did You Know?

Terrorist offenders are ineligible for parole for half of the sentence imposed, unless the offender can show that this is not in the public interest.

Percentage of Paroles Completed Successfully, Year Ending in 2000

Parole	Day Parole	Full Parole
Completed successfully	82.5%	72.8%
Revoked (violation of conditions)	11.9%	14.3%
Revoked (commission of non-violent offence)	4.8%	11.1%
Revoked (commission of violent offence)	0.8%	1.8%

Figure 9-14

What does the data indicate about the success rate of conditional release programs?

There are more than 170 inmates over the age of 65 in federal institutions. Some are in their 80s. In many cases, they stay past their parole eligibility dates because prison is the only home they know.

- Should different programs and release procedures be available to those inmates over 65 years of age? Explain.

e activity

Visit **www.law.nelson.com** and follow the links to learn more about parole.

a parole supervisor is assigned. Parole is a conditional system. If the **parolee** (the person who has been granted parole) violates any conditions set by the board, he or she may be brought back to serve the rest of the sentence. If the conditions are respected, parole ends when the original sentence would have ended.

Parole for Murder

Offenders who have committed murder are subject to different parole rules and conditions. The *Criminal Code* says that those convicted of first-degree murder and sentenced to life in prison are not eligible for full parole for 25 years. Thus, a life sentence does not mean that the offender will spend life in prison—indeed, most who receive a life sentence are released. However, they are under parole supervision for the rest of their lives. Those convicted of second-degree murder have their parole eligibility established by the judge at the time of sentencing, between 10 and 25 years. In a trial by jury, the jury meets again after delivering a verdict to decide whether it will recommend an appropriate time length for parole eligibility. The judge does not have to consider the jury's recommendation, but must consider the factors outlined in *R. v. Shropshire* (see Case, below).

Both groups may be eligible for unescorted temporary absences and day parole three years before their full parole eligibility date. As well, those sentenced to serve more than 15 years before being eligible for full parole may apply for a judicial review after 15 years. This is referred to as the **faint hope clause.** For example, someone who would not be eligible for parole for 20 years could apply to have the 20-year limit reviewed after 15 years. This clause was introduced to recognize that an inmate may be rehabilitated after 15 years. Offenders convicted of more than one murder are not eligible for judicial review.

When such an appeal is made, a judge must consider the character of the applicant, the offender's conduct in prison, the nature of the offence, any victim impact statements, and any other relevant information. If the judge approves the review, a superior court judge holds a hearing with a jury. If the jury unanimously decides that the parole eligibility period should be reduced, a majority of jury members must decide by how many years. In the year ending in 2000, of 103 parole reviews, 84 offenders had their parole eligibility date brought closer.

Case

R. v. Shropshire

[1995] 4 S.C.R. 227
Supreme Court of Canada

Shropshire, Buffam, and Lang were together at Shropshire's home dealing marijuana. Without any warning, Shropshire shot Buffam three times in the chest as they were about to complete the deal. He then chased Lang in his car, shouting that another

person had told him to do it. Two days later, Shropshire gave himself up to the police. He expressed remorse, but was unwilling or unable to explain his actions. No motive was ever given. Shropshire was 23 years of age and had a wife and two children.

Shropshire had a criminal record that included two convictions in Youth Court for robbery, a conviction for impaired driving, and two narcotic

continued

offences as an adult. The Crown and defence presented a joint submission, asking for the minimum of 10 years for parole ineligibility. The trial judge then sentenced Shropshire to life imprisonment without eligibility for parole for 12 years. He said that denunciation (condemnation) was the reason for the increase. A majority of the British Columbia Court of Appeal allowed Shropshire's appeal against his sentence and reduced the parole ineligibility to 10 years, the minimum. The Crown appealed this reduction to the Supreme Court of Canada, which upheld the original trial judge's sentencing.

The *Criminal Code* states that the sentencing judge should consider the character of the offender, the nature of the offence, and the circumstances under which the offence was committed when considering the eligibility period for parole.

Commenting on the appeal court's reduction of the sentence, the Supreme Court of Canada stated: "An appellate court should not be given free reign to modify a sentencing order simply because it feels that a different order ought to have been made. The formulation of a sentencing order is a profoundly subjective process; the trial judge has the advantage of having seen and heard all of the witnesses whereas the appellate court can only base itself upon a written record. A variation in the sentence should only be made if the court of appeal is convinced it is not fit. That is to say, that it has found the sentence to be clearly unreasonable."

For Discussion

1. In your opinion, what facts should the trial judge have included in this case when considering the following factors?
   a) the character of the offender
   b) the nature of the offence
   c) the circumstances surrounding the offence
2. Would you consider this offence to be a more severe example of a second-degree murder? Explain.
3. Why would the Crown appeal the decision of the British Columbia Court of Appeal to reduce the parole ineligibility to 10 years when that is what the Crown asked for in the joint submission to the sentencing judge?
4. What advantages does a sentencing judge have over an appeal court when determining an appropriate sentence?
5. According to the Supreme Court of Canada, under what circumstances should an appeal court modify a trial judge's sentence?

Accelerated Review

Offenders who are serving their first term in a penitentiary, and who did not commit a violent offence, a drug offence, a sexual offence, or a criminal organization offence, are eligible for an **accelerated review,** provided that the judge did not set parole eligibility at one-half of the sentence. They must be released on full parole unless the parole board can find reasonable grounds to believe the offender is likely to commit an offence involving violence before the end of the sentence.

Statutory Release

By statute, prisoners are entitled to statutory release—to spend the final one-third of their sentence in the community under supervision. The exceptions are offenders serving life or indeterminate sentences. Although statutory release is automatic for most offenders, the parole board can add conditions to the release. The inmate can be ordered to stay in a community correctional centre, a community residential centre, or a psychiatric facility. For provincial inmates, there are no conditions on release. If the offender is likely to commit an offence causing death or serious harm to another person, a sexual offence involving a child, or to commit a serious drug offence before the end of the sentence, even statutory release can be denied.

Royal Prerogative of Mercy

The federal government has the power to grant a **Royal Prerogative of Mercy.** Applications are made to the National Parole Board, which investigates and makes recommendations to the solicitor general. Under a Royal Prerogative of Mercy, an inmate may have a fine or prison sentence rescinded (revoked) or may be issued a free pardon or an ordinary pardon. A **free pardon** is granted when evidence shows that the convicted person is innocent. An **ordinary pardon** is usually granted on compassionate grounds. All alternatives release the offender from the conviction and related penalties. One of the most celebrated cases of pardons in Canada involved Donald Marshall Jr., who spent 11 years in prison for a crime he did not commit. A royal commission cleared Marshall of any responsibility.

Criminal Records

More than 2.5 million people in Canada have criminal records. For some people, the penalty for having a criminal record may be only embarrassment. For others, it may mean the loss of job opportunities. For instance, many jobs require **bonding**—insurance that guarantees the honesty of a person who handles money or other valuables. A person with a record usually cannot be bonded. Also, some countries refuse to admit persons with a criminal record.

If an accused is given an absolute or a conditional discharge, the RCMP will automatically remove the record from its computer system following the court decision. This applies to cases after July 24, 1992. For removal of records prior to that time, applications must be made to the RCMP. Those with other convictions can apply to the National Parole Board for a pardon. If successful, the offender's criminal record is kept separate from other criminal records. The offender must be free of other convictions during the waiting period (three to five years after completing the sentence). The *Human Rights Act* of each province also prohibits employment discrimination against anyone with a criminal record. The *Canadian Human Rights Act* forbids discrimination based on a pardoned conviction.

Figure 9-15

Security guards are bonded if they are required to work with cash or other valuables. What other jobs might require bonding?

Review Your Understanding (Pages 274 to 278)

1. a) Who has jurisdiction over conditional release?

   b) What factors are considered in a release review?

2. Compare escorted absences to unescorted absences.

3. What is the purpose of the faint hope clause?

4. a) Who may receive an accelerated review? When must they be released?

   b) Explain the circumstances under which statutory release is allowed.

5. Discuss the alternatives available when the Royal Prerogative of Mercy is granted.

6. a) What effect does a criminal record have on bonding?

   b) Who is eligible to have a criminal record erased?

   c) Describe the process for having a criminal record removed.

Chapter Review

Chapter Highlights

- The defence and the Crown can both make submissions on sentencing.
- A judge uses a variety of information to establish an appropriate sentence.
- There are four basic sentencing objectives.
- Parliament has given guidance to judges by enacting sentencing principles.
- The *Criminal Code* directs judges to increase or reduce a sentence if there are any relevant aggravating or mitigating circumstances.
- Sentences are to be proportional: They are to reflect the degree of harm caused.
- The principle of totality states that an offender should not be sentenced to an overlong prison term.
- Sentences for multiple offences may be served consecutively or concurrently.
- Violent offenders may be classified as dangerous offenders or long-term offenders.
- Restorative justice focuses on the healing of relationships.
- Circles are used as means of healing the offender, the victim, and the community.
- Victims of crime have new rights at the time of arrest, trial, sentencing, and parole.
- The rules for appealing judgments and sentences are very specific.
- There are many types of release available to inmates: day parole, escorted absences, unescorted absences, work release, full parole, statutory release, and a Royal Prerogative of Mercy.
- The time for parole eligibility for murderers is specified at the time of sentencing.
- Free pardons and ordinary pardons can be granted by the federal government.
- An offender can apply to have his or her criminal record removed from the police computer system.

Review Key Terms

Name the key terms that are described below.

a) the return to prison of repeat offenders

b) a sentence that discourages a person from committing the same offence

c) a sentence that keeps an offender in an institution until the offender can show that he or she will be able to return to society and display normal behaviour

d) the right to be released back into the community under supervision after serving two-thirds of a sentence if the offender has not already been released on parole

e) the principle that a person who is convicted of several violations of the same offence should not be sentenced to an overlong prison term

f) a sentence with more than one penalty served at the same time

g) to be discharged with no conditions and no conviction recorded

h) imprisonment

i) programs directed at keeping offenders out of the prison system

j) a report prepared prior to sentencing

k) a statement made by the victim outlining the impact of the offence on his or her life

l) circumstances that lessen the responsibility of the offender

m) the party requesting an appeal

n) a sentence to be served on weekends

o) repaying the victim

p) the party opposing an appeal

Check Your Knowledge

1. Distinguish among deterrence, retribution, rehabilitation, and segregation as goals of sentencing.

2. Outline the various sentencing options available and provide an example of each.

3. Explain the role of victims at the time of sentencing and during the parole application process.

4. Explain the various forms of conditional release and provide an example of each.

Apply Your Learning

5. For each of the following situations, indicate whether or not you would impose a conditional sentence, and if so, what additional requirements you would add on as part of a conditional sentence order. Give the reasons for your decision.

a) *R. v. Bogart* (2001), (Ontario Superior Court of Justice)

A doctor, described as being very gifted in psychotherapy treatment for patients with HIV, is convicted of defrauding the Ontario Health Insurance Plan of $922 780. The fraud was the largest single fraud against the plan. He used much of the money to go on expensive trips with his lover, who turned the doctor in when the relationship ended. The doctor claimed that it was an abusive relationship.

b) *R. v. Habib* (2000), 147 C.C.C. (3d) 555 (Ontario Court of Appeal)

A babysitter was convicted of aggravated assault of an 18-month-old child. The child had a brain injury, a skull fracture, and serious injuries to her eyes, caused by shaken-baby syndrome. The babysitter had acted responsibly when it first appeared that the child required medical assistance. The babysitter was a first-time offender and exemplary reports were given about her child care. The child had recovered well from her injuries.

c) *R. v. Bates* (2000), 35 C.R. (5th) 327 (Ontario Court of Appeal)

A man is found guilty of 11 offences, including one count of criminal harassment, one count of uttering a death threat, three counts of assault, and six counts of failing to comply with the terms of various judicial interim release orders. He harrassed a woman with whom he had an affair while married, and despite judicial orders to stay away from her, he continually bothered her. A doctor's report indicated that he needed to take part in anger management therapy.

d) *R. v. Dharamdeo* (2000), 149 C.C.C. (3d) 489 (Ontario Court of Appeal)

A young man is convicted of one count of impaired driving for an incident that involved the car he was driving hitting a lamppost, splitting it in two, and demolishing a bus shelter. He was found guilty of impaired driving causing bodily harm for another incident in which he lost control of the car; it became airborne and struck two other vehicles. One person was injured. In the first incident, he was in contravention of his learner's permit, which required that he drive with a licensed driver.

6. For each of the following cases, decide upon a sentence for the offender. Outline the rationale for your decision, including which sentencing objective is most important. (The maximum sentence allowed for the offence is shown in parentheses at the end of each case.)

a) Welch was an 18-year-old when he and several others robbed a grocery store of $3200. Weapons and disguises were used. He robbed a small country store 30 days later, and the victim was treated roughly. Welch was apprehended, and while out on bail, he and others robbed two Calgary service stations at gunpoint, departing from the crime scenes in Welch's car. Evidence at trial indicated that Welch came from a stable, supportive family, and he had done well in school and in community activities. He had hung around with friends who had a bad influence on him, and he had been somewhat out of control for four years. (life imprisonment)

b) Travis was charged with the theft of just over $17 worth of pens, markers, and other items from the University of Western Ontario bookstore. At the time of the offence, Travis had already purchased $125 worth of goods and had $36 in his wallet. He was enrolled in an M.B.A. program after completing his undergraduate work. Evidence indicated that he had been under emotional stress because of problems with his family and with his university studies. Prior to his trial, Travis apologized to the bookstore management and offered to work in the store on a voluntary basis as a penalty for his offence and as a form of compensation. (2 years)

c) Campbell had been drinking in a bar all evening when he exchanged words with the 59-year-old victim. The words led to blows, and the two men had to be separated by bar staff. Later that evening, the victim left the premises, Campbell followed him out, and a fight started. Witnesses testified that, after the victim was on the ground and defenceless, Campbell punched and kicked him in the face. The force of the blows caused the cheekbone to break away from the base of the victim's skull and he died. It was determined that both men were heavily intoxicated while fighting. Campbell pleaded guilty to the lesser charge of manslaughter. His lawyer asked for leniency in Campbell's sentencing because he had no prior convictions for violent crimes and he had been slightly provoked by the victim. Also, he acknowledged his alcohol problem, showed genuine remorse for what happened, and had been in detention for nine months pending trial. (life imprisonment)

d) *R. v. Millar* (1994), 31 C.R. (4th) 315 (Ontario Court, General Division)

Millar was charged with first-degree murder in the killing of his father. In a frenzied state and blind with rage, Millar struck the fatal blow. For over 25 years, Millar had been dominated and humiliated by his father. The court found that Millar had been physically, sexually, and psychologically abused in ways that can only be described as cruel, insensitive, inhumane, and unthinkable. The judge noted that in more than 20 years in the practice of criminal law, this case stood out as one of the most tragic. Shortly before the killing, Millar's father menaced him with a knife and castigated him in a cruel and inhuman fashion for his inadequacies. The father's rage was due to Millar's failure to respond to his father's suggestion that it would "be nice to have a glass of milk." The jury found Millar not guilty as charged but guilty of the lesser offence of manslaughter. After being released on bail pending sentencing, he faithfully attended treatment sessions. (life imprisonment)

Communicate Your Understanding

7. Some people think that inmates have too many comforts while in prison. In some jurisdictions, they enjoy colour television, pool tables, and other recreational games. Critics suggest that prison should not be a comfortable place. Write a position paper outlining your opinion on whether inmates enjoy a life that is too comfortable. Consider the objectives of sentencing in your response.

8. Write an argument and a counterargument for the following statement: "The answer to community safety is longer sentences and bigger prisons." Support your argument and counterargument with examples. Share your opinions. As a class, generate a list of the key issues in support of the statement and the key issues that go against the claim.

9. In recent years, victims have been given more access to the criminal justice system. They are provided with aid at the time of the incident, information during the trial, opportunity to provide input on sentencing, knowledge of the inmates' imprisonment, and opportunity to provide input at the time of a parole application. Summarize these rights by drafting your own Victims' Bill of Rights. Outline rights that would provide recognition and support for victims at all stages of the criminal justice process.

Develop Your Thinking

10. California has a three-strikes law by which a person convicted of three offences receives life imprisonment. Steven White, a two-time offender, stole a $146 videocassette. Rather than face life in prison, he committed suicide. Another person faced life in prison for having stolen four cookies. Do you think that Canada, like California, should institute more severe penalties for repeat offenders? Explain. Support your opinion by researching rates of recidivism in Canada.

11. Some people believe that too many inmates are given some form of conditional release, and that there are too many offences committed by those on release. Is the use of conditional release a valuable use of resources in preparing offenders to return to society? Use the data given in this chapter on release, as well as information from current print and online sources, to develop and support your opinion on this issue.

The Youth Justice System

Focus Questions

- In what ways are the *Juvenile Delinquents Act,* the *Young Offenders Act,* and the *Youth Criminal Justice Act* different?

- What aspects of youth justice laws are controversial?

- How are young people treated differently from adults when they break the law?

- What areas of criminal law outside the *Youth Criminal Justice Act* apply to youths?

Chapter at a Glance

Figure 10-1

In 2000, Montreal hacker "Mafiaboy" paralyzed Web sites around the world. Because he was 16 years old, he could not be identified in the media. Do you agree with this legal protection for youths? Would he be protected in this way now, with society's concerns about security?

10.1 Introduction

In Canada, anyone between the ages of 12 and 17 who commits a criminal offence is dealt with under the *Youth Criminal Justice Act*. This new Act, passed in February 2002, states that youths have the same rights as adults under the *Canadian Charter of Rights and Freedoms*. It also gives young people additional rights and protection in certain types of arrest. The *Youth Criminal Justice Act* was drafted over several years to replace the *Young Offenders Act*. That Act defined anyone between the ages of 12 and 17 who committed a criminal offence as a **young offender.**

Over the years, the broad powers of the *Young Offenders Act* led to demands that it be changed. Some critics said it was too "soft" on young offenders. Others said it abused the rights of young people. As the *Youth Criminal Justice Act* takes effect, critics will be looking at it closely. Is it too tough, or not tough enough? Is youth crime worse than ever, or are fears exaggerated? This chapter will help you to answer these and other questions. It will also give you a better understanding about how Canada's youth criminal justice system works and evolves.

Looking Back · The Juvenile Delinquents Act

For most of its history, Canada's legal system has treated young people and adults differently. Under English common law, children between the ages of seven and 13 often were not charged for criminal offences. It was believed they could not understand the seriousness of their actions. If it could be proved that a child could form criminal intent, he or she would be charged and tried in the same courts as adults. Children 14 or older were tried in adult courts and faced adult punishments: hanging, whipping, or imprisonment. Children and teenagers were forced to serve their sentences alongside petty thieves, the "insane," and hardened criminals in filthy, overcrowded prisons.

In 1892, Canada changed the *Criminal Code* so that children were tried privately and separately from adults. Special laws, child welfare agencies, and a separate justice system were developed. In 1908, the federal government passed the *Juvenile Delinquents Act*. The age limit for a "juvenile" varied, but most provinces set it between the ages of 12 and 16. Nonetheless, children as young as seven could be criminally charged under the new Act.

The objective of the *Juvenile Delinquents Act* was to rehabilitate and reform, not to punish. Young people who broke the law were "delinquents," not criminals. They were viewed as victims of poverty, abuse, and neglect. Their parents had failed to raise them well—so the state would take over training and controlling the delinquent. Not surprisingly, the legal rights of juveniles were mostly ignored.

Figure 10-2

In 1910, teenagers and men had to "break stones for breakfast" in a house of industry. These institutions—known as poor houses—were feared by homeless and impoverished youths.

continued

Juveniles seldom had lawyers in court. Judges, police, and probation officers could impose whatever they thought was best for the youth. Because there were no formal guidelines, sentences ranged from incredibly harsh to extremely lenient. The definition of "delinquency" was so broad that youths could be charged for breaking minor municipal bylaws, even for truancy, coming home late, or loitering.

If found to be delinquent, juveniles could be sent indefinitely to correctional or training institutions. Staff decided when the delinquent was rehabilitated and could be released. There was no *Charter* to protect a juvenile's rights, and no right to a lawyer. Problems with the Act led to demands for changes, and it was revised in 1929. In 1984, the *Young Offenders Act* replaced the *Juvenile Delinquents Act*.

For Discussion

1. In a chart, compare the treatment of children and young people under English common law and under the *Juvenile Delinquents Act.*

2. Why was the *Juvenile Delinquents Act* replaced by the *Young Offenders Act?*

10.2 Ages of Criminal Responsibility

activity

Visit **www.law.nelson.com** and follow the links to learn more about the *Youth Criminal Justice Act.*

The *Young Offenders Act* drastically changed the criminal justice system for young people. Much of it is still contained in the *Youth Criminal Justice Act.* Both Acts reflect the fact that how Canadians view the role of young people in society changes constantly. Indeed, the *Youth Criminal Justice Act* is the third major federal plan designed to deal with young people who come into conflict with the law.

Objectives of the Youth Criminal Justice Act

The *Youth Criminal Justice Act* was created to address complaints about the *Young Offenders Act.* Its purpose is to improve the youth justice system by
1. promoting accountability, responsibility, and consequences for all youth crimes
2. supporting long-term solutions to youth crime and reinforcing social values such as respect, responsibility, and accountability
3. respecting national and international human rights protections for children, while protecting public safety
4. streamlining and making youth justice more flexible so that cases take less time and so that provinces can develop their own unique measures

activity

Visit **www.law.nelson.com** and follow the links to learn how the United Nations promotes youth justice through the *Convention on the Rights of the Child.*

Declaration of Principle

The *Youth Criminal Justice Act* is criminal law. It applies to young people between the ages of 12 and 17 who are charged with *Criminal Code* offences. It also applies to other federal laws, such as the *Controlled Drugs and Substances Act.* These other laws define the offence, while the *Youth Criminal Justice Act* outlines how youths are to be dealt with if charged. Violations of provincial or territorial laws, such as drinking while under age and traffic violations, or municipal bylaws, are dealt with under provincial or municipal legislation. Anyone aged 18 or older who commits a criminal offence is considered an adult and faces adult trial procedures and penalties.

The Youth Criminal Justice Act

In its preamble, the *Youth Criminal Justice Act* recognizes the United Nations *Convention on the Rights of the Child* as its guide. The Convention's principles are reflected in the Act's "core values," which have been defined by the Department of Justice Canada:

- Protection of society is the paramount [most important] objective of a youth justice system, which is best achieved through prevention, meaningful consequences, and rehabilitation.
- Young people should be treated separately from adults under criminal law.
- The youth justice system must hold the offenders responsible.

- Parents and victims must have a role to play in the youth justice system.

For Discussion

1. Why do you think the *Youth Criminal Justice Act* acknowledges the *Convention on the Rights of the Child*?
2. In your opinion, which of the four points are the most and least important? Explain.

■ Age and Degree of Criminal Responsibility

Age	Classification	Responsibility
0–11 years	child	none
12–17 years	youth	partial
18 years +	adult	full

Figure 10-3

These classifications apply in Canada today.

Under the *Juvenile Delinquents Act,* the minimum age for criminally charging a youth was seven years of age. The *Young Offenders Act* raised the minimum to 12 years of age. This reflected the view that younger children could not form criminal intent and should not be dealt with in the criminal justice system. Today, children younger than 12 who get into trouble are dealt with under provincial or territorial laws, such as child-welfare legislation.

The *Youth Criminal Justice Act* kept these ages of criminal responsibility, even though there were demands to lower the age. Some critics are concerned that police still cannot charge children younger than 12, even if they commit serious crimes. Some critics want the limit set back to age seven.

Changes Brought in by the Youth Criminal Justice Act

The *Youth Criminal Justice Act* expanded the role of rehabilitation programs for nonviolent, violent, and repeat offenders. It also introduced much stiffer penalties and sentences for violent youth crimes.

Youth justice court judges must impose a period of supervision in the community for youths who serve time in custody. The period is usually equal to half the time spent in custody. In this way, it is hoped these youths will get the treatment and rehabilitation needed to return successfully to the community. The provinces and territories have been encouraged to expand community services. Making more child-care, health, and educational services available to young people is seen as a way to stop youth crime from happening in the first place.

Did You Know?

The *Youth Criminal Justice Act* recognizes the hardships of Aboriginal youth. It states that these hardships should be considered when sentencing Aboriginal young offenders.

Because nonviolent offenders also have more access to rehabilitation programs, many cases will be diverted from court. These programs are designed to reintegrate youth into society before they are drawn into criminal courts and penalties. Families of offenders, victims, and communities are directly involved in dealing with youth crime under the new law.

The *Youth Criminal Justice Act* responded to public fears about violent youth crimes. Under the *Young Offenders Act,* only 16- and 17-year-olds accused of murder, manslaughter, and aggravated sexual assault could face adult sentences. Now, any youth over the age of 14 accused of a violent act can be treated and sentenced as an adult. Youth justice courts can give out adult sentences to youths convicted of offences that are punishable by more than two years in jail. Law makers believe that the lower age limit will act as a deterrent and help to prevent violent youth crimes from occurring.

Figure 10-4

How has the *Youth Criminal Justice Act* responded to public fears about violent youth crimes?

Review Your Understanding (Pages 284 to 287)

1. **Who is a young offender?**

2. **What is the purpose of the *Youth Criminal Justice Act*? Why was it passed?**

3. **Identify the four basic objectives of the *Youth Criminal Justice Act*.**

4. **What types of offences can a youth be charged with under the *Youth Criminal Justice Act*?**

5. **Why was the minimum age for charging a youth with a crime raised from seven to 12?**

6. **Why was a distinction made between nonviolent and violent offenders in the *Youth Criminal Justice Act*? In your opinion was this distinction valid? Explain.**

7. **Compare how violent and nonviolent crimes are treated in the *Youth Criminal Justice Act*.**

8. **What was the purpose of lowering the age at which youths can be charged for serious violent crimes under the *Youth Criminal Justice Act*?**

> **Did You Know?**
>
> Statistics Canada reported that youth crime rose 1 percent in 2000 from 1999, after falling in the previous eight years. Violent offences increased by 7 percent. Sexual assault was up by 18 percent from 1999, but 24 percent below its 1993 level.

10.3 Rights of Youths

Police do not have to arrest youths who are suspected of breaking the law. They have other options. For example, if the offence is shoplifting, police may simply talk to the young person and then take him or her home or call the parents or guardians. Police record these incidents, however, so that charges may be laid if the youth gets into trouble again. Retail stores may want all shoplifters prosecuted, regardless of age, but they cannot force police to lay charges. Police consider several factors, including the youth's attitude and the value of the stolen items.

Extrajudicial Sanctions—Alternative Measures Programs

Nonviolent first-time offenders who are unlikely to reoffend can avoid trial in a youth justice court by taking part in programs of **extrajudicial sanctions.** These are similar to the adult diversion programs that you read about in Chapter 9 and are designed to work outside the court system. Under the *Young Offenders Act,* they were called **alternative measures programs.** Because existing crime and justice information refers to the old Act, both terms will be used in this chapter.

In the period 1998 to 1999, 93 percent of the youths involved in alternative measures programs were first-time offenders. Seventy percent had committed property offences, the most common of which was theft under $5000. The next most common offences were mischief, other property offences, and common assault.

Extrajudicial sanctions are designed to help youths learn from their mistakes before they get criminal records. In some programs, the young person apologizes to the victim and returns stolen goods. In others, youths work for victims to compensate them for damages done. Other programs include community service, counselling, drug and alcohol treatment, and special school programs. The most common program is community service. Youths must work a set number of hours in the community and follow this up with apologies to the victims.

These programs increase the involvement of parents and neighbourhoods and cost less to run than the youth justice court system. The intention is to rehabilitate youths who have come into conflict with the law. Approximately one out of three youths who are caught committing offences go through these programs rather than through youth justice courts.

▌ Alternative Measures Assigned to Youth

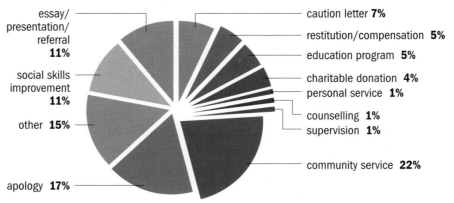

- essay/presentation/referral **11%**
- social skills improvement **11%**
- other **15%**
- apology **17%**
- caution letter **7%**
- restitution/compensation **5%**
- education program **5%**
- charitable donation **4%**
- personal service **1%**
- counselling **1%**
- supervision **1%**
- community service **22%**

Figure 10-5

Assignment of these programs in Canada from 1998–1999

To enter a program of extrajudicial sanctions, a youth must admit some involvement in the offence. Although this is an acceptance of some responsibility, it is not a confession of guilt. It cannot be used as evidence against the youth in any later court appearance. Youths must be told of their right to consult a lawyer before they take part in a program. Otherwise, they might confess to something they did not do simply to avoid a trial.

Youths who successfully complete these programs may have all charges against them stayed or dropped. No criminal conviction is recorded. Those who fail to complete the program can be tried on the original charge in a youth justice court. Youths can refuse to participate in these programs. If they have a valid defence, they should choose to be tried in a youth justice court.

Arrest and Detention

For serious offences, police must arrest youths, just as they would adults. From the moment the police decide to arrest a youth, however, certain legal rights and protections come into effect. The legal rights listed in the *Charter* apply to all youths. For example, a youth has the right to know the reason for the arrest, the automatic right to obtain free advice from a legal-aid lawyer, the right to apply to be released from custody, and the right to a fair trial.

During an arrest, the police officer or person in authority—including school principals—must describe a youth's rights in clear, understandable language. The youth must be told that he or she does not have to make a statement and that any statement that is made could be used against him or her in court. Youths must be told of the right to consult a lawyer. They must also be told of the right to have a parent or another adult present during any questioning. A youth who decides to ignore these rights must sign a statement to that effect.

These rights are very important. Youths often have no idea of their legal position or rights. They may be so frightened by authorities—especially the police—that they may say things they do not mean. In situations where police have failed to respect these rights and requirements, the Supreme Court of Canada has found confessions by youths to be inadmissible evidence.

Case

R. v. I.(L.R.) and T.(E.)
(1994) 109 D.L.R. (4th) 140
Supreme Court of Canada

Three young offenders, L.R.I., E.T., and A., and a young adult were charged with the first-degree murder of a taxi driver. If convicted in adult court, they could be sentenced to life imprisonment. The Crown attempted to transfer the case to adult court, but failed. During the youth court trial, the Crown's case depended largely on statements that E.T. had made to the police just hours after the killing.

E.T. lived with his 62-year-old great-aunt and was driven by police officers with her to the station. During the ride, his great-aunt looked for her lawyer's card in her purse. The police officer told her "all of that" would be taken care of at the station. Instead, E.T. and his great-aunt were taken to an interview room, where a statement was taken from E.T. during questioning that lasted more than four hours. In a form required under the *Young Offenders Act*, the officer reported E.T. had been given an opportunity to speak to a lawyer or parent or adult relative. E.T., the officer wrote, had chosen

continued ▶

instead to speak in front of his great-aunt, who had little formal education. After completing a statement, E.T. gave police a knife and the taxi driver's keys. Only then did he speak to his lawyer.

The next morning, after talking to his lawyer again, E.T. told the police he wanted to add some things to his first statement. He indicated that he did not wish to speak to anyone other than the officer or to have anyone else present.

At trial, the judge excluded E.T.'s first statement, but admitted the second. L.R.I. was convicted of manslaughter, while E.T., A., and the young adult were all convicted of second-degree murder. E.T. appealed his conviction, seeking to have his second statement excluded. The British Columbia Court of Appeal dismissed his appeal. E.T. appealed that decision to the Supreme Court of Canada, which ruled that his second statement should have been excluded, and acquitted E.T.

For Discussion

1. All statements made by an accused youth to a person in authority must be voluntary to be admitted in court. Why might it be difficult to determine if a young person's statement is, in fact, voluntary?

2. Explain why a young person is entitled to have an adult present when giving a statement to the police.

3. Is it likely that E.T. and his great-aunt understood and appreciated his act of confession? Explain.

4. Why did the trial judge exclude the first statement as evidence?

5. Why did the Supreme Court of Canada exclude the second statement and enter an acquittal against E.T.'s second-degree murder conviction? Do you agree? Explain.

Figure 10-6

What other disadvantages are there to house arrest?

Detention and Bail

The *Criminal Code* gives youths and adults the same right to bail. The terms of release for youths, however, often impose curfews and forbid contact with victims and certain friends. For many offences, youths are released into the custody of parents or other responsible adults. Generally, youths are not released on their own recognizance. If they are at risk of reoffending or not appearing for trial, youths may be sent to **foster homes** (see page 301) or placed under **house arrest** before trial or sentencing. House arrest is a court order that forces the youth to remain at home during set hours. In some cases, the youth must wear an electronic device so that his or her movements can be monitored.

As much as possible, youth offenders are kept separate from adult offenders. Youths can only be fingerprinted and photographed when they have been charged with indictable offences. To protect the rights of youths, police must destroy the photos and fingerprints if the youth is acquitted, the charge is dismissed, or proceedings are discontinued.

Case

R. v. M.C.

(2001) 191 N.S.R. (2d) 72
Nova Scotia Supreme Court, Family Division

M.C. was 15 years old when he was charged with robbing a bank and using and possessing an imitation firearm. He was arrested in Halifax and taken to a police station, where two police officers informed him of his right to have a parent or other adult present during questioning. One officer and the youth discussed his previous convictions and talked about the time M.C. might get for this offence.

M.C. then consulted with his mother for about two hours. He was told in her presence that any statement he gave had to be made in her presence, unless he wished otherwise. The officer testified that both M.C. and his mother knew that the interview would continue after she left and

that neither objected. About an hour after she had left, M.C. confessed.

At trial, M.C. argued that his confession was inadmissible because police had failed to tell him for a second time that he had a right to consult with a parent or adult. As a result, it had not been voluntary. The Nova Scotia Supreme Court ruled the statement admissible.

For Discussion

1. **Why was it important for M.C. to clearly understand his rights on arrest and detention?**

2. **Why did the court rule that M.C.'s statement was admissible?**

3. **If you were the judge in this action, what would you decide and why?**

Victims, schools, and police have access to youth justice court records. They are not destroyed automatically when a convicted youth reaches the age of 18. These records are often used later in adult bail hearings and sentencing. However, after certain periods of time, they are not made available. The records of youths who receive adult sentences are treated in the same way as adult records.

Notice to Parents

Parents must be notified as soon as possible after their child is detained or arrested. They are encouraged to be present during all steps of the legal process. If their child is found guilty, parents must be given opportunities to provide input prior to sentencing.

Because their role is so important, a judge can order parents to attend hearings. Parents who do not appear may be found in contempt of court and the judge can issue a warrant for their arrest. Any parent or adult who promises the court to supervise a youth placed in his or her care and who deliberately fails to carry out these duties can face criminal charges.

Review Your Understanding (Pages 287 to 291)

1. **What choices do police have when dealing with a youth who has committed a minor offence?**

2. **Identify three factors that police may consider before laying charges for shoplifting.**

3. **What are extrajudicial sanctions programs, and what are they designed to do?**

You Be the JUDGE

In 1997, Manitoba was the first province to pass a *Parental Responsibility Act*. It permits victims of property crime to sue the parents of youths who committed the offences. (See Agents of Change, page 341.)

- Should parents be held responsible for the criminal actions of their children? Explain.

e activity

Visit **www.law.nelson.com** and follow the links to find recent statistics on youth crime.

4. **What two conditions must be met before a youth offender can participate in an extrajudicial sanctions program?**
5. **What rights are available to youths who are arrested?**
6. **What must be considered before a youth's statement can be admitted as evidence at trial?**
7. **When may a young person be fingerprinted and photographed?**
8. **What rights and obligations do parents have when their children are arrested?**

10.4 Trial Procedures

Trials under the *Youth Criminal Justice Act* may be held in either a family court or a youth justice court, depending on the province or territory. Youth and adult trials are often held in the same facilities, but at different times. The same judge might hear adult criminal cases some of the time and youth criminal cases at other times. Ontario's youth court system, for example, has two levels. Youths aged 12 to 15 are tried in family court; youths aged 16 to 17 in provincial court.

Trials for youths and adults follow the same rules of evidence and are equally formal. Defence lawyers usually represent both youths and adults. Both youths and adults have access to legal aid. There are differences, however.

Youths do not have the right to decide in which court system they will be tried. All trials occur in a youth justice court or family court, unless the case is transferred to adult court. No preliminary hearing is held, and a judge alone, regardless of the offence, conducts all trials. There are no jury trials. The intent of the youth justice system is to deal with youth as rapidly as possible and to let them return home quickly.

Did You Know?

It takes more than twice as long for a case to make its way through an adult court than through a youth justice court. From 1999–2000, 80 percent of youth court cases concluded within six months.

Privacy of Hearings

The *Youth Criminal Justice Act* lets the public and the media attend trials or hearings involving youths. Proceedings may be reported, but the identity of the youth can be disclosed only under certain conditions. Usually, the name of any youth involved in the case as a witness or a victim cannot be disclosed.

The names of 14- to 17-year-olds who are convicted of serious, violent crimes, such as murder, attempted murder, manslaughter and aggravated sexual assault, can be reported in the media. If youths who are considered dangerous are at large, their photographs can be published in the media along with their names.

A Crown attorney may tell the court at the beginning of a trial that the Crown will not seek an adult sentence in a particular case—even for a serious, violent offence. This means that even if the young person is found guilty, he or she will receive a youth sentence. In this case, the name of the youth must not be reported or published.

Re F.N.

[2000] 1 S.C.R. 880
Supreme Court of Canada

F.N., a young offender, was charged with two counts of assault and breach of probation. He appeared in Provincial Court, Youth Division, in St. John's, and his name and the alleged offences appeared on the youth court docket, or list. Unlike dockets in other provincial courts, youth court dockets in Newfoundland were not posted in a public area. They remained in the court clerk's possession. The court had a practice of sending a copy of the court docket to psychologists at two St. John's school boards.

F.N. sought a court order to prevent the youth court from supplying copies of its weekly dockets to the school boards. His application to the Newfoundland Supreme Court, Trial Division, and his next appeal to the Newfoundland Court of Appeal were dismissed. His final appeal was to the Supreme Court of Canada, which heard the appeal and ruled in his favour. It ordered the practice of sending youth court dockets to both school boards to stop.

For Discussion

1. Why did F.N. object to the youth court's distribution of the court docket to the school boards?

2. Why do you think the two Newfoundland courts dismissed F.N.'s appeal?

3. Why do you think the Supreme Court of Canada ruled in favour of F.N.?

Transfer to Adult Court

Under certain circumstances, cases involving youths may be transferred to adult court. For such a transfer to be permitted, the youth must have been 14 or older at the time the offence was committed and be accused of a serious violent crime or be a repeat offender of such crimes. When cases are transferred to adult court, accused youths are tried as adults and can receive severe adult sentences. Even if these conditions are met, transfers to adult court are not automatic. The decision to transfer the trial must be made before the accused's plea is heard.

A transfer hearing is held to determine which court—adult or youth justice (or family)—will best suit the case. This hearing is not intended to determine the accused's innocence or guilt. During transfer hearings, witnesses are often asked for their opinions about the benefits and harm of custody under the *Youth Criminal Justice Act* as compared to imprisonment under the *Criminal Code*. Parents can present their views. Victims can also give impact statements and testify how the crimes have affected their lives. In making a decision regarding a transfer, a judge must consider both the interests of society and the needs of the young person.

Usually, the Crown applies to transfer a case to adult court when it believes the offence requires an adult punishment. An accused youth may also request a transfer to adult court, but this rarely happens. If a youth feels that a jury may be more sympathetic, however, he or she might apply for a transfer to adult court. If several co-accused are charged with the offence, and only one is a youth, the defence lawyer for the youth may also want to transfer the case to adult court. In this way, the same judge would hear all the cases.

The transfer process is controversial. Because individual judges decide which cases are transferred, some critics say that youths are being treated differently for similar offences. Some judges are reluctant to send youths to adult court because they may face longer sentences that will be served in adult jails and penitentiaries. As well, the cases of 12- and 13-year-olds who commit very serious offences cannot be considered for transfer to adult court. Many Canadians feel that all youths who commit serious violent offences should be tried in adult court.

Agents of Change   The Taber Shooting

Figure 10-7
Horrified students leave the high school in Taber, Alberta, just after the fatal shooting.

He has been called a copycat killer, a geek, a "punching bag," and a kid who got away with murder. One thing he has not been called—at least in the media—is his real name. That's because under the *Young Offenders Act,* he could not be identified

On April 28, 1999, 14-year-old T.C.S. entered his former high school in Taber, Alberta, hiding a sawed-off rifle. He had come for revenge and he quickly started shooting, killing one 17-year-old student instantly and wounding another.

It was eight days after two students with sawed-off guns had killed 12 students and a teacher in Littleton, Colorado. Some experts saw the Taber killing as a copycat act inspired by the media frenzy. But was it? The case of T.C.S. raised tough questions that law makers have to deal with when considering youth justice.

T.C.S. was a killer, but he was also young—and a victim himself. He was bright and created his own computer games. As early as age six, however, he had been picked on at school. A group of students had dowsed him with lighter fluid and threatened to set him on fire. The bullying continued for years. One student described T.C.S. as "everybody's best punching bag."

By the age of 14, T.C.S. had left school for fear of the beatings. He was often depressed and angry. But victim or not, T.C.S. had killed another human being. The Crown and many parents wanted the case transferred to adult court, but the judge said no. During the trial, T.C.S. had a heart operation and suffered a stroke. He pleaded guilty to first-degree murder and to two charges of attempted murder. The judge sentenced T.C.S. to three years in prison, to be followed by seven years under community supervision.

The sentence was meant to reflect T.C.S.'s health, his youth, his guilty plea, and a previously clean record. Many people were outraged by this "light" sentence and by the fact that T.C.S.'s identity was protected. What about the victim? He had no protection.

This case and others like it contributed to demands for tougher sentences and to the *Youth Criminal Justice Act.*

For Discussion

1. **What factors may have led T.C.S. to start shooting on April 28, 1999?**

2. **Is bullying a problem at your school? What can be done to prevent it?**

3. **Why do you think the judge refused to transfer this case to adult court? Do you agree? Why or why not?**

Case

R. v. J.A.B. et al.

(2000) 270 A.R. 389
Alberta Provincial Court, Youth Division

The two accused, 17-year-old J.A.B. and J.C.S., did not like the way B.M. had treated some of their female friends. Allegedly, late one night in Edmonton, J.C.S. pulled a knife and made threats, while J.A.B. kicked and punched B.M. and stole his sweater, shirt, and shoes. They also held a cigarette lighter against B.M.'s bare stomach, leaving a burn that was scabbed over for several weeks. The accused were later arrested and charged with robbery, assault, and assault with a weapon.

Both youths had long records. J.A.B. had five prior convictions in youth justice court and had been diagnosed with attention deficit hyperactivity disorder (ADHD) and fetal alcohol syndrome. He had threatened teachers with scissors, scared a young girl with a knife, and threatened violence to others. J.C.S. had 16 prior convictions, plus this charge, in a 26-month period.

The Crown applied to have the two youths transferred to adult court, and the application was granted.

For Discussion

1. Give two reasons why the Crown would want to have J.A.B. and J.C.S. tried in adult court.

2. Why do you think the application to transfer to adult court was granted?

3. Do you agree with the decision to try the two youths in adult court? Why or why not?

Case

R. v. C.G.M.

(2000) 189 Sask. R. 103
Saskatchewan Court of Appeal

C.G.M. was 15 years old and charged with the first-degree murder of an operator of a community home to which she had been sentenced for an earlier offence. C.G.M. had struck the victim over the head twice with a cast-iron frying pan, and then the co-accused in the case stabbed the victim to death. Notes found at the crime scene indicated the attack had been planned, and the murder scene was gruesome.

The Crown successfully applied to a youth court judge for an order to transfer the accused to adult court. C.G.M. then appealed that order, but the Saskatchewan Court of Appeal dismissed her appeal.

For Discussion

1. Why did the youth court judge order the transfer to adult court?

2. Why would C.G.M. appeal the transfer order?

3. In its judgment, the Court of Appeal stated: "The interests of society, which includes public protection and rehabilitation of the offender, was best served by raising this offender to adult court." Argue in support of or against this judgment.

Review Your Understanding (Pages 292 to 295)

1. Identify the similarities and differences between trial proceedings in an adult court and a youth justice court.

2. Why do youth court cases usually take less time than adult court cases?

3. Under what circumstances will the identity of an accused youth be made public?

4. What conditions must exist for the transfer of a case from youth justice court to adult court to be considered?

5. Describe the purpose of a transfer hearing. Who has input and why is their input important?

6. Why are transfers to adult court of cases involving youths controversial? What is your opinion of such transfers?

10.5 Sentencing

Under the *Young Offenders Act,* youths found guilty in youth court were given "dispositions." These were similar to a sentence in adult court. Under the *Youth Criminal Justice Act,* the term "dispositions" disappeared and youths now receive sentences.

A wide variety of sentencing options allows youth justice court judges to consider the needs and circumstances of each youth. They also let judges look at the needs and concerns of the victim and at public safety. Balancing these different demands makes the judge's task very difficult. Even if the Crown or the defence recommends a specific sentence, the judge makes the final decision.

While the judge must consider the needs of the community, the sentence must also help the youth to take responsibility for breaking the law. It is generally assumed that youths are more easily rehabilitated than adults to become

▌A Century of Federal Legislation for Youth Justice

	Juvenile Delinquents Act	Young Offenders Act	Youth Criminal Justice Act
Dates	1908–1984	1984–2002	2002–
Philosophy	Juveniles are not criminals but children who need guidance.	Youths are less responsible for crimes than adults.	Tougher sentences prevent crimes, but rehabilitation is important.
Ages covered	7–18, depending on province	12–17, inclusive	12–17, inclusive; youths 14 and older treated more like adults
Youths' rights	no right to a lawyer	must be advised of right to lawyer	must be advised of right to lawyer
Court/trial procedures	*Canadian Charter of Rights and Freedoms* generally did not apply; hearings closed; transfers to adult court possible	*Charter* applied; hearings open; publication ban on names; transfer to adult court possible for offenders aged 14 and older	*Charter* applies; parents may have to attend; hearings open; no publication ban on names for adult sentences, serious violent offences, or youths considered dangerous
Sentencing	fine up to $25; placed in foster home or in the care of the government	many dispositions, including closed and open custody; usual terms 2–3 years, but up to 5 for murder	many sentences, including closed and open custody; up to 10 years for first-degree murder

Figure 10-8

Key differences and similarities in three Acts of youth justice legislation law-abiding citizens. The judge, then, must choose a sentence that will help the youth to become rehabilitated and reintegrated into society.

Before making a final decision, the judge may hold a sentencing hearing, just as in adult court. The more serious the offence, the more likely such a hearing will take place. During this hearing, the judge will usually review a pre-sentence report. This report is prepared by a probation officer or youth justice court worker and is similar to a pre-sentence report in adult court.

The pre-sentence report provides information about the young person, including

- interviews with the youth, the parents, and the victim
- any intention by the offender to change his or her conduct
- records of school attendance and performance
- a history of any previous criminal offences
- the offender's attitude toward the offence
- any background that will provide insight into the offender's character

Where there is concern for a youth's state of mind, a medical and psychiatric profile may also be included in the pre-sentence report.

In the following pages, you will look at the different sentences available to judges in a youth justice court. They range from the most lenient to the most severe.

Case

R. v. P.L.D.

(2000) 196 Nfld. & P.E.I.R. 181
Prince Edward Island Supreme Court, Trial Division

P.L.D., a first-time offender, pleaded guilty in youth court to six charges of joy riding. He was 15 and 16 when he committed the offences with two other youths.

Before appearing in court, P.L.D. prepared and delivered letters of apology to the car owners involved. His pre-sentence report was very positive. P.L.D. was an honours student, captain of his hockey team, and through his part-time work, had saved $10 000. His mother described P.L.D. as a responsible young man and expressed great surprise at his involvement in the offences.

The youth court judge imposed a sentence of 45 days open custody (see page 301) plus 22 months of probation, including 120 hours of community service. The accused appealed the open custody disposition. The Supreme Court of Prince Edward Island, Trial Division, allowed the appeal and deleted the custody provision.

For Discussion

1. In your opinion, what would motivate someone like P.L.D. to commit these offences?

2. Why do you think the youth court judge ordered open custody?

3. Why do you think the custody provision of the sentence was deleted?

Absolute Discharges

An absolute discharge may be given to a youth for a first-time offence if it is relatively minor, such as theft under $5000. Such a sentence is given when it is in the youth's best interest and does not go against the public interest. An absolute discharge means the youth has been found guilty, but that no formal conviction will be entered and the court will take no further action. If the same youth is later found guilty of another offence, however, the judge will be informed of the earlier discharge in the pre-sentence report.

Fines

Under provincial and municipal legislation, youths may be fined up to $1000 for summary offences. These include minor property damage, trespassing, and driving offences. In imposing a fine, the judge must consider the youth's ability to pay. If the youth has no way of earning money and has no savings, imposing a fine may be senseless. The youth, not the parents, must pay the fine as a penalty for the crime. The youth may ask the court to extend the payment deadline. If the fine is not paid in reasonable time, the judge may place the youth in custody. Judges may also combine fines with other sentences, such as probation or community service work.

Compensation

A youth may be required to pay monetary compensation to the victim or to make up for any damage to property or lost income caused by the offence. For example, a youth who stole $50 from a friend's purse could be ordered to repay that sum. If a youth commits a crime of mischief by deliberately breaking a neighbour's window, appropriate compensation would be the cost of replacing the window.

Personal and Community Service

Youths who commit crimes often cannot afford to pay fines or compensation to their victims. In the place of money, judges may order youths to work for the victims. For example, if Herman damages his neighbour's prize-winning garden, the judge could order him to do gardening tasks for the victim for a certain period. The victim, however, must agree. Because victims are often frightened or angered by an offence, few want further contact with offenders. As a result, personal service orders are uncommon. When used, they are usually the result of property offences.

When the victim rejects a personal service order, or when the youth has harmed the community in some way, the judge may impose a community service order. The purpose is to have the youth put something back into the community. For instance, if 15-year-old Sheila spray-paints slogans on city property, she may have to work for a certain number of hours with the city's maintenance department. She might also be asked to work in a day-care or seniors' centre.

Police and Community-Based Programs

Across Canada, community-based programs are working with children and youths. The Ottawa Police Youth Centre, for example, operates in a public housing community. It offers everything from simple recreational facilities to alternative measures programs for youths who have been charged with drug-related offences. The number of drug-related charges in the area has dropped significantly since the program started.

In British Columbia, the Sparwood Youth Assistance Program is a police-run diversion program that involves youths, their families, and victims in working together to help youths fit back into the community. Because of its work, the rate of reoffending for enrolled youths was about 9 percent in 2001, which is very low. The program is also used as a model to deal with problems in local high schools. In Regina, Saskatchewan, the Atoskata Victims' Compensation Project gets work opportunities for youths who have committed crimes. This means they can pay damages to their victims.

As these examples show, police participation can be an important part of community-based rehabilitation programs. Police are often the first to deal with at-risk youths in schools and neighbourhoods and have the necessary experience and knowledge to deal with them.

Figure 10-9

The Ottawa Police Youth Centre involves the community in preventing crime.

Case

R. v. B.J.K.

(2000) 270 A.R. 312
Alberta Provincial Court, Youth Division

Wearing masks, a 16-year-old offender, B.J.K., and another youth robbed a Calgary convenience store. B.J.K. carried a knife as they approached two female employees and robbed them of money, cigarettes, bus tickets, and phone cards. After police investigations, both youths were caught and confessed. B.J.K. pleaded guilty to three offences related to the robbery.

Following his guilty plea, in which he expressed sincere remorse, B.J.K. participated in two community conferences. Each conference lasted three hours and brought the victims and offenders together in a group that was supervised by a social worker. This was done in hopes of repairing the financial and emotional damages the robbery had caused. As well, B.J.K.'s family was very supportive.

The court ordered B.J.K. to serve 12 months' probation, do 30 hours of personal service under the store manager's supervision, perform 50 hours of community service, and pay compensation to the victims.

For Discussion

1. **What is the purpose of a community conference? What is meant by "emotional damage"?**

2. **How would you feel about participating in such a conference as (a) the accused, and (b) the victim?**

3. **The judge stated that the youth's participation in the community conference justified a non-custodial sentence. Why do you think the judge took this factor into consideration?**

Probation

A judge can limit a youth's freedom by issuing a probation order. This means the youth will be placed under the supervision of a probation officer for up to two years. There is no limit to the number of conditions a probation order can contain. One basic condition is that the youth must stay out of trouble while on probation. Other conditions depend on the kind of offences committed and the youth's background.

▌ Standard Conditions of Youth Probation

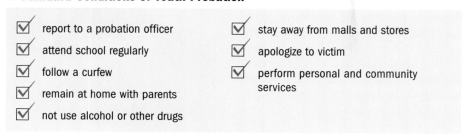

- ☑ report to a probation officer
- ☑ attend school regularly
- ☑ follow a curfew
- ☑ remain at home with parents
- ☑ not use alcohol or other drugs
- ☑ stay away from malls and stores
- ☑ apologize to victim
- ☑ perform personal and community services

Figure 10-10

Which conditions do you think would be most effective in making an offender take responsibility? Explain.

To be fully aware of the conditions, youths must be given copies of their probation orders. Breaking the terms of probation is a criminal offence, and it may lead back to court and a longer sentence.

Case

R. v. F.D.C. et al.

(2000) 153 Man. R. (2d) 69
Manitoba Court of Appeal

Two 16-year-old females and a 14-year-old female, all first-time offenders, took part in an unprovoked attack on a 21-year-old newcomer to Pukatawagan, Manitoba. The victim was kicked while lying on the ground and suffered bruising and swelling to her face and body. At trial, the youths showed no remorse and were unresponsive to the sentencing judge's questions and concerns about this act of violence.

The accused pleaded guilty to a charge of assault causing bodily harm and were sentenced to six months' open custody, followed by 18 months of supervised probation. The Manitoba Youth Centre, in Winnipeg, was the only facility in the province for young females sentenced to both open and secure custody (see page 302). This was a considerable distance from where the girls lived.

The youths appealed their sentences and the Manitoba Court of Appeal set aside the six-month custodial sentences, substituted time served (44 days), and imposed tighter curfew hours, 50 hours of community service, and greater restrictions in the probation orders.

In setting aside the custodial sentence, the court considered that the youths' parents were unable to visit them because transportation to Winnipeg was limited and very expensive. As well, the youths had no other relatives in Winnipeg to visit them or give support.

For Discussion

1. Although first-time offenders are seldom sentenced to custody, why did the trial judge impose six months' custody on these youths?

2. What does it mean when the Court of Appeal set aside the six-month sentence and substituted time served?

3. Should the ability of family and relatives to visit have been a factor for the appeal judge in this case? Explain.

Custody

Custody is the most serious sentence in the youth justice system. It is used when a youth is seen as a danger to society and when other types of sentences have failed. It is also used when the court finds that youths need to be supervised or when violent crimes have been committed. Custody can be either open or secure (closed). Judges decide the kind of custody in which youths will be held.

Open Custody

Open custody is ordered for offenders who need more supervision and structure in their lives than they are getting at home. Access to the community is available, but it is limited and supervised. Open-custody facilities are designed to rehabilitate youths and include foster or **group homes,** child-care facilities, and residential wilderness programs.

In a foster home, a youth lives with another family. Only a few restrictions, perhaps including a curfew, are in place. Foster parents receive payments from provincial governments for their services. They are usually people who are genuinely interested in children and youths but have no special professional training.

A group home is designed to house several offenders at the same time and is operated by trained staff. The setting is meant to help youths learn how to behave responsibly and get along with others. Group homes also link up to community resources, such as schools, and certain rehabilitation programs, such as alcohol- and drug-abuse counselling, anger management, and life-skills training. Youths may also be placed in the care of the Children's Aid Society or the appropriate government department, for example, the Ministry of Community and Social Services.

Case

R. v. G.R.H.

(2000) 189 Sask. R. 250
Saskatchewan Court of Appeal

G.R.H., a 16-year-old student, was caught selling marijuana to another student from a car parked near an entrance to a high school in Swift Current, Saskatchewan. As a result of being caught, G.R.H. was suspended from school for a period of time.

Although G.R.H.'s home influence and support were unsatisfactory, G.R.H. had the ability to be a good student. Evidence at trial indicated he had stopped using drugs and associating with people who did. He had earlier been convicted of theft and

had been ordered to perform 30 days of community service.

G.R.H. was convicted of trafficking in marijuana, contrary to the *Controlled Drugs and Substances Act,* and was ordered to serve a three-month term in open custody. He appealed his sentence to the Saskatchewan Court of Appeal, but the appeal was dismissed.

For Discussion

1. **Why did G.R.H. appeal his conviction?**
2. **What aspects of his behaviour could he use as evidence of good character?**
3. **Why do you think his appeal was rejected?**

Secure Custody

Youths who have committed serious violent offences or who have a history of offences may be judged a threat to society and sentenced to **secure custody.** This is a last resort, and it means freedoms are totally restricted, with little community contact. Secure facilities usually have barred windows and locked doors. Some are located in separate wings of adult jails or prisons in isolated rural areas. If this is the case, youth and adult offenders are totally separated.

Educational upgrading and skills training are important goals in custodial facilities. Youths may be granted a temporary absence or day release for educational (as well as for medical and family) reasons. Even with a sentence to secure custody, youths are often sent to an open facility near the end of their sentence to make the transition back into the community easier.

If a young person turns 18 while in custody, correctional officials may apply to a youth justice court judge to transfer the offender to an adult facility for the rest of the sentence. Again, the judge must balance the best interests of the youth with the needs of society. Unlike adults in prison, youths in custody are not eligible for parole or for time off for good behaviour. This is because the sentencing has already given youths special consideration and protection.

Figure 10-11

Life behind bars is the end of freedom.

Figure 10-12

Sentences handed out by youth justice courts, listed by significance

▌ Youth Court Cases by Category of Sentences in Canada

Sentences	Number of Cases Heard in Youth Courts				
	1995–1996	1996–1997	1997–1998	1998–1999	1999–2000
All sentences	**72 945**	**74 797**	**74 527**	**71 961**	**68 184**
Secure custody	10 850	11 772	12 199	12 312	11 610
Open custody	13 462	13 506	13 470	12 857	11 605
Probation	35 783	37 960	35 913	34 451	33 028
Fine	4 226	3 574	4 295	4 081	4 062
Community service order	5 020	4 594	5 256	4 988	4 750
Absolute discharge	2 094	1 464	1 160	1 130	1 094
Other sentences*	1 510	1 927	2 234	2 142	2 035

* Includes restitution, prohibition, compensations, and other sentences such as apologies, counselling programs, and conditional discharges

Appeals and Reviews

Under the *Criminal Code,* youths and adults have similar rights of appeal. The *Youth Criminal Justice Act* gives both the offender and the Crown the right to appeal a sentence that seems unfair. Either party may also appeal a decision to transfer a youth case to adult court.

R. v. J.L.Z.

(2000) 181 N.S.R. (2d) 281
Nova Scotia Court of Appeal

A 14-year-old youth, J.L.Z., was charged with two counts of robbery with violence, two counts of aggravated assault, break and enter, and breach of probation following a planned home-invasion style robbery. He committed the offences with an adult at the Halifax home of an elderly couple. The 77-year-old wife broke her hip and the 79-year-old husband suffered permanent brain damage after they were severely beaten by the adult. The robbery and attack lasted about an hour and, as they ransacked the house, the accused ignored the wife's pleas to help her husband.

Background information on J.L.Z. was mixed. He was a person who did not respond well to authority and was described as both a leader and a follower. J.L.Z. was described as having "street smarts," but

also as being emotionally immature. He was polite at times, obnoxious at others.

The Crown applied to transfer the proceedings to adult court, and the Nova Scotia Family Court approved the application. The youth appealed the transfer to adult court, but the Court of Appeal dismissed his appeal.

For Discussion

1. Was deterrence, retribution, or rehabilitation the most important legal principle in deciding to transfer this case to adult court? Explain.

2. What is meant by "a person who did not respond well to authority"? Why could this be a problem?

3. Why do you think the Court of Appeal dismissed the accused's appeal?

The *Youth Criminal Justice Act* allows for court reviews of all sentences. A review may be requested by youths, their families, or by provincial authorities. Application for a review may be made up to six months after the sentence has been imposed. The situation of any youth in custody for more than one year is automatically reviewed at the end of one year. This is intended to allow the courts to change a sentence to reflect any progress the youth may have made. The judge conducting the review may keep or reduce the sentence, but never increase it. The review makes it possible for a youth to avoid serving the complete sentence if his or her behaviour shows evidence of reform.

Review Your Understanding (Pages 296 to 303)

1. What demands must a judge balance in considering sentencing options?

2. What is the purpose of a pre-sentence report? What kind of information does it contain?

3. What is the most lenient sentence a youth can receive? Why is it the best option for the youth?

4. Distinguish between a personal service order and a community service order. Give examples to support your answer.

5. In your opinion, what are the most effective probation conditions? Least effective? Explain.

6. Using examples, distinguish between open and secure custody.

7. Distinguish between an appeal and a review. What are their purposes?

Should Violent Students Be Expelled from School?

Dawn-Marie Wesley was 14 years old when she committed suicide. She was afraid of being beaten up at school and did not know where to turn. "If I try to get help, it will get worse," she wrote in her suicide note. "They are always looking for a new person to beat up and they are the toughest girls. If I ratted, they would get suspended and there would be no stopping them."

Another 14-year-old in British Columbia, Hamed Nastoh, had committed suicide a few months earlier by jumping off a bridge. In a seven-page suicide letter, he too wrote that he could no longer stand being bullied at school. These two tragic cases made headlines in 2000, and sadly they were not alone.

Violence and bullying are serious problems in Canada's schools. In 1994, *Weapons Use in Canadian Schools,* a major federal report, found that school violence had increased. Incidents of students carrying weapons—clubs, knives, machetes, and handguns—had become a fact of life in some schools, especially in larger cities. The study found that students carry weapons to class to impress or intimidate other students or for protection. Some people believe that there has been a dramatic increase in classroom violence that reflects greater violence in society in general. Statistical data, however, indicates that violent crime has not increased within the last decade—neither among youths nor adults in society at large.

Governments and educators, however, have taken action to deal with school violence and bullying. In 1999, Alberta's *School Act* was amended. Section 28(7) states: "A board shall ensure that each student enrolled in a school

Figure 10-13

School programs to deal with bullying and violence are much more common and strict than they used to be.

... is provided with a safe and caring environment that fosters and maintains respectful and responsible behaviours." In 2000, British Columbia announced that it would spend millions of dollars on anti-bullying programs in order to reduce school violence.

In some classrooms and hallways, there is a general air of disrespect and misbehaviour, which sometimes leads to violent incidents. Educators, concerned about the increasing level of violence, are divided about how to deal with the problem. Some school boards have adopted a zero-tolerance policy to deal with violent teenagers. Offenders are kicked out of school and are not permitted to return.

In September 2001, Ontario's *Safe Schools Act* came into effect. It requires school principals to expel any student who is in possession of a weapon on school property or while engaged in school activities. Any student who uses a weapon to cause or threaten bodily harm must also be expelled. Once expelled, a student must complete a **strict-discipline program** before being able to attend a publicly funded school in Ontario.

One such program, also called a "boot camp," is Turnaround. With military-style drills, uniforms, exercise, and classes, its purpose is to instill discipline and respect for authority, and to raise confidence.

On One Side

Educators who support get-tough policies believe that teaching methods that allow students to discover and develop their own morals are too lax. This approach, they say, has created violence problems in schools and society at large. They want schools to teach and enforce what is right and wrong, even if that means calling in police. If rules are enforced, troublemakers will think twice about bullying. Rigidly enforced rules will also create a safer environment for students who might otherwise have carried weapons to protect themselves. Young people, they say, only respect standards if there are punishments to enforce them.

On the Other Side

Critics of the get-tough approach view students as confused and alienated, not as mindless or violent thugs. They argue that counselling can help students develop a healthy sense of self-esteem and self-worth, and this will achieve better results than rigid discipline. They also support programs that teach anger and stress management and that involve peer mediation. Such programs, they say, help students in conflict with one another to reach a solution or agreement. Teaching these life skills will help students in school and also later in the workplace. Supporters of student service programs feel they are far more effective in the long run than stern penalties, such as expulsion.

The Bottom Line

If school violence escalates, some people fear Canadian schools could require armed guards to patrol the hallways. Before Canadian schools reach this extreme, measures must be taken to control school violence. The question remains: What measures? Should violent teens be expelled or sentenced to fines and community service? Or should schools implement more counselling and treatment programs to help troubled teens—including those who are terrified of being bullied?

What Do You Think?

1. What evidence is there to indicate that violence in Canadian schools is increasing?

2. Do you agree that "there has been a dramatic increase in classroom violence that reflects greater violence in society in general"? Explain.

3. What are educators and governments doing to deal with school violence? Is it enough? Explain.

4. Do you think that zero-tolerance policies work? Why or why not?

5. How is "self-esteem" related to violence in the schools?

6. What programs do you think would be most effective to reduce school violence and why?

Chapter Review

Chapter Highlights

- Youths have the same rights as adults under the *Canadian Charter of Rights and Freedoms*.
- The *Youth Criminal Justice Act* is criminal law that outlines the rights of youths and procedures for dealing with them.
- The *Youth Criminal Justice Act* changes the youth justice system in four ways.
- A child under the age of 12 is considered to be too young to be dealt with in the criminal justice system.
- The *Youth Criminal Justice Act* expands the role of rehabilitation services for dealing with young offenders.
- Youths aged 14 years and over can be treated as adult offenders if they commit serious violent crimes.
- Programs of extrajudicial sanctions (alternative measures) are designed to deal with youths outside the court system.
- Youths have the same right to a lawyer and bail as adult offenders.
- The names of youths aged 14 to 17 can be published if they have been convicted of a serious indictable offence under the *Youth Criminal Justice Act*. This was banned under the *Young Offenders Act*.
- Youths convicted of a criminal offence can be placed in custody when considered a danger to society.
- Youths have the right to appeal a conviction, but not to parole.

Review Key Terms

Name the key terms that are described below.

a) programs for nonviolent first-time offenders to avoid trial in a youth justice court

b) a professionally run facility that houses youth offenders, with access to rehabilitation programs and community resources

c) anyone between the ages of 12 and 17 who committed a criminal act

d) a court order that forces offenders to stay at home during specific hours and that may include electronic monitoring

e) a form of custody ordered for offenders who need more supervision than they could get at home but who should have community access

f) detention that totally restricts the freedom of violent and dangerous youth offenders

g) a program under the *Young Offenders Act* that was similar to adult diversion programs

h) a program for youth offenders that stresses military-style discipline, drills, and physical exercise

i) the home of another family into which a youth offender is placed

Check Your Knowledge

1. Outline the key differences between the *Juvenile Delinquents Act*, the *Young Offenders Act*, and the *Youth Criminal Justice Act*.

2. Summarize controversial aspects of youth justice laws.

3. Explain the legal rights of youths when they are arrested.

4. Outline the sentencing options available to a youth court judge, and provide an example for each.

Apply Your Learning

5. Section 146 of the *Youth Criminal Justice Act* sets the conditions for a statement made by a youth to be admissible in court. The statement must be (a) voluntary, and (b) the peace officer or authority arresting or detaining the youth must communicate in clear, understandable language. Furthermore, any written or oral statement will be admissible only if, according to section 146(2):
   (c) the young person has, before the statement was made, been given a reasonable opportunity to consult
       (i) with counsel, and
       (ii) with a parent or, in the absence of a parent, an adult relative or, in the absence of a parent and an adult relative, any other appropriate adult chosen by the young person.
   a) Summarize the conditions that must be met before a statement from a youth is to be admitted in court.

b) Why do you think there are so many conditions on statements made by youths? If these conditions are not met, what will happen?

6. Section 42(2) of the *Youth Criminal Justice Act* sets out youth sentences for first- and second-degree murder as defined in section 231 of the *Criminal Code*. Under paragraph (q), the youth justice court must

> order the person to serve a sentence not to exceed
> (i) in the case of first degree murder, ten years ...
> (ii) in the case of second degree murder, seven years ...

a) The sentence for first-degree murder is more severe than the sentence for second-degree murder (see page 128). What elements in the offence of first-degree murder support the rationale for a longer sentence?

b) Are there circumstances that would justify a youth receiving a life sentence for committing acts of murder? Support your opinion.

7. Manny is 16 years old and has been charged with robbery for the third time. He lives with his father, who is on social assistance. Neither can afford to pay for a lawyer for Manny's court appearance next week.

a) What options are available to Manny if he can't afford to pay his own legal costs?

b) Would the fact that his father is on social assistance have any bearing on the help offered to Manny? Explain.

8. Angie, who is 13 years old, stole $12 worth of cosmetics from a department store. She was caught by the store's security officer and turned over to the police. This is Angie's first offence.

a) What possible options are available to the police officer?

b) Would the fact that this is her first offence have any bearing on the case? Explain.

9. In 2001, a 16-year-old Montreal teenager, known as "Mafiaboy," pleaded guilty in youth justice court to 58 charges related to attacks and security breaches of Internet sites in Canada, the United States, and elsewhere in February 2000. This series of acts comprised the most expensive act of computer vandalism in history. Sites breached included Amazon, Yahoo, CNN, and eBay. The FBI estimated the youth's activities cost the U.S. economy over $1 billion because targeted sites lost six hours' worth of revenue when legitimate users were prevented from accessing them.

The Crown prosecutor recommended a one-year sentence in a secure facility, while the defence counsel recommended no time in detention. The maximum sentence the teen could have received was two years in a secure facility.

Form a group of three. One student will be the Crown prosecutor; one will be the defence counsel; one will be the judge.

a) As Crown prosecutor, prepare a sentencing argument against Mafiaboy.

b) As defence counsel, prepare a sentencing argument on behalf of Mafiaboy.

c) As judge, decide what sentence you would impose, and why.

Communicate Your Understanding

10. Between 1999 and 2000, youth courts in Canada handed down slightly more than 68 000 guilty verdicts. Of these, 48 percent resulted in a sentence of probation and 34 percent resulted in custody. In your opinion, are these adequate sentences, or should they be more severe? Support your opinion.

11. Debate the following topics in class. Prepare a brief introduction, identify facts and arguments that support your stance, anticipate points against your view and prepare counter-arguments to defend your viewpoint, and conclude with a statement that summarizes your position.

a) The age of criminal accountability should be lowered to 10 years of age.

b) Youths should get lighter sentences than adults for committing the same crimes.

c) Offenders aged 16 and older should automatically be tried in adult court.

d) Any extra protection for youths who break the law is a violation of section 15 of the *Canadian Charter of Rights and Freedoms*.

e) Delinquents are made, not born, and parents must share the responsibility for the actions of their children.

12. Principals are required to report criminal acts to police. For example, the Ontario Ministry of Education and Training requires school principals to report the following criminal acts:

- possession of prohibited weapons
- threats of serious physical injury
- physical assault causing bodily harm
- sexual assault
- gang or group assault
- repeated aggressive behaviour
- robbery
- extortion
- hate-motivated violence
- vandalism
- mischief or arson
- criminal harassment, including stalking
- prostitution
- possession of drugs or alcohol
- trafficking of drugs or alcohol

In a small group, prepare a report that analyzes the safety of your school environment. Gather information in response to the following questions:

a) Which actions or behaviours would be considered a violation of your school code of conduct?

b) Which actions could result in criminal charges?

c) In your school, are there activities that pose a threat to a safe school environment? Explain. Are teachers and principals aware of them?

d) What is being done to address the issue of safety in your school? Explain.

e) What should be done to address the issue of safety in your school?

13. In 1997, Ontario established a strict-discipline facility called Turnaround for young offenders (see Issue, page 304). Youths wear uniforms and their 16-hour days consist of military-style drills, physical exercise, and classes in anger management and drug rehabilitation. No television is permitted. It has been found that 60 percent of cadets released from this program do not commit additional crimes within one year.

With a partner, outline the advantages and disadvantages of military-style "boot camps" like Turnaround. Compare your results with other pairs of students. Attempt to reach a class consensus on the issue.

Develop Your Thinking

14. Lisbet Palme, chairperson of the Swedish UNICEF committee, made this statement in 1997: "Children in many countries face the wrath [anger] of the law for the 'crimes' of being poor, neglected or abused. Regardless of the reasons for their offences, young people are entitled to fair treatment at the hands of juvenile justice systems that are designed to aid youngsters' return to productive society as quickly as possible."

a) Why is the word "crimes" in quotation marks?

b) Why are attitudes of people important in a society that is trying to achieve justice for everyone? Explain.

15. On the whole, do you think the *Youth Criminal Justice Act* is effective in balancing the interests and protection of society with the rights of youths who come into conflict with the law? Justify your opinion.

> The mission of tort law in the next millennium should be
> empowering the injured.
>
> Allan M. Linden
> Justice, Federal Court of Canada
> Excerpt from *Torts Tomorrow* (1998)

Tort and Dispute Resolution

Chapter
11

Resolving Civil Disputes

Focus Questions

- What is the difference between criminal (public) and civil (private) law?
- What is a tort?
- In what courts are civil disputes tried?
- What are the procedures involved in bringing a civil action to trial?
- What are the types of damages and other remedies available for resolving civil disputes?
- What is alternative dispute resolution (ADR)?
- What are the most common forms of ADR?

Chapter at a Glance

Figure 11-1

Why would Small Claims Court often be called "The People's Court"?

11.1 Introduction

Civil law is also known as private law. It regulates disputes between individuals; between parties, such as business or government; and between individuals and parties.

Society does not have an interest in regulating civil disputes as it does crime. Civil disputes are really only important to the parties involved. While the main purpose of *criminal* law is to punish the offenders and to protect society from dangerous people, the main purpose of *civil* law is to compensate victims. When a crime occurs, anyone can help to bring the offender to justice. When a civil dispute arises, only the victim can take action. However, there is a significant public interest in ensuring that these disputes are settled fairly.

Civil actions include claims arising from accidents; injuries done by one person to another's body, property, or reputation; divorces, child custody, and support claims; adoptions; failure to pay for work done; nonpayment of rent; and unpaid debts. The victim may bring an action against the person who committed the civil wrong for **damages** (monetary compensation), or some other civil remedy. Review Chapter 1 for the various areas of civil law.

Tort law, the subject of this unit, is a major division of civil law. The word "tort" means "a wrong" that could be either intentional or unintentional (negligent). Civil procedure is also examined in this unit, while important aspects of family law, contract law, and labour law follow in later units.

11.2 Crimes and Torts

As you know, Canada's justice system involves both criminal and civil law, which both concern wrongs and, in some cases, the same wrong. Some actions may involve both a crime and a tort, as you can see in Figure 11-2.

▌ Crimes and Torts

If a person ...	It may be a crime of ...	And also the tort of ...
hits another person	assault	battery
breaks into someone's property	break and enter	trespass to land
takes someone's belongings	theft	trespass to goods

Figure 11-2

Some actions involve a crime and a tort.

Assume that Andrea tries to drive home while under the influence of alcohol. She runs a red light, hits Pavel's car, and seriously injures him. Society, represented by the Crown, may begin criminal action against Andrea on the grounds of impaired or dangerous driving. If convicted, Andrea will find her punishment outlined in the *Criminal Code.* At the same time, Pavel can begin a civil action to sue Andrea for **compensation.** Tort law entitles Pavel to receive compensation (usually money) for the injuries he sustained and other losses suffered.

Should an Athlete Who Intentionally Injures Another Athlete Face Criminal or Civil Action?

Canadians have become increasingly vocal about violence in team sports such as hockey. Many Canadians, for example, were shocked when, on February 2, 2000, Marty McSorley of the Edmonton Oilers slashed Donald Brashear of the Vancouver Canucks in what seemed like a deliberate attack (see photos on pages 4 and 243). The NHL disciplinary committee suspended McSorley for 23 games—the longest suspension in league history. That move cost McSorley $100 000 in lost wages.

The Crown also charged McSorley with the crime of assault with a weapon. On October 11, 2000, he was found guilty and given an 18-month conditional discharge. Brashear could have also launched a civil suit against McSorley for battery, but did not.

Violence in sports is not confined to players. Fans also have been guilty of outbursts of violence. In Europe, incidents of spectator violence have been a relatively common occurrence at soccer matches. Many fans expect violence, and players and coaches have tried not to disappoint them. Sometimes, outbreaks of violence between teams spark fights between their respective supporters in the audience.

Such incidents have provoked Canadians to consider how to deal with them and how to prevent them.

Figure 11-3

The Pittsburgh Penguins and Toronto Maple Leafs get into a scuffle. Is this "a natural part of the game"?

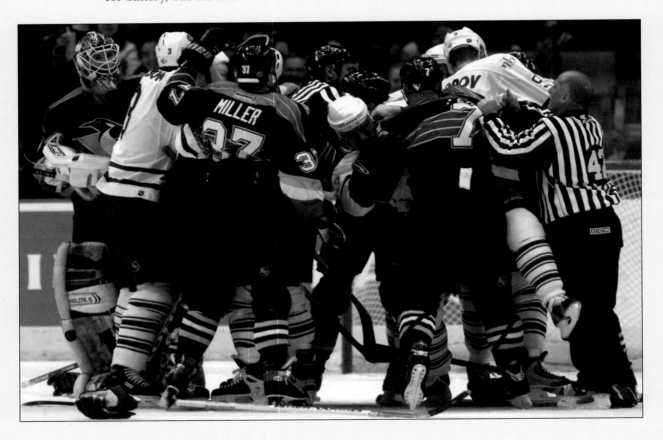

On One Side

Some fans and players maintain that a certain amount of violence is a natural part of the game. They say that risking injury during a hockey game is as much a part of the game as winning and losing. Those who criticize the bodychecking and occasional fights do not really understand the game. Aggression is a basic human condition and it is natural for athletes to let off steam. Players may be upset by questionable calls, heckling fans, pressures of the game, or all three. If violence were eliminated, fan support would decrease and the game would suffer. There are enough rules and penalties in games like hockey to punish those who use excessive force, and there is no need for criminal or civil action.

On the Other Side

People who oppose violence in sports say that violent behaviour is learned and can be unlearned. At an early age, children who play hockey are taught how to bodycheck to get control of the puck. They see their heroes and role models involved in violent acts and want to copy them. Phrases like "taking him out" and "playing the man" are commonplace. Players are expected to engage in fighting, to resist backing down, and to support team members who are involved in a fight. There is a fear that this learned violence will become part of their daily lives.

Fans who oppose violence in sports believe it overshadows the skills of the game. They want criminal and civil action taken against those who use intentional violence. They point out that, if this type of violence were to occur outside the game, it would be subject to criminal or civil action. They propose large fines and lengthy suspensions to deter athletes from engaging in violence.

The Bottom Line

Efforts are being made to understand the nature of violence and to deal with it effectively. Violence in sports is no exception. Sports clubs are being pressured to make and enforce tougher rules and penalties for violence in sports. The media are moving away from sensational coverage of violence in sports. Failure to address the problem at the grassroots level may lead to government action to deal with it.

Although some Canadians approve of violence in sports and consider it part of the game, others feel that violence takes away from the game. In hockey, some violence falls within the rules; the rest is penalized within the game. Society needs to consider which acts are outside the game rules and require legal action.

⊖ activity

Visit **www.law.nelson.com** and follow the links to learn more about the issue of violence in sports.

What Do You Think?

1. What is the relationship between tort law and violence in sports?

2. How has the traditional attitude toward violence in sports changed?

3. Assume you are a participant in a body-contact sport. Prepare an argument in favour of the use of violence in contact sports. Prepare a counterargument that supports criminal or civil action for acts of intentional violence.

4. In your opinion, is violence in sports a reflection of violence in society? Explain.

5. Under what circumstances should players be encouraged to press charges and sue for damages? Explain.

It is Pavel's personal responsibility to bring this action. A civil court will award him suitable damages for his injuries; that is, "suitable" in the court's view. Each action, criminal and civil, proceeds independently of the other. Each case is tried in a different court with a different judge, and there is no set order in which the cases must be tried.

People who can prove that they have suffered injury or loss through another person's fault deserve some remedy. Although compensation is the most important purpose of tort law from the victim's viewpoint, some tort actions also contain elements of punishment and deterrence. Interesting tort cases are often followed closely by the media. The resulting publicity may affect the future behaviour of many people, including the parties involved in the suit and the public.

For example, an action against a fast-food outlet by a customer who finds human hair or a fingernail in a hamburger might have a negative effect on the company's sales and public image. The company itself would probably try to avoid another similar lawsuit. Most likely, the negative publicity from this case would cause other manufacturers to review and improve their production facilities and quality-control inspections.

Likewise, if a court awarded Pavel a substantial amount of cash in the motor vehicle scenario, this could have a deterrent effect on other negligent drivers.

Review Your Understanding (Pages 311 to 314)

1. Define "tort" and give three examples of torts.
2. How can an offence be both a crime and a tort? Provide an example.
3. Identify the main purpose of tort law.
4. Explain how a tort action might also consider the element of deterrence.

11.3 Civil Courts

In Chapter 4, you learned about Canada's criminal courts. This section examines Canada's civil courts. Although it is a civil court, Family Court will be discussed separately in Unit 4: Family Law.

Small Claims Court

Sometimes called "The People's Court," **Small Claims Court** provides a simple and relatively inexpensive way to settle disputes concerning money or property. Cases are tried informally by a judge without a jury. Both parties are given the chance to tell their story and are not usually represented by lawyers. In fact, Quebec has barred lawyers from its Small Claims Courts.

All provinces issue free, easy-to-read booklets with step-by-step procedures for filing a claim. In addition, court staff are available to answer questions and explain how to fill out the proper forms, most of which follow a fill-in-the-blank format.

Typical small claims include failure to pay rent, consumer complaints, unpaid bills, unpaid wages, claims for minor accidents, and consumer debts.

Many businesses use this court to collect unpaid accounts from customers. The dollar limit for such claims varies from province to province and currently ranges from $3000 to $10 000. The maximum claim for each province is shown in Figure 11-4. Procedures for settling civil disputes are discussed in Section 11.4.

Provincial Supreme Court

All civil cases above the small claims limit go directly to the Supreme Court of the province or to the Court of Queen's Bench. Disputes that reach this level are usually argued by lawyers since the cases may be very complex and may require several years of preparation. Examples include serious motor vehicle accidents, medical malpractice or injury, breach of contract, division of property after a divorce, and so on. Cases at this level may be tried by a judge alone or by judge and jury. Unlike a criminal trial jury, a civil trial jury in most provinces has only six members, and they can reach a decision by majority vote. In recent years, jury trials in civil cases have become rare because of the cost and complexity of the cases.

Court of Appeal

All provinces have Courts of Appeal that hear appeals from their lower courts. Appeals are heard by three or more judges, depending on the case, and their decisions may be either unanimous or majority judgments. A split 2 to 1 judgment is not uncommon from these courts. The court will release its decision and provide explanations for the majority vote. Dissenting judges will also provide their reasons for disagreeing with the majority vote.

Federal Court of Canada

The Federal Court of Canada's Trial Division deals with civil cases involving the federal government and its employees; disputes over federal income tax; and patents, copyrights, and trademarks. The Appeals Division hears appeals from the court's Trial Division.

Supreme Court of Canada

The Supreme Court of Canada, the highest court in the country, is an appeal court that hears only those cases from the Federal Court of Canada and provincial Courts of Appeal that it believes are of national importance or in which an important issue or question of law must be decided or interpreted. There is also an automatic right of appeal when there is a split decision from a provincial Court of Appeal. Like the provincial Courts of Appeal, the Supreme Court of Canada may issue unanimous or split decisions.

▮ Small Claims Court Maximums, January 2002

Province	Maximum Claim $
Alberta	7 500
British Columbia	10 000
Manitoba	7 500
New Brunswick	6 000
Newfoundland & Labrador	3 000
Nova Scotia	10 000
Ontario	10 000
Prince Edward Island	8 000
Quebec	3 000
Saskatchewan	5 000

Figure 11-4

The provincial Small Claims Court maximums range from $3 000 to $10 000. Why do you think limits are set?

Review Your Understanding (Pages 314 to 315)

1. What dollar limit exists for cases tried in Small Claims Court?
2. Give four examples of cases that could be tried in your province's Small Claims Court.
3. Why are juries seldom used in civil suits?
4. What types of appeals will the Supreme Court of Canada hear?

11.4 Trial Procedures

Balance of Probabilities

A civil lawsuit involves two parties: the **plaintiff,** who is suing, and the **defendant,** who is being sued. If more than one person or party has suffered the harm, all injured parties should sue together as plaintiffs in one action. If more than one person is responsible for causing the loss, they all should be sued as defendants. The process of suing is called **litigation,** and the parties in the action are the **litigants.**

In Ontario, minors may sue on their own for up to $500. A minor is a person under the age of 18 or 19, depending on the province. If a minor sues for more than $500, a responsible adult or **litigation guardian** must act for the minor. Usually, the child's parent or guardian will act in this capacity, but any responsible adult can serve.

As in a criminal procedure, the litigants prepare and present the facts of the case. The burden of proof is on the plaintiff; he or she must prove the case. However, the plaintiff is not required to prove the case beyond a reasonable doubt, as is the case in a criminal trial. Instead, the plaintiff must prove the case on the **balance of probabilities.** This means that as the plaintiff, you must prove that the events took place in the way you claim. The defendant will then try to show that his or her version is what really happened. The judge will then determine which side is more credible or believable.

Case

Lewis v. Robinson

2001 BCSC 643
British Columbia Supreme Court

The plaintiff, Kenneth Lewis, was a delivery person. He knew that the defendants, Will Robinson and Marci Salach, were the new owners and occupants of the property, but Lewis didn't know that the defendants had a dog. Lewis entered the property and was confronted by Salach and her dog. She was holding the dog's leash at the time.

Most times, the dog was chained to its doghouse on the defendants' property. However, on this particular day, Lewis arrived on the property, startling Salach and the dog. Salach asked Lewis to identify himself, received no response, and then warned him that the dog did not like strangers and to be careful. Lewis saw the defendant speaking, but claimed he

continued

couldn't hear her as the dog was barking. He tried to pet the dog and then tried to move out of the dog's range when the dog bit his hand. Prior to this incident, the dog had never attacked, bitten, or lunged at strangers, and there was no evidence of complaints from neighbours or friends.

Lewis brought an action for damages, but his action was dismissed.

For Discussion

1. **Why did Lewis bring an action against the defendants?**
2. **Summarize the conflicting evidence.**
3. **Based on the evidence presented, why do you think the plaintiff's action was dismissed?**

Figure 11-5

Who is at fault when, despite warnings, someone approaches a dog and is injured?

▌ Criminal and Civil Procedures Compared

Case Factors	Criminal/Public	Civil/Private
Parties involved	Crown prosecutor versus accused (defendant)	Plaintiff versus defendant
Grounds/reason	To determine innocence or guilt of accused	To resolve a dispute
Purpose of action	To punish offender	To compensate victims
Onus of proof	On Crown prosecutor	On plaintiff
Burden of proof	Beyond a reasonable doubt	Balance of probabilities
Result of action	Accused is guilty or not guilty	Defendant is liable or not liable
Action taken if defendant is guilty or liable	Defendant sentenced	Plaintiff awarded some compensation or remedy

Figure 11-6

What are the similarities and differences between criminal and civil law procedures?

Filing and Serving a Claim

What actually happens during a civil procedure? Assume that Bjorn runs a red light and hits Penny's car. As in the earlier example involving Andrea and Pavel, the Crown may lay criminal charges against Bjorn for the accident. Penny, too, must decide whether to take legal action against Bjorn. She must determine if she has a **cause of action;** that is, a valid reason for suing. If Penny finds she has a cause, she must then decide on the proper court in which to proceed. As you have learned, the court in which a civil action is tried depends on the amount of money involved. As you will learn later in this chapter, going to court is not the only option, but it is often the only way when the parties have very different versions of the same event.

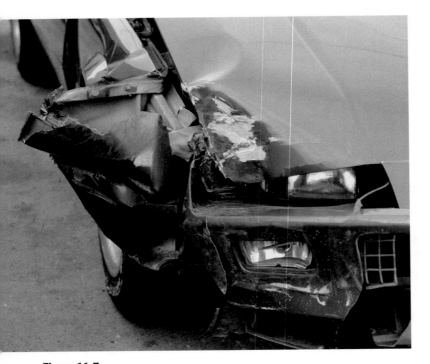

Figure 11-7

The Crown may lay criminal charges against Bjorn for running a red light and hitting Penny's car. Penny can lay civil charges against Bjorn, too, if she can determine the cause of action.

Assume that Penny's action will begin in Small Claims Court. Her first step is to file a **claim** that must include
- her full name and address
- Bjorn's full name and address
- the amount of money she is claiming
- a brief, clear summary of the reasons for the claim

If more than one defendant is involved, each one must be named and identified correctly.

After completing the claim, Penny mails or hand-delivers it to the court clerk, along with the required filing fee. The fee is the cost of handling the claim, and the amount depends on the amount the plaintiff is claiming. The fee the plaintiff pays is added to the claim by the court.

At this time, Penny must choose a location to file her action. It may be a Small Claims Court near the accident location, near Bjorn's residence, or near her residence. Penny receives a copy of the summons, and the court clerk keeps a copy. Bjorn must be served with a copy as well. The document may be delivered personally by Penny, by a friend or business associate, or by a private process serving agency so that the court is assured that the defendant, or a responsible adult, has received the claim.

Penny must also ensure that she files her claim within a certain period of time following the event. This is called the **limitation period.** Also, the claim must be served within six months from its date of issue. If it cannot be served within six months, it can be renewed by a judge.

When Bjorn receives the claim, he has several options. If he agrees that he owes Penny the full amount of the claim, he can pay the amount plus court costs to the Small Claims Court office. He must do so within 10 to 30 days, depending on the province. The court clerk will then pay Penny, ending the dispute.

Defence or Reply

If Bjorn feels that he does not owe Penny anything, he prepares a **defence** (**reply**), a document that clearly outlines his reasons for disagreeing with her claim. Bjorn may have a number of reasons. He might argue that the light was not red when he went through it and hit Penny's car. Or he might say that the brakes on his car failed and he could not stop in time to prevent the accident. If Bjorn intends to dispute the claim, he must do so within 10 to 30 days of receiving the summons or claim. A copy of the defence will be sent to the plaintiff by the court office.

Payment into Court

If Bjorn feels that Penny is entitled to some part of the claim, he can pay that amount to the Small Claims Court office. Penny will then be notified and can either accept the amount and drop the balance of her claim, or pursue the case in the hope of obtaining the full amount.

Counterclaim

The defendant may also make a **counterclaim,** saying that it was actually the plaintiff who was at fault for the accident. Bjorn will attempt to claim damages from Penny for his own loss. A counterclaim must relate to the problem that caused the plaintiff's claim. When a civil action involves damage to vehicles, the defendant will often counterclaim.

In this scenario, Bjorn defends against Penny's claim and makes one of his own against her, arguing that she began to move before her traffic light had turned green and that she was driving too quickly to stop. The judge will examine the counterclaim and the plaintiff's claim at the same time if the case comes to trial and decide who is at fault and who will receive what from whom.

Third Party Claim

Another option available to the defendant is to involve a third party who the defendant feels is partly or completely responsible for the dispute. If Bjorn had his brakes repaired just before the accident, and if the failure of the brakes was responsible for the accident, Bjorn might involve the repair garage as a third party to share some of the blame and the cost. Taking this action saves time and money, because the case can proceed in the presence of all three parties. Otherwise, Svend would have to sue the repair garage separately.

Default Judgment

If Bjorn does not reply to the claim within the required time period, a **default judgment** is automatically made against him. This means that Penny wins her action. She is awarded a judgment against Bjorn by default, since he has not responded to the claim. The court considers that the defendant agrees with the claim. Penny is entitled to recover the amount she claimed, plus any related costs.

Out-of-Court Settlement

At any point, either party can make a formal or informal offer to settle the dispute instead of proceeding to trial. The litigants should make every effort to negotiate an **out-of-court settlement.** The plaintiff must balance the proposed offer with the chance of winning the full claim at trial. Penny might prefer to settle for a portion of her claim rather than involve herself in a trial. Settling before a trial saves time and money.

Pre-Trial Conference

A **pre-trial conference** (settlement conference) is the last chance for the parties to resolve the dispute before trial. Both litigants will have an informal

activity

Visit **www.law.nelson.com** and follow the links to learn more about small claims actions.

meeting with a judge or a court-appointed referee who encourages the parties to settle the claim. The conference allows each party to hear a basic summary of the other's case so there are no surprises at trial. Based on discussions, the judge may give an opinion of the possible judgment if the case moves to trial. Many cases are settled on the basis of this opinion, without going to trial. The parties can discuss matters openly and honestly since the pre-trial conference judge is not the trial judge. If the parties cannot reach an agreement during the pre-trial conference, a trial date will be set.

Civil Procedure in Higher Courts

For actions in higher courts, there are additional procedures to help the parties settle their dispute without a trial. In higher courts, the claim is known as a "statement of claim" and the defence is known as a "statement of defence." The litigants send legal documents back and forth over several months, or even years, in an attempt to define and narrow the disputed issues and to assist the judge in understanding the details of the dispute. Because of this, many cases tried in provincial superior courts take four to six years before reaching trial. Then, the discovery process begins.

The **examination for discovery** is a question-and-answer session for the litigants and their lawyers. Its purpose is to limit the possibility of surprises at trial by providing information about each side's case and to reach agreement on certain issues. This reduces court time, saves money, and makes settlement easier. Both parties must disclose *all* relevant documents. Either party can question the other under oath; the questions and answers are transcribed by the court reporter and are available at trial. Either party can also ask the court to issue an order permitting inspection of physical objects in the case. In our scenario, Penny's and Bjorn's cars and photographs from the accident scene might be inspected. If Penny claimed for serious injuries from the accident, Bjorn could request X-rays and the medical report. Often, the parties settle the case after discovery.

The Trial

If no settlement can be reached, the parties go to court for a trial by judge alone or by a judge and a civil jury of six people, except in Small Claims Court. However, as mentioned earlier, juries for civil actions are no longer common.

Procedures in a civil trial are similar to those used in criminal trials. Each party has a chance to present his or her case by calling witnesses; parties can also testify themselves if they choose. The plaintiff goes first, followed by the defendant. When all the evidence has been presented, each party sums up his or her case and makes a final argument to the judge. The judge will make a decision and may allow none, part, or all of the claim.

In a trial by jury, the judge instructs the jury members on the law applicable to the facts of the case. The jury must consider the evidence, as well as questions such as these: Who was at fault? Is that person totally at fault, or are both parties somewhat to blame? How should damages be determined? How much should the damages be? All these factors must be considered in reaching a judgment. (If there is no jury, the judge does all of the above.)

activity

Visit **www.law.nelson.com** and follow the links to learn about civil case management as a method of improving access to the civil justice system.

1. **Distinguish between the plaintiff and the defendant.**
2. **What does the "balance of probabilities" mean in a civil action? How does it differ from the burden of proof in a criminal trial?**
3. **Identify four key pieces of information that must appear on a plaintiff's claim.**
4. **Briefly outline the four options available to a defendant who disputes a plaintiff's claim.**
5. **Explain the significance of a default judgment.**
6. **Outline the benefits of an out-of-court settlement.**
7. **Explain the purpose of a pre-trial conference.**
8. **Outline the benefits of an examination for discovery.**

11.5 The Judgment and Civil Remedies

After the trial, the judge delivers a judgment. In Small Claims Court, the judge often gives an oral judgment while all the parties involved are still present. In higher courts, the judge usually needs some time to review the evidence and to consider the case itself and the relevant law. The judge is then said to be "reserving judgment"; that is, delaying a decision until all the evidence has been examined.

Civil Remedies

Damages for the plaintiff's injury or loss are the remedy most often awarded in tort actions. The intent is to return plaintiffs, as much as possible, to the same position they were in before the loss or injury occurred. In the case of injury (e.g., paralysis), no amount of money can adequately compensate victims, but a major purpose of awarding damages is compensating plaintiffs for the cost of future care and future loss of income. Courts consider these factors, if applicable, and refer to past cases and precedents to determine awards.

There are five types of damages, and plaintiffs may be awarded one or more of them.

Figure 11-8

Anne Poulin (left), pictured with her sister and mother, was awarded almost $3 million in damages after she was left partially paralyzed by gallbladder surgery. Poulin's pursuit of justice took 11 years.

General Damages

General damages are damages that cannot be calculated easily or precisely and require a judge's or a jury's discretion. There are two main categories:
- damages for loss of income and future earnings and the cost of specialized future care
- damages for pain and suffering and for loss of enjoyment of life

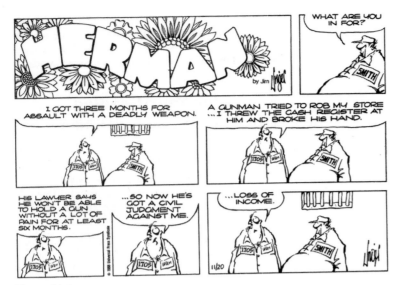

Figure 11-9

What is unfair about this settlement?

For loss of income, the judge must consider what the plaintiff was earning at the time of the accident and what he or she would earn in the future. The longer the injured plaintiff is expected to live, the greater the compensation. If the victim has a job or had definite plans to enter a specific profession or trade, then the average earnings for that occupation may be used. The settlement must, moreover, be fair to both the plaintiff and the defendant.

Determining adequate compensation is extremely difficult when the injured plaintiff is very young or has not yet entered the workforce. For example, if you were injured, would you be able to say with certainty what you intend to do after high school? Are your school marks high enough to enter college or university or a particular trade? Have you seriously thought about what type of employment you intend to seek? If so, who knows about these decisions, and who could testify on your behalf at a trial to support your claims if you were an injured plaintiff?

Costs for future care cover professional help, equipment, facilities, and medication necessary to assist the injured plaintiff in performing daily activities.

While damages can be difficult to determine, placing a price on pain and suffering is even more difficult. What is the loss of enjoyment of life worth to a person permanently injured in an accident? Should an athletic, socially active youth be given more money for loss of enjoyment of life than a quiet, less active one? Money cannot always restore what has been injured or lost; however, it can provide substitutes for pleasures that are no longer possible. Compensation can, for instance, make it possible for an injured plaintiff who can no longer skate or ski to enjoy a winter vacation.

Looking Back — The Supreme Court of Canada Trilogy

Because of highly publicized American legal cases in which plaintiffs are awarded millions of dollars, many Canadians feel that they will receive equally high awards for personal injury lawsuits. However, this is not the case. Canadian courts take a more cautious approach in determining damages.

In three precedent-setting decisions in 1978, the Supreme Court of Canada set out the factors to consider for awards for pain and suffering in very serious cases—those resulting in severe, life-long physical incapacity. The court set $100 000 as maximum compensation for pain and suffering in most cases, excluding "exceptional circumstances," based on the severity of injuries and the victim's disability. In today's dollars, this amount is roughly worth between $275 000 and $300 000.

Two of the three cases were *Thornton v. Prince George School District No. 57* (1978) and *Arnold v. Teno* (1978). In the first case, Gary Thornton, a high school student, was injured during a gymnastics class, leaving him a

continued ▶

quadriplegic (paralyzed in all four limbs). He had minimal use of his hands and some use of his arms up to his shoulders, but he would require constant care for the rest of his life and his life expectancy was 54 years. His mental faculties were unimpaired. He and his parents sued the teacher and the school board, and the Supreme Court of Canada ultimately awarded Thornton $810 000.

In the second case, Diane Teno, a four-year-old child, was hit by a car while crossing the street to buy an ice-cream cone from a vendor in her neighbourhood. Her speech, physical abilities, and mental capacity were left severely handicapped, and she would require full-time assistance to perform even ordinary tasks for the rest of her life. Her life expectancy was 67 years. On the child's behalf, the parents sued the driver of the car, the ice-cream vendor, and the company for whom he worked. The Supreme Court of Canada ultimately awarded the Tenos $540 000.

In each of these judgments, along with another case involving a quadriplegic young adult—*Andrews v. Grand and Toy Alberta Ltd.* (1978)—the Supreme Court established the ceiling of $100 000 for pain and suffering and loss of enjoyment of life.

Figure 11-10

In *Arnold v. Teno*, the court considered whether negligence occurred by the simple fact that some children had to cross the street to buy ice cream. Some handbooks for vendors recommended that a sign be posted on the left-hand side of the truck, warning children not to cross the street.

For Discussion

1. What factors do the courts consider when awarding damages for pain and suffering?

2. In the case of permanent disability, a key issue for courts to determine is whether the victim's future care should be in an institution or a modified home. Although home care is preferable, it is more expensive. In a chart, outline the advantages and disadvantages of an institutional versus modified-home environment.

3. Discuss the merit of having a ceiling for pain and suffering in the 21st century.

Case

Tran v. Financial Debt Recovery Ltd.

(2000) 193 D.L.R. (4th) 168
Ontario Superior Court of Justice

The plaintiff, Mark Tran, had a student loan that remained unpaid. He graduated from the University of Toronto with a commerce degree in 1996. Collection of Tran's loan had been transferred from the original lender to the defendant collection agency. Tran questioned the amount owing and refused to make any payments until the issue was cleared up.

The defendant agency and its employees then began a planned campaign of harassment. They lied about their identities, harassed Tran at work, threatened him with physical harm, and repeatedly telephoned Tran and other employees at his office. After receiving seven abusive calls within 30 minutes, the receptionist threatened to call the police if the callers didn't stop. The agency also lied to Tran's employer, claiming that he was looking for work with a competitor, that there was a court judgment he had not paid, and that he was financially irresponsible.

As a result of these events, Tran's employer did not give the plaintiff his annual raise or bonus. Tran, unrepresented by counsel, brought an action for $15 000 for damages to his reputation,

continued ▶

for humiliation and emotional suffering, and for economic loss. The trial judge found in Tran's favour and awarded him $25 000 plus court costs.

For Discussion

1. Briefly summarize the main issues in this case.
2. How was Tran's reputation damaged from this incident?
3. Tran based his action on three factors: his loss in income; the time he spent daily doing exercise and meditation to relieve the stress caused by the defendant; and a modest amount to compensate him for the loss of weight and humiliation caused by the defendant. Although he felt his damages were about $40 000, he reduced that amount to $15 000 because he did not want to appear unreasonable. What factors do you think the trial judge took into consideration in awarding $25 000 plus court costs?

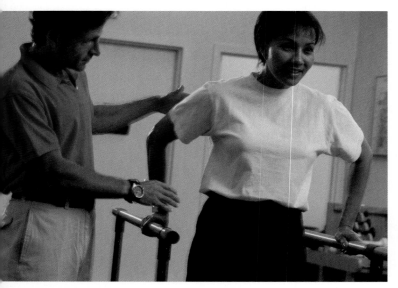

Figure 11-11

The cost of physiotherapy may be recovered through the awarding of special damages.

Special Damages

Special damages compensate for out-of-pocket expenses already spent before trial because of the injuries suffered. Although they are not essential, it is helpful to produce receipts for these expenses. A plaintiff may be hospitalized after an accident, lose income, and/or pay expenses for ambulance service, drugs, therapy, rehabilitation, car repairs, and so on. Lost wages between the accident and the trial are also special damages because they can be calculated exactly.

Punitive Damages

Punitive damages (exemplary damages) are additional damages awarded to punish the defendant for bad, insensitive, or uncaring behaviour. The intention is deterrence: to discourage both the defendant and the public from committing similar actions. However, punitive damages are seldom awarded in cases where the defendant has already been punished by the criminal courts for the same action. They are most commonly awarded for intentional torts, discussed in Chapter 12.

Aggravated Damages

Aggravated damages are similar to punitive damages. These damages are awarded when the defendant's behaviour is so outrageous, it harms the plaintiff. For example, the plaintiff suffers serious emotional shock or suffering because of the defendant's behaviour. While punitive damages are intended to punish or deter defendants, aggravated damages compensate the plaintiff for the defendant's outrageous conduct. Assume, for example, that a drug company markets a morning-sickness pill that is later revealed to cause birth defects. If investigation shows that the pill was not adequately tested, the company could be assessed for punitive damages. If, on the other hand, investigation reveals that the company executives knew the pill could cause birth defects but marketed it anyway, the court could award aggravated damages because of the company's outrageous behaviour.

Nominal Damages

Nominal damages are awarded when a judge wants to indicate support for a plaintiff and awards a small sum, such as $1 to $100. Such an award suggests that, although the plaintiff has suffered little or no loss or harm, he or she has won a moral victory. If, for example, someone trespasses on another person's property but does not actually damage the property, nominal damages may be awarded to tell trespassers that they have affected the owner's right of property use.

Injunctions

In a small number of civil actions, the plaintiff is not interested in cash compensation as a remedy. Suppose that Jack and Arnie are band members who rehearse late each evening at their home. Their neighbours, the Harrises, feel that their right to quiet enjoyment of their property is being disturbed. The Harrises might ask the courts to prevent the continuation of late-night

Case

Dunne v. Gauthier

2000 BCSC 1603
British Columbia Supreme Court

The plaintiff, David Dunne, was a school-bus driver who drove the four children of the defendant, David Gauthier. One November morning in 1996, the children boarded the bus. One child told Dunne that they would not be taking the bus home. However, at the end of the day, three of the four children caught the bus. Dunne didn't ask about the fourth child, a six-year-old boy, nor did the Gauthier children say anything about their brother. About 60 children were on the bus for the ride home.

Shortly after school dismissal, Gauthier heard a recorded phone message from his young son, upset about missing the bus. The father then phoned the school and said he'd break both of the driver's legs if his son was not on the bus when it got home. The school arranged for a ride home for the boy and called the boy's home with that news. When the bus arrived at the Gauthier home, however, the defendant entered the bus, tore the telephone from Dunne's hand, and threw it out the bus door. Then, Gauthier put his arm around Dunne's neck, twisted it, and forced the driver down while he was

still strapped in his seat belt. Fifteen children were still on the school bus and witnessed this attack.

As Gauthier left the bus, he told Dunne that if he ever saw him on the road, he would "take" him and the bus "out." Dunne completed his route and then went to hospital for emergency care. He sued the father for personal injuries, psychological and emotional problems, and depression, and was awarded $10 000 general damages, $5000 aggravated damages, $3425 for lost wages, and $1600 special damages.

For Discussion

1. In his defence, Gauthier claimed that the plaintiff's reaction to the assault was unreasonable and that he shouldn't have been so affected by what happened. What argument could the plaintiff make to counter this claim?

2. Gauthier also argued that he was broke and couldn't pay any award, even if the court found in the plaintiff's favour. Should this be a concern of the court in reaching a judgment? Explain.

3. What factors do you think the court considered in awarding aggravated damages?

Figure 11-12

These striking public service workers are blocking entry to a government building in Ottawa. Should an injunction be granted in this situation?

rehearsals by requesting an **injunction**—an order for a person to do or not do something. The courts could respond by issuing a court order to Jack and Arnie, restricting the rehearsals to reasonable hours.

Similarly, a factory that is dumping its waste into a lake, thus polluting it, might be subject to an injunction requiring the owners to stop this activity. The most common use of injunctions is to require striking workers to return to work. Failure to comply with an injunction might result in a charge for contempt of court, followed by a fine or jail sentence.

Costs

If the plaintiff wins the case, the judge must determine whether court costs will be allowed. Usually, the losing party is required to pay the legal fees and other expenses of the successful party. These costs are based on a fee schedule published by the courts and vary somewhat by province. The winning party prepares a bill of costs and gives it to the losing party for payment. However, the amount the judge awards may cover only part of the costs, especially for a long trial in a higher court. The rest might have to come from the award of damages, leaving little for the plaintiff.

Because of the expense of civil actions in provincial superior courts, a **contingency fee** system exists everywhere in Canada except Ontario. This system allows people who cannot afford to pay legal fees in advance to take legal action. If the client loses the case, the lawyer receives nothing. If the case is successful, the lawyer receives a fee based on a percentage of the damages the plaintiff receives. In most provinces, there is no cap (limit), but rules state that a lawyer's fee must not exceed a fair and reasonable limit. Where provincial limits exist, clients pay their lawyers between 30 and 40 percent of a successful judgment. Although this may seem high, it is based on the complexity of the cases tried in superior courts. However, opponents of the system fear that it will result in too many actions and multimillion dollar lawsuits, as has happened in the United States.

Enforcing a Judgment

In a civil case, it is up to the successful party to collect on the judgment. The court has no responsibility to ensure that the losing party—the debtor—pays the damages. The loser may have little money or may be reluctant to pay. So, being awarded a judgment is one thing; collecting on it is quite another. However, the following options are available to plaintiffs to enforce payment.

Garnishment

Garnishment is a remedy that involves a third party. If the losing defendant is owed money by a third party, the successful plaintiff can obtain a court order forcing the third party to pay the debt to the court. In turn, the court will give the money to the plaintiff as a payment on the judgment. The third party is responsible only for the amount owed to the unsuccessful defendant, not for the total amount of the judgment.

Bank accounts, unpaid rent, money owing on contracts, and a portion (20 to 30 percent) of a defendant's wages can be the subjects of a garnishment order. The percentage differs from province to province. If the defendant cannot afford to have this percentage of wages taken, an application may be made to the court to have the amount altered. In most provinces, a garnishment remains in effect for six months, but can be renewed if the entire amount is not paid within that time.

Seizing Assets

Another option is to apply to the courts to take legal possession of the debtor's property and sell it to settle the judgment. The **bailiff** or sheriff seizes the assets and notifies the defendant of the seizure. The assets are held for a certain period, to give the defendant an opportunity to settle the judgment and redeem (get back) the goods. If this is not done, the goods are sold at public auction. The court deducts all its costs from the sale and then pays the plaintiff the amount of the judgment, or as much as possible. Any money remaining is returned to the debtor. Certain goods, such as clothing, furniture, utensils, and workers' tools, cannot be seized. One difficulty in seizing goods is that it is necessary to be certain that they belong to the person from whom they are seized.

Examination of the Debtor

If the defendant still refuses to pay, the plaintiff can request an **examination of the debtor.** The defendant is ordered to appear in court to satisfy the judge that he or she has the available resources to settle the claim. The debtor is examined under oath regarding income, assets, and any money owing from others. An agreement is usually reached as to how much, if anything, the debtor can afford to pay. Installment payments can be arranged, if necessary.

Review Your Understanding (Pages 321 to 327)

1. Distinguish between the two main categories of general damages.
2. Why is it difficult to determine what damages to award a young child?
3. Distinguish between special and nominal damages.
4. Distinguish between punitive and aggravated damages.
5. What is an injunction, and when might it be awarded in a civil judgment?
6. What is a contingency fee system? Identify one advantage and one disadvantage of this system.
7. Briefly outline three remedies available for enforcing a judgment.

11.6 Alternative Dispute Resolution

As you have seen, civil litigation often takes considerable time and money. Courts all across Canada are backlogged, and it may take several years and many thousands of dollars before a case reaches trial. Although the court system has traditionally managed disputes, there are new ways of resolving conflict that give more control over the outcome to the parties themselves. The pre-trial conference discussed earlier is one such way. As Canadians become frustrated with the excessive costs and delays in civil courts, they are considering other means of resolving disputes. As you learned in Chapter 1, negotiation, mediation, and arbitration are methods used in **alternative dispute resolution (ADR).** In this chapter, you will examine ADR in more detail.

ADR avoids the cost and risks of litigation and usually results in a win/win situation, with both parties gaining some benefit.

Negotiation

Resolving disputes happens all the time. You may have to negotiate with a family member for the use of the family car, and part of the discussion may involve when you'll be home with the car. You may try to negotiate a new deadline with your teacher for handing in a major project. **Negotiation** is an informal and voluntary dispute resolution process between the parties involved without

▌ ADR Communication Models

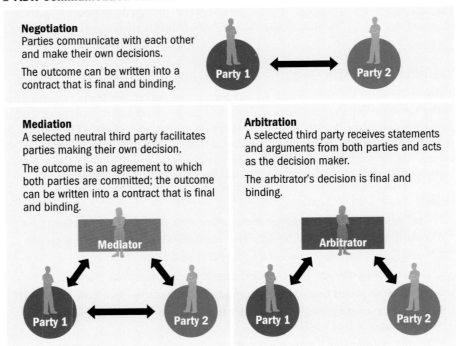

Negotiation
Parties communicate with each other and make their own decisions.

The outcome can be written into a contract that is final and binding.

Mediation
A selected neutral third party facilitates parties making their own decision.

The outcome is an agreement to which both parties are committed; the outcome can be written into a contract that is final and binding.

Arbitration
A selected third party receives statements and arguments from both parties and acts as the decision maker.

The arbitrator's decision is final and binding.

Figure 11-13

If you were resolving a dispute with friends, which model would you choose? Explain.

involvement of a third party. The two parties determine the process, communicate with each other, and reach mutually acceptable decisions. Discussions may relate to proof, witnesses and evidence, and problem solving to consider available options. Any agreement reached can be written into a contract. If negotiation doesn't work, mediation is often the next step.

Mediation

Mediation is a process in which the parties appoint a neutral third party to help them reach a mutually acceptable solution to their dispute. Mediation is the most rapidly growing form of ADR, with success rates that range from 80 to 85 percent. In some provinces, certain categories of cases must attempt mediation before a trial is scheduled. Mediation is becoming a major factor in family relationship disputes, such as child custody, visitation, support, and division of property. These issues will be examined in Chapters 14 and 15.

The mediator's role is advisory only. He or she involves the parties in a cooperative decision-making process to settle their dispute. The mediator's main role is to provide a relaxed, informal, and comfortable environment in which the parties are free to discuss their conflict openly and honestly, and arrive at possible solutions. Discussion should flow between the parties, rather than via the mediator, as they attempt to develop an understanding of the unresolved issues. The process takes place in private, which provides confidentiality for the parties involved. Mediation leaves the parties in control of their own decision making and emphasizes cooperation instead of confrontation. The cost of mediation is usually shared between the parties. Once an agreement is reached, it can be included in a written contract.

Arbitration

Arbitration is a more formal process in which the parties involved select a neutral third party or a panel of people with specific technical knowledge. Although arbitration is more formal than negotiation or mediation, it is still less formal than litigation in a courtroom. It is also much less costly than litigation, and it can make a difference of many thousands of dollars to the disputing parties.

Unlike mediation and negotiation, the parties no longer have control over their decision making. The arbitrator's role is to receive statements of key issues and hear arguments. Both parties have the chance to present evidence and to examine and cross-examine witnesses. Communication here flows mainly between the parties through the arbitrator. With his or her specific knowledge, the arbitrator will consider the two positions and usually make a final, binding decision or ruling on both parties. Binding arbitration is often used between professional hockey and baseball players and their teams when resolving salary disputes. Striking workers and their employers turn to binding arbitration to resolve their contract disputes. Unlike mediation, there is a winner and a loser with arbitration.

You Be the JUDGE

"In a trial, there is a winner and a loser. In mediation, there are two winners."

- In your own words, explain the meaning of this statement.

▋ Arbitration and Litigation Compared

Factor	Arbitration	Litigation
Speed	Takes days to weeks	Takes months to years
Expertise	Involves an expert	Involves a judge and a jury with limited expertise
Procedures	More business-like but less formal than litigation	Follows formal, complex rules and procedures
Costs	Significantly less expensive than a trial	Can be costly, depending on length of trial
Privacy and confidentiality	Conducted in private; not publicly disclosed	Proceedings conducted in public and may be reported by media
Finality	Resolution may permanently satisfy both parties	Resolution may result in divided feelings; there is a winner and a loser

Figure 11-14

Factors to consider when deciding to pursue arbitration versus litigation

Choosing an appropriate ADR option depends upon the interests of both parties. Mediation can be used at any time when a neutral third party can bring fresh perspectives to deadlocked negotiation. Arbitration is effective if negotiation and mediation have failed, and neither party is ready to sue in court.

Review Your Understanding (Pages 328 to 330)

1. What is ADR? What three options to litigation are available?
2. List two reasons why ADR is being used more often to resolve civil disputes.
3. Distinguish between negotiation and mediation.
4. Distinguish between mediation and arbitration.

Figure 11-15

James Savary, Chair, CAMVAP Board of Directors

Founded in 1994, the Canadian Motor Vehicle Arbitration Plan (CAMVAP) helps to arbitrate disputes between vehicle owners and manufacturers. Usually, these disputes hinge on the quality of the vehicle or how the manufacturer is implementing the vehicle's warranty. CAMVAP is a free service, fully funded by the automobile manufacturers.

Most domestic and imported passenger cars, trucks, sports utility vehicles, and vans bought or leased in Canada since 1996 are covered by CAMVAP. Currently, it is the largest consumer product arbitration plan in Canada. It is a working partnership among all the provincial and territorial governments, the Canadian Automobile Dealers' Association, the Canadian Vehicle Manufacturers' Association, the Association of International Automobile Manufacturers of Canada, and the Consumers' Association of Canada.

Imagine that you've pulled over to the shoulder of a major highway on a hot, humid afternoon. Your new car—only three months old—has stalled again. Your local dealer and the manufacturer have been very helpful and have tried unsuccessfully to correct the problem. You are furious and upset and think about legal action, but you've just heard about CAMVAP as an alternative. You may go to court, or you may use CAMVAP, but you can't do both.

With CAMVAP, consumers resolve disputes with manufacturers in a fair, free, and friendly manner. From start to finish, the process takes about 70 days. Once a decision has been reached, it is final and binding for both parties.

Consumers choose the arbitrator from a list provided. The arbitrator can order such remedies as repairs to the vehicle, buy-back, and reimbursement for repairs or out-of-pocket expenses up to $500. Engine, transmission, steering/suspension, and exterior complaints are at the top of the list of consumer complaints arbitrated by CAMVAP.

For Discussion

1. **Explain the significance of CAMVAP.**
2. **Who are the sponsors of CAMVAP, and why do you think they would want to be involved?**
3. **Outline the advantages and disadvantages of using CAMVAP.**

⊜ activity

Visit **www.law.nelson.com** and follow the links to learn more about CAMVAP.

CAREERS

Figure 11-16
Deputy sheriff

Figure 11-17
Small Claims Court clerk

In Civil Law

Employment opportunities in Canada's court system can be rewarding. Court officers, deputy sheriffs, and clerks operate at the heart of the justice system. Job requirements include a strong sense of responsibility, excellent organizational skills, and the ability to respond tactfully to awkward or difficult situations.

(e) **Visit www.law.nelson.com and follow the links to find out about the employment prospects and average earnings for court officers, deputy sheriffs, and court office clerks.**

In Focus

Court Officer

Court officers have many administrative duties. They arrange pre-trial conferences and hearings, and schedule trials. They maintain court records, including trial proceedings and judgments, and manage the collection of court-ordered fees and fines. As a court clerk at a criminal trial, you would read the charge against the accused, swear in witnesses, and tag evidence. As a court registrar or manager, you might administer the operation of a range of court services in both civil and criminal matters.

Deputy Sheriff

Deputy sheriffs perform several trial-related duties. At criminal trials, they arrange for prospective jurors and supervise the safety of persons in the courtroom, assisting the judge when needed. They also escort prisoners to and from the courtroom. Following a trial, they enforce court orders, such as orders to pay maintenance, or to seize or sell property and distribute the proceeds as the court has directed.

Clerk, Small Claims Court Office

Clerks at Small Claims Court offices assist members of the public in filing a claim, a defence against a claim, or a counterclaim. They receive all completed paperwork, such as forms from the plaintiff or the defendant, and supporting documents, such as bad cheques or contracts. Court office clerks are responsible for filing all original claim forms and photocopying all paperwork and documents. They also collect fees for filing claims and notify the litigants of trial dates and times.

Career Exploration Activity

1. As a class, visit the local law courts and observe the activities of the various court officers, deputy sheriffs, and clerks. Outline the roles and responsibilities of the various positions.

2. For extended research, use the Internet to conduct research on the various positions. As part of your career exploration in the course, compile the information for a guidance bulletin-board display or use it in a law-related career fair.

Chapter Review

Chapter Highlights

- Civil (private) law involves disputes between individuals, or between individuals and businesses or governments.
- The main purpose of civil law is to compensate victims for harm or loss suffered.
- Tort law, family law, contract law, and labour law are examples of civil law.
- Small Claims Court provides a simple, inexpensive way to settle many civil disputes by a judge without a jury.
- The litigants (persons suing) in a civil action are the plaintiff (the person suing) and the defendant (the person being sued).
- The process of suing is litigation.
- In civil actions, plaintiffs must prove their case on the balance of probabilities.
- The claim is the document the plaintiff files to begin a civil action.
- Defendants who receive a claim may enter a defence, make a payment into court, or make a counterclaim or a third party claim.
- A default judgment is a decision made in the plaintiff's favour when the defendant has not replied to the claim within the required time.
- A pre-trial conference is the last chance for the litigants to reach a settlement without a formal trial, and many cases are now settled on this basis.
- There are five types of damages that may be awarded to a successful plaintiff: general, special, nominal, punitive, and aggravated damages.
- An injunction is a court order requiring the defendant to do or not do something.
- Legal remedies available to a plaintiff to enforce a judgment against a defendant are garnishment, seizing assets, or an examination of the debtor.
- Alternative dispute resolution (ADR) has become a practical and popular alternative to civil litigation.
- The three ADR models are negotiation, mediation, and arbitration.

Review Key Terms

Name the key terms that are described below.

a) party who is being sued in a civil lawsuit

b) person who is suing in a civil lawsuit

c) legal document in a civil action outlining the plaintiff's case against the defendant

d) a court order requiring a person to do or not do something

e) money awarded to a plaintiff for pain and suffering and for cost of future care

f) money awarded to a plaintiff for specific out-of-pocket expenses

g) money awarded to a plaintiff to punish the defendant for bad or uncaring behaviour

h) proof needed in a civil action

i) a process more formal than mediation for resolving disputes between persons through a third party

j) an attempt by a neutral third party to get two opposing parties to come to an agreement

k) an informal and voluntary dispute resolution process between the parties involved without the involvement of a third party

l) a defendant's response to a plaintiff's claim

m) decision made in the plaintiff's favour when the defendant does not reply to the plaintiff's claim within the required time period

n) the procedure by which a defendant's money in the hands of a third party is claimed by a plaintiff to settle an unpaid judgment

o) the process of suing

p) a valid reason for suing

Check Your Knowledge

1. Outline the main differences between a civil and a criminal action.

2. Summarize the procedures used in a small claims action.

3. Summarize the types of damages available for resolving civil disputes, and provide an example of each.

4. Summarize the remedies available to enforce a judgment against a defendant, and provide an example of each.

Apply Your Learning

5. The British Columbia government granted a 21-year lease on some land to the District of North Saanich. The lease covered the foreshore around the upper portion of a peninsula on Vancouver Island, for a distance of some 300 m from the high-water mark to the ocean. The Murray brothers built wharves partly situated on the foreshore without first obtaining the district government's permission. The district took action against the Murrays and was awarded nominal damages.
   a) Why did the district take action against the Murray brothers?
   b) Why was the district awarded only nominal damages?

6. *Grant v. Dempsey* (2001), 190 N.S.R. (2d) 392 (Nova Scotia Supreme Court)

   On October 14, 1995, the 18-year-old plaintiff, Adrian Grant, was lying in the middle of a street in Middleton, Nova Scotia, severely intoxicated, wearing dark clothing. At 1:30 A.M., he was run over and seriously injured by a van operated by the defendant, Garth Dempsey. The defendant had been working on renovations with a fellow worker until close to 1:00 A.M. that morning, and was driving home at a speed between 40 and 50 km/h. It was a dark, but dry, night, and there were no streetlights in the area. Shortly before the accident, Dempsey met a pickup truck coming down the road. He put his van's lights on low beam before meeting the oncoming vehicle. As he looked ahead, Dempsey had no time to put his headlights back on high beam because he immediately "saw an object right there in front of him." He testified that he thought it was a duffle bag or a garbage bag. When he realized he had run over a person, he called 911. Evidence at trial indicated that the plaintiff had a blood–alcohol level of about 193 (about two and one-half times the legal limit for driving) at the time of the accident, and he had no recollection of how he came to be lying on the road. He testified that he would sometimes drink a case of beer in a couple of hours. The judge concluded that Grant was lying on the road as a result of severe intoxication and remained in that state. The plaintiff sued for damages for personal injuries, but the court dismissed the action.
   a) Can you find any fault in Dempsey's driving? Explain.
   b) To what extent was Grant responsible for his own injuries? Explain.
   c) Why do you think the court dismissed Grant's action?

7. *Davis v. Charles*, 2001 BCSC 698 (British Columbia Supreme Court)

   In the early morning hours of March 15, 1993, a brief fistfight broke out between the plaintiff, Jack Davis, and the defendant, Shayne Charles, outside the Ocean Beach Hotel in White Rock, British Columbia. Charles produced a knife and stabbed the plaintiff, leaving him with a deep cut to the lower right forearm, severing an artery, a nerve, and tendons. Davis required three surgeries to repair and improve the function of his right hand. Evidence indicated that the defendant's attack on the plaintiff was excessive and unwarranted, and Charles had started the fight. Davis, the plaintiff, claimed damages for injuries from the assault and battery. He is a helicopter mechanic and missed a total of 12 weeks for his surgeries. Although Davis returned to work 9 weeks after his first surgery, he was limited to light duties for the first year. He had good functional use of his right hand, but he could not perform fine manual work because of muscle weakness. After the surgeries, Davis had several physiotherapy treatments on a doctor's advice. Davis was also trained as an auto mechanic, but his hand problems prevented him from handling small bolts and small tools. As a result, he was less able to take advantage of all job opportunities previously available to him. Finally, before the injury, the plaintiff was actively involved in playing baseball and hockey, but two years later, he could play only hockey.

a) Assume you are a lawyer for the plaintiff. Outline the specific losses for which Davis should be compensated.

b) Outline an argument in favour of damages for lost future earning capacity.

8. *Thomas v. Hamilton (City) Board of Education* (1994), 20 O.R. (3d) 598 (Ontario Court of Appeal)

Jeffry Thomas, an athletic 16-year-old student at Scott Park Secondary School, was one of the best and most experienced players on his school's junior football team. He also played in the Steel City Peewee League and was named the most valuable offensive player in the league. Football skills were taught as part of the regular classroom physical education program and as an extracurricular activity in Hamilton high schools. Games were coached by teachers selected by school principals. Students were eligible to play junior football if they were not older than 15 years at the beginning of the school year, and if they provided a permission form signed by their parents and a medical certificate indicating that they were fit to play football.

Between 1980 and 1982, Thomas played football and basketball, rode his bike, jogged, and lifted weights four times a week. By the fall of 1982, he was 183 cm tall and weighed about 68 kg. In October 1982, during a football game, Thomas tackled an opposing player, headfirst, crashing into the punt returner's hip. Thomas was running at jogging speed or faster; the punt returner was running at full speed. All witnesses agreed that the contact between the two players was substantial, and that Thomas's body was extended but his head was not up at the point of contact. He and the other players had been taught to tackle with their shoulders, not their heads, and contact should be made with a shoulder. Thomas suffered serious injury to his cervical spine, which left him quadriplegic. Thomas and his family sued the school board and the school football coaches. The action was dismissed at trial, and Thomas and his family appealed to the Ontario Court of Appeal. In a 3 to 0 judgment in late 1994, the appeal was dismissed.

a) Outline the arguments that could be made on behalf of the plaintiff.

b) Why did the plaintiff sue the Hamilton Board of Education?

c) What factors do you think the court took into consideration in dismissing the plaintiff's appeal?

Communicate Your Understanding

9. Explain the meaning of the following quotation from former American president Abraham Lincoln:

> Distinguish litigation. Persuade your neighbours to compromise whenever you can. Point out to them the nominal winner is often a loser—in fees, expenses, and waste of time.

In your explanation, consider the advantages outlined for the various alternative dispute resolution mechanisms you have studied.

10. Collect at least five newspaper or Internet articles over a seven-day period that discuss or describe civil actions, civil courts, damage awards, and any other issues studied in this chapter. For each article

a) summarize the article in your own words

b) highlight the issue(s) involved

c) state and justify your opinion on the issue(s) discussed in the article

11. Imagine and describe in detail a scenario that involves a plaintiff suing a defendant in a civil action. Your scenario must provide information that supports a claim for the various types of damages discussed in this chapter. Create an answer key that indicates which evidence supports a claim for general, specific, punitive, and aggravated damages. Share your scenario with another classmate and have him or her identify the evidence that could support each particular damage claim.

Develop Your Thinking

12. Although the primary function of tort law is to compensate victims, some people feel that it also acts as a deterrent or a penalty. Using original examples from cases you have found in the news, describe two situations in which tort law serves each of these functions.

13. As you have learned, juries in criminal trials must reach unanimous decisions, while juries in civil cases only have to reach majority decisions. Provincial Courts of Appeal also reach split decisions. Should Canadian law be changed so that all three groups of decisions are the same, either all unanimous or all majority judgments? Discuss with a partner, and be prepared to defend your decision in class.

14. Punitive damages function like fines in criminal law. How are they similar? How are they different?

15. Assume that you are involved in an accident today that leaves you permanently disabled.
   a) What evidence would you bring to justify your claim for loss of future income?
   b) How would such evidence differ for the following?
      (i) a five-year-old
      (ii) a 40-year-old CEO (chief executive officer)
      (iii) a single parent with an eight-year-old child

Negligence and Other Torts

Chapter

12

Focus Questions

- What is the difference between an intentional and an unintentional tort?
- What is negligence, and why is it the most important part of tort law?
- What are a "reasonable person," foreseeability, and causation in negligence?
- What are the legally acceptable defences for negligence?
- What are some special types of negligence?
- What are the most common examples of intentional torts?
- What are the main legal remedies and defences for intentional torts?
- How can individuals protect themselves against civil liability?

Chapter at a Glance

Figure 12-1

Linda Hunt and her lawyer, Roger Oatley, break from court proceedings in Barrie, Ontario, in October 2000. Hunt sued her former employer and a local pub, claiming they were partly responsible for serving her alcohol and not physically stopping her from driving home following a Christmas party. She was later involved in an accident. How do you think this case turned out?

12.1 Introduction

In Chapter 11 you learned that a tort means "a wrong," which can be either intentional or unintentional. Tort law entitles you to sue for damages in a civil court of law. Tort law involves many aspects of your daily life—your personal property, your pets, the sports you play, even your personal freedom and reputation.

Like criminal law, tort law changes with society. For example, people used to drive without seat belts and ride on motorcycles and bicycles without wearing helmets. However, accident prevention research showed that using seat belts and helmets reduced injuries. As a result, provincial governments made such safety devices compulsory. Failure to comply with these laws can reduce or even eliminate compensation to the injured. Although tort law may differ slightly from province to province, the principles are similar. Modern tort law is largely the result of decisions made by judges over many years.

12.2 Negligence and Intent

The tort of negligence is one of the most important areas of tort law. **Negligence** has three key characteristics:
- The action is unintentional.
- It is unplanned.
- An injury results.

Anyone who carelessly injures a person or a person's property should compensate the victim for that injury. But carelessness alone does not make someone liable for negligence; someone must actually be injured by the careless conduct.

For instance, if Liam does not clear his slippery sidewalk after a winter storm, he will not be liable for negligence unless somebody actually falls and is injured. If Alden does slip and fall, Liam might be liable in any legal action that occurs. Other examples of negligence include car accidents, injuries to consumers caused by defective products, and medical and legal malpractice (misconduct).

There are also intentional torts. When a person deliberately causes harm or loss to another person by assault and battery or false imprisonment, it is an intentional tort. Trespassing, causing a nuisance, and defaming (damaging) a person's reputation are other intentional torts. Intentional torts are the oldest wrongs recognized by the courts.

If one person hits another, is it an intentional tort? The answer depends upon a number of factors. The most important element of an intentional tort is intent. **Intent** is the true purpose of an act, a person's hope or desire for a result of an action. If Matt punches Josh squarely in the jaw, harm is clearly intended. But foreseeability (see page 342) is also a factor. If your friend Renu throws a snowball at you and it hits you in the face causing damage to your eye, that is an intentional tort. Renu should have realized that the snowball could hit you *and* that injury could result. She would be responsible for the damage to your eye. Renu was in control of her actions. Thus, the tort would be considered intentional. The result would be the same if Renu hit a passerby, even if she did not intend to hit that person.

However, many acts do not result in torts. A certain amount of interference with individuals' rights occurs on a daily basis and is considered acceptable in a busy society. Brushing against bodies on a crowded bus or subway, touching someone lightly to get his or her attention, or taking a shortcut across someone's property are actions that are accepted as a normal part of life. Unless they are done in a hostile manner and cause serious harm or fear of harm, they are not considered torts.

Figure 12-2

Beware the consequences of throwing an icy snowball.

Review Your Understanding (Pages 338 to 339)

1. **Why should all Canadians know something about tort law?**
2. **What is negligence, and why is it the most common form of tort law?**

You Be the JUDGE

"Law must be stable, and yet it cannot stand still."
—Roscoe Pound, lawyer and dean of Harvard Law School, 1922

- What does this quotation mean? How does it apply to tort law?

12.3 The Elements of Negligence

The elements of negligence are shown in Figure 12-3 and are described in more detail on the following pages.

▮ The Potential for a Negligence Action

Elements	Examples in ...			
	a car	a store	a hospital	a law office
Plaintiff is owed a duty of care.	Duty to avoid accidents	Duty to ensure store is safe	Duty to provide competent treatment	Duty to provide competent legal advice
Defendant breached duty of care.	Drove unsafely; went through a red light	Failed to clean up jam spilled on floor	Amputated the wrong limb	Gave faulty legal advice; client lost right to sue
Plaintiff suffered resulting harm or loss.	Plaintiff and/or plaintiff's car suffered damage.	Plaintiff slipped on mess and broke hip.	Plaintiff endured unnecessary pain and suffering.	Plaintiff lost money arising from potentially successful lawsuit.

Figure 12-3

When someone unintentionally harms or injures you, a negligence action may arise. Do you know what is needed to prove negligence?

Duty of Care

In a negligence suit, the plaintiff must show that the defendant owed the plaintiff a **duty of care.** You have a duty of care to people when a legal duty has been placed upon you. Your actions must not cause harm to people or to their property. This principle is central to the study of the laws governing negligence. In our earlier example, the municipality placed upon Liam a duty of care owed to pedestrians—he must keep his sidewalk clear of ice and safe for anyone walking by his home.

Breach of Duty of Care

Once a duty of care has been established, the court must determine if the defendant breached it. This happens when the defendant fails to meet the expected **standard of care** of a "reasonable person."

The Reasonable Person

The **reasonable person** is an image of someone who has neither physical nor developmental disabilities and who people agree is careful, thoughtful, and considerate of other people in all dealings. The reasonable person is never expected to be perfect. Are all reasonable people exactly the same? No. What is reasonable for a person in downtown Vancouver, for example, may not necessarily be reasonable for a person in Milk River, Alberta, or in Iqaluit, Nunavut. In addition, what was "reasonable" 50 years ago is often not reasonable today. If the defendant was repairing car brakes, the "reasonable person" would be a reasonably competent mechanic. If the defendant was performing surgery, the standard would be that of a reasonably competent surgeon.

A person or company whose conduct falls below the expected standard of care is liable for the results of the negligence, even if the party was acting within the law. For example, Anya drives at the posted speed limit during a snowstorm and hits a pedestrian. If a "reasonable person" would have driven slower, Anya is liable.

Minors and a Duty of Care

A child cannot be judged by the standards of an adult "reasonable person." You learned in Chapter 10 that minors under the age of 12 cannot be charged with a criminal offence under the *Youth Criminal Justice Act.* However, there is no legislation that clearly outlines the

Figure 12-4

According to Canadian law, children below the age of six or seven do not understand the consequences of their actions.

tort liability of minors. In each case, the court must determine liability on the basis of the facts and the minor's background. The older the minor, the greater his or her responsibility.

A child under the age of six or seven is seldom held liable for negligence. Children below this age are not equipped to understand the consequences of their actions. In any incident involving an older child, the courts will consider what a child of similar age, experience, and intelligence might have done. Children must provide the duty of care expected from reasonable children of a similar age. But minors involved in adult activities, such as driving a car or riding a trail bike, are expected to meet the adult standards of care. The potential danger from the activity makes it unfair to society to apply a lower standard of care.

Agents of Change | The Parental Responsibility Act

In 1997, Manitoba Justice Minister Rosemary Vodrey introduced Bill 58, the *Parental Responsibility Act*. It allows the victim of a child's vandalism or another crime to sue the child's parents or legal guardians in Small Claims Court for damages up to $7500. The bill covers children who live at home and are under age 18.

After Manitoba passed its legislation, other provinces followed suit. British Columbia introduced similar legislation in August 2001, and Ontario's *Parental Responsibility Act* became law on August 15, 2000. Under Ontario law, victims can sue for damages up to $10 000 in Small Claims Court against parents of minors who intentionally take, damage, or destroy property.

Punishing parents was not the intent of Manitoba's legislation, says Vodrey. "But parents must become involved and aware of their young people's activities, and I hope this legislation accomplishes that."

In all three provinces, victims need prove only the amount of the damage; that the child caused the property loss or damage; and that the defendants are the child's parents. The defendant's parents are liable for damages unless they can prove that the damage was not intentional, or that they exercised reasonable supervision over the child and made reasonable efforts to prevent the damage from occurring.

By 2001, the *Parental Responsibility Act* has been used successfully only once.

For Discussion

1. What can victims do if the amount of the property loss or damage exceeds the Small Claims Court limit of $10 000?

2. "This new legislation will create new business for lawyers in defending Small Claims Court actions on behalf of families." Discuss with a partner the extent to which you agree or disagree with this statement.

3. Should all provinces have a *Parental Responsibility Act*? Why or why not?

Figure 12-5
Rosemary Vodrey

Foreseeability

The concept of **foreseeability** is related to the concept of a reasonable person. Asking the question: "Would a reasonable person in similar circumstances have foreseen the injury to the victim as a result of his or her action?" determines to a large extent tort liability. If the answer is "yes," fault and liability exist; if the answer is "no," there is no liability. If the defendant has not met the reasonable person's standard of care, then the defendant has breached his or her duty of care. In our earlier example, Liam should have foreseen that somebody might slip and fall and be injured because of the ice on the sidewalk.

Foreseeability is a difficult standard to apply. The courts have tended to follow the principle that defendants should not be held responsible for any results of actions that could not reasonably be expected. For example, if Alden carries a gun that discharges as he falls, shooting a neighbour, Liam is not liable for the neighbour's injuries.

Causation

Once it is established that the defendant has breached the required standard of care, the plaintiff must prove that the defendant's negligent conduct caused the plaintiff's harm. There must be a direct causal connection between the defendant's negligent act and the plaintiff's claim; for example, Liam's failure to shovel and Alden's injury. This relationship is called **causation;** without it, liability for negligence does not exist.

Once it has been established that the defendant's action was a cause of the plaintiff's injury, the court must decide how direct a connection there was between the action and the injury. In our example, the connection is very direct. There is no doubt that Liam's actions caused Alden's injury.

Now suppose that, as Alden slips on the ice, Chandra is driving by and is startled to see the pedestrian falling toward her car. To avoid an accident, Chandra swerves and loses control of her car on the slippery road. She hits a telephone pole, knocking out service to the subdivision and damaging her car. Because the telephone lines are out of order as a result of the accident, Lisa is unable to call an ambulance for her husband, who is having a heart attack. Since she cannot drive and is unable to get an ambulance, Lisa's husband dies. Is Liam responsible for this man's death, or for the damage to Chandra's car?

To answer this question, the court must examine the connection between Liam's actions and the various losses. Even if his negligence ultimately caused the damage to Chandra's car and the death of Lisa's husband, Liam would not be held liable if the court decides that these losses are too far removed to be recoverable in damages. Causation depends on the facts of each case, judged on its own merits.

Actual Harm or Loss

Finally, in a negligence suit, the plaintiff must prove that real harm occurred because of the defendant's negligence. If nobody had been injured as a result of Liam's actions, no loss would have been suffered by anyone, and legal action would not succeed.

Case

Prevost (Committee of) v. Vetter

(2001) 197 D.L.R. (4th) 292
British Columbia Supreme Court

On June 19, 1998, at around 11 P.M., the 18-year-old defendant, Desiree Vetter, and about 15 other teenagers arrived at the home of her aunt and uncle, Shari and Gregory Vetter, in Enderby, British Columbia. The aunt and uncle had gone upstairs and were asleep when the group arrived, but their 17-year-old son Scott was there with a few friends. He did not see his cousin Desiree or any of her friends bring alcohol or consume it on the premises, but Desiree admitted to drinking in the backyard. No liquor was supplied by Scott. At about 11:30 P.M., the 17-year-old plaintiff, Adam Prevost, arrived with a group of intoxicated young adults. By then, there were about 30 people in the Vetters' yard.

Around 1:00 A.M., the police arrived in response to neighbours' complaints. They told Scott to quiet the group and clear everyone out. Scott woke his mother to advise her of this; she asked if he needed help in breaking up the party. He said no, and she went back to sleep. Evidence indicated that Shari and Gregory regularly permitted Scott to host such parties, and they were aware that minors sometimes brought their own liquor and drank it there. In the past, but not this evening, Shari was protective of drinking minors, offering to have them sleep over, taking away their car keys, or driving them home.

Everyone had left by about 1:30 A.M. Desiree was one of the last to leave, and the plaintiff asked her for a lift. Desiree drove with five passengers in her car. She lost control of the vehicle, and Adam was thrown through the sunroof, leaving him with a severe brain injury. Desiree underwent a breath test and registered a blood–alcohol level of 120.

Prevost and his parents brought an action for negligence against Desiree and her aunt and uncle. His action succeeded, and the court awarded $2.5 million in damages, but a new trial was ordered on appeal.

For Discussion

1. Did Shari and Gregory Vetter owe the plaintiff any duty of care and, if so, was it breached?

2. Why would Shari and Gregory be held liable when they were unaware of the party and were asleep upstairs?

3. Is there anything that Shari could have done as a "reasonable person" to have prevented this accident?

4. Was the accident foreseeable? Why?

Looking Back   The Snail in the Bottle

Negligence was not recognized as a tort until the landmark judgment in *Donaghue v. Stevenson* (1932) from England's highest court. A friend bought May Donaghue a ginger beer in a dark bottle. Pouring the drink into a glass, Donaghue found a dead snail in the bottle. The sight of the snail caused Donaghue nervous shock, requiring medical treatment. She sued David Stevenson, the drink manufacturer, claiming he was negligent. He claimed that she couldn't sue him or his company. There was no contract between them because Donaghue's friend bought her the drink. Donaghue lost at trial but won at appeal.

England's highest court ruled that every person has a duty to take reasonable care for the safety of anyone who might foreseeably be harmed by the person's actions. Since the manufacturer allowed a harmful or

continued ▶

Figure 12-6

How would you react if you found a snail in your drink?

defective product to be sold, it was only reasonable to hold the company responsible for consumers' safety. The manufacturer should have been able to foresee that its products would be used by people other than the actual purchasers.

In its judgment, the court stated: "The rule that you are to love your neighbour becomes in law, you must not injure your neighbour. You must take reasonable care to avoid acts or omissions which you can reasonably foresee would be likely to injure your neighbour."

This ruling on duty of care marked the beginning of negligence law. Even today, many lawyers claim this decision is the common law's best-known and most important precedent. Today, anyone involved in producing consumer goods may be held liable for negligence if consumers are injured by products when using them routinely. This is the legacy of this landmark case.

For Discussion

1. **Why would Donaghue claim the manufacturer was negligent?**
2. **What must a manufacturer be able to prove to avoid liability?**
3. **Why do many lawyers feel this case is a most important precedent?**
4. **Explain the meaning of the quotation from the judgment.**

The Burden of Proof

As you learned in Chapter 11, the burden of proof is on the plaintiff, who must prove all the required negligence elements. If the plaintiff fails to prove any of the elements, the action fails. The defendant does not have to prove anything, but many defendants do present evidence to show that the plaintiff did not suffer any harm or that the harm was not reasonably foreseeable. Proof exists on a balance of probabilities, and the plaintiff's version of the incident must be viewed as "more likely than not" to succeed.

Case

McQueen v. Alberta

2001 ABQB 220
Alberta Court of Queen's Bench

The 32-year-old plaintiff, David McQueen, went to Sikome Lake Provincial Park with his three children and some friends in June 1994. Sikome Lake, near Calgary, is one of two artificial swimming lakes in Alberta. Carrying his two- and three-year-old sons, McQueen waded into the lake a distance of 3 to 5 m toward a skimmer platform (a water-intake mechanism to recycle and clean the water). On reaching the platform, he put each child on the edge of the platform and stepped up to the top. He then dove in headfirst, breaking his neck, which rendered him a paraplegic.

The plaintiff sued the province and the city of Calgary for damages for his injuries. Evidence at trial indicated that McQueen and his children had been at Sikome Lake on previous occasions. Several lifeguards were on duty at the time of the accident, and No Diving signs were posted.

McQueen testified that he did not know how deep the water was, and he thought it was safe to dive when he looked down and couldn't see the bottom of the lake. He also admitted that he had

continued ▶

consumed about 750 mL of rum the night before, had finally gone to bed at 4:30 A.M., and was up at 7:00 A.M. with his sons. McQueen's blood–alcohol level was 148 when he was treated in hospital for his accident. McQueen claimed the province and the city were negligent and he sued for damages for his injuries. His action was dismissed.

For Discussion

1. What duty of care did the defendants owe McQueen, and was there a breach of it? Explain.

2. What was the cause of this accident? Was it reasonably foreseeable?

3. The trial judge stated: "Although this Court is very sympathetic to Mr. McQueen in relation to the tragedy that has befallen him and his family, there is no basis at law upon which this Court can attribute any responsibility to the defendant for that loss." Why do you think the action was dismissed?

Figure 12-7

The beach at Sikome Lake, outside Calgary, Alberta. Should lifeguards bear any responsibility for accidents?

Review Your Understanding (Pages 339 to 345)

1. Identify the key elements that a plaintiff must prove to succeed in a negligence action.

2. What is an intentional tort? Provide three examples.

3. Why do many potential tort actions not result in legal action?

4. Distinguish between a duty of care and a standard of care in a negligence action.

5. When is a minor expected to meet an adult standard of care?

6. What is the connection between foreseeability and a reasonable person?

7. Why is proof of causation so important in a negligence action?

8. Why was "the snail in the bottle" case so important in the development of negligence law?

12.4 Defences for Negligence

People sued for negligence have a number of available defences. The best defences are that negligence did not exist or that the defendant did not owe the plaintiff any duty of care. Even a plaintiff who is able to prove that negligence exists may not be able to recover as much as expected. If the plaintiff has also been negligent in the incident or has assumed a risk voluntarily, then damages may be reduced or not awarded at all.

Contributory Negligence

At one time, under common law, a plaintiff found to be in any way at fault for an accident was denied the right to claim damages. Society's attitude was that the law should not protect people who do not look after their own safety. However, such treatment seemed harsh for plaintiffs who were only slightly at fault for their loss or injury.

Today, if both the plaintiff and the defendant are negligent to some degree, damages are divided between them, according to the principle of **contributory negligence.** The court must determine which party was more negligent, or whether both parties were equally at fault. In making this decision, the judge considers the elements of negligence discussed earlier in this chapter. The burden is on the defendant to prove the plaintiff's contributory negligence. Each province has a Contributory Negligence Act or a Negligence Act that allows courts to divide responsibility between the parties.

For example, a motor vehicle accident results in damages of $80 000. The court finds the defendant 75 percent at fault for driving well above the speed limit and through a red light. The plaintiff, however, is found 25 percent at fault for driving through the intersection on an amber light and not wearing a seat belt. As a result of this finding of contributory negligence, the plaintiff will receive $60 000 from the defendant. The plaintiff is liable for the remaining $20 000 and will not receive it. The damages calculated are those that the judge or jury believe are required to fully compensate the injured

Case

Jordan v. Poirier

(2000) 231 N.B.R. (2d) 170
New Brunswick Court of Queen's Bench

In July, 1998, the plaintiff, James Jordan, and the defendant, Ulysse Poirier, each headed to a corner store to buy cigarettes at around 11:30 P.M. Jordan was on his bike and was wearing a brown leather jacket, jeans, and a baseball cap because it was raining heavily. Poirier drove his parents' car. The young men went to the same corner store but did not see each other there.

On their way home, the parties were travelling in the same direction on parallel streets. They both stopped at the stop signs at the intersection with a through street. As Jordan entered the intersection, Poirier made a left turn into the intersection, proceeded along the through street, and struck Jordan, severely injuring him. Evidence indicated that Poirier's car windows were fogged up and he had trouble seeing. It was raining so hard that he had his wipers on full speed and his headlights on high beams. There was no evidence that Poirier was

speeding, although Jordan thought he was driving fast. Jordan was wearing dark clothing, and his bike didn't have the required headlight or bell. There were no other vehicles on the roadway, and there were streetlights illuminating both streets and the intersection.

Jordan sued Poirier for damages for negligence, but the Court of Queen's Bench held that both parties were equally negligent as either party could and should have been seen by the other.

For Discussion

1. **What arguments could the plaintiff use to establish negligence on the part of the defendant?**

2. **How did each of the parties contribute to the negligence for this accident?**

3. **Under New Brunswick's *Contributory Negligence Act,* the judge found the parties equally at fault. Why do you think the judge found equal fault?**

person for loss suffered. In other words, contributory negligence does cost the victim. Contributory negligence is often used as a defence in accidents when the plaintiff is not wearing a seat belt.

Voluntary Assumption of Risk

For the defence of **voluntary assumption of risk** to succeed, the defendant must prove that the plaintiff clearly knew of the risk of his or her actions and made a choice to assume that risk. For example, a fan struck and injured by a baseball at a game will probably not succeed in an action against the player who hit the ball because the fan should be aware of the risks of the game. On the other hand, if an angry player threw the bat or ball into the stands and injured a fan, the fan might well succeed in a legal action. In this case, injury does not arise from an ordinary risk of the game. Generally, risk is stated on the ticket. The ticket holder enters into a contract to attend the event and assumes this risk. If risk is not stated on the ticket, there may be an implication that the person voluntarily assumes the risk merely by observing the activity.

Conditions of Acceptance: By using this ticket, the holder hereof (the "Holder") agrees to and accepts all Conditions of Acceptance ("Conditions") contained herein and all Stadium Rules and Standards of Conduct ("Standards") posted in or about the stadium. Any violation of the Conditions or Standards may result in denial of admission to or immediate removal from the stadium without refund. This ticket is valid only for the event held on the date and at the time shown on the front hereof. A valid ticket must be produced upon entering the stadium and at any time thereafter upon request. This ticket cannot be replaced if destroyed, lost or stolen. This ticket is not redeemable for cash. NO REFUNDS – NO EXCHANGES. The resale or attempted resale of this ticket at a price greater than the price printed on the front hereof is strictly prohibited and is grounds for seizure and cancellation of this ticket without compensation. Tickets obtained from unauthorized sources may be lost, stolen or counterfeit and, if so, are void. The Holder will not use this ticket for advertising, promotion (including contests and sweepstakes) or any other trade purpose without the prior written consent of Toronto Blue Jays Baseball Club. The Holder will not transmit or aid in transmitting any description, account, picture or reproduction of the game to which this ticket admits the Holder. The Holder acknowledges that damages may not be an adequate remedy for breach of the Conditions or Standards and consents to injunctive or relief which may be sought to enforce same. Advance copies of the Standards may be obtained at SkyDome, Gate 9 or by telephone (416) 341-1000. WARNING: The Holder voluntarily assumes all risks of any injury or other loss incidental to any game for which this ticket has been issued (including, without limitation, injury suffered from balls or other objects projected into the stands), and releases the management of the Club and/or stadium, Major League Baseball, the Commissioner, the participating clubs and their respective agents and employees from any and all liability therefore, regardless of whether such injury or loss occurs before, during or after the actual playing of the game and whether such injury or loss is caused by any person's negligence or otherwise.

™ Rogers Communications Inc.
Used under license.

Someone who causes injury to passengers while driving impaired may also use the defence of voluntary assumption of risk. The burden of proof is on the defendant. The court assumes that a plaintiff who gets into a car knowing that the driver is drunk voluntarily assumes a risk of injury. The plaintiff will therefore receive reduced damages.

Figure 12-8

The waiver of risk is clearly visible on this baseball ticket.

Inevitable Accident

Injury or loss may result from a situation that is unavoidable, no matter what precautions the reasonable person would have taken under the circumstances. If lightning strikes Hannah's moving car, causing her to lose control and to collide with oncoming traffic, Hannah would not likely be held liable since she could not foresee such an occurrence and could not prevent it. This is an inevitable accident.

Case

Hagerman v. Niagara Falls (City)

(1980) 29 O.R. (2d) 609
Ontario High Court

The 66-year-old plaintiff and avid hockey fan, Hagerman, and her friend Bruce Harris attended the Niagara Falls Memorial Arena to watch a Junior A hockey game. They requested seats at the south end of the arena behind a plexiglass screen, 1.5 m high. They usually sat there, since Hagerman preferred this view of the ice surface, and she also had protection from flying pucks.

During the game, a player shot a puck from the blue line in the direction of the goal. Harris saw the puck coming and thought it would hit the plexiglass, but it just cleared the top of the screen and came toward them. He raised his arm to protect himself and leaned to his left to protect the plaintiff, who had been distracted from the play and did not see the puck coming toward her. The puck shattered the left lens of Hagerman's glasses, resulting in the loss and removal of her eye.

Hagerman sued the city of Niagara Falls and others for damages. However, her action was dismissed.

For Discussion

1. On what grounds did the plaintiff base her claim?
2. What duty of care did the defendants owe the plaintiff and others attending the game?
3. Explain the meaning of the following statement: "Flying pucks are an inherent risk of the game of hockey." Does it apply to this case? Explain.
4. Why did the defendants argue the defence of voluntary assumption of risk?
5. Why do you think the action was dismissed?

Review Your Understanding (Pages 345 to 348)

1. What are the two best defences in a negligence action?
2. What is contributory negligence? Explain, using an original example.
3. How do the courts divide the fault between the parties when both are at fault?
4. What is voluntary assumption of risk?
5. Identify the two factors that the defendant must prove for the defence of voluntary assumption of risk to succeed.

12.5 Special Types of Negligence

Among negligence suits, the most common involve occupiers' liability, motor vehicle negligence, and professional negligence. Each is discussed in this section.

Occupiers' Liability

Occupiers' liability concerns responsibility toward people who enter a property. An **occupier** is any person who has control and physical possession of a property and who owes a duty of care to make the property safe for people. The occupier, as a reasonable person, should foresee that some harm could come to persons entering the property. Occupiers are responsible for keeping their sidewalks and steps reasonably free of snow and ice. Store owners are responsible for keeping their floors reasonably dry and free of obstructions that could cause customers to slip or fall and injure themselves. Also, clear glass panels and doors should be clearly identified.

To establish the standard of care and the occupier's liability, the common law established three classes of persons who could enter another's property: invitees, licensees, and trespassers.

Invitees

An **invitee**—any person on the property for a purpose other than a social visit—is owed the highest standard of care. Invitees include students attending school, store customers, persons making deliveries, and service personnel coming to make repairs. This high standard of care is placed on invitees in the belief that an occupier and an invitee will likely do business, so that each may obtain some material benefit from their meeting.

Licensees

A **licensee** is a person who enters property with the implied permission of the occupier; for example, a friend who has been asked to dinner. A licensee is a guest at the occupier's premises and is usually there for a social, not a business, purpose. Since no economic benefit is expected to flow to either party, a lesser standard of care is required than for invitees.

Trespassers

A **trespasser** is a person who enters property without permission or without a legal right to be there. This would include anyone from a burglar to a wandering child. Guests who overstay their welcome may also be trespassers. Occupiers cannot set traps or cause deliberate harm to trespassers. In fact, once occupiers are aware of a trespasser's presence, they must exercise a reasonable standard of care. Even for trespassers, occupiers owe a duty of common humanity to act with at least a minimal degree of respect for the safety of all others who come onto the property.

Trespassing children are recognized as having special rights because of their age. A special duty is imposed on an occupier when the property includes play equipment, such as a swimming pool or a jungle gym. While alluring to children, such equipment may also pose dangers. What is considered an **allurement** varies from case to case. However, an occupier must be able to show that all reasonable precautions have been taken to prevent any accident that could reasonably have been foreseen as arising from a possible allurement. Taking reasonable precautions may help to reduce, but not eliminate, liability.

Figure 12-9

This sign protects a store from lawsuits arising from negligence. Why are these signs usually so prominent?

Did You Know?

In Saskatchewan, farmers must clearly mark farm equipment left in fields over winter so that trespassing snowmobilers don't mistake any snow-covered equipment for a small hill.

Legislators have accepted that many items are naturally attractive to children. As a result, there are laws requiring the owners of such allurements to take specific precautions to protect children. For instance, municipalities must erect fences of a certain height around swimming pools and construction sites, and other dangerous premises must be marked and barricaded.

Occupiers' Liability Acts

Sometimes it is difficult to decide if a person is an invitee or a licensee. For example, if Tom invites his business associate Serge to dinner, is Serge an invitee or a licensee? Since Tom and Serge might settle a business transaction during dinner, thus benefiting both economically, it might be argued that Serge is an invitee. On the other hand, Serge is coming to dinner at Tom's invitation, and the meal is a social occasion.

Figure 12-10

Municipalities insist that fences around construction sites be a certain height. Why would a construction site be considered an allurement?

Because of these difficulties, several provinces have passed Occupiers' Liability Acts that abolish the old common law and create new codes for all visitors. The legislation eliminates the difference between invitees and licensees and provides a common duty of care to all visitors, regardless of why they are there. Alberta was the first province to introduce such legislation in 1973. Since then, British Columbia, Ontario, Manitoba, Prince Edward Island, and Nova Scotia have passed similar legislation. The remaining provinces still follow the common law categories, but they are reviewing this issue.

The Law   Alberta's Occupiers' Liability Act

Excerpts from Alberta's *Occupiers' Liability Act*

5.
An occupier of premises owes a duty to every visitor on his premises to take such care as in all the circumstances of the case is reasonable to see that the visitor will be reasonably safe in using the premises for the purposes for which he is invited or permitted by the occupier to be there or is permitted by law to be there.

15.(1)
When the occupier does not discharge the common duty of care to a visitor and the visitor suffers damage partly as a result of the fault of the occupier and partly as a result of his own fault, the *Contributory Negligence Act* applies.

[Note: The statute also requires every visitor to act in a reasonable manner when warned of a particular danger or hazard.]

For Discussion

1. **To whom is a duty of care owed under section 5 of Alberta's *Occupiers' Liability Act*?**

2. **Describe the care required of an occupier of premises under section 5.**

3. **According to section 15(1) of Alberta's *Occupiers' Liability Act*, when does the *Contributory Negligence Act* apply?**

Barnfield v. Westfair Foods Ltd.

(2000) 258 A.R. 183
Alberta Court of Queen's Bench

The 77-year-old plaintiff, Eileen Barnfield, was shopping at one of the defendant's stores, Real Canadian Superstores, in Calgary in January, 1995, where she shopped twice a week. As she was moving from one side of the tomato bin to another, she caught her foot in the gap between the tomato bin and a protruding bumper corner. She slipped, fell, and broke her hip. At the time, she was wearing winter boots with good grip soles. The corner was bolted to the floor at the base of the bin to protect the bin from being damaged by shopping carts.

The plaintiff sued for damages for pain and suffering caused by the injury. Evidence at trial indicated that there had been only one other reported accident in that store involving a customer tripping on these protective corners. Also, the plaintiff admitted that she had noticed these corners in the past but didn't remember specifically looking for them the day of this accident.

Although the plaintiff won her action, the court awarded her an agreed amount of damages, reduced by 25 percent for her contributory negligence.

For Discussion

1. **Did the defendant owe the plaintiff a duty of care? Explain.**
2. **If so, how did the defendant breach the duty of care?**
3. **Did the plaintiff take reasonable care for her own safety while in the store? Explain.**
4. **How would you have decided the case? Use negligence law concepts to support your answer.**

Commercial and Social Host Invitees

An emerging area of tort law involves the possible liability of commercial and social hosts. This means that bar and restaurant owners, service-club volunteers, or even private citizens hosting parties in their own homes could be sued if someone is hurt or killed after being hit by a drunk driver leaving their functions. Courts have recognized that people who drink and drive do not consider the duty of care for their own safety, let alone anyone else's safety.

Bar and tavern employees must observe if their customers are intoxicated and take steps to prevent them from driving. This may involve refusing to bring any more drinks, calling a taxi for the customer, or even calling the police. Restaurant and bar owners now have a specific duty of care and must take positive steps to prevent intoxicated customers from driving, or they will be held liable for any resulting injuries to third parties. A person's liability as an alcohol provider begins when that person serves someone who is already intoxicated.

The liability of commercial hosts is just now being extended to social hosts, although there is very little Canadian case law to date. *Prevost (Committee of) v. Vetter* (see page 343) is one of the first examples. Based on that decision, it appears that a social host will only be held liable for injuries that are reasonably foreseeable as a result of the activity that takes place on the host's property.

Figure 12-11

Bartenders must observe whether a customer is intoxicated and take steps to prevent him or her from driving.

Case

Hunt et al. v. Sutton Group Incentive Realty Inc.

(2001) 196 D.L.R. (4th) 738
Ontario Superior Court of Justice

The 44-year-old plaintiff, Linda Leigh Hunt, attended a Christmas office party organized by her employer, a real estate company, in December 1994. The defendant, Sutton Realty, held the party at its business establishment where there was an open, unsupervised bar. Hunt was a part-time employee working as a receptionist, and she regularly answered the phone while attending the party that began at 1:00 P.M. At about 4:00 P.M., her employer was so concerned about Hunt's intoxication that he offered to call her husband to drive her home. She refused. When the party ended around 6:30 P.M., he asked if anyone needed a ride home and offered to provide cabs. Again, Hunt declined.

On her way home, the plaintiff stopped at P.J.'s Pub with some co-workers and had two more drinks. Around 8:00 P.M., she turned down offers to give her a ride home and a bed for the night.

Driving home in a bad storm with a blood–alcohol reading of 175, Hunt lost control of her car and crashed into an oncoming truck. The crash left her with severe head injuries causing personality changes. She was unable to work.

The plaintiff brought an action against her employer and the pub, and was awarded $1.1 million, the judge finding the plaintiff 75 percent responsible for the accident and the defendants liable for the remaining 25 percent. However, the pub, which was uninsured, was out of business, so Sutton Realty was fully responsible for the nearly $300 000 awarded to Hunt. Notice of appeal was filed in the Ontario Court of Appeal on March 2, 2001, by the defendant and its insurance company.

For Discussion

1. Did the defendant pub owe the plaintiff a duty of care? Explain.

2. Why was the plaintiff found 75 percent contributorily negligent?

3. In his ruling, the trial judge stated: "I find that the defendant Sutton not only owed its employee an obligation to take reasonable care to avoid acts or omissions which it could reasonably have foreseen would likely cause her some harm.... He ought to have anticipated the possible harm that could have happened to her and ... taken positive steps to prevent her from driving home." What did the judge feel Hunt's employer should have done?

4. What arguments do you think will be made by the defendant on appeal?

ⓔ activity

Visit **www.law.nelson.com** and follow the links to learn more about civil liability in alcohol-related cases.

Motor Vehicle Negligence

Motor vehicle accidents often lead to both criminal and civil actions. Each province has a Highway Traffic Act or Motor Vehicle Act that provides a variety of regulations; for example, speed limits and seat-belt laws. Violating any section of an Act usually suggests driver negligence. As you have learned, the burden of proof usually rests on the plaintiff in a negligence action. However, this burden has been shifted to the defendant in some motor vehicle cases. Once a plaintiff proves that he or she was struck by another vehicle, the burden of proof shifts to the defendant to prove that any loss or injury did not result from the defendant's negligence. If there is evidence that both drivers are responsible for an accident to some extent, liability will be split between them. Thus, motor vehicle accidents often involve contributory negligence.

Liability for Passengers

The driver of a motor vehicle is liable for the safety of passengers. However, a passenger who accepts a ride knowing that the driver is intoxicated, or that the driver engages in dangerous activities such as excessive speeding, is presumed to have voluntarily accepted the risk by riding in the vehicle. Drivers often use voluntary assumption of risk as a defence in negligence actions brought by passengers injured under such circumstances. The burden is on the defendant to prove that the plaintiff understood the risk involved and willingly assumed it. If the defendant can prove this, the plaintiff will receive reduced damages.

If, however, the plaintiff is unaware of any danger, there is no voluntary assumption of risk. Suppose, for instance, that Melanie accepts a ride from Calvin, without knowing that his car has faulty brakes. If Calvin has an accident because of the faulty brakes and Melanie is injured, he cannot argue voluntary assumption of risk as a defence, since Melanie did not know about the problem.

Figure 12-12

Do you think this driver would be able to mount an "assumption of risk" defence if his passengers accept a ride in his car and are injured in an accident caused by his impaired driving? Explain.

 activity

Visit **www.law.nelson.com** and follow the links to learn more about seat-belt legislation.

Seat Belts and Negligence

When worn properly, seat belts reduce the severity of injuries from motor vehicle accidents. They can even prevent a person from being thrown from a vehicle and killed. It is true that seat belts sometimes injure the ribs and abdomen, or trap people in burning or submerged cars. However, most studies conclude that the benefits far outweigh the disadvantages and that wearing seat belts gives more protection to the public. All provinces and the territories now have seat-belt laws that require both drivers and passengers, with few exceptions, to wear seat belts while a car is being driven. In fact, highway traffic statutes require that drivers have a specific duty of care to ensure that passengers in their vehicles, especially passengers under 16 years of age, wear seat belts.

Case

Galaske v. O'Donnell

(1994) 89 B.C.L.R. (2d) 273
Supreme Court of Canada

In August 1985, the eight-year-old plaintiff, Karl Galaske, and his father, Peter, were riding as passengers in a pickup truck owned and driven by one of the defendants, Erich Stauffer. Stauffer was a close family friend. Karl sat in the middle between his father and Stauffer. Although the truck was fitted with seat belts, none of the occupants were wearing them. Stauffer testified that he would have insisted that Karl wear his seat belt if the boy had been in the truck alone with him. However, he said he did not order the child to buckle up because that was the responsibility of Peter Galaske, the child's father.

Stauffer was aware of the importance of seat belts, having been warned and ticketed on three occasions for failing to wear his belt. British Columbia's *Motor Vehicle Act* states that a driver shall not drive unless children under age 16 wear their seat belts. While driving through an intersection, Stauffer was

continued ▶

hit by another vehicle, driven by the defendant, Columcille O'Donnell. The Galaskes were thrown from the truck; the father was killed and Karl was rendered paraplegic.

The plaintiff and his litigation guardian brought a negligence action for damages for personal injuries against the defendants O'Donnell and Stauffer to the Supreme Court of British Columbia. Although the trial judge found that the Galaskes would not have suffered any serious injuries if they had been wearing their seat belts, he ruled that it was reasonable to expect Karl's father would ensure that the boy wore his seat belt. Finding that the accident was caused solely by O'Donnell's negligence, the judge held that Stauffer was not negligent. A 1992 decision from the British Columbia Court of Appeal agreed with the conclusions of the trial judge.

The plaintiff appealed this decision to the Supreme Court of Canada where a 5 to 2 decision ruled that Stauffer was liable to share some of the liability. The case was referred back to the trial judge to determine the degree of contributory negligence of Stauffer and the Galaskes.

For Discussion

1. **Why did the two lower courts find that Stauffer had no liability for this accident?**
2. **Did a duty of care exist between Erich Stauffer and Karl Galaske? Explain.**
3. **Did the presence of Peter Galaske relieve Erich Stauffer of any responsibility? Explain.**
4. **Why do you think the majority of the Supreme Court of Canada found Stauffer contributorily negligent?**
5. **Why do you think two judges wrote a dissenting judgment?**

Drivers or passengers who fail to wear seat belts are not acting as reasonable persons because it can be foreseen that injury can result from this action. Increasingly, judges are ruling that contributory negligence exists when a person fails to "buckle up." Generally, damages are being reduced by 15 to 40 percent for those failing to wear a seat belt, even when an accident is totally the other driver's fault.

Vicarious Liability

In tort law, holding a blameless person responsible for the misconduct of another is known as the principle of **vicarious** (substitute) **liability.** Vicarious liability and motor vehicle negligence are based on the assumption that owners of vehicles have a duty of care to society to lend their vehicles only to individuals who are competent to drive them safely. It is clearly intended to encourage owners to be careful when lending their vehicles.

Provincial statutes place liability on both the driver of a vehicle and the owner. The owner is liable for the negligence of any driver when the vehicle is being used with the owner's permission. Even if the owner was not driving or was not present when an accident occurred, both parties are held responsible for any negligence. However, if the owner can prove that the vehicle was stolen and that the person driving it did not have permission to use the vehicle, the owner may avoid liability.

The concept of vicarious liability applies also to the workplace. Employers are personally liable for torts committed by their employees during working hours. Although this may seem unreasonable or unfair, there are two main reasons for this principle. First, employers usually have large amounts of liability insurance to compensate victims for injury or loss, while employees have limited resources or insurance available. Second, society believes that the company that hires employees and makes the profit should be responsible for its employees' actions. Thus, although employees remain personally liable for their torts, their employers may, or may not, also be sued because of vicarious liability (see *John v. Flynn*, page 187).

Professional Negligence

Recently, tort law has been updated to better reflect people's expectations of professionals and the services they provide. "Professionals" include doctors, dentists, engineers, architects, accountants, and lawyers. These experts have specialized knowledge and skills, and they must exercise a certain standard of care. This does not mean that these professionals are perfect and never make mistakes. It does mean, however, that a professional's actions can be evaluated against the standards of similar professionals—members of the profession who have the same rank, qualifications, and skills.

The more specialized and qualified the person, the higher the standard of care the law and society expects. For example, a heart surgeon will be held to a higher standard of care than a family doctor in dealings with patients. Although actions have occurred against many types of professionals, the largest body of case law is in the area of medical negligence.

Case

Posca v. Sotto

(1999) 43 O.R. (3d) 420
Ontario Court of Appeal

On May 26, 1989, the plaintiff, Rosario Posca, went to the emergency department of Peel Memorial Hospital where he was treated for a scalp laceration by the defendant, Dr. Alain Sotto. Sotto was an independent physician and not a hospital employee.

Posca was treated on an operating table without side rails. After his wound was cleaned and sutured, he sat up on his own with his legs dangling over the side of the table. He complained of dizziness but declined Dr. Sotto's advice to lie down, saying he felt better sitting up. The doctor then told the plaintiff, "Just sit there, don't move, I'll be back in a couple of minutes" and then left the room, leaving Posca unattended. In the doctor's absence, Posca fell off the operating table and suffered a fractured nose, damaged teeth, and lacerations to his face.

The plaintiff brought an action for negligence against Dr. Sotto and the hospital. The trial judge dismissed the action against the hospital but found for the plaintiff against the doctor. Posca was awarded nearly $40 000 in August 1997. This represented $30 000 in general damages, future dental care of $9500, and special damages of $137.77. The defendant doctor appealed this judgment, and the Court of Appeal dismissed his appeal in April 1999.

For Discussion

1. **How did the doctor breach the duty of care owed to the plaintiff? Explain.**
2. **What should the doctor have done regarding his patient? List at least three options.**
3. **Why was the action against the hospital dismissed?**
4. **Why do you think the Court of Appeal dismissed the doctor's appeal?**

Medical Negligence

Medical negligence concerns a doctor's duty of care to the patient; that is, whether he or she has provided an adequate standard of care. Surgery, for example, always involves some risk, and even surgery that has been performed with the greatest duty of care may result in new problems. For example, the patient may not respond as expected and may be worse, rather than better, after surgery. A doctor who agrees to provide any medical service has a duty of care to meet a reasonable standard of care.

Figure 12-13

Former Reform MP Sharon Hayes sued her local hospital following her husband's stroke in 1997. She alleged that nurses breached the duty of care when they didn't monitor her husband's neurological signs after giving him a certain drug. The British Columbia Supreme Court dismissed her claim, saying the stroke made her husband's injuries inevitable.

If the doctor fails to meet this standard, this is medical negligence. If, however, the patient cannot prove negligence, no damages for injuries will be awarded, even if the harm is serious and permanent.

Patients who are to undergo treatment have the right to know the truth about their medical condition, their treatment options, and the risks involved in order to decide whether or not to accept or reject a medical procedure. A doctor's ignorance of a particular risk may not be a successful defence: the law expects such a high standard of care from doctors that a court may rule that the doctor *ought to* have known about that particular risk.

Figure 12-14

Doctors can be sued for medical negligence if they do not live up to the required standard of care. What standard of care would you expect from your health-care professional?

If the patient lacks sufficient information to give **informed consent,** the doctor may be liable for negligence—even assault and medical battery. Negligence may exist if the doctor did not fully inform the patient about the risks involved. Medical battery may exist if the doctor treated the patient without any consent at all, or if aspects of treatment had no consent. Assault and battery are discussed on page 359. Both torts are breaches of a doctor's duty of care to a patient. In determining whether a tort has been committed, the courts must answer this question: Would a reasonable patient, knowing all the risks, have decided against the treatment? If the answer to the question is "yes," then the physician has been negligent.

ⓔ activity

Visit **www.law.nelson.com** and follow the links to learn more about medical negligence cases.

Looking Back   The Need for Informed Consent

Doctors have no right to touch any patient, no matter how sick or close to death, without that person's consent. Medical emergencies are exceptions to this principle, but the situation must be life threatening. In all but these cases, the consent must be informed.

Exactly what must physicians tell patients? This issue was settled with the landmark Supreme Court of Canada judgment in *Reibl v. Hughes* (1980). Reibl accepted Dr. Hughes's advice about the need for surgery, but the doctor neglected to tell his patient that there was a slight risk of stroke or death during the operation. Although the doctor performed the operation with proper care and competence, Reibl suffered a massive stroke and was left with partial paralysis. Reibl sued for damages and was awarded $225 000, a judgment later upheld by the Supreme Court of Canada.

Since that judgment, doctors must fully disclose any significant or **material risks** involved in the proposed treatment. Doctors must inform patients of known side effects, length of recovery time, recovery rates, and expected quality of life after surgery. The patient has to be sufficiently informed about all risks to make a reasoned decision about whether or not to submit to the treatment. Only then can the patient give informed consent to the doctor for the proposed treatment.

For Discussion

1. Why did the courts find the defendant doctor at fault?

2. Does this decision mean that doctors must tell patients even obvious information? For example, an appendectomy will probably result in some pain and leave a scar. Explain.

3. The Supreme Court judgment stated: "Even if a certain risk is only a mere possibility that ordinarily need not be disclosed, if its occurrence carries serious consequences it should be regarded as a material risk and the patient informed of it." What risk should have been disclosed in the *Reibl v. Hughes* case? Why?

Case

Brushett v. Cowan

(1990) 3 C.C.L.T. (2d) 195
Newfoundland Court of Appeal

The plaintiff, registered nursing assistant Sheila Brushett, consulted the defendant, Dr. Cowan, an orthopedic surgeon, in connection with a leg injury.

When her condition did not respond to treatment as hoped, and a noticeable lump appeared on her right thigh, the doctor advised a muscle biopsy, to which Ms. Brushett consented. The signed hospital consent form also contained a statement that the patient consented to "such further or alternative measures as may be found necessary during the

continued ▶

course of the operation." As the muscle biopsy progressed, Dr. Cowan became suspicious of possible malignancy in the bone tissue, and he biopsied a portion of the bone also. The plaintiff was released from hospital later that same day without crutches.

Two days later, after a further visit to Dr. Cowan, arrangements were made to provide Ms. Brushett with crutches. She claimed she received no instructions telling her to avoid placing any weight on the leg. Nor, she said, was she informed that bone tissue had been taken during the operation. However, the doctor claimed otherwise. Several days later, while not using her crutches, Brushett fell and broke her leg at the point where the bone biopsy had occurred.

She brought an action to the Newfoundland Supreme Court, Trial Division, for injury, alleging both battery and negligence in the provision of post-operative care. The trial judge found the defendant doctor liable for both torts, but found the plaintiff 20 percent negligent for her injuries. The doctor appealed this judgment, and the Court of Appeal set aside (dismissed) the finding of battery, but upheld the finding of negligence.

For Discussion

1. Why did the plaintiff claim that battery and negligence had occurred?
2. Why was Brushett found 20 percent at fault for her accident?
3. Why did the Court of Appeal dismiss the battery claim?
4. One of the appellate court judges felt that Brushett should be held 50 percent liable for her own accident. With which of the appellate court judges do you agree? Why?

Review Your Understanding (Pages 348 to 358)

1. Who is an occupier, and what duty of care does this person have for persons entering his or her property?
2. Name the three common-law classes of persons who may enter another's property. Outline the duty of care that occupiers owe to each class.
3. What are occupiers required to do to prevent children from being harmed around an allurement?
4. How does some provincial legislation on occupiers' liability abolish the old common law?
5. Why does the burden of proof shift to the defendant in motor vehicle cases?
6. What trends have developed in judgments regarding passengers who fail to wear seat belts?
7. What is the principle of vicarious liability? How does it relate to negligence and tort law?
8. Identify five types of professionals, and give an example of negligence for each.
9. What is informed consent and why is it so important?
10. Distinguish between medical negligence and medical assault and battery.

12.6 Trespass to Persons and Land

You have learned that there are two main types of torts: unintentional (negligence) and intentional. The main intentional torts are trespass to another person (assault and battery, false imprisonment), trespass to land, and nuisance.

Assault and Battery

Assault as defined in tort law differs from assault as defined in the *Criminal Code*. In tort law assault occurs when the victim has reason to believe or fear that bodily harm may occur. Any threat of apparent or immediate danger or violence is an assault. The essential element is the victim's fear. No actual physical contact is necessary. Assault can occur without battery. If someone swings a fist at another person and misses, an assault has occurred. The victim may be awarded damages for the fear and dread experienced as a result of that action. Pointing an unloaded gun is assault if the victim believes the gun is loaded or feels fear or danger. Threatening words, such as "I'm going to knock your head off" is assault if the threatened person has a reasonable belief that the other person intends to carry out the threat. Other examples of assault include unleashing a barking dog, shaking a fist, or a group of people swarming around a person in a hostile manner.

Battery is the follow-through of assault and is the most common form of trespass to another person. Battery is the unlawful and intentional touching of a person without that person's consent. The actual physical contact can be offensive or harmful. It may exist even if no injury results. Kissing or hugging someone without the person's consent can be battery, especially if the action is offensive or upsetting to the recipient.

Case

Arthur v. Wechlin

[2000] B.C.W.L.D. 1150
British Columbia Supreme Court

The 38-year-old plaintiff and longtime Elton John fan Shelley Arthur and a friend attended an Elton John concert at Vancouver's Pacific Coliseum in September 1995. The 43-year-old defendant, Jerry Wechlin, his girlfriend, and two friends were seated behind them. During a ballad sung by Mr. John, the defendant yelled out insults and profanity at the performer. The plaintiff asked the defendant to take his party to the lobby so she and others could enjoy the concert.

Although no smoking was allowed in the arena, Arthur had a lit cigarette in her hand. When Wechlin told Arthur that smoking was not allowed, she agreed to put it out if he stopped yelling and disrupting the concert. As she dropped the cigarette, Wechlin thought she was throwing the butt at him. He grabbed her wrist, held it for a couple of seconds, lifted her out of her seat, and turned her around, causing immediate pain. Wechlin believed that Arthur was trying to burn him with her cigarette.

Arthur brought an action for damages. Evidence at trial indicated that Arthur's shoulder and neck were seriously injured by this incident. Her ability to work as a court reporter was severely restricted. The trial judge awarded her nearly $500 000, mainly for lost future income because Arthur was one of the few people in her community skilled in this field.

For Discussion

1. **On what grounds would the plaintiff base her action?**

2. **What defence or explanation would Wechlin use to justify his actions?**

3. **On the balance of probabilities, which version of this incident is more credible? Explain.**

4. **What is your opinion of the trial judgment? Explain.**

Figure 12-15

This scenario could lead to both civil and criminal proceedings. What legal options does the victim have? Do you think punitive damages would be awarded in the civil action?

Assault and battery are usually tried together, since assault often occurs before or with battery. In fact, the distinction between these two torts is disappearing. Most cases based on assault include battery. The damages awarded in such actions compensate the victim for harm or loss. If an assault was extremely vicious or committed without reason, the court may also award punitive damages.

False Imprisonment

False imprisonment involves confining or restraining a person without consent in a specific area. The word "false" means "wrongful" or "unauthorized"; "imprisonment" refers to a particular area that is not necessarily a prison. "Wrongful confinement" might be a better term for this tort. Confinement may be through physical restraint, barriers, or legal authority. Imprisonment must be a total not a partial restriction. A plaintiff must attempt every reasonable means of escape before bringing an action for false imprisonment.

A common example of false imprisonment occurs when store detectives mistakenly detain an innocent person whom they suspect of shoplifting. Actual physical restraint is not necessary for false imprisonment to exist. If a suspect is stopped by store security and has a genuine fear that an embarrassing scene will occur if he or she tries to leave, false imprisonment exists. In fact, it is enough for a store employee to shout, "Grab that thief!" for false imprisonment to exist.

Collins v. Clowater

(2000) 224 N.B.R. (2d) 12
New Brunswick Court of Queen's Bench, Trial Division

The plaintiff, David Collins, was arrested by Constable Roger Clowater of the Saint John City Police Department in the parking lot of a car dealership. Collins was frisked, handcuffed, and placed in the police cruiser. He was told he was being detained and that he was a suspect in a child abduction investigation; he was read his rights.

It is police policy to handcuff anyone taken into the back seat of a police car. About 15 to 20 people gathered around the parking lot to observe what was happening, and these witnesses confirmed that the plaintiff did not resist and acted in a polite and cooperative manner. After about 30 minutes,

Collins was released once the police realized that there had not been an attempted child abduction.

The plaintiff sued the police officer, the police department, and the city of Saint John, and was awarded $1000 damages.

For Discussion

1. **Why did the plaintiff sue all three defendants instead of just the police officer?**

2. **On what grounds did the plaintiff base his action?**

3. **Do you think it was necessary to handcuff the plaintiff? Why?**

4. **Why do you think the plaintiff was successful in his claim for damages?**

You saw in Chapter 7 that, if the police arrest a person without a warrant or without reasonable and probable grounds for believing that a crime has been committed, the arrested person may sue for false arrest. Like "assault" and "battery," the terms "false arrest" and "false imprisonment" are often used together to mean the same thing.

Trespass to Land

Trespass is the act of entering and crossing another person's land without permission or legal authority. As in battery, no specific damage needs to occur for trespass to exist. Simply going on a person's property without permission is a trespass, whether or not trespass was intended. Remaining on that land when asked to leave is also trespass. So is throwing an object onto another person's land, or bringing an object onto another's land and not removing it. Cutting down a tree, letting it fall onto a neighbour's land, and not removing it is a trespass. As long as the tree remains on the land, there is a continuing trespass.

Ownership of land gives the owner the right to use the land both above and below the surface of the earth. So, if Iris tunnels through to Kevin's land to access oil there, Kevin can successfully sue for trespass. Similarly, stringing wires or lines over another person's land is trespass.

However, statutes permit the use of all space at certain distances above land. This allows aircraft to fly on regulated flight paths above private property.

Figure 12-16

Do signs keep people from trespassing? Explain.

The right of occupiers to use property is also recognized by provincial land-lord and tenant statutes. For example, a landlord wishing to enter a tenant's rented property must notify the tenant in advance.

Nuisance

What is a **nuisance,** and how does it differ from trespass? A nuisance involves one person's unreasonable use of land that interferes with the enjoyment and use of adjoining land by other persons or a community. Although tres-pass is always an intentional tort, a nuisance may be intentional or unin-tentional. Trespass laws protect the possession and use of property, while nuisance laws protect the quality of that possession and use. For example, if a farmer enters her neighbour's property without permission and without reason, she is guilty of trespass to land. If the same farmer sprays her fruit trees and the spray drifts onto a neighbour's property, causing him to fall ill, the neighbour can claim damages for nuisance. Nuisance has been used to try to prevent, or to obtain damages for, excessive odours, noise, pollu-tion from factories, and the malfunctioning of sewage systems.

In recent years, nuisance has been highlighted because society has become more concerned about environmental pollution. Growing awareness of envi-ronmental problems has resulted in more government regulations. Local zoning bylaws attempt to keep land for industrial and residential use some distance apart, in the best interests of both groups. Despite these laws, a cit-izen still has the right to take civil action. Every occupier is entitled to make reasonable use of his or her property.

▌ Nuisance Actions Against Polluters

Advantages	Disadvantages
Individuals may sue polluters without waiting for government to act.	Usually, a plaintiff must have a property interest in the land being harmed by pollution in order to sue.
The courts will award compensation to successful plaintiffs for losses suffered.	It is difficult to prove that a polluter's activities are directly linked to the harm and that such harm could be foreseen.
It may be possible to obtain a permanent injunction to stop a polluter. In some cases, temporary injunctions can be obtained quickly.	The costs of bringing a civil action can be very high.
An action in tort law may be the only legal remedy for a plaintiff against a polluter.	Many serious environmental problems are global and cannot be addressed through tort law.
	The case may not be tried for a long time.

Figure 12-17

Launching a nuisance action against polluters has its pros and cons. How difficult would it be to prove unreasonable interference with the use and enjoyment of your land?

Nuisances are not always linked to environmental concerns. Picketers who protest illegally outside the entrance to a hospital or a factory are a nuisance because they interfere with the free movement of other people in and out of these buildings.

It is a matter for the courts to determine what is reasonable and to bal-ance that right against the rights of other occupiers. Courts should only

Gleneagles v. BCFC

2001 BCSC 512
British Columbia Supreme Court

Figure 12-18

Members of the Gleneagles Committee opposed to British Columbia Ferry Corporation's terminal expansion display a plan of the proposed work outside the British Columbia Supreme Court.

In February 2001, the Gleneagles Concerned Parents Committee Society tried to stop the British Columbia Ferry Corporation (BCFC) from expanding its Horseshoe Bay ferry terminal in West Vancouver. The parents' committee sought a court injunction to halt the expansion until a proper environmental review had been conducted. The terminal formed part of a link between the British Columbia mainland and Vancouver Island.

The BCFC had been working on the project since 1995. One thing it proposed to do was to double the size of the parking lot for vehicles waiting to board ferries. A larger parking lot would address the problem of overflow parking on the shoulder of the highway leading to the terminal. During peak travel periods, this line-up of cars extended 8 km along the highway. The overflow parking was not only inconvenient, but unsafe.

In planning the project, the BCFC had anticipated the impact of construction activities on air quality. It had also commissioned Cirrus Consultants, a private firm, to conduct an environmental study. This study concluded: "The proposed project is not expected to have any significant environmental or health effects related to air quality."

At court, the plaintiff—the Gleneagles Concerned Parents Committee Society—made the following arguments in support of its application for an injunction:

- The environmental study conducted by Cirrus Consultants was not comprehensive and could not anticipate the impact of construction.
- There was evidence that both the construction and the completed parking lot would produce air pollution harmful to the children attending Gleneagles Elementary School and to the residents of Horseshoe Bay. One local doctor had concluded that the existing ferry operation was producing pollution that had already caused a critical health problem among area residents. Another doctor argued that the proposed construction would produce more respiratory illness. Because the parking compound would come within 35 m of the school, there was heightened concern about health issues connected to the project.
- The project would create a **private nuisance.** The air pollution from the project would interfere with students' use and enjoyment of Gleneagles Elementary School. Because the British Columbia *School Act* required the students to attend the school, this gave students and parents rights as "occupiers," with a legal standing in relation to the school property. This satisfied the requirement that plaintiffs claiming private nuisance have a legal interest in the property affected.
- The project would create a **public nuisance.** Private citizens claiming a public nuisance must prove that they are suffering, or will suffer, special harm in comparison to the general public. The fact that local area students were required by law to attend Gleneagles Elementary made them unlike any other residents, and they thereby met this prerequisite.

continued ▶

The court ruled in favour of the defendant and denied the plaintiff's application for an injunction. Below are excerpts from the judgment:

"The courts in deciding whether an interference can amount to an actionable nuisance have to strike a balance between the right of the defendant to use his property for his own lawful enjoyment and the right of the plaintiff to the undisturbed enjoyment of his property."

"A private nuisance is a wrong only to the owner or occupier affected. This is still the test.... The plaintiff is in fact a society. It has no occupancy interests at all relative to property, including the school site adjacent to the proposed expansion. It is not sufficient to argue the mandatory attendance provisions found in the *School Act*."

"[The plaintiff] has not established, and in my view it cannot establish that damage the Society has suffered or will suffer differs in degree from that suffered by the public or is a different type than that suffered by the public at large."

For Discussion

1. Identify the competing rights argued by the plaintiff and defendant.
2. Distinguish between private nuisance and public nuisance.
3. What argument did the court consider in rejecting the plaintiff's claim of private nuisance?
4. On what basis did the court reject the plaintiff's claim of public nuisance?
5. Would the plaintiff's legal position have been different if Gleneagles Elementary School had been a private school? Explain.

You Be the JUDGE

A group of citizens bring an action for nuisance against a pulp and paper mill for its unpleasant odours and air pollution. The citizens seek an injunction from the court.

- How will a court injunction forcing a company to stop its operation affect the community?
- Should the court award damages for the nuisance, but allow the defendant's activity to continue?
- In a small group, debate both sides of this issue and reach a group decision with reasons. Compare your decision with that of other groups.

become involved when occupiers in the vicinity can reasonably show they have been inconvenienced. Compensation will not be awarded for occasional minor annoyances; the harm must be serious and continue for some time. One golf ball landing in a person's yard from a neighbouring country club is an annoyance; golf balls hit regularly into the same yard are a nuisance. The normal remedy for a nuisance is an injunction, although damages may be awarded.

Review Your Understanding (Pages 358 to 364)

1. What is an intentional tort? Identify five examples.
2. Why do many potential torts not result in legal action?
3. Distinguish between assault and battery.
4. When might punitive damages be awarded for assault and battery?
5. What two conditions must exist for a false imprisonment action to succeed?
6. How are trespass to land and battery similar?
7. Why is propelling an object onto another's property considered trespass?
8. Explain the tort of nuisance.
9. In what two ways do trespass and nuisance differ?

12.7 Defences for Trespass

People who commit intentional torts may not be liable if they have a legal defence for their actions. Once the plaintiff has established that the defendant

has committed a trespass, the defendant has a number of defences that might explain the trespass. The most common defences are
- consent
- self-defence
- defence of others or property
- legal authority
- necessity

A defendant may use more than one defence in the same lawsuit.

Consent

Consent is the defence most often used in cases involving trespass to the person, especially battery. This defence must be established by the defendant. A defendant who can show that the plaintiff willingly consented to the action is excused from liability for any injury that results. Suppose a group of teenagers play a friendly neighbourhood game of football. During a tackle, Felix is injured, and his arm is broken. Felix will not succeed if he sues for damages because he voluntarily agreed to play, and no anger was displayed during the game. Also, he consented while being aware of the possible risks of the game. This defence is similar to the defence for negligence of voluntary assumption of risk.

Recently, court cases involving separate issues—contact sports and medical treatment—have tried to resolve the extent to which consent applies. Courts assume that players who participate in certain contact sports have consented to the bodily contact permitted by the rules of the sport. A football player expects to get tackled, a boxer punched, a hockey player checked, and so on. Bodychecking is considered a normal or reasonable part of a hockey game. However, if Robin deliberately slashes Michelle's face with her hockey stick, she is using excessive force and is committing an intentional tort. Michelle could succeed in a tort action, and a criminal charge could also be laid against Robin, the overly aggressive player. (See Issue, page 312.)

As discussed earlier, a doctor who treats a patient without consent is committing battery. An exception is if a doctor provides emergency treatment for an unconscious patient, and the treatment is limited to only what is necessary to protect the patient's life.

Self-Defence

Self-defence is a valid defence as long as the force used is not excessive *and* it is reasonable and necessary in the circumstances to prevent personal injury. What is reasonable and necessary depends on the facts of each case. Suppose Julian claims he was defending himself against Scott. Julian must convince the court that he genuinely feared being injured by Scott, and that Scott was struck in self-protection against the threat. The burden of proof rests with Julian: he must prove that his actions were necessary to prevent the attack and that excessive force was not used. Self-defence may even be used as a successful defence if Julian struck the first blow. Julian must convince the court that striking out was the only means of self-protection.

de Groot v. Arsenault

(2000) 150 Man. R. (2d) 154
Manitoba Court of Queen's Bench

The plaintiff, Karen de Groot, and the defendant, Wilma Arsenault, accompanied their husbands to a Winnipeg arena where their sons, Wesley de Groot and Michael Arsenault, played hockey. Both boys played on the same team. The younger de Groot son, Steven, told his mother that he had been kneed in the groin by Michael a day earlier at a bus stop. After the game, Wilma Arsenault left the arena quickly to start up her car because it was a very cold night. Outside the arena after the game, Karen de Groot carried Wesley's hockey gear while encouraging him to deal with Michael to avenge the assault on Steven.

A fight started between Wesley and Michael. Michael was pushed down, and Michael's father separated the boys and stopped the fight. Karen de Groot pulled Michael's father away, telling him to leave the boys alone to settle the incident. Wilma Arsenault came quickly toward the boys, spun Wesley around to break up any further fighting, and then moved toward Karen de Groot. Carrying two hockey sticks, Karen de Groot yelled and pointed her finger at Wilma Arsenault, telling her to leave the boys alone. Wilma Arsenault grabbed Karen de Groot's hands, pushed her backward, and twisted and broke her index finger. The finger required two minor surgeries, and Karen de Groot was left with some minor permanent disability and periodic pain. But, she retained good use of her finger.

Karen de Groot sued for damages for her broken finger, but her action was dismissed.

For Discussion

1. **On what grounds did the plaintiff base her action?**

2. **What two defences would Wilma Arsenault plead, and why?**

3. **Why do you think the plaintiff's action was dismissed?**

Provocation, which Chapter 5 outlines as a possible defence for murder, is not a defence for an intentional tort. If Petra hits Bill for provoking or annoying her to the point where she loses her temper, she has no legal defence. She may be held liable for any injury she causes Bill. But, provocation may reduce the damages that the defendant must pay.

Defence of Others

A third party can come to the aid of a person if it is reasonable to assume that the person is in some degree of immediate danger. This defence occurs most often when a parent comes to the assistance of a child or close relative, or one spouse defends the other. The same principles apply to this defence as to the defence of self-defence.

Defence of Property

Property owners may use reasonable force to eject intruders from their property. The owner must first ask the trespasser to leave. If the request is ignored, then a reasonable amount of force may be used to expel the intruder. However, if the trespasser made a forcible entry onto the property, no request to leave is necessary before force can be used. Again, the amount of force used must be reasonable. The property owner cannot set a deadly or dangerous trap to harm trespassers.

Case

Runcer v. Gould

2000 ABQB 25
Alberta Court of Queen's Bench

In May 1994, Eric Gould's wife hired a landscaping company to do some work on their property. The 18-year-old plaintiff, Ryan Runcer, was one of the employees. While working at the Gould home, Runcer saw two all-terrain vehicles. On May 4, the vehicles disappeared. Eric Gould suspected that Runcer had stolen them and questioned him about the theft. The youth denied stealing them. Then, Gould and a friend, Anthony Hunley, threw Runcer to the ground, duct-taped him, forced him into a helicopter that had no door, and, while in the air, threatened to throw Runcer from the helicopter unless he confessed. Runcer was scared, began to cry, and was still vomiting three days after the incident.

Back on the ground, Runcer led the defendants to one of the vehicles; however, the second vehicle had been sold. At a criminal trial, Runcer pleaded guilty to the theft and was sentenced to one day in jail plus a $700 fine. Unable to pay the fine, he spent another two weeks in jail. In a separate criminal trial,

Gould was fined $3000 for assaulting Runcer. The Crown withdrew the assault charge against Gould's friend Hunley.

Runcer then brought an action for general and aggravated damages and punitive damages for trespass to the person, mental stress, and intimidation (threatened force). He was awarded $7000 general and aggravated damages jointly between the defendants. As well, the judge awarded punitive damages—$7500 from Gould and $3500 from Hunley.

For Discussion

1. **What specific torts were committed by the defendants?**
2. **What defence would the defendants plead?**
3. **Why was Runcer awarded aggravated damages?**
4. **Why was he awarded punitive damages as well?**
5. **Since Runcer committed a crime, should he receive compensation for what happened to him? Why?**

Legal Authority

In limited situations, certain individuals, such as law enforcement officers, have the legal authority to do what could otherwise result in legal actions for assault and battery or false imprisonment. For example, the police can detain individuals in the course of a valid arrest. Many civil actions against officers have been decided in their favour because they were carrying out a legal duty to arrest suspects in a criminal case. Store detectives likewise have the legal authority to arrest shoplifters, but they have no higher rights of arrest than a private citizen. (To review arrest rights, see page 195.)

Police officers with a search warrant can use legal authority as a defence if someone claims that the officers have trespassed on the plaintiff's property. Prior to entry, except in an emergency, the officers should identify themselves, show the search warrant, and request entry to the premises. An unexpected arrival on a person's property could lead to serious misunderstanding and possible injury. The personal safety of both the homeowner and the police are at stake.

By law, certain industries are given the legal right to emit a reasonable amount of smoke, noise, and effluent (liquid watse) without being liable. Similar regulations apply to aircraft and vehicles with sirens. In passing such legislation, the government attempts to balance the right of society to enjoy land against the need of industry to generate pollution in the course of providing products and services. However, if a business exceeds the level considered reasonable in law, a nuisance action may be brought against it.

Necessity

Necessity is also a defence against trespass. A defendant is excused from liability for trespass to land if the action is strictly necessary. The necessity to use another's property may arise unexpectedly, as when a sudden storm forces boaters to seek safety on nearby land. Although the boaters are trespassing by being on the land without permission, their defence of necessity would likely succeed. But if they caused damage while on the property, they could be held liable for any losses. A person trespassing on another's property to reclaim goods that rightfully belong to him or her could also argue that the action was necessary.

Review Your Understanding (Pages 364 to 368)

1. Identify six defences for trespass.
2. When is consent not a valid defence in a contact sport?
3. When is self-defence a valid defence against battery?
4. When may defence of another person be used?
5. Who may use the defence of legal authority, and in what situations?
6. Explain necessity as a defence against trespass to land.

12.8 Defamation of Character and Its Defences

Defamation is an unjustified or untrue attack on a person's reputation. The attack may be intentional or unintentional, and it must lower the person's reputation, cause people to avoid him or her, or expose the person to hatred, contempt, or ridicule. A damaged reputation may result in difficulty in finding or keeping jobs, or strained friendships. A person whose reputation has been harmed through defamation can sue for damages. In such an action, the plaintiff must establish that the defendant's statements have seriously injured his or her reputation. Otherwise, only nominal damages are possible.

Protection of a person's reputation, however, may conflict with another person's right. Freedom of thought, belief, opinion, and expression, including freedom of the press and other media of communication, are guaranteed in section 2(b) of the *Canadian Charter of Rights and Freedoms*. Across Canada, the laws governing defamation attempt to balance the rights of individuals. People should be free to seek and share information and all kinds of ideas without fear of censorship or legal action. Yet, people should not be allowed to make groundless or unproven statements about others without being subject to defamation of character laws.

For a statement to be defamatory, it must be false, be heard or read by a third party, and bring the person defamed into ridicule, hatred, or contempt.

The more malicious or vicious the remarks, the more serious the tort. Defamation may take the form of slander or libel. The difference between them has been abolished by legislation in Alberta, Manitoba, New Brunswick, Prince Edward Island, and Newfoundland and Labrador.

Slander

Slander is defamation through spoken words, sounds, physical gestures, or facial expressions. Slander may be unintentional. If, for example, Niko is making negative comments to Istvan about Istvan himself, and Laura enters the room and overhears the conversation, then slander may have occurred. Even though Niko did not intend anyone but Istvan to hear the criticism, she took the risk of having her defamatory remarks overheard.

Libel

Libel is defamation in a more permanent visual or audible form than slander, such as in radio or television broadcasts, publications, cartoons, photographs, tape recordings, films, or videotapes. Like slander, libel does not have to be intentional. If a person writes defamatory statements about another in a private diary, the remarks are not libel. However, if someone else reads them, libel may exist.

Newspapers publish the names and addresses of persons arrested for criminal offences so that persons with the same names are not defamed. If a publication is sued for libel, the reporter, the editor, the publisher, and the owner are all liable for defamation. Often, however, it is the publisher or owner who pays the damages. The award may be reduced if the defendant makes an apology or prints a correction in another issue of the newspaper.

Defences for Defamation

The most common defences for defamation of character are the truth, absolute and qualified privilege, and fair comment. These defences help ensure a balance between the protection of a person's reputation and the guarantees of freedom of speech and expression.

Truth

The best defence against defamation is to prove that the statements made are the **truth.** The law protects persons from false statements only. An action for damages will fail if the defendant can show that the statements made are absolutely true and justified. This is a complete defence, even if the remarks have harmed the plaintiff's reputation. However, truth is not an adequate defence if a person repeats statements that he or she believes to be true when they are actually false. Repeating remarks that harm a person's character is just as serious as making the remarks in the first place. As a result, editors and publishers of newspapers and magazines have great responsibility to ensure that their reporters' stories are completely accurate.

Case

Langille et al. v. McGrath

(2000) 233 N.B.R. (2d) 29
New Brunswick Court of Queen's Bench

The defendant, Odette McGrath, and her neighbours wanted the city of Saint John, New Brunswick, to close a gravel pit in their neighbourhood. They felt that the safety of their neighbourhood and the value of their homes were threatened by the operation of the pit. The plaintiffs, the operators of the pit, wanted the city to license the pit. They felt that opposition to the pit threatened their livelihood and economic future.

During a televised city council meeting, McGrath stated she'd heard rumours to the effect that if she didn't "watch herself," she would be bumped or clipped walking on the streets. She repeated this statement during a televised interview, further stating that she felt threatened and believed that the plaintiffs might do her serious bodily harm.

The plaintiffs sued the defendant for damages for defamation, and the defendant counterclaimed for alleged threats. The court allowed the plaintiffs' action and awarded them $500 plus $200 for costs. The counterclaim was dismissed.

For Discussion

1. What defamation occurred here?
2. What defence would the defendant plead?
3. Why do you think the damages awarded were so small? Do you agree? Why?

Figure 12-19

In May 2001, Tory MPP Gary Guzzo said he would name suspected pedophiles when in the Ontario Legislature. Although protected by absolute privilege, he never did.

Absolute Privilege

Members of Parliament, members of the provincial legislatures, and all persons participating in courts, coroners' inquests, and judicial hearings are given **absolute privilege.** This means that they may make statements openly, honestly, and freely, without the fear of being sued. The statements must be made within the confines of where the proceedings take place. The principle of absolute privilege is based on the belief that society's interests are best served by open debate, even at the cost of someone's reputation.

However, if a defamatory statement is repeated outside the protected locations, the defamed person may take civil action. For example, if an MP makes a defamatory statement to reporters on the front steps of the Parliament Buildings in Ottawa, which is later found to be untrue, the member could be sued for slander. If the same statement had been made within the House of Commons, absolute privilege would have protected the MP.

Qualified Privilege

People who are required to express their opinions during the course of their work are protected by **qualified privilege.** Its purpose is to encourage free speech on matters of public importance. Qualified privilege will succeed as a defence if the defendant can prove that the statements were made in good faith and without **malice.** If malice is involved as a motive, qualified privilege is not a valid defence.

The law believes that there are certain times when open and honest communication is more important than protecting a person's reputation. For instance, employers and teachers are often asked to write letters of reference for former employees and students. Also, credit-reporting agencies are required to provide information on a person's credit rating and ability to meet loan payments. Qualified privilege enables such people, acting in good faith, to provide honest, but negative, references without fear of legal action, even if the statements turn out to be untrue and defamatory. This defence is also available to doctors, nurses, and teachers who have a legal duty to report suspected child abuse.

Unlike elected federal and provincial politicians, who are granted absolute privilege in Parliament and provincial legislatures, government officials who take part in local or municipal council meetings are only granted qualified privilege.

Fair Comment

Media critics who review plays, theatre performances, sports events, and concerts provide information to the general public. **Fair comment,** the right to criticize openly and honestly, is an accepted part of our society. Critics should be able to comment on matters of general interest to the public without concern for legal action. However, if the comments are not fair and can be proved to be malicious, then the defendant can be held liable. It is fair comment for a critic to offer an opinion that a particular actor has just given the worst performance of her life in her new film. It is not fair comment to make untrue statements about an actor's performance or malicious comments about a performer's private life.

Figure 12-20

Pet Shop Boy Neil Tennant (above) along with Chris Lowe sued British philosopher Roger Scruton when he implied they did not write their songs but owed their trademark sound to "sound engineering." Scruton was forced to pay £10 000 for the remarks, as well as court costs, and he had to apologize in court to Tennant and Lowe.

Case

Pliuskaitis v. Jotautas

(1999) 47 O.R. (3d) 227
Ontario Superior Court of Justice

The plaintiff, Michael Pliuskaitis, was head swimming coach with the Cobra Swim Club in Brampton from 1990 to 1996. Over the years, he had raised the swim club to a highly competitive level. Pliuskaitis was a national team coach for Canada between 1993 and 1995, and he was named Canadian Coach of the Year in 1994. However, his approach to competitive swimming brought him into conflict with a largely volunteer board of

directors. The defendant, Jotautas, was a director of the club and resigned because of an ongoing legal dispute with the plaintiff.

That dispute arose from a letter that the plaintiff wrote and publicized, criticizing the actions of the defendant. The defendant brought an action for libel against Pliuskaitis, but it was settled after a pretrial conference. The settlement required Pliuskaitis to write a letter of apology to all club members and to pay damages and costs. The defendant then wrote to the Canadian Swimming Coaches Association, of which the plaintiff was a member, stating that the plaintiff operated in a manner that contradicted the

continued ▶

beliefs of that organization, that he set a bad example for the coaching staff and children of the club, and that he had no place in coaching.

The plaintiff brought an action for damages for libel, but his action was dismissed.

For Discussion

1. **What defence would the defendant plead and why?**

2. **In his decision, the judge stated: "While there has been adequate proof of libel ... I find that the defendant is entitled to his defence. As a consequence, the plaintiff's case fails, may I say by a narrow margin." What does this mean?**

Review Your Understanding (Pages 368 to 372)

1. **What is defamation, and what are its two forms?**
2. **Which of the two forms of defamation is considered the more serious?**
3. **What is the best defence to the tort of defamation, and why?**
4. **Distinguish between absolute and qualified privilege.**
5. **When can fair comment be used as a defence?**

12.9 The Need for Insurance

As you have learned, awarding damages to a plaintiff is the most common form of compensation in tort law. You have also seen several cases in which defendants were required to pay judgments in the thousands of dollars—money that few defendants can pay themselves. For this reason, most people purchase liability insurance to protect against the possibility of expensive legal actions.

Motor Vehicle Liability Insurance

Today, disputes arising from motor vehicle accidents are the source of many civil actions. Lawyers specializing in civil lawsuits probably spend more time dealing with negligence actions arising from car accidents than from any other type of tort. It can take several years to resolve such actions, from the time of the accident to the completion of the trial and the awarding of damages. As you know, a person injured in an automobile accident can claim both special damages and general damages from the driver responsible. More recently, the courts have determined that persons who were not directly involved in the accident may also claim damages on such grounds as mental anguish and loss of companionship of a relative or a loved one. Statutes in several provinces allow such claims.

Even minor accidents in which no one has been seriously injured can result in damage claims so high that most people would be unable to pay them. For this reason, all car owners in Canada are legally required to purchase motor vehicle liability insurance. The insurance company pays any claims

Automobile Damage Claims in Canada, 1984–2000

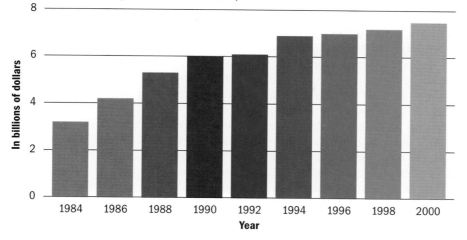

Figure 12-21

Automobile damage claims have more than doubled since 1984. What factors might account for this?

for damages arising from an accident, up to a certain maximum. This type of insurance is called **third-party liability** insurance, because three parties are involved when a claim is made: the person who caused the accident, that person's insurance company, and the victim who claims damages.

The minimum amount of insurance coverage required by law in all provinces and the Northwest Territories is $200 000. Because damage awards for automobile accidents have recently been quite high, many drivers have been motivated to buy insurance coverage of $1 million or more—far higher than the required minimum.

Some drivers have no insurance, although this is illegal in Canada and carries severe fines. People who suffer loss in an accident with an uninsured driver are compensated through special arrangements. In some provinces, a fund run by the insurance industry handles such claims; in the other provinces, the fund is administered by the government. Because victims of motor vehicle accidents often have to wait years for damages, a limited form of **no-fault insurance** has been instituted in some provinces. It is designed to put money in the hands of victims immediately, whether or not they are at fault in the accident.

A person who suffers loss beyond that covered by no-fault insurance can still bring a tort action for damages. However, if the person wins additional damages from the courts, any no-fault insurance benefits are deducted from the award. Motor vehicle insurance regulations differ from province to province, and their details are too complex to be discussed here. You can obtain information about the specifics of your provincial or territorial regulations from a local insurance agent.

Figure 12-22

Several hundred people attend a rally criticizing no-fault insurance in Vancouver, British Columbia.

activity

Other Liability Insurance

In recent years, it has become common practice for people and businesses to minimize losses from possible civil actions by buying insurance. Any type of liability insurance policy has an upper dollar limit for insurance coverage. If a court awards damages greater than the maximum, the defendant must pay the difference. This may require the sale of possessions or the garnishment of wages. Often, the damages can never be paid fully because the sum is too large to repay in a person's lifetime.

When all forms of damages are considered, awards in civil actions can involve millions of dollars. Although such large awards occur far more often in the United States, personal injury accidents, ranging from cut fingers to paralysis for life, now cost Canadians at least $3.5 billion a year in medical treatment and future care, lost wages, and pain and suffering.

The number of medical malpractice suits and the size of the settlements is increasing in Canada. Most Canadian doctors pay fees to the Canadian Medical Protective Association. This organization provides medical insurance that covers legal costs and damage awards for doctors who are sued successfully for malpractice. Malpractice insurance is also available from insurance companies.

Many Canadian lawyers also purchase malpractice insurance from insurance companies to protect themselves against civil actions from dissatisfied clients. Retail outlets, shopping centres, schools, churches, clubs, municipalities, and community organizations purchase insurance coverage to protect themselves in the event of lawsuits arising from injuries to persons on their property. Both homeowners and tenants who rent property also buy liability insurance to cover damages in case of injuries to visitors. The increasing readiness of many people to sue makes it wise for all businesses and individuals to carry liability insurance.

Review Your Understanding (Pages 372 to 374)

1. What is third-party liability insurance? Who are the three parties involved?

2. Why might a motorist purchase more insurance than the provincial legal requirement?

3. What is no-fault insurance?

4. What is the purpose of the Canadian Medical Protective Association?

5. Identify three other groups, besides doctors and lawyers, who should purchase liability insurance. Explain why in each case.

No-Fault Insurance: Does It Work?

Automobile liability insurance gives financial protection to it holders. This kind of insurance protects drivers from people who might sue them for injuries or losses resulting from automobile accidents. It is compulsory in all the provinces and territories.

Some provinces, such as Saskatchewan, Manitoba, Quebec, and Ontario, have no-fault insurance. This means that persons injured in automobile accidents are paid for loss of wages and for rehabilitation costs, regardless of who was at fault. No-fault insurance does not pay for any damage to vehicles arising from the accident. The other provinces have a tort or negligence system through which injured parties sue for damages in the courts and do not get automatic payments from their insurance companies.

On One Side

Those in favour of no-fault insurance say that the tort system of suing for damages is slow and costly. It means that people injured in motor vehicle accidents often have to wait months or years to collect damages for their injuries. For those injured and unable to work, such delays can be ruinous. Under no-fault insurance, claims are settled quickly and there are no expensive civil actions, which can increase insurance premiums.

Provinces with no-fault insurance have almost completely eliminated the claim of pain and suffering (usually associated with whiplash) as grounds for collecting damages. As a result, there has been a dramatic decline in the number of claims for personal injury. From July 1, 1994, to December 31, 1995, in Saskatchewan (during the last 18 months of the tort system), 9006 claims were made. Eighty-three percent of these claims were for whiplash injuries involving pain and suffering. Such claims are no longer allowed. This has helped to reduce insurance premiums even further.

On the Other Side

Opponents of no-fault insurance argue that it limits people's rights to sue for damages in court. Damages awarded under no-fault insurance often are inadequate and do not properly compensate the injured. It limits their civil liberties to achieve justice. It protects the guilty parties, even drunk drivers, who are also paid compensation for their injuries.

Provinces with no-fault insurance are sometimes taken advantage of by people who stage accidents and then submit insurance claims for phony injuries. In 1995, 19 people in Ontario were arrested and charged with defrauding 29 insurance companies of $1.1 million. Police suspect that law clerks, doctors, and body-shop employees may have been involved in this scheme as well. In 1996, Ontario changed its no-fault insurance scheme and greatly reduced the benefits for people only slightly injured in motor vehicle accidents. It also restored the right to sue a guilty party for economic losses suffered.

The Bottom Line

Insurance companies need to recover their claims paid out with premiums. Whether the no-fault system is more efficient and less expensive than its predecessor, or whether it encourages fraudulent claims that penalize honest policyholders, remains to be seen.

What Do You Think?

1. **Should automobile liability insurance be compulsory? Explain your answer.**
2. **What is no-fault insurance?**
3. **Create a two-column organizer. Identify the advantages and disadvantages of no-fault insurance.**
4. **Why would lawyers be opposed to no-fault insurance?**
5. **In your opinion, should the no-fault insurance system be abandoned or changed? Present your conclusions to the class.**

Chapter Review

Chapter Highlights

- Torts fall into two classes: intentional and unintentional.
- Negligence is the most important and best-known part of tort law.
- A duty of care, foreseeability, and the "reasonable person" are important concepts in negligence.
- The plaintiff must prove his or her tort action on the balance of probabilities.
- Contributory negligence and voluntary assumption of risk are the main defences to negligence.
- Occupiers of property must take reasonable care to make their property safe for visitors.
- Occupiers must take extra precautions to protect children from accidents around allurements such as swimming pools and playgrounds.
- Everyone from bar and restaurant owners to private citizens hosting parties in their homes could be sued if someone is harmed by a drunk driver leaving any of these places.
- The driver of a motor vehicle is liable for the safety of passengers.
- Contributory negligence may exist when passengers in motor vehicles don't wear seat belts.
- Vicarious liability—holding a blameless person responsible for the misconduct of others—affects liability for motor vehicle owners and employers.
- Doctors must receive informed consent before they touch any patient unless the patient is unconscious, or to save a life.
- Trespass to a person, such as assault and battery, is a common intentional tort.
- Trespass laws protect the possession and use of property, while nuisance laws protect the quality of that possession and use.
- Consent, self-defence, defence of others or property, legal authority, and necessity are the main defences to trespass to a person or land.
- Defamation of character may take the form of slander or libel.
- Truth, absolute and qualified privilege, and fair comment are the main defences for defamation.
- The purchase of various types of insurance helps protect against expensive lawsuits.

Review Key Terms

Name the key terms that are described below.

a) a person's failure to exercise reasonable care that results in harm to others

b) intentional physical contact harmful or offensive to another person

c) using land in a way that interferes with another's enjoyment and use of neighbouring land

d) holding a blameless person responsible for another's actions

e) to enter another's property without consent

f) a person who has control over property and owes visitors a duty of care

g) true purpose; the person's state of mind that causes him or her to perform an action

h) defamation in printed or other more permanent form

i) defamation in oral form

j) the obligation to ensure that others are not harmed by one's actions

k) an object that attracts, such as a swimming pool

l) the fact of being the cause of something that happened

m) a defence against defamation in which the defendant shows comments were made without malicious intent

n) the principle that a plaintiff may not recover damages for harm from risks to which he or she consents

o) the ability of a reasonable person to anticipate what might occur from his or her actions

p) someone who has neither physical nor mental disabilities and who people agree is careful, thoughtful, and considerate

q) the best defence against defamation of character

Check Your Knowledge

1. Outline the elements that are necessary to prove a negligence action, and provide an example for each.

2. Identify the acceptable defences for a negligence action, and provide an example for each.

3. Outline the intentional torts in this chapter, and provide an example for each.

4. Identify the legally acceptable defences for intentional torts, and provide an example for each.

Apply Your Learning

5. *Mohamed v. City of Vancouver,* [2001] B.C.W.L.D. 737 (British Columbia Court of Appeal)

A Vancouver police constable, on patrol in a cruiser with his police dog, received information that three men were involved in a robbery. A few minutes later, the constable saw three men fitting the description. He stopped his vehicle and got out with his dog, Czar. He called, "Stop, police!" twice, and two of the men stopped. The third man, plaintiff Asad Mohamed, ran into a lane, and the constable sent Czar after the suspect while he radioed for help. The plaintiff was trying to jump a small retaining wall when Czar caught him. Mohamed fell over the wall and broke his leg, and Czar bit the plaintiff's arm and held it until the constable arrived a minute or two later once help arrived. A large knife was found by the wall.

Mohamed brought an action for personal injuries against the city and the police, but the action was dismissed. The plaintiff appealed to the British Columbia Court of Appeal where his action was again dismissed.

a) In his action, Mohamed claimed that the police use of Czar was excessive force. What argument could the police make to counter this claim?

b) The plaintiff also claimed that the officer was negligent in failing to follow Czar immediately after letting him loose. Also, the city was negligent in failing to train police dogs in other than the "bite and hold" method of apprehension. What arguments could the police make to counter these claims?

c) Why do you think the plaintiff's action was dismissed in both courts?

6. *Rai v. Koziar* (2000), 275 A.R. 145 (Alberta Court of Queen's Bench)

The plaintiff, Gurmeet Rai, took her husband's work clothing to Annie's Laundromat, owned by the defendants, Annie and Frank Koziar, in March 1995. Rai's husband had presoaked his clothes in gasoline to help remove dirt and oil, but Rai was not aware of this. There was nothing about the clothes to cause her concern, and Annie Koziar did not detect the odour of gasoline. Rai loaded the washing machine, which contained this warning sign: "Do not wash articles containing flammable fumes or materials." As the machine was filling, the plaintiff lifted the lid, causing a flash explosion. The plaintiff suffered burns to her face, hands, and legs.

The plaintiff sued for damages for negligence, while the defendants counterclaimed for damages. However, both actions were dismissed.

a) What duty of care did the defendants owe the plaintiff, and was it breached?

b) Was this accident foreseeable? Why?

c) What is a counterclaim, and why do you think the defendants counterclaimed for damages?

d) Why do you think both actions were dismissed?

7. *Tabaka v. Greyhound Lines of Canada Ltd.* (1999), 252 A.R. 373 (Alberta Court of Queen's Bench)

In February 1995, the plaintiff, Andrea Tabaka, was a paying passenger on a Greyhound bus driven by the defendant, Steve Howitt. The bus was travelling from Prince George, British Columbia, to Jasper, Alberta. Howitt was driving at 90 km/h, the legal speed limit, at about 2:20 A.M., when he collided with a mother and calf moose. Before seeing the moose, Howitt had seen signs with a picture of a moose with "Suggested night speed 80 km/h" clearly marked. There were also several other signs, warning of "the possibility of moose in the next 35 km." The road conditions were good: the road was dry, there was no ice or snow, and visibility was good. Howitt was keeping a reasonable lookout and applied his brakes as soon as he saw the moose in his high beams. But, he was unable to stop in time to avoid hitting the moose.

The plaintiff brought an action for negligence against Greyhound Lines and the driver, but her action was dismissed.

a) Why did Tabaka claim that Howitt was negligent?

b) Tabaka also claimed that the driver owed a high duty of care to his paying passengers. Should this have any bearing on the duty of care? Explain.

c) If Howitt had been driving at the suggested speed limit, do you think the accident could have been avoided? Explain.

d) Why do you think the plaintiff's action was dismissed?

8. *Hanson v. Wayne's Café Ltd.* (1990), 84 Sask. R. 220 (Saskatchewan Court of Queen's Bench)

The plaintiff, Shelley Hanson, was a waitress at the China Inn Restaurant in Saskatoon. The restaurant was operated by the defendant company. Suspecting that she was pregnant, Hanson placed a urine sample in a styrofoam cup and put a top on it to take the sample for analysis. She then put the cup in a paper bag and hid it under her coat as she left the restaurant because she was embarrassed by the personal nature of its contents. The restaurant owner, Wayne Mak, thought she was sneaking something out under her coat and demanded to see what it was. Being somewhat embarrassed, the plaintiff refused. When Mak touched her arm and asked her to sit down while he called the police, Hanson ran out the back door of the restaurant and fell in the parking area, scraping her knee. She did not return to her job.

Hanson then brought an action for damages for assault and false imprisonment against Mak and the defendant company, but her action on both counts was dismissed.

a) Why did Hanson claim that she had been assaulted?

b) Why do you think the assault claim was dismissed?

c) Why do you think the claim for false imprisonment was dismissed?

d) Was Hanson in any way to blame for what happened? Explain.

9. *Gambriell v. Caparelli* (1974), 54 D.L.R. (3d) 661 (Ontario County Court)

One July day, Fred Caparelli, the 21-year-old son of the defendant, was getting a hose to wash his car when the 50-year-old plaintiff, Gambriell, accidentally backed his car into the rear of Caparelli's vehicle, giving it a small dent in the bumper. An argument developed between the two, and Caparelli threatened to call the police. When Gambriell started to get back in his car, Fred Caparelli grabbed him. Gambriell then hit Fred Caparelli in the face. Fighting broke out, with blows being exchanged.

Attracted by the shouting, Mrs. Caparelli, the 57-year-old defendant, saw her son fighting with their neighbour. Her son was on the ground, and Gambriell had his hands on Fred Caparelli's neck. Thinking that her son was being choked, the defendant ran into her garden and got a metal three-pronged garden cultivator tool with a wooden handle 1.5 m long. After yelling at Gambriell to stop, she struck him three times on the shoulder and then on the head with the tool. As soon as Gambriell saw blood flowing from his head, he released Fred Caparelli. Gambriell was taken to the hospital, where he received nine stitches for lacerations.

Gambriell claimed damages in County Court. The action was dismissed, because the court found Mrs. Caparelli's actions reasonable under the circumstances.

a) On what grounds did the plaintiff base his action?

b) What defence did the defendant plead?

c) Was the use of force by Mrs. Caparelli justified in this case? Explain your reasoning.

d) In the decision, the judge observed: "Gambriell was the author of his own misfortune and ... even had I found for the plaintiff, I would not have awarded damages in excess of $1." Explain the meaning of this statement.

Communicate Your Understanding

10. In August 2001, 24-year-old inmate and acknowledged heroin user, Jason Pothier, filed a claim in Ontario Superior Court against Correctional Services Canada and the wardens of two penitentiaries for $25 million. Pothier alleged that, despite frequent requests, he was denied access to clean needles and methadone, a drug used to help addicts on heroin. And, as a result, he contacted HIV and the hepatitis C virus because public health measures in Canadian prisons are so abysmal that they constitute negligence. With a partner, argue both sides of Pothier's case, and them compare your arguments with those of another group.

11. In pairs, choose one of the debate topics below, which reflect opinions in the trial judgment in *Hunt v. Sutton Group,* page 352. Prepare a brief introduction; identify facts and arguments that support your stance; anticipate points against your view and prepare counterarguments to defend your viewpoint; and conclude with a statement that summarizes your position.
    • The trial decision in this case means that even if an employee takes foolish risks, his or her employer can be held accountable.

• The ruling in this case extends liability for serving alcohol to absurd limits. It turns employers into babysitters.

12. In pairs, choose one of the debate topics below, which reflect opinion on the *Parental Responsibility Act.* Prepare a brief introduction; identify facts and arguments that support your stance; anticipate points against your view and prepare counterarguments to defend your viewpoint; and conclude with a statement that summarizes your position.
    • I think that parents should definitely be responsible for their children's actions. They bring them up, so they should be punished if they do a bad job.
    • I think the act is crazy. Kids should be responsible for what they do. Parents try their best to teach their children the best way to live. Kids know what's right or wrong, and it's their fault.

13. *Toews v. Weisner and South Fraser Health Region,* 2001 BCSC 15 (British Columbia Supreme Court)

    A young girl, age 11, was vaccinated at school against the hepatitis B virus by a public health nurse. Although the child suffered no physical harm, her parents brought an action against the public health unit and the nurse for assault and battery. Neither parent had signed a consent form for the immunization. The public health nurse testified that verbal consent had been obtained. Both parents denied giving verbal consent. Outline the argument the plaintiff could use to substantiate the claim of battery. Outline the counterargument for the defendant. With a partner, debate both sides of this case and reach an appropriate decision.

14. Working with a partner, collect editorial cartoons or film, theatre, or book reviews from five editions of a daily or weekly newspaper or the Internet. Analyze the material and determine

if it is fair comment, libel, or questionable. Prepare a bulletin-board display of the material you have gathered, and be prepared to defend your choices before the class.

Develop Your Thinking

15. Given the tort law standard of the "reasonable person," what standard would people of low or very low intelligence be expected to meet, and why?

16. A person attending a sporting event voluntarily assumes certain risks, but not all risks. Using your favourite sport as an example, identify guidelines for which risks are assumed and which are not.

17. Negligence law has reached the point where social hosts are now being held liable for injuries caused by or to drunken guests. With a partner, brainstorm what a host of a party might do to reduce possible liability from any guests who leave the party when intoxicated and cause harm to others. Compare your ideas with those of other groups.

18. Someone who punches another person in the face may be liable for both the tort of battery and the crime of either assault or assault causing bodily harm. (See page 136 regarding assault causing bodily harm.) What factors determine whether one or both charges will proceed to trial?

19. Whether a nuisance exists and there has been unreasonable interference with the use and enjoyment of land is often left to the courts to determine. As a judge, what factors would you consider in reaching a decision on this issue?

As you all know, this young generation is close to my heart. They are special not only because they are vulnerable, and are the first to suffer whenever we adults get things wrong, but also because of their remarkable spirit, their ability to heal not only themselves but their societies as well.

Nelson Mandela

Family Law

13

Marriage, Divorce, and Family Mediation

Focus Questions

- Is there a "typical" family in the 21st century?
- How are federal and provincial powers divided for marriage and divorce?
- What are the legal (essential and formal) requirements of a valid marriage?
- What is the difference between an annulment and a separation?
- What are the grounds for divorce?
- What are the purpose and benefits of family mediation?

Chapter at a Glance

Figure 13-1

Gilbert and Winnie Chingee got married at McLeod Lake near Prince George, British Columbia, in 2000. It was the first traditional Native wedding ceremony held at the site since 1866. Why do you think some couples opt for traditional weddings while others decide to move away from traditions?

13.1 Introduction

Family law deals with the relationships among family members—between husband and wife, between same-sex partners, between parents and children, and sometimes between other parties, such as grandparents and stepparents. Family members are required to register births, marriages, and deaths; pay taxes; feed and clothe their children (if they have any), educate them, protect them from harm; and be law-abiding citizens. If these functions are fulfilled, governments do not interfere in family lives.

The primary sources of family law in Canada are found in federal, provincial, and territorial statutes. The *Constitution Act* divides the power of making marriage laws between the federal and the provincial governments. Section 91(26) gives the federal government jurisdiction over the *essentials* of marriage and divorce. In other words, there is national recognition for the standard procedures of marriage and divorce. If these were provincial responsibilities, there would be no guarantee that procedures in one province would be valid in another.

Section 92(12) gives the provincial governments jurisdiction over the **solemnization of marriage,** the formal requirements of the marriage ceremony. In turn, the provinces have delegated the responsibility for issuing marriage licences to the municipal governments. Section 92(13) also gives the provinces authority to enact laws dealing with property and civil rights; for example, laws governing support, adoption, and division of property on marriage breakdown. For this reason, some aspects of family law differ somewhat from province to province.

13.2 The Changing Family Structure

Family Structures in Canada

The family has been the basis of our social structure since earliest times. The **nuclear family** (father, mother, their children) has come to mean a breadwinning husband/father, a home-caring wife/mother, and children sharing the same household. This family type was the common living model in most industrialized countries, including Canada, for much of the 20th century. However, family life has changed so dramatically in the past four decades that it is probably impossible to talk about a "typical Canadian family" anymore. Statistics Canada now defines a family as (1) married couples with or without never-married children; (2) unmarried couples who have lived together for longer than one year; and (3) lone parent (single parent) with never-married children.

In recent years, the diversity of family structure has become obvious. High divorce and remarriage rates, more common-law and same-sex relationships, and two-income families with and without children have reshaped the definition of family. Canadian family types are shown in Figure 13-2.

You Be the JUDGE

For nine years, the province of Quebec offered cash bonuses to have babies. They ranged from $500 for a first baby to $8000 for a third. During this time, birth rates increased by 12 percent. The government ended this practice in 1997.

- Why would the Quebec government make this offer? Should all provinces offer baby bonuses to people who have children? Why?

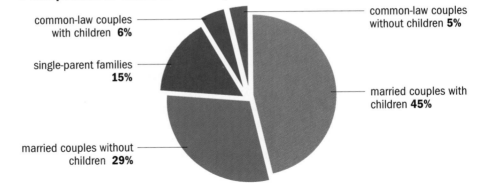

▌ Composition of Canadian Families, 1996

common-law couples with children **6%**

single-parent families **15%**

married couples without children **29%**

common-law couples without children **5%**

married couples with children **45%**

Figure 13-2

What trends seem to be indicated by these statistics?

Today, Canadian families are likely to be any one of the following:
- traditional nuclear family
- married couple without children
- **blended family**—a married or common-law couple with at least one stepchild
- **extended family**—children, parents, and grandparents sharing a dwelling and cooperating economically
- common-law relationships with or without children
- single parent with biological or adopted child
- same-sex partner relationships

▌ Canadian Families in Private Households, 1991 and 1996

Family Types	1991	1996
Total husband–wife families	6 402 090	6 700 360
Families of married couples	5 682 815	5 779 720
Families of common-law couples	719 275	920 640
Total lone-parent families	953 635	1 137 505
Female Parent	788 395	945 230
Male Parent	165 240	192 275

Figure 13-3

What is the overall trend in the data? Compare the 1996 data with current census statistics.

 activity

Visit **www.law.nelson.com** and follow the links to learn about the current composition of the Canadian family.

Family structure may also reflect social factors. Because the Canadian population is aging rapidly, there may be more families in the future consisting of several generations living under the same roof. Until the 1960s, a majority of immigrants to Canada came from European countries. Today, one out of every two immigrants comes from Asia, Africa, the Caribbean, or Central America. These new Canadians bring their family customs, traditions, and values with them. Family law is rapidly changing in response to changing family relationships. In fact, during the past 25 years, probably no other area of law has undergone such major changes.

Marriage and the 21st Century

Recently, Statistics Canada has estimated that 28 to 30 percent of all marriages will end in divorce, but 75 percent of all divorced men and women will marry again or live with another partner. Marriage is still a popular institution, and most Canadians will marry at least once during their lifetime.

Traditionally, a family is formed in our society through marriage. Dictionaries define marriage as "the voluntary union between one man and one woman, to the exclusion of all others, joined in a special kind of social and legal dependence for the purpose of founding and maintaining a family." Couples are marrying later in life and sometimes delay having children for various reasons. Families are smaller, often with only one or two children, and some couples remain childless, either by choice or for medical reasons.

When two people marry, they enter into a legally binding contract, provided certain requirements are met. If they divorce, they terminate that contract. Like all contracts, marriage involves both rights and responsibilities, some of which come into effect only upon divorce:

- Marriage is a partnership in which each party is expected to make an equal contribution.
- If there are children, partners must determine care, custody, access, and child support. This topic is discussed further in Chapter 14.
- Each spouse has the right to live in the family home; the couple must decide about the possible sale of the home and other assets.
- One spouse may be obliged to support the other. These obligations are discussed in Chapter 15.

Domestic contracts (marriage contracts, cohabitation agreements, and separation agreements) are discussed in detail in Chapter 15.

Figure 13-4

David Gaucher and his partner, Maria Piccolo, have been married for over two decades and are childless by choice. In the 20th century, this kind of family unit gained more social acceptance, and the number of childless couples grew.

Looking Back — Common-Law Marriages

Until the mid-1700s, people under British law were often united in common-law marriages rather than through formal ceremonies. The requirements for such unions were a private agreement and an exchange of promises between a man and a woman. The couple then began to live together as husband and wife. Once sexual intercourse had occurred, the marriage was valid.

However, the Church of England did not approve of such marriages. After considerable debate, the British Parliament passed the first Marriage Act in 1753. This legislation stated that common-law marriages were no longer valid and outlined certain requirements for a valid marriage. Its effect was to recognize only those unions that met the requirements.

Common-law marriages still exist when a man and woman choose to live together without undergoing a formal marriage ceremony. However, the term "marriage" in this context is misleading since such a relationship does not confer the same rights or responsibilities of a legal marriage upon the couple, no matter how long they live together.

Recently, as more and more couples have chosen this living arrangement, the law has started to recognize the common-law relationship and to provide some legal protection for the parties. The rights of common-law spouses to support, and the law governing property division are discussed in greater detail in Chapters 14 and 15.

continued ▶

For Discussion

1. What were the requirements for common-law marriages under British law?
2. How is the term "common-law" used today?

Figure 13-5

This carefree British couple probably lived during the passage of the Marriage Act of 1753. Some couples found their formerly valid marriages declared invalid by this law.

Review Your Understanding (Pages 383 to 386)

1. Which level of government has jurisdiction over (a) marriage and divorce, and (b) solemnization of marriage?
2. What type of issues does family law address?
3. What is a nuclear family? What percentage of Canadian families does it represent?
4. What trend seems apparent with single-parent families?
5. What is a common-law relationship?

13.3 Essential Requirements of Marriage

Although the federal government has jurisdiction over the **essential requirements for marriage,** there is little statute law in this area. Instead, the requirements are determined by common-law principles, which are outlined in this section. Because of this lack of federal legislation, each province has included any omissions in its own Marriage Act. In fact, most laws concerning marriage have been enacted by the provinces. If any essential requirement is lacking at the time of the marriage, the marriage contract cannot be legally recognized and is, therefore, **void** (without legal standing).

Capacity

To have the **capacity** to marry, you must have the mental and legal ability to marry. No person who lacks mental capacity by reason of illness, drugs, or alcohol can legally marry. At the

Figure 13-6

Although you must have the legal and mental ability to marry, Canadian law does not require you to be in love. However, it helps.

time of the marriage, both parties must have the ability to understand not only the nature of the ceremony, but also the duties and responsibilities created by the marriage. If mental capacity exists at the time of the marriage, but ceases to exist afterward, the marriage remains valid.

Case

Re McGill

(1979) 21 A.R. 449
Alberta Court of Queen's Bench

An elderly woman, Norah McGill, was diagnosed with multiple sclerosis in 1939. Over the years her condition deteriorated, and she stayed in a bed or a wheelchair most of the time. McGill developed a close friendship with David Peal, an 80-year-old man with whom she lived and who had cared for her for five years. When the couple announced that they wished to marry, McGill's two married sisters obtained an injunction to stop the marriage. They also applied to the court for an order confining their sister to a hospital or nursing home.

Medical evidence was presented suggesting that McGill was not able to conduct her own affairs or to make a decision as to her marital status. Evidence was also given that she required nursing care 24 hours a day, either in an institution or at home. This evidence was strongly supported by the two sisters. McGill's personal physician of many years gave opposing evidence that the marriage to Peal was important for her psychological welfare, and that Peal could care for her properly. The doctor further stated that, in his opinion, McGill understood and appreciated the nature of marriage. His evidence was supported by testimony from David Peal. McGill applied to the court to have the injunction removed and the application for her confinement dismissed. Her action succeeded.

For Discussion

1. **On what requirement of marriage did McGill's sisters base their actions?**
2. **Which side's medical evidence do you think the court considered more convincing? Why?**
3. **Why did McGill win her action? Do you agree with the judgment? Explain.**

Minimum Age

A valid marriage also requires the parties to be old enough to marry. In Canada, the federal government has not established any minimum age for marriage but has adopted the minimum ages under English common law: 14 years for males, 12 years for females. However, all the provinces and territories have legislation requiring a higher minimum age, and parental consent for a child under a certain age, for marriage. These restrictions are discussed on page 393.

Close Relationships

A marriage between two people who are too closely related either by **consanguinity** (blood), by adoption, or by **affinity** (marriage) is not valid. These restrictions were first codified by King Henry VIII in England in the 16th century, and some still remain today. In 1990, Canadian Parliament enacted the *Marriage (Prohibited Degrees) Act*, which came into force in 1991. It lists persons who may not marry because they are too closely related by blood or adoption.

Did You Know?

In Canada, the average age of brides and grooms has been rising steadily over the last two decades. In 2000, grooms were 33.7 years old while brides were 31.1 years old. In your opinion, why are couples marrying later in life?

Marriage (Prohibited Degrees) Act

Excerpts from the *Marriage (Prohibited Degrees) Act*

2.

(2) No person shall marry another person if they are related

   (a) lineally by consanguinity or adoption;

   (b) as brother and sister by consanguinity, whether by the whole blood or by the half-blood; or

   (c) as brother and sister by adoption.

For Discussion

1. What is the meaning of the term "lineally"?

▌Degrees of Consanguinity and Affinity

A man may not marry his	A woman may not marry her
grandmother	grandfather
mother	father
daughter	son
sister	brother
granddaughter	grandson

Figure 13-7

Why would marrying a blood or adopted relative be prohibited?

Did You Know?

In March 2000, Alberta passed the *Marriage Amendment Act* defining marriage as a union between a man and a woman. The bill invokes the *Charter*'s notwithstanding clause to ensure the law endures any future *Charter* challenge. What does this legislation prevent?

Before 1991, there were even more restrictions on marriage partners, but these have been abolished. It is now possible, for example, for a woman to marry her divorced husband's brother or nephew, or for a man to marry his divorced wife's sister or niece.

Furthermore, on June 8, 1999, Parliament passed a resolution related to the protection of marriage. It stated: "That, in the opinion of this House, it is necessary, in light of public debate around recent court decisions, to state that **marriage** is and should remain the union of one man and one woman, to the exclusion of all others, and that Parliament will take all necessary steps to preserve this definition of marriage in Canada."

Genuine Consent

Since marriage is a contract, the parties must consent to it freely. If either party is forced or tricked into getting married, the marriage may be declared void. Whether the marriage ceremony is religious or civil, performed before a member of the clergy or a judge, the bride and groom and all those present will be asked if any reason exists to prevent the marriage. Usually, nothing is said. If either spouse then says after the ceremony that consent was not freely given, the evidence must be very strong for the marriage to be annulled. Lack of consent may result from either a mistake or duress.

Mistake

A **mistake** in marriage law refers to (1) mistaken identity of one of the parties, and (2) mistake as to the nature of the ceremony. Although mistaken identity is quite unusual, it might occur if the face of one party were covered for some reason, or when one identical twin takes the place of the other at the ceremony. Mistake as to the nature of the ceremony might occur when one of the parties does not speak the language used in the ceremony and genuinely believes that the ceremony is something other than marriage, such as an engagement ceremony. Being mistaken or deceived concerning other matters involving the marriage partner, such as wealth, religion, age, health, or personal habits, is not a valid reason for declaring a marriage void.

Duress

Duress occurs when one person marries another out of fear for his or her life, health, or freedom. It does not require the use of physical force. The most common example of duress related to marriage occurs when a pregnant girl's parents threaten to take legal action against the girl's partner if he does not marry their daughter. In any situation involving duress, the courts will annul the marriage if asked to do so by the party forced into the marriage.

Case

S. (A.) v. S. (A.)
(1988) 15 R.F.L. (3d) 443
Ontario Unified Family Court

The female applicant in this action was 16 years old when she was pressured into marriage by her mother and stepfather. The parents received $500 for arranging this marriage to enable the respondent, a visitor to Canada, to remain here.

When the young woman expressed unwillingness to marry, the parents applied even more pressure. No physical force was used to persuade her to enter into the marriage, and none was threatened.

The marriage was not consummated, and the applicant did not live with her husband after the marriage ceremony. The female applicant sought an annulment of her marriage in Hamilton's Unified Family Court, and her application was granted.

For Discussion

1. **On what grounds did the applicant seek an annulment?**
2. **Did the applicant willingly agree to the marriage? Explain.**
3. **Why do you think the annulment was granted?**

No Prior Marriages

In Canadian law, **monogamy** is the only accepted form of marriage; that is, a person can be married to only one spouse at a time. It is illegal for a person to enter into a second marriage while still married. A person who does so commits the crime of **bigamy,** which makes the second marriage illegal and void. A person convicted of bigamy can be sentenced to a maximum punishment of five years, although very few charges have been laid in recent years. Before a person can remarry legally, he or she must present a document showing that the earlier marriage ended by annulment, divorce, or the death of a spouse.

If a spouse disappears for a certain period of time, usually seven years, and no one knows his or her whereabouts, the surviving spouse can apply to the courts for a "presumption of death" certificate. Once presumption of death has been declared, the surviving spouse is free to marry again. In some situations, this seven-year limit can be reduced by the courts. This might occur after a plane crash, for example, where many victims' bodies cannot be found.

It is presumed that any person missing from the airplane has been killed. A victim's spouse is, therefore, usually free to remarry without waiting for seven years. Another option for a spouse whose partner has disappeared without a trace is to obtain a divorce in order to marry legally.

It is a difficult situation when a missing spouse, legally presumed dead, is still alive and returns home. This has occurred when people have been injured and suffered long periods of amnesia (loss of memory). The second marriage is then declared void by law. However, the courts do not consider that bigamy has occurred in these cases.

Sexual Capacity

A valid marriage also requires **consummation** of the marriage. The partners must be physically able to have sexual intercourse to consummate the marriage. If either party lacks sexual capacity—for example, if the man or woman is impotent—the marriage may be dissolved.

Impotence may arise from a physical problem or a psychological fear of sexual intercourse. It is the inability of one or both spouses to engage in sexual intercourse with each other. This lack of capacity must exist at the time of the marriage. If it develops afterward, it does not affect the validity of the marriage. Impotence should not be confused with **sterility,** the inability to have children. A sterile person can consummate the marriage.

Review Your Understanding (Pages 386 to 390)

1. **Identify the six essential requirements for a valid marriage.**
2. **What effect does the lack of one or more of the essential requirements have on a marriage?**
3. **What must a marrying couple have the mental capacity to understand?**
4. **Under common law, what are the minimum ages of marriage?**
5. **Whom can you not marry under the federal *Marriage (Prohibited Degrees) Act*?**
6. **What is genuine consent? In what two situations might consent to a marriage not be genuine?**
7. **What two types of mistakes might affect the validity of a marriage?**
8. **Define (a) monogamy and (b) bigamy. What effect does bigamy have on a second marriage?**
9. **Distinguish between impotence and sterility. Which affects the validity of a marriage?**

13.4 Formal Requirements of Marriage

Provincial and territorial governments have jurisdiction over the procedures involved in getting married. These include such formalities as
- issuing marriage licences
- designating who can perform the ceremony

- establishing the formalities for the marriage ceremony
- registering the marriage

These **formal requirements of marriage** are outlined in the Marriage Act of each province and territory. If any one of the requirements is not met at the time of marriage, the marriage could be made void. If spouses fulfill the essential requirements, marry in good faith, and live together, the courts may consider them legally married even if a formal requirement is lacking. Suppose, for instance, that a couple was married in good faith by a person they believed to be properly licensed to marry them, but later discovered that the person was not authorized to perform marriages. The couple would be considered legally married despite the lack of this formal requirement. This problem does not occur very often.

Marriage Licence or Banns

Provincial and territorial statutes require that any couple planning to marry must either obtain a marriage licence or have the **banns of marriage** read in their place of worship. (The reading of banns is an option only in Ontario, Manitoba, and Saskatchewan.) A marriage licence may be purchased for a fee at any city hall, civic centre, or township office. (In New Brunswick, a marriage licence is obtained through a provincial office.) A couple must wait no fewer than three days and no more than three months to one year (varying by jurisdiction) after obtaining a licence to get married. The cost of a licence varies from province to province.

Couples who regularly attend a place of worship may prefer to have their banns of marriage announced instead of, or as well as, buying a licence. In the announcement, the member of the clergy asks the congregation whether anyone is aware of any reason why the couple cannot legally marry. The banns are read at two or three successive weekly services, depending on the province. A couple must wait at least five days after the last banns are read before getting married. Banns may not be announced when either intended partner has been previously married. In this situation, a marriage licence must be purchased.

Marriage Ceremony

A marriage ceremony must be performed by someone with legal authority to conduct marriages. This can be a minister, priest, rabbi, or any other person registered to perform a religious ceremony; or a judge, justice of the peace,

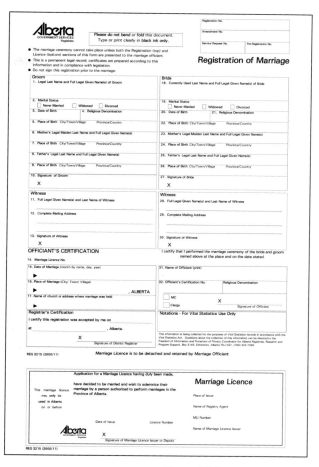

Figure 13-8

Copy of an Alberta marriage licence

 activity

Visit **www.law.nelson.com** and follow the links to learn more about the formal requirements for marriage, including the cost of a marriage licence in your province or territory.

Chapter 13 Marriage, Divorce, and Family Mediation

or marriage commissioner for a civil ceremony. The marriage must take place before at least two witnesses who sign (witness) the Certificate of Registration of Marriage.

The couple may marry wherever they wish and may have the ceremony conducted as they wish. They may even write their own ceremony, or portions of it, with the permission of the person officiating at the ceremony. However, the statutes require both parties to make a solemn declaration during the ceremony that they know of no legal reason why they cannot marry. Each must state that he or she takes the other to be his or her lawful wedded spouse, and the person conducting the ceremony must then pronounce them husband and wife.

Figure 13-9

Nick Skalkos and Sarah LeRiche were married at a Tim Hortons doughnut outlet by a minister of the Universal Life Church. Their rings were honey crullers, which they ate after the ceremony.

Case

Re Lin

(1992) 44 R.F.L. (3d) 60
Alberta Court of Queen's Bench

Shun Liang Lin, a Chinese resident, met Teresa Tang, a Canadian resident in China, and they agreed to marry in Canada. However, it was a condition of Lin's entry into Canada that he marry Tang within 90 days. About two weeks after arriving in Canada, the couple went through a traditional, non-religious Chinese wedding ceremony, presided over by the eldest member of the family, 76-year-old Pak Lun Lau. The couple did not apply for, or obtain, a marriage licence.

In a Chinese wedding ceremony, it is a tradition to honour the family members. The bride and groom are surrounded by family, while the eldest family member performs the ceremony. Mr. Lau was neither a member of the clergy or a marriage commissioner authorized to perform marriages.

After the ceremony, the couple lived together intermittently for two months, and it was unclear whether their marriage had been consummated. Lin brought an application to the Alberta Court of Queen's Bench for an order declaring the marriage to be valid and directing the Director of Vital Statistics to issue a marriage licence. However, Lin's application did not succeed.

For Discussion

1. Why was it so important for Lin to have this marriage declared valid?
2. Were the essential and formal requirements of this marriage met? Explain.
3. Does Lin's ignorance of Alberta marriage law affect this case? Why or why not?
4. Why did Lin's application not succeed?

Age Requirement

As you have already learned, the federal government has adopted the minimum ages for marriage from English common law: 14 years for males, 12 years for females. These ages were based on the fact that, generally speaking, females are more mature at 12 than males, and these were the ages at which males and females reached puberty. Although these minimum ages stand across Canada (except for Ontario) most provinces and territories have passed legislation modifying them.

As Figure 13-10 shows, a person must be at least 18 or 19 years old to marry. Between this age and 16, a teen must have written consent from one or both parents to marry. If parental consent is unreasonably withheld, the young person may apply for a court order dispensing with parental consent. The court's function is to review the parents' objections and to decide whether or not they are reasonable. However, case law in this area is very limited.

Below age 16, marriage is permitted by court order only, and only when the young woman is pregnant or has a child. In Ontario, however, no matter what the circumstances, no person under 16 may legally marry. In Quebec, males as young as 14 and females as young as 12 may marry with parental consent.

▌ Minimum Ages for Marriage in Canada

Province	Age without Parental Consent	Age with Parental Consent
Alberta	18	16
British Columbia	19	16
Manitoba	18	16
New Brunswick	19	16
Newfoundland & Labrador	19	16
Nova Scotia	19	16
Ontario	18	16
Prince Edward Island	18	16
Quebec	18	14 male 12 female
Saskatchewan	18	16

Figure 13-10

Why isn't there a common age to marry without parental consent all across Canada? Research the minimum age in Canada's three territories.

Case

Re Al-Smadi

(1994) 90 Man. R. (2d) 304
Manitoba Court of Queen's Bench

In 1993, a 14-year-old girl, Emman Al-Smadi, and her father, representing her because of her age, applied to the court for permission for her to marry a 27-year-old Jordanian student, Ra'a Ahmed Said. Both were of the same religious faith. At the time of the application, Said was a doctoral student in electrical engineering at the University of Manitoba, hoping to obtain his degree in 1994.

Evidence was presented to show that it is a belief of their faith that a girl, having reached puberty, may marry if she wishes, with her father's consent. Emman assumed a major role in cooking, cleaning, and caring for her younger sister as her parents were divorced, and custody of the two girls had

continued ▶

been awarded to her father. She also confirmed her consent to the proposed marriage and stated that she was doing so freely and of her own choosing. As well, her father consented to the proposed marriage. The Director of Child and Family Services opposed the application as it was not in the best interest of the child to marry under the age of 16 simply because of parental, cultural, or religious consent.

The Manitoba Court of Queen's Bench dismissed the application. However, several months later, a second application, on the same grounds as the first, was brought to court with the additional ground that the now 15-year-old girl was pregnant with Said's child. This time the court consented to the marriage.

For Discussion

1. **Why was it necessary to apply to the court for this couple to marry?**

2. **What concerns might the judge have had in considering this application?**

3. **In the initial trial judgment, the judge stated: "In Canada, the rights of all people are recognized and carefully protected. Nevertheless, certain basic values now exist that are the product of hundreds of years of development ... to protect all citizens. From time to time they may conflict with specific religious, moral, or cultural practices and beliefs ... and any such conflict must be resolved in favour of the general public interest." Do you agree or disagree with this statement? Explain.**

Name Change upon Marriage

It is not a legal requirement for the bride to adopt the groom's surname when they marry. It is simply a custom or tradition. A woman may assume her spouse's name, keep her own birth name, or combine her name and her husband's into a surname with or without a hyphen. Whichever choice she makes becomes her legal name. The latter two options are becoming very common. Many women feel that keeping their own surnames is an important indication of their identity as equal partners in marriage. As well, many women may have established professional careers and want to keep their birth name for business purposes. Men have similar options when they marry, but more women change their names than men. Procedures for doing this are outlined in provincial and territorial Change of Name Acts.

A child born to a married couple is usually given the husband's surname or the hyphenated names of both parents. An unmarried woman can choose between giving her child her own surname or the father's name if he grants permission or paternity is proven. However, since court challenges in the 1980s under section 15, the equality rights section of the *Canadian Charter of Rights and Freedoms,* a married woman in most provinces may now legally give her child her own surname if both parents consent. In the event of a dispute, a child will be given both names, hyphenated, in alphabetical order.

Same-Sex Marriages

Although the provinces are responsible for issuing marriage licences and deciding who can preside over weddings, the federal government has total control over the capacity to marry and who can marry whom. As you have learned, Parliament passed a resolution in 1999 reaffirming marriage as a voluntary union between a man and a woman. Yet, in recent years the media has given great attention to the issue of same-sex marriages.

Though same-sex couples can live together, adopt (in some provinces) or raise children, and qualify for spousal benefits such as health care and pensions, they still cannot legally marry anywhere in Canada. In other words, same-sex couples enjoy many of the legal rights enjoyed by heterosexual couples, except for the right to marry. As a result, some gay men and lesbians have turned to the courts to change what they see as a basic injustice. Since they have the same level of love and commitment as heterosexual couples, and since they are often already raising children, they feel that being denied the right to marry is a form of discrimination. It is, they believe, a violation of their equality rights under the *Canadian Charter of Rights and Freedoms.*

Did You Know?

As late as the 1960s, some U.S. states prohibited interracial marriage because it was thought to be unnatural. This is no longer the case. In your opinion, will same-sex marriages become legal in Canada? Why or why not?

Issues in Same-Sex Partnerships

Why are same-sex partners asking for the right to form legally recognized marriages? They want the same rights that heterosexual couples have, including
- the right to choose a marriage partner
- the right to visit their partner in hospital, even if the partner's blood family doesn't approve
- pension benefits and other spousal benefits such as company medical, dental, and drug plans
- income-tax deductions for the couple
- the right to inherit without a battle from the partner's blood family
- the right to custody of children by a former heterosexual marriage or former gay relationship
- the right to adopt children
- the term "spouse" as it appears in law to apply also to gay couples who have a legally recognized union

Figure 13-11

David McKinstry (left) and his partner Michael have adopted two children. They were married by clergy, but their marriage has no legal standing in Ontario.

Should Same-Sex Marriages Be Made Legal?

Figure 13-12

Judy Lightwater (left) and Cynthia Callahan of British Columbia applied for a marriage licence in 2000. Their application was put on hold while the court reviewed the ban on same-sex marriage.

Recent opinion polls show that Canadians are becoming more accepting of same-sex relationships. In 2001, a Leger Marketing opinion poll revealed that 75.7 percent of Canadians agreed that gay men and lesbians deserve the same rights as heterosexuals. But that same poll also showed that only 53.1 percent believed that gay men and lesbians should have the right to adopt children.

As you learned in Chapter 3, the Supreme Court of Canada ruled in the 1999 case of *M. v. H.* that laws in Ontario concerning couples living together without being married were discriminatory. It ordered the Ontario government to change its laws so that all heterosexual and same-sex couples are treated equally. In 2001, a Nova Scotia Supreme Court judge ruled that same-sex couples have the right to adopt children in that province.

However, one important legal right is still out of reach for gay men and lesbians living in Canada: the right to be legally married. No government in Canada recognizes same-sex marriages.

In Canada, the federal government controls marriage law for all the territories and provinces, except Quebec. But the provinces actually issue marriage licences and register the marriages. Section 5 of the Ontario *Marriage Act* makes same-sex marriages illegal. However, it also permits any two adult persons to marry provided they give notice of their intent to marry during a religious ceremony (reading of the banns). Recently, the Metropolitan Community Church of Toronto used the Christian tradition of publishing marriage banns to marry two same-sex couples: Kevin Bourassa and Joe Varnell, and Elaine and Anne Vantour (Anne Vantour legally changed her last name to that of her partner) on January 14, 2001. The Ontario government refused to register these marriages, resulting in the constitutional challenge described on page 398.

On One Side

Many Canadians believe that marriage is a sacred tradition uniting a man and a woman for the purpose of **procreation.** They believe that this family unit is in children's best interests and should be passed on to successive generations. They argue that same-sex marriage is an attack on time-honoured values and customs.

Furthermore, a relaxation of sexual values has already undermined marriage, evidenced by the high divorce rate. This group believes that recognizing common-law relationships and same-sex marriages as legal unions further weakens traditional family values.

The federal *Marriage Act* specifically states that a marriage is restricted to one man and one woman. Therefore, there can be no recognition of same-sex marriages. Critics of same-sex marriages applaud the House of Commons vote in 1999. By a vote of 216 to 55, members of Parliament approved the following: "[A] marriage is and should remain the union of one man and one woman, to the exclusion of all others."

On the Other Side

In 1967, Pierre Elliott Trudeau stated that governments should keep out of the "bedrooms of the nation." Relationships are private affairs and the government has no right to approve or disapprove of them. Marriage is a personal and private matter and a celebration of the relationship of two people regardless of their sexuality.

Figure 13-13 shows that 55 percent of Canadians support the legalization of same-sex marriages. Attitudes are changing, and some people believe for the law to be fair for everyone, the laws must also change. The *Canadian Charter of Rights and Freedoms* specifically states that persons cannot be discriminated against because of their gender. The Supreme Court of Canada has also ruled that individuals cannot be discriminated against because of their sexual orientation.

▌ Canadian Views of Same-Sex Marriages

Support Same-Sex Marriages	Percentage of Canadians
Strongly	29%
Somewhat	26%
Do not support	45%

Figure 13-13

This survey was conducted in April 2001 by Environics Research Group.

The Bottom Line

Strong arguments are presented by both sides in the debate about same-sex marriages. Arguments are presented to preserve important traditions by one side while the other stresses individual equality rights. Is it inevitable that same-sex marriages will become legal?

What Do You Think?

1. Why do you think legal rights for same-sex couples have become an issue only in recent years?

2. Is there a contradiction in the 2001 Leger Marketing opinion poll? Explain.

3. In 2000, Holland became the first country to recognize same-sex marriages as being legal. What effect do you think it will have on Canadian law? Explain.

You Be the JUDGE

"Ottawa is not discriminating against anyone by denying official marital status to same-sex couples. The federal government has come to court to defend the historic definition of marriage, that being an opposite-sex institution."

—Lawyer for the federal government, 1999

• Explain the significance of this comment.

You Be the JUDGE

In June 2001, Nova Scotia became the first Canadian province to register common-law and same-sex partnerships. The new legislation brings same-sex couples under matrimonial laws, but does not actually allow them to marry. Quebec introduced a similar bill in December 2001.

• Should the Nova Scotia legislation be adopted by other provinces? Why?

Recent Challenges to Marriage Law

After the Supreme Court of Canada's landmark judgment in *M. v. H.* in 1999, challenges to traditional marriage began (see pages 90, 448, and 477). Federal legislation passed in June 2000, which provided same-sex couples with benefits identical to those of heterosexual couples, also encouraged court challenges in this area.

In May 2000, two gay couples applied to a Toronto city clerk for marriage licences. Instead of refusing the applications, the clerk referred the issue to the Ontario Superior Court for a ruling. One year later, an action was launched by two Montreal men who had been together for 17 years; they were denied a marriage licence on the grounds that they did not have the capacity to marry under federal law. When licences were denied, these couples then had a reason to begin court actions claiming discrimination.

Eight same-sex couples launched an action in the British Columbia Supreme Court in July 2001. They, too, were challenging marriage law after being denied marriage licences. The couples stated that common law—now more than a century old—is outdated and must change with the times. In October 2001, the trial judge ruled that preventing same-sex couples the right to marry breaches equality rights under the *Canadian Charter of Rights and Freedoms;* however, this discrimination is justifiable under section 1 of the *Charter* as "the main purpose of marriage is to provide a societal structure for the raising of children in order to perpetuate [continue] Canadian society." The decision, not binding on other provinces, is the first time a Canadian judge has ruled that forbidding same-sex couples to marry is discrimination under the *Charter.* This decision is being appealed.

In November 2001, several Ontario same-sex couples launched a constitutional challenge, claiming that the government's refusal to register their marriages violates several provisions of the *Charter,* including equality rights, freedom of expression, freedom of conscience and religion, and freedom of association. As with the other cases discussed in this section, the Ontario government's position was that these couples did not have the capacity to marry under federal law.

Whatever the outcome of these challenges to marriage laws from the trial courts, there likely will be appeals to provincial appeal courts and, then finally, to the Supreme Court of Canada years from now. (See Issue, page 396.)

Countries that have granted legal status to same-sex couples include France, Denmark, Norway, Sweden, and Iceland. As of July 1, 2000, Vermont became the first U.S. state to allow gay civil unions. As you learned in Chapter 3, the Netherlands legalized same-sex marriages in April 2001, and Germany in August 2001. Italy, Israel, and Spain are considering similar legislation.

Review Your Understanding (Pages 390 to 398)

1. Identify the formal requirements for a valid marriage.
2. How does the lack of a formal requirement affect the validity of a marriage?
3. What is the purpose of having the banns of marriage read?
4. Describe the requirements for a valid marriage ceremony.
5. When is parental consent needed for a couple to marry?

6. Identify at least two reasons why many women keep their birth surname after marriage.

7. Identify five reasons why same-sex partners argue they have the right to marry.

8. On what grounds is the ban on same-sex marriages being challenged?

13.5 Annulment and Separation

Marriage is a legally binding contract between a man and a woman. If the spouses want to end their marriage, it must be dissolved by the courts through a legal procedure: an annulment or a divorce. The death of either spouse also terminates a marriage.

Annulment

An **annulment** is a court order stating that two spouses were never legally married. It allows them to void the marriage, ending the partnership without a divorce. Annulments are usually sought to end marriages that have lasted for a very short time.

Grounds for an annulment are very specific and arise from the requirements for a legal marriage. The cause for the annulment must have existed at the start of the marriage—in other words, it must be shown that the parties could not have married in the first place. For example, one of the essential requirements for entering a marriage contract might not have been met. Genuine consent might not have been given; for example, one spouse might have been too immature to understand what was being promised. Or there might have been a major defect in the marriage ceremony; for example, the officiator might not have had the authority to conduct marriages at all. For any of these reasons, the marriage would be declared void, and a judge would issue a **decree of nullity,** a court order declaring that a marriage never existed.

An annulment may also be granted when one spouse is unable to consummate the marriage. If, however, a spouse refuses to have sexual relations, though physically capable of doing so, an annulment will not be granted.

Occasionally, a couple marries to allow one of the parties to remain legally in Canada, and neither party really intends the marriage to last. When this happens, the courts will usually consider the marriage valid and will not annul it because of nonconsummation.

The Roman Catholic, Jewish, and Islamic faiths also dispense religious annulments, which allow a person to marry again within his or her faith. These annulments do not have legal standing, and anyone who obtains an annulment through a religious court must also obtain one through a civil court to remarry legally in Canada. By the same principle, a legal annulment does not satisfy the requirements established for the followers of these faiths.

Case

Aisaican v. Kahnapace

(1996) 24 R.F.L. (4th) 143
Saskatchewan Court of Queen's Bench

The applicant, Shelley Marie Aisaican, sought to annul her marriage on the ground that the respondent, Sheldon Kahnapace, was impotent and could not consummate the marriage. Two weeks prior to the marriage, Kahnapace was shot by unknown persons and left a quadriplegic. The couple did not engage in sexual intercourse at all after the marriage. No medical evidence was presented to suggest that quadriplegics are incapable of having sexual intercourse. The applicant's request for a decree of nullity was denied.

For Discussion

1. Should the fact that the applicant knew of her husband's condition at the time of the marriage matter? Why?
2. Should the fact that the respondent didn't oppose the application matter? Explain.
3. Why do you think the applicant's request was denied?

Case

Juretic v. Ruiz

(1999) 49 R.F.L. (4th) 299
British Columbia Court of Appeal

The plaintiff, Nedjelko Juretic, advertised for a bride in a Honduran newspaper. He was interested in finding a Spanish-speaking woman who wanted to marry and be a homemaker. The defendant, Brenda Ruiz, answered the advertisement.

In 1995, Juretic spent two weeks visiting Ruiz and her family. With her parents' approval, she returned with him to Vancouver on July 28, 1996, and moved into his apartment. They were married on October 5, 1996. He was 66; she was 23.

On two occasions following the marriage, the defendant wife said that her husband could have sex with her as long as "he did not embrace and touch her." Juretic said that sex under those circumstances would be like rape, and he gave up trying. The couple continued to sleep in the same bed until they separated on March 12, 1997. During their short marriage, they ate together, lived together, and represented themselves as a couple among their friends.

The plaintiff sought an annulment in the British Columbia Supreme Court, but his application was denied. His further appeal to the Court of Appeal was also denied.

For Discussion

1. On what grounds would the plaintiff base his application?
2. How valid was his application? Explain.
3. Why were Juretic's applications denied by both courts?
4. What would the plaintiff now have to do to end his marriage?

Separation

Separation is an intermediate step between marriage and divorce. It occurs when a couple decides not to live together as husband and wife; they "live separate and apart." Sometimes the parties go no further than this; they live out their lives separately, without getting divorced. This most often occurs when one or both spouses belong to a faith that does not recognize divorce.

The statutory phrase "living separate and apart" means that the spouses have separated physically and do not intend to live together again. Usually, one spouse moves out of the family home. But, a couple could still be separated while living under the same roof. If either spouse can prove that they slept separately, shared little or no communication, had no common activities, and lived independent lives, Canadian law considers that a valid separation exists. Unless they obtain a divorce, the couple is still legally married. A separation does not end a marriage.

Separation Agreement

Couples do not need a legal document to separate, but most enter into a written separation agreement. "Do-it-yourself" separation agreement forms and divorce kits can be obtained from book and office supply stores and the Internet. However, since this agreement is a legal contract that is written, signed, and witnessed, each spouse should ask a lawyer for help in preparing a separation agreement. It is important that each spouse consult his or her own lawyer so that each person's best interests are fairly and objectively represented. A separation agreement outlines the position of each spouse on such issues as the ownership and division of property and debts, who gets to stay in the family home or if it will be sold, support for either spouse and any children, and child custody and visitation rights. These issues are discussed in Chapters 14 and 15.

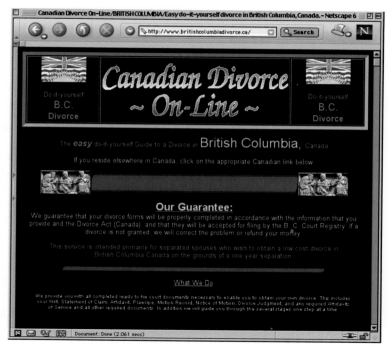

Figure 13-14

Do-it-yourself separation-and-divorce kits can be ordered over the Internet. These agreements are binding contracts when completed and signed.

Although the spouses determine the contents of the agreement, the lawyers will probably advise them. The contract must be prepared carefully, or the couple may insert terms or conditions that become unacceptable in the future. It is essential to include provisions that will allow sections of the document to be changed if either party's situation changes. The agreement must also be signed by both spouses in front of a witness. The witness's signature makes the agreement legally binding.

The courts are not involved in the preparation of a separation agreement. Once the lawyers have prepared the document with the approval of the spouses, it becomes as enforceable as any other private contract. Spouses should be allowed to determine their own affairs without interference from the legal system. Since a separation agreement is a legally binding contract, each party can sue the other party for a breach of contract. For instance, if one spouse agrees to pay a certain amount of support each month to the other, but does not do so, the spouse who suffered the loss may ask the courts to enforce payment. Contract law is discussed in Chapters 16 and 17.

A separation agreement does not give either party the right to remarry or to have sexual relations with another person. To remarry without a divorce is bigamy; to engage in voluntary sexual intercourse with another person outside the marriage is **adultery.**

Review Your Understanding (Pages 399 to 402)

1. **Identify three ways of ending a marriage.**
2. **What are an annulment and a decree of nullity?**
3. **Under what circumstances is an annulment obtained?**
4. **Why might some couples prefer to obtain an annulment rather than a divorce?**
5. **When does separation legally occur?**
6. **Identify three issues arising from the separation that are usually included in a separation agreement.**

13.6 Divorce

Divorce is the legal procedure that ends a valid marriage. You only need a divorce if you want to remarry. Otherwise, you could live forever, legally married, to someone from whom you are separated.

The procedures followed in a divorce case are similar to the civil procedures described in Chapter 11. The process begins with a document called a **petition for divorce,** outlining the grounds for the divorce and other essential information. The two parties involved in the action are the **petitioner,** the spouse seeking the divorce, and the **respondent,** the spouse being sued for divorce. If the divorce is based on the respondent's adultery, the **co-respondent** is the person with whom the respondent may have committed adultery.

Divorce actions are heard in the superior courts of each province, but about 90 percent of cases are settled before trial after many months of discussion and negotiation. There are self-help books and divorce kits readily available that outline the steps and procedures for a divorce. However, most people consult a lawyer if the divorce is likely to be at all complicated.

A divorce is final 31 days after judgment is pronounced. Either party may remarry after paying for a Certificate of Divorce from the court. This is the final step in the divorce. The purpose of the waiting period is to give the spouses one last opportunity to get back together. If this happens, the couple must apply to the courts to have the divorce judgment set aside. Another reason for the delay is to let either party appeal the judgment. If either spouse does so, the divorce is not final until the appeal has been heard. If both parties agree, and if there is a very good reason, the 31-day waiting period may be reduced. This may happen, for instance, if the woman is pregnant and wishes to remarry as soon as possible. However, the judge must be convinced of a special need before reducing the waiting period.

The *Constitution Act* gave the federal government jurisdiction over divorce. However, before 1968, there was no federal law concerning divorce. Divorce law varied somewhat from province to province, although most of Canada followed England's divorce laws. In Newfoundland and Quebec until 1968, a federal Act of Parliament (passage of a private statute) was necessary to get a divorce, and most divorces were granted for adultery. This posed a problem for people who sought a divorce because they were unhappily married.

As a result of changes in social attitudes toward divorce and the need for additional grounds for divorce, the federal government passed the *Divorce Act* in 1968. This statute established a divorce law that applied fully and equally for the first time in all parts of Canada. The Act provided two main grounds for divorce: matrimonial fault or blame and marriage breakdown. Within these categories, there were 15 specific grounds, including adultery, mental or physical cruelty, bigamy, homosexuality, addiction to alcohol or drugs, imprisonment, and desertion. In each case, the petitioner had to find fault with the respondent before petitioning for divorce. The 1968 *Divorce Act* also recognized a three-year separation or a permanent marriage breakdown as a new ground for divorce. This new ground made divorce more acceptable to those who previously were reluctant to petition for divorce on a fault ground.

The legislation also outlined procedures for trying to save the marriage. Both lawyers and judges were specifically required by the Act to discuss the possibility of **reconciliation** (getting back together) between the spouses. The courts had the authority to adjourn divorce proceedings where there seemed to be a possibility that the couple might get back together. Judges could even recommend marriage counselling if they felt that it would assist the couple.

Figure 13-15

Before 1968, this couple could not have obtained a divorce. What is the cartoonist saying about marriage in this cartoon?

As time passed, legal and other experts continued to criticize the grounds for divorce. Pitting spouses against each other and finding fault with one party created much pain and suffering during the divorce process. Also, when both spouses agreed that the marriage had broken down and could not be repaired, a three-year waiting period was too long and created unnecessary hardships on the couple. These issues led to the *Divorce Act, 1985*.

For Discussion

1. **Which level of government has jurisdiction over divorce?**
2. **What significant change did the 1968 *Divorce Act* bring to Canadian divorce law?**
3. **Why was it necessary to amend the 1968 *Divorce Act*?**

Barbour v. Barbour

(1980) 18 R.F.L. (2d) 80
Newfoundland Supreme Court, Trial Division

The Barbours were married in March 1973 in a tiny village in Newfoundland. There were two children from the marriage: a daughter born in 1974 and a son born in 1976. The couple separated in December 1978. The daughter lived with the father in the family home, and the son lived with the mother in her parents' home. Mrs. Barbour intended to petition for divorce in three years.

After the separation, Mr. Barbour was seen on many occasions in the company of another woman, Myrtle Sinclair. Mr. Barbour and Ms. Sinclair generally met in the family home or in the Horse Shoe Lounge, where Mrs. Barbour worked part-time. On several occasions, Mr. Barbour would hug and kiss his girlfriend in front of Mrs. Barbour. As well as being intimate in the lounge in front of his wife, Mr. Barbour and his girlfriend spent the night together in a motel. On a number of occasions, the girlfriend's car was seen in Mr. Barbour's driveway.

Mrs. Barbour petitioned for divorce before the end of the three-year period and she succeeded in her action.

For Discussion

1. **Why do you think Mrs. Barbour intended at first to wait three years before petitioning for divorce?**

2. **Based on the facts of the case, why was Mrs. Barbour successful in petitioning for divorce early?**

Before the 1968 *Divorce Act,* Canada's divorce rate was 8 percent. By 1987, the rate had jumped to 44 percent. Why do you think there was such an increase in the divorce rate?

The Divorce Act, 1985

The *Divorce Act, 1985,* was an attempt to simplify the law, streamline the many grounds for divorce, and respond to social change and pressure for reform. It came into effect on June 1, 1986. Under current divorce law, there is only one ground for divorce: **marriage breakdown.** This is the origin of the term **no-fault divorce,** which states that neither party is totally at fault or to blame for the divorce—the marriage has simply broken down. This occurs when one of the following conditions exists:

- The spouses have separated for at least one year and were living apart when the divorce petition was filed.
- The respondent has committed adultery.
- The respondent has treated his or her spouse with such serious physical or mental cruelty that it is impossible for them to continue to live together.

The Law   The Divorce Act, 1985

Excerpts from the *Divorce Act, 1985*

8.

(1) A court of competent jurisdiction may, on application by either or both spouses, grant a divorce to the spouse or spouses on the ground that there has been a breakdown of their marriage.

(2) Breakdown of a marriage is established only if

    (a) the spouses have lived separate and apart for at least one year immediately preceding the determination of the divorce proceeding and were living separate and apart at the commencement of the proceeding; or

    (b) the spouse against whom the divorce proceeding is brought has, since celebration of the marriage,

        (i) committed adultery, or

continued

For Discussion
1. Identify the one ground for divorce in Canada.
2. Summarize the circumstances under which marriage breakdown can occur.

Separation Leading to Divorce

Most couples now use separation of at least one year as proof of a marriage breakdown and the ground for divorce. The one year provides a balance between rushing into a divorce and requiring spouses who know their marriage is over to stay together longer. It does not matter which spouse left or why. Either spouse can begin divorce proceedings immediately upon separation, but the court will not grant the divorce until the year is up. The law also gives the couple the choice of applying to the court together for their divorce.

During the separation period, the *Divorce Act, 1985,* allows the couple to reconcile to try to save their marriage. However, they can reunite only for 90 days or less without affecting their one-year separation time. This can occur for one period of no more than 90 days, or on several occasions, provided the total number of days does not exceed 90 days. If the reconciliation does not work out within the 90 days, this time together does not affect the one-year period. If the couple stays together for more than 90 days, but then separates again, they begin counting another one-year separation period.

Did You Know?

According to the federal Department of Justice, over 90 percent of divorces in Canada are based on a one-year separation. Why do you think this is the most common ground?

Adultery

Adultery and cruelty have been grounds for divorce for many years. It is the petitioner's responsibility to prove that adultery actually occurred. The courts usually recognize that adultery took place on the basis of reasonable probability. For example, if the respondent and the co-respondent spend a weekend alone in a hotel room, the judge may assume that adultery occurred, unless the respondent can prove otherwise. It is adultery if sexual intercourse with someone else happens while a couple is separated.

Cruelty

Cruelty is of two types, physical and mental, and represents very serious conduct that makes living together impossible. Physical cruelty is often easier to prove than mental cruelty. Evidence in the form of medical reports and photographs of injuries can be entered by the injured spouse. Witnesses may also testify about the spouse's physical condition. In today's courts, physical violence by one spouse against the other is not tolerated.

Mental cruelty is more difficult to determine because certain kinds of conduct are open to interpretation. Which actions are so heartless or insensitive that they make living together impossible or intolerable? The daily arguments that arise in most marriages are not mental cruelty. Over the years, the courts have ruled that mental cruelty includes constant criticism, serious alcoholism, psychiatric disorders, and refusal to have sexual relations. The

ⓔ activity

Visit **www.law.nelson.com** and find out more about divorce proceedings in Canada.

definition of mental cruelty is very subjective and may differ from spouse to spouse and from judge to judge.

If one spouse has committed adultery or treated the other spouse with cruelty, the offended spouse can sue for divorce immediately. The offending spouse must wait for a one-year separation period. However, if you apply for a divorce on these grounds, your spouse may be more likely to oppose the application. This could lead to a longer and more expensive process.

Contested and Uncontested Divorces

As long as a marriage has broken down, either spouse may ask the court to grant a divorce. A judge won't refuse a divorce just because one spouse wants to stay married. If one spouse wants a divorce and the other spouse doesn't, the marriage has obviously broken down. If the spouses cannot agree on terms, such as custody of the children and support, this is a contested divorce. If this happens, the couple and their lawyers will need to work out these matters. As a result, the divorce may take longer to complete, but it will only delay, not stop, the divorce.

In Canada, most divorces are uncontested or resolved without having a trial before a judge. Usually, spouses have lawyers representing them, and the lawyers work out a fair and equitable agreement. Once an agreement has been reached, a judge will look it over. The judge wants to know that the arrangement is fair to both parties and especially to any children of the marriage.

If the spouses do not dispute any issues, such as property division, support, or custody, the *Divorce Act, 1985,* makes it possible to obtain a divorce without appearing in court. In this procedure, the lawyer can present the evidence to the court. A judge reads all this documentation, along with the petition for divorce. If the judge is satisfied with the evidence, the divorce will be granted. Today, nearly 90 percent of divorces are uncontested.

A divorce also affects such issues as custody of, and access to, children, and child and spousal support. However, the *Divorce Act* does not govern property matters, which fall under provincial jurisdiction. Property matters are covered by provincial statutes, such as Ontario's *Family Law Act,* British Columbia's *Family Relations Act,* and Alberta's *Matrimonial Property Act.* Often, property matters are brought to court with the petition for divorce and are heard together. Unlike a divorce, which is final once the certificate of divorce is issued, custody, access, and support are never final and may be changed by the courts. You will read more about custody and access in Chapters 14 and 15.

▮ Marriage and Divorce in Canada

Year	Marriages	Divorces
1990	187 737	78 463
1991	172 251	77 020
1992	164 573	79 034
1996	156 691	71 528
1997	153 306	67 408
1998	153 190	69 088

Figure 13-16

What trends do you see here? What is the relationship between marriages and divorces during these 6 years?

You Be the JUDGE

"The decline in divorce could be due to ... the increase in common-law unions and also the increase in the average age of marriage, which increases the chance of stability."

—Statistics Canada

• Do you agree or disagree with this statement? Explain.

Children and Divorce

Marriage breakdown can be very difficult, especially if children are caught in the crossfire of their parents' anger. Research indicates that children may be negatively affected by a divorce if parents use them to attack and wound each other. Children are often faced with losing one parent, spending less time with both parents attending to their needs, and adjusting to a lowered standard of living. Some may suffer depression, long-term behaviour problems, low self-esteem, poor school performance, and truancy.

A 1998 report, *For the Sake of the Children,* prepared for the federal justice department, recommended changes to the *Divorce Act, 1985,* that would make divorce easier on children. A key suggestion, if adopted, would allow both divorcing parents the automatic legal right to be involved in all aspects of their children's upbringing. In theory, this concept of shared parenting could eliminate, or greatly reduce, confrontation between divorced parents and give children proper access to both parents. Parenting plans would establish who is going to pick up the child and take him or her to the doctor or to school, or even to activities such as a sports practice or music lessons. In short, these plans divide up parental responsibilities to provide the best possible arrangements for the children.

Some provinces also offer courses to help divorced parents raise well-adjusted children. In Alberta, a government course called Parenting After Separation has been compulsory for divorcing parents since 1996. In addition, the Canadian Bar Association has recommended that parents be required to take parental education courses. Most major Canadian cities already have these courses, but they differ widely in scope and content. Also, most are voluntary, not compulsory.

For the Sake of the Children also recommends more public education programs, better child-counselling services, and more mediation services. Another recommendation is a change in language. Many divorcing parents are bothered by terms such as "custody" and "access," which seem to suggest a winner and a loser parent. Instead, "shared parenting" and "parental responsibilities" are suggested as terms that focus more appropriately on the children.

Possibly the report's most important recommendation, and one supported by the Canadian Bar Association, is the enhancement of Unified Family Courts across Canada. Divorcing parents should be able to access this court system to obtain a variety of services, including legal advice, counselling, and parent education. Federal and provincial Justice Ministers are studying these recommendations, and changes to the *Divorce Act* are expected in 2002.

You Be the JUDGE

In August 2001, Virginia joined other U.S. states such as Connecticut, Florida, Massachusetts, and Utah in requiring divorcing parents to take a course on understanding divorce from a child's viewpoint.

- Should such courses be compulsory all across Canada? Discuss.

Agents of Change — Ontario's Unified Family Court System

Until the late 1970s, family law matters in Canada were heard in many courts. In Ontario, for example, family law disputes were divided between the Ontario Court of Justice and the Superior Court of Justice. Divorce and division of family property were heard in the Superior Court, while child protection and adoption cases began in the Ontario Court of Justice. Each of these two courts had control over child and spousal support, as well as custody and access claims. This system was confusing and expensive for separating or divorcing families.

In July 1977, the first Unified Family Court (UFC) of Hamilton–Wentworth opened as a three-year pilot project. The UFC approach to family law was straightforward. Now one court would deal with all aspects of family law. The cost and confusion associated with

continued ▶

settling family disputes would be reduced and children would be better served. This more user-friendly court became permanent in 1982.

The concept of the UFC was created as a result of a joint initiative by the federal and provincial governments to help divorcing families solve their disputes peacefully and to help parents make informed decisions in the best interests of their children. Chief Justice Patrick LeSage of the Superior Court of Justice has called UFC "a model for early intervention and quick resolution of the difficult and emotional issues affecting people involved in family crisis."

In late 1999, the Ontario government added even more courts. Since 1995, the number of Ontario UFCs has tripled. Today, there are 17 UFCs in many jurisdictions in Ontario dealing with all aspects of family law and hearing all family law cases involving

- divorce
- child and spousal support
- custody of, and access to, children
- division of family property
- adoption
- child protection

In early 1998, the federal Justice Minister provided support and funding for expanding UFCs into Saskatchewan, Nova Scotia, and Newfoundland. This brought UFCs to half the residents of Ontario and Newfoundland, most of Saskatchewan, and portions of Nova Scotia. Other provinces are considering the benefits of Unified Family Courts.

Figure 13-17

Former Justice Minister Anne McLellan worked to expand the Unified Family Court system. She noted: "Having a single place where family members can find judicial and other services to help them resolve all legal issues is an excellent way of helping families, especially children."

For Discussion

1. **Identify the main benefit of a Unified Family Court.**
2. **The Canadian Bar Association is recommending the expansion of UFCs across Canada. Do you think this is a good recommendation? Why?**

Review Your Understanding (Pages 402 to 408)

1. What are the legal names for the parties involved in a divorce action?
2. When can a person remarry after being granted a divorce?
3. When was Canada's first *Divorce Act* passed? What were its two main grounds?
4. What were the two main reasons for amending Canada's first *Divorce Act*?
5. What is the only valid ground for divorce under the *Divorce Act, 1985*? Identify the three ways this can be proven.
6. What is an uncontested divorce, and how common is it?
7. In a contested divorce, what are some of the key issues?
8. What are the benefits of a Unified Family Court?

13.7 Family Mediation

The *Divorce Act, 1985,* established reconciliation as an important objective for couples experiencing a marriage breakdown. It includes a section that encourages **family mediation** to resolve issues that cause conflict between the spouses. In Canada, family mediation is firmly established because it reduces the emotional and economic costs to the partners and is certainly preferable to litigation.

In 1984, Canada established a national organization, Family Mediation Canada, and divorce mediation is now available everywhere in Canada. This growth in family mediation is part of a new approach to handling disputes over a marriage breakdown outside of the traditional court setting.

The Law — The Divorce Act, 1985

Excerpts from the *Divorce Act, 1985*

9.

(1) It is the duty of every barrister, solicitor, lawyer or advocate who undertakes to act on behalf of a spouse in a divorce proceeding

  (a) to draw to the attention of the spouse the provisions of this Act that have as their object the reconciliation of spouses, ...

(2) It is the duty of every ... lawyer ... to discuss with the spouse the advisability of negotiating the matters that may be the subject of a support order or a custody order and to inform the spouse of the mediation facilities known to him or her that might be able to assist the spouses in negotiating those matters.

(3) Every document presented to a court ... that formally commences a divorce proceeding shall contain a statement ... certifying that he or she has complied with this section.

For Discussion

1. Summarize the obligations of a family lawyer who acts on behalf of a spouse in a divorce proceeding.

2. Why do you think the availability of mediation is suggested when support or custody is at issue?

Family mediation is a voluntary conflict-resolution process. The spouses meet (usually without their lawyers) with a trained mediator to resolve family disputes once they have decided to divorce. Some level of reasonable and positive communication between the spouses is necessary for mediation to succeed. Mediators are usually social workers, psychologists, lawyers, or other trained personnel. Their expertise allows them to help the couple negotiate mutually satisfactory solutions in the following areas:
- if, how, and when to separate
- spousal support
- child support
- custody of, and access to, the children
- resolving disputes between parents and children about school work, curfews, rules, and so on
- division of property

The family mediator
- provides a safe and supportive setting for the spouses and their family
- identifies and clarifies the issues to be resolved

You Be the JUDGE

"When a marriage ends, mothers and fathers remain parents to their children."

- Identify some of the implications of this statement.

- ensures that each spouse freely communicates his or her needs to the other to allow for a fair and informed basis for the negotiations
- assists the couple to identify their needs and reach decisions that are satisfactory to all and in the best interests of the entire family, and especially the children
- facilitates positive communication and problem solving
- refers clients to appropriate information for effective decision making
- ensures that discussions are respectful and non-threatening
- acts in an unbiased, neutral manner to help reach a positive agreement
- does not give legal advice

The couple meets several times with the mediator. Usually about six to eight sessions are necessary, depending on the number and complexity of the issues. There is an hourly fee for mediation sessions, and costs are shared between the participants. In most provinces, the couple pays from $5 to $100 an hour, depending on family income. Successful mediation requires the cooperation of both spouses. In most cases, it is still a good idea to consult with lawyers throughout the mediation process to protect the interests of all family members. Lawyers are also needed after mediation to review the legal aspects of the agreement and to present it in court.

Family mediation is encouraged by governments and the courts. Its benefits are as follows:

- It is a voluntary process.
- It keeps decision making with those who know the children best: their parents.
- It promotes cooperation and compromise, not competition. It reduces hostility and conflict between the parties.
- It provides results that can be mutually satisfying to all parties in the dispute. They are more likely to honour personal commitments rather than imposed solutions.
- It helps protect family relationships by hopefully improving communication and reducing conflict between the parents.
- It may improve parenting because the parents and their children need to reach mutually agreeable decisions.
- It is a confidential process. Information learned in mediation cannot be used in other court proceedings, unless the parties agree otherwise.
- It is cost-effective and is much less costly than litigation. In turn, this leaves more money for the children and their parents.

However, mediation is not appropriate for every couple, especially if there is a history of violence or abuse between the partners. Also, mediation may not work when one partner is intimidated by the other partner.

Review Your Understanding (Pages 409 to 410)

1. What is family mediation? Why is it so firmly established in Canada?
2. What groups of professionals often become mediators?
3. Identify five areas of family law in which mediation may be helpful.
4. Who pays for family mediation?
5. Identify five benefits of family mediation.
6. When might mediation not be appropriate?

In Family Law

Careers in family counselling, social work, and mediation can be both rewarding and exhausting. People entering these fields should be non-judgmental and have the ability to empathize and establish rapport with people of all ages. They should enjoy the challenge of negotiating or mediating situations in which emotions run high.

(e) Visit www.law.nelson.com and follow the links to find out about the course requirements for a Bachelor of Social Work degree at a major university.

Figure 13-18
Social worker

Figure 13-19
Marriage counsellor

In Focus

Social Worker

Social workers assist people who are having difficulty functioning well in society. They interview clients to understand their problems and to determine the types of services they require. As a social worker, you would interact closely with individuals, families, or groups. Your clients could include the elderly or people with mental and physical disabilities.

Social workers help clients build skills to overcome their problems. They work with community agencies to arrange for financial assistance, housing, medical treatment, or legal aid. They also investigate alleged cases of child abuse or neglect and take children into protective custody, if necessary.

Family or Marriage Counsellor

These counsellors help clients overcome personal problems affecting a relationship with a spouse or family member. They may provide therapy to just one person or to the other family members, if required. Through therapy, clients identify their problems and explore possible solutions to problems. They learn about their family dynamics, and how certain behaviours can cause a family to break apart.

Mediator

Mediators in divorce proceedings are skilled individuals who draw on a background of psychology, counselling, and possibly social work. They work with divorcing couples to help them arrive at mutually satisfying solutions for their divorce. They act as a neutral third party to help the couple agree on division of property, spousal and child support, and matters of custody and access if there are children. They foster cooperation and ensure that the legal rights of all parties affected by the divorce are protected.

Career Exploration Activity

As a class, explore career opportunities in family counselling, social work, and mediation. The information you compile can be used to profile the various law-related careers for a guidance bulletin-board display, or you may choose to run a law-related career fair.

1. Briefly outline the role and responsibilities of a social worker, a family or marriage counsellor, and a mediator.
2. For extended research, interview someone who works in the family counselling, social work, or mediation field. Outline which aspects of his or her work are most rewarding, and which are more demanding and frustrating. Share your information with the class.

Chapter Highlights

- Family law deals with such concerns as marriage and divorce, marriage procedures, spousal and child support, adoption, and division of property upon marriage breakdown.

- The federal government has control over marriage and divorce, while the provincial and territorial governments have control over marriage procedures.

- Families today come in many different forms: married couples with and without children, blended families, single-parent families, common-law couples with or without children, and same-sex partner relationships.

- The essential requirements for marriage deal with a person's capacity, or ability, to marry.

- The federal *Marriage (Prohibited Degrees) Act,* 1990, lists persons who may not marry because they are too closely related by blood or adoption.

- Since marriage is a contract, the parties must freely and willingly consent to the union.

- Parliament passed a resolution in 1999 stating that marriage is a union between a man and a woman to the exclusion of all others.

- The formal requirements for marriage deal with the procedures of the marriage ceremony.

- With few exceptions, no one under the age of 16 may marry in Canada.

- Same-sex partners are asking for the right to form legally recognized marriages.

- An annulment is a court order stating that two persons were never legally married and allows them to end a partnership without divorce.

- Separation is a middle step between marriage and divorce; the couple lives separate and apart.

- Separation agreements deal with ownership and division of property, spousal and child support, and child custody and visitation rights.

- Divorce is the legal procedure that ends a valid marriage. The petitioner begins the divorce action against the respondent.

- In Canada today, the only ground for divorce is marriage breakdown, evidenced by a one-year separation, adultery, or mental or physical cruelty.

- Over 90 percent of divorces are uncontested and are granted on the basis of a one-year separation.

- Family mediation is a new approach to handling disputes over a marriage breakdown outside of the traditional court setting.

- Some level of reasonable and positive communication between the spouses is necessary for mediation to succeed.

Review Key Terms

Name the key terms that are described below.

a) a court order declaring that a marriage never existed

b) relationship by blood

c) spouse who begins a divorce action

d) being married to only one spouse at a time

e) relationship by marriage

f) validation of a marriage by sexual intercourse between spouses

g) being married to two persons at the same time

h) inability to consummate the marriage and a ground for annulment

i) voluntary sexual intercourse by a married person with someone other than his or her spouse

j) only valid ground for a divorce in Canada

k) the ability to understand the nature and effect of one's acts, such as marriage

l) has no legal standing

m) a family with a mother, father, and their children

n) a court order stating that two spouses were never legally married

o) the person being sued for divorce

p) spouses getting back together, salvaging the marriage

Check Your Knowledge

1. Identify the essential and formal requirements of a valid marriage.

2. Distinguish between an annulment and a separation.

3. Identify the three specific ways to show marriage breakdown has occurred.

4. Outline the purpose and benefits of family mediation.

Apply Your Learning

5. Louise Vandervliet and Robert Brisebois had been dating for one year and planned to marry. During their engagement, Robert assumed, from comments made by Louise, that she came from a wealthy family and that her mother was chief executive officer of a large national corporation. A week after the marriage, Robert realized that none of this was true. Was their marriage invalid? Why or why not?

6. Sam Bukowski and Bill Stahoviak rented a small plane to fly to northern British Columbia for a hunting trip. The plane crashed in a sudden storm. Sam's body was found by searchers the next day, but even after two separate searches, Bill's body was never located. When will Bill's widow be able to remarry? What court process would be required?

7. *Norman v. Norman* (1979), 9 R.F.L. (2d) 345 (Ontario Unified Family Court)

   The parties in this action were married in April 1978, when Mrs. Norman was 63 years of age and Mr. Norman was 64 years of age. Both had been previously married, but their spouses had died. During their six months of courtship, they were good companions. They did not engage in sexual relations. When the couple married, their prime reason was companionship. In fact, Mrs. Norman testified that sexual intercourse was not an important part of the marriage from her viewpoint. During their marriage, the couple never had sexual intercourse with each other. After a serious argument, the parties separated in late August 1978. Mrs. Norman sought an order declaring the marriage void. Her application was dismissed.
   a) On what grounds did Mrs. Norman base her claim?
   b) Was this a valid reason? Why?
   c) Why do you think her application was dismissed?

8. *Khan v. Mansour* (1989), 22 R.F.L. (3d) 370 (Ontario Unified Family Court)

   In January 1989, Sophia Khan, aged 23, entered into a marriage ceremony with the respondent, Mansour. After the ceremony, the wife returned to her parents' home, and her husband returned to his own residence. This was not unusual as members of the Islamic faith usually allow the husband four months following the ceremony to set up a home under the families' supervision. Then, the couple would begin living together as a married couple. However, at the end of the four months, Mansour told his wife that he had no intention of living with her as he had no feelings for her. Khan applied for an annulment of the marriage.
   a) On what ground did the petitioner base her application?
   b) What conditions must exist for this application to succeed?
   c) Based on the facts, do you think Khan's application for an annulment succeeded? Why?

9. *Bailey v. Bailey* (1994), 119 Sask. R. 71 (Saskatchewan Court of Queen's Bench)

   The parties in this action, Gail Christine Bailey and Ted Harold Bailey, had been married for several years and lived in the same house. However, as time passed, they ate in separate rooms, although their meals were prepared together. They travelled together to social events, but they did not have sexual relations. In late 1993, Ted moved out, and the parties lived in separate accommodations for about three months. In February 1994, Gail sought a divorce.
   a) Who was the petitioner, and who was the respondent in this action?
   b) On what ground was the divorce petition based?
   c) Was this ground valid? Explain.
   d) Do you think the court granted the petitioner a divorce? Why or why not?

Communicate Your Understanding

10. Using the Internet, research various legal requirements and marriage customs from countries around the world, and prepare a report to share with the class. If possible, obtain visuals to illustrate your report, or prepare a bulletin-board display. In an organizer, compare and contrast these requirements and customs to those of a Canadian marriage.

11. Who should determine the age at which a person can marry—the person, his or her parents, statute law, the courts, or another party? In groups of four, examine this issue and prepare arguments for and against each option. As a group, reach consensus and compare your conclusion with that of other groups.

12. With a partner, discuss the financial, social, and emotional issues of getting married. Make a list of the positive and negative factors involved. Try to reach consensus or agreement on the issues.

13. Many people believe that the state has no business trying to persuade a couple to attempt reconciliation if they want to divorce and that the *Divorce Act* should not require lawyers to recommend reconciliation. With a partner, prepare arguments for and against this principle of reconciliation.

14. Debate one of the following topics. Prepare a brief introduction; identify facts and arguments that support your stance; anticipate points against your view and prepare counterarguments to defend your viewpoint; and conclude with a statement that summarizes your position.
    - All couples planning to marry must take a life-skills and family planning course.
    - Women who marry should assume their husband's surname.
    - Divorce in Canada is much too easy to obtain.

Develop Your Thinking

15. Why is marriage considered a legally binding contract? Should it be? Why or why not?

16. Should a marriage entered into in Ontario between two persons aged 15 be valid if the teens somehow managed to obtain a marriage licence and persuade an authorized person to perform the ceremony? Support your opinion.

17. Assume the role of a family mediator listening to a divorcing couple with two children, aged 7 and 12. What concerns or issues related to the children would you expect the couple to have? Identify these items, and then compare your list with that of a partner. As a mediator, how would you conduct yourself in a family mediation session in order to facilitate communication between the parties?

Children and Family Law

Focus Questions

- How are federal and provincial powers divided in the area of children and the law?
- What are the main factors considered in determining custody and access?
- Why are custody and access orders never permanent?
- What is joint custody or shared parenting?
- What are the factors involved in determining parental obligations for child support?
- What can the state do to enforce child support payments?
- What are the most common forms of child abuse?
- What are the two main types of adoption in Canada?

Chapter at a Glance

Figure 14-1

Children are dramatically affected by family law and, for the most part, parents have the right to raise their children as they see fit. What kinds of situations warrant legal intervention in family life? What kinds of situations might be resolved through assistance, not intervention?

14.1 Introduction

Today's Canadian children have their own rights and freedoms. They also have responsibilities, and they can both sue and be sued. Except for federal law dealing with youth crime, and some *Criminal Code* protection from assault, abuse, or being denied the necessities of life, most laws concerning children are provincial.

The courts determine the fate of children when their parents separate or divorce. Courts also help to determine the parents' joint obligations to support their children's basic needs. Courts can remove children from a home if they are being neglected or abused. In some cases, the courts arrange adoptions. Children can also be brought before the courts in both civil matters and criminal matters. In all cases, the courts consider the best interests of the child. This chapter will discuss the role of the courts in administering the relationship between children and their family.

Looking Back Changing Directions in Child Welfare

Figure 14-2

These children toiled in Britain's coal mines during the Industrial Revolution (about 1750–1850). In the past, children had few rights and were generally treated as slave labour. Their situation improved toward the end of the 19th century.

Laws dealing with child–parent relationships were revolutionized during the 20th century. For many years, English common law regarded children as property belonging to the father. This was a carryover from Roman law, where a father (or the oldest male relative) had the power of life and death over his children. This included the right to sell the children into slavery or even put them to death. No thought was given to the children's welfare. Although some provision was made for the care and protection of orphans, there was little legislation to protect children living with their family. There was no law, as there is today, to punish parents who beat their children.

In England, during the 1800s, children of poor families worked long hours under the worst conditions in factories and mines for very little pay. Serious illness and death were common because of the poor working conditions. Though conditions in Canada were never as bad as in England, there was greater protection for animals than for children. Legislation regarding cruelty to animals was first passed around 1825. By contrast, the first legislation in Canada to protect children was passed by the Ontario government in 1893. Young children worked in factories and mines and on farms, and child abuse and neglect were common.

By the end of the 19th century, concern was mounting for the welfare of children. This concern was reflected in compulsory education for children, the gradual disappearance of inhumane working conditions, and the establishment of juvenile courts. In Ontario, the *Act for the Prevention of Cruelty to and Better Protection of Children* (1893) created Canada's first Children's Aid Societies. It gave courts the right to intervene in the fate of neglected children and marked the first time in Canada that the state became actively involved in the protection of children. Manitoba passed similar legislation in 1898, and the other provinces followed. As the 20th century began, courts dealing with family separation started to emphasize the value of children, especially young ones, growing up in their mother's care. By the middle of the century, provincially regulated child protection agencies operated across Canada.

continued ▶

In the early 1960s, doctors became aware of the "battered baby" issue and recognized the problem of physical child abuse. The result was passage of the first child-abuse legislation, in the mid-1960s. In the late 1970s, society became conscious of the extent and effects of sexual abuse. Before then, victims of sexual abuse were often too frightened or felt too guilty to disclose their abuse. With the release of the *Badgley Report on Sexual Offences Against Children* in 1984, it was evident that child sexual abuse was greatly unreported in Canada. The result was a massive increase in the reporting of childhood sexual abuse in the 1980s and 1990s and in criminal trials.

In the late 1990s, attention in Canada was focused on child-abuse deaths. Most Canadians were concerned about the inability of the system to protect abused children. In 1995 in British Columbia, Family Court Judge Tom Gove held a public inquiry into the tragic death of five-year-old Matthew Vaudreuil. The child had been tortured and starved before his mother killed him by putting her hand over the boy's mouth and nose to stop him from yelling. The *Gove Report* resulted in new legislation in that province and the creation of a new Ministry for Children and Families. In April 2001, after 63 days of hearings, an Ontario coroner's inquest produced more recommendations for detecting children in need. The case in question involved a young mother, Renée Heikamp, whose five-week-old son, Baby Jordan, literally starved to death in downtown Toronto, weighing less at death than at birth.

For Discussion

1. **How has child-protection legislation changed during the past 100 years?**
2. **What major changes occurred around the beginning of the 20th century?**
3. **Describe the trends in child-welfare concerns in the 1990s.**

14.2 Custody

Every year in Canada, couples separate or divorce. If children are involved, a judge may have to make a decision about **custody** (which parent the children of the marriage will live with) and **access** (which parent will be given visitation rights). Although parents are ending their relationship, they are not ending their relationship with their children; they remain mother and father. Custody and access disputes are the part of family law that affects children most directly. These disputes are among the most difficult for courts to resolve.

Sometimes, both parents want custody of the children. Each parent has equal custody rights to children born of their relationship until there is a contrary order. In determining custody and access, courts must determine what is in the **best interests of the child.** Parliament has adopted "the best interests of the child" principle as the *only* test on which custody and access disputes are to be resolved (see The Law, page 418). What a particular parent wants or a parent's conduct is not a factor, unless violence or abuse has occurred.

This principle requires the courts to consider the emotional, intellectual, physical, and moral well-being of the child. Over time, judges have taken the following factors, among others, into account when deciding on the best interests of the child:

- the home environment
- the parent–child relationships and bonding
- the parenting abilities of each parent
- the emotional, mental, and physical health of each parent
- the support available from relatives, grandparents, neighbours, and friends
- the parents' and child's schedules

Excerpts from the *Divorce Act, 1985*

16.

(8) In making an order under this section, the court shall take into consideration only the best interests of the child of the marriage as determined by reference to the condition, means, needs, and other circumstances of the child....

(10) In making an order under this section, the court shall give effect to the principle that a child of the marriage should have as much con-tact with each spouse as is consistent with the best interests of the child....

For Discussion

1. Why is the "best interests of the child" the only test to consider in determining custody?

2. Should the *Divorce Act* have included guide-lines to assist judges in custody decisions? Why?

- the belief that keeping siblings together as often as possible is a good thing
- the child's wishes

More children live in single-parent families than ever before. In fact, the single-parent family is now the fastest growing lifestyle in North America. In Canada, women now head 83 percent of single-parent families.

▌ Marital Status of Single-Parent Mothers

Year	Divorced	Separated	Never married	Widowed
1951	3.1%	28.9%	1.5%	66.5%
1991	32.5%	24.6%	19.5%	23.4%
1996	34.0%	21.0%	24.0%	21.0%

Figure 14-3

What trends can be observed from these statistics? What is the most surprising information? Explain.

Did You Know?

Mothers are more than five times as likely as fathers to obtain sole custody. Joint custody is awarded to about one in four couples. About 2 percent of the time, custody is awarded to a non-parent (such as a grandparent or other relative) who is close to the child.

Because male and female roles are changing, the courts can no longer rely on tradition to assist them in determining custody. As mothers enter the work force, and fathers assume some of the home management respon-sibilities, the courts have realized that the traditional reason for giving the mother custody has disappeared. Proof that society's attitude on this sub-ject has changed is seen in the increasing number of fathers awarded cus-tody of their children.

Many courts offer parent-education sessions that present options for resolving custody disputes. The sessions also discuss the impact of separa-tion and divorce on the children. Children of any age can react strongly to divorce and may display their anxiety in different ways. Whenever possible, parents should try to reach an agreement that is acceptable to themselves and to their children. Family mediation often plays a major role in helping parents reach such an agreement (see Chapter 13). Usually, courts will not interfere with an agreement made by the parents about custody and access. Asking the court to resolve custody is often expensive, unpredictable, and very emotional for all involved, especially the children.

H. (J.) v. B. (W.)

(1999) 49 R.F.L. (4th) 263
Ontario Superior Court of Justice

For 29 years, J.H. and A.H. lived in a common-law relationship. J.H. had already raised three children and was 56. A.H. was an active 72-year-old. He snowplowed, cut wood, and had the time and energy to care for a grandson, R., who was born in February 1997 to parents J.T.-B. and W.B. (B), who was J.H.'s son.

Following the child's birth, the Children's Aid Society (CAS) visited the parents' home as a result of concerns expressed by a public-health nurse and the family's doctor. In July 1997, when it became apparent that J.T.-B. would need to be hospitalized because of her schizophrenia, B. asked his mother to care for the baby, and the grandmother was given interim custody. After the baby had been with J.H. and A.H. for three months, he was returned to his parents on a trial basis. But, after a five-day stay, he was returned to the grandparents (J.H. and A.H.) because a CAS worker noticed a hairline fracture in his arm. CAS was concerned and gave the parents a choice—a foster home or J.H. (with A.H.). The parents chose J.H.

A family feud developed. The grandparents initially took the child to help the new parents. Unfortunately, the grandparents lived some distance from the baby's parents, and the parents did not have a vehicle. They did, however, live close to the mother's family, whose members began to think that J.H. and A.H. were plotting to seize control of the baby.

J.H. applied for **sole custody** with generous access to the parents. The parents also sought sole custody. Failing that, the parents wanted custody to go to J.T.-B.'s sister, not J.H. The court ruled in J.H.'s favour, with supervised access granted to the parents.

For Discussion

1. **Should the grandparents' ages be a major factor to consider in this action? Explain.**

2. **Do you think the grandparents' actions were a plot to seize control of the baby? Explain.**

3. **Why do you think the judge ruled in favour of the grandparents?**

Factors Determining Custody

All the provinces and territories have statutes governing custody. Alberta's *Domestic Relations Act,* British Columbia's *Family Relations Act,* and Ontario's *Children's Law Reform Act,* for example, govern custody and access applications processed under provincial or territorial law. Other provincial or territorial statutes contain the same principles. The *Divorce Act, 1985,* governs such applications under federal law.

Stability of Home Environment

The stability of a child's home environment is probably the most important factor to consider when determining custody. An abrupt move from one home to another may cause children a great deal of stress, especially since they are also experiencing the emotional stress of the separation or divorce. The parent who has **interim** (temporary) **custody** during the separation often gets permanent custody of the children after the divorce. Courts seldom change children's home environments if they have a stable and steady routine with one parent. Interim custody remains in effect until the spouses reach a final custody agreement or the issue is resolved in court.

Figure 14-4

The parent who was the child's primary caregiver before the separation is usually awarded custody of the child. Often, the primary caregiver is the mother, but fathers have also been awarded custody. The stability of the child's home life with the custodial parent is the critical factor.

Judges often decide that it is in the best interests of the children to award interim custody to the parent who was the **primary caregiver** for the children prior to the separation. This is the parent who was responsible for most of the child-care jobs, such as

- attending to the children's educational, cultural, religious, and social development
- taking the children to medical appointments
- planning and preparing the children's meals
- buying, cleaning, and caring for the children's clothing
- interacting with the children after school

Shuffling children back and forth between contesting parents is never recommended by the court. Neither is changing a satisfactory custody arrangement. The parent who assumes responsibility for the children at separation is usually awarded final custody. The children are settled into that home. Courts are reluctant to disturb children who are settled and doing well because it is not in their best interests. The parent with interim or temporary custody, therefore, has an advantage when the court rules on final custody.

You Be the JUDGE

There is an old saying that "possession is nine-tenths of the law."

- What does this mean? How does it apply to the awarding of custody?

Case

Levine v. McGrath

(2001) 11 R.F.L. (5th) 337
Ontario Superior Court of Justice

The applicant father, Mr. Levine, and the respondent mother, Ms. McGrath, lived in London with their two daughters, Amy, aged 13, and Sarah, aged 10. The mother changed jobs and moved to Toronto with the girls so that Amy could receive athletic coaching in synchronized swimming, estimated to involve 25 to 30 hours a week. Although the mother initiated the idea, both parents agreed

continued ▶

that Amy ought to move to pursue her athletic career. The father tried to be accommodating and flexible, but his primary concern related to Sarah's wishes. He believed if she wanted to stay in London, she should be able to do so. Sarah felt that she could turn to both parents when she was troubled or wanted advice.

A few weeks after the move, while visiting her father, Sarah told him she wanted to stay in London with him in the family home and be with her neighbourhood and school friends. When Mr. Levine advised his wife of Sarah's wishes, she ordered him to leave. The father then applied for an interim court order that Sarah reside primarily with him. His application was granted. In addition, an access order gave each parent access on alternate weekends to the daughter not living with them.

For Discussion

1. In a two-column chart, identify the arguments in favour for and against Sarah's move.
2. Why was separating the sisters not the main concern in this case? Do you agree? Why?
3. Why do think the father's application succeeded?

Separation of Siblings

Siblings (brothers and sisters and stepbrothers and stepsisters) are seldom separated unless there is a good reason. Because divorce is a major crisis for most children, keeping siblings together is believed to maintain some sense of security and family. Children are usually good companions for one another in this time of need. They spend time together, they share experiences, and they provide mutual support as they grow up. Of course, there are occasions where it is better to separate siblings; for example, if there is serious friction among them or if they are so far apart in age that bonding is unlikely to occur. In such cases, the mother often gets custody of the girls, or the younger children, while fathers get custody of the boys, or the older children.

Case

Poole v. Poole

(1999) 45 R.F.L. (4th) 56
British Columbia Court of Appeal

Arthur and Christine Poole married in July 1978, both at a very young age. When this case was heard, the father was 41 and the mother 39. Four children were born: three sons, aged 18, 16, and 13, respectively; and a daughter, Samantha, aged 6. After almost 17 years together, the Pooles separated in March 1995, and the mother and the four children left the family farm. However, within a few days, the three boys returned to the farm and remained there.

Since 1987, the father had been operating a farm in Vanderhoof, British Columbia, with his father and brother. In addition to attending school, the boys assisted with the farm's cattle operation. They were also actively involved in the 4-H Club. When the mother left the farm, she moved into an apartment in Vanderhoof and remained there with Samantha.

The two became well established in the neighbourhood, and Samantha attended the local school.

In 1998, the British Columbia Supreme Court granted the Pooles a divorce, divided the family assets, and awarded custody of the daughter to the father. Custody of the three sons had previously been granted to the father with the mother's consent. The mother appealed the custody order for the daughter to the Court of Appeal where she was awarded custody of young Samantha.

For Discussion

1. What factor in determining custody do you think was most important to the trial judge?
2. Should the sons' ages have been given much consideration in the court's decision? Explain.
3. Why did the Court of Appeal overturn the trial judge's custody decision?

Children's Preferences and Wishes

In deciding custody, the courts may seriously consider the children's preferences and wishes. If a child is old enough to express his or her opinion, that opinion is usually weighed carefully. (The wishes of very young children, who may be manipulated by one parent, are also evaluated as reasonable or unreasonable.) The wishes of children between the ages of 8 and 13 years may be considered but not isolated from other factors. The wishes of children 14 years of age or older are very seriously considered. The older the child, the more weight is usually given to that child's preferences. In fact, custody disputes seldom occur over older children because any court order made contrary to a teen's wishes is likely to be ignored.

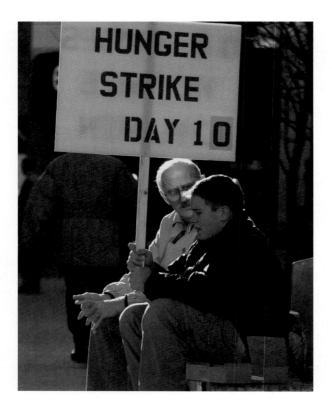

Figure 14-5

In January 2001, Clayton Giles of Calgary, Alberta, went on a hunger strike to protest a judge's order that he live with his mother. Giles said that part of his protest was directed at the court for failing to make a decision in the best interests of the child. Despite the order, Giles ran away to live with his father.

Case

Lidkea v. Jarrell

(1999) 49 R.F.L. (4th) 324
Ontario Court of Appeal

The appellant, Leonard Lidkea, and the female respondent were married in Montreal on November 7, 1987. They had one child, Shakyra Langille, born February 19, 1988. After the couple separated in March 1989, the mother moved with the child to New Brunswick, where she obtained a divorce from Lidkea in February 1991. In the divorce judgment, the respondent was granted custody of Shakyra with reasonable access given to Lidkea on reasonable notice. He was living and working in Toronto at that time. Lidkea was also ordered to pay monthly child support of $300.

After the divorce in 1991, the respondent married David Jarrell, and they had a son in 1993. In 1996, the Jarrells and the two children moved to the Toronto area. At this time, access to Shakyra, then eight years old, began to be a problem. Lidkea felt as though his daughter was being manipulated by her mother, while the mother claimed that Lidkea showed no concern for their daughter's wishes, and that he exercised access in an uncaring manner. Shakyra was coping poorly with the difficulties between her parents, and she wanted her father's access to end. In fact, she resisted being made to see her father.

As a result, Lidkea's access was suspended in May 1997. The applicant father appealed this decision, but his application was dismissed in a unanimous 3 to 0 decision.

For Discussion

1. How much importance should the judge give to Shakyra's wishes, and why?
2. Do you think that the girl's mother was willfully trying to frustrate the father's access rights? Why or why not?
3. Why was the father's application dismissed?

Parental Conduct

Canadian courts generally do not consider a parent's past conduct in deciding on custody unless that conduct is relevant to that person's ability to act as a parent. For example, if parents separated because of the adultery or unusual lifestyle of one of them, this is not likely to influence the court in a custody application. On the other hand, parental abuse of drugs or alcohol, or episodes of violence, rage, and abuse would be major factors.

Case

Van de Perre v. Edwards
2001 SCC 60
Supreme Court of Canada

Figure 14-6

Kimberly Van de Perre, pictured here with her son, Elijah, smiles after the Supreme Court of Canada awards her sole custody of her son.

Kimberly Van de Perre, the 27-year-old appellant and former beauty queen, was a single woman living in Vancouver. Theodore "Blue" Edwards, the 35-year-old respondent, was a professional basketball player earning $2 million a year with the NBA's Vancouver Grizzlies from 1995 to 1998. Kimberly is white; Theodore is African American. Race was to become a factor in this case.

Theodore had been married to his wife, Valerie, since 1991, and they had twin daughters, born in 1990. They maintained their home in North Carolina. Kimberly and Theodore met in the spring of 1996 in a Vancouver sports bar and had an affair that lasted about 18 months. At the end of the 1996 to 1997 basketball season, the Edwards family returned to North Carolina. In June 1997, Elijah, the son of Kimberly and Theodore, was born. Valerie accidentally learned of her husband's affair in 1996, just as she had with two earlier affairs.

In September 1997, Theodore returned to Vancouver for the new basketball season, and he resumed his affair with the appellant. When Elijah was three months old, Kimberly began an action against Theodore for custody and child support. After a 26-day trial in 1999, the trial judge awarded her sole custody, with four one-week access periods a year being granted to the father. Theodore appealed this decision to the British Columbia Court of Appeal. Valerie joined her husband as a party seeking joint custody of Elijah.

In a 3 to 0 judgment in March 2000, the Court of Appeal granted the joint custody application, giving Kimberly generous access. The court ruled that Elijah would be better off growing up in a Black culture in the United States because he would always be perceived as "being Black." The court questioned Kimberly's lack of higher education and her spotty

continued ▶

employment record. Every three weeks for the next year, Elijah jetted between his mother's Vancouver apartment and his father's home in North Carolina.

Kimberly appealed this decision to the Supreme Court of Canada, where the case was heard in June 2001. On September 28, in a unanimous, 9 to 0 decision, the Supreme Court reversed the British Columbia Court of Appeal decision and restored the trial judgment.

For Discussion

1. Why do you think the trial judge and the Supreme Court of Canada awarded custody to Elijah's mother?

2. In its decision, the British Columbia Court of Appeal stated: "It would obviously be in Elijah's best interests to live with a parent or family who can nurture his identity as a person of colour and who can appreciate and understand the day-to-day realities that black people face in North American society—including racism and discrimination in various forms." Prepare an argument for and against this position.

3. In its decision, the Supreme Court of Canada stated: "Race is connected to the culture, identity, and well-being of the child.... Bi-racial children should be encouraged to positively identify with both racial heritages." Discuss with a partner.

In recent years, judges have struggled with the issue of parental sexuality in custody decisions. Although most judges cannot ignore sexual orientation completely, many are more interested in the quality of parenting and the children's response to a parent's sexuality. A homosexual parent may have more difficulty than a heterosexual parent in obtaining custody. However, both gay and lesbian parents have been granted custody of their children in contested cases. The main question considered by the courts is not whether a parent is homosexual but, rather, how that parent handles his or her sexuality. As well, the parent's love for his or her children, interest in their welfare, and involvement in the children's academic and recreational activities must be considered. In other words, it is the best interests of the children that will determine custody, not the parent's sexuality or sexual preference.

Religion

Disputes over a child's religious upbringing, especially in cases of interfaith marriages, are making custody negotiations more difficult. Traditionally, the courts have recognized the custodial parent's right to determine a child's religion. However, this tradition is changing as judges look closely at the non-custodial parent's relationship with his or her children. Can a Jewish father who takes his children to temple on Friday nights prevent his former wife, a Roman Catholic, from taking the children to church regularly every Sunday? Adapting to two religions can be confusing to children, but they can cope if each parent does not mock or ridicule the other parent's religion. As with other custody issues, the children's best interests are still the major consideration. The Young case judgment is a landmark that courts still follow as precedent today.

Case

Young v. Young

(1993) 49 R.F.L. (3d) 117
Supreme Court of Canada

Irene and James Kam Chen Young were married in 1974. When they separated in 1987, they had three daughters, aged 6, 11, and 13. In 1985, James converted to the Jehovah's Witness faith; this conversion became a source of conflict between the parents. The mother and the two older children objected to the father's insistence on sharing his religion with them.

In 1988, Irene began divorce proceedings in which she was granted sole custody of the daughters; the father could have access only on specific occasions. Under the court order, the father could not discuss his religion with the children or involve them in religious activities without their mother's consent. Furthermore, he could not prevent the children from having any necessary blood transfusions. Both parents were also ordered not to make negative remarks about each other's beliefs.

Arguing that this order infringed on his freedom of religion, James appealed this decision to the British Columbia Court of Appeal in 1990. In a 2 to 1 decision, the court held that the father should not be restricted from discussing his religion with his children because it was in their best interests to know their father fully, including his religious beliefs. There could be exceptions to this rule only if it could be shown that the children were harmed by such discussions.

Irene appealed this decision to the Supreme Court of Canada where, in a 4 to 3 judgment, the Court upheld the Court of Appeal's decision, reinforcing "the best interests of the children" principle.

For Discussion

1. What does the trial judgment suggest about the custodial parent's right to make decisions regarding the couple's children?

2. Should a non-custodial parent have the right to share his or her everyday lifestyle with the children, including religious beliefs, regardless of whether the custodial parent approves? Discuss.

3. What principle does the majority judgment seem to establish about a non-custodial parent's right to share his or her lifestyle with the children?

Tender-Years Principle

In the first part of the 20th century, the tender-years principle was a main factor in custody decisions. This principle was drawn from a society in which women stayed home to care for the children and men worked outside the home. It was generally thought that mothers were better suited to care for children in their "tender years" than were fathers. This belief meant that the mother was almost certain to get legal custody of very young children, unless she was found to be a totally unfit parent. The tender-years principle applied to children up to about the age of six or seven. In the second half of the 20th century, this situation changed dramatically, and the tender years principle is much less important than it once was. Today, both parties are equally entitled to custody of their children, and the parenting abilities of mothers and fathers are assessed carefully by the court.

Determining custody is never an easy decision for a judge. Moreover, a custody decision is never final because children's needs change. A decision that was in the best interests of a three-year-old may not be in the best interests of the child when he or she is 16. Conditions change, and a custody order can always be brought back to court for further review. This may occur several years after the original custody order, but the courts are concerned about the best interests of the children at all times.

Joint Custody/Shared Parenting

Joint custody (**joint parenting** or **shared parenting**) is a custody plan in which both parents have a shared responsibility for the children. Together, they control their children's upbringing and make the major decisions that affect their children—much as they did before the separation. Such decisions may include the following:

- where the children will live
- which schools they will attend, along with extracurricular activities
- their daycare and after-school care arrangements
- health care, such as surgery and braces on teeth
- social contacts and friends
- religious upbringing

The concept of shared parenting is intended to protect the children's rights to an ongoing relationship, as much as possible, with both parents. The *Divorce Act, 1985,* stresses that children's best interests are served if they can maintain contact with both parents. Indeed, several provincial statutes have had a joint-custody provision for years. The parents must have a history of shared decision making that worked during their marriage in order for joint custody to succeed. This doesn't mean that the parents must agree on everything, but they must be able to compromise and resolve disputes. Joint custody will not be recommended, or may break down, if parents are so stung by the divorce that they constantly criticize the other parent in front of the child.

Neither the *Divorce Act, 1985,* nor any provincial statute actually defines joint custody. Different forms of joint custody/shared parenting have evolved over time. In **joint physical custody,** the children spend equal, or nearly equal, amounts of time with each parent, and both parents make the major decisions. The children alternate between the permanent home of each parent. Obviously, this form of joint custody may present major problems for the children. However, when both parents live in the same neighbourhood, joint physical custody can be easier for everyone. It is becoming more common for children to divide their time between both parents' homes rather than living full-time with one parent and visiting the other for weekends.

Joint legal custody is still the more common form of joint custody. Children remain with one of the parents while the other parent has generous access rights. However, both parents have an equal voice in all major decisions concerning the children. (If the parents cannot agree, the primary custodial parent usually has ultimate decision-making power.) This situation may be less stressful for children, but it does require cooperative parents who will put the children's welfare ahead of their own personal disagreements. They must be willing to work together with some degree of mutual respect and have a high degree of communication, cooperation, and trust. In Canada, the courts generally will not impose joint custody unless it appears that the parents are able to cooperate and communicate with each other to make decisions and resolve differences.

Joint custody gives the non-custodial parent a significant parenting role and gives the children a sense of being cared for by both parents. Both parents feel like equal partners in raising their children. Studies also indicate that divorced fathers whose children do not live with them but who have frequent contact with their children are much less likely to avoid their support obligations.

Future Changes in Custody and Access

Many countries have been reassessing their custody and access legislation. In 1997, the Canadian Parliament struck a committee to analyze these issues and to ensure better outcomes for children of divorcing parents. The committee's report, *For the Sake of the Children*, was released in December 1998. It made recommendations that greatly altered the course of custody and access

Figure 14-7
Senator Landon Pearson co-chaired the committee that drafted the report *For the Sake of the Children.* She once said that she wanted to be known as the "senator for children." The committee held months of hearings before it released its report and heard from many individuals who complained about custodial parents defying access orders.

decisions. The report recommended that the *Divorce Act* be amended to remove the concept of custody and access. Instead, upon a divorce, parents would be required to create a shared parenting plan that would enable them to share responsibility for raising children of the marriage. As well, the report urged a more flexible approach to custody and access issues that would be less adversarial and more effective in responding to the best interests of the children.

Since then, the federal government has consulted with the provinces and has listened to the feedback of the public and legal community. Suggested amendments and a new framework for custody and access decisions are expected to be debated in Parliament before 2003.

Review Your Understanding (Pages 417 to 427)

1. What is the only test in determining custody and access, and why?
2. Why are increasing numbers of fathers being awarded custody of their children?
3. Why does the parent with interim custody have an advantage when final custody is determined?
4. Why do courts try to keep siblings together as much as possible?
5. When might a judge consider a child's preferences in a custody case?
6. To what extent is a parent's lifestyle considered in determining custody?
7. What is the tender-years principle? Why has it become less important in determining custody?
8. Why are custody decisions never permanent?
9. Why is joint custody or shared parenting becoming more common?

You Be the JUDGE

For the Sake of the Children recommends that a list of "best interests" criteria be introduced into the *Divorce Act* to better direct judges in making custody and access decisions.

- What would be the advantages and disadvantages of including a list of "best interests" criteria in the *Divorce Act*?

e activity

Visit **www.law.nelson.com** and follow the links to learn more about the issues and factors involved in weighing the best interests of the child.

Did You Know?

In 1997, Alberta was the first Canadian province to pass a law enabling grandparents to apply for access to their grandchildren. The legislation was modelled on a U.S. law.

You Be the JUDGE

In 2000, a British Columbia man tried to stop his former wife from taking their seven-year-old son on a holiday to Arizona because she and her new boyfriend smoked in the car. The boy was highly sensitive to cigarette smoke.

- As a judge, would you grant the injunction? Why or why not? Discuss with a partner.

10. Briefly outline the two forms of joint custody. Which is more common, and why?
11. Identify two advantages and one disadvantage of joint custody.
12. Why is it necessary to make changes in custody and access laws in Canada?

14.3 Access and Mobility Rights

When one parent has been granted custody of the children, the courts usually award access, or visiting rights, to the other parent. Under the *Divorce Act, 1985,* a non-parent, such as a grandparent, may also apply for an access order.

Access to a child by the non-custodial parent is usually in the child's best interests. A parent with access usually has the right to

- spend time with the children, such as on a weekday evening, weekends, and on special occasions like birthdays and major holidays
- receive information about the children's health, well-being, and progress in school
- receive advance notice (of at least one month) if the custodial parent intends to move

However, if a judge feels that a child might be harmed emotionally, physically, or morally, access might be very strictly controlled or even denied. These situations are rare. An example is a parent whose smoking severely affects a child's asthma.

Types of Access

The courts encourage parents to work out reasonable terms of access when the spouses have parted on good terms. If, however, the separation or divorce has resulted in a courtroom battle, the court may outline specific conditions for access. There are three common types of access orders, described below.

Reasonable access involves time spent with the non-custodial parent that is quite flexible and occurs on a regular basis. Sometimes, this parent spends almost as much time with the children as the custodial parent. The parents have worked out an acceptable agreement that is preferable to having access strictly outlined, as in specified access.

Specified access involves precise times spent with the non-custodial parent, such as after school, on certain weekends, on special occasions such as birthdays, and on major holidays, including summer holidays.

Supervised access also involves a specified time, but it must be spent in the presence of a supervisor, such as a grandparent, another relative, a family friend, or a social worker, so that the child is safe. It might be ordered if the non-custodial parent is addicted to alcohol or drugs, is mentally ill, or has a history of violent or abusive behaviour. Supervised access may even be ordered for a baby when the access parent has little experience in caring for an infant.

Some provinces offer supervised-access programs through organizations such as the YMCA, Children's Aid Societies, and neighbourhood support centres. These facilities provide a safe, neutral setting for visits between a child and a non-custodial family member. Usually, trained staff and volunteers are on hand to assist both parent and child.

Supervised Access in Ontario

Years	Families Served	Children Served	Number of Visits
1997–1998	8 952	16 860	14 592
1998–1999	11 293	19 765	15 647
1999–2000	12 088	20 358	16 108

Figure 14-8

These statistics were gathered from 36 districts across Ontario. What do these statistics indicate?

Case

Hartwick v. Stoneham

(2000) 8 R.F.L. (5th) 74
Ontario Superior Court of Justice

Joseph Hartwick and Allison Stoneham lived together briefly before the birth of their son, Brandon Stoneham, on February 9, 1991. The couple was not married, and they did not cohabit after the child's birth. They signed a separation agreement on June 3, 1994, giving custody of the boy to the mother with increasing access given to the father until he was able to enjoy nine hours every other Sunday "unless it was not in the child's best interests."

In September 1999, the mother ended access visits after Brandon expressed a preference not to visit his father because the father took little interest in him. The boy was no longer interested in the activities his dad proposed for their visits, and he felt he was "getting too old to go there." Brandon also told a psychologist that his father didn't ask about friends, school, or sports activities, nor did he attend his son's hockey or soccer games. Hartwick claimed that when he saw Brandon he was always rushed, and he could only see his son at times dictated by the mother. However, Stoneham denied that claim.

Hartwick brought an application to restore access, and his motion was granted.

For Discussion

1. What is the significance of the 1994 separation agreement in this decision to restore access?

2. If Hartwick's access was permanently terminated, what would this do to the father–son relationship?

3. How much consideration should the judge give to Brandon's comments and feelings? Why?

4. Why did the judge restore access? Do you agree? Why?

Mobility Rights

As more families separate and as society becomes even more mobile, **mobility rights** have become an issue before the courts. The right of mobility is a custodial parent's right to move to another location with his or her children—often away from the non-custodial parent. Access orders, like custody orders, are open for review if conditions change. Why might the custodial parent want to move? Some common reasons include

- plans to marry someone who lives elsewhere

Figure 14-9

Francine accepts her job promotion, which means moving the children to a city a significant distance away from their father. The courts generally allow the children to move with the custodial parent, even if it interferes with the non-custodial parent's access.

- desire to return to a former community to be with family and friends
- transfer by an employer
- pursuing better job opportunities
- experiencing serious problems with the non-custodial parent

For example, Francine has custody of her two children, and generous access has been granted to her former husband, Luc. Francine has just been promoted to systems operations manager of a major corporation and is now required to move from Halifax to Vancouver. Luc's right to access will be greatly reduced because of the cost of travel and the distance between the two cities. The law generally allows children to move with custodial parents as long as the move is reasonable and in the best interests of the children. If Luc asks the court to stop Francine from moving, she will have to prove that the benefits of moving are greater than the loss of the children's ability to visit with their father as regularly.

Canadian courts have ruled that the custodial parent has the right to move the children for reasonable purposes, even if this interferes with the other parent's access rights. Courts will look closely at the reasons for the move. In our example, Francine can show that she is moving in order to maximize her career and earning potential—factors directly affecting her children's quality of life. The move is not simply an attempt to deny access to Luc, and so the court will probably allow her move. What is good for the custodial parent is often presumed to be good for the children. This implies that the right of the custodial parent to create a happy home for the children may be greater than the right of access for the non-custodial parent. The Supreme Court of Canada considered parental mobility rights in the 1996 landmark judgment in *Gordon v. Goertz*.

Case

Gordon v. Goertz

(1996) 19 R.F.L. (4th) 177
Supreme Court of Canada

Robin James Goertz and Janet Rita Gordon, formerly Janet Goertz, lived in Saskatoon, Saskatchewan, until their separation in 1990. In a mediated agreement, the parents agreed that their daughter, Samantha, would reside with each of them on a rotating basis, and that if one party moved, the child would remain in Saskatoon with the other. In 1993, the mother petitioned for divorce and was granted permanent custody of the seven-year-old child, while the father received generous access. Both parents enjoyed a warm and loving relationship with Samantha, and the father saw the child frequently.

In 1994, when Goertz learned that Gordon planned to move to Australia to study dentistry, he applied for custody of the child, or an injunction preventing the mother from moving from Saskatoon. The mother cross-applied to allow her to move to Australia with Samantha.

continued ▶

Relying heavily on the divorce judgment and the Unified Family Court judge's decision that the mother was the appropriate custodial parent of Samantha, the trial judge dismissed the father's application. The judge varied the access order, allowing the mother to move while granting the father very generous access on one month's notice to visit in Australia. Mother and daughter moved there in early 1995.

A further appeal to the Saskatchewan Court of Appeal by the father was dismissed, and he appealed this decision to the Supreme Court of Canada. Because of the time involved in hearings, the mother and daughter had already been living in Australia for over a year before the Supreme Court ruled 7 to 2 in favour of the mother, again dismissing the father's appeal.

For Discussion

1. **When these parents separated, what benefit did family mediation provide them?**

2. **Why do you think all courts ruled in favour of the mother?**

3. **Although the mother was successful, the Supreme Court decision placed the welfare and best interests of the child well ahead of the rights and interests of the mother. A representative from the Women's Legal Education and Action Fund (LEAF) said: "With this decision, the risk of losing custody will effectively deter [discourage] women from ever raising the issue of moving." Discuss the meaning of this quotation with a partner.**

Because of the decision in *Gordon v. Goetz,* courts are more inclined to examine the impact of the move on the children and not just the needs of the custodial parent. They may also consider other changes that have occurred in the lives of parents and children between the granting of the original custody order and the proposed move. For example, the father may have remarried with a new family into which the child could easily fit. In addition, it might be in the child's best interests to remain with the father instead of leaving the city, province, or country to go with the mother.

As the issue of mobility rights appears in courts more often, some couples are adding a clause in their agreements, preventing the custodial parent from leaving a certain location with the children without the other parent's consent. The *Divorce Act, 1985,* says that the court may require the custodial parent to give 30 days' notice, or other period as the court specifies, before changing the child's residence.

When problems arise and legal access is denied, the non-custodial parent's only option is to go back to court and charge the former spouse with breach of access provisions. The judge can impose a jail sentence or a fine for contempt of court, but these measures are seldom used. A jail sentence for the custodial parent leaves the children on their own, while a fine takes money out of a household that usually has little to spare. On application, the judge may award increased or makeup access as remedies for access denial.

In extreme cases, the court may change the primary residence of the child as a remedy for repeated denial of access. That parent is then responsible for facilitating access between the child and the other parent.

Child Abduction

In Chapter 5, you learned that most child abductions are not committed by strangers, but by a parent embroiled in a custody dispute. This kind of abduction occurs when a parent decides to take a child not legally in his or her custody. A parent who illegally removes a child under the age of 16 from the care of the custodial parent commits a criminal offence. Child abduction is an indictable offence under the *Criminal Code,* for which the offender is liable to imprisonment for a maximum of 10 years, even if that person is a parent. Parents sometimes abduct their own children because they expect to lose the court custody decision or because they have already lost it and cannot accept the court's decision.

Many parents who abduct their children remove them to another province or territory. As a result, all provinces and territories have passed legislation to enforce custody orders from other provinces and territories. As well, federal information banks may be searched under the *Family Orders and Agreements Enforcement Assistance Act.* Provincial data banks, such as motor vehicle registration, must be searched first. The court, and not the parent, receives any information available from the federal data banks. To ensure confidentiality, information released is limited to the address of the missing person and the name and address of an employer. It is hoped that such a procedure will assist in locating a missing child taken by a parent contrary to a custody or access arrangement.

The problem becomes more difficult if the parent and child have left Canada. Extradition, or getting the other country to send the parent and child back, is possible only if child abduction is also an offence in the other country. On December 1, 1983, *The Hague Convention on the Civil Aspects of International Child Abduction* came into effect at The Hague in the Netherlands. It is the main international treaty to help parents whose children have been abducted to another country, but it ceases to apply when the children turn 16 years of age. Fifty-five countries now follow the Convention.

The Convention aims
- to deter child abductions
- to ensure the prompt return of abducted children to their home countries
- to promote cooperation among countries and their respective authorities

In Canada, child custody is a provincial and territorial responsibility, and each province and territory has established a central authority (normally the Ministry of the Attorney General or the Ministry of Justice). The federal government has also established the Department of Justice as a central authority to assist the provinces. When a child is abducted, the parent files an application with a central authority, which tries to locate the child, prevent harm to the child, and secure the child's return.

Canada also has an "our missing children" program with the joint cooperation of the RCMP, Canada Customs and Revenue Agency, Citizenship and Immigration Canada, and the Department of Foreign Affairs and International Trade. All four agencies work to locate and return missing and abducted children to the custodial parent.

Review Your Understanding (Pages 428 to 432)

1. **When might a parent be denied access to his or her child?**
2. **Identify the three common types of access orders, and describe how they differ.**

3. Outline four reasons why a custodial parent might want to move.

4. Discuss why courts should look at what happened between the granting of the original custody order and the custodial parent's application to move.

5. What penalties can a court impose on a custodial parent who denies child access to the other parent?

6. Why do some non-custodial parents abduct their children?

7. Outline the three aims of *The Hague Convention on the Civil Aspects of International Child Abduction*.

8. Identify the partners in Canada's "our missing children" program.

14.4 Child Support

Both parents have an obligation to contribute to meet their children's needs, whether or not there is a court order. Even a parent who remarries and starts a new family is still responsible for supporting the children of a previous marriage. The federal *Divorce Act, 1985,* outlines procedures for determining child support amounts if the parents are already divorced or planning to divorce. Provincial laws apply if the parents have never married, or are separated or planning to separate, but do not intend to divorce.

Federal Child Support Guidelines

In the early 1990s, the provincial, territorial, and federal justice ministers created the Child Support Guidelines Project. The committee's purpose was to study the existing child-support guidelines, to evaluate the effectiveness of these guidelines based on economic research, and to make recommendations to improve problem areas. The main goal was to increase child support for children who most needed it. Judges needed guidelines that were realistic and reflected the true cost of raising a child, as support awards varied widely among the provinces and even among judges of the same court. Before these reforms, courts all across Canada determined child support on a case-by-case basis, based on the children's needs and the parents' abilities to meet these needs. Reform was necessary.

The May 1, 1997 amendments to the *Divorce Act, 1985,* and the introduction of Child Support Guidelines resulted in one of the most significant reforms in family law in many years. The guidelines were instituted to
- establish a fair standard of child support to ensure that children continue to benefit from the financial means of both parents after divorce
- reduce conflict and tension by making the calculation of child support simpler and more objective
- improve the efficiency of the legal process by giving courts and parties guidance in setting awards and encouraging settlement
- assure more consistent treatment of support-paying parents, while providing sufficient flexibility to ensure that awards are fair in individual family circumstances

The main features of the reform were (1) the introduction of child support guidelines, (2) changes to the tax treatment of child support, and (3) additional enforcement measures. The highlights of these features are summarized below.

Determining Child Support

The appropriate level of child support depends upon these factors: (1) the non-custodial parent's total income, (2) the number of children to be supported, and (3) the appropriate federal child support table for the province or territory in which the non-custodial parent lives.

Usually it is the non-custodial parent who pays all, or most, of the child support to the custodial parent. The amount to be paid is now based on federal, provincial, and territorial tables, which order payments based on income and number of children. There is a separate table for each province and territory, but they are very similar. The differences are the result of different provincial income-tax rates. The paying parent must consult the table for the province or territory in which he or she lives. In limited circumstances, payments may vary from these amounts, but this would be unusual since the guidelines are intended to provide consistency, fairness, objectivity, and predictability in court decisions on child support.

ⓔ activity

Visit **www.law.nelson.com** and follow the links to learn more about child support and enforcement measures in Canada.

▌ Typical Monthly Support Payments

Annual Income ($)	Typical support ($) for			
	1 Child	2 Children	3 Children	4 Children
20 000	163	285	390	476
30 000	266	446	568	672
40 000	345	570	748	894
50 000	429	700	917	1094
60 000	507	823	1076	1283
70 000	572	927	1212	1444
80 000	639	1031	1346	1603
90 000	706	1136	1480	1761
100 000	773	1240	1613	1919
125 000	940	1500	1948	2315
150 000	1108	1761	2283	2711

Figure 14-10

Shown are typical monthly child support payments under the federal Child Support Guidelines. How does this table compare to your province's or territory's child support table?

Exceptions to the Tables

Of course, not all children and families are the same. Most families spend more on their children as family income increases, and spending changes with each parent's income. The tables reflect the amount that an average parent with a certain income would spend on his or her children. As well, the custodial parent is expected to contribute a similar share of his or her income to meet the costs of raising the children. In this way, children share in increases and decreases in either parent's income, just as they would have if their parents were still married.

Although these tables are followed very closely by the courts, exceptions are sometimes made. Courts may require additional payment for special or extraordinary expenses, including such items as

- reasonable child-care expenses that the custodial parent must pay because of work, school, or illness
- medical and health-related expenses over $100 not covered by insurance, including dental care and glasses
- extra expenses for extracurricular activities that allow a child to pursue a special interest or talent, or attend a specialized program
- post-secondary education expenses

In addition, the court can order payments to be reduced if standard payments would cause undue (excessive) hardship to the parent. Undue hardship can only be claimed if the person making payments has a lower standard of living (SOL) than does the recipient. The SOL test takes into account a number of variables, including how many people are being supported in each household. For example, a paying parent who has to support other children in a new marriage might be able to claim undue hardship. The court must look at the facts of each case to determine undue hardship. It must also examine in detail the financial circumstances of the two households, including any new partners for either parent.

In joint custody, the guideline amounts may similarly not apply if the paying parent cares for the children at least 40 percent of the time. Here, the court looks at the costs of a shared custody arrangement, including both parents' incomes and the children's needs. As a result, the parent who pays support could pay less than the table amount.

Finally, if the paying parent's annual income is over $150 000, the court must first order the table amount for the $150 000. However, the court is free to order more or less payment, depending on the circumstances. The first test of the Child Support Guidelines in the Supreme Court of Canada occurred in the Court's 9 to 0 judgment in *Francis v. Baker*, although it will not affect the majority of divorcing Canadians.

Case

Francis v. Baker
(1999) 177 D.L.R. (4th) 1
Supreme Court of Canada

Thomas Baker, the appellant, and Monica Francis, the respondent, were married in 1979. He was a lawyer in a large Toronto law firm; she was a high school teacher. Their first daughter was born in 1983. In July 1985, when their second daughter was five days old, Baker left the family, leaving the children with their mother. Since the separation, the mother had been struggling financially and had to return to full-time teaching three months later, contrary to the parties' original plans. Under the terms of a separation agreement, she received $30 000 a year in child-support payments and a lump-sum payment of $500 000 to ease her financial problems. The couple was divorced in 1987.

continued ▶

Figure 14-11
Monica Francis in her lawyer's office in 1999

In 1988, Francis applied for an increase in child support from $2500 monthly for both girls. At trial in 1997, she changed her claim for child support to be made under the federal Child Support Guidelines, which were to come into effect shortly. At that time, the mother was earning $63 000 yearly. The father had prospered since the separation; he had become the chief executive officer of a large company and was earning $945 538 yearly. His net worth was estimated at $78 million. When his daughters were in his care, Baker took them on European vacations and to luxury box seats at Blue Jays games, and gave them expensive gifts. As well, he paid about $25 000 yearly to send his daughters to private school.

In 1997, the Ontario Superior Court of Justice awarded Francis $10 000 a month in child support, which was in line with the guideline table amounts. The amount was upheld on appeal and reaffirmed unanimously by the Supreme Court of Canada.

For Discussion

1. **The Ontario Court of Appeal's judgment stated: "Children are entitled to live at the standard permitted by all available income, even if that means living better than your basic needs demand." Argue in support of or against the Court of Appeal judgment. Share your view with a partner.**

2. **What is the significance of these decisions? Do you agree with them? Why or why not?**

3. **The Supreme Court's judgment stated: "Parliament did not choose to impose a cap or upper limit on child support payments .... In my opinion, child support undeniably involves some form of wealth transfer to the children, and will often produce an indirect benefit to the custodial parent." What does this mean?**

Did You Know?

In Alberta, a parent who fails to pay support can have a driver's licence suspended or wages garnisheed (a portion legally deducted). Money is then forwarded to the spouse in need. Newspapers may also print the names and photos of people owing a "significant" amount of support. What are the advantages and disadvantages of this plan?

Tax Treatment

Before 1997, Canadians who paid child support were able to deduct the payments from their income for tax purposes, while the parent receiving child support had to include it as income at income-tax time. Many people questioned the fairness of this law. Since May 1, 1997, child support is no longer deductible for the paying parent and no longer taxable for the receiving parent.

Enforcement Measures

The federal government has amended other federal laws to give provinces and the territories the means to enforce support payments. Federal law allows the provinces to request permission to have federal data banks scanned, such as those of the Canada Customs and Revenue Agency, to locate parents who are behind in their support payments. To receive help from an enforcement program, a parent must register a child-support agreement with the appropriate program in his or her province or territory. That office then monitors all support payments by either arranging for payments to be sent to the office or by automatically deducting payments from the parent's pay. The office then turns the money over to the parent who is entitled to payment. See Chapter 15 for further discussion of the enforcement of support orders.

Children of the Marriage

Under provincial and territorial legislation, parents are obliged to support unmarried children living at home until they reach the age of majority—either 18 or 19, depending on the province or territory. In addition, some provinces may order continued support as long as the children are enrolled in a full-time educational program. For example, child support may be granted to an adult child for post-secondary education; however, support usually lasts only for the first undergraduate diploma or degree, or until the child turns 23, whichever is first. If a child between 16 and the provincial age of majority leaves home and withdraws from parental control, this obligation ends.

Figure 14-12

Depending on the province or territory, parents must support their unmarried children who live at home until they are 18 or 19. Even older children living at home can be the recipients of child support.

Case

P.T. v. R.B.

2001 ABQB 739
Alberta Court of Queen's Bench

The mother, T., and the father, B., are the biological parents of a daughter born on June 16, 1982. The couple was never married, but a paternity agreement was reached in 1983. In 1988, B. was ordered to pay child support for their daughter. This support continued in some fashion until 2000, when the daughter turned 18. The mother sued to have the court order B. to pay university education support for their daughter.

When the case was heard, B. was living alone on a disability pension, had two grown sons from an earlier marriage, and a 16-year-old daughter from another relationship. He saw his sons every weekend and had a good relationship with them when they were growing up. He had not seen his then-19-year-old daughter for more than two years, or his younger daughter for 10 years. Evidence at trial indicated that the older daughter left her mother's home in Vancouver at 17, lived with her father in Edmonton for one month, and then left to live with her boyfriend. The father offered to give her $400 a month to help her through university, but instead a legal action was started.

In August 2001, the trial judge ruled that the daughter was "destitute" because she could not go to university and work at the same time and, so, required support. B. launched an appeal to the Alberta Court of Appeal, which has not yet been heard.

For Discussion

1. Why did the trial judge rule in favour of the mother?

2. Do you think parents should be required to support their adult children? Why?

3. In an interview, B. said: "If this ruling stands, it could mean that parents of students could be faced with kids refusing to work part-time and demanding money to go to school. Nor does the ruling place any age limit on a student." Do you agree with his comments? Discuss.

If the parents of the child are, or were, married, the definition of child under section 2(1) of the federal *Divorce Act, 1985,* may apply. It allows a court to make an order beyond the provincial or territorial age of majority. A test of this section of the *Divorce Act* was resolved in a 7 to 0 decision from the Supreme Court of Canada in *Chartier v. Chartier.*

The Law — The Divorce Act, 1985

Excerpts from the *Divorce Act*

2.

(1) In this Act, ... "child of the marriage" means a child of two spouses or former spouses who, at the material time,

(a) is under the age of sixteen years, or

(b) is sixteen years of age or over and under their charge but unable, by reason of illness, disability or other cause, to withdraw from their charge or to obtain the necessaries of life;

...

(2) For the purposes of the definition "child of the marriage" in subsection (1), a child of two spouses or former spouses includes

(a) any child for whom they both stand in the place of parents; and

(b) any child of whom one is the parent and for whom the other stands in the place of a parent.

For Discussion

1. In your own words, explain the meaning of "child of the marriage."

Case

Chartier v. Chartier

(1999) 43 R.F.L. (4th)
Supreme Court of Canada

The appellant, Sharon Chartier, and the respondent, Gerald Leo Chartier, started living together in 1989 and were married in June 1991. Their child, Jeena, was born in August 1990. The parties separated in May 1992, later reconciled for two months, then permanently separated in September 1992. While the couple lived together, Gerald played an active role in caring for Jeena and Jessica, Sharon's daughter from a previous relationship. He was a "father figure" for Jessica, and although there was some discussion of adoption, it never happened. But the parties changed Jessica's birth registration, listing Gerald as her father and changing Jessica's last name.

After separation, the parties agreed that Gerald could have access to Jessica, and he consented to an order that acknowledged her as a "child of the marriage." Although he agreed to pay support for Jeena, he contested the claim for support for Jessica. In divorce proceedings in 1995, an interim order

ordered him to pay support for both girls until a final report was prepared. That report clearly indicated the husband's desire to sever his relationship with Jessica, and the trial judge found that he was not obligated to pay support for her.

In 1997, the Manitoba Court of Appeal dismissed the wife's appeal for child support. However, her appeal to the Supreme Court of Canada was allowed, and a 7 to 0 judgment set aside the Court of Appeal's judgment, ordering interim support of $200 a month for Jessica until the Manitoba Court of Queen's Bench (Family Division) could determine the appropriate amount to recover from the date of the trial judgment.

For Discussion

1. Summarize the decision of the trial and appeal courts.

2. What precedent does the Supreme Court of Canada judgment establish?

3. Which decision do you support? Why?

Future Directions

Although the 1997 Child Support Guidelines were introduced to bring consistency, equity, and simplicity to court decisions granting child support, this has not always been the case. The determination of child support under the new system can be time-consuming, as it often involves detailed inspection of the parents' living standards. These guidelines continue to be reviewed.

In August 2001, the provinces and territories agreed to pass legislation to make it easier to collect support payments from non-custodial parents across Canada. The government leaders agreed it would be easier to enforce court-ordered support payments if legislation was passed in each jurisdiction. Once such legislation is passed, it will be much easier to collect unpaid child support in other jurisdictions.

Parental Support

Every province and territory has passed laws that can be used to make adult children responsible for their parents. However, the statutes are not worded or interpreted in exactly the same way in every province and territory. Making adult children support their needy parents saves the government money and maintains the family unit as a social unit. On the other hand, some people believe that these types of actions should be judged on the quality of care provided by the parent while the children were young. For example, should adult children of abusive parents be forced to support them? Can such private family matters be decided in a courtroom? These cases highlight the role of the family in Canadian society and, given Canada's aging population, it is likely that more such cases will be heard.

Review Your Understanding (Pages 433 to 439)

1. Outline the four main reasons for the introduction of Child Support Guidelines in 1997.

2. Identify the three main factors that help determine the appropriate level of child support.

3. Describe four situations in which a court may award more than the table amount of support.

4. What is "undue hardship"? Give some examples that represent this concept.

5. Why may the support tables not automatically apply to parents who have at least 40-percent custody of their children?

6. Does the paying parent stop paying child support when the child reaches the age of majority? Explain.

7. How will the collection of support payments be improved in the future?

8. Outline an argument for and against adult children being held responsible for their needy parents.

14.5 Children in Need of Protection

Parents have a right to raise their children according to their own personal values and beliefs. All families should have the right to have little government involvement in their lives. In the past, many children, especially Aboriginal children, were removed from their homes without good cause. In the 1950s and 1960s, the child welfare system tended to regard white families as ideal families. It failed to see the cruelty of separating children from their parents and community. The fallout from this policy was a renewed effort in the 1970s to keep families intact.

Now the pendulum has swung the other way. In recent years, society has recognized that some parents are not raising their children in an acceptable fashion. What is "unacceptable" is not easy to decide, since one parent's punishment may be another parent's abuse. Individual values within society vary widely, and methods of child rearing vary with these values (see Issue, page 442). In certain cases, however, the legal system has the authority to protect the child from his or her family.

Child abuse is any behaviour that endangers the development, security, or survival of a child. Forms of abuse may be physical, sexual, emotional, or neglect.

▌ Types and Examples of Child Abuse

Types	Definition and Examples
Physical	Deliberate physical force used against a child; for example, shaking, choking, hitting, biting, kicking, burning, or poisoning
Sexual	Sexual activity with a child; for example, incest, touching and fondling genitals, juvenile prostitution, intercourse, sexual exploitation, and involving a child in the production of pornography
Emotional	Attacks on a child's sense of self-worth; for example, constant yelling, insults, rejection, terrorizing, or humiliation. Can be the most difficult type to identify and prove.
Neglect	Lack of attention to a child's physical, emotional, and psychological needs; for example, failure to provide adequate food, clothing, shelter, sleep, medical care, and emotional warmth

Figure 14-13

The four main types of child abuse and examples to recognize each. Which do you think is the most common type of abuse? Why?

Child abuse is one of society's most serious problems. Abused children suffer, often silently, and the damage may last a lifetime. Even worse, children abused today may become future child abusers. Abuse is not confined to any one group of people or any age group. Children from babies to teenagers, and from all kinds of homes and from all types of educational, religious, ethnic, social, and economic backgrounds, may be abused. Family members are responsible for the majority of assaults against very young children. This includes immediate and extended family members related by marriage, blood, common law, or adoption, as well as people who have been named legal guardians.

Most parents are caring and loving. However, caring for children is often stressful and sometimes becomes overwhelming for one or both parents. Young and immature parents may not understand a child's behaviour or may have few support systems. When parents have financial problems, or a major illness occurs in the family, or personal difficulties arise, parents often "take it out" on their children. In these cases, the law will seek to protect the child while recognizing that the parents may need help with their problems.

Society's concern about neglect and child abuse is reflected in specific legislation. Canadian children are protected by offences in the *Criminal Code,* including failing to provide the necessaries of life, assault, sexual assault, sexual exploitation, sexual touching, and child pornography, discussed in Chapter 5.

All provinces and territories have legislation, such as Child Welfare Acts or Child and Family Services Acts, to protect neglected children. The British Columbia legislation is called the *Child, Family and Community Service Act.* In May 1999, the Ontario legislature unanimously passed the *Child and Family Services Amendment Act,* resulting in the most significant change to Ontario's child protection laws in a decade. This Amendment Act became law on March 31, 2000. These statutes are based on two main principles:

- The "best interests" of the child are the most important concern of the law and the courts.
- The child must be protected, and the family must be supported as the basic unit of society.

In most provinces and territories, child protection services are provided by provincial/territorial employees, typically from the Ministry of Community and Social Services or Child and Family Service Agencies, or by Children's Aid Societies (CAS).

Did You Know?

According to the federal Department of Justice, abuse of children under age three is most often neglect, while abuse of children aged 12 to 15 is most often physical.

Did You Know?

In 2000, Ontario's 52 Children's Aid Societies handled 195 000 referrals of child abuse. Of these, 72 000 required investigation. About 19 000 of these children were taken under the protection of CAS.

Reporting Child Abuse

If you know or suspect that a child is being abandoned, emotionally mistreated, neglected, or physically abused, you must report your information or suspicion, no matter where in Canada you live. People who may have close contact with children, such as doctors, dentists, nurses, teachers and other school staff, counsellors, social workers, daycare workers, clergy, and peace officers must immediately report any actual or suspected child abuse to the authorities. In some provinces, such as British Columbia, Saskatchewan, and Prince Edward Island, the law places a broad duty on "every" or "any" person to report. This includes relatives, friends, neighbours, and even strangers who suspect child abuse. Failure to do so may result in a fine of up to $1000 to $10 000, depending on the province or territory.

Procedures for reporting abuse vary throughout Canada. Figure 14-14 outlines the basic procedures.

▮ Child Abuse Reporting Procedures

Responsible Authority	What to Report
Children's Aid Society	Child's name, address, age, and sex
Provincial child welfare agency	Parent/guardian's name and address
Social worker	Alleged offender's name and address
Police officer	Details of alleged incident
Crown attorney	Your name and address

Figure 14-14

Depending on your province or territory, you would report child abuse to one of the authorities in the left-hand column. You would report some or all of the information in the right-hand column. What other information could be reported? Why?

Is Spanking Child Abuse?

Figure 14-15

Reverend Henry Hildebrandt, a pastor of the Church of God, maintains that "the word of God advocates corporal punishment."

Section 43 of the *Criminal Code* states: "Every schoolteacher, parent or person standing in the place of a parent is justified in using force by way of correction toward a pupil or child ... who is under his care, if the force does not exceed what is reasonable under the circumstances."

In 2000, an Ontario Superior Court judge ruled that spanking does not violate the constitutional rights of children and upheld section 43 of the *Criminal Code*. Children's rights groups had been trying to declare section 43 unconstitutional because it trespasses upon the rights guaranteed in the *Canadian Charter of Rights and Freedoms*. The judge ruled that parents must have the authority to discipline their children, but he also observed that perhaps it is time for Parliament to define "reasonable force." The judge cautioned that any injury caused to children is child abuse and is a criminal offence. While the law allows parents to spank their children with their bare hands, implements (sticks, rods, paddles) are considered to be evidence of unnecessary force. In 2002, the Ontario Court of Appeal upheld this decision.

In 2001, child welfare officials forcibly removed seven children from their Aylmer, Ontario, home because their parents refused to stop spanking them. The family were members of the Church of God, an international order made up mostly of Mennonites. Church of God followers believe that the Bible allows for the use of corporal punishment. In Proverbs, for example, it is written: "He that spareth the rod hateth his son." Church of God followers support the use of implements to spank children.

Many neighbours were horrified to see the children dragged kicking and screaming from their home. Other members of the Church of God fled to the United States and Mexico because they feared their children would also be removed. A total of 25 mothers and their 93 children are trying to get refugee status in the United States on the grounds of religious persecution. There was no evidence of any injury to the children who were removed. Three weeks after they had been removed, the children were returned to their parents on the understanding that no further corporal punishment would be used.

The pastor of the Alymer parish, Reverend Henry Hildebrandt, took exception to the actions of the child welfare authorities, and may have counselled the family to violate the court order to refrain from spanking. As a result, in December 2001, child welfare authorities sought a restraining order against him. Hildebrandt stood firm. "To maintain a good conscience, we must express that the Church believes that the word of God advocates corporal punishment under certain circumstances," Hildebrandt said.

On One Side

"Spare the rod and spoil the child."
—Samuel Butler, poet

Some people believe that spanking is good discipline for children and that parents have the right to use corporal punishment on their own children. Many point to the fact they were spanked themselves and turned out just fine. They regard spanking as an essential part of raising a child well. Some parents maintain that spanking is helpful in disciplining rebellious children. They believe that if certain behaviours are not corrected, the child may grow up into a dysfunctional adult.

Spanking is done for the child's sake and it is part of the loving relationship that exists between parents and their children. Some groups think that the government has no right to interfere with the private affairs of families. They applaud the 2000 ruling by the Ontario judge stating that section 43 of the *Criminal Code* is constitutional. They believe that those who are trying to overturn this law are weakening the authority of parents. Removing section 43 from the *Criminal Code* would also turn parents who use corporal punishment into criminals.

On the Other Side

"Children need discipline but not hitting."
—Dawn Walker, Canadian Institute of Child Health

In 1979, Sweden became the first country to ban corporal punishment of children. Since then, eight other countries have passed similar laws. A Canadian Medical Association journal reported that children who experience less corporal punishment have lower rates of depression, anxiety, and alcohol abuse when they become adults. They also have better education results and higher incomes. Serious criminal offenders have a history of abuse as children.

Some groups think corporal punishment does not persuade children to become better people—it just makes them angrier and more stubborn. Children learn better through cooperation and rewards, not through threats and violence. Parents have a duty to explain to their children what they did wrong and why it is not acceptable. Section 43 does not give children the protection and rights that are granted to all other Canadians. It allows one group of citizens to be assaulted. Children need the protection of the law, and this will only occur when section 43 is removed by Parliament or declared unconstitutional.

The Bottom Line

One of the important questions about section 43 of the *Criminal Code* is what is considered "reasonable force." Neither Parliament nor the courts have defined it. Do small spanks lead to larger ones and does spanking damage the child? Do parents have the right to use force when disciplining their children? Or is spanking a violation of basic human rights that should be outlawed altogether?

What Do You Think?

1. Summarize the significant aspects of section 43 of the *Criminal Code.*
2. Why did the judge uphold section 43 as being legal? What caution did the judge issue?
3. How did children's rights groups react to the 2000 Ontario Superior Court ruling?
4. Why did the removal of seven children from their home in 2001 create controversy?
5. Answer the questions asked in The Bottom Line and support your opinions.

To encourage people to report suspected cases of neglect and abuse, provincial and territorial legislation treats the information received as confidential. The identity of the person making a report will not be revealed unless it should prove necessary for a court hearing. As well, the person supplying the information is protected from legal action, unless the report was made without reasonable grounds or with malicious intent. In that case, the informant may be liable for damages.

Extreme cases of abuse are easy to identify, but they represent only a small percentage of the total picture. Even cases of severe abuse may not be readily identifiable. (The injuries may be covered by clothing, or the child may have carefully rehearsed explanations for bruises and cuts.) A child's behaviour may indicate a form of abuse. Signs of withdrawal, truancy from school, aggression, depression, overtiredness, and a strong need to control others may be evidence that the child is in trouble. Emotional abuse and neglect are the most difficult to identify and to prove.

Child Abuse Registry

Most provinces and territories have established a child abuse registry, a record of information about reports of abuse, including details of the incident, the child's identity and that of the alleged abuser, and the relationship between them. These registries have made it harder for parents to cover up acts of abuse; for example, by taking the child to a different doctor on each occasion to avoid detection. If medical personnel suspect child abuse, they have quick access to information files about suspected abusing parents. A person whose name is entered into the registry must be notified of this fact. Suspects who can prove that no abuse occurred can request to have their names removed from the registry. Access to registry information is restricted; it is not available to the general public. In Ontario, for example, the law prohibits police from obtaining information without a search warrant. In some provinces, a person applying for a job involving contact with children may be asked to consent to a name search in the registry.

Removal of Children

Authorities can obtain a search warrant to enter a home and remove children when there is a strong suspicion that they need protection. If there is a very strong reason to have children removed without waiting for a warrant, it can and will be done to protect the children. In October 2000, the Supreme Court of Canada ruled in a 5 to 2 decision in *Winnipeg Child and Family Services v. K.L.W.* that social workers who reasonably believe a child or children need protection should be able to remove them without warrants. The dissenting judges warned that giving such powers to social workers could lead to abuse in removing children.

Children who are taken from their parents are brought before a Family Court judge, usually within seven days in most provinces. Parents must be notified of this hearing. The decision to provide protection for a child ultimately rests with the courts. If a court finds that a child is in need of protection, the court may issue one of the orders discussed on the next page.

Supervision Order

A **supervision order** allows the children to remain in the custody of their parents, under the supervision of the Children's Aid Society or other child protection agency. This might occur when the children require some professional care and attention yet are still best off at home.

Society Wardship

A **society wardship** allows the legal custody and guardianship of the children to be transferred to a child protection agency on a temporary basis. In most provinces, the period is 12 months. Children are usually placed in a foster or group home during this time, and parents are allowed some visiting rights. At the end of this time, children must either be returned home, made a Crown ward and enter long-term care, or be adopted.

Such an order might be required when the child needs medical care contrary to the parents' religious beliefs. It could also be required when a child is born addicted to drugs because of the mother's addiction during pregnancy. Since there is a risk that these children might not receive adequate care and treatment at home, an order will be issued for support services. A society wardship suggests that a positive child–parent relationship will be restored within time. Parents may usually request a review of supervision or temporary wardship orders, similar to the procedure with custody and access decisions.

Crown Wardship

A **Crown wardship** enables a child to become a permanent ward of a Children's Aid Society. The CAS becomes responsible for the child's care until age 18 (in Ontario, until age 16). The parents lose all rights of control over their child. An example of such a situation would be parents who leave very young children alone, exposing them to possible danger. The children become wards of the state and can be placed with foster parents or given up for adoption. In such circumstances, the consent of the child's parents is not required. Once adoption occurs, the parents have no right to visit their children.

Damages for Child Abuse

Civil actions for cash damages by survivors of childhood abuse are becoming more common. Most of these cases involve adults bringing actions against abusing parents, stepparents, siblings, or other relatives for damages in the torts of assault and battery, and negligence. These torts were discussed in Chapter 12. Although most lawsuits for damages involve female victims suing male offenders, often for incest committed by a father, some actions have involved claims by male victims against either male or female offenders.

An area of increasing controversy and concern is the abuse reported by Aboriginal children who attended residential schools from 1930 until 1996. The schools were funded by the government and operated by several different churches. About 8500 former residents have filed claims alleging

Did You Know?

In 2000, Statistics Canada estimated that 500 000 Canadian children have been exposed to domestic violence in the past five years. A study shows that more than half of them suffer from stress disorders after witnessing this type of violence.

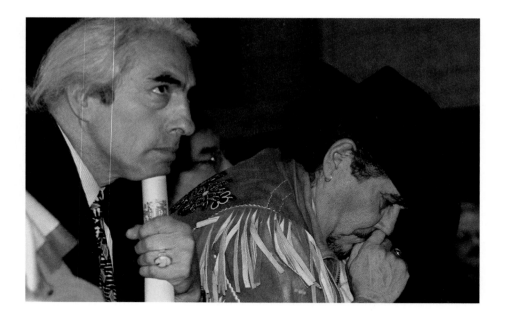

Figure 14-16

Phil Fontaine (left), representing the Assembly of First Nations, and Harry Daniels, representing the Congress of Aboriginal Peoples, listen as federal officials apologize to the Aboriginal peoples for their treatment in residential schools.

ⓔ activity

Visit **www.law.nelson.com** and follow the links to find out about the Law Commission of Canada's *Institutional Child Abuse Report*.

abuse. Government officials estimate that the claims could be worth between $1 and $1.5 billion. In October 2001, the federal government offered to pay 70 percent of the amount owed jointly by the government and churches to Aboriginal men and women with valid claims.

As you read in Chapter 11, most civil actions must begin within a certain time frame. Until recently, this has prevented abused children from taking action years after the event. However, in 1992, the Supreme Court of Canada ruled in *M. (K.) v. M. (H.)* that the allowable period should begin only when the adult victim understands the harm caused by the childhood abuse. Often, this does not occur until the victim obtains counselling and treatment as an adult. A child victim may also sue a parent for breach of care in failing to protect him or her.

Case

J. (L.A.) v. J. (H.)

(1993) 13 O.R. (3d) 306
Ontario Court, General Division

The 20-year-old plaintiff, L.A.J., brought an action against her mother and father for negligence, and against her mother for breach of duty of care as a parent. Evidence presented in court indicated that the father, H.J., started sexually molesting the plaintiff when she reached the age of 12. She was told that such activity was natural, and H.J. gave his daughter money and gifts to obtain her cooperation and silence.

When the mother caught her husband having sexual intercourse with their daughter, she accepted her husband's promise that it would never happen again because she feared losing him and his financial support. Over the next six years, the abuse continued. At one point, the mother and daughter left home for a shelter for abused women. However, when the Children's Aid Society inquired about possible sexual abuse, the mother denied any problem.

At trial on the criminal charges, the defendant father assumed responsibility for his actions and characterized his wife as an unwitting victim of his misconduct. He was sentenced to a four-year prison

continued ▶

sentence for the sexual assaults. In a separate civil action, the plaintiff daughter was awarded $90 700 in general damages jointly from her mother and father, and an additional $45 000 in punitive damages from the mother alone. (See page 321 to review general and punitive damages.)

For Discussion

1. What choices were available to the mother when she discovered that the sexual abuse was occurring?

2. Why was the mother ordered to pay an additional $45 000 in punitive damages to her daughter?

3. Why do you think the father was not required to pay punitive damages as the abuser?

4. What is the significance of this judgment concerning a parent's duty of care toward his or her children?

Review Your Understanding (Pages 440 to 447)

1. Describe the four main types of child abuse, and provide examples.
2. Outline the two main goals of child protection legislation.
3. Who is responsible for reporting suspected child abuse cases?
4. What is the purpose of a child abuse registry? If a name has been incorrectly placed in the registry, what can be done about it?
5. Distinguish between a society wardship and a Crown ward. Which is the more permanent?
6. Why are civil actions by survivors of childhood abuse becoming much more common?

You Be the JUDGE

In *T. (L.) v. T. (R.W.)* (1997), the British Columbia Supreme Court ordered a father to pay damages to his adult daughter for childhood sexual abuse. The court dismissed the woman's claim against her mother because of the mother's "limited education and imagination."

- How is this case similar to and different from *J. (L.A.) v. J. (H.)*?

14.6 Adoption

Adoption is the creation of a legal relationship between a child and adoptive parents, and the ending of that child's legal ties to the **birth parents.** A birth parent is an adopted child's biological mother or father, and someone who consents to the adoption.

Until the early 1970s, many infants were available for adoption in Canada. Since then, there has been a marked decline in the number of babies available because it is now socially acceptable for a young single mother to keep her baby, and many more single parents are raising their own children. As well, birth control and legalized abortion have reduced the number of unplanned births. Currently, there are many more people wanting to adopt a young child than there are young children available to adopt. Because of the limited number of infants and young children available for adoption today, older children, children from other countries, and differently abled children are being adopted by couples who want to build their families.

Each province's adoption laws are part of a comprehensive plan for child care. In Alberta, adoption procedures are found in the *Child Welfare Act,* in Ontario in the *Child and Family Services Act,* and in British Columbia and Manitoba in recently passed Adoption Acts. Since adoption in British Columbia is run by the provincial government, a province-wide database exists. Thus, the characteristics of every approved person or family can be instantly compared to the needs of every child waiting to be adopted. Results can be quickly ranked, listing the top 10 provincial homes for each child. On the other hand, adoption in Ontario is run through each of the 52 Children's Aid Societies, compiling a list of adoptive parents only for its own use.

Eligibility

Generally, a person to be adopted must be under the provincial or territorial age of majority, 18 or 19, and unmarried. In most provinces, adopting parents must be at least the age of majority and may be married or single. As recently as the early 1990s, most adoptive parents were married. Then, in 1994, British Columbia changed its adoption rules to give single people the right to adopt, and other provinces soon followed.

Although Canadian gay men and lesbians have adopted children as single parents for many years, only recently have same-sex couples been able to adopt. The 1999 landmark Supreme Court of Canada decision, *M. v. H.* (see pages 90 and 477), caused most provinces to rewrite many of their laws and to provide same-sex couples the same rights and responsibilities as opposite-sex couples, although a few provinces still excluded adoption from this process.

Agents of Change   Gloria Epstein

She once owned and operated a fishing camp and is now justice of the highest trial court in Ontario. She is a former civil litigator and an active member of the Canadian Equestrian Federation. In June 1998, Ontario Premier Mike Harris entrusted her with the delicate task of reviewing the province's treatment of the Dionne quintuplets. Yet this is merely a glimpse into the busy life of the Honourable Madam Justice Gloria J. Epstein.

Epstein graduated from Queen's University with an Honours Bachelor of Commerce degree in 1972. After graduation, she lived in Temagami, Ontario, where she owned and operated the Camp Manito Hotel Resort for two years. In 1974, she began studying law at the University of Toronto. She was called to the Ontario bar in 1979, and appointed Queen's Counsel in 1992. After practising law with two Toronto firms, Epstein launched her own law firm, Gloria Epstein & Associates. She kept her practice until she was appointed Justice of the Ontario Superior Court of Justice in late 1993. Since then, she has presided over cases in civil, commercial, criminal, and family law.

Figure 14-17

Justice Gloria Epstein

In February 1996, Justice Epstein released her landmark decision in *M. v. H.* (see page 477), reaffirmed by the Ontario Court of Appeal and the Supreme Court of Canada. She held that it was unfair to exclude

continued ▶

same-sex couples from the remedy of spousal support under Ontario's *Family Law Act* because it violated section 15 of the *Canadian Charter of Rights and Freedoms* and was not saved by section 1. As a result, Ontario altered the definition of "spouse" in 67 of its statutes, and provided same-sex couples the same treatment under the law as common-law couples. The federal government also amended all federal statutes including the words "of the opposite sex" and replaced those words with the term "survivor" to ensure equal treatment under the law for opposite- and same-sex relationships.

For Discussion

1. Justice Epstein once said of *M. v. H.*: "With my decision, I understood that I was a mere speed bump on the way at least to the Court of Appeal and, perhaps, to the Supreme Court of Canada." Explain what she meant by this statement.

Some studies have shown that the traditional nuclear family unit is no longer the only acceptable framework for children; the most important factor in healthy child development is a stable and loving relationship between a child and his or her caregiver. These studies suggest that long-term relationships are basically similar, whether the partners are of the opposite or the same sex. Allowing same-sex partners to adopt is still a very sensitive issue, and court challenges are likely to occur because many provinces do not yet allow same-sex couples to adopt.

Placement

The process of selecting adoptive parents, placing a child in their custody, and monitoring the situation for a period of time is known as **placement.** Before placing a child with adoptive parents, a social worker from the Children's Aid Society or a related government agency, such as the Department of Social Services, usually conducts a number of interviews with each parent and visits their home. This home study acquaints the worker with the couple and their home environment, and includes references, a doctor's medical report, and a criminal record check. This gathering of information is necessary for making a placement in the child's best interests. The process usually takes 6 to 12 months. It is also necessary for the child to live with the adoptive parents for a certain length of time, usually 6 to 12 months depending on the province or territory, before the adoption is final. If approval is given for final adoption, an adoption order is made in Family Court.

Figure 14-18

A new spin on an old idea?

Parental Consent

In most cases, a child's birth (biological) parent(s) must give consent for adoption to occur. The parent must be completely informed of all the implications of this action. Adoption severs the link between that parent and the child and is final. The consent must be honest, informed, and freely given. Any adoption that occurs as a result of uninformed consent is not legally binding. In certain situations in which consent is being unreasonably withheld or when biological parents cannot be located, the courts can issue an order dispensing with consent.

In many provinces, legislation now requires a child to be a certain age before parental consent to adopt can be given. It ranges from 7 to 14 days, depending on the province. This period gives the baby's mother time, following childbirth, to consider at length this serious decision. The birth father's consent is also usually required. The sooner an infant is placed in a secure, loving environment, the better.

Withdrawal of Consent

A parent who has given consent may have a change of heart. For this reason, a period of 21 to 30 days during which consent may be withdrawn generally applies. During the waiting period, the child is usually placed in a foster home so that the adoptive parents do not have to give the child up should the birth mother change her mind. A birth mother's revocation must be in writing. If there is a good reason, courts may allow a parent to withdraw consent any time up to the final adoption hearing.

Case

Sawan v. Tearoe

(1993) 84 B.C.L.R. (2d) 223
British Columbia Court of Appeal

Figure 14-19
The Tearoes with their adopted son, David.

A baby son, Jordan, was born to Cecilia Sawan, a status Indian, in Alberta on December 3, 1991, following a brief relationship with a non-Native man. She was a single, 18-year-old woman at the time. In early February 1992, Sawan decided to give up her son for adoption to James and Faye Tearoe, a couple from Victoria, British Columbia, and she signed the required consent forms.

Within 10 days, Sawan changed her mind. She mailed a written revocation to the Alberta Ministry of Family and Social Services, as required by Alberta law. However, the revocation was never received. With the support of the Woodland Cree Band Council at Cadotte Lake, Alberta, Sawan began legal proceedings to regain custody of her son. Sawan and the Woodland Crees believed that the child should be raised in a Native culture.

Meanwhile, the Tearoes applied in British Columbia to adopt the child, now named David, and to dispense with Sawan's consent. At the time of this application, the baby boy had been in his mother's care for a total of 22 days, while he had been in the Tearoes' care continuously for

continued ▶

16 months. The Tearoes, who had married in 1978, adopted their first child, a daughter named Heidi, in 1984.

At trial in the British Columbia Supreme Court, the judge ruled in favour of Sawan, believing that it was in the child's best interests to be raised in a Native culture with his birth mother and that the bond between Sawan and her son had not been irretrievably broken. The Tearoes appealed this trial decision to the British Columbia Court of Appeal where, in a 3 to 0 judgment, the court allowed the appeal and ruled in favour of the Tearoes. Leave to appeal to the Supreme Court of Canada was dismissed in February 1994.

For Discussion

1. Upon which factors did the trial judge base the decision?

2. What do you think would be the impact of the Court of Appeal's decision on the relationship between Sawan and her son? Why?

3. Prepare a list of arguments for and against the Tearoes retaining custody of David.

4. The Court of Appeal's judgment stated: "To remove David from the Tearoe home would destroy the family bonds that have been established between the child and the adoptive parents.... Therefore, it is not in the best interests of this child to revoke Ms. Sawan's consent to adoption." Do you agree with the Court of Appeal's decision? Why or why not?

Domestic Adoptions

Once the probation period has ended and all consents have been obtained, a private hearing is held to grant an adoption order. If the child is over the age of 7 in Ontario or the age of 12 in British Columbia or Manitoba, he or she must also give consent to the proposed adoption. In granting the order, the court must be completely satisfied that the parents applying for the order are suitable parents for the child. At this point, the child becomes the legal child of the adoptive parents and assumes all the rights of a natural child. All ties with the child's natural parent(s) are terminated. Even the child's birth certificate is changed to identify the adopting parents as the biological parents of the child.

A domestic adoption is not as expensive as a private or international adoption. There is no fee for the home study or for registering the adoption. However, there may be a charge for medical reports, criminal record checks, and travel and accommodation.

Private Adoptions

Private or direct placement adoptions can also be arranged by an individual or agency licensed by the appropriate government ministry. Licences are renewed on a regular basis as long as the licensee meets the required standards.

Private adoptions can occur when a pregnant woman seeks a licensed individual or agency to help her find a family for her baby, or when a prospective adoptive parent asks a licensee to help make arrangements with a woman planning to give up her child. Home studies are also required, and the licensee must arrange for a government-approved social worker to conduct the home visit. In recent years, private adoptions have overtaken those occurring through social agencies and Children's Aid Societies.

Two major differences exist between agency adoptions and private adoptions. In an agency adoption, there are many approved people available to adopt the child; in a private adoption, only one set of parents is usually proposed. The birth parent may select the child's adoptive parents after reviewing case profiles of approved parents. Agency adoptions are handled without cost, while private adoptions can cost up to $10 000 for fees and services rendered. In spite of this cost, private adoptions may be more appealing to some couples because the waiting period for an infant is much shorter, usually within three years.

International Adoptions

In recent years, it has become more popular to adopt children overseas. Each year in Canada, about 2000 children are adopted from such countries as China, Vietnam, Guatemala, Russia, Romania, and Ukraine. The cost of adopting differs from country to country, but Canadians can expect to pay up to $35 000 for a child, including airfare and a visit to that country, which usually lasts several weeks.

A person considering an international adoption must first contact the appropriate government ministry or department; for example, Ontario's Ministry of Community and Social Services or Manitoba Family Services. Citizenship and Immigration Canada is responsible for the immigration process that allows the adopted child to come to Canada. In most provinces, adopting parents must hire an agency licensed by the provincial government to facilitate adoptions from the child's country of origin.

Adoption Disclosure Register

In the past, many experts believed it was best for everyone involved in an adoption to keep the information totally secret. The confidentiality of adoption records was intended to protect the adoptive parents, the birth parents, and the adoptee. This attitude is changing dramatically. Birth parents may want to be assured that the adoption decision they made was a good one. In addition, adoptive parents are appreciating the many benefits to the adoptive child of developing an ongoing contact with birth parents.

Since July 1987, Ontario has had an Adoption Disclosure Register (ADR). The ADR is maintained by the Ontario Ministry of Community and Social Services and provides two essential services: (1) It serves as a register for those adult adoptees, birth parents, and birth relatives (siblings and grandparents) who wish to contact each other and/or exchange updated information; and (2) It conducts searches for birth parents and specific birth relatives at the request of an adoptee who is 18 years of age or older.

Adopted children under age 18 may request this procedure with their adoptive parents' consent. At the request of an adoptee 18 years of age or over, the Ministry of Community and Social Services will make a "discreet search"

Figure 14-20

Simone Lai Ming and her adoptive mother, Jessica Pegis, residents of Toronto, Ontario. China was one of the first countries in the world to permit single-parent international adoption.

e activity

Visit **www.law.nelson.com** and follow the links to learn more about adoption procedures in your province or territory and for international adoptions.

for a natural parent or birth relative. Non-identifying information, such as the birth family's ethnic origin, religion, medical history, type of occupation, level of education, and reasons for the adoption will be released on request. Similar information about the adoptive family's background will be provided to a birth parent. To begin a search, a person should start with the Children's Aid Society or the licensed individual or agency that arranged the adoption.

Information about the identity of an adult adoptee or birth relative will be shared only if both parties have submitted their names to the Adoption Disclosure Register and consent to disclosure. Consent of the adoptive parents is not required. Because the issues surrounding adoption are so complex, emotional, and often sensitive, professional counselling is provided before the possible reunion takes place. There is no fee for this service. Once you have registered, you are not required to proceed; you can stop the process at any point. The interest in these procedures is so high that thousands of adopted people face a possible five- to eight-year wait because of the enormous backlog in the ministry conducting the searches. Not all provinces have similar adoption registers.

Figure 14-21

Ontario MPP Marilyn Churley (right), pictured here with NDP leader Alexa McDonough, is a strong advocate of adoption reform. Churley wants to amend current adoption disclosure legislation so that birth parents and adoptees can obtain records and information directly, without government involvement.

Review Your Understanding (Pages 447 to 453)

1. Outline three reasons why there is a shortage of infants available for adoption in Canada today.
2. How has the eligibility to adopt changed in recent years?
3. Briefly describe what happens in the placement process for an adoption.
4. Why is parental consent so important before an adoption is finalized?
5. Describe the major differences between agency adoptions and private adoptions.
6. What is the Ontario Adoption Disclosure Register? Briefly describe how it operates.

Chapter Review

Chapter Highlights

- Custody and access disputes are areas of family law that seriously affect children.
- Both parents are equally entitled to custody of their children.
- The "best interests of the child" is the only test on which custody and access disputes are resolved. A stable home environment is probably the most important factor to consider.
- Courts try to keep siblings together as often as possible, unless there is a good reason to separate them.
- Joint custody or shared parenting gives both parents an opportunity to maintain contact with their children.
- There are three types of access: reasonable, specified, and supervised.
- Access and custody orders are always open for review if conditions change.
- Mobility rights are an increasing concern in court applications.
- Child abduction, in which a parent decides to take a child not legally in his or her custody, is on the rise.
- The 1997 federal Child Support Guidelines were one of the most significant family law reforms in many years. These guidelines are intended to provide consistency, fairness, objectivity, and predictability in court decisions of child support.
- Although the Child Support Guidelines are closely followed by judges, exceptions may occur for undue hardship or extraordinary expenses.
- The four types of child abuse are physical, sexual, emotional, and neglect.
- Civil actions for monetary damages by survivors of childhood abuse are increasing.
- Adoption is the creation of a legal relationship between a child and new parents and the ending of legal ties between the child and his or her birth parents.

Review Key Terms

Name the key terms that are described below.

a) the care and control of a child
b) time spent with the non-custodial parent in the presence of another person
c) a custody order in which the children remain with one parent while the other parent has generous access rights
d) an adopted child's natural or biological mother and father
e) any behaviour that endangers a child's development, security, or survival
f) brothers and sisters
g) the only factor used to determine custody and access to a child
h) the process of selecting adoptive parents with whom to place a child, and monitoring the match for a short time
i) the parent most responsible for basic child-care jobs
j) a custody order in which the children spend equal, or nearly equal, time with both parents
k) the right of the non-custodial parent to visit his or her child
l) an order that a child be removed from his or her parents' custody and become a permanent ward of the CAS or other child services agency
m) selected time spent with a non-custodial parent
n) regular and flexible time spent with a non-custodial parent

Check Your Knowledge

1. Outline the main factors considered in determining custody and access.

2. Identify factors involved in determining the parental obligation for child support.

3. What can the state do to enforce child support payments?

4. Summarize the various types of child abuse.

Apply Your Learning

5. *Hanmore v. Hanmore* (2000), 4 R.F.L. (5th) 348 (Alberta Court of Appeal)

The appellant, Dorothy Hanmore, and the respondent, Charles Hanmore, were married in 1980, divorced in 1986, and had two children who were in their mother's custody. At the time of the divorce, the father was ordered to pay $75 a month per child. He fell behind in his payments and then paid $300 a month for some years until he had paid back payments in full. He then voluntarily continued to pay $300 a month until late 1998, when the mother applied for an increase in child support, seeking the Child Support Guidelines table amount of $562 a month for the two children and extraordinary expenses of $76.

The father opposed her application, claiming financial hardship if he had to pay the guideline amounts. He was supporting a second wife and two children, earned about $32 000 a year, received a supplement between $300 and $500 a month from his father-in-law, and received medical and dental benefits through work. He and his new family lived in a single family dwelling with a large mortgage. The mother, who worked on contract basis and had no medical or dental benefits, had a net annual income of about $29 000. She lived in a rented basement suite with the two children, now aged 15 and 17.

The trial judge ruled that there would be an undue hardship on the father's part if he had to pay the guideline amounts. If the increased support asked for was granted, the respondent would have to support his new family of four on a net income of about $24 000, while the appellant would have about $29 000 to support three people. The mother appealed this decision to the Alberta Court of Appeal where the father's claim of hardship was rejected. He was ordered to pay a total of $637 child support per month, representing the table amount of $562 plus $76 for extraordinary expenses.

a) What factors did the father include in his application claiming financial hardship?

b) Why did the trial judge rule in the father's favour?

c) Why do you think the Court of Appeal ruled in the mother's favour? Explain.

6. *Marsland v. Gibb* (2000), 5 R.F.L. (5th) 406 (British Columbia Supreme Court)

Janice Marsland and Geoffrey Gibb had a daughter, Jennifer, born September 18, 1980. The parents separated when the child was three years old, and the father had access to his daughter until she was 11. He continued to pay support for her throughout this time. In 1991, Jennifer began to refuse to see her father or to go with him on access visits. She even returned her father's Christmas cards and birthday gifts. In 1998, Gibb tried to attend Jennifer's graduation, but Marsland had contacted the school telling them that there was a court order preventing him from having contact with Jennifer. This was not true.

Gibb's other attempts to see his daughter were either rejected by the mother or by the daughter herself. Finally, Jennifer wrote her father stating, "I do not want to see you, nor do I want you phoning me or showing up at events such as my recital.... I am nearly 18 years old and fully capable of making up my own mind. I do not want to hear from you or see you. If at any time my feelings change, I will contact you."

The father, who had been paying child support since 1983, applied for an order terminating child support, while the mother applied for an order requiring continued support under the Child Support Guidelines for their daughter for ongoing educational costs. The court ruled in the father's favour.

a) On what grounds did the father base his application?

b) If you were Jennifer, would you expect support for your education from your father? Why?

c) Why did the trial judge rule in favour of Gibb?

Communicate Your Understanding

7. With a partner, assume the roles of siblings whose parents have divorced. You live with your mother and her new partner; your father has remarried and has more children.

a) Prepare an argument for your father continuing to make the same level of support payments as before his remarriage.

b) Prepare an argument for your father reducing the level of support payments.

c) Objectively determine which set of reasons is better for all concerned.

d) With other groups, compare your conclusions.

8. In small groups, create an advertising campaign that could be used in your school to focus attention on the issue of child abuse. This activity could include posters, school announcements, and video presentations. Highlight what constitutes child abuse and the necessity of reporting child abuse, and provide information on agencies that deal with child abuse.

9. From a newspaper or the Internet, collect at least five articles dealing with issues relating to children and family law as discussed in this chapter.
   a) Summarize the articles in your own words.
   b) Highlight the issue(s) involved.
   c) State and justify your opinion on the issue(s) discussed in the articles.

10. If a divorce is final and property division at that time is final, should custody of children decisions also be final? Express your opinion and support your answer.

11. Instead of following the tender-years principle slavishly, the courts are now considering each parent's parenting abilities. Do you agree or disagree with this direction in awarding custody? Defend your position.

12. Should children be placed with adoptive parents who are of the same race, cultural background, and religion as the child? Discuss with a partner, arguing both sides of the issue.

Develop Your Thinking

13. For many children, the problem with access is that the non-custodial parent visits too rarely or not at all. Should the courts do something to force or encourage unwilling non-custodial parents to visit? Would educational programs help? Discuss in small groups, and try to reach consensus.

14. a) Imagine that you are the custodial parent of two children, aged six and nine. Think of a valid reason not mentioned in this chapter for moving out of the province with your children, thereby making access difficult for your former spouse. Support your right to mobility before the court that is hearing your application for a custody and access change.
    b) Now take the role of the non-custodial parent in this scenario, and present your side of the issue to the judge.
    c) Have the class determine a fair resolution to this conflict, keeping in mind "the best interests of the children."

15. A baby born out of wedlock was offered for adoption by the birth mother. A year after the baby was adopted, the biological father demanded his child, claiming his consent had not been given for the adoption. The adoptive parents claim the child is theirs since they have provided a secure and loving environment.

    Work in groups of three to role-play a judge and two lawyers (one representing each side in the dispute). The lawyers must present arguments to the judge, who must then decide the case, hand down a decision, and explain the legal reasoning behind the decision.

Chapter 15

Division of Family Property and Spousal Support

Focus Questions

- How does the law regard marriage today?
- Why were new laws needed for dividing family property?
- How is family property divided on a marriage breakdown?
- When partners separate, how is spousal support determined?
- How does the law regard common-law relationships?
- What domestic contracts are recognized in law?

Chapter at a Glance

Figure 15-1

Following a divorce, it is impossible to cut the couple's home in two, so there are provincial and territorial laws to ensure that both spouses are treated fairly. This was not always the case, however. What do you think happened in the past?

15.1 Introduction

In Chapter 13, you learned that there is one divorce law for all Canadians because the *Constitution Act* gives the federal government jurisdiction over marriage and divorce. However, the provinces and territories have jurisdiction over property and civil rights. These provincial and territorial laws regulate

- child custody and access
- division of family property
- spousal support

When a marriage breaks down today, provincial and territorial laws control the fair and equal division of the value of the property between married couples. This kind of legislation does not currently exist for common-law or same-sex partners, no matter how long they have lived together. Some legislation provides certain rights for these partners and is discussed later in this chapter.

During a marriage, both spouses have financial obligations to support each other and any children of the marriage. When the spouses separate, these obligations do not disappear. Provincial legislation deals with support during separation. When couples divorce, the federal *Divorce Act, 1985,* regulates support obligations.

Some couples may want to specify their rights, responsibilities, and obligations to each other in the event that they divorce. Or they may want to opt out of provincial legislation that would dictate the division of property upon marriage breakdown. To accommodate these couples, provincial and territorial legislation now recognizes domestic contracts made by both married and unmarried couples.

15.2 Family Property: A History

Over time, marriage has come to be viewed as an equal partnership. This was not always the case (see Looking Back, below). During the late 1970s and early 1980s, provincial and territorial laws for dividing family property changed significantly. The new laws acknowledged that women contributed to the marriage and to the accumulation of family property even if they did not work outside the home.

Looking Back | Married Women and Property

Under English common law, married women could not own property. When they married, the husband and wife became a single person, or "one being," in the eyes of the law. This one person was always considered to be the husband, who was also in charge of the family property.

This injustice was finally addressed in 1882 with the passage of the *Married Woman's Property Act*. The new British law granted wives the right to own and control property as though they were single. In Canada, provinces that followed the common law used this statute as the basis for similar legislation. But the **separate-property system** often resulted in hardship for women if a marriage ended.

Until the early 1970s, husbands were generally the breadwinners and wives usually looked after the home

continued ▶

and the children. In the event of marriage breakdown, the most common attitude was, "What I paid for is mine and what you paid for is yours." Since many wives earned little, if any, money, they could buy few goods. As a result, husbands owned most of the family property and walked away with it following divorce. The courts did not give the wife an interest in property that was registered in her husband's name, or recognize her contribution in the form of household management and home-care duties.

Even if both spouses worked outside the home, the husband usually earned much more than his wife. Often, his wages were used for the mortgage payments on their home, while her wages paid the household expenses. When the marriage broke down, the husband was considered to be the sole owner of the home if it was registered in his name only, as often happened. Although the wife's wages paid for the family's expenses, which allowed her husband to pay for their home, her financial contribution was not recognized. At best, she might be permitted to keep some items she had actually paid for; for example, her own car.

Clearly, the old property system presented problems—the existing law did not recognize a woman's material contribution to marriage. This injustice became the focus of public attention in the landmark case *Murdoch v. Murdoch* (1975). Legal observers and average Canadians alike were outraged by the Murdoch judgment (see page 460). Over the next decade, all provinces and territories passed new legislation to establish a more equal division of property rights between spouses upon separation or divorce.

For Discussion

1. How did the *Married Woman's Property Act* benefit women?

2. What is the separate-property system? Why did it often result in hardship for women in the event of marriage breakdown?

3. What impact did the *Murdoch v. Murdoch* decision have on the division of property law?

Figure 15-2

Was this her property, too? Not likely.

Case

Murdoch v. Murdoch

[1975] 1 S.C.R. 423
Supreme Court of Canada

Figure 15-3
Irene Murdoch

Irene Murdoch and her husband were married in 1943. They worked together for hire on various ranches, receiving about $100 a month. In 1947, Murdoch and his father-in-law purchased a guest ranch for $6000. When they sold it four years later, they divided the profit equally between them. In 1952, Mr. Murdoch purchased additional property from money borrowed, in part, from his mother-in-law. The loan was repaid. Over the years, Murdoch bought and then sold bigger and better ranch properties, always in his name. At all times, the Murdochs lived on and operated one or more of these properties. Irene did not make a direct financial contribution to any of these purchases.

During this period, Mr. Murdoch got a job at a cattle stock association. While her husband was away for up to five months of the year working for the association, Irene performed or supervised many of the necessary chores, including driving trucks and tractors; haying; mowing; vaccinating,

branding, and dehorning cattle; and working with horses. In effect, while her husband was absent, she ran their properties.

Marital problems arose, and in 1968, Irene left her husband after 25 years of marriage. She brought actions for separation, support, and custody of their son, as well as a one-half interest in all lands and assets owned by her husband, on the basis that they were equal partners. Irene claimed that payments from her bank account were contributions to the partnership agreement. Mr. Murdoch claimed that the money he received from time to time usually came from his in-laws and was always repaid. As well, all land, livestock, and equipment were held in his name, and income-tax returns were filed in his name only. No formal partnership declaration existed between them.

The trial court granted Irene a separation and support of $200 a month. The father was awarded custody of their son, and Irene's claim for the one-half interest was dismissed. Irene appealed to the Appellate Division of the Supreme Court of Alberta, and her action was again dismissed. She then brought a further appeal to the Supreme Court of Canada. In a 4 to 1 decision, the Supreme Court ruled that Irene was not entitled to any interest in her husband's land and assets because there was no evidence of either a direct financial contribution on her part or a partnership agreement between them. All the work she had done was merely the work "that would be done by any farm wife."

For Discussion

1. Outline three reasons why all three courts dismissed Irene's claim to a one-half interest in the land and assets.

2. Was the work done by her typical of that done by any farm or ranch wife? Discuss.

3. What is your opinion of the federal Supreme Court's decision and why?

4. Should marriage be considered a partnership that recognizes contributions in the form of household management and home-care duties? Why or why not?

Agents of Change   Bora Laskin

Bora Laskin, legal scholar, judge, and civil rights advocate, was born in Fort William, Ontario (now Thunder Bay), on October 5, 1912. He pursued law degrees at the University of Toronto and Osgoode Hall and received an LL.M. (a master's degree in law) from Harvard University in 1937. Although he never practised law, he was destined to become one of Canada's great law teachers.

In 1940, Laskin became a founding member of the University of Toronto's Faculty of Law. Despite graduating from Harvard University with a brilliant record, he had battled anti-Semitism to gain this position. As a faculty member, he was an outstanding scholar, particularly in the areas of labour and constitutional law. His example and life work of fighting racism helped break down barriers for others.

Laskin's teaching career ended in 1965 when he was appointed to the Ontario Court of Appeal. He was named to the Supreme Court of Canada in 1970. In 1973, Prime Minister Pierre Elliott Trudeau named him the 14th Chief Justice of the Supreme Court of Canada, a position he held until his death on March 26, 1984. He was the first Jewish judge appointed to the Court.

One of Laskin's most significant judgments was his dissenting opinion in the Murdoch case. He was the only one of the five male Supreme Court justices who supported Irene Murdoch's claim to a share of the ranches she and her husband had owned for 25 years. Many Canadians felt that Irene Murdoch had been let down by the Supreme Court, and Laskin's judgment focused national attention on the legal inequities faced by Canadian women. Within a few years, all provinces and territories had passed legislation that recognized women's rights to an equal share of family property.

In 1985, the Bora Laskin National Fellowship was established by the Social Sciences and Humanities

Figure 15-4

Bora Laskin, Chief Justice, Supreme Court of Canada

Research Council of Canada to encourage research and development of Canadian expertise in the field of human rights. The annual fellowship is worth $45 000, plus an allowance for research and travel expenses. In March 1991, the Bora Laskin Law Library at the University of Toronto opened in his honour.

For Discussion

1. Why is Bora Laskin considered an agent of change?

2. What is the legal significance of Laskin's lone dissenting decision in the Murdoch case?

Review Your Understanding (Pages 458 to 461)

1. Which aspects of the divorce process are regulated by the provinces and territories?

2. Did married women have a right to property under common law? Explain.

3. Name one person mentioned in this section who had a major impact on family law. Support your choice with reasons.

15.3 Dividing Family Property

The provincial and territorial statutes that deal with the division of property following divorce have different names in different provinces and territories. For example, British Columbia passed the *Family Relations Act*, Alberta and Saskatchewan the *Matrimonial Property Act*, and Ontario and several Atlantic provinces the *Family Law Act*. However, the basic intent of the statutes is similar. Each recognizes marriage as an economic partnership to which the spouses contribute equally. All forms of contribution are considered equally significant. This text does not provide a detailed analysis of each statute. Since the Ontario legislation is the most detailed, it is the focus of this section.

activity

Visit **www.law.nelson.com** and follow the links to learn more about property division in your province or territory.

The Family Law Act, 1986

In 1978, after the Murdoch decision, Ontario passed the first major division-of-property legislation in Canada, recognizing marriage as an equal partnership. This law led to passage of Ontario's *Family Law Act* in 1986. Legally married spouses in all provinces and territories are now entitled to share the value of everything acquired during the marriage, with a few exceptions. Common-law and same-sex partners do not have the same automatic division of property rights. However, they do have some rights to claims for support if certain conditions are met. These claims are discussed in greater detail in Section 15.5 of this chapter.

Calculating Family Property and Equalization Payments

The *Family Law Act* provides steps for dealing with property following a marriage breakdown. The legislation does not divide specific property, only the value of the property. The process is fairly complicated and usually requires couples to seek legal advice.

First, the law requires the spouses to calculate the total net value of all their assets on the date they separated. Almost everything of value to the couple is included, such as furniture, appliances, personal property, bank accounts, savings and investments, pensions, registered retirement savings plans (RRSPs), and business interests. Determining the value of most of these assets is easy. Complications may arise in the valuation of pension plans or in calculating the future worth of a spouse, such as a doctor or dentist who has professional training and substantial business interests. In these cases, the couple might need to consult an accountant or a lawyer to assist with the calculations.

Once the value of everything owned by each spouse has been established, the couple must subtract the value of the following:
- the value of gifts (from someone other than the spouse), or inheritances received
- damages from personal injury lawsuits
- proceeds from insurance policies

The next step involves adding up all the debts on the date of separation. This includes debts such as car loans, mortgages, credit-card payments, and so on. If these debts belong to both spouses, then half their value belongs to each spouse. The couple subtracts the total debts from the value of the total assets to determine the total value of the property on the day of separation. Next, each spouse creates a list of property owned and debts held on the day of the marriage. The value of the items is on the date of marriage, not the current value. Then each spouse subtracts the value of all debts on the day of marriage to determine the total marriage-date value of properties.

After the couple totals their individual property values, the spouse with the greater value of **net family property** gives the other spouse an **equalization payment** in cash, property, or investment shares, to make up one-half the difference between the two figures. For example, if Alexi has a net family property of $20 000 while Michelle has a net family property of $50 000, the difference between the two totals is $30 000. The *Family Law Act* states that the spouse with the higher total has to pay the spouse with the lower total half of the difference between them. Half of $30 000 is $15 000, so Michelle would have to pay Alexi $15 000 as an equalization payment.

Usually, each spouse keeps the property that he or she is using or that is registered in his or her name. The balancing payment often comes from the proceeds of the sale of their home, a transfer of RRSPs, or a loan. If the equalization payment is a large amount, it may be paid over time instead of in a lump sum.

Figure 15-5 summarizes the steps in calculating family property.

▌ Steps in Calculating Family Property and Equalization Payments

Step 1	List and calculate the value of your assets on the date of separation.
Step 2	Subtract from the value of assets the value of inheritances, gifts, personal injury awards, and life-insurance proceeds.
Step 3	Subtract your total debts on the date of separation to provide a total property value on the date of separation.
Step 4	List and calculate the value of your assets, less debts, on the date of marriage.
Step 5	Subtract amount #4 from amount #3 to calculate each spouse's "net family property."
Step 6	Deduct the lower "net family property" from the higher one and divide the difference by two to determine the amount of the equalization payment.

Figure 15-5

The steps to be followed in calculating net family property and determining the amount of an equalization payment

Figure 15-6 shows how this process could be used for an actual couple, Isabella and Ethan.

▌ An Example

Steps in the Process	Isabella	Ethan
1. Value of assets at separation	$60 000	$300 000
2. Less: Exemption for inheritance received	35 000	0
3. Less: Debts/liabilities at separation	0	100 000
= Total property value at separation	25 000	200 000
4. Less: Value of assets at marriage	5 000	50 000
5. Net Family Property	20 000	150 000
6. **End result:** Isabella deducts her net family property from Ethan's net family property and is entitled to one-half the difference. Half of $130 000 equals $65 000.	$150 000 20 000 $130 000 $65 000	

Figure 15-6

This example shows the calculation of net family property and the determination of an equalization payment.

Spouses can opt out of an equal division of property sharing by having a marriage contract that exempts certain assets from division. (Marriage contracts are discussed later in this chapter, on page 481.)

Figure 15-7

It may be mobile, but the law says it's still the matrimonial home, provided it meets the basic requirements.

The Matrimonial Home

The **matrimonial home**—the home in which spouses live while married—is generally their most valuable asset. The *Family Law Act* says the matrimonial home applies only to legally married spouses and must be located in-province. The provincial statutes say that the matrimonial home can be a house, a mobile home, a condominium, or any dwelling owned by one or both spouses. If, for example, Ethan and Isabella spend part of the year in their Vancouver condominium and the rest at their chalet in Whistler, then both homes may be considered matrimonial homes. Places that are used only a few times each year for recreational purposes probably are not matrimonial homes.

Each spouse has an equal right to live in the matrimonial home and to share equally in the proceeds if the couple agrees to sell it (unless a marriage contract states otherwise). Because the right to possession of the home does not depend on ownership, the spouse who may be the legal owner cannot force the other spouse to leave. However, if one spouse unreasonably withholds consent, or cannot be located, or is mentally incompetent, the court has the power to order the sale of the home without consent.

On separation, the courts may grant one spouse exclusive possession of the matrimonial home and its contents for a certain period. This spouse must first convince the court that sharing the home is a practical impossibility. Second, this spouse must show that his or her claim should be preferred over the other's; in other words, that remaining in the home is extremely important to him or her. In such a situation, the courts consider the financial position of both spouses, the availability of other accommodation, and the best interests of any children. This option is most often used when one spouse has custody of the children and wants to remain in the matrimonial home until they have grown up and finished school.

After the period of exclusive occupancy ends, the spouses usually divide the value of the matrimonial home. (This will not occur in a situation where the couple has signed a marriage contract and one party has released his or her property interest in the home.) This division may involve selling the property and dividing the sale proceeds; alternatively, one spouse may buy out the other's interest. If there is no end date on the exclusive occupancy order, the parties must eventually set one or the court will order one to be set. At that time, the asset must be divided.

Significant Legislative Differences

The assets that may be divided upon separation differ among provinces and territories. In provinces other than Ontario, these assets are known as **matrimonial property** (marital property). For example, legislation in Alberta, Saskatchewan, Manitoba, and Quebec states that all property acquired by the spouses during marriage is to be divided equally. The Atlantic provinces and Yukon Territory, on the other hand, distinguish between family assets and non-family (business) assets associated with one spouse only.

A **family asset** is the matrimonial home and property owned by one or both spouses that is "ordinarily used or enjoyed by the spouses or one or more of their children for family purposes." Examples include the family cottage, the family car or cars, and money in a joint bank account normally used to run the household (e.g., paying bills). Art works displayed in the family home are also family assets. The intent of the law, in most cases, is to allow family assets to be divided equally between the spouses.

British Columbia's *Family Relations Act* states that each spouse is entitled to a one-half interest in all family assets after the marriage breaks down. However, family assets are more widely defined in British Columbia than in other provinces or territories, and include such items as pension plans and RRSPs. In addition, property owned by either spouse before the marriage that is later used by the family is considered a family asset. For example, a cottage and a boat owned by the wife prior to marriage and used frequently by the whole family would be a family asset. Furthermore, one spouse's interest in a business might be considered a family asset if the other spouse made some contribution to it.

Non-family assets (business assets) include stocks and bonds, pension funds, RRSPs, and most business interests. These assets are not divided equally because they are not family property. Instead, they belong to the spouse who purchased them. They would only be divided with the other spouse if he or she helped to build up the assets and could prove it. Such a situation might arise, for example, when one spouse works to put the other through university or gives up a career opportunity to stay in the home and raise children, thereby contributing to the future success, earnings, and investments of the other spouse.

In summary, there are three principles of law for the division of marital property in all provinces and territories:

1. The property of the marriage is to be divided equally between the spouses unless injustice or inequity would result.
2. The contribution of the spouse who is primarily responsible for child care and home management should be legally recognized. Such a contribution gives the other spouse an opportunity to acquire property that might not be a family asset.
3. The contribution of each spouse should be legally recognized, whether in the form of money or work, toward the acquisition of property. This principle does not apply to provinces or territories that still distinguish between family and business assets.

Exemption from the Equal Division Rule

Every province and territory has the intention of distributing the marital property equally. However, there are situations in which this might be very unfair. Consider the following:

- **Length of the Marriage**
  Mark and Lynn have not been married long, and dividing the value of family assets equally may be unfair to Lynn. She brought much more property into the marriage than Mark.

- **Length of the Separation**
  Nabil and Hannah separated many years ago. Subsequently, they bought furnishings for their separate accommodations. It would be unfair to divide these assets equally because both Nabil and Hannah bought them for personal use after they separated.

- **Date When an Asset Was Acquired**
  Gary bought an expensive Ming vase for himself just before separating from Danielle. He wishes to keep this asset. Depending on the circumstances, Gary might not have to divide the value of the vase with Danielle.

- **Gifts and Inheritances**
  Thalia received an inheritance from a wealthy uncle while she was married to Todd. This inheritance may be specifically excluded from equal division. It is unfair to require a spouse to share a valuable family heirloom given as a present by a close relative or left as an inheritance in a will. (This could change, however, if Thalia invests her inheritance in the matrimonial home.)

The courts will consider other relevant circumstances when determining one spouse's contribution to any property that might be considered a marriage asset. Still, while legislation gives courts discretion to make an unequal division of property, this may not happen. Judges do not have to use this discretion, but it is available to be used when appropriate.

Most provincial and territorial statutes have removed judicial discretion in property division, unless a strict application of the law of equal division would lead to an **unconscionable judgment.** The term "unconscionable" means grossly or shockingly unfair and is likely to be applied only in extreme cases; for example, when the marriage was very brief, or when one spouse has intentionally and recklessly depleted or squandered his or her assets prior to the separation.

 activity

Visit **www.law.nelson.com** and follow the links to research a case in which an unequal division of property was awarded.

Review Your Understanding (Pages 462 to 466)

1. Outline how property is divided under Ontario's *Family Law Act.*

2. What are "net family property" and an equalization payment?

3. What can be considered a matrimonial home, and what rights of possession and ownership does each spouse have concerning that home?

4. How does the division of property in other provinces differ from procedures in Ontario?

5. Summarize the three principles all provinces and territories follow in the division of marital property.

6. Outline four situations in which an equal division of the value of property might be unfair.

15.4 Spousal Support

Couples who separate often encounter financial problems. This is especially true if one spouse has been dependent on the other during the marriage. As you learned in Chapter 14, dependent children also require support, especially if they live with the dependent spouse. The general purpose of **spousal support**—money paid by one spouse to another after marriage breakdown—is to compensate one spouse for any financial losses suffered as a result of the marriage breakdown and to assist that spouse until he or she gains **self-sufficiency;** in other words, becomes self-supporting. Spousal support is *not* intended to punish or blame the other spouse. It is also not automatic—the spouse in need must apply for support.

Why should one spouse have to support the other spouse after their marriage has ended? For how long should support be paid? Each case is different and is decided on its own merits. It is usually difficult to compare or even predict the amounts a court awards.

Both the federal *Divorce Act, 1985,* and provincial and territorial legislation contain provisions for the support of spouses and children. In the case of divorce, the federal law applies; in the event of separation, provincial and territorial legislation applies. Although support rights and obligations differ from province to province, the principles are similar.

▌ Provincial Support Legislation

Province/Territory	Name of Act
Alberta	Domestic Relations Act
British Columbia	Family Relations Act
Manitoba	Family Maintenance Act
New Brunswick	Family Services Act
Newfoundland & Labrador	Family Law Act
Northwest Territories	Family Law Act
Nova Scotia	Family Maintenance Act
Nunavut	Domestic Relations Act
Ontario	Family Law Act
Prince Edward Island	Family Law Act
Quebec	Civil Code of Quebec
Saskatchewan	Family Maintenance Act
Yukon Territory	Family Property & Support Act

Figure 15-8

Notice that all the provinces have different legislation affecting support obligations. Why isn't there a single piece of legislation for all the provinces?

Factors Affecting Support

As you learned in Chapter 13, the federal government introduced the *Divorce Act* in 1985. It outlines four objectives for awarding spousal support (see The Law, page 468).

The federal *Divorce Act* and provincial and territorial laws guide judges in determining if support should be awarded and, if so, how much. Judges weigh the following factors when considering support:

- assets and financial status of each spouse, including present and future earning ability
- ability of each spouse to be self-supporting
- ability of each spouse to provide support to the other spouse, if necessary
- age and physical and mental health of each spouse
- length of time the spouses were married or lived together
- length of time required by the spouse in need to acquire or upgrade job skills
- length of time one spouse spent at home raising the family instead of contributing financially by working outside the home

Notice that the behaviour of the spouses is not included in this list. The obligation to provide support for a spouse exists without regard to the other spouse's conduct. The *Divorce Act, 1985,* entirely eliminated conduct (behaviour) from consideration as an issue of support. Only if a spouse's behaviour is so shocking or unconscionable as to cause public concern would it become a factor under some provincial or territorial law. Few cases exist in which this has occurred.

Judges may order one spouse to pay the other spouse indefinitely or for a certain period. A judge may order the support to be paid in the form of one lump sum or weekly, monthly, or yearly payments. Either party can apply to the court to have the spousal support order increased, decreased, or stopped if circumstances change. This may arise from a change in salary, remarriage, unemployment, or poor health. A change in circumstances does not mean that the order for maintenance will vary or end.

Judges recognize that one spouse cannot be expected to support two families equally. Indeed, financial problems can strain second and third marriages more than some of the human problems associated with blended families. When a second marriage results in a blended family, obligations to the first family generally have some priority over obligations to the second family. If the paying parent remarries and establishes a new second family, those obligations do not exempt that person from paying child support to the first family. As a result, if there is insufficient income to support both families equally, most judges will at least ensure that the two families are treated equally.

The Law   The Divorce Act, 1985

Excerpts from the *Divorce Act, 1985*

15.2

(1) A court ... may, on application by either or both spouses, make an order requiring one spouse to secure or pay ... such lump sum or periodic sums ... as the court thinks reasonable for the support of

   (a) the other spouse; ...

(7) An order ... that provides for the support of a spouse should

   (a) recognize any economic advantages or disadvantages to the spouses arising from the marriage or its breakdown;

   (b) apportion [divide] between the spouses any financial consequences arising from the care of any child of the marriage over and above the obligation apportioned between the spouses pursuant to subsection (8) [for the support of any child of the marriage];

   (c) relieve any economic hardship of the spouses arising from the breakdown of the marriage; and

   (d) in so far as practicable, promote the economic self-sufficiency of each spouse within a reasonable period of time.

For Discussion

1. **Outline, in your own words, the meaning of each of the objectives in section 15.2(7).**

2. **Which do you think is the most important and why?**

Self-Sufficiency

After 1985, Canada's legal system began to focus on the goal of economic self-sufficiency. It was believed that individuals could quickly gain the necessary skills they had lost or set aside during the marriage to raise a family and become self-sufficient within a reasonable time period, usually two or three years.

Once the marriage ends, each spouse has an obligation, if necessary, to seek additional education, employment, or retraining as quickly as possible to become self-supporting. Today, both spouses are likely to be employed, particularly if they are younger people. If they earn similar salaries, and if each spouse receives a fair share of all assets upon separation, then support may not even be an issue.

If one spouse is unable to achieve self-sufficiency, then the other spouse has a duty to provide support, according to his or her ability to pay. Thus, the need of one spouse and the ability of the other spouse to pay are key elements for the court to consider in granting support.

Most commonly, support is necessary when one spouse has stayed home to care for children and manage the household while the other spouse has been the primary wage earner. An older spouse who has been out of the work force for many years while raising a family may find it especially difficult, even impossible, to gain self-sufficiency. For example, a woman who has been married for 30 years and has few marketable skills may only be able to find part-time work. Such a job is not likely to allow her to become self-sufficient. In such a situation, the courts generally do not place a time limit on a support award. Court orders are often left open, to be reviewed after a certain period of time.

However, if the homemaking spouse is young and has only recently left the work force, support will be given for a limited time only. During this time, that spouse is expected to upgrade employment opportunities or acquire new job skills. Once the spouse receiving support reaches this goal, there is no further need for support. A spouse cannot refuse to work and expect to receive support. If the spouse needing support does not try to become self-sufficient, the other spouse may reduce or stop support payments upon applying to the courts and receiving a ruling.

In the landmark judgment in *Moge v. Moge* (1992), the Supreme Court of Canada rejected the idea that self-sufficiency is the most important consideration in determining support. Instead, all four factors must be considered when spousal support is claimed or an order for support is changed (see The Law, page 468). The self-sufficiency objective is only one of the listed objectives, but nothing in any legislation suggests that it should be given priority. *Moge v. Moge* involved a traditional marriage in which the husband worked and the wife raised three children (see page 470).

The Court was presented with a different set of circumstances in the case of *Bracklow v. Bracklow* (1999). This case involved a professional couple (with two children from a previous marriage), who had similar incomes and who divided expenses equally. One spouse became seriously ill and was not able to work again (see page 471).

These two cases suggest that there are basic reasons for spousal support. First, support compensates people for the economic sacrifices they make for their marriage or the contribution made to a partner's career. Second, support compensates people such as Marie Bracklow, who were married and who now need spousal support from a spouse who can afford it. This second reason for support is still controversial. As you can see from these decisions, support obligations may never be final or permanent. This principle was reaffirmed in *Miglin v. Miglin* (2001) (see page 472).

Case

Moge v. Moge

[1992] 3 S.C.R. 813
Supreme Court of Canada

Andrzej Moge and Zofia Moge were married in Poland in the mid-1950s. The couple moved to Manitoba in 1960. Throughout the marriage, he worked full-time as a welder and learned to speak fluent English. Zofia stayed at home during the day to raise their three children and care for their home. She worked at regular part-time jobs in the evening, cleaning offices. She had a Grade 7 education and spoke little English.

When the couple separated in 1973, she was awarded custody of the children and $150 a month for spousal and child support. In 1980, Andrzej petitioned for divorce; Zofia did not contest the action. During this time, she was unable to find the time to improve her education or find a job that would pay her enough money to raise her family above the poverty line. Although she was able to provide the children with the necessities, she was unable to acquire any assets. Meanwhile, her former husband bought a home and car, accumulated savings, and invested his money. He remarried in 1984.

In 1987, after losing her job when her employer closed down, Zofia sought an increase in support for herself and the one child still living with her; the court awarded her $400. Between 1987 and 1989, Zofia secured some part-time work with the province of Manitoba. Her gross pay was about $800 a month, while Andrzej earned about $2200 a month.

In 1989, Andrzej brought an application to terminate support payments, since he believed that his former wife had had enough time to become financially self-sufficient. In granting Andrzej's application, the trial court judge stated: "She cannot expect that Mr. Moge will support her forever. He has contributed to her support since 1973."

Zofia appealed this decision to the Manitoba Court of Appeal where, in 1990, a 2 to 1 judgment ruled that Andrzej must continue indefinitely paying his former wife $150 a month since she remained economically disadvantaged as a result of her role as caregiver in a traditional marriage. This decision was appealed to the Supreme Court of Canada, and, in a landmark 6 to 0 judgment in December 1992, the court ruled that Andrzej must continue his support payments indefinitely, even though he and his former wife had separated nearly 20 years earlier.

For Discussion

1. Why did Andrzej bring a court action against his former wife in 1989 to terminate support payments?

2. Why did both the Court of Appeal and the Supreme Court of Canada rule in Zofia's favour?

3. Should Zofia be entitled to ongoing support from her husband for an indefinite period of time, or should spousal support be terminated? Discuss with reasons to support your position.

Case

Bracklow v. Bracklow

[1999] 1 S.C.R. 420
Supreme Court of Canada

The appellant, Marie Bracklow, and the respondent, Frank Bracklow, began living together in 1985 and were married in late 1989. During their first two years together, Marie paid two-thirds of the household expenses because she was earning more money as an accountant and a data processor than Frank, a heavy-duty mechanic. In addition, her two children from a previous marriage were living with them. After 1987, they shared the expenses equally until Marie became disabled with mental and physical problems and was forced to stop work completely. Except for periods when she was too ill, the couple shared all household duties. Although her health problems were not related to the marriage, it was unlikely that she would ever work again because of them.

In December 1992, the couple separated. They divorced in early 1995. Frank remarried, and his new wife was employed. Meanwhile, Marie obtained an interim support order of $275 a month, which was later increased to $400 a month in 1994 but ended in 1996. She lived in subsidized housing in Burnaby, British Columbia, and received a monthly federal disability pension of about $800 since a trial court had allowed her ex-husband to stop her monthly support payments. She appealed this decision to the British Columbia Court of Appeal, which upheld the lower court decision, ruling that marriage vows did not include an implied agreement to support each other indefinitely in times of financial need.

Marie then appealed this decision to the Supreme Court of Canada where, in a 9 to 0 judgment in November 1999, the Court ruled that she was entitled to spousal support based on "the length of cohabitation, the hardship the marriage breakdown imposed on her, her needs, and the husband's financial ability to pay." The Court referred the case back to a British Columbia trial court to decide how much support, if any, Frank Bracklow owed his

former wife. The trial judge ruled that Marie was entitled to $400 a month for five years, but was not eligible for indefinite support. In reaching this decision, the judge considered the Bracklows' relatively short relationship and that Frank's new wife depends on him financially.

For Discussion

1. Outline Marie's arguments before the courts.
2. Outline Frank's arguments before the courts.
3. The Court stated: "While it may not prove to be till death do us part, marriage is a serious commitment not to be undertaken lightly. It involves the potential for lifelong obligations. There is no magical cutoff date." Discuss the significance of the Supreme Court's decision.

Figure 15-9
Marie Bracklow

Miglin v. Miglin

(2001) 16 R.F.L. (5th) 185
Ontario Court of Appeal

The appellant, Eric Miglin, and the respondent, Linda Miglin, were married in 1979. In 1981, the Miglins bought Killarney Lodge in northern Ontario for just over $1 million, and each of them owned one half of it. He managed the business while she looked after the administrative and house-keeping tasks. Both worked hard and the hotel thrived—it grossed about $1.5 million a year.

The first of four children was born in 1985, and the last child was born in 1991; there were three daughters and one son. Linda was the primary care-giver of the children. The family spent the summers at the lodge, but she would return to Toronto with the children when school started. At the end of the season, in November, Eric took extended vacations by himself.

In 1993, the marriage failed, and the Miglins' lawyers eventually negotiated a settlement. Three agreements were signed on June 1, 1994. A parenting agreement gave Linda $60 000 yearly in child support. The parents "shared responsibility" for raising the children, but their primary residence was in Toronto with Linda. A consulting agreement ordered the lodge to pay Linda $15 000 annually for her services for a fixed five-year term, subject to cost-of-living increases, and renewable after five years. The separation agreement ordered Linda to trade her share of the lodge for Eric's share of the family home, both worth about $250 000. As well, Linda gave up all rights to spousal support "at no time, now or in the future, ... under any circumstances."

The couple remained separated for the next three years and followed their separation and consulting agreements, but not the parenting one. Eric did not assume his one-half of the parenting duties, as he had promised. The Miglins divorced in early 1997. A few months later, Linda sold the Toronto house to repay substantial debts that had accumulated since the separation, and she and the children moved to a new home north of Toronto. Eric's attitude toward his former wife and her custody of the children changed abruptly, and the couple ended up in a custody battle. He then cancelled her consulting agreement with the lodge.

In June 1998, in spite of the agreements she had signed, Linda applied for sole custody, child support in accordance with the Child Support Guidelines, and spousal support. In February 2000, the trial judge awarded Linda monthly child support of $3000, and monthly spousal support of $4400 for five years, and both parties agreed to joint custody. Eric appealed this judgment to the Ontario Court of Appeal. In a 3 to 0 decision in April 2001, the court upheld the amounts established by the trial judgment and removed the five-year limit on spousal support, ordering it for an indefinite period of time.

Leave to appeal this decision to the Supreme Court of Canada was granted in late 2001.

For Discussion

1. Outline the basis for Linda's case.
2. Outline the basis for Eric's appeal.
3. Why did the courts rule in favour of Linda?
4. Why did Eric appeal this decision to the Supreme Court of Canada?

Enforcement of Support Orders

A support order, like any court judgment, may be enforced by various means. For many years, up to 75 percent of spouses—mostly men—defaulted on their court-ordered support payments. The result was that many households affected by default would end up on social assistance.

Furthermore, the victims of default (usually mothers and children) had to return to court for a remedy, which took both time and money but did not guarantee success. Even if the judge ordered payment, this did not guarantee collection.

Case

Manis v. Manis

(2001) 148 O.A.C. 127
Ontario Court of Appeal

The appellant, Warren Manis, and the respondent, Gail Manis, were married in 1985. They had two children, Erica and Jay, born seven years apart. The couple separated in early 1997, two months after Jay's birth. In 1999, Gail was diagnosed with breast cancer, which later spread to her bones. By 2000, she required weekly chemotherapy treatments.

In late 2000, Warren was ordered to pay Gail an equalization payment of just over $415 000, monthly child support of $2300, and monthly spousal support of $4750. As well, Warren was ordered to pay off the mortgage on the matrimonial home and a joint line of credit. He was ordered to provide drug insurance to Gail for her cancer treatment. Finally, he was ordered not to deplete his assets until the equalization payment had been made and the mortgage had been removed from the matrimonial home.

Warren did not comply with any aspect of the court order. He stopped making payments on the mortgage. As a result, the home was sold by the bank in August 2001. He depleted his assets and defaulted on the line of credit. He voluntarily declared bankruptcy, even though there was no evidence that any creditors had made demands on him. As a result, he could no longer practise as a chartered accountant and securities dealer.

Gail brought contempt-of-court proceedings against Warren for his failure to comply with the lower court order. He was sentenced to six months in jail for failing to make payments totalling more than $500 000 to Gail. He appealed this decision to the Ontario Court of Appeal where, in a 3 to 0 decision in September 2001, the court dismissed his appeal.

For Discussion

1. **What is contempt of court, and why was Warren convicted of that charge?**
2. **Why do you think he appealed the trial judgment?**
3. **What message does this decision send out to people who refuse to meet their spousal obligations?**

Provincial Enforcement

Both the federal government and some provinces passed legislation in the 1980s to make it easier to collect payments from defaulting spouses. The new legislation was designed to reduce child poverty and the need for social assistance. Manitoba and Quebec were the first provinces to address this serious social problem by establishing an enforcement system for defaults on spousal and child support. Support enforcement statutes now exist in all the provinces and territories. Examples include Alberta's and Nova Scotia's *Maintenance Enforcement Act,* British Columbia's *Family Maintenance Enforcement Act,* and Ontario's *Support and Custody Orders Enforcement Act.* The provinces and territories also cooperate with one another and with other countries to locate defaulting spouses.

Ontario's Family Responsibility Office

In 1992, Ontario's Family Support Plan (now the Family Responsibility Office, or FRO) became Canada's first automatic wage-deduction program. This means that court-ordered support payments are automatically deducted from a parent's paycheque or other income sources. Quebec introduced a similar system in late 1995, and the other provinces and territories have followed

Did You Know?

In 2000, Ontario's FRO administered about 170 000 cases.

Figure 15-10

Even with wage deduction programs, support orders are sometimes hard to enforce. Margaret Yanish of Port Coquitlam, British Columbia, has been trying to collect child support for her son, David, for 17 years. Why do you think it is so hard to enforce some support orders?

ⓔ activity

Visit **www.law.nelson.com** and follow the links to find out more about your province's or territory's procedures for enforcing child and spousal support payments.

the Ontario model. All court-ordered support is automatically deducted through a Support Deduction Order that deducts the support at source and forwards it to the FRO.

In Ontario, support orders are automatically registered with the FRO, which ensures that families receive the support payments they should be receiving. Once the case is registered, the FRO will collect support payments from the partner paying support, from his or her employer, or from both. These payments are then deposited directly into the recipient's financial institution. If support is not being paid, FRO acts legally to collect money that is owed.

Federal Enforcement

Although support enforcement is primarily a provincial or territorial concern, Parliament passed the *Family Orders and Agreements Enforcement Assistance Act* in 1988. It allows the federal government to assist in the enforcement process by

- tracking down people who have defaulted on their support orders and agreements
- deducting certain federal monies payable to debtors
- refusing to issue important documents, such as a passport, to debtors

Finding such individuals is not too difficult. Authorities can search data banks listing Canada Pension Plan payments and social insurance benefits, and locate the address of a missing spouse or that of his or her employer. Authorities can also search the Canada Customs and Revenue Agency for tracing information. The federal statute also permits garnishment of federal payments to the defaulting spouse—such as employment insurance cheques, income-tax refunds, Canada Pension Plan payments, and interest from Canada Savings Bonds—to redirect them to the spouse owed money. (See Chapter 11 for more information on garnishment.)

Review Your Understanding (Pages 467 to 474)

1. What are the two key factors that courts consider in determining support orders?
2. Identify the four objectives that spousal support orders should consider.
3. Why were the Supreme Court decisions in *Moge v. Moge* and *Bracklow v. Bracklow* considered landmark judgments?
4. Are spousal support orders permanent? Why or why not?
5. How are the courts determining support orders for blended families?
6. What are governments doing to assist in the enforcement of unpaid support orders?

15.5 Common-Law Relationships

Many people believe that if you live with a partner for a certain length of time, you have a common-law marriage and the same rights as married couples. This is untrue. No amount of time together—2, 5, 10, or 50 years—will transform a common-law relationship into a legal marriage. To be legally married, a man and a woman must have a recognized marriage as outlined in Chapter 13. The relationship ends when the partners stop living together. Unlike a marriage, a divorce is not necessary to end a common-law relationship.

Today's laws recognize common-law relationships to some extent because more and more couples are choosing to live together and not marry. In all provinces and territories, if a couple lives together without the benefit of a legal marriage, they may have some automatic rights under the law.

Did You Know?

According to Statistics Canada, 57 percent of first live-in relationships in Canada are common-law.

Property

When married couples separate, they have an automatic right to property division and claims between them. This principle does not apply to common-law couples. No matter how long couples live together, each partner can only ever claim the property owned individually. The partners separate as though they were business partners.

In a common-law relationship, property belongs to the person who paid for it. For example, if the partners bought something together, then it belongs to both of them. If one partner pays 30 percent of the price and the other pays 70 percent of the price, then 30 percent of the item's value belongs to one party and 70 percent to the other. If the item was a gift, then it belongs to the person to whom it was given.

The partners may have some property rights based on contributions of work and household maintenance. For instance, if a woman's contribution helped her common-law partner to build a successful and prosperous business, she may be entitled to a share or an interest in the business. However, she will have to prove her claim in court to obtain a portion of the asset's value. To prove this claim, the following questions must be considered by the courts:

- How many years have the partners lived together?
- What agreements, if any, did the couple have about each person's contributions and obligations?
- Is there proof that a valid contribution was made?

In 1980, the Supreme Court of Canada made a landmark judgment in the case of *Pettkus v. Becker* (see page 476). This judgment provided the first major recognition of the rights of common-law partners by Canadian courts. It is still widely used as a precedent.

Pettkus v. Becker

[1980] 2 S.C.R. 834
Supreme Court of Canada

Rosa Becker and Lothar Pettkus met in Montreal in 1955 shortly after they arrived from Europe. She was 29 and he was 24. After a few dates, he moved in with her. She paid for the couple's rent, food, clothing, and other living expenses from her salary, while he saved his entire salary in his own bank account. Becker expressed a desire to be married; Pettkus said he might consider marriage after they knew each other better. By 1960, Pettkus had saved a large sum of money. He used some of it to buy a farm at Franklin Centre, near Montreal. The property was in his name only.

Becker moved to the farm with Pettkus and participated fully in a very successful beekeeping operation over the next 14 years. In the early 1970s, Pettkus bought two pieces of property in Hawkesbury, Ontario, with funds from the Franklin Centre operation. He transferred the bees to the new property and built a house for himself and Becker there. The couple never married, but they lived together for 19 years. In 1974, Becker moved out permanently, claiming she was being mistreated. She then filed for a one-half interest in the land and business, which by then was worth about $300 000.

In the original action in 1977, the trial court judge awarded her 40 beehives, minus the bees, and $1500 cash. In his decision, this judge claimed: "Rosa's contribution to the household expenses during the first few years of the relationship was in the nature of risk capital invested in the hope of seducing a young man into marriage."

Becker appealed this decision to the Ontario Court of Appeal, where three judges overturned the trial decision, stating that Becker's contribution to the beekeeping operation and her relationship with Pettkus had been greatly underrated by the trial judge and that her contribution to the success of the business and acquisition of property was significant. Thus, Becker was awarded a one-half interest in all lands owned by Pettkus and in the beekeeping business.

Pettkus was then granted leave to appeal this decision to the Supreme Court of Canada. A landmark judgment in December 1980 awarded Becker a one-half interest in the assets accumulated by Pettkus during the 19 years of their relationship, and all court costs.

In November 1986, Rosa Becker committed suicide. In a suicide note, she stated that her death was a protest against the legal system; she still had not received any of her $150 000 court award because Pettkus refused to recognize the decision. He had married and placed his property in his wife's name, thereby avoiding paying the settlement.

Six years after her 1980 landmark judgment, Becker had received very little, if anything, from Pettkus. One payment of $68 000 was claimed by her lawyer for his fees. In May 1989, Becker's estate received $13 000 from Pettkus. This money was paid to two of Becker's friends whom she had named as beneficiaries.

For Discussion

1. Do couples in a common-law relationship have an automatic right to a division of property upon separating? Explain.

2. Why did the Supreme Court of Canada rule that Becker was entitled to a one-half interest in Pettkus's assets?

3. The Supreme Court decision stated: "Pettkus had the benefit of 19 years of unpaid labour while Miss Becker had received little or nothing in return.... This was not an economic partnership or a mere business relationship, or a casual encounter. These two people lived as 'man and wife' for almost 20 years. Their lives and their economic well-being were fully integrated." Do you agree or disagree with this decision? Support your opinion.

4. Explain the meaning of the following statement: "Becker's suicide was the final, desperate act in a life that had become a bitter symbol of the shortcomings and limits of the law."

Support

As you saw in Chapter 14, all parents, whether married or not, have an obligation to support their children. All provinces and territories also now recognize the right of common-law partners to support from each other. In other words, partners who live together for a certain period of time or have a child have the same right to support as married couples.

However, the right to claim support from a common-law partner is not the same in every part of Canada. In some provinces, such as Manitoba and Newfoundland, couples must live together for one year in order to claim support. In other provinces, such as Ontario and Alberta, the period is three years. In Nova Scotia, since June 2001, couples have the option of registering their partnership—whether opposite- or same-sex—with the government. Registering the partnership immediately provides partners with many of the rights and obligations of married spouses under Nova Scotia law, including the *Maintenance and Custody Act,* the *Matrimonial Property Act,* and the *Pension Benefits Act.* (If Nova Scotia couples do not register their partnerships, they must live together for one year before being entitled to support.)

Moreover, all provinces allow partners with children who have lived common-law for less than the required period to claim spousal and child support. This provision is specifically intended to ensure the welfare of children.

The principles of support were developed further in the May 1999 Supreme Court of Canada's judgment in *M. v. H.* (also discussed on pages 90 and 448).

Case

M. v. H.

[1999] 2 S.C.R. 3
Supreme Court of Canada

Two women, M. and H., began a relationship in 1982. They lived in a home owned by H. since 1974. They shared living expenses and financial responsibilities equally and launched their own advertising business. The business became successful and provided the couple with income sufficient for a comfortable lifestyle that included a fine home, a farm, several cars, trips, entertaining, and the like. This business and several related businesses started by the couple provided them with their main source of income. Although H.'s direct contribution to this business was greater than that of M.'s, they continued to be equal owners. M. assumed more of a role managing the home and contributing indirectly through her assistance to H., including a good deal of business entertaining. When the advertising business was adversely affected by the economy in the late 1980s, the couple found themselves in financial difficulty. H. felt M. was taking advantage of her because M. was not actively in the workforce. The business downturn seriously affected the personal relationship of the two women.

By late 1992, their relationship had fallen apart completely, and H. presented M. with a draft agreement to settle their affairs. The challenge of trying to resolve their complicated financial interdependency caused a great deal of bitterness. M. left with some personal belongings after which H. changed the locks on the home and excluded M. from the business. M. suffered financial hardship while struggling to become self-sufficient once again. In October 1992, M. initiated court proceedings, claiming partition and sale of the home, a share of the business and cottage, and spousal support, challenging the validity of the definition of "spouse" under Ontario's *Family Law Act.* The Act did not allow spousal applications from persons in same-sex relationships.

continued ▶

In a landmark judgment in early 1996, Justice Gloria Epstein of the Ontario Court (General Division) ruled that the "opposite sex" definition of "spouse" violated section 15 (equality rights) of the *Canadian Charter of Rights and Freedoms* and could not be saved under the *Charter's* section 1. Justice Epstein declared that the words "a man and a woman" were to be read out (deleted) from the definition of "spouse" and replaced with the words "two persons." H. appealed this judgment to the Ontario Court of Appeal, where the trial judgment was upheld in a 2 to 1 decision in December 1996. Shortly afterward, M. and H. privately concluded a settlement of their financial issues.

In March 1998, the Supreme Court of Canada heard the appeal of the Ontario Court of Appeal decision. This appeal was launched by the Ontario government. Although M. and H. were no longer interested in the result, the government felt it important to resolve the constitutional issue of whether same-sex couples were generally entitled to equality and specifically had a right to seek spousal support. In May 1999, in a 9 to 0 decision, the Court affirmed (agreed with) both earlier judgments and gave the Ontario government six months to rewrite provincial laws to ensure equal treatment for same-sex spouses.

For Discussion

1. **On what basis did M. initiate court proceedings under Ontario's *Family Law Act*?**
2. **Explain the meaning and significance of Justice Epstein's trial judgment.**
3. **Why is this case such a landmark judgment?**
4. **Should a court be able to order a government to rewrite its laws that violate *Charter* rights? Why or why not?**

You Be the JUDGE

M.'s lawyer stated: "Until gays and lesbians are in our human family, we will never put an end to discrimination."

- Explain the meaning of this statement.

The Impact of M. v. H.

The Supreme Court of Canada found that gay and lesbian couples were similar to heterosexual couples, forming relationships of emotional and economic dependency. The Court observed that it was unfair to exclude same-sex couples from the remedy of spousal support. The Court's decision was restricted to the issue of spousal support under Ontario's *Family Law Act*. However, the Court sent a clear message to all provincial and territorial governments that laws excluding same-sex couples would likely contravene (go against) section 15 (equality rights) under the *Canadian Charter of Rights and Freedoms*.

The Ontario government responded to this decision quickly, although reluctantly. In October 1999, Bill C-5 was proclaimed in order to amend 67 statutes in Ontario. Now same-sex couples would be treated the same under law as common-law couples. The statutes amended wide-ranging legislation governing, for example, name change, consumer protection, credit unions, organ donations, property ownership, insurance, adoption, and employment and pension benefits. While the Ontario legislation created a category of same-sex relationships separate from common-law relationships, British Columbia

Figure 15-11

British Columbia expanded the definition of spouse to include common-law and same-sex couples. Introducing the new legislation, former BC Attorney General Ujjal Dosanjh noted that supporting a variety of family types "is essential in the healthy, thriving, and diverse society that forms British Columbia."

decided to include opposite-sex and same-sex relationships in the definition of "spouse." Other provinces are currently updating their family law legislation to bring it in line with the *M. v. H.* decision.

In July 2000, the federal government passed Bill C-23, the *Modernization of Benefits and Obligations Act.* This legislation ensures that opposite- and same-sex relationships are treated equally under federal law. Throughout all federal statutes, the words "of the opposite sex" were removed and replaced with the term "survivor." Among other things, this allowed same-sex couples to claim survivor pension benefits, but only if a partner had died as of January 1, 1998, or later (the cutoff date established by Ottawa for same-sex spouses to claim benefits).

In November 2001, a $400 million lawsuit was filed in the Ontario Superior Court of Justice against the federal government on behalf of up to 10 000 gay and lesbian survivors whose partners died before the cutoff date. This lawsuit, launched in all provinces except British Columbia and Quebec, says Ottawa is discriminating against surviving spouses not eligible to receive benefits. This action seeks benefits for all applicable same-sex spouses retroactive (dated back) to April 17, 1985, when section 15 of the *Charter*—equality rights—came into effect. A separate action was launched in British Columbia at the same time; Quebec residents contribute to a different pension plan.

These decisions have given same-sex partnerships new legal status. However, it is important to remember the definition of marriage has not changed. It is still a union between a man and a woman, unless court challenges on attempted same-sex marriages overturn this principle.

activity

Visit **www.law.nelson.com** and follow the links to learn about the *Modernization of Benefits and Obligations Act* and the impact on federal legislation.

Pensions

Both the Canada Pension Plan and provincial workers' compensation legislation recognize common-law relationships to some degree. For example, if one partner dies in a work-related accident, benefits may be paid to the surviving partner. Other statutes, such as the *Employment Insurance Act,* also recognize common-law partners' rights to benefits. To qualify for benefits, partners must have lived together for a certain time, which varies from place to place. As well, the federal government passed legislation that granted survivor benefits to the same-sex partners of federal public service employees. Finally, a number of major Canadian cities and over 200 private sector Canadian companies currently provide benefits to the same-sex partners of their employees.

Inheritance

A surviving common-law partner, unlike a married survivor, has no automatic claim to the estate of the deceased. The deceased must leave a will leaving everything to the survivor. However, full title (right of ownership) to any assets owned jointly by common-law partners—real estate, furnishings, vehicles, bank accounts—goes automatically to the survivor.

Review Your Understanding (Pages 475 to 479)

1. What is the major distinction in family law between a married couple and a common-law relationship?
2. Outline the questions that a court must consider in dividing property rights between common-law partners.
3. Why was the *Pettkus v. Becker* case such a landmark judgment?
4. Why was the *M. v. H.* case such a landmark judgment?
5. Compare the rights of married and common-law spouses with respect to the following: property, support, and inheritance.

15.6 Domestic Contracts

One way for partners to ensure that they agree on the division of assets and other legal matters is to draw up a legally binding contract. Twenty years ago, the courts seldom recognized such contracts. Legal authorities thought they threatened the stability of marriage and the family unit. However, domestic contracts only determine how assets are divided if the relationship has broken down.

Today, these contracts are recognized by the courts, provided each couple has contributed to the agreement after seeking legal advice. (Each partner must retain a separate lawyer.) If the couple agrees on the key issues before notifying their lawyers, it is likely that the contract will be easily negotiated. The lawyers must explain how the agreement affects each party before it is signed and dated.

Domestic contracts are becoming more popular—they allow couples to air their views on many issues; for example, how property should be divided if they were to separate, career plans, raising children, and so on. Contracts help couples anticipate future problems and disputes and arrive at solutions in advance. Sometimes the very process of negotiating a domestic contract allows couples to understand that they should not live together or marry after all.

Types of Domestic Contracts

Under provincial and territorial law, a **domestic contract** is a general term that refers to any of three types of contracts made between the partners in a relationship: a **marriage contract,** a **cohabitation agreement,** and a **separation agreement.** The contents of each depend on a couple's particular needs. To be legally binding, the contract must be dated, written, signed by the two parties, and witnessed by at least one person who is not related to either spouse. Any changes to the contract must also be made in writing. Although people sometimes refer to these contracts as prenuptial agreements, this term is not recognized in Canadian law.

Marriage Contract

A marriage contract is a legally binding contract between two people who plan to get married or who are already married. The purpose of the marriage contract is to detail the financial impact of separation on each spouse. For example, the couple may wish to specify that the earnings of one may be used for mortgage or rental payments and utility expenses, while the salary of the other may be spent on household expenses such as food, clothing, entertainment, and miscellaneous items. They might want to decide whether to have separate bank accounts or a joint account. If they buy a car, in whose name will the ownership be registered? By making these decisions, the couple also ensures what happens to these assets upon separation. No one enters a marriage with the idea that it will end in divorce, but marriages do fail. A marriage contract may be useful for a variety of reasons.

First among the reasons, one partner may have a lot more money or financial assets than the other. That spouse may not want to divide assets equally if the marriage breaks down. For example, Bob's wealthy parents may want to prevent family money from going to Sarah if the marriage breaks down. Or perhaps Sarah owns art, antiques, or family valuables that have great sentimental value to her. She may feel that Bob should not share in the rising value of those assets.

Next, partners entering a second or third marriage and who have children from an earlier marriage may want a contract to protect specific assets for those children. In other words, assets intended for their children would go to them instead of being part of property division. Marriage contracts are becoming very common for second marriages.

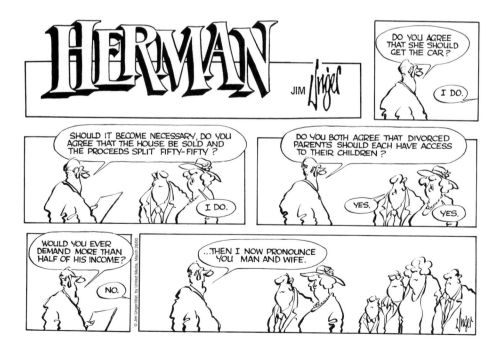

Figure 15-12

This cartoon seems to suggest that a marriage contract might make a good marriage vow.

Finally, a marriage contract can be used to make arrangements for dividing property and money earned during the marriage. This allows couples to make decisions about the division of property that may not line up with the provincial statutes. Provincial legislation provides that, under most circumstances, married spouses are entitled to an equal share of the marital property when they separate. However, one spouse or both may own property that is not to be shared in the event of separation. In such situations, the couple can include their own property division in their marriage contract.

Suppose, in our earlier example, Isabella owned a piece of property prior to her marriage to Ethan. She may want to draw up a contract with a clause stipulating that Ethan has no right to any share of the property. In the absence of such a contract, the value of the property may be divided between them if they separate, regardless of who owned it before the marriage. Spouses who are also business partners are entering into domestic contracts to keep their business out of any marital dispute. However, domestic contracts cannot limit a spouse's right to live in the matrimonial home or share in its value.

When a couple draws up a marriage contract, each partner must be honest about his or her financial situation, assets, and liabilities. Although the courts now recognize all forms of domestic contracts, judges tend to set aside unfair contracts that are one-sided and that favour the interests of one party over the other.

Cohabitation Agreement

A cohabitation agreement is a legally binding contract between common-law or same-sex partners who are cohabiting (living together) or who plan to cohabit and want to make their wishes clearly known to family and friends. It is the common-law equivalent of a marriage contract. A cohabitation agreement may be useful to couples who are not legally married and who want a process for dividing their property on separation or death. If the parties to a cohabitation agreement marry, their agreement automatically becomes a marriage contract.

Unlike married spouses, common-law partners do not have any automatic right to share property when they separate. Whatever assets each person brings into the relationship remain that person's property. However, as you saw in the case of *Pettkus v. Becker* (page 476), the court revisited this position and awarded Rosa Becker an equal share of the property because of her contributions made during her long-term relationship.

Separation Agreements

Separating couples that do not have a marriage contract or cohabitation agreement must settle their issues with a separation agreement or in court. As you saw in Chapter 13, a separation agreement is a legally binding contract between separating partners. It usually deals with such issues as property division; child and spousal support; custody of, and access to, the children; the children's education; and any other matter of importance to the couple. As a contract, a separation agreement can be enforced against either party in the same way a court order can be enforced. Contract law is discussed in greater detail in Chapters 16 and 17.

Terminating Domestic Contracts

Married or common-law spouses may terminate (end) and destroy their contract by mutual agreement. Alternatively, the contract may include a term ending it automatically, such as the day when the last child reaches the age of majority. Some contracts include plans for review or revision at the end of a certain number of years. This allows the spouses to adjust their contract to reflect changes in their circumstances as children are born, career changes are made, and property is bought and sold.

Review Your Understanding (Pages 480 to 483)

1. Why have the courts only recently recognized the validity of domestic contracts?
2. Why should partners drawing up domestic contracts each have a different lawyer?
3. Identify the three main types of domestic contracts. Why is no standard form available for such contracts?
4. Outline three key reasons why a couple planning to marry might want a marriage contract.
5. Describe why partners living together might want a cohabitation agreement.
6. Describe the more common ways to end a domestic contract.

Should Canadians Have Universal Daycare?

Figure 15-13

Many experts think that quality preschool experiences contribute to later academic achievement. Whether such experiences are best provided through a daycare or by parents is widely debated.

Shona and Dave have three young children, and both parents work outside the home. The daycare costs are very high, but the couple's two salaries can accommodate them—for now.

Joy is the single parent of Ezra and has no child support or spousal support. She has gained new skills and is looking for paid work.

Rohan and Patty have two children. They decided early in their relationship to "shelve" one career until both children are in school.

Joy finds paid work but must scramble to find safe, affordable child care. Patty and

Labour Force Participation Rates of Mothers of Children 0–15 Years, Canada

Age of Youngest Child	1995	1998
Less than 3	62%	64%
3–5	68%	70%
6–15	77%	78%

Figure 15-14

More women participate in the workforce as their younger children become school age.

Rohan separate and so must maintain two homes, relaunch the second career, and find child care. Dave and Shona dread each monthly reckoning of family expenses.

As you can see, child care plays a central role in the life of a young child's family—and is a significant concern in court orders. Daycare costs are often as high as rent and may pose a particular burden after a marriage breakdown. As a result, Canadians have been debating whether the government should provide universal daycare—free or affordable daycare for all Canadian children.

In many countries, such as Sweden, Finland, Holland, France, and Cuba, government-funded daycare is already available to all families with young children. Each country has developed its own system for delivering daycare, but in every case the government oversees the program and provides substantial funding.

The province of Quebec leads Canada in providing affordable, high-quality daycare for a range of income earners. In 1997, it introduced a flat $5.00/day rate for each child enrolled in its daycare system. Before this program was introduced, the average cost per child each day was $25. Today, 100 000 children benefit from this program.

Salaries for daycare work have traditionally been very low, even when the people employed are skilled in child care. The Quebec government doubled the salaries of daycare workers to attract more trained child-care specialists. Raising the salaries signalled the importance of quality daycare in the healthy development of young children. The cost of the program for Quebec taxpayers is $1 billion a year.

Despite the high demand for quality daycare, less than a quarter of Canadian children have a spot in a licensed daycare or preschool program. This means that most families who need child care rely on arrangements with babysitters, nannies, and family members to supervise their children. Occasionally, private arrangements, such as unlicensed care offered in a private home, have proven unsafe.

On One Side

Supporters of government-funded daycare believe that free or heavily subsidized child care is similar to free education and health services—the right of all Canadians. Society has an obligation to provide all young children with a healthy and stimulating environment. Studies show that children who experience early childhood education go on to do better in school. Since children are the adults of the future, it seems only right to invest in high-quality daycare. In addition, parents—mothers and fathers alike—benefit from the peace of mind afforded by reliable daycare. All provincial and territorial governments should follow Quebec's example and commit the money needed for government-funded daycare programs. Single parents in particular often require low-cost daycare in order to achieve economic self-sufficiency.

On the Other Side

Critics of government-funded daycare believe that those who choose to have children have the responsibility of paying the costs of raising them. Taxpayers are already paying enough in taxes and should not have to assume financial burdens such as daycare expenses that properly belong to parents. They point out that the federal government already allows parents who work outside the home to deduct a portion of their child-care expenses from their income at tax time. They reject the legal argument that single parents should be entitled to low-cost daycare for economic reasons.

A few critics angrily reject the whole notion of daycare. They hold to a traditional view that men should be breadwinners and women should stay at home to raise young children. They say that universal daycare is an inadequate substitute for home-based child care and may even serve to undermine the family.

The Bottom Line

The pressure on parents with young children to find suitable daycare continues to increase. Although some employers now provide flexible work hours and part-time work to help meet the needs of the changing family, only 4 percent of employers provide daycare centres for their employees.

Parents continue to pressure the government to pass laws to provide universal daycare. They want daycare facilities that are properly regulated and staffed by qualified child-care workers. The debate continues over who should pay for this expensive service. Should parents be responsible for these expenses? Or is this the responsibility of all Canadians?

What Do You Think?

1. Why has the issue of universal daycare become important in recent years?
2. How has Quebec taken a leadership role on daycare?
3. Support or argue against this statement: "Access to daycare is a right of all parents."
4. Do you think that governments and society have "a responsibility to ensure that all young children have a healthy and stimulating environment"? Explain.
5. What would be the advantages and disadvantages of employers providing daycare services to their employees?

Chapter Review

Chapter Highlights

- Provincial and territorial governments have control over property and civil rights.
- The *Murdoch v. Murdoch* case highlighted injustice to women in property division following divorce.
- Provincial legislation considers marriage as an economic partnership to which the spouses contribute equally.
- Equal-division-of-property legislation does not apply to separating common-law or same-sex partners.
- Each spouse has an equal right to live in the matrimonial home and to share equally in the proceeds if the couple agrees to sell it.
- Spouses can opt out of an equal division of property by drawing up a domestic contract, but the matrimonial home cannot be included in such a contract.
- Although the intent of provincial legislation is to divide the value of property equally, there are some situations in which this might be unfair.
- When a couple divorces, federal law applies to child and spousal support; when a couple separates, provincial or territorial law applies.
- Self-sufficiency of each spouse is one of the main objectives after marriage breakdown.
- Spousal support is ordered to compensate spouses for the economic sacrifices made during the marriage or for ill spouses who need it and whose former partners can afford it.
- All provinces have procedures in place to collect support payments from defaulting parents.
- A common-law relationship is not a legal marriage, no matter how long the partners have lived together.
- Common-law and same-sex partners may be entitled to support if they have lived together for a certain length of time or have a child.
- The *M. v. H.* case has resulted in changes in legislation, ensuring that same-sex relationships are treated equally with common-law relationships.
- There are three types of domestic contracts: marriage contracts, cohabitation agreements, and separation agreements.

Review Key Terms

Name the key terms that are described below.

a) a domestic contract between two unmarried persons living together

b) the residence in which the spouses live during their marriage

c) a domestic contract between a man and a woman who are married and living together

d) assets owned by one spouse and used primarily in the course of business carried on by that spouse

e) property owned or ordinarily enjoyed by both spouses and/or their children

f) grossly or shockingly unfair

g) financial assistance paid by one spouse to another on marriage breakdown

h) the basic value of a spouse's assets, less any debts, at the date of separation

i) the consideration that each spouse has an obligation to support himself or herself within a reasonable period of time after marriage breakdown

j) system in which property is owned by a partner or spouse in his or her own name during a relationship

Check Your Knowledge

1. Explain briefly the ruling of the court in the judgment of *Murdoch v. Murdoch*. What major changes have been made in legislation regarding division of property since that time?

2. Summarize the factors that are often considered in the determination of spousal support.

3. Briefly explain the significance of the Supreme Court of Canada ruling in the case of *M. v. H.*

4. Marriage contracts take some control away from the government and give individuals more control over their personal relationships. What are the advantages and disadvantages of this?

Apply Your Learning

5. *Ferreira v. Ferreira* (1998), 41 R.F.L. (4th) 101 (Ontario Court, General Division)

A man and a woman divorce in 1983. They later cohabit from 1994 to 1996. Their adult son also lives in their home with them. Although the couple discusses the possibility of remarriage, they never do. Are they legal spouses? Why or why not?

6. *Boston v. Boston* (2001), 201 D.L.R. (4th) 1 (Supreme Court of Canada)

Willis and Shirley Boston separated in 1991 after 36 years of marriage. Shirley was a wife and homemaker, raising seven children, while Willis pursued his career and financially supported the family. Willis worked in the public education system and was a director of education at his retirement in 1997.

In 1994, the Bostons divorced and divided their assets. Shirley received about $370 000 in assets, including the matrimonial home, its contents, and RRSPs, while Willis received $385 000 of which $333 000 was the value of his pension. As required under Ontario's *Family Law Act*, the value of Willis's pension was included in the calculation of the couple's assets. As well, he agreed to pay Shirley $3200 a month in spousal support indexed annually to the cost of living. At the time, his annual income was just over $115 000, while his wife had no employment income as she served in high-profile volunteer positions once their children had grown up.

Willis remarried, retired in 1997, and began receiving a monthly pension of $8000. In 1998, he applied to the court to reduce the amount of spousal support, claiming that his retirement and reduced income represented a material (major) change in his financial circumstances. He also argued that he was paying support from his pension, which had already been considered in the original division of assets, and that his

former wife would be "double dipping," or accessing his pension twice. The trial judge agreed and reduced the monthly support from $3200 to $950, not indexed.

On appeal by Shirley, the Ontario Court of Appeal raised this amount to $2000 a month, indexed again. Willis appealed this decision to the Supreme Court of Canada, where in July 2001, in a 7 to 2 judgment, the Court restored the trial judgment.

a) Explain Willis Boston's argument in your own words.

b) With which court's decision do you agree and why?

c) The Supreme Court's majority judgment stated: "It is generally unfair to allow the payee spouse (the wife) to reap the benefit of the pension both as an asset and then again as a source of income, particularly where she received assets which she uses to grow her estate." Explain the meaning of this statement in your own words.

7. Karen and Russ were married for seven years. Long before the marriage, Russ won a sum of money in a provincial lottery and purchased $35 000 worth of Canada Savings Bonds in his name. The couple accumulated a home worth $250 000, property worth $75 000, a sailboat worth $28 000, and some works of art worth $50 000. All these assets were registered in Russ's name. Because of some disastrous business investments, Russ needed cash quickly and sold the art, the boat, and the property. Because of this and other marital problems, the couple separated. Karen later petitioned for divorce.

a) Would the court divide the value of the matrimonial home equally between them? Why or why not?

b) In your province or territory, does Karen have a claim to any of Russ's $35 000 worth of Canada Savings Bonds? Explain.

8. After the Wilsons married, Carol Lynn was the main breadwinner, earning $40 000 a year as nurse and hospital director. Her husband, Larry, had a grade 11 education and worked only occasionally, playing trombone in a band. For 13 years, Larry stayed at home looking after their three children, aged 7, 9, and 10, and cooked and cleaned. When the couple separated, Larry claimed monthly support payments from his wife to allow him to become self-supporting.
   a) What factors would be considered in Larry's argument for support payments?
   b) Would he succeed in his action? Explain.

Communicate Your Understanding

9. If the Murdoch case (see page 460) appeared before the Supreme Court of Canada today, what decision do you think the Court would reach? Assume you are a judge hearing the same facts in a courtroom today, and create a judgment based on your understanding of the current law.

10. When a former spouse remarries, for how long should that spouse continue to pay support to his or her first spouse and family? Should a person's first or second family receive economic priority? In your response, detail the factors that should be considered in making this determination and justify your answer.

11. Should provincial and territorial laws be changed to give common-law partners the same automatic rights to property division as married spouses? Defend your position.

12. Regarding the Miglin decision (see page 472), debate either of the following reactions:
    a) "This case depreciates the value of separation agreements to an all-time low." (a family law lawyer)
    b) "It's fantasy to think that you are not going to have a lifetime obligation to someone who has taken herself out of the workforce to wash the socks and raise the kids." (another family law lawyer)

13. From newspapers or the Internet, collect at least five articles dealing with issues in this chapter.
    a) Summarize the articles in your own words.
    b) Highlight the issue(s) involved.
    c) State and justify your opinion on the issue(s) discussed in the articles.

Develop Your Thinking

14. Assume that you and the person whom you have been in a relationship with for five years decide to marry in a civil ceremony. Would you prepare a marriage contract, or would you depend on your province's division of property legislation to settle any disputes if the two of you decide to separate or divorce? Prepare arguments for and against each of these two positions.

15. Explain the meaning of the following statement: "Just because an applicant is a spouse does not create an automatic right to support."

Whether common law or civilian, good law of contract promotes freedom of contract—the freedom of people and groups of people to enter into new transactions and create new wealth.

Beverley McLachlin
Chief Justice of the Supreme Court of Canada

Contract Law

Chapter
16

Elements of a Contract

Focus Questions

- How does a contract differ from other kinds of agreements?
- What elements must be in place for a contract to be valid?
- How can minors, as opposed to those who have reached the age of majority, make contracts?
- What groups of people are offered special protection in contract law?
- In what situations will consent to a contract be declared invalid?
- To be valid, what standards must a contract in restraint of trade meet?
- What is the legal status of gambling in Canada?

Chapter at a Glance

Figure 16-1

Canadian Estella Warren presents MTV awards with Usher. A supermodel since her teens, Warren is no stranger to contracts. Neither are you—you make them every day. Do minors need special protection when making contracts?

16.1 Introduction

As a consumer, you have entered into many contracts, often without knowing it. Every time you go to a movie or a concert, ride a bus or subway, buy perfume or a CD, you have made a contract. If you have ever been hired for a job, a contract was formed. Contract law is a fact of everyday life and the basis of business.

Because contracts are so important, the courts have established rules to determine exactly when they are valid. Contract law is mainly judge-made common law. It has developed over many years as courts heard cases and reached decisions. In this chapter, you will look at the elements that make up a contract.

16.2 Agreement or Contract?

To be a **valid contract,** an agreement must impose rights and responsibilities on the parties involved. However, the courts will not always recognize an agreement as being legally binding and enforceable even if the parties have agreed to the duties imposed. For example, Ingmar offers to take Anita to dinner and a movie and Anita accepts. Later, Ingmar backs out of the invitation. Anita has no basis to take Ingmar to court. Although Ingmar made a promise, the agreement cannot be enforced in court: it was simply a social or moral obligation.

All contracts involve agreements, but not all agreements are contracts. A **contract** can be defined as an agreement or promise that the law will enforce. To be a valid contract, these essential elements must be in place: offer and acceptance, consideration, capacity, consent, and lawful purpose.

▍ Elements of a Valid Contract

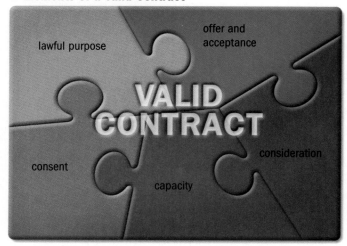

Figure 16-2

It's elementary; every piece of the contract must be in place.

For example, at a local store you find a snowboard that you want to buy. When you take the snowboard to the sales clerk, an **offer and acceptance** takes place. You offer to buy the snowboard at the price advertised and the sales clerk accepts your offer. After you give your money to the clerk, the clerk gives you the snowboard. Another essential element of a contract has occurred here: **consideration,** the exchange of something of value between the parties.

The other elements of a contract are also involved. Both you and the clerk have the legal **capacity** (ability) to enter into the contract. You are of sound mind and old enough to make the purchase. You both freely give **consent** to the contract, in good faith. The clerk does not pressure or trick you into making your purchase, and you do not force the clerk to sell you the snowboard. Finally, the contract has a **lawful purpose** (object)—there is nothing illegal about buying a snowboard.

A contract that lacks one or more of these essential elements cannot be enforced by either party in the courts.

Types of Contracts

All contracts are either express or implied. An **express contract** can be verbal or written, and it clearly defines all terms and conditions. An **implied contract** is only suggested by a person's actions—nothing is precisely stated or written. Ordering a meal in a restaurant is an example of an implied contract. Your order suggests to the server that you will pay for the meal once you have eaten it. Hailing a taxicab is also an implied contract: the driver assumes you will pay the fare once you arrive at your destination.

Contracts can be classified as simple or under seal. Most day-to-day transactions are **simple contracts.** They can be verbal or written, or implied. A verbal contract can be hard to enforce. Without witnesses, it may be impossible to prove that a contract exists at all. Therefore, if possible, contracts

Figure 16-3

What kind of contract is this?

should be in writing. Simple contracts need not be very detailed, but they must include basic terms, the date, and the signatures of the parties involved.

Some transactions require **contracts under seal.** These contracts must be in writing and signed and witnessed "under seal." The use of a seal dates back to when people pressed family rings or signets into sealing wax to finalize a contract. Today, the seal is a red dot or the word "seal." This indicates that the parties have given the contract serious thought, are aware of their rights, and have accepted their responsibilities. In some provinces, deeds to property and mortgages must be signed under seal to be legally binding.

Any changes made to a written contract should be in writing and initialled by all parties. The courts can ignore any verbal changes or agreements made after a contract is written if these changes contradict or alter the original document. If there is a dispute, the court would have to be convinced that any verbal agreement was a genuine agreement to change the terms of the original contract.

Review Your Understanding (Pages 491 to 493)

1. Explain what makes an agreement a legally enforceable contract.
2. Identify the essential elements of a contract.
3. What forms can a simple contract take?
4. Distinguish between an express contract and an implied contract, using original examples.
5. What is the significance of a seal on a contract?

16.3 Offer

As you learned in the example of the snowboard, the essential elements of a legally binding contract include a valid offer and acceptance. One party, the **offeror,** must make a clear, precise offer, and the other party, the **offeree,** must accept the offer. In the example of the snowboard, you were the offeror and the clerk was the offeree. As you prepared to pay for the snowboard, a **meeting of the minds** took place: both parties (you and the clerk) clearly understood the rights and responsibilities in the contract that developed.

As with contracts, offers must contain certain elements to be valid.

Serious Intent

To be valid, an offer must be definite and seriously intended. Salman says to Karen, "I'll sell you my blue 18-speed mountain bike for $375." Karen replies, "That's a deal. I'll take it for $375." Both a definite offer and a definite acceptance have taken place. If Karen says, "It looks like a good deal and I'd like to have it," this is not a valid acceptance. Only the offer is valid, and no contract has been made.

Offers made as a joke or in anger are not valid. An automobile stalls in the driveway and the frustrated owner shouts, "I'll sell this piece of junk for a loonie!" Any neighbour who takes this as a serious offer will not be able to force the owner to sell the automobile for that price. The owner obviously had no serious intent.

An offeror's words or conduct must indicate both the clear intention and the willingness to carry out the promise if the offer is accepted. "I think I might sell my old CD player for $60," for example, is a vague statement of possible intent. It is not a definite offer.

Definite Terms

The terms of an offer must also be clearly stated. If goods are being sold, then quantity, price, size, colour, terms of sale, and delivery date should be defined. Salman, for example, described his bicycle in detail because he has more than one bike. Some terms are implied, or assumed to be known. Many goods and services, for example, have a standard price. Consumers are unlikely to ask the price when buying a newspaper or riding the bus. Similarly, patients may not ask their regular dentist what the fee is before having dental work done.

Case

Frecon Construction Ltd. v. DiGirolamo & Son Ltd.

(September 2, 1997) Docket 92560/95
Ontario Court, General Division

General contractor Frecon Construction Ltd. intended to bid on a school renovation project and asked DiGirolamo & Son Ltd., a subcontractor, to quote on some work related to the project. A few days later, Frecon received a two-page proposal from DiGirolamo. Page one showed a price of $165 000. The second page listed four separate prices (which added up to $117 050), but the final line, titled "total consideration price," was blank.

Frecon concluded that $165 000 was the total quote, but called to confirm this. Someone who identified himself as Gord answered the phone at DiGirolamo & Son and confirmed that $165 000 was the total price. Relying on this information, Frecon made a successful bid on the school renovation project.

Later, DiGirolamo claimed its total price was $282 050. It also declared that no binding contract had been formed because the two parties had not reached agreement on the total price. Frecon then sued DiGirolamo in the amount of $125 000 for breaking the contract.

The court found in favour of Frecon, for the following reasons:

- Given the way DiGirolamo presented the proposal, it was reasonable for Frecon to conclude that $165 000 was the total quote.
- Gordon Lee, an employee of DiGirolamo, claimed he would not have answered Frecon's questions on the telephone because he did not have the authority. The court, however, was convinced by evidence presented that Gordon Lee had given Frecon the impression he could speak for DiGirolamo and that he had confirmed $165 000 as the total price being quoted.

For Discussion

1. Why did Frecon stand to lose money when DiGirolamo refused to do any work on the school renovation project?

2. Summarize the arguments put forward by Frecon and DiGirolamo on the question of whether a contract existed between them.

3. How would you have decided this case? Explain your position.

Invitations to Buy

Are newspaper and magazine advertisements clear and definite offers? What about merchandise featured in a store's retail displays and catalogues? When you go into a supermarket, select goods, and present the goods and your money at the cash register, has a contract been formed?

According to the courts, the answer to all these questions is no. The advertisements, displays, and catalogues are merely invitations by sellers for customers to make an offer to buy the products advertised. This is also known as **invitation to treat.** A retailer does not expect everyone who sees an advertisement to buy the item.

The basic rule is that customers make definite offers to purchase once they select advertised items or goods from the store's stock. The store's cashier

---

Case

Carlill v. Carbolic Smoke Ball Company

[1893] 1 Q.B. 256
England, Court of Appeal

The defendant company made and sold a medical preparation called the Carbolic Smoke Ball. The company advertised its product in various English newspapers stating that a "£100 reward will be paid by the Carbolic Smoke Ball Company to any person who contracts the increasing epidemic influenza, colds, or any disease caused by taking cold, after having used the ball three times daily for two weeks according to the printed directions supplied with each ball. £1000 is deposited with the Alliance Bank, Regent Street, showing our sincerity in the matter."

Mrs. Carlill, the plaintiff, read the advertisement, bought the product at a chemist's store, and used it as directed three times a day from November 20, 1891, to January 17, 1892. Then she caught influenza. When the company refused to pay Mrs. Carlill the £100, she sued successfully. The defendant company appealed the trial judgment, but the appeal was dismissed. The court held that the reference in the advertisement to the £1000 deposit indicated the serious intention of the Smoke Ball Company to pay.

For Discussion

1. Must an offer be made to one specific person, or is it valid and legal to make an offer to an indefinite number of people? Explain.

2. What argument do you think the defendant company used in its attempt to avoid paying the plaintiff?

3. Was it necessary for Mrs. Carlill to communicate to the company her intention to purchase the smoke ball and use it as directed? Why or why not?

4. Why did the court rule that the advertisement was a valid offer?

Figure 16-4

This advertiser had to pay up. Why?

Did You Know?

Each year, every person in Canada receives one-and-a half-trees' worth of junk mail (unsolicited, bulk-mail advertising). Polls show that the majority of Canadians want more control over this. Should legislation be passed to regulate junk mail? Explain.

then has the right to accept or reject those offers. In most cases, the cashier accepts the customer's money and hands over the merchandise. Only after all these actions have occurred has a contract been formed and completed.

Newer forms of advertising are being used to present consumers with countless invitations to buy. Telemarketing promotes goods and services through unsolicited, or uninvited, phone calls and has become very popular with advertisers. Online advertising using the Internet is also quickly gaining in popularity. Both telemarketing and online advertising keep consumers informed, but they can also be an invasion of privacy. Computer files known as "cookies" allow online marketers to create detailed files on individual consumers. Online shoppers may find their computers flooded with unsolicited e-mails, or "spam."

Federal and provincial governments have passed laws that identify unfair, deceptive, and misleading selling practices. These laws also provide consumers who have been victimized by these practices with remedies and compensation. This area of law will be examined in detail in Chapter 17.

Normally, advertisements are not considered to be promises that are legally binding on the advertiser. However, the courts may consider advertisements that are worded very precisely, and with a serious intent, to be offers. The case of *Carlill v. Carbolic Smoke Ball Company* (page 495) was the first to illustrate this point.

Communicating an Offer

Obviously, the offeror must communicate the offer to the offeree before acceptance can occur. This can be done in person or by mail, courier, fax, and so on. Because an offer is not valid until it has been received, it is important to know when the offeree becomes aware of it. What happens, for example, if identical offers cross in the mail?

Suppose that Tom writes Erin, offering to sell her a painting for $750. Unaware of this, Erin writes to Tom, offering to buy the same painting for the same price. At first glance, it would seem that Erin's letter could be considered an acceptance of Tom's offer and that a contract had been formed. But what if Tom changes his mind after sending the letter? What if one letter never arrives at the intended address? In either case, two separate offers exist.

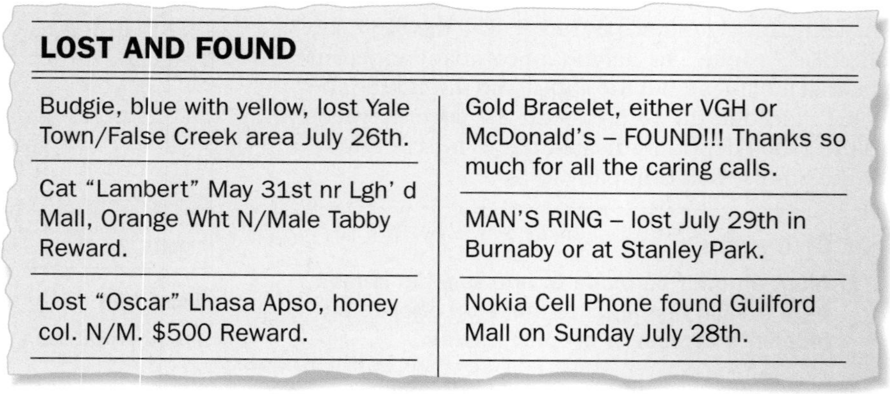

LOST AND FOUND

Budgie, blue with yellow, lost Yale Town/False Creek area July 26th.

Cat "Lambert" May 31st nr Lgh' d Mall, Orange Wht N/Male Tabby Reward.

Lost "Oscar" Lhasa Apso, honey col. N/M. $500 Reward.

Gold Bracelet, either VGH or McDonald's – FOUND!!! Thanks so much for all the caring calls.

MAN'S RING – lost July 29th in Burnaby or at Stanley Park.

Nokia Cell Phone found Guilford Mall on Sunday July 28th.

Figure 16-5

For each of these notices, what is the finder's entitlement to a reward?

To form a valid contract, an acceptance must be an unconditional reply to a specific offer. The courts would thus assume that no contract was formed between Tom and Erin.

An offer can legally be communicated to a specific person or to people in general, as in a reward notice. Suppose you find a lost dog, look at its name and address tag, and then return Vasco to his owner. Later, you read a notice the owner had placed in the newspaper offering a $500 reward for Vasco's return. Are you entitled to the reward? No, not legally. When you returned Vasco, you did not know of the reward. Therefore, you could not have intended to accept the offer. If you had read the notice first, you would have been entitled to the reward. In this case, by returning Vasco you would have been accepting the offer, thus forming and **performing** (completing) a contract.

Terminating an Offer

Unless an offer is accepted, no legal rights or obligations can arise from it. When making an offer, offerors can protect themselves by including a deadline for acceptance. If not accepted by that date, the offer will automatically **lapse** (end). An offer may also be terminated by **revocation,** which means it is withdrawn before being accepted.

If an offer includes no deadline, it remains open for a reasonable length of time before lapsing. How long this is depends on the nature of the transaction. An offer to sell stocks, for example, is open for a much shorter period than an offer to sell a house. Stock prices can change minute by minute.

A verbal offer lapses when the parties leave one another, if it is reasonable to assume that the offeror intended this. For example, Leroy offers to sell Freda his old laptop computer for $350. If Freda does not accept the offer before they part company, it lapses. The offeror can also decide to give the offeree time to consider the offer. Leroy could give Freda seven days to make up her mind. In this case, the offer would be valid until that period had passed, or until Freda accepted or rejected the offer.

An offer also lapses if one party dies or is declared incapable before acceptance takes place. If any of these events occurs after acceptance, the contract is valid, as long as the other elements are in place.

The offeror can also terminate the offer by revoking it. On the fourth day, Freda still has not accepted the offer. Leroy changes his mind and clearly communicates to Freda that the offer is revoked: his laptop is no longer for sale. It does not matter that only four days have passed. Leroy can legally change his mind because Freda has not accepted the offer.

An offer, however, cannot be revoked if the parties have a separate contract that states the offeror cannot withdraw it for a specific period of time. Also, if Freda gives Leroy a deposit toward purchasing the laptop to show sincerity in considering the offer, then Leroy cannot withdraw his offer until the seven days have passed. Usually, a purchaser of a house will make a deposit to keep the house available to him or her alone. This is called "placing an option." If the purchase is completed, the deposit is applied to the house price. If the offeree does not complete the transaction, the deposit may or may not be returned. This depends on the original terms of the agreement.

Review Your Understanding (Pages 493 to 497)

1. Distinguish between an offeror and offeree in a contract.
2. Explain the term "meeting of the minds."
3. Identify four things wrong with the following offer: "I offer to sell you one of my watercolours at a fair price on generous terms with a quick delivery."
4. What are the benefits and dangers of telemarketing and online marketing?
5. Why must an offer be communicated before it may be accepted?
6. If Louise returns a lost watch to its owner, is she legally entitled to a reward of which she is unaware? Explain.
7. For what period of time does an offer remain open?
8. Distinguish between the lapse and revocation of an offer.

16.4 Acceptance

Acceptance can be communicated either in words or by conduct and must follow certain legal rules. For example, you leave your bicycle for repair, the service person agrees to fix it, and you agree to pay the charges. This is acceptance by words or agreement. Many offers are also accepted by performance; for example, in the Carlill case and with the rewards. Most offers made over a store counter are accepted without negotiation. To be valid, an acceptance must be unconditional. It must also be made within a specified time and in the manner specified by the offeror.

An offeree may want to accept an offer, but not exactly as presented. In this case, the offeree could make a **counteroffer,** which changes one or more terms of the original offer. For example, Katya offers to sell her car to Dino for $4000. Dino replies, "I'd really like to have the car, but I'll give you $3500 for it." Dino has made a counteroffer, which ends the original offer. It is really a new offer to Katya, who can accept or reject it. Of course, Katya can then make her own counteroffer. This process can go back and forth many times. If these negotiations are done through written documents, the exchange is commonly referred to as the "battle of the forms."

Case

Hunter v. Baluke

(1998) 42 O.R. (3d) 553
Ontario Court, General Division

Wayne Gretzky and Janet Jones Gretzky (with Hunter acting as the purchaser in their stead) exchanged offers and counteroffers with the owners (Baluke) of a cottage property. On January 12, 1998, the Gretzkys told their real-estate agent that an offer from the owners dated January 11 was acceptable

except for the date of possession of a boathouse on the property. The Gretzkys' agent told the owners' real-estate agent that the Gretzkys agreed to let the owners keep their boats, but not their furniture, in the boathouse until May 8, 1998. The Gretzkys' agent wrote up an offer to this effect and sent it to the owners.

On January 14, the owners signed the offer, adding the words "supplies and furniture" to the provision about the boathouse. The Gretzkys told their

continued ▶

agent this was unacceptable. Soon after, according to the Gretzkys' agent, the owners' agent indicated that the owners were prepared to change their January 14 offer to reflect the Gretzkys' wishes. The Gretzkys then made and initialled changes to their copy of the owners' January 14 offer: the owners could keep only their boats in the boathouse. A copy of this document was forwarded to the owners' agent. The Gretzkys also wired a deposit to the account of the real-estate firm acting for the owners.

After seeing the amended document, the owners declared that no enforceable agreement had been reached. The Gretzkys later sued the owners to close the deal according to the terms of the Gretzkys' last counteroffer. The court found in favour of the owners, stating that there was no evidence that they had agreed to the changes to the January 14 offer. Furthermore, there was no evidence that the owners had appointed the purchasers (the Gretzkys) as their agents for the purpose of changing the offer.

For Discussion

1. **What was the main problem between the owners and the Gretzkys?**

2. **Why did the Gretzkys believe that they had formed a binding agreement with the owners?**

3. **Why did the court find in favour of the owners?**

Communicating Acceptance

No contract exists until acceptance is communicated to the offeror. It is assumed that offer and acceptance will be communicated in the same way, unless the offer specifies another method of communication. For example, a written offer is usually accepted in writing.

Acceptance by Mail

Offers sent and accepted by mail are a part of everyday business; hence, there are legal rules to determine when acceptance is valid. An offer made and accepted by mail becomes a binding contract once a properly addressed and stamped letter of acceptance has been mailed. The postmark is proof of the mailing date. If the acceptance is lost or delayed in the mails, the parties are still bound to the contract, as long as the offeree can prove the acceptance was mailed in time.

If the acceptance is lost or doesn't arrive on time, the offeror may make the offer to someone else. An offeror who fails to specify that acceptance is not complete until the letter is received assumes the risk of loss by Canada Post. The offeree, however, may find it impossible to prove that he or she mailed the acceptance. Because of this, it may be wise for both parties to use registered mail or couriers.

If an offer does not specify a method of acceptance, a "reasonable method of acceptance" must be used. The courts have interpreted this to mean any method that is at least as fast as the offeror's method of communication. Thus, a mailed offer could be accepted by mail, telephone, or fax. Courts have recognized the importance of fax machines in business today. As evidence in contract disputes, signed faxed documents appear to be as legal as originally signed documents.

When acceptance of a mailed offer is made in some reasonable manner other than mail, the contract is not formed until the acceptance reaches the offeror. If the mailed offer specifies that acceptance must be by mail, then a faxed or telephoned acceptance is not valid.

Electronic Contracts

Commerce conducted over the Internet (**e-commerce**) is transforming business. Around the world, law makers are creating new laws to deal with the realities of buying, selling, and forming contracts online. Technology has made it possible to create a digital signature that is personal, verifiable, and protected by encryption (coding). This is a major breakthrough because all formal contracts must be signed.

In 1996, the General Assembly of the United Nations adopted the *Model Law on Electronic Commerce.* Drafted by the UN Commission on International Trade Law, it has set international standards that allow electronic communications to have the same legal weight as paper documents.

Because the provinces and territories regulate contracts in Canada, it is important that they work together in this area. In the years 2000 and 2001 alone, for example, British Columbia, Yukon, Saskatchewan, Manitoba, Ontario, Quebec, New Brunswick, Prince Edward Island, and Nova Scotia passed or introduced legislation that deals with e-commerce, digital signatures, and contracts.

Ontario's *Electronic Commerce Act, 2000,* is a good example and deals with these key areas of concern:

- Section 3 states that persons are not obliged to use electronic communication, but their consent to do so may be inferred from their actual use of electronic communication.
- Section 4 states that electronic communication can be legally equal to paper documents.
- Sections 5 to 13 set out conditions for electronic communication to satisfy the legal requirements for written communication.
- Sections 19 to 22 establish rules for contracts made electronically. These rules decide such questions as when a message has been sent and received and where the sending and receiving took place.

The need to define and protect electronic contracts will continue to concern law makers as well as computer and software designers, Internet service providers, businesses, and consumers. In Chapter 17, you will look at federal and provincial consumer-protection legislation that also touches on this area of contract law.

Silence and Inaction

An offeror might be tempted to say, "If you don't notify me within five days, I'll assume you've accepted my offer." Unfortunately, this would not be legally valid. Acceptance must be expressed actively in words or action.

Negative-option marketing is an exception to this rule. It means that a consumer must take an action in order not to receive an item or service. For example, some book and music clubs automatically send selections unless members return a form before a specified due date. Silence and inaction—in this example, not returning the form—is considered valid because members have signed a pre-existing agreement with the club.

In 1995, Rogers Cablesystems Inc. announced it was increasing the number of TV channels it offered to subscribers. This offer was negative-option marketing, and subscribers had to notify Rogers if they did *not* want to receive the new channels. Subscribers who did nothing would automatically receive and be billed for the expanded service. More than 2500 people complained to the Canadian Radio-television and Telecommunications Commission (CRTC), and Rogers cancelled the plan.

Other businesses have used this kind of marketing with similar results. In 1996, British Columbia became the first province to specify that consent to receive unsolicited services, such as cable programming, must be clear and cannot be inferred from use or payment.

Unsolicited Goods and Services

In the past, it was common for unsolicited credit cards to be mailed to consumers. If consumers used the cards, it was seen as acceptance by performance. If a third party stole such a card, the original addressee was held liable, even though he or she had done nothing to receive the card. Today, Alberta, Manitoba, New Brunswick, Prince Edward Island, and Quebec prohibit the issuing of unsolicited credit cards. In British Columbia, Newfoundland, Nova Scotia, Ontario, and Saskatchewan, any person who receives an unsolicited credit card is under no obligation unless he or she gives written acknowledgment of intent to accept the card.

Consumers receive many other kinds of unsolicited goods. Where no consumer-protection legislation is in place, anyone who receives unsolicited goods is liable only if he or she uses the goods. Consumers can mark "refuse to accept; return to sender" across any package containing unsolicited goods and return it to the sender, without liability. Consumers may also keep the goods and simply not use them. There is no obligation to return them. This also applies to members of book and music clubs who have fulfilled their contract and sent a cancellation.

Review Your Understanding (Pages 498 to 501)

1. What is a counteroffer, and what effect does it have on the original offer?

2. a) When is acceptance by mail legally binding?

   b) What happens if an acceptance letter is mailed but never received by the offeror?

3. If an offer does not specify the method of acceptance, what options are available to the offeree?

4. What is the legal status of offers and acceptances sent by fax?

5. What is the basic intent of Ontario's *Electronic Commerce Act, 2000*, and what are its main provisions?

6. Explain the meaning of this statement: "Remaining silent is not a valid acceptance."

7. What basic rule of acceptance does negative-option marketing appear to ignore?

16.5 Consideration

The next essential element after offer and acceptance is consideration: the exchange of something of value. In most contracts, consideration for one party is the purchase of a particular item or service; for the other, it is the money paid.

There are two forms of legal consideration: present and future. **Present consideration** occurs at the time the contract is formed. **Future consideration** occurs when one or both of the parties promise to do something in the future. Buying on credit is an example of this because the seller will not receive payment (or consideration) until a later date. Another example of future consideration occurs in sports; a team may trade a player this season for a player to be selected from another team next year.

A promise by one person to pay another for services that have already been performed for free is **past consideration.** Such a contract is not legally binding. (See *Pickett v. Love,* below.)

Courts assume that if the parties have taken the time to prepare a contract under seal, they are gaining benefits of some sort. Thus, the courts assume that consideration exists. In fact, the seal satisfies the requirement for consideration.

Adequacy of Consideration

The courts are not concerned with the amount of consideration exchanged, as long as one party gives something to the other. The courts

You Be the JUDGE

A rock collector found a rock at a roadside display in Arizona and asked the vendor in surprise: "$20?" The vendor reduced the price to $10 and the collector bought it. Later, the collector sold the stone—an uncut emerald—for $2 million.

- Can the roadside vendor legally force the buyer to renegotiate the deal? Explain.

Case

Pickett v. Love

(1982) 20 Sask. R. 115
Saskatchewan Court of Queen's Bench

Gordon Pickett, the plaintiff, and Brenda Love, the defendant, entered into a romantic relationship in June 1981 and exchanged keys to one another's apartments. Their relationship continued until December 31. Love's feelings started to cool in October, and she told Pickett she wanted only to be friends. Pickett, however, persisted in his advances and gave Love presents, including a watch and the offer of a plane ticket to New Orleans.

Later, Pickett offered to renovate Love's bathroom. She indicated that she would like this but could not afford to pay him for the work. In February 1982, after the renovations were completed, a conversation took place between the parties. Pickett claimed that Love had agreed to pay him what she could each month until the bill was

paid, although he was not sure what that amount was. Love indicated to Pickett that their friendship was over and that he was to return the key.

After discovering that Love was seeing his friend, Pickett placed a claim on Love's property for $759. The court was not certain as to what had been agreed between the parties, but the judge believed that the plaintiff had done the work in a bid for the defendant's continued affection. Pickett's claim was dismissed.

For Discussion

1. **Was there a legally binding contract between the parties? Why or why not?**

2. **Did the defendant have an obligation to pay the plaintiff for the renovations? Give reasons.**

3. **Why did the plaintiff's action fail?**

will not bargain for you. If someone freely sells something for much less than it is worth, the contract is still binding since both parties received something of value and benefit. Parties are free to make good or bad bargains, unless evidence suggests that one of the parties was pressured or the consideration is grossly inadequate.

The courts do not regard love, affection, respect, and honour as valuable legal consideration. If your aunt promises to give you a car on your birthday and changes her mind, this is not a contract. It is a gift, and promises of gifts are generally not enforceable.

Case

MacKenzie v. MacKenzie

(1996) 139 Nfld. & P.E.I.R. 1
Prince Edward Island Supreme Court, Trial Division

In May 1977, David MacKenzie began building a home for himself and his wife, Linda. David's father, Hanford MacKenzie, helped him build the house. A year later, in June 1978, David and Linda signed a mortgage agreement for David's father to lend them $25 000. This agreement was not registered with a bank. Hanford, however, did not transfer money, or anything else, to David or Linda on or after this date. David and Linda moved into their new home in October 1978.

Three months after David died in an accident, in 1994, Hanford MacKenzie formally registered the 1978 mortgage agreement. He demanded that Linda pay him the principal of $25 000 and interest of $85 000. Linda MacKenzie applied to the courts to have the mortgage agreement declared void and unenforceable.

Linda testified that she had never seen her father-in-law pay for anything during construction of the house. His contribution, she said, had been his labour. She also said she did not realize what she was doing when she signed the 1978 mortgage agreement. Hanford testified that he had advanced the mortgage funds to his son by paying for the construction costs on the house and through earlier loans.

The court held that the mortgage was void for lack of consideration and that any money Hanford MacKenzie had given to his son was given prior to the execution of the mortgage and "as a gift out of love and concern for his son."

For Discussion

1. What motive might Hanford MacKenzie have had for having David and Linda MacKenzie sign the 1978 mortgage agreement?

2. a) Outline the argument of Linda MacKenzie.
   b) Why was the mortgage agreement declared void?

3. Explain how this case illustrates the principle of "past consideration."

Review Your Understanding (Pages 502 to 503)

1. Explain the significance of consideration in a contract.

2. With examples, distinguish between past, present, and future consideration, and discuss the validity of each type.

3. Does a contract under seal require consideration? Why or why not?

4. Why are the courts not concerned that both parties in a contract obtain equal value for consideration?

16.6 Capacity

After offer, acceptance, and consideration, the next essential element is capacity, or the ability to enter into a contract. All sane and sober adults can form contracts. There are laws, however, to protect certain groups of people from being exploited in contract situations. As a result, contracts involving minors or persons with a developmental disability or impaired judgment will not be legally binding under certain circumstances.

Minors and Contracts

A minor is any person under the age of majority, the age at which a person gains full rights and responsibilities in legal matters, including contracts. Canada's provinces and territories have set the age of majority at either 18 or 19 years of age. Each province or territory can also restrict the rights and responsibilities that attach to the age of majority. In Ontario and Saskatchewan, for example, the age of majority is 18, but you must be 19 to legally purchase alcohol and cigarettes.

Over the years, the courts have developed laws that determine when and if a minor's contract is valid and enforceable.

■ Minimum Drinking Ages

Country	Age
Australia	18
Canada	18 or 19, depending on province or territory
China	none
France	16
Germany	16, for beer and wine 18, for spirits
Italy	16
Japan	20
United States	21 (in 31 of 50 states)

■ The Age of Majority in Canada

18 Years of Age	19 Years of Age
Alberta	British Columbia
Manitoba	New Brunswick
Ontario	Newfoundland & Labrador
Prince Edward Island	Northwest Territories
Quebec	Nova Scotia
Saskatchewan	Nunavut
	Yukon Territory

Figure 16-6

The age of majority is not always the same as the age at which a person can legally drink, marry, or drive a car. Why do you think this is the case?

Valid Contracts

Minors are obligated to fulfill contracts for **necessaries,** which are goods and services that everyone needs: food, clothing, shelter, education, and medical services. If this were not so, businesses would not enter into any contracts with minors. This situation might be harmful or damaging to minors in times of need, especially those minors nearing the age of majority.

To be considered a necessary, a good or service must reflect a minor's **station in life** (social position). For example, a mayor's teenaged son may need to have a tuxedo to attend important functions and formal banquets with his parents. Other students in the same classroom would not have the same need. Even in contracts for necessaries, a minor may not be obligated to pay the contract price if the courts find that terms of the contract were not in the minor's best interests. Only a "reasonable" price must be paid. What is reasonable? Suppose Becky, a minor, needs a winter coat and buys one for $400. If she finds an identical coat for $250 at another store, Becky may be obligated to pay only $250, the reasonable price, to the store from which she purchased the coat originally.

Apprenticeship and employment contracts are also considered necessary, if they are beneficial and do not take advantage of minors. However, if the court feels that the minor was overwhelmed by the bargaining power of the other party, the contract will be judged unenforceable (Chapter 19 deals with Employment Law).

Void Contracts

Contracts that are not in a minor's best interests are said to be **void** (to have never existed). If a person has taken unfair advantage of a minor to have the youth enter into a contract, courts will rule that the contract is prejudicial and has no legal effect.

Voidable Contracts

Contract law has always offered special protection for minors, but it also protects persons and businesses that deal with minors. A **voidable contract** is one in which one party has the right to make the contract binding or not binding. The general rule is that a minor's contracts are voidable at the minor's option; that is, the minor decides whether or not to be bound by the contract. Most minors do complete such contracts, since they entered them in good faith.

It is in the area of **non-necessaries** that voidable contracts for minors sometimes become an issue. For example, Fiona, who is a minor, purchases a camcorder at the mall, makes a down payment, and takes it home. A week later, she decides she really does not want it. Fiona is not legally bound to complete the payments on her contract, but she must return the purchase to the retailer and cancel the contract. The retailer has the right to keep Fiona's down payment, since she obtained some benefit from the use of the camcorder. If there is damage to the camcorder that Fiona did not cause deliberately, the retailer cannot recover the cost from her. The cost of any "wear and tear" is also not recoverable. However, the cost of any deliberate damage may be recovered.

If the retailer learns over the weekend that Fiona is a minor, he or she cannot cancel the contract without Fiona's permission. An adult who enters into a contract with a minor is bound by it if the minor wishes to fulfill its terms.

Figure 16-7

The *Tobacco Act, 1997,* restricts the sale of tobacco to persons over the age of 18.

Misrepresentation of Age

If a minor lies about his or her age, this does not change the legal rights of the minor or retailer. It also does not remove the minor's protection under the law. As a result, retailers deal with minors at their own risk. Because of the great protection given to minors, most retailers will only sell to minors for cash. Retailers know that a contract is voidable at the minor's option.

Parental Liability

To protect themselves, many retailers require a parent or other adult to cosign any contract involving a minor. The parent or other adult is responsible for full payment if the minor does not pay. If a minor uses a credit card belonging to a parent and the parent pays the account, it is implied that the parent will continue to do so in the future. A parent who wishes to cancel this arrangement must notify the retailers involved. Parents are also responsible if they expressly tell a retailer that their child may purchase items for which they will pay. Generally, however, parents are not responsible for the contracts or debts of their children.

Case

Staples (Next friend of) v. Varga (c.o.b. True Legends Sports Cards and Comics)

(1995) 27 Alta. L.R. (3d) 442
Alberta Provincial Court, Civil Division

Fourteen-year-old Mark Allan Staples made cash advances on his parents' credit cards without their permission. He then bought $4233.75 worth of vintage comic books from True Legends Sports Cards and Comics. When Mark's parents found out, they tried to return the comics to True Legends for a refund. The owner, Archie Varga, refused, but suggested ways to sell the comics and offered to help sell them. Eventually, Mark's parents sold some of the comics at a flea market.

Figure 16-8

Mark used his parents' personal identification number (PIN) to get cash advances.

Mark went to court to void the contract he had made with True Legends. He argued that since he was a minor, and because the comics were not "necessaries," his contract with True Legends was either void or voidable. Therefore, he was entitled to a refund.

The court dismissed Mark's action. The judge ruled that the contract was not void. There was no evidence that True Legends had pressured Mark into buying the comics, or that he had been defrauded or penalized in any way.

The judge also ruled that the contract was not voidable because Mark had paid a reasonable price for the comics and had received a financial benefit from them. The judge pointed to evidence that many of Mark's comics had, in fact, increased in value.

For Discussion

1. **The court did not concern itself with how Mark had obtained the money to make his purchases. Should it have? Defend your point of view.**

2. **Summarize the argument Mark made in claiming he was entitled to a refund.**

3. **The court gave different reasons for finding that the contract between Mark and True Legends was neither void nor voidable. How did the court justify its finding in each situation?**

4. **Research the meaning of "Next friend of," used in the citation of this case.**

People with Impaired Judgment or a Disability

Contract law treats people with impaired judgment and developmental disabilities in much the same way that it treats minors: it offers them protection. Impaired judgment may be temporary or permanent. It may be caused by illness, disability, hypnosis, or by the effects of alcohol and drug use. If a person's mental impairment requires institutionalization, the person cannot enter into contracts. All others having impaired judgment are still responsible in contracts for necessaries.

As with minors, people with impaired judgment are obligated to pay only a "reasonable" price for necessaries. Any contract for non-necessaries is voidable if the person with impaired judgment can prove that he or she was incapable of understanding what was happening at the time the contract was formed and that the other party knew of this condition. Even then the contract must be voided within a reasonable time after recovery, and the goods must be returned. If a person with impaired judgment recovers and continues to benefit from a contract, he or she is bound by the contract.

Review Your Understanding (Pages 504 to 507)

1. What groups are protected from being taken advantage of when they enter into contracts?
2. What types of contracts are binding for minors?
3. Distinguish between void and voidable contracts made by minors.
4. As a retailer, what would you do to reduce the risk when entering into contracts with minors? Why would you do so?
5. When are parents liable for contracts that their children may enter?
6. What two points must be established before people with impaired judgment can avoid liability for signed contracts?

16.7 Consent

Each party in a contract must understand and freely agree to complete it. This is consent. Four situations may prevent consent from occurring: misrepresentation, mistakes, undue influence, and duress.

Misrepresentation

If you are purchasing a good or service, the principle of *caveat emptor* (buyer beware) applies. This means that the seller is not legally obligated to disclose negative facts that might stop you from buying. You are responsible for checking out claims for the product or service. If either party enters a contract willingly and later discovers they have made a bad deal, the contract cannot be voided on that fact alone. Parties who enter a contract must accept the consequences of their actions (see page 534).

If misrepresentation takes place, however, a contract can be voided. **Misrepresentation** is a false statement made by one person concerning a material fact, which is a fact that is so important that it causes the other person to enter a contract. Misrepresentation makes genuine consent impossible and is the most common reason that contracts are voided. There are two kinds of misrepresentation: innocent and fraudulent.

Innocent Misrepresentation

When a person makes a false statement about a material fact that he or she believes to be true, **innocent misrepresentation** exists. A seller may be repeating facts provided by a usually reliable source, such as a manufacturer. For example, Clorinda sells hair colouring to Shamir, repeating the manufacturer's claim that it will last for seven or eight washings. In reality, the colour washes out the second time Shamir shampoos his hair. In another example, a travel agent makes a genuine error while reading a brochure and tells two clients that their total cost for a cruise is $3500. The clients later discover that there is a $750 charge for airfare to get to the cruise ship.

In both cases, the seller is innocent, and the buyer can legally rescind, or cancel, the contract. **Rescission** is the basic remedy for innocent misrepresentation. It restores the parties to the positions they were in before forming the contract. In other words, Shamir and the clients for the cruise would be entitled to a refund, but not to damages.

Fraudulent Misrepresentation

e activity

Visit **www.law.nelson.com** and follow the links to learn more about fraudulent misrepresentation.

If a seller makes a statement about a material fact knowing it to be false, **fraudulent misrepresentation** has occurred. This is far more serious than innocent misrepresentation because the seller is lying to cheat, or defraud, the buyer. Not only can a buyer rescind a contract formed under such circumstances, he or she can be awarded damages. The buyer must, however, prove to the court that he or she has suffered some loss from entering into the agreement as a result of the misrepresentation.

Suppose that Lisa DeLuca owns a service station on a busy two-lane highway. She learns that a multilane highway will be built nearby, jeopardizing her business. She lists her property for sale. A prospective buyer hears about the proposed highway and asks Lisa about it. She tells the purchaser that the mayor has told her the highway will never be built. This is a lie, fraudulent misrepresentation. If a contract is formed on this basis, the purchaser can later rescind it and also sue Lisa for damages. The courts will protect innocent parties from fraud.

Case

Willoughby v. Gallant

(2000) 582 A.P.R. 179
Prince Edward Island Supreme Court, Trial Division

In August 1999, David Willoughby went to the home of David Gallant to inspect a sea-doo that Gallant had advertised for sale. Gallant showed Willoughby maintenance records and a 1998 repair invoice that noted "the motor sounds rough." Willoughby asked about this and Gallant said the problem had been repaired. The sea-doo, Gallant said, had been in excellent condition the last time he had used it.

continued ▶

Willoughby purchased the sea-doo without taking it for a test run, despite Gallant's suggestion that he do so, and without having it inspected. Two days later, Willoughby had the sea-doo out no more than 20 minutes when the engine stopped. An inspection revealed the engine was corroded and in need of extensive repairs. Willoughby sued Gallant for damages.

At trial, the court considered two key questions: Had Gallant made any misrepresentations to Willoughby? Did *caveat emptor* apply?

The court ruled that, on the balance of probabilities, Gallant had not used innocent or fraudulent misrepresentation. It accepted that when Gallant had stated the sea-doo was working well the last time he had used it, he was expressing an honest opinion. Also, there was no evidence to connect the 1998 report that the engine sounded "rough" to finding that the engine was corroded in 1999. The court found that Willoughby had no right to complain when he could have tested the sea-doo and had it inspected. For these two reasons, *caveat emptor* applied. The court dismissed the plaintiff's claim.

For Discussion

1. What argument would Willoughby have presented to support his case?

2. What argument would Gallant have presented to support his case?

3. Willoughby explained to the court that he had not taken the sea-doo for a test run because a storm was approaching. Should the court have considered this fact a point in Willoughby's favour? Explain.

Agents of Change   The Bre-X Mining Scandal

Michael de Guzman, a trained geologist, left the Philippines for Indonesia in 1987, hoping to make a rich mineral discovery. Instead, he found hard times. By 1992, he was desperate for work and accepted a job from William McLucas to check out the Busang property, a gold claim in the remotest rain forest of Borneo. There, Guzman tested core samples from old test holes and reported promising results. This was a big change from earlier findings.

In May 1993, Bre-X Minerals Ltd., owned by John Walsh of Alberta, bought the Busang property from McLucas for US$80 000. By October, Bre-X began explorations at Busang with de Guzman as chief geologist and his friend John Felderhoff as general manager in charge of drilling. Tests in 1993 and 1994 showed significant amounts of gold. Then, on June 20, 1995, Felderhoff made a stunning announcement: Busang could be "one of the world's great ore bodies." Respected Canadian analysts soon recommended Bre-X, and the stock soared. From $1.50 in 1994, Bre-X stock was hitting $280 a share in September 1996.

Then disaster struck:
- In October 1996, an ownership fight became public and Bre-X stock plunged.

Figure 16-9

Paul de Guzman attends his father's funeral in the Philippines in 1997.

continued

- In January 1997, fire destroyed vital maps, drilling results, and core samples.
- On March 10, 1997, independent tests showed insignificant amounts of gold at Busang.
- On March 19, 1997, de Guzman either fell or jumped from a helicopter over Borneo.
- On May 3, 1997, an independent study declared the Busang gold claim to be of little economic value.

On May 7, 1997, Bre-X was taken off major stock exchanges. Once worth $6 billion, it was now worthless. Investigations showed what many had suspected: fraud. A person or persons had added gold to the core samples. In the wake of the scandal, shareholders' launched a lawsuit. It went nowhere. The RCMP investigated, but no charges were laid. Walsh died of a heart attack, and Felderhoff was believed to be living in the Cayman Islands.

The Bre-X scandal embarrassed Canada's mining industry around the world and led to demands for reforms to prevent future frauds.

For Discussion

1. Is the Bre-X scandal simply a reminder of caveat emptor? Explain.
2. Did Canadian analysts and stock exchanges fail to protect investors from fraudulent misrepresentation? Research this story further before drawing your conclusions.

Mistake

Once a contract has been formed, the law states that it should be carried out whenever possible. It is generally assumed that each party has read and understood the contract and will be bound by his or her signature. Ignorance of the law is no excuse, with the following exceptions.

Common Mistake

Common mistake occurs if both parties are mistaken about the same fundamental fact of a contract. Suppose Shani is negotiating with Matt to buy his 2000 Pontiac Grand Prix car, which Shani keeps in her garage. Unknown to them both, the garage burns down and destroys the car as they are negotiating. This is an example of a common mistake, and the contract would be void. In fact, there was no car to sell when the contract was made.

Unilateral Mistake

A contract will also be void and unenforceable if one party has made a mistake and the other party knew of the mistake but made no attempt to correct it. This is known as a **unilateral mistake.** For example, you select a utility knife for purchase and tell the store clerk that you want to cut masonite with it. The clerk, however, knows that the knife will not cut masonite but says nothing and sells it to you. This is a unilateral mistake, and it makes the contract void and unenforceable.

The courts have recognized two common types of unilateral mistakes: **clerical mistake** and *non est factum.*

Suppose Séguin and Kirilenko have been discussing the sale of a tractor for some time. Kirilenko offers to sell it to Séguin for $15 000 and agrees to put the offer in writing and to mail it. Kirilenko later writes up the offer and writes the price as $1500, not $15 000. He does not catch the mistake before he mails the offer. When Séguin receives the offer by mail, the error is obvious to him. Séguin cannot hold Kirilenko to selling the tractor for the price of $1500. The clerical mistake makes the agreement void and unenforceable.

Freeman v. General Motors Acceptance Corp. of Canada Ltd.

(1999) 186 Sask. R. 104
Saskatchewan Court of Queen's Bench

In the fall of 1994, Les Freeman bought a new truck through General Motors Acceptance Corporation of Canada Limited (GMAC). In January 1995, he purchased a 1994 car, again through GMAC's credit department.

Freeman defaulted on payments, and GMAC served notice that it intended to seize both vehicles unless he made good on his debts. In November 1997, through computer error, GMAC mailed Freeman a letter saying he owed $558.16 on the truck. Through the same error, GMAC later mailed Freeman a letter saying it had received the final car payment. At the time, Freeman still owed GMAC approximately $35 000 on the two vehicles.

On December 22, 1997, Freeman sent a certified cheque for $558.16 to GMAC. GMAC immediately advised Freeman by mail of the computer mistakes and its intention to seize the vehicles. GMAC received no payments from Freeman after January 1997 and took possession of the two vehicles in July 1998.

In 1999, Freeman sought a court order to stop GMAC from selling the vehicles. In court, he claimed that he had settled his debts and reached an "accord" with GMAC on the amount owing. GMAC rejected these assertions and asked the court to dismiss Freeman's claim.

The court found no evidence that the debts had been paid or that a settlement had been reached. Even if such a settlement had been reached, the court said, it would "be voidable under the doctrine of unilateral mistake." Instead of trying to correct the error, the court noted, it was clear Freeman had tried to "take advantage of GMAC's mistake."

For Discussion

1. What prompted GMAC to take action to repossess Freeman's truck and car?

2. What GMAC mistakes did Freeman try to take advantage of?

3. What contradictory claims did Freeman make in his 1999 court submission?

4. How were the rules of "unilateral mistake" applied in this case?

Non est factum means: "It is not my deed." This type of mistake was more common in Canada when few people were literate. For example, a person might be presented with a document to sign and be told it was a will when, in fact, it was a loan guarantee. Later, if the signer went to court over the loan, he or she could plead *non est factum*. The actual document had nothing to do with the signer's intended action (deed). *Non est factum* is rare today, since most people know how to read and write. Although a person might be illiterate, *non est factum* may not serve to void a contract if evidence exists that the party was aware of what he or she was doing in signing the contract.

Undue Influence

Undue influence occurs when one person applies improper mental or emotional pressure to induce another to enter and form a contract involuntarily. It usually takes place when one party dominates another. Dominating relationships typically exist between husbands and wives, parents and children, doctors and patients, lawyers and clients, invalids and home-care workers, and so on. Anyone in need can be influenced by the person who can meet that need. A contract formed through undue influence lacks genuine consent and is voidable at the option of the victim.

Generally, a person who claims that he or she entered a contract because of undue influence must prove that such influence was possible. Action to void the contract must be taken promptly; otherwise, the right to void the agreement may lapse. Once such a legal action goes to court, the burden of proof shifts to the dominant party, who must then prove that he or she did not take advantage of the dominant position or use undue influence.

Case

Berry v. Nencescu Estate

(June 27, 1997) Docket Regina S.U.R. 595/95
Saskatchewan Court of Queen's Bench

In his will, lifelong bachelor George Nencescu left most of his large estate to his sister Phoebe Langley, her husband, Sid Langley, and her son Garth. After Nencescu died in 1995, a distant relative, Francis Berry, went to court to have the will declared invalid on the grounds that Sid Langley had exerted undue influence on Nencescu at the time the will was executed.

Berry, who had seen Nencescu only three times between 1990 and 1995, testified that he seemed intimidated by Langley. Several other relatives, and a neighbouring family that had rented land from

Figure 16-10

What contract laws protect disabled seniors from being exploited?

Nencescu, also testified that Langley seemed to dominate the relationship.

Other evidence contradicted Berry's claim. A nurse, who saw Nencescu regularly, described Sid Langley's relationship with Nencescu as "good" and "caring." A home-care worker who visited Nencescu weekly described Nencescu as being strong-willed and independent. The lawyer who helped draw up the will testified that Nencescu was fully capable of managing his affairs.

The judge quoted two previous cases to establish the law with respect to undue influence:

It is only when the will of the person who becomes a testator is coerced into doing that which he does not desire to do, that it is undue influence.

Moreover, it is not sufficient to establish that a person has the power unduly to overbear the will of the testator. It is necessary to prove that, in the particular case, the power was exercised, and that it was by means of exercise of that power that the will, such as it is, has been produced.

The judge found that Berry had "fallen far short" of proving that Sid Langley had exerted undue influence on Nencescu. The claim, the judge stated, was based on little more than Berry's suspicions.

For Discussion

1. **What evidence did the applicant bring to court to show that Nencescu had executed his will while under the undue influence of Sid Langley?**

2. **Explain the meaning of the judge's second quotation.**

3. **Identify several reasons the judge gave for deciding against the applicant.**

4. **What would have been the legal consequences if the applicant had won her case?**

The spousal relationship presents a special legal situation. For example, if a wife tries to void a contract that she either entered into with her husband or entered into for his benefit (such as guaranteeing his debts), she must prove that her husband exerted undue influence. If the wife in such a situation did not receive independent advice (from a lawyer other than her husband's), the courts may accept this as evidence that she was subjected to undue influence. For this reason, some lending agencies require a wife who is guaranteeing her husband's loan to sign a statement indicating that she has consulted her own lawyer about her guarantee.

The courts developed the concept of undue influence to provide remedies for situations not covered by fraud or duress. As a result, it is more flexible and wider ranging in its application.

Duress

Duress is similar to undue influence, but more extreme. It occurs when one party uses threats or violence to force another to enter into a contract. The threats may be of physical punishment or detention, or they may include some form of blackmail. The person entering the contract may be the victim, but the person's spouse, children, or parents may also be targeted. Obviously, a person who has been threatened or beaten into a contract cannot be said to have consented and should be able to avoid any responsibilities under it. As with undue influence, a victim should act to void the contract as soon as possible once he or she is free of the duress.

Review Your Understanding (Pages 507 to 513)

1. Identify the four conditions that may prevent genuine consent from occurring in a contract.
2. Using original examples, distinguish between innocent and fraudulent misrepresentation.
3. Distinguish between a common and a unilateral mistake.
4. What types of unilateral mistakes do the courts recognize?
5. What is undue influence? Identify four examples of special relationships in which undue influence might arise.
6. What is duress? How does it differ from undue influence?

16.8 Lawful Purpose

The last essential element in a legally binding contract is lawful purpose (object). Any contract that amounts to a crime under the *Criminal Code* or that breaks federal or provincial laws is illegal and, of course, void. For example, a contract to sell state secrets to a foreign power or terrorist organization would be a crime and unenforceable. Other contracts may not break any laws but still may be illegal and void because they go against **public policy.** This means that the private good of the contracting parties cannot be considered to be more important than the general good of society. Contracts that offend the public good are simply not enforceable.

Should Commercial Surrogacy Contracts Be Allowed?

In the 1970s, the term "surrogate mother" entered the language. It was used in connection with in vitro fertilization (IVF), a reproductive technology that allows a human embryo to be conceived outside the mother's body. In IVF, an ovum (egg) taken from the mother, or donor, is placed in a petri dish. Sperm from the father, or donor, is added to the ovum. If fertilization occurs, the embryo is transferred to the mother's body. If the mother cannot carry a developing fetus in her body, the embryo can be implanted in another woman—a surrogate mother—who has agreed to bear the child.

There are two types of surrogacy: commercial and altruistic. In commercial surrogacy, a woman is paid to be a surrogate mother. Agreements with the surrogate mother involve a signed contract and consideration. By 2001, fees paid to surrogate mothers averaged $20 000. In altruistic surrogacy, the surrogate mother is not paid. In this case, she likely is a friend or relative.

Commercial surrogacy contracts raise legal and ethical questions. Are they moral? Should they be strictly regulated? Should fees be allowed or outlawed? After four years of study, the Royal Commission on New Reproductive Technologies recommended outlawing commercial surrogacy in 1993. It stated that reproduction involves all of society, not simply the individual choice of a woman willing to be a surrogate. In May 2001, the federal government introduced draft legislation on assisted human reproduction that would outlaw commercial surrogacy. Anyone convicted of violating the law would face a prison term of up to 10 years and a fine of up to $500 000.

On One Side

Those who support commercial surrogacy stress that it benefits couples who would otherwise be unable to have children. They view surrogacy as an act of compassion. They point out that often the husband of the couple receiving the child is the child's biological father, and that the mother may also be the biological mother.

Figure 16-11

Sally Rhoads (right) says she brought great joy to the couple who hired her.

Supporters argue that women must have control of their own bodies. It must be the woman's choice to decide if she wants to be a surrogate mother. Furthermore, if a woman does make that choice, it is only fair that she be paid. Sally Rhoads, an Ontario surrogate mother who gave birth to twins in 2000, told the press: "I love being pregnant." Rhoads, who was 23 years old at the time, first learned about commercial surrogacy in her high school law class. She feels it has allowed her to make a valuable contribution to society.

Supporters claim that a formal contract between the surrogate mother and the couple is better than pressuring a friend or a relative to provide the service. A contract also protects the couple from lawsuits over child custody once a child is born. With a commercial surrogacy contract, they say, everybody benefits.

On the Other Side

Opponents argue that commercial surrogacy contracts focus on the rights of the contracting parties, but to the detriment of the children involved. They point out that contracts are meant to deal with the exchange of goods and services, not human life. Surrogacy contracts, they argue, have transformed infants into commodities that can be bought and sold. Such contracts, they say, deny children the dignity and respect to which they have a right as human beings.

Opponents also point out that surrogate mothers tend to be younger and less educated, and come from lower income groups than the couples seeking surrogacy. This raises the possibility that the surrogates will be exploited.

All surrogate mothers face some physical risks during pregnancy. In some cases, they may find themselves being pressured to continue with a difficult pregnancy that endangers their own health. Surrogate mothers may also experience psychological problems after giving up a child to whom they may have developed a close emotional attachment.

The Bottom Line

The draft legislation on assisted human reproduction would prohibit commercial surrogacy. This means criminal law would be used as a means to deal with commercial surrogacy. Is legislation that criminalizes commercial surrogacy justifiable in a free and democratic society? Should adults be free to form contracts that involve human reproduction? Would making commercial surrogacy contracts illegal result in the exploitation of surrogate mothers?

What Do You Think?

1. What is commercial surrogacy and why has the federal government taken steps to make it illegal?

2. What is the purpose of a surrogacy contract?

3. Summarize arguments in favour of surrogacy contracts and counterarguments. Which side of the issue do you support? Why?

Restraint of Trade

Business contracts may be challenged on grounds of public policy if they are in **restraint of trade.** Because competition is considered to be necessary to Canada's economic health, the courts limit the time that a contract can restrain or restrict trade to a reasonable period. If the time period is too long, or if the restriction is unreasonable, the contract may be void.

For example, Victor Paslowski owns the only pharmacy in a small community of 3000 people. He enters into a contract to sell his business to Chung Sing Chen. Chung will purchase the business only if Victor promises not to operate another pharmacy within a radius of 100 km of the existing store for 20 years. It is understandable that Chung would want to limit competition, but are these conditions reasonable?

▮ Questions for Contracts Challenged in Court on Restraint of Trade

☑ Is this contract a restraint of trade?

☑ Is the restraint against public policy and, therefore, void?

☑ Is the restraint reasonable for the parties involved?

☑ Is the restraint reasonable for the public interest?

Figure 16-12

Questions to ask of contracts challenged in court on restraint of trade

In this example, the contract might be considered an unreasonable restraint of trade and, therefore, void. The distance involved is probably too great. Potential customers are unlikely to travel more than 50 km. Also, the 20-year time limit seems unreasonable. It should take Chung only a few years to establish a successful business with the existing customers.

The reasonableness of a restraint depends on the size of the community the business serves, the type of business, the available competition, how necessary the business is to the community, and the time period of the restriction. Courts will only support restraints of trade that give a person buying a business a reasonable amount of time to establish a reputation.

Case

Miller v. Toews

[1991] 2 W.W.R. 604
Manitoba Court of Appeal

Frederic and Brenda Toews, the defendants, sold a restaurant in Altona, Manitoba, to the plaintiff, Robert Miller. As part of the contract, they promised not to open another restaurant or catering business within 16 km of Altona for five years. Three years later, in June 1990, the Toews bought a fast-food outlet in Altona.

The plaintiff immediately sought an injunction in court. The trial judge dismissed the application,

saying that Miller would not suffer "irreparable harm" if the injunction was denied. Miller appealed this decision to the Manitoba Court of Appeal where, in a 3 to 0 judgment, the injunction was granted.

For Discussion

1. **Why did Miller build a restraint-of-trade clause into the contract with the Toews?**

2. **In your opinion, was this an unreasonable restraint of trade and against public policy? Explain.**

After a reasonable period of time, the original seller should be able to start a similar business.

The courts are similarly reluctant to restrict an employee's ability to earn a living by moving from one business to another similar business. Employees who have access to confidential information or trade secrets, however, may have to accept certain restraints in their contract. Such a contract is called a **restraint of employment** contract. A promise not to work for a competitor for a certain period of time after leaving the place of present employment is likely to be binding.

Restraint of Competition

The federal *Competition Act* prohibits contracts between businesses if they restrict competition and are contrary to the public interest. The Act protects the public against any agreement that involves price fixing, eliminates or reduces competition, or reduces production in order to restrict competition. Business mergers that would unreasonably reduce competition and be against the public good may also be prohibited under the Act.

ⓔ activity

Visit **www.law.nelson.com** and follow the links to learn more about restraint of trade.

Bets and Wagers

Gaming and betting are popular activities in which something of value is exchanged for the chance to win something of greater value. Because these activities may be addictive and, thus, damaging to society, they are strictly controlled by statute law. Provincial and territorial authorities grant licences that allow charitable groups to raise funds through gaming events such as lotteries, bingos, and so on, for worthwhile projects. Most of the proceeds, however, must go back to customers as winnings. Under the *Criminal Code*, it is illegal to operate an unlicensed gambling business.

Betting (making a wager) on the outcome of an event is also allowed under statute law. All territories and provinces have acts that regulate it. Betting on horseraces, for example, is allowed and regulated by governments. It is also legal for two coworkers to bet on the outcome of a football game, for example, but the courts will not help the winner to collect. Contracts for bets are not considered important enough to be heard by the courts.

Private businesses can set up slot machines, pinball machines, and video games wherever governments have authorized them. These slot machines can only pay out tokens or merchandise, however, and the pinball and video games can only give free games as winnings, not money. Many municipalities have bylaws to keep game parlours from locating near schools.

Regardless of these restrictions, gambling in Canada is a multibillion dollar industry, which is controlled and dominated by provincial and territorial governments. Government-run lotteries, casinos, and video lottery terminals (VLTs) raised more than $9 billion in 2000. The profits from government-run gambling help fund social, athletic, and cultural groups and projects. However, many critics have accused governments of taking advantage of people who cannot afford to gamble and who may become addicted to gambling, especially through the use of VLTs.

ⓔ activity

Visit **www.law.nelson.com** and follow the links to learn more about legal and illegal gaming.

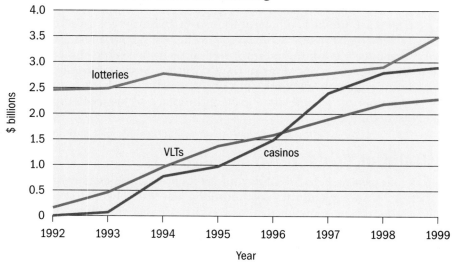

Net Revenue from Government-Run Gambling

Figure 16-13

This graph shows how widespread and profitable government-run lotteries, VLTs, and casinos have become.

Review Your Understanding (Pages 513 to 518)

1. Distinguish between "illegal" and "void" as these terms relate to contract law.
2. Give an example of a contract that might be against public policy.
3. Summarize the four questions that must be considered if a contract is challenged in court as a restraint of trade.
4. Why are courts reluctant to enforce restraint of employment contracts? When would such a contract be enforceable?
5. List three practices restricting competition that are prohibited under the federal *Competition Act*.
6. Will the court help a winner to collect a bet? Explain.

Chapter Review

Chapter Highlights

- The law of contracts is the basis of business and is founded on judge-made common law.
- The essential elements of a valid contract are offer and acceptance, consideration, capacity, consent, and lawful purpose.
- The legal requirements of a valid offer and acceptance are serious intent, definite terms, and proper communication of the offer and acceptance.
- Telecommunications technology has created new tools that benefit business and consumers and that also create new areas of contract law.
- Present and future consideration create a legally binding contract, but past consideration does not.
- Minors and people with impaired judgment enjoy special protections in contract law.
- Contracts formed through undue influence or duress are void.
- Contracts in restraint of trade cannot impose unreasonable restrictions or be against public policy.

Review Key Terms

Name the key terms that are described below.

a) a binding agreement that is enforceable in court

b) legal ability to make a contract on one's own behalf

c) the legal purpose of a contract

d) a contract that is unenforceable because it lacks at least one essential element

e) the act of withdrawing an offer before it is accepted

f) statement by an offeree rejecting an offer and creating a new offer

g) "buyer beware"

h) a fact that persuades a person to enter into a contract

i) termination of an offer when an offeree does not accept within a reasonable time

j) something of value that the contracting parties promise to exchange

k) promise by one person to pay for services that another has already performed for free

l) when a person makes a false statement about a material fact that he or she believes to be true

m) a contract that one party can choose to make binding or not binding

n) a contract situation in which one party knows the other has made a mistake but does nothing to correct it

o) improper emotional pressure used to induce a person to sign a contract

p) the limiting of competition in business

Check Your Knowledge

1. Identify the elements that must be present for a contract to be valid, and provide an example of each.

2. Identify the groups of people that are provided with extra protection in contract law, and provide an example for each.

3. Outline circumstances in which consent to a contract can be declared invalid.

4. In a restraint-of-trade action, what factors are considered in determining the reasonableness of the contract?

Apply Your Learning

5. Cranston offers to sell a sailboard to Parker for $1000. Parker is prepared to pay the price and mails a properly stamped and addressed envelope with his acceptance by return mail. Cranston does not receive Parker's letter of acceptance. What must be established to prove a binding contract between the parties?

6. While sitting in the lobby of the Playa Tambor resort hotel, Andrea hears cries for help coming from the swimming pool. She jumps into the pool and rescues an elderly man. The grateful gentleman asks her to return later that afternoon for a $100 reward for saving his life. However, instead of paying her the reward, he simply thanks her once again.

   Is Andrea entitled to the reward? Why or why not?

7. While Marg is trying to adjust her snowmobile engine, her neighbour, Anton, offers to help. Anton owns and operates the local snowmobile agency and he makes the adjustments. Neither of them discusses money.
   a) Can Anton later sue Marg for the cost of his services? Explain.
   b) If Marg had offered to pay Anton at the end of the month, would this be legally enforceable? Explain.

8. Kirk, 17 years of age, leaves home to live in Winnipeg. He finds lodging there and pays his landlord room and board regularly for some time. Then Kirk is laid off and fails to pay his weekly rent because he cannot find employment. Kirk's mother sends him money, and he pays his back rent. Later, Kirk falls behind again and the landlord demands money directly from Kirk's mother. She claims she has no responsibility in this matter.
   a) What factors should be considered in reaching a decision in this case?
   b) What could the landlord have required before entering into the contract with the minor?

9. Bates, 53 years of age, is subject to periods of mental illness during which he must receive medical help. During one of his periods of lucidity, he enters into a contract to purchase a new television set and a DVD player.

   Can Bates later repudiate the contract during an attack of depression, citing his problems as grounds for repudiation? Explain.

10. Rachelle contracts to build a cabinet for Greg by a certain date for $800. As time passes, Greg begins to doubt that Rachelle will meet the deadline. He promises her another $100 in return for her promise to finish the project by the agreed-upon date. Rachelle finishes the cabinet on time and sends Greg a bill for $900.

Is Greg legally bound to honour his promise to pay Rachelle the extra $100? Give legal arguments on both sides of this question.

Communicate Your Understanding

11. Consider the following statement: "If they do things right, the parties to a contract create their own legal rights and duties." Create a written contract in which you agree to cut a neighbour's lawn for the summer. Make sure that it includes the following: (a) a definite time period; (b) how often the lawn is to be cut; (c) whether any other maintenance is involved, such as raking; (d) the amount of payment and when it is to be received; (e) any circumstances that may cause the contract to end early; and (f) the scheduled termination date for the contract.

Develop Your Thinking

12. Explain the following statement: "The use of a seal on a contract answers for the failure to satisfy all essentials of a binding contract."

13. Explain the following statement made by an English judge, Sir George Jessel (1824–1883): "A creditor might accept anything in satisfaction of a debt.... He might take a horse, or a canary if he chooses, and that was accord and satisfaction."

14. Interpret the following statement: "The protection afforded to a minor should be used as a shield, not a sword."

15. Assume you are a young entrepreneur who is considering setting up a new business using the Internet. Outline the attractions and potential problems of operating your business electronically. As an extended activity, research items you should consider in order to protect your interests and those of your customers.

Carrying Out the Contract

Focus Questions

- How are contracts discharged?
- What civil remedies are available for breach of contract?
- How do warranties and disclaimers protect all parties to a contract?
- What protections are available to buyers and sellers regarding transfer of ownership?
- What federal and provincial laws protect consumers?

Chapter at a Glance

Figure 17-1

You run a company called Omnitainment and this storm means the outdoor rock concert you have planned cannot go on. Can you be sued for breach of contract? Will the concert have to be rescheduled? Should you give ticket holders a refund?

17.1 Introduction

Once a contract exists, each party has rights and responsibilities to carry out. When these are completed as planned, the contract is successfully **discharged.** Sometimes, circumstances arise that make this impossible. At other times, one party may decide not to live up to the terms of the contract. In this case, a **breach of contract** occurs.

Because contracts are the basis of all business relationships, they must be binding and enforceable. This chapter will help you to understand how contract law deals with such questions as the following: How can contracts be discharged? Should parties be held to a contract at all costs? What legal steps can you take if a contract is not honoured?

This chapter also explores how the provinces and territories deal with a specific area of contract law: the sale of goods.

In a world in which technology advances and businesses grow bigger every day, governments recognize the need to protect consumers. Provincial, territorial, and federal laws try to create equal bargaining powers between buyers and sellers. But business is changing very quickly. As e-commerce continues to grow, governments are struggling to create new laws to protect consumers. Will the huge multinational business that built your new computer fix it if it breaks down? Can you trust that unbelievable offer you just got in an e-mail or on the telephone? This chapter will help you to answer questions like these and to better understand the fine print of contracts.

17.2 Discharging the Contract

Once the parties have agreed and the essential elements (described in Chapter 16) are in place, an enforceable contract exists. However, all contracts must come to an end. This usually happens after the parties fulfill their obligations, or through **performance.** Contracts can also be ended by mutual agreement, impossibility of performance, and breach of contract.

Performance

Performance is the most common way to discharge a contract. For example, a promoter contracts a rock group to give an outdoor concert during Canada Day celebrations. The group puts on its show and the concert sells out. The promoter then pays the group, as agreed. Because all parties have fulfilled their obligations (performed), the contract has been discharged. If the group has been contracted to give six shows over the summer, the contract will be discharged once they have done so and been paid by the promoter.

What if one party to the contract offers to perform and the other party refuses to accept? According to contract law, the first party is no longer obligated to attempt to perform his or her part of the contract and may take legal action against the other for breach of contract.

Mutual Agreement

Parties to a contract may agree to cancel it. For example, if few tickets sell for the Canada Day rock concert, both parties could decide it is not worthwhile to continue the contract. Parties may also cancel one contract by agreeing on a new one. The promoter could negotiate a new agreement with the rock group to perform on another date. Some contracts may include a provision that foresees an event that will end the contract. For example, the contract between the promoter and the rock group will be cancelled if a certain number of tickets are not sold by a certain date.

Impossibility of Performance

Under English common law, parties to a contract once were responsible for meeting all its obligations even if events later made this impossible. It was felt a contract should anticipate all circumstances that could make performance impossible and cover these in specific terms or conditions. For example, a farmer's contract to sell wheat might include a term covering the destruction of the crop by an early frost, flooding, or drought. Insurance is now sometimes purchased as protection against unforeseen circumstances.

Today, the courts sometimes excuse parties from performing their contracts when events after agreement make this impossible. For example, the Canada Day rock concert cannot take place because a huge storm erupts on the night it is scheduled. When a contract cannot be performed because of this kind of situation, or because the subject matter has been destroyed, the contract is said to be **frustrated** (impossible to perform).

Figure 17-2

These students signed a contract to paint this house. Once they finish and the owner pays them, each party will have performed its part of the contract.

Case

KBK No. 138 Ventures Ltd. v. Canada Safeway Ltd.

[2000] 5 W.W.R. 588
British Columbia Court of Appeal

KBK No. 138 Ventures Ltd. was interested in buying an $8.5-million property that Canada Safeway Ltd. advertised as a prime redevelopment opportunity with commercial zoning. KBK made an offer and paid Safeway a $150 000 deposit, clearly stating in the contract that it intended to redevelop the property as a condominium project.

Soon after, the city of Vancouver rezoned the property. This cut the amount of floor space that could be built by more than 70 percent. KBK could no longer develop the condominium at a profit. KBK felt the contract had been frustrated through

continued ▶

a fundamental change in circumstances and asked for the deposit to be returned. After Safeway refused, KBK launched a civil action.

The trial judge ruled that the contract for the sale of the land had been frustrated by the rezoning and that Safeway must return the $150 000 deposit. Safeway appealed. The appeal judge agreed with the trial judge and dismissed the appeal. In his summary, the appeal judge stated: "There is an intervening event and change of circumstances so fundamental as to be regarded as striking at the root of the agreement and as entirely beyond what was contemplated by the parties when they entered into the agreement."

For Discussion

1. What circumstance allowed KBK to successfully argue that the contract had been frustrated?

2. How did KBK communicate its intention to develop a condominium property?

3. If the rezoning had changed the floor space by only 10 percent, what would your decision have been in the case?

4. How could Safeway have safeguarded its interests?

You Be the JUDGE

In the landmark case of *Taylor v. Caldwell* (1863), a music hall rented to hold a concert was destroyed by fire before the concert could be held.

- How could you argue that the contract had been frustrated?

The existence of a law can also make certain transactions impossible to perform. Suppose that real-estate developers draw up a contract to build an apartment complex on a piece of land. Before construction begins, they learn the property lies on Aboriginal burial grounds. By law, nothing can be built here. The contract is frustrated. As you learned in Chapter 16, a contract must have a lawful purpose if it is to be enforceable.

Review Your Understanding (Pages 522 to 524)

1. Explain the difference between discharge by performance and discharge by mutual agreement.

2. How can a contract be terminated by mutual agreement?

3. To what extent were parties to a contract obligated to fulfill it under English common law?

4. What condition must exist for a contract to be discharged by impossibility of performance?

17.3 Breach of Contract

Breach of contract is the opposite of performance. It occurs when one party does not fulfill its obligations. If a fundamental part of the contract is breached, it is a **breach of condition.** In this case, the injured party can end or terminate the contract and sue for damages. If the rock group did not show up for the Canada Day concert because it accepted a better offer from another promoter, this would be a breach of condition. As the original promoter, you could sue the group

If the breach of contract is minor, a **breach of warranty** exists. In this case, the injured party cannot rescind or terminate the contract. For example, Asher orders a specific make and colour of car with a racing stripe painted on each side. The car that is delivered to him conforms in every respect except for the racing stripes. This is a breach of warranty, and the omission is minor. Asher has several choices. He can ask the dealer to paint the stripes; he can deduct the cost of the stripes when he pays for the car; or he can sue for damages to obtain the money to have someone else do it.

The amount of damages awarded will depend on the financial losses the injured party suffers. It would likely be more for a breach of a condition than for a breach of a warranty. As you learned in Chapter 11, legal actions are often costly and time-consuming. This means that it often makes more sense for parties in contract disputes to use alternative dispute resolution procedures (see pages 32 and 328).

Substantial Performance

The law protects the party inconvenienced by the breach. However, the rule of **substantial performance** also protects a party who has fulfilled most, but not all, parts of the contract. In the case of Asher's missing car stripes, this means the dealer is protected. What if Asher simply no longer liked the car? The rule of substantial performance prevents him from using the missing racing stripes as an excuse to break the contract. Because the dealer fulfilled most of the terms of the contract, so must Asher.

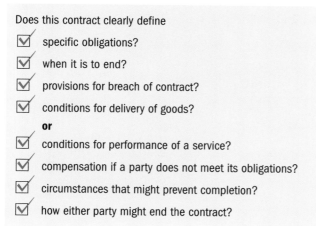

Figure 17-3

Tanaquil was rear-ended. The body shop repairs are excellent, but she says the paint colour is wrong. Is this a breach of condition or a breach of warranty?

▌ Contract Checklist

Does this contract clearly define

- ☑ specific obligations?
- ☑ when it is to end?
- ☑ provisions for breach of contract?
- ☑ conditions for delivery of goods?
  or
- ☑ conditions for performance of a service?
- ☑ compensation if a party does not meet its obligations?
- ☑ circumstances that might prevent completion?
- ☑ how either party might end the contract?

Figure 17-4

Key clauses that should be in a contract

Did You Know?

The most common remedy in breach-of-contract cases is monetary compensation.

You Be the JUDGE

Gabriella's roofer failed to fix her roof and she had to hire another roofer. She sued the original roofer, claiming damages to cover the cost of finishing the work and also punitive damages for stress leave she took from work.

- Which of Gabriella's claims for damages would more likely be awarded? Explain.

Remedies for Breach of Contract

Once parties have entered into a legally binding contract, they are bound to perform the agreement. Still, breaches of contract do occur. The following remedies are available to the party injured by the breach.

Damages

Damages are awarded to compensate the injured party for any losses, not to punish the party that breached the contract. They are meant to place the injured party in the same position as if the contract had been completed. Specific types of damages that might be awarded—such as general, special, punitive, and nominal—were discussed in detail in Chapter 11.

Mitigation of Loss   The courts expect whoever is injured by a breach of contract to take "reasonable steps" to reduce or prevent any losses that the breach may cause. This is known as **mitigation of loss.** For example, Rimma refuses to accept a truckload of vegetables that she ordered from Omar. Omar must try to find another buyer. Not only that, he must do this quickly to reduce spoilage and prevent greater damages. If Omar has to sell the vegetables for a lower price, he can sue Rimma for the difference. He cannot, however, simply leave the produce to rot and then sue Rimma. Similarly, if an employee sues for damages after being wrongfully dismissed or fired, he or she must make an effort to mitigate losses by seeking alternative employment.

Case

Wilson v. Sooter Studios Ltd.

(1988) 55 D.L.R. (4th) 303
British Columbia Court of Appeal

Thelma Battaglia and Chris Wilson booked Sooter Studios Ltd. to photograph their wedding. The $399 contract included 102 photos to be taken at two different locations, albums, and thank-you cards. The couple paid a deposit of $280, with the balance to be paid on completion.

On the day of the wedding, the photographer arrived late, and only after Chris Wilson telephoned him. He was inappropriately dressed, took photos at one location only, and was indifferent about the composition of the pictures. In fact, the bride's brother-in-law suggested many of the poses. When the Wilsons finally received their photos, there were

Figure 17-5

A day to remember? How far would you go for justice if this were the best photograph of your wedding?

continued ▶

47 instead of 102. Only 10 were focused. The others were double-exposures over shots of another wedding.

The plaintiffs brought a court action in early 1988 for breach of contract, mental distress, and the cost of reassembling the wedding to pose for new photos. Because some guests had come from as far away as Brazil and Australia, it was estimated this would cost about $7000, including airfare and accommodation. The trial judge disagreed with this and awarded the plaintiffs $1000, plus their deposit. The Wilsons were determined to have their wedding rephotographed properly, however, and appealed to the British Columbia Court of Appeal. In late December 1988, the court dismissed their appeal in a 3 to 0 decision.

For Discussion

1. Did this action involve a complete breach of contract, a breach of condition, or a breach of warranty? Explain your choice.

2. What is the benefit of the Wilsons seeking the remedy they did?

3. Why did the trial judge award the plaintiffs only $1000?

4. Explain the meaning of the following statement from the court decision: "On legal principles, one cannot justify an award based on the cost of reconstituting the wedding as a proper measure of damages. These were not expenses incurred by the Wilsons, nor was a photographer to necessarily assume that a majority of the wedding guests were from out of town. Whatever he contracted for, he never contemplated that the cost of a breach would be to fly back six adults from Toronto."

5. Under what conditions do you think a plaintiff should be awarded damages for mental distress? Explain.

Liquidated Damages   To avoid court disputes, many contracts specify **liquidated damages.** This is a sum of money that the parties agree to in advance to settle any breach of contract that might occur. For example, a renovation contract might include a term that sets the sum of money the renovator will pay for each day that work continues beyond the contract completion date. The sum is meant only to compensate the injured party, not punish the renovator.

Specific Performance

In most cases of breach of contract, monetary damages are an adequate remedy. But what happens when money is not enough? For example, you find a piece of heritage jewellery on the Internet and your bid of $500 wins the auction. Later, the dealer returns your cheque and says she is keeping the piece for herself. In this breach, the court may order **specific performance.** This means that the precise terms of the original contract must be honoured. The dealer would have to sell you the piece of jewellery for $500, as promised.

The courts will likely award an injured party specific performance if a breach involves one-of-a-kind items such as homes, art, antiques, and so on. Since no two pieces of land are the same, the courts often award specific performance as a remedy in a breach of contract involving land. However, if the land is being purchased for development or investment, the courts are less likely to award specific performance. This is because the purchaser could buy a different parcel of land for these purposes.

Specific performance is not available if the courts would have to supervise the carrying out of the order to determine if it is satisfactory. For this reason, a contract for a personal service, such as painting a family portrait, cannot be specifically enforced. As well, an employee cannot be forced to work for an employer, and an employer usually cannot be forced to keep a particular employee. In cases involving these kinds of services, either an injunction or money damages are awarded.

Case

Chan v. Chadha Construction & Investments Ltd.

(2000) 74 B.C.L.R. (3d) 396
British Columbia Court of Appeal

The defendant, Chadha Construction, sold a home that it had built for the Chan family in 1989. It did not, however, make all the changes and repairs that it agreed to do at the time. Later, the Chans sued, saying Chadha had breached the contract by providing an incomplete house. In 1998, the trial judge ordered specific performance, instructing Chadha to do the repair work under the supervision of an engineer of the Chans' choice.

The plaintiffs appealed, saying that specific performance was inappropriate. It would, in effect, require the original builder to do the repair work 10 years after the original construction. The appeal was allowed. In March 2000, the British Columbia Court of Appeal ruled that the proper remedy in this case was an award for damages. It awarded damages in the amount of $65 729.92 for repairs. Because the repairs would require the plaintiffs to leave the residence for a period of time, the judge awarded $1000 in moving, storage, and accommodation expenses.

For Discussion

1. Why was specific performance deemed inappropriate in this case?

2. What is the purpose of an award for damages?

3. Why did the judge award Chan additional damages of $1000?

4. In your opinion, would the decision have been different if only one year had passed, rather than 10? Explain.

Injunctions

When ordered as a remedy for a breach of contract, an injunction is the opposite of specific performance: it requires the defendant not to do something. For example, Ziyi's employment contract contains a **non-competition clause.** It states that she may not conduct research for any other laboratory during the term of her contract and for a period after the contract ends. If Ziyi breaks the contract and does research for the competition, her initial employer may seek an injunction to stop her from doing this. Injunctions are usually granted at the discretion of the court when damages would be considered inappropriate.

Privity of Contract

To succeed in a court action over breach of contract, the plaintiff must be able to prove **privity of contract**—a contractual relationship with the defendant. Normally, a person who is not directly involved in the contract, or a third party, cannot take legal action. There are exceptions. The beneficiary of a life insurance policy, for example, can sue the insurance company if it refuses to pay the benefit. The original contract, however, would have been between the insured person, who is now the deceased, and the insurance company.

Rescission

In situations involving the breach of a major condition, the injured party can sometimes seek to have the contract rescinded. As you learned in Chapter 16, rescission restores the parties to their original positions before the contract was formed.

Case

Kitchen Craft Connection v. Dennis

(1999) 50 C.L.R. (2d) 239
Ontario Superior Court of Justice

Dennis, the defendant, contracted Kitchen Craft Connection to build and install kitchen cabinets. After they were installed, however, it was clear that the cabinets and the installation were defective. The plaintiff was given the opportunity to fix the problems on two occasions, but was unable to complete the contract within the agreed-upon time. Dennis declined to make the payments under the contract.

The plaintiff, Kitchen Craft, sued for the money owed. The defendant then made a counterclaim seeking to have the contract rescinded and to have the money that had been paid returned. The court dismissed the action by Kitchen Craft and allowed the Dennis counterclaim. The contract was rescinded and the defendant was given a full refund of the $3698.32 that had been paid, plus interest.

For Discussion

1. Was there a fundamental breach of the contract? Explain.

2. What purpose does rescission of the contract serve?

Limitation of Actions

If an injured party has the legal right, he or she should take court action as soon as possible after a breach of contract has occurred. As time passes, evidence may get lost or forgotten; witnesses may move or die.

Certain laws also impose specific time limits. The *Statute of Limitations*, provincial Limitations Acts, and limitations sections in certain federal and provincial laws set fairly similar time limits that apply to contracts. If action is not taken within the time allowed, the claim is barred; that is, the courts will not help to enforce it. The standard time limit for contracts, other than real estate, is six years from the time of the breach.

Review Your Understanding (Pages 524 to 529)

1. Distinguish between a breach of condition and a breach of warranty. How does each affect a contract?

2. Distinguish between the various remedies for breach of contract.

3. What is meant by this statement: "A party must mitigate its losses"?

4. What is the importance of a statute of limitations?

5. What remedy could a plaintiff use if suing over non-delivery of a rare painting? Why?

6. Explain the advantage of using an injunction for a remedy.

Should Governments Be Sued for Breach of Contract When They Reduce Services?

During the 1990s, most provinces cut spending. The media was full of stories about the hardships people experienced as welfare payments were slashed, along with funding for health care, education, the environment, and other programs. There were howls of protests, but governments who made the cuts were popular and got reelected.

Then, in April and May of 2000, a disaster struck in Walkerton, Ontario. Seven people died and thousands became ill after drinking the town's water. Many blamed the tragedy on government cutbacks. They believed the government had a legal obligation, or contract, to make sure the public's drinking water was safe. Failing to do so was a breach of contract, and a government that breaches a contract must pay damages. By the summer of 2000, lawyers representing Walkerton victims announced a $13-million class action lawsuit against the Ontario government.

On June 13, 2000, the Ontario government announced an inquiry. Headed by Ontario Court of Appeal Justice Dennis O'Connor, public hearings were held about events surrounding Walkerton. During these hearings, which ended in October 2001, many witnesses blamed Ontario government cutbacks. Other witnesses, however, pointed to local causes that had nothing to do with government or cutbacks.

Figure 17-6

A boy poisoned by the water in Walkerton, Ontario, is rushed to hospital in May 2000. One child had already died.

On March 19, 2001, the Ontario government set up the Walkerton Compensation Plan. Under this plan, any person who can prove he or she was harmed by consuming Walkerton's water will receive a minimum of $2000. Those seeking higher damages will be compensated in accordance with Ontario law. Anyone who participates in this plan must waive, or give up, the right to sue the government.

In 2002, Justice O'Connor submitted his report to the government. He agreed that government cutbacks and dishonest practices by Frank and Stan Koebel, who were in charge of testing the water at Walkerton for contamination, were jointly responsible for the Walkerton tragedy.

On One Side

Those who blame cutbacks for Walkerton point out that the Ministry of the Environment budget was cut by 40 percent. Many of the employees that the ministry let go had a very important job: checking Ontario's drinking water.

These critics insist that cutbacks were responsible for the deaths and injuries of innocent people. Walkerton, they say, was a time bomb waiting to explode. Cutbacks are unacceptable when it comes to providing basic services to Canadians. They cause irreparable harm to the health and welfare of Canadians and are a breach of contract.

On the Other Side

Those who support cutbacks say government has no place in providing basic services, such as water, to begin with. Private business can do it more efficiently and for less. Why should taxpayers pay for services they might not use? Let people who use these services make contracts with businesses and pay them. Communities must take responsibility for themselves.

Canadians have come to believe that safe drinking water is a cheap natural resource. They are wrong. In parts of Britain and Europe, many water systems are operated by private businesses, and they do a fine job. Consumers pay more, but this may raise awareness of water safety and prevent future Walkertons. Some people believe this is what must happen in Canada.

The Bottom Line

Are governments legally contracted to provide essential services to the public? Or do governments have the right to reduce essential services in order to reduce deficits and taxes?

What Do You Think?

1. If a contract exists when a government service is created, what type is it: express or implied? Explain.

2. Do you think people and groups should have the legal right to sue the government for breach of contract when cutbacks take place? Explain.

3. Why has safe drinking water become an issue in recent years? In your opinion, should water systems be placed in the hands of private business? Why or why not?

4. How did the Ontario government respond to the Walkerton tragedy? Was the response reasonable and sufficient given the circumstances? Explain.

5. Research further developments in the Walkerton Inquiry. What final conclusions have been drawn?

17.4 Sale-of-Goods Legislation

In 1893, the British Parliament passed the *Sale of Goods Act*. This was its first legislation to regulate the sale of goods. Since then, each common-law province and territory in Canada has passed similar Sale of Goods Acts. In Quebec, these laws are part of the *Civil Code*.

The sale of goods is a very specific area of contract law. It deals with contracts in which the seller transfers the ownership of goods, in the present or in the future, to the buyer for monetary consideration. In an **absolute sale,** ownership passes to the buyer when the contract is fulfilled. Because **barter** transactions exchange only goods and services, not money, they are not covered by sale-of-goods laws. In these Acts, "goods" refers only to personal property, such as furniture, clothing, appliances, and other movable possessions. Such items as stocks, bonds, and cheques—and services—are covered by other Acts.

Title, Delivery, and Payment

Most written contracts specify the time when ownership of goods (**title**) passes to the buyer. This is important because the owner must accept the burden of loss if the goods are lost, stolen, damaged, or destroyed. If no agreement is made, the provincial or territorial sale-of-goods legislation outlines how to deal with these situations.

Delivery involves the transfer of ownership from seller to buyer, and it usually takes place at the seller's place of business. There may be agreements that state otherwise; however, it is usually the seller who is responsible to deliver the goods to the buyer at the location specified in the contract.

Most contracts state the time and method of payment, but sale-of-goods legislation provides for payment at the time of delivery. If no price is agreed upon, a "reasonable price" is due. Late payment does not automatically allow the seller to reclaim the goods. The seller can, however, charge interest and take legal action against the buyer. If the buyer has breached the contract, the seller must attempt to mitigate any loss.

Express Conditions and Warranties

As you read earlier, it is important in a breach of a sales contract to know whether a condition or a warranty is involved. If it is difficult to determine which of the two is involved, the courts will decide.

An **express condition** is both essential to the contract and clearly outlined in it. For example, Miyoshi draws up a contract with Lingaard, a carpenter, to build her a maple cabinet. If he builds a walnut cabinet, Miyoshi can refuse to accept it. Lingaard has broken the express condition, which makes the contract void.

Express warranties are specific promises that manufacturers and retailers make to consumers about the performance, quality, and condition of goods. Also known as **guarantees,** they are usually given to a buyer in the form of a certificate along with the purchase. Limited warranties last for a certain period; for instance, six months or one year. A car warranty, for example, will generally cover the cost of parts and repairs for a certain number of kilometres or years, whichever comes first.

When a contract in writing contains express warranties, any verbal promises the seller makes will not be binding. There is an exception, however. If a buyer makes a purchase relying solely on advice and information from the seller, any verbal promises the seller makes are binding. Such a contract may be rescinded under provincial consumer protection legislation.

Warranties and conditions that are not written into a contract but that are stated clearly in displays and advertisements are also binding on the seller. If it is the manufacturer who makes the warranty promises, not the seller, then a contract exists between the buyer and the manufacturer.

Secret warranties also exist. For example, a certain model of automobile has a defect but the manufacturer alerts only dealers, not the public. It promises dealers to cover repair work related to the defect. Even though the defect may not be identified in the buyer's warranty, and even if the buyer's warranty has expired, this secret warranty may still be in effect. It is up to the consumer to find out if such a warranty exists and then to complain to the dealer or manufacturer about the problem.

Figure 17-7

What terms regarding title could be implied in this retail transaction?

❚ Warranty Checklist

When buying a product that has an express warranty, or guarantee, check to see

☑ who holds it

☑ what it covers

☑ how long it lasts

☑ if it can be extended

Figure 17-8

What other terms would you add?

Implied Conditions and Warranties

Implied conditions and **implied warranties** are promises in law that sellers make to buyers through implication or suggestion. They are described in sale-of-goods legislation and include the following basic promises:

- The seller has title to the goods and the right to sell them.
- The articles or goods are of merchantable quality and suitable for the required purpose.
- The goods supplied correspond to the samples or descriptions provided to the buyer.

Because each of these is a part of every sale of goods, they are examined more closely on the following pages.

Title

It is implied that the seller has title to the goods and, therefore, the right to sell them. If the goods belong to someone else, the true owner can demand that they be returned—even from a buyer who has paid for them in good faith. To be compensated, the buyer would have to take legal action against the seller for breach of condition. This is one reason you should search title before buying a used car, for example.

If a seller has clear (good) title to the goods, they legally belong to the buyer after the contract of sale has been fulfilled. The buyer can then use the goods in any way, including reselling them. It is further implied that the seller does not give the right to anyone else to use the goods.

Quality and Suitability

When making purchases, buyers should check goods carefully, even though in some cases there is an implied condition that they will be of good quality and fit for use. Buyers often know very little about a product and must be able to depend on sellers to be honest. If a buyer indicates to the seller how the goods are to be used and that he or she is relying on the seller's knowledge and judgment, then there is an implied condition that the goods will be fit and suitable for the buyer's purpose.

A buyer may be able to obtain a refund if a product is not of **merchantable quality** (fit to be used for its normal purpose). For example, a lawnmower must be able to cut grass, a CD burner to make CDs. Goods of merchantable quality are normally saleable, but not always. For example, electrical goods must be approved by an accredited certification organization—such as the Canadian Standards Association (CSA)—and display a certification mark. For example, if you buy a desktop computer in the United States, then pay the duty and taxes to bring it back to Canada, it may not have been certified according to the standards set by certification organizations in Canada. This would mean that it goes against provincial regulations and is not saleable in Canada, even though it works perfectly.

▌ CSA International Certification Marks

Figure 17-9

In each instance, a sample of the product has been tested against applicable standards and found to meet those requirements for the particular market.

CSA®	certified for the Canadian market
CSA® US **CSA® NRTL**	certified for the U.S. market
CSA® C US **CSA® NTRL/C**	certified for both the Canadian and U.S. markets

Vargek v. Okun

(1997) 118 Man. R. (2d) 35
Manitoba Court of Appeal

Robert and Anne Vargek bought a used vehicle from a dealer, Almey Autobody Ltd. On the agreement of purchase and sale, the odometer reading was 82 000 km. Unknown to the dealer, however, the odometer had been tampered with and should have read 182 000 km.

After using the vehicle, the Vargeks sued in small claims court and won a judgment against the dealer for $1000. The dealer appealed this decision to the Court of Queen's Bench, which viewed the case as one of innocent misrepresentation. It ruled that the Vargeks were not entitled to restitution because they had kept and driven the vehicle for an extended length of time.

The Vargeks appealed to the Manitoba Court of Appeal. It held that the Court of Queen's Bench had made an error in treating the issue as being innocent misrepresentation. Instead, the case should be viewed as breach of warranty. In applying section 58 of the *Consumer Protection Act,* the Manitoba Court of Appeal held that there was an express condition in the agreement. In other words, the goods should correspond with the description under which they were sold. Because the odometer reading description was inaccurate, the appellants were successful suing for damages under the *Sale of Goods Act.* They were awarded $2200.

For Discussion

1. Why did the Vargeks sue the dealer?
2. Why did the Court of Queen's Bench not order restitution?
3. Why do you think the case was not argued on the basis of merchantable quality?
4. Explain why the Manitoba Court of Appeal held that there was a breach of warranty.

Sale by Description or Sample

If you buy a product based on a description or sample, or both, there is an implied condition that the goods you receive will match the description and/or sample. The seller must tell the buyer that the goods are samples, however, and these must be of merchantable quality and visibly free of defects. In any sale by description or sample, a buyer must be allowed to compare the delivered goods with the sample.

An example of sale by sample is buying certain grades of lumber after looking at sample pieces displayed in the retail outlet. A sale by description might involve buying a sofa online based on photographs and descriptions displayed on the retailer's Web site. If you later visit the retailer's store to select your fabric from samples, this would be an example of sale by description and sample.

If delivered goods do not match the description and/or samples, the buyer has the right to return them and rescind the contract. The buyer, however, must examine the goods and act as quickly as possible. A buyer who accepts goods without examining them does so at risk. It is probably too late to do anything if the buyer discovers later that the goods are not exactly what was ordered.

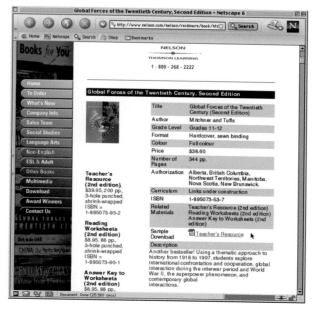

Figure 17-10

This is a Web site for ordering books. Would this be sale by description or sample or both? Explain.

If you buy a product without asking the seller's advice—for example, a brand-name product—the seller cannot be held responsible if you, the buyer, are dissatisfied with the purchase. The manufacturer, however, can be held liable for the tort of negligence if the product is faulty and the buyer is injured through its use (see page 338).

▌ Checklist for Buying a Used Car Privately

Legal points to consider:

☑ *Caveat emptor*, or buyer beware, applies.

☑ Generally, the sale is "as is."

☑ Implied warranties generally exist regarding fitness for the purpose.

☑ If the seller makes any representations, get them in writing.

☑ Check the vehicle's registration and accident history.

☑ Check title: Are there any liens on the vehicle?

Figure 17-11

When buying a car privately, take time to check the title, condition, and history of the vehicle.

Disclaimer Clauses

Many sellers try to reduce the risk of being sued for breach of implied warranties and conditions by adding **disclaimer clauses** to contracts. You will often find these on the back of standard printed sales contracts. Typical wording might be: "There are no conditions, express or implied, statutory or otherwise, other than those contained in this written agreement." A contract might also stipulate that the sale is "as is."

Because these clauses seek to remove protections from the buyer, they are not binding unless the seller brings them to the buyer's attention. For example, if the disclaimer appears on the back of a contract, there must be an indication on the front of the contract that additional terms are to be found on the back. Or, if the disclaimer clause is in "fine print," it may have to be highlighted in some way. Most provinces and territories carefully regulate these disclaimers in consumer contracts.

Case

Mayer v. Big White Ski Resort Ltd.

(1998) 112 B.C.A.C. 288
British Columbia Supreme Court

In March 1995, Bernard Mayer was injured while skiing at Big White Ski Resort in British Columbia. He collided with a snowmobile operated by resort employee Eric Bobert. Mayer sued Big White for negligence. Big White successfully moved to have the action dismissed, relying on a waiver (release clause) that Mayer had signed.

Mayer appealed, arguing that Big White had failed to take reasonable steps to bring the release to his attention. He also argued that there was no present consideration (see page 502): his wife had completed the season's pass application form and included a cheque earlier. Mayer testified that when he picked up the pass at the busy resort, he signed the agreement without reading the release, just as he had in previous seasons.

continued ▶

The release clause indicated in large type and heavy black ink:

> Waiver of claims, Assumption of Risk and Indemnity Agreement. By signing this document you will waive certain legal rights, including the right to sue. Please read carefully!

Signing of the release was a condition on the application form for the pass.

The court held that the plaintiff made no effort to read the release despite opportunities to do so. Not only did he sign the release, Mayer had to print his name and address just below the printed summary. The court concluded that Big White had taken reasonable steps to bring the release to Mayer's attention and that it was a condition of the contract. There was consideration for the contract and the passes were issued. The release was held to be binding and enforceable, and Mayer's appeal was dismissed.

For Discussion

1. Why did Mayer bring an action against Big White Ski Resort Ltd.?
2. Outline Mayer's arguments against the ski resort in his appeal.
3. What was the consideration for the contract?
4. The *Occupier's Liability Act* of British Columbia states that reasonable steps must be taken to bring a release of liability to the attention of the party signing the agreement. Outline the steps that Big White took in this regard.

Figure 17-12

Why do you think ski resorts have to include disclaimers in contracts with skiers?

Remedies of the Buyer and Seller

If a sales contract is breached, there are remedies for both buyers and sellers. If goods are not delivered, or if goods do not match the samples or descriptions, the buyer need not pay for the goods. As discussed earlier, the buyer can also rescind the contract or sue for damages or specific performance.

For the seller, breach of contract usually means that the buyer has not paid for the goods. Under the Sale of Goods Acts, the seller has certain remedies that reflect who has title to the goods: seller or buyer.

Non-delivery If the goods have been sold but not delivered, the seller can keep them until the buyer pays. This is often referred to as the **right of lien.**

Stoppage in Transit If the goods are in transit and the seller learns the buyer is unable to pay the amount owing, the seller can order the carrier not to make delivery. If the goods are intercepted, they can be returned to the seller or redirected to another location.

Resale Goods stopped in transit are often resold. First, however, the seller must notify the buyer of the intended resale so that he or she has one last opportunity to pay to obtain the goods.

Damages If the buyer has the goods, the seller can sue for the full price. If the goods are still in the seller's possession, the damages sued for might represent the expenses involved in finding a new buyer and any difference in the resale price of the goods.

Review Your Understanding (Pages 532 to 538)

1. What types of transactions do the Sale of Goods Acts cover?
2. Why is it important to determine when title to goods passes from seller to buyer?
3. Distinguish between express and implied conditions and warranties, using original examples of each.
4. List three implied obligations that sellers have to buyers under Sale of Goods Acts.
5. Define "merchantable quality." What can a purchaser of goods do if the goods are not of merchantable quality?
6. If goods purchased do not match the samples or description provided, what options are open to the buyer?
7. What is a disclaimer clause, and when may it have no legal effect?

Did You Know?

The *Competition Act* applies to online advertising and marketing. Why might it be hard for the federal government to enforce the Act on the Internet?

17.5 Consumer Protection

Technology is changing how and where goods are made and how and where consumers buy them. Because business today is more global and complex, consumer protection laws are becoming more important and controversial. Telemarketing fraud and Internet fraud, for example, have raised consumer concerns about deceptive and unlawful activities in the marketplace. They have also forced police and intelligence agencies to cooperate internationally; borders alone cannot stop these activities (see Agents of Change, page 540).

As you have learned, provincial and territorial Sale of Goods Acts only cover transactions between buyers and sellers; they do not extend to manufacturers. As a result, they are not enough to control deceptive or unfair business practices. Since the late 1960s, federal and provincial governments in Canada have been enacting legislation to protect consumers. These laws are meant to
- ensure that consumers are given accurate information
- protect consumers from hazardous or dangerous products
- regulate activities around the sale of goods

Sometimes federal and provincial laws overlap, which gives consumers some choice in seeking help or compensation. Because these laws differ from province to province, they cannot be covered in detail in this textbook. Federal and provincial governments, however, do provide information on their Web sites and through free booklets. You may want to refer to these if you need detailed, up-to-the-minute information.

e activity

Visit **www.law.nelson.com** and follow the links to learn more about consumer protection in your province or territory.

Federal Laws

Federal laws treat dishonest business conduct and misleading advertising as offences against society. The Competition Bureau, a department of Industry Canada, oversees consumer protection under these laws. It looks into complaints that fall under various federal acts, including the *Competition Act*.

As you learned in Chapter 16, the *Competition Act* is the main federal law that deals with misleading advertising and unfair business practices. It prohibits agreements among businesses that unfairly limit competition. Violations can result in civil or criminal sanctions. Offences outlined in the Act fall into three general areas: conspiracy, misleading advertising, and deceptive marketing.

■ Federal Laws That Protect Consumers

Law	Application
Consumer Packaging and Labelling Act	Stipulates information that must be included on product packages and labels, including contents and warnings
Hazardous Products Act	Imposes safety requirements on products and can take goods off market
Textile Labelling Act	Requires labelling on clothing, household textiles, and fabrics
Food and Drugs Act	Imposes safety standards and regulations on food and drugs and can recall goods

Figure 17-13

In addition to the *Competition Act,* the federal government has a broad range of laws and regulations that protect consumers.

Conspiracy

Conspiracy can include price fixing, market sharing, and bid rigging. **Price fixing** occurs when two or more parties enter into an agreement to set prices so that consumers have no choice. In **market sharing,** competitors split up the market geographically, or by customer, to reduce competition. **Bid rigging** happens when suppliers or bidders reach a secret agreement among themselves. For example, paving companies might secretly coordinate their bids on a highway project to guarantee that one of them gets the contract at an inflated price.

Misleading Advertising

Advertisers are allowed to be creative in describing products, but they cannot mislead consumers. Sometimes, though, sales clerks, store displays, and advertisements do make misleading claims. For example, a store might advertise a "great sale price" for a new computer system. Buried in the fine print of the warranty, however, is a requirement to send the computer to Japan for any servicing—at the buyer's expense. In this case, the advertisement could be considered misleading. A seller who knowingly or recklessly makes a false or misleading representation can be criminally charged under the *Competition Act*. Civil action can result in orders to cease the activity or pay monetary compensation.

activity

Visit **www.law.nelson.com** and follow the links to learn about recent cases of misleading advertising.

visit **www.law.nelson.com**
and follow the links to
find out about the recent
telemarketing scams and
how consumers can pro-
tect themselves.

Deceptive Marketing

Deceptive marketing involves unfair business practices and fraud. **Telemarketing schemes** to defraud people, commonly called "scams," have become so widespread that one Montreal judge has called them an epidemic. One project, Operation PhoneBusters, reveals how police and consumers have come together to fight the problem (see Agents of Change, below).

The Law — The Competition Act

Excerpts from the *Competition Act*

False or misleading representations

52.(1)

No person shall, for the purpose of promoting, directly or indirectly, the supply or use of a product or for the purpose of promoting, directly or indirectly, any business interest, by any means whatever, knowingly or recklessly make a representation to the public that is false or misleading in a material respect.

Deceptive telemarketing

52.1(3)

No person who engages in telemarketing shall

(a) make a representation that is false or misleading in a material respect.

_____

For Discussion

1. **Representation is "material" if it is necessary to a consumer's decision to purchase something. Provide an example of a claim that a telemarketer might make that would be considered false or misleading in a material respect.**

▌ Advertisers' Checklist

☑ Use only terms that the ordinary person can understand.

☑ Always charge the lower of two prices appearing on a product.

☑ Have a reasonable supply of a product advertised at a bargain price.

☑ Use the words "sale" or "special" only if the price has been significantly reduced.

☑ Do not increase a price to cover the cost of a product or service advertised as "free."

☑ Do not make a performance claim unless you can offer proof.

Figure 17-14

Under the *Competition Act*, advertisers must follow these rules. What rules would you like to see added?

Agents of Change — Telemarketing Scam Protection Programs

Telemarketing is big business. Each year it sells billions of dollars worth of goods and services in Canada. It is indispensable to everything from hospital charities to polling firms, from environmentalist groups to the makers of acne cream. It is such a growth industry that provinces compete to attract new call centres and the jobs associated with them.

Unfortunately, telemarketing fraud is also big business. Telemarketing scams defraud thousands of Canadians each year. How do they work? First, marketing research pinpoints prospects, often elderly people who live alone on fixed incomes. Then the telemarketer phones the potential victim with wonderful news: he or she has just won a major prize, for example. There is one catch—a small payment must be made to claim it. Of course, the marketer takes credit cards and personal cheques. Then there is another payment, or the winner has to buy a product, or.... The deceptions go on and on. But there is no prize at the end. Then the call centre vanishes.

One successful initiative to protect consumers is a program called PhoneBusters. It was started in 1993

continued ▶

by the Ontario Provincial Police (OPP) to prosecute people who were running call centres in Quebec and Ontario to defraud people in other provinces and in the United States. Collaboration with American police agencies, business and consumer organizations, and the RCMP have led to spectacular arrests and a crackdown on international telemarketing scams.

Today, PhoneBusters has a national call centre and Web site to take reports and complaints of deceptive telemarketing. It spearheads national efforts to educate the public on how to spot telemarketing and Internet fraud and what to do about it.

For Discussion

1. **Why do you think international collaboration is needed to crack down on telemarketing and Internet fraud?**

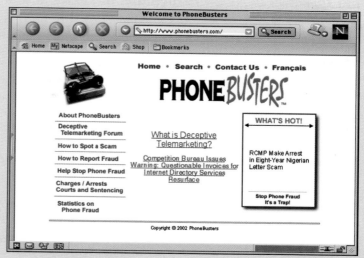

Figure 17-15

The home page for the PhoneBusters' Web site. Who usually gets trapped in telemarketing scams?

Case

R. v. Nichols

(2001-08-08) ONCA C32022;C32127
Ontario Court of Appeal

Nichols, a young Toronto telemarketer, was charged with defrauding an 82-year-old woman in Chicago. In November 1995, he had contacted the woman to tell her she had won a US$13-million lottery prize. To claim it, she had to secretly pay him US$1million for insurance and taxes. The victim gathered her investments together and sent him a cheque for US$900 000, followed by cheques totalling US$105 000.

Nichols pleaded guilty to fraud. At the sentencing hearing, the judge commented on the way in which "cowardly" telemarketers defraud their victims. "The basic plot in this case is so old and so obviously fraudulent that some might think it would amount to stupidity or worse to fall for it. Those who might think so fail to understand the increasing fragility of mind that comes with age; the loneliness of a single older person that can be manipulated by the crafty and the devious; and the persuasive practised tones of the professional, both male and female, who mar-

kets by voice alone." The judge also commented on the growing cross-border fraud industry and the difficulties it presents for prosecution.

The maximum sentence for fraud is 10 years, but the trial judge decided that the appropriate sentence would be seven years. Because the accused had returned US$772 000 to the victim, the sentence was lessened to five years and three months.

Nichols appealed his sentence. On appeal, the court considered the trial judgment excessive, given that Nichols had no previous record, most of the money had been returned, and other cases of serious fraud had resulted in lesser sentences in the courts. The sentence was reduced to four years.

For Discussion

1. **What factors did the trial judge consider in sentencing Nichols?**

2. **Should Nichols have received the maximum sentence of 10 years for fraud? Explain.**

3. **Should the fact that Nichols targeted an elderly, vulnerable woman weigh heavily in the sentencing decision? Explain.**

Know?

n 2001, identity theft was the fastest growing crime in North America. It happens when thieves steal personal information, often via the Internet. With this information, criminals do everything from transfer funds to forge passports. Why would it be hard to prosecute?

Protection of Personal Information

As Canadians do more business over the Internet, more and more private and personal information enters cyberspace. To protect consumers, the federal government has enacted the *Personal Information Protection and Electronic Documents Act.* As of January 2001, it applied to all businesses regulated by the federal and territorial governments, including banks, airlines, broadcasters, and telecommunications companies.

The Act protects Canadians by regulating when personal information about customers and employees can be collected, used, and disclosed. It generally requires organizations to get the person's consent before using or disclosing any personal information while doing business. Under the Act, businesses must also have effective security measures in place to protect personal information, and these measures must be current and accurate. Consumers and employees must also be able to check the information for themselves.

The Act is being phased in. By January 1, 2004, it will also apply to all commercial activities regulated by the provinces. The only exemption will be if the province has passed similar legislation of its own.

▌ Personal Information Checklist

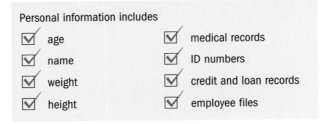

Personal information includes

☑ age   ☑ medical records

☑ name   ☑ ID numbers

☑ weight   ☑ credit and loan records

☑ height   ☑ employee files

Figure 17-16

Information that can be found in a telephone book is not considered to be personal information. Why?

Provincial Laws

The provinces and territories have Consumer Protection Acts or the equivalent (see Figure 17-17). The names vary, but the Acts provide consumers with a basis for seeking compensation in civil actions against offenders. Provinces and territories also have the equivalent of the federal Consumer Protection Bureau. It is normally a branch of the ministry that deals with consumer affairs and commercial relations.

Provincial and territorial legislation also protects consumers in areas such as door-to-door sales, loan scams, credit reporting, disclosure of credit costs, and **unconscionable** (completely unreasonable) transactions.

℮ activity

Visit **www.law.nelson.com** and follow the links to find out more about direct sales in your province or territory.

Door-to-Door Sales

Door-to-door (direct) sales have offered buyers convenience and ease for generations. On the other hand, some door-to-door sellers have been using high-pressure tactics for just as long. This is one reason why sellers have to register with the provincial Consumer Protection Bureau. Once an aggressive seller gets a foot in the door, he or she might not leave until the resident has signed up to buy the goods. Laws recognize this and have established a **cooling-off period.** During this time, a buyer can cancel a contract with a door-to-door

Consumer Protection Across Canada

Province or Territory	Consumer Protection Legislation
Alberta	*Fair Trading Act; Direct Sellers Act; Unconscionable Transactions Act*
British Columbia	*Consumer Protection Act; Trade Practices Act; Credit Reporting Act; Cost of Credit Disclosure Act*
Manitoba	*Consumer Protection Act; Business Practices Act; Trade Practices Inquiry Act; Unconscionable Transactions Relief Act*
New Brunswick	*Direct Sellers Act; Unconscionable Transactions Relief Act; Cost of Credit Act, Consumer Product Warranty and Liability Act*
Newfoundland & Labrador	*Consumer Protection Act; Direct Sellers Act; Consumer Reporting Agencies Act, Unconscionable Transactions Relief Act*
Northwest Territories	*Consumer Protection Act*
Nova Scotia	*Consumer Protection Act; Direct Sellers Licensing and Regulation Act; Collection Agencies Act; Unconscionable Transactions Relief Act*
Nunavut	*Consumer Protection Act*
Ontario	*Consumer Protection Act; Business Practices Act; Consumer Reporting Act; Consumer Protection Bureau Act*
Prince Edward Island	*Consumer Protection Act; Direct Sellers Act; Business Practices Act; Consumer Reporting Act; Unconscionable Transactions Relief Act*
Quebec	*Consumer Protection Act; Civil Code*
Saskatchewan	*Consumer Protection Act; Direct Sellers Act; Collection Agents Act; Credit Reporting Agencies Act; Cost of Credit Disclosure Act*
Yukon Territory	*Consumer Protection Act*

Figure 17-17

Laws to protect consumers are always changing. Research what your government is doing to protect you in the marketplace.

seller without giving any reason whether or not the goods have been received and/or paid for. The Consumer Protection Acts of Ontario and British Columbia, for example, set their cooling-off period at 10 days.

If the consumer wishes to cancel after the cooling-off period, he or she can do so if the goods or services are not delivered within 30 days of the date promised. To cancel, the buyer must notify the seller of the desire to cancel within the cooling-off period. The best way to do this is by registered mail, or by delivering the letter personally.

Loan Scams

Consumer ministries also try to protect consumers against fraudulent lending and borrowing practices. Often, this is done through public education campaigns and by providing consumers with free advice. In Ontario, for example, the Ministry of Consumer and Business Services has warned consumers against advance-fee loan scams. In Ontario, as in many other provinces, it is illegal for lenders to charge consumers a payment fee before they receive the loans. In these scams, loan brokers charge the consumers fees, reassuring them that the loans have been secured. As it turns out, the loans are never delivered.

Did You Know?

Between 1985 and 2001, Ontario's Ministry of Consumer and Business Services laid more than 1400 charges against advance-fee loan brokers.

Credit Reporting

Consumers are also encouraged to know their credit rights as a form of consumer protection. Equifax Canada and Trans Union of Canada are the two businesses that collect credit information on individuals and report it to credit-granting institutions such as retailers and banks. Some provinces have legislation to regulate this area. In Ontario, for example, the *Consumer Reporting Act* states that a consumer must be notified when his or her credit file is being accessed for a check by an appropriate credit-granting firm. Individuals or organizations that unlawfully access your credit bureau file can be fined. Recently, a private investigator was fined $2500 under the *Consumer Reporting Act* for unlawfully accessing a consumer's credit file.

Disclosure of Credit Costs

To make sure consumers know the cost of buying goods on credit, provincial legislation requires **full disclosure** of all credit costs. This means that consumers must receive a detailed statement of the cost of credit in dollars and cents and as a true annual rate of interest expressed as a percentage. This lets consumers compare credit terms so that they can shop around for the best interest rates. Consumers are not bound to contracts that do not provide full disclosure.

Unconscionable Transactions

Most regulations that govern interest rates are set at the federal level. Each province, however, also has legislation that allows the courts to look into loan agreements to determine if interest charges are too high. If they are, the court can order the lender to repay the consumer the excess amount. This applies to all loans, even those that have been paid in full. In making its decision, the court looks at the costs of similar loans from other lending sources, the reputation of the lender, and the position of the two parties involved. In many provinces, the statute governing these matters is called the *Unconscionable Transactions Relief Act*. In British Columbia it is part of the *Consumer Protection Act*.

Review Your Understanding (Pages 538 to 544)

1. Why are criminal penalties available under the *Competition Act*?
2. Why are elderly people often victims of telemarketing fraud?
3. What part of securing a loan for someone could result in an offence?
4. How does a cooling-off period protect consumers?
5. Why is registered mail a good way to cancel a direct sales contract during the cooling-off period?
6. Explain the meaning of "full disclosure" in terms of its significance to credit sales.

Chapter Review

Chapter Highlights

- Contracts can be discharged by performance, mutual agreement, impossibility of performance or frustration, or breach of contract.
- Civil remedies available for breach of contract include damages, specific performance, injunctions, or rescission.
- A breach of condition is the breaking of a fundamental term of the contract; a breach of warranty involves the breach of a minor term.
- In assessing damages, courts will determine whether a party has attempted to mitigate its loss.
- The *Statute of Limitations* or the Limitations Act in each province sets up the time periods within which a claim under contract law must be acted upon.
- Sale-of-goods legislation is designed to offer protection to the buyer and seller by codifying implied conditions and warranties.
- Sellers often use disclaimers in an attempt to exempt them from liability.
- There are remedies available to a buyer and seller if a breach occurs over a sale of goods.
- Federal and provincial legislation is available to protect the consumer against unfair, harmful, or deceptive business practices.

Review Key Terms

Name the key terms that are described below.

a) the completion of all obligations under a contract

b) the breach of a fundamental term of a contract, entitling the injured party to treat the contract as ended

c) attempting to reduce the damages caused by a breach of contract

d) a sum of money, agreed upon in advance, in case the contract is breached

e) a specific promise made by a manufacturer or retailer concerning performance, quality, and condition of an item

f) marketable condition; suitable for sale

g) contract that is impossible to perform

h) a court order that requires the person guilty of a breach of contract to complete the obligations under the contract

i) a clause in a contract denying that guarantees or other representations have been made

j) being told by phone that you have won a prize and must pay money upfront when, in fact, there is no prize

k) a period of time in which you can cancel a door-to-door sales contract

l) a minor breach of contract

m) right of ownership to goods or property

n) a contract term assumed to exist, but not clearly set out, by the buyer and seller

o) when two or more parties enter into an agreement to set prices so that consumers have no choice

p) a required statement of costs of credit to be given to a customer

Check Your Knowledge

1. Briefly describe the various methods used to discharge a contract.
   a) Which is the most cost effective?
   b) Which is most likely to lead to legal action?

2. What civil remedies are available for breach of contract? Provide an example of the appropriate use of each remedy.

3. Briefly outline the main remedies available to the buyer of goods if the seller fails to deliver them.

4. Outline actions that would be considered offences under the *Competition Act* and provide an example to illustrate each type of offence.

Apply Your Learning

5. Katco Manufacturing sold plastic pipe to the Centre '99 arena to be used as part of the ice-making equipment at the hockey and skating rink. The diameter of the pipe supplied was smaller than called for in the purchase order. After installation, the pipe cracked and split in several places. The arena owners took legal action for damages.
   a) On what grounds would they base their claim?

b) Outline the arguments the arena owners would make in their claim for damages.

c) What arguments would Katco Manufacturing likely make in their defence?

6. Billingsley purchased several cases of canned lobster for his specialty food store from the defendant seafood company, a Prince Edward Island processor of frozen and canned fish products. Several customers who purchased the lobster from Billingsley returned the products as inedible. After being examined by federal food inspectors, the entire lot of canned lobster was destroyed. Billingsley claimed damages from the processor for his loss.

a) Under what area of law would Billingsley sue?

b) What argument would substantiate his claim?

7. A door-to-door seller, Kirk Wilson, called on an elderly couple and tried to persuade them to buy some aluminum siding for their home. The home had been newly painted and was in good repair. When the couple said that they didn't need any siding, Kirk told them he had a great deal for them. The couple listened to the deal and then signed the contract. A day later, they realized that they really didn't want the siding.

a) What can the couple do, if anything, about the contract they signed?

b) How should they go about communicating their intention to end the contract? How long do they have to change their minds?

Communicate Your Understanding

8. You have been hired by a consumer protection agency to produce a pamphlet that will alert the public to the dangers of telemarketing fraud. Contact your local Better Business Bureau or use the Internet and other media to research the following:

a) some examples of deceptive telemarketing scams

b) some signs that you might be the potential target of this fraud

c) how consumers can protect themselves

9. Assume you are working for a local Better Business Bureau and your job is to educate your local community on issues of consumer protection. Create a bulletin-board display that highlights consumer protection issues. For an extension, hold a Consumer Awareness Day in your law class that highlights the material you have researched. Invite other business classes to attend.

Contact your local Better Business Bureau or Consumer Protection Agency, or use the government Internet sites to research consumer protection issues.

a) Indicate the agencies that offer consumer protection assistance.

b) Highlight areas under which consumers are provided with protection.

c) Highlight examples of cases that have resulted in the protection of consumer rights.

d) Create a category of tips that could be used to warn people about potential scams.

Develop Your Thinking

10. The law has changed from the time when *caveat emptor* was the main defence a seller used in contractual dispute with a buyer.

a) In what situations does *caveat emptor* still apply today?

b) Where has it been superseded by legislation?

c) Should statutes protect consumers or should it be a responsibility for consumers to educate themselves before entering into contract relationships? Explain.

11. Explain the meaning of the following statement: "Consumers must be honest and must be prepared to accept their responsibilities in the marketplace."

Landlord and Tenant Law

Focus Questions

- What are the different classes of tenancy?
- What are the rights and duties of a tenant?
- What are the rights and duties of a landlord?
- What is the difference between an assignment of a tenancy agreement and a sublet?
- What are the implications of giving a notice of termination?

Chapter at a Glance

Figure 18-1

Moving into your first apartment may be one of the most exciting moments of your adult life. What steps might lead up to signing the lease? List as many as you can.

e activity

Visit **www.law.nelson.com** and follow the links to learn more about the United Nations *Habitat Agenda*.

Did You Know?

A familiar saying among landlords is "No tenant is better than a bad tenant." Why would no tenant possibly be better than a bad tenant?

18.1 Introduction

In its *Habitat Agenda*, the United Nations established the goal of adequate shelter for all as a basic human right. This 1996 declaration supported the expansion of many types of housing, including rental housing. It states that "the rights and obligations of both tenants and owners" must be respected. For many Canadians, shelter means renting, not owning. Not too many years from now, you will probably be searching for your first apartment. When you find one, you will begin to understand more about these rights and obligations.

Landlord and tenant law applies to people who rent property and those who rent it to them. A **landlord** is a party that owns property and agrees to allow another party to use it in return for payment. A **tenant** is a party that rents a piece of residential or commercial property. (A party can be a person or a corporation.) This chapter examines residential tenancies only. The term "residential tenancy" generally does not apply to rental accommodation in hotels; rooms with shared facilities in private homes, educational institutions, or correctional facilities; or boarding houses for lodgers and boarders. In some provinces and territories, however, residential tenancy legislation does include roomers and boarders, mobile-home owners, and people who have rented a plot of land for their trailer.

Law governing the landlord and tenant relationship developed from English common law and was adopted by Canada's first provinces and territories. Each province or territory has enacted legislation that applies to residential tenancies. This legislation brings together the relevant case law and tries to reduce the number of disputes the courts must resolve. Each province or territory has also enacted human rights legislation, which prohibits landlords from discriminating among prospective tenants.

The laws governing residential tenancies in one province or territory may differ from the laws of another province or territory. Therefore, it is important to understand the laws of the jurisdiction in which you live in order to know your rights and responsibilities as a landlord or tenant.

Residential tenancy legislation tries to balance the rights and duties of the landlord and the tenant. In most disputes, a resolution is needed quickly. To encourage the resolution of disputes and reduce the number of cases that go to court, most provinces and territories provide a system of justice to resolve disputes outside the courts. In Yukon Territory, landlord and tenant matters go before a Rentals Officer. In Saskatchewan, decisions are made by the Office of the Rentalsman. In Ontario, matters are adjudicated (studied and settled) by the Ontario Rental Housing Tribunal. If neither party is satisfied with the decision, the matter can go before a court.

18.2 Types of Tenancies

The contract between a tenant and a landlord is called a **tenancy agreement (lease)**. In it, the landlord is called the owner **(lessor)** and the tenant is the occupier **(lessee)**. The lease identifies the parties to the lease, the property to be rented, the amount of the rent, and the period of the tenancy. The tenant is entitled to use the property exclusively for the length of the lease.

A lease can be verbal or written. Many people prefer a written lease because it details the rights and duties of both parties. However, even without a written lease, a tenancy agreement can still exist. A critical aspect of landlord and tenant law is that the Residential Tenancy Acts of each province and territory outweigh other agreements entered into by a landlord and tenant. In other words, landlords and tenants cannot "opt out" of the provincial or territorial statutes that created their relationship.

Many of the provincial and territorial statutes are so detailed that people sometimes question the need for a lease. Each province or territory requires the landlord to provide the tenant with a copy of the signed lease.

You Be the JUDGE

Newfoundland and Labrador, Nova Scotia, and Nunavut require landlords to give tenants, without charge, a copy of the relevant Landlords and Tenants Act.

- What would be the advantages and disadvantages of every province and territory giving a copy of the Act to all tenants?

Classes of Tenancy

There are several types of tenancy, known as classes of tenancy. Two will be discussed here. It is important to know the kind of tenancy you are entering into, because this will determine how much notice you or your landlord must give to terminate the lease.

Fixed-Term Tenancy

A **fixed-term tenancy** is also known as a "tenancy for a term certain"; that is, it expires (ends) on a specific date. For example, Hakim and Miranda are renting a winter cottage for a three-month period beginning January 1. The parties know that the tenancy will end on March 31.

Periodic Tenancy

A **periodic tenancy** is one that runs from day to day, week to week, or month to month. This kind of tenancy often arises when a tenant stays on and makes rent payments after a fixed-term tenancy expires. If rent is paid monthly, the periodic tenancy is month to month.

Joint Tenancy

When more than one person enters into a tenancy agreement, a **joint tenancy** is created. All parties entering into the agreement are liable not only for their own portion of the rent, but also for the total amount if the other renters do not pay. Therefore, if one tenant leaves before the termination of the lease, the remaining tenants must pay that person's share of the rent.

Figure 18-2

Young renters are often enthusiastic about sharing the rent, but under a joint tenancy agreement, each person is liable for the whole rent if one person fails to pay. How do you think such a situation could be prevented?

You Be the JUDGE

Mohammed and Wilma decide to live together in a rented apartment, each paying one half of the rent. Only Wilma signs the 12-month lease. After eight months, Mohammed moves out and refuses to pay any more rent

- In this situation, what are the rights of the landlord, Mohammed, and Wilma?

activity

Visit **www.law.nelson.com** and follow the links to learn more about dispute resolution in landlord and tenant matters.

Figure 18-3

Fixing a leaky faucet is the landlord's obligation, but if the repair is not made, it doesn't necessarily mean that you can withhold rent. How would you raise the subject of repairs with your landlord?

If only one person enters into a tenancy agreement, he or she is liable for rent under the agreement. The status of the other persons living in the rental property is less clear—they may be occupants or people paying money to the main tenant who entered into the agreement. The security of their arrangement would depend on whether the landlord recognized them as tenants in their own right. If the landlord did not accept their tenancy, they could be forced to vacate along with the person who entered into the tenancy agreement.

Review Your Understanding (Pages 548 to 550)

1. What is a tenancy agreement? Who are the parties to it?
2. Distinguish between a fixed-term tenancy and a periodic tenancy. When does a fixed-term tenancy change into a periodic tenancy?
3. What is a joint tenancy? What are the special implications for parties to a joint tenancy?

18.3 Entering into a Tenancy Agreement

Terms of a Tenancy Agreement

As you read earlier in the chapter, the parties in a landlord and tenant relationship cannot opt out of their jurisdiction's residential tenancy laws. Leases (tenancy agreements) must, therefore, reflect the laws of the jurisdiction in which the rental property is located. Terms that do not reflect these laws are void. They may even be used as evidence of harassment, misrepresentation, or fraud against the party that proposed them.

If a term of a residential tenancy agreement is broken, the landlord or tenant can take the matter before an adjudicator (such as a Rental Housing Tribunal) to resolve the dispute. You are probably already familiar with the ways in which agreements are broken. The landlord could raise the rent without reason or refuse to do repairs or provide sufficient heat. The tenant could be failing to pay rent on time or disturbing others in the building on a regular basis. If a breach occurs, the innocent party may not be freed from his or her obligations even if he or she takes legal action. For example, if John takes legal action to force Kim, his landlord, to fix his leaking faucet, he may still be obliged to pay rent. The landlord may also take legal action to evict the tenant but is similarly obliged to fulfill all his or her responsibilities to the tenant until the tenancy is terminated.

A tenancy agreement should specify at least the following:
- name and address of the landlord
- name of the lessee
- period of possession of the rented accommodation
- statement that the lessee is granted exclusive possession
- specific address of the property to be rented
- amount of rent to be paid and when it is to be paid
- services or utilities included in the rent (e.g., water, snow shovelling)

It is possible to use a form available at stationery stores to complete a lease—you simply buy the form and fill in the blanks. In Manitoba, New Brunswick, Nova Scotia, and Nunavut, the legislature has approved a standard form lease, which must be used. Leases will usually contain clauses pertaining to rent, security deposit, repairs, liability for injury, quiet and privacy, and utilities and taxes.

Rent

The exact amount of the rent, and when it is due, should be specified in the tenancy agreement. Tenancy agreements usually specify that payment is due at the beginning of the month. The tenant is responsible for delivering the rent payment to the landlord. Rent is overdue the day after it should have been paid. Some leases state that a penalty will be charged (so much per day) until the rent payment is received. Tenants may decide, for convenience, to provide postdated cheques to their landlords, but they do so at their own risk. The practice of insisting tenants provide postdated cheques has been abolished in some provinces and territories to protect the tenant.

If the tenant does not pay the rent that is due, the landlord sometimes gives him or her a brief grace period. If payment is still not received, the landlord can give notice of termination (eviction notice). However, the tenant can still remain in the premises. The landlord must apply for an order from the appropriate adjudicating body (e.g., Rental Housing Tribunal or Office of the Rentalsman) to have the tenant evicted. The landlord *cannot* forcibly remove the tenant—only a legal authority, such as the sheriff, can evict the tenant by acting on an order issued by the adjudicating body.

If the landlord intends to increase the rent at the end of the periodic or fixed-term lease, then notice in writing must be given to the tenant. The notice period varies according to the type of tenancy. In Alberta, for example, a fixed-term tenancy means a rent increase is not allowed until the end date. Three months' notice of a rent increase is required, however, for monthly leases.

Residential Tenancy Agreement (Ontario)

THIS AGREEMENT made the_____ day of_____, 20_____.

BETWEEN:

_____

_____
(hereafter referred to as "the Tenant(s)")

AND

_____
(hereafter referred to as "the Landlord")

_____
(Address)

1. The rental premises are [   ] a single family dwelling, [   ] a unit in a duplex, triplex, or fourplex, or [   ] an apartment in an apartment building, located at_____
(Apt./Suite no.)

_____
(Street address)

2. The term of this agreement shall be as follows:
This shall be a
[   ] week-to-week tenancy which shall begin on_____, 20_____.
[   ] month-to-month tenancy which shall begin on_____, 20_____.
[   ] fixed term tenancy which shall begin on_____, 20_____ and end on
_____, 20_____.

3. The rent shall be $_____ [   ] per week [   ] per month, and shall be payable in advance on or before the_____ day of each [   ] week [   ] month. The first [   ] week's [   ] month's rent shall be payable on_____.

4. The following person is authorized to act on behalf of the Landlord and is specifically authorized to accept notices of the Tenant's complaints and to accept any service of legal process or notice. (Complete if different from Landlord.)

_____
(Name)

_____
(Address)

_____

_____
Initialled

SELF-COUNSEL PRESS-RTA (2-1) 00

Figure 18-4

The first page of a tenancy agreement from a stationery store

Figure 18-5

Issuing an eviction notice is the last step in the process of removing an undesirable tenant.

Rent control was originally legislated in many jurisdictions across Canada as a temporary measure to control and regulate the amount of rent increases. However, rent control has now become a permanent part of the legislation of many provinces and territories, so that rents may only increase by a certain percentage each year.

Security Deposits

Tenants are usually required to pay a **security deposit** when they enter into a tenancy agreement. The laws of the province or territory clearly specify how these deposits should be used, as shown in Figure 18-6. The security deposit is held in trust by the landlord (except in New Brunswick) until the termination of the tenancy. Usually, the landlord must pay the tenant yearly interest on the deposit; the rate varies depending on the location in Canada. If the tenant fails to pay all rent owing, the deposit can be used to cover the amount owing, provided the jurisdiction permits this.

In some provinces and territories, the security deposit can be used to pay for damage done by the tenant. This often leads to disputes because the two sides often disagree on what constitutes damage, or what it will cost to fix the damage. If the two sides cannot agree, the matter can be referred to an adjudicator.

Did You Know?

New Brunswick is the only province that requires the security deposit to be deposited with the province and paid into a security-deposit fund. The interest from the deposit is kept by the government to pay for the Office of the Rentalsman.

e activity

Visit **www.law.nelson.com** and follow the links to learn more about security deposits in your province or territory.

Tenants' Security Deposit: Amount and Use

Province/Territory	Legislation	Amount of Deposit	Use of Deposit
Alberta	*Residential Tenancies Act*	one month's rent	as agreed with the tenant
British Columbia	*Residential Tenancy Act*	one-half of one month's rent	unpaid rent, damage
Manitoba	*Residential Tenancies Act*	one-half of one month's rent	unpaid rent or other compensation
New Brunswick	*Residential Tenancies Act*	one month's rent	unpaid rent, damage
Newfoundland & Labrador	*Residential Tenancies Act*	one-half of one month's rent	unpaid rent, damage
Nova Scotia	*Residential Tenancies Act*	one-half of one month's rent	unpaid rent, damage
Northwest Territories	*Residential Tenancies Act*	one month's rent	unpaid rent, damage
Nunavut	*Residential Tenancies Act*	one month's rent	unpaid rent, damage
Ontario	*Tenant Protection Act*	one month's rent	rent for last period
Prince Edward Island	*Rental of Residential Property Act*	one month's rent	unpaid rent, damage
Quebec	*Civil Code*	one month's rent	rent for last period
Saskatchewan	*Residential Tenancies Act*	$125 or one-half of one month's rent, whichever is less	security for performance of tenant's obligations; payment of a liability to a landlord
Yukon Territory	*Landlord and Tenant Act*	one month's rent	rent for last period

Figure 18-6

A summary of legislation concerning the amount and use of tenants' security deposits

Repairs

Generally, landlords must maintain the rental unit and the residential complex in a good state of repair so that it is "fit for habitation." The building and the units must comply with local health, safety, and housing standards. This includes getting rid of mice, cockroaches, and other pests on the premises. Since the dwelling is the landlord's investment, maintenance and most repairs are considered his or her responsibility. It would be unfair to have tenants make repairs that would benefit the landlord and future tenants.

Figure 18-7

Appliances that don't work or are unsafe belong in the garbage dump, not in a rental unit. Most of the time, landlords must repair or buy new appliances for a tenant.

Generally, tenants are responsible for ordinary cleanliness of the rental unit. They are also responsible for any undue or willful damage they cause to their own unit or to the complex, or for damage caused through negligence. In addition, they are responsible for damage caused by other occupants in their apartment or by guests. For this reason, tenants often get insurance not only to cover their own possessions, but also to protect themselves from third-party damages or injuries to guests. For example, if Sam's young nieces and nephews visit him and cause the bathtub to overflow, damage may result. If Sam is insured, his insurance company may agree to pay for the damage. Similarly, if one of Sam's guests is injured because of his negligence, a claim may also be made against Sam's insurance.

Tenants have the right to a well-maintained property, and residential tenancy laws help them enforce that right. However, tenants must first tell the landlord about any needed repairs or deficiencies that the landlord should address. If the landlord fails to respond, tenants should complain in writing. This provides them with a dated, written record of their notification to the landlord.

If nothing is done to address the tenant's issues after a reasonable amount of time, tenants can pay for repairs and deduct the cost from the next month's rent. However, the tenants can later be found liable if the repairs were not really required, or if repairs cost too much. For this reason, tenants may decide to apply to an adjudicator for a termination of the tenancy, for an abatement (lowering) of rent, or for an order to have the repairs done. Tenants may be entitled to a reduction of their rent if they lose privileges or are inconvenienced by repairs.

Keep in mind that landlords and tenants bring different interests to residential tenancy agreements. Landlords are running a business and trying to realize a profit; tenants are contracting for an essential service for themselves and their families, often in a very tight marketplace. Because disputes happen frequently, it is important for the parties to deal with each other in writing and to keep copies of correspondence and records of conversations. In this way, landlords can help to protect their business investments and tenants can help to protect their homes.

You Be the JUDGE

The *Residential Tenancies Act* of Alberta requires landlords and tenants to inspect the premises within a week before or after the tenant takes possession and within a week before or after a tenant vacates. The landlord must give the tenant a report of the inspection.

- Should all provinces and territories adopt this regulation? Why or why not?

MacLeod v. Yong

(1999) 26 R.P.R. (3d) 13
British Columbia Court of Appeal

Brenda MacLeod leased a Vancouver house from the Yongs in January 1992. The house had been designed in 1949. The main floor had one bedroom, so she rarely used the upstairs. A carpeted stairway from the kitchen was the means of access to the upper floor. Because the stairway was narrow, MacLeod had to walk sideways when using it, and it did not have a handrail. The area at the bottom of the staircase was slightly lower than the kitchen floor.

In August 1993, MacLeod washed the kitchen floor, read in the living room for 45 minutes, crossed the kitchen floor (which she claimed was now dry), and went upstairs. When she came downstairs, the left side of her body was facing the bottom of the stairs, and the right side was facing the top. Her right hand was sliding along the wall. As she put her left foot onto the kitchen floor at the bottom of the staircase and raised her right foot, she slipped and fell. Her right ankle was broken. A thin layer of water had accumulated at the bottom of the stairwell.

MacLeod gave evidence that she was not aware that the floor sloped slightly toward the bottom of the stairs before washing the floor. Also, she had not complained to the Yongs about the stairway. A home renovator provided evidence for the tenant. He said

the stairwell violated the Vancouver *Building Code* because it had no handrail.

In finding for the tenant, the judge found that other *Building Code* infractions also existed:

- The width of each step was too small.
- The rise (height of the stairs) was too high.
- The depth of each step was too narrow.
- The headroom was much too low.

The judge noted that if conditions are unsafe, owners must comply with the specifications of the *Building Code* even if a property was built before the Code came into effect. The judge found the conditions in the tenant's unit to be unsafe and awarded her damages. The Yongs appealed, but the British Columbia Court of Appeal upheld the decision of the lower court.

For Discussion

1. **For leased residential property, who is responsible for repairing it and ensuring that it meets local building codes?**

2. **Summarize the arguments that you would make if you were MacLeod's lawyer.**

3. **Summarize the arguments that you would make if you were the Yongs' lawyer.**

4. **Should the fact that MacLeod had not complained about the stairway mean that the Yongs are not liable? Why?**

Quiet Enjoyment and Privacy

Quiet enjoyment is the right to enjoy your rental property free from interference by someone else. This right can be upheld against the landlord and other tenants.

The law says that the landlord cannot enter your rented premises unless there is an emergency, unless proper notice has been given, or unless you agree

Figure 18-8

Playing the drums is perfectly legal, but not if it interferes with someone else's right to quiet enjoyment of the rental property. How would you schedule drum practice if you shared a house with other tenants?

to let the landlord in. Entry is usually only allowed during daylight hours or as otherwise agreed between the landlord and tenant. Saskatchewan and New Brunswick prohibit entry on holidays and Sundays.

One reason a landlord may give notice of entry is to show the unit to prospective renters or buyers. The law says that the landlord has the right to show the premises to prospective new tenants during reasonable hours, provided the tenant or the landlord has given notice to terminate the tenancy. The landlord has no right to prevent political canvassers from entering the building, although tradespeople can be restricted. Neither the landlord nor tenants can alter the locks without the consent of the other. This is intended to prevent a landlord from evicting a tenant or to prevent the tenant from obstructing a landlord's lawful access.

Case

Caldwell v. Valiant Property Management

(1997) 9 R.P.R. (3d) 227
Ontario Court, General Division

In 1993, Frank and Cindy Caldwell signed a residential lease for a high-rise apartment unit. The lease was renewed year by year. They were not told that major repairs were about to begin on the complex, and the lease did not say anything about quiet enjoyment. The Caldwells' side of the building was repaired in 1995. They were given notice to keep their windows and balcony door shut because of dust. They could not use their balcony or air conditioner, or the building's swimming pool, or park in their usual place.

In 1996, repairs were made to the opposite side of the building. The Caldwells were disturbed by the noisy repairs. Cindy worked shifts and sometimes had to sleep during the day. A number of times, she had to go to a relative's home in order to sleep. The repairs took eight months in 1995 and three months in 1996. A judge found that the repairs undertaken in 1995 were more disruptive than the repairs done in 1996.

The Caldwells did not complain to their landlord in writing as required by their lease. They did, however, frequently complain to the building superintendent. The work was generally done during business hours, but on occasion started early and extended into weekends. The Caldwells applied for

an abatement (reduction) of rent. They relied on the right to quiet enjoyment, set out in the *Landlord and Tenant Act* of Ontario. (In 1997, this Act was replaced by the *Tenant Protection Act*.) The *Landlord and Tenant Act* also stated that "neither a landlord nor a tenant may waive rights under [the Act]."

For Discussion

1. Why did the Caldwells apply for an abatement of rent?

2. The lease did not contain any clause concerning quiet enjoyment. How would the Caldwells argue that their right to quiet enjoyment was breached?

3. The court departed from historical cases on abatement, which held that physical interference with use of the property must exist for there to be interference with quiet enjoyment. Should physical interference be the only grounds for interference with quiet enjoyment? Why?

4. Valiant Property Management argued that it would be unfair to grant a tenant an abatement when the landlord was repairing the building in good faith to fulfill its obligation to keep the premises safe and in good repair. Give your opinion on its position.

5. Would you award the Caldwells an abatement of rent for loss of quiet enjoyment? Why or why not?

Figure 18-9

Before you sign a lease, it's a good idea to determine which services the landlord will provide and which ones you will have to provide yourself.

ⓔ activity

Visit **www.law.nelson.com** and follow the links to find out more about landlords' and tenants' rights and obligations in your province or territory.

Utility Services and Property Taxes

Municipal bylaws require certain services to be provided to a tenant to make the premises habitable. These vital services include water, adequate heat, electricity, garbage collection, and sewage. Other services are provided at the discretion of the landlord or the tenant, such as telephone, cable, and snow clearing. If services to which the tenant is entitled by law are not provided, the tenant should first notify the landlord. If there is no response, municipal inspectors should be notified. After inspecting the premises, they can order the services to be provided or order the landlord to do the necessary repairs. If the landlord refuses to comply, the tenant can apply to an adjudicator for a remedy. It is a serious offence for a landlord to withhold vital services.

The lease should state who is responsible for paying for optional services. If the lease does not state the payment responsibilities for services, or if there is no lease, the person who hires someone to provide a service—for example, snow clearing—is liable for payment. In multi-unit dwellings, the landlord might pay for water and heat, and the tenant might pay for electricity, telephone, and cable. The landlord is also responsible for paying the property taxes to the local government. The tenant's share of the taxes is included as part of the rent.

Discrimination

Prejudice and discrimination are as unacceptable in landlord and tenant relations as they are in many other legal relationships. Federal, provincial, and territorial governments have enacted human rights legislation that tries to eliminate discrimination in the rental housing market on the basis of a variety of characteristics, including religion, race, sex, age, or marital status. The human rights statutes have primacy over all other provincial or territorial statutes, meaning if there is a conflict between the human rights statute and a residential housing statute, it will be resolved in favour of the human rights statute.

Landlords want to protect their investments and often hesitate to rent to someone with a low income. Under human rights legislation, a prospective tenant's low income is not a legitimate reason for denying him or her a rental unit (see Issue, page 558). In Ontario, for example, the *Human Rights Code* explicitly states that prospective renters have the right to equal treatment even if an applicant is receiving public assistance. Someone who believes that he or she has been denied housing for this reason can file a complaint with the Human Rights Commission in the jurisdiction of the dispute.

Case

Watson v. Antunes

[1998] O.H.R.B.I.D. No. 9
Ontario Human Rights Commission Board of Inquiry

Watson, a member of a visible minority, went to see an apartment that she wanted to rent for herself and her daughter. Satisfied with the apartment, she later phoned the number listed on the advertisement and spoke with the person who had shown her the apartment. She was then informed that the apartment was not available. Watson thought that she may have been denied the apartment because of her race, so she had a friend call the number. The friend was told that the apartment was still available.

Watson took the matter to the Ontario Human Rights Commission on the basis of discrimination because of race. Section 2(1) of the Ontario *Human Rights Code* states: "Every person has a right to equal treatment with respect to the occupancy of accommodation, without discrimination because of race, ancestry, place of origin, colour, ethnic origin, citizenship, creed, sex, sexual orientation, age, marital status, same-sex partnership status, family status, handicap or the receipt of public assistance."

The respondent, Antunes, did not participate in the proceedings of the Board of Inquiry.

For Discussion

1. On what ground did Watson file a complaint?
2. What does "occupancy of accommodation" mean under the Ontario *Human Rights Code*?
3. Why would Watson take the case to the Human Rights Commission rather than sue Antunes in a court?
4. Why would the respondent have chosen not to participate in the proceedings?
5. The Board of Inquiry, as part of its judgment, ordered that the landlord provide the Commission with a written policy and non-discriminatory tenant application form for its approval. Why do you think the Commission made this order?

Review Your Understanding (Pages 550 to 557)

1. What types of clauses should be included in a lease?
2. What is a standard form lease?
3. What is a security deposit? What can it be used for in your province or territory?
4. Summarize which repairs are the responsibility of the landlord and which are the responsibility of the tenant.
5. What services is a tenant entitled to receive? Where should the responsibility for paying for these services be specified?
6. If there is a conflict between a residential housing statute and a human rights statute, which legislation prevails?

Did You Know?

Some companies offer a unique video service— they make a video of the premises being rented, both at the beginning and at the end of a tenancy. Why do you think such a service would appeal to landlords and tenants? Who should pay for it?

Should the Government Ensure That Low-Income Canadians Have Access to Affordable Housing?

The Canada Mortgage and Housing Corporation (CMHC) has a rule about shelter: If you spend more than 30 percent of your income on housing, "you can't afford to live there."

The Federation of Canadian Municipalities, however, reports that one in five renters spends at least 50 percent of his or her income on rent. It also reports that for every one of the estimated 200 000 homeless people in Canada, another four are on the brink of losing their homes because of rising rents. Those most threatened by this situation are senior citizens and single-parent families.

Jane Jenson of Canadian Policy Research Networks, Inc., calculates that the lack of adequate low-cost housing has put half a million Canadian children at risk:

- Poor housing affects children's health and exposes them unnecessarily to physical hazards.
- Crowded housing affects children's performance at school, as they have no quiet space to read, or be read to, or to do homework.
- Rising rents mean that children may become malnourished, as parents are forced to cut back on food budgets. High rents may also deny children opportunities for recreational and cultural activities.

Figure 18-10

In July 2001, about 200 protesters took over a building in Montreal to raise awareness of the lack of affordable housing in that city.

In the past, the federal, provincial, and territorial governments invested in social (subsidized) housing, such as public housing projects and nonprofit cooperatives. In the 1970s, provincial governments introduced rent controls to limit rent increases.

However, in 1993, the federal government stopped the funding of new social housing, and the provinces and territories soon followed suit. Most provinces and territories have now either lifted or relaxed rent controls. For example, in 1997 the Ontario government enacted the *Tenant Protection Act*. This Act allows landlords to set rents at any price once a unit becomes vacant. Tenants who continue to occupy their units are protected from unregulated rent increases. However, in this type of situation, tenants have fewer places to move to and are more vulnerable to eviction since landlords gain more from evicting a tenant protected by rent control than from working out problems.

Are these changes in government policy justified in light of evidence that fewer low-income people are now able to find affordable housing?

On One Side

Many in the private sector argue that governments should not be involved in the housing business. They reject rent controls and government spending on social housing. They believe that Canadians are already taxed too heavily, and that spending on social welfare programs should be kept to a minimum. Once government gets out of the way, private developers will move in and will do a better job of filling the demand for low-cost housing.

Most developers say that governments still have a role to play in low-cost housing. They say that governments must provide incentives to developers such as cheap land, lower property taxes, and loan guarantees so that new housing units get built. Governments should also set and monitor housing standards, and in some cases, manage and operate completed housing projects. Others reject any form of government subsidy on the grounds that such spending encourages people to remain dependent on government assistance.

Landlords strongly oppose rent controls. They want rental rates set by the market forces of supply and demand. They argue that rent controls make it impossible to keep up with the rising cost of maintenance and repairs, heating, and taxes. Because rent controls artificially limit the returns that landlords get from rental properties, some leave the business and put their money into investments that give them a better return.

As a result, many landlords have converted their rental properties into condominiums aimed at the higher end of the real-estate market. Unfortunately, these conversions have reduced the number of rental apartments available to low-income people, who now make up the largest number of renters. Some landlords have proposed the creation of a "shelter allowance program" to address this problem. People with low incomes would pay what they could afford, and the government would pay a shelter allowance to landlords to ensure a fair return on their investment.

On the Other Side

Advocates for social housing say that the private sector has failed to fill the gap left by government in the 1990s. As it turns out, private developers have not built enough affordable rental housing for low-income Canadians. At the same time, the demand for such housing has increased because of cuts in employment insurance and social assistance, and high levels of unemployment that persist in certain regions of the country.

A number of social activists have called on government to reintroduce strong rent controls.

They say controls are necessary to keep greedy landlords from charging high rents. In the absence of rent controls, many low-income people will suffer. They simply cannot afford to pay skyrocketing rents produced by tight rental markets. This means low-income people face the real possibility of being evicted from their homes and becoming homeless. Rent controls will help reduce the anxiety and feelings of fear and powerlessness that afflict many poor and low-income Canadians.

For many citizens, the government's decision to reduce its involvement in affordable housing goes against the democratic tradition of this country. Public spending on health care, education, pensions, and social welfare shows that governments are working to maintain the well-being of all Canadians. Affordable, decent housing should be on this list. It is essential for achieving equality of opportunity. As such, it is a right, not a privilege.

The Bottom Line

At a time when low mortgage rates have allowed many Canadians to afford to buy homes, Canada's low-income communities are in a housing crisis. Finding a solution requires cooperation among all levels of government—federal, provincial, and municipal—as well as the private sector.

Recent opinion polls show that two-thirds of Canadians want more government spending on housing for the homeless even if it means higher taxes. In 2001, the federal and provincial governments agreed to a $1.4 billion plan to subsidize the building of rental units across the country. It is the first time in 10 years that such an agreement has been reached. But the issue remains: Should governments spend taxpayers' dollars to provide affordable housing to persons of low income?

What Do You Think?

1. Distinguish between rent controls and social housing. Are they connected? Explain.

2. What is the evidence that many low-income Canadians are experiencing a housing crisis?

3. Working in groups as landlords or tenants, develop arguments in support of, or against, rent controls.

4. Do you believe that governments should be in the business of providing social housing to persons of low income? Defend your point of view.

18.4 Changing or Terminating the Tenancy

A tenancy can end in a number of ways. The tenant can move out at the end of the lease or move out during the lease period. The tenant can sublet or assign the tenancy to another person. The landlord can terminate the tenancy for reasons specified in the residential tenancy legislation. Or the tenancy can be terminated because both the landlord and tenant agree to it. These scenarios are examined below.

Surrender of the Lease

After entering into a lease, a tenant's circumstances may change—he or she might lose a job, drop out of school, or experience some other change in circumstances. If the tenant decides to surrender the lease and leave the premises, that person is still responsible for the rent during the period of the tenancy agreement. However, a landlord has a responsibility to mitigate (minimize) the tenant's losses; that is, the landlord has a duty to rerent the unit as quickly as possible. In a tight rental market, the unit may be rented as soon as the former tenant vacates. In that case, the former tenant may only be responsible for reasonable out-of-pocket expenses to the landlord, such as advertising the availability of the unit.

Assignment and Sublet

The terms **assignment** and **sublet** have different meanings. An assignment occurs when a tenant succeeds in getting a replacement tenant during the period of the tenancy agreement and waives the right to repossess (regain possession of) the rental unit. The new tenant makes rent payments directly to the landlord. The original tenant, however, is still liable for the terms of the lease (such as the obligation to pay rent) if the new tenant defaults.

A sublet occurs when a tenant either rents out part of the premises, or all of the premises, but keeps the right to repossess. For example, Troy, a university student, rents an apartment on an annual basis. He sublets to other students in the summer with the agreement that he will move back into the apartment in the fall, when the school year starts. Troy is liable for all the terms of the tenancy agreement, including the obligation to pay rent, until

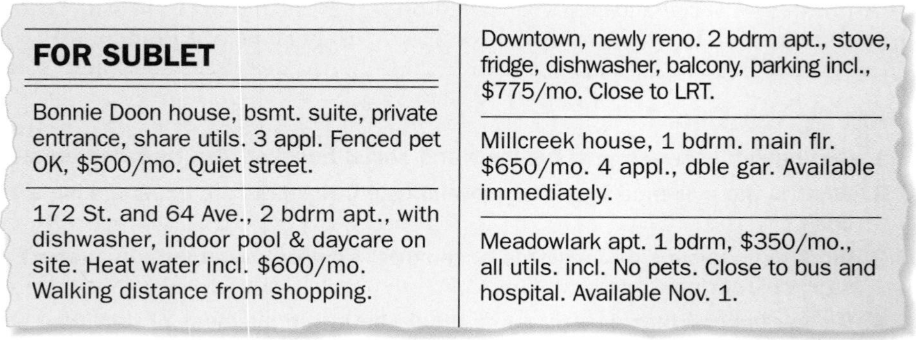

FOR SUBLET

Bonnie Doon house, bsmt. suite, private entrance, share utils. 3 appl. Fenced pet OK, $500/mo. Quiet street.

172 St. and 64 Ave., 2 bdrm apt., with dishwasher, indoor pool & daycare on site. Heat water incl. $600/mo. Walking distance from shopping.

Downtown, newly reno. 2 bdrm apt., stove, fridge, dishwasher, balcony, parking incl., $775/mo. Close to LRT.

Millcreek house, 1 bdrm. main flr. $650/mo. 4 appl., dble gar. Available immediately.

Meadowlark apt. 1 bdrm, $350/mo., all utils. incl. No pets. Close to bus and hospital. Available Nov. 1.

Figure 18-11

What would be the advantages and disadvantages of subletting?

the lease term ends. The summer tenants, called the subtenants, pay the rent to Troy, who then pays the landlord. If Troy fails to make his rent payments, the subtenants can be evicted. Troy has the right to give notice to vacate to the landlord according to the terms of the lease. If this happens, the subtenants have to move out unless they can enter into a new lease with the landlord.

Case

Raymond v. Byrapaneni

(2001) 39 R.P.R. (3d) 1
New Brunswick Court of Appeal

Raymond and Bennett signed a one-year lease for a basement walkout apartment, starting in August 1997. In December 1997, they vacated the apartment, breaking their agreement. Since the landlord, Byrapaneni, was required by the *Residential Tenancies Act* to minimize his tenants' losses, he advertised the apartment in Fredericton's daily newspaper. The apartment remained vacant until July 1, 1998. Byrapaneni filed in Small Claims Court for losses that included six months' rent. He won his claim, but Raymond appealed that decision.

Byrapaneni had three other vacant apartments available in the same building at the same time that he was trying to rent the Raymond apartment. Though the lease did not allow Raymond to sublet the apartment, Byrapaneni contacted Raymond and Bennett and gave them permission to do so, on condition that they remain liable if the subtenant did not pay rent.

Raymond gave evidence at the Small Claims Court trial that he had met with two prospective tenants, McCarty and Fournier. They told him that they were interested in renting a walkout basement because of safety concerns that they had for their infant child. In January, the family rented an apartment on the third floor of the building despite the fact that Raymond had advised them that his unit was available. When asked at trial why they did not take the Raymond apartment, McCarty testified that when he asked to see the basement unit, the landlord told him it was not available. The landlord disputed McCarty's statement.

For Discussion

1. **What type of tenancy existed for Raymond?**
2. **How does Byrapaneni benefit from renting the legally vacant apartments before finding a subtenant for Raymond's apartment?**
3. **Why are landlords required by Tenancy Acts to mitigate the loss of an abandoning tenant?**
4. **Should Raymond have to pay the six months' rent that was owing while the apartment was vacant? Why?**

For an assignment or sublet, the landlord is permitted to charge the original tenant a reasonable fee for any actual expenses incurred, such as drawing up a new lease for the new subtenant.

Although tenants have a right to assign or sublet, the landlord is usually interested in meeting the person who will occupy the premises. The landlord can thus require the original tenant to obtain permission to assign or sublet. In the past, landlords often withheld such permission, preferring to rent an empty apartment to a new tenant rather than to have someone take over an existing lease. Today, however, if the tenant finds a person who will sublet the apartment or to whom the contract can be assigned, the landlord cannot unreasonably withhold permission. If the landlord does so, the tenant can apply to the courts for permission to sublet to a specific person. The only tenants who do not have the right to sublet or assign are residents of public housing because of the long waiting lists.

Termination by Notice

Neither a landlord nor a tenant can terminate a lease on a whim. Termination is allowed only on certain grounds (which must be set out in the written notice). For example, each province and territory requires a certain length of notice.

Situations that allow a landlord to terminate a tenancy are usually one of two kinds:

- The tenant has committed a serious breach. For example, Pat has caused undue damage, has failed to pay rent to Len (the landlord), or disturbs others.
- Len wants to change the use of the premises; for example, convert the building to condominiums or move in his immediate family members.

If the landlord serves notice to terminate a tenancy because the tenant has committed a breach of the tenancy agreement, the tenant may be given some time to correct the situation. If the tenant does not correct the problem and does not vacate, the landlord can apply to an adjudicator or the court to obtain a **writ of possession.** This document allows the landlord to regain possession. If necessary, the landlord can call the sheriff to enforce the writ.

Landlords cannot invent excuses to terminate tenancies. Termination is a legal process and must have a legitimate basis. A judge may refuse to issue an eviction order if it can be shown that the landlord

- is in serious breach of his or her obligations
- is retaliating against a tenant who tried to exercise his or her legal rights
- wants to evict a tenant because he or she belongs to a tenants' association or is trying to organize one

When the landlord wants to change the use of the premises, the tenant may be able to challenge termination of the lease. Usually, the landlord must prove that he or she will be changing the use of the rental unit according to what is set out in the notice of termination.

Figure 18-12

Sometimes, landlords become upset when tenants form associations and hold regular meetings, but it is not a legitimate reason for evicting someone.

Case

Gonte Construction Ltd. v. Williams

(1997) 15 R.P.R. (3d) 120
Ontario Court, General Division

Williams and her two young children occupied a Toronto apartment for almost four years. Justin, aged six, was at school in the mornings and went to daycare in the afternoon. Brandon, nearly five, had a form of autism. He could not express himself well and had a hard time controlling his behaviour. He was enrolled in a program for developmentally challenged children. Both boys usually arrived home around 6:00 P.M.

The landlord, Gonte Construction Ltd., sought to terminate the tenancy, alleging the following:

- There were constant problems with noise, loud music, shouting, fighting, and screaming. The source was Williams, her guests, and her children.
- The children's father had half-hour access visits. He would stand outside the building and shout until Williams let him in, or would bang at the door demanding entry.
- Another tenant witnessed at least one instance of physical violence.
- On more than one occasion, Williams had moved her belongings into the hall, blocking hallway access.
- Gonte Construction Ltd. had warned Williams, but she had failed or refused to remedy the situation.
- Several tenants had moved out because of the noise, and others threatened to do so.

Evidence suggested that a lot of disturbances resulted from the tenant's relationship with the children's father, Francis. Williams testified that the situation had improved. As well, Williams testified that she had investigated moving but found the requirements of first and last month's rent and job references impossible to fulfill.

The *Landlord and Tenant Act* (now the *Tenant Protection Act*) gives the landlord the right to give the tenant notice of termination and seven days in which to remedy the problems. Gonte Construction Ltd. took action because it alleged that Williams did not remedy these complaints. The lawyer for the tenant argued that the judge could refuse the landlord's application for eviction if, under the circumstances, the eviction would be unfair. The judge did not accept that there were circumstances that should halt the eviction. He allowed the landlord's application and Williams was evicted.

For Discussion

1. Many people cannot afford to pay a month's rent and a security deposit at the beginning of a tenancy. Should the right to collect a security deposit be abolished by legislatures? Why?

2. In this case, what are the relevant circumstances that the judge should consider in deciding whether the tenancy should be saved?

3. Would you grant the landlord's application to evict the tenant? Why?

In addition, it is an offence for a landlord to harass a tenant with the objective of getting the tenant to vacate.

At one time, the landlord had the **right of distress.** This is a common law right of the landlord to seize a tenant's possessions for arrears of rent. This right has been abolished in residential tenancy statutes.

A tenant may also give the landlord notice of termination if the landlord is not following the conditions of the tenancy agreement. The tenant could move out but would still be liable for rent if the landlord took action and the tenant's case proved to be unfounded. As in the case of surrendering the lease, discussed earlier, if the tenant moves out before the tenancy period has ended, the landlord must try to find a new tenant in order to mitigate the tenant's losses.

Case

Murray v. Kerton

(1997) 15 R.P.R. (3d) 300
Ontario Court, General Division

The landlord, Murray, tacked a letter to tenant Kerton's door on February 20, 1997, informing him that his month-to-month tenancy could be renewed if he paid the statutory rent increase of 2.8 percent, beginning June 1, 1997. The tenant refused to pay the increase because he alleged that the landlord's notice was not in the prescribed legal format. The notice did, however, set out the current rent and the amount of the increase. The notice also stated that the increase was within government guidelines. Kerton refused to pay the increase, so Murray sent him two notices of early termination by registered mail, telling him to vacate the premises.

The landlord then brought an eviction application against the tenant. He also alleged that the tenant was interfering with his right of quiet enjoyment by

- using the front lawn as a turnaround
- keeping raw kitchen garbage in open containers and other trash on the front veranda
- keeping a pile of old chairs and a rusty table in the back yard
- refusing to discuss problems with the tenancy without resorting to abuse or threats

At trial, the landlord gave evidence that Kerton conducted a sale of appliances on the front lawn over a two- to three-week period, did not return drapes that had been loaned to him, stored tires and bottles near the front of the home, stored a bicycle in an area he was not supposed to use, and installed an air conditioner contrary to the terms of the lease. Kerton removed the air conditioner when informed that it was contrary to the lease, moved the bicycle, and relocated the open garbage pails.

In dismissing the landlord's application, the judge held that the notice of rent increase provided to the tenant complied with the notice requirements set out by law, and that the tenant was neither misled nor prejudiced by it. He further held that there was insufficient evidence to find that the tenant had interfered with the landlord's quiet enjoyment. However, the tenant was ordered to pay the rent increase from June 1, 1997.

For Discussion

1. According to the judge, did Murray meet the legal requirements for providing notice for the rent increase?

2. Why would Murray seek a court-ordered writ of possession when he had already sent Kerton a notice of early termination?

3. Was there sufficient evidence to indicate that the landlord's quiet enjoyment was interfered with? Explain.

Review Your Understanding (Pages 560 to 564)

1. What are the responsibilities of the tenant and the landlord when the tenant surrenders the lease?

2. Distinguish between sublet and assignment of a lease.

3. What are the rights of the tenant and landlord in subletting?

4. What are the rights of the tenant and landlord when an assignment occurs?

5. What steps must the landlord follow to evict a tenant?

Chapter Review

Chapter Highlights

- The term "residential tenancy" does not apply to rental accommodation in hotels or to rooms with shared facilities in private homes.
- The provincial and federal Human Rights Acts apply to the renting of accommodation.
- The lease should outline the rights and duties of the landlord and the tenant as set out in the province's or territory's residential tenancy legislation.
- Two classes of tenancy are fixed-term and periodic tenancy.
- Each tenant who signs a joint tenancy is liable for the total rent.
- The landlord and tenant must look to the common law, the statute law, and the lease for conditions that apply to their relationship.
- The tenant is responsible for delivering the rent to the landlord on time.
- Each province or territory specifies how a security deposit can be used.
- The landlord is responsible for providing and maintaining the premises in a state fit for habitation.
- The tenant is responsible for ordinary cleanliness.
- The tenant has a right to quiet enjoyment from other tenants and the landlord.
- The landlord or tenant should give a notice of termination if he or she wishes to end the tenancy before the due date.
- The landlord must get a court or adjudicator's order to evict a tenant.

Review Key Terms

Name the key terms that are described below.

a) use of one's property free from interference by another party

b) another name for a tenancy agreement between a landlord and tenant

c) tenancy created by two or more persons signing a lease

d) tenancy for a particular period

e) an agreement whereby a tenant rents out all or part of the premises to another person but reserves the right to repossess

f) person who grants a lease of a property to another person

g) person who rents property from the owner

h) a tenancy that runs from day to day or week to week

i) an amount of money deposited by the tenant with the landlord

j) a tenant finds a new replacement tenant and waives the right to repossess the premises

k) a common law right of a landlord to seize a tenant's possessions for failure to pay rent

Check Your Knowledge

1. Briefly explain the classes of tenancy and provide an example for each.

2. Identify some of the conditions that a tenant should check when entering into a lease.

3. Summarize the rights and duties of a landlord.

4. Summarize the rights and duties of a tenant.

Apply Your Learning

5. *Bramar Holdings Inc. v. Deseron* (1996), 1 R.P.R. (3d) 287 (Ontario Court, General Division)

Sandy Deseron leased a new residential unit in an eight-unit townhouse complex. The landlord's practice was to have a real-estate agent provide tenants with a copy of the lease. The tenant would sign it, and then the agent would have the landlord sign. The agent would then give a copy of the lease to the tenant. The *Landlord and Tenant Act* (now *Tenant Protection Act*) of Ontario required that the landlord provide a fully executed lease to the tenant within 21 days after it had been signed and delivered by the tenant to the landlord.

Shortly after Deseron moved into her townhouse, heavy rain caused the city's sanitary sewer to create a sewer backup in her basement. A cleaning crew was immediately brought in, and a device was installed to prevent another backup. Another heavy rain caused the laundry tub to fill with sewage and overflow. The landlord again brought in cleaning crews and had repairs done. A public health inspector was brought in to inspect and, despite detecting a slight odour in Deseron's townhouse, he declared that the premises were habitable.

Deseron left the unit for a month to live with relatives, during which time repairs were made and a pump installed that disconnected the unit from the city's main sewer. Deseron maintained that her townhouse continued to smell months later, and so she did not pay her rent. As well, her children could not use the basement as a play area. She also maintained that she never received a copy of the lease and, therefore, had no obligation to pay the rent. The landlord sued.

a) What responsibility does the landlord have for maintenance of the building?

b) Why do the Acts relating to landlords and tenants in most provinces and territories require that the landlord give the tenant a copy of the lease? In your opinion, should the fact that Deseron did not receive a copy of the lease allow her not to pay rent?

c) Was Deseron's quiet enjoyment interfered with? Explain.

d) What award, if any, would you make to Deseron?

6. *Fulber v. Doll*, 2001 BCSC 891 (British Columbia Supreme Court)

Ralph and Ron Fulber were tenants in separate houses owned by Copper Beach Estates Ltd. The tenants were criminally charged on June 21, 2000, with growing marijuana in their respective homes. The landlord immediately issued notices to terminate the tenancies.

Section 36(1)(f) of British Columbia's *Residential Tenancy Act* states that the landlord could issue a notice of termination if "the safety or other lawful right or interest of the landlord or other occupant in the residential property has been seriously impaired by an act or omission of the tenant." The arbitrator, Doll, ruled that growing marijuana in itself would not necessarily constitute grounds for ending a tenancy. However, because there was evidence that the tenants were stealing electricity (Ralph's meter was upside down) to cultivate their plants and

that the operation itself caused some risk to the landlord's premises, there were grounds for ending the tenancy.

The tenants brought an application for judicial review of the arbitrator's decision. They argued that they were denied procedural fairness, that essential findings were made on the basis of hearsay evidence, and that the decision was unreasonable. Because the arbitrator did not specify the nature or magnitude of the risk related to the growing operation, Ron's tenancy was saved. Ralph's tenancy, however, was terminated because the electricity issue was found to interfere with the landlord's economic interests.

The appeal court judge noted: "I am persuaded on a balance of probabilities that electrical alterations have been made to House #160 and #161 in the form of additional lights and sockets."

a) Under British Columbia's *Residential Tenancy Act,* when can a notice of termination be issued?

b) What was the decision of arbitrator Doll at the initial hearing?

c) Why did the Fulbers apply to a court for a judicial review of the arbitrator's decision?

d) Should the use of a rented premises for illegal activities be automatic grounds for terminating a lease, even if the landlord has not suffered loss? Explain.

e) Should Ralph's lease be terminated? Explain.

7. *Pajelle Investments Ltd. v. Herbold* (1976), 62 D.L.R. (3d) 749 (Supreme Court of Canada)

The Herbolds, mother and daughter, rented an apartment in Toronto. The landlord had advertised that the premises were air-conditioned and that there was an indoor swimming pool and sauna available. These items were not, however, mentioned in the lease.

Some time after the Herbolds moved in, the landlord failed to supply air conditioning for one month in the summer, and the swimming pool and sauna were not usable for nearly five months. The landlord indicated that the facilities in question were unusable because of mechanical breakdown, and large sums of money were required for repairs. The Herbolds contended that the building in which their apartment was located was in a serious state of disrepair. Other tenants called as witnesses for the landlord countered many of the Herbolds' arguments.

The Herbolds filed an affidavit setting out the problems, and the matter was heard by the County Court. It was eventually appealed to the Divisional Court, the Court of Appeal for Ontario, and the Supreme Court of Canada.

a) Where would the courts look to find the responsibilities of the landlord and tenant regarding repairs?

b) Should the courts grant the Herbolds relief for not having the use of recreational facilities when these items were not specified in the lease? If so, what compensation should be given?

c) What would be your decision in this case? Why?

Communicate Your Understanding

8. Use the Internet to access the laws that apply to landlord and tenants in your province or territory. Prepare a report for one of your classmates, on the understanding that he or she will be renting an apartment in the future. Indicate the specifics for each of the following:

a) time period that the landlord has to deliver a copy of the lease to the tenant

b) time period that the landlord must give the tenant before taking action when the rent is not paid

c) who is responsible for repairs and maintenance

d) what a security deposit can be used for, and the amount of interest that must be paid on it

e) title of the office in the province or territory to whom complaints must be addressed

f) length of notice that must be given to terminate each type of tenancy

9. For each of the following situations, prepare a paragraph to indicate what you would do to resolve the problem.

a) The landlord refuses to raise the heat above 18°C.

b) The landlord states that you must leave at the end of your tenancy agreement, but you want to stay.

c) The landlord states that a security deposit must be paid, equal to one and one-half month's rent.

d) The landlord refuses to fix the stairs leading to your apartment, which are in a dangerous state of disrepair.

e) The landlord decides to raise your rent by an amount greater than allowed by law.

f) The landlord refuses permission to sublet.

g) The landlord makes frequent, unannounced visits to the apartment, even while you are not there.

10. Role-play each of the following situations:

a) a tenant trying to get the landlord to fix the sink in the bathroom of the apartment

b) a landlord trying to make the tenant aware that the surrounding tenants have complained of noise from the apartment

c) discrimination by a landlord who is renting an apartment

11. Write a letter to your landlord indicating that you want to end your tenancy on April 30, the end of your one-year lease. Include all information that you think is essential.

12. Using reference materials in your resource centre, including CD-ROMs and the Internet, research one of the following topics: public housing, the effect of the economy on availability of accommodation, rent control, or discrimination by landlords. Create an informative poster based on your findings.

Develop Your Thinking

13. Landlords have a large investment in their properties. It is sometimes said that the laws favour the tenant too much. Imagine that you are a landlord. What tenancy laws would you change to protect your investment? Why would you change them?

14. The provincial and territorial acts relating to landlords and tenants have become very prescriptive (authoritative) in what a lease must contain. Rules are made for, among other things, notice for termination, security deposits, and responsibility for maintenance and repairs. The municipalities have bylaws that apply to maintenance of the outside of the property and smoke detectors on the inside of the property. In your opinion, is there too much government regulation concerning leasing residential property? Explain.

Employment Law

Focus Questions

- What is the nature of the employer–employee relationship?

- What duties do employers and employees have under common law?

- Why are statutes needed to govern the terms of employment?

- What laws deal with discrimination in employment contracts, interviews, and advertisements?

- What procedures must unions and employers follow when they cannot agree during contract negotiations?

Chapter at a Glance

Figure 19-1

A job fair for information technology. Employers are eager to hire these skilled workers. What kind of terms could skilled workers expect compared to unskilled workers?

19.1 Introduction

Unless you are independently wealthy or unable to work, you will spend most of your adult life working for others or running your own business and hiring people. Employment contracts will probably be the most important contracts in your life. They will determine what you earn and what kind of lifestyle you can afford.

In this chapter, you will look at employment contracts and how employment law has developed over the years. Today, most employees negotiate contracts with their employers either directly or indirectly. They may do this as individuals or through **unions,** organizations that represent groups of employees in contract negotiations. Unions were once illegal in Canada, at a time when employers were all-powerful and could dismiss employees without notice or explanation.

Employers and employees still come into conflict, which can result in changes to employment law. To balance the powers of employers and employees, and to bring peace to the workplace, statutes have been enacted. Minimum wages, hours of work, occupational health and safety, and human rights are some key areas of employment law now governed by federal, provincial, and territorial legislation.

This chapter also examines the situation of **independent contractors,** who have very different relationships with businesses. Independent contractors are not in an employer–employee relationship at all, but have **clients** for whom they do business. This kind of contractual relationship has become much more popular in the last 30 years.

19.2 The Employment Relationship

Figure 19-2

An employer must provide the employee with supervision, a workplace, and equipment.

All employment relationships are based on contracts, which must have all the essential elements that you studied in Chapter 16. This is true even if the work is casual or part-time or the employment contract was made informally or verbally. It is important to distinguish between the employer–employee relationship and the relationship between an independent contractor and client.

In the employer–employee relationship, a person is hired to work under someone's direction, for certain hours, usually in the employer's workplace, and using the employer's equipment. The law governing this is employer–employee (employment) law. It covers the majority of workers in Canada today and is the main focus of this chapter.

About 70 percent of contracts between employers and employees are negotiated individually. Terms usually include whether the job is permanent or for a limited period of time, rate of pay, work hours, holidays, and benefits. Benefits can include medical and dental insurance, life insurance, pension plans, and so on. Usually, the employer pays all or part of the costs of benefits for the employee. The remaining 30 percent of employer–employee contracts are negotiated between employers and unions, which will be discussed later in this chapter.

An independent contractor is someone who is hired by a business or person to do a specific job. The independent contractor establishes the work hours, uses his or her own equipment, and is self-directed. To earn money during summer vacation, for example, Hanuf builds landscaped retaining walls for his clients. He creates his own designs and uses his own supplies and equipment. Independent contractors are not in an employer–employee relationship with clients and, so, are not covered by employment (employer–employee) law.

Common Law, Statute Law, and Employment Contracts

Francisco has finished high school and is working at his first full-time job as an assistant in information technology at a small business. He has disagreed with his boss about overtime pay. Where should he look to confirm the terms of his employment? If he has a written contract, he should check that first. But his contract is informal and unwritten. If Francisco were a union member, he could check with his union. But his workplace is not unionized.

Francisco has one other option. He could look to statute law: legislation that has been passed by governments to establish basic employment standards. These laws set minimums for wages, work hours, overtime, vacation pay, and so on. Employment legislation also sets standards for occupational safety and working conditions. Francisco discovers that his boss must pay overtime if Francisco works on the next public holiday. This quickly settles the dispute. All employment contracts must meet the minimums set by these statutes.

▌ Areas of Employment Law

Terms of employment may be defined by

☑ human rights legislation

☑ employment standards and safety legislation (statutes)

☑ trade union legislation (often called "labour law")

☑ common law of employment contracts

activity

Visit **www.law.nelson.com** and follow the links to learn more about employment contracts.

Figure 19-3

Employment terms must not contravene human rights laws.

If Francisco had not found what he was looking for in legislation, he would have looked next to common law (except in Quebec). This is mainly contract law that has developed over many years as courts have heard employment disputes. In settling these disputes, judges have dealt with both verbal and written contracts. They have also interpreted terms that were both implied (understood to exist) and express (clearly written out).

The common law of employment is interpreted by the courts. Labour laws in the provinces and territories are enforced by labour relations boards and tribunals. Employment-related statutes, such as employment standards legislation, human rights legislation, and occupational health and safety legislation, provide their own scheme of enforcement.

Review Your Understanding (Pages 570 to 571)

1. What is the difference between an employee and an independent contractor?
2. What areas of law can an employee consult to find the terms of employment?
3. Who enforces the common law of employment? Who enforces labour law?

19.3 Laws Affecting Employers and Employees

For many years, employer–employee law was referred to as the **law of master and servant.** The employer was the master and the employee the servant. Although the term is no longer used, it does describe a key fact: employees work for employers. Employers direct employees in what, how, where, and when work is to be done. Employers also provide the means to do the job. A complex network of common law and federal, provincial, and territorial legislation now applies to the employer–employee relationship.

Common Law and Employment

Common law lays out the basic duties of the employer and employee in terms of the employment contract.

Under common law, the employer must
- pay the agreed-upon wage or salary
- pay agreed-upon employee expenses
- provide a safe workplace, which includes hiring workers with necessary skills
- provide the type of work the employee was hired to do
- let the employee have a second job, as long as it is non-competitive
- assign work that is legal
- honour the terms of the contract
- give reasonable notice of an intention to terminate the contract of employment

The employee can sue an employer who fails in these duties.

Under common law, the employee must
- be punctual and take only permitted leaves of absence
- obey legal and reasonable orders
- be loyal, honest, and competent

An employee who does not perform his or her common-law duties has breached a fundamental part of the employment contract. This gives the employer the legal right—or **just cause**—to dismiss (fire) the employee. Termination and dismissal will be looked at in detail later in this chapter.

Did You Know?

Through vicarious liability (see page 354), an employer is responsible for any torts that an employee commits while acting in the course of his or her employment.

Gilmour v. Mossop

[1951] 4 D.L.R. 65
Supreme Court of Canada

Gilmour, the plaintiff, agreed to be the housekeeper for Mossop, the defendant. During Gilmour's first two weeks of employment, Mossop's daughter, who lived in Mossop's bungalow, showed Gilmour her duties. She told Gilmour that Mossop had two dogs and that they were "rather fond of lying on the basement stairs." Gilmour grew attached to the dogs and let them stay in the kitchen with her as she worked.

One night, as she was having dinner with Mossop and his son, Gilmour realized she had left food in the basement. At the top of the stairs, she switched on the basement light, which was located on the ceiling at the foot of the stairs. Gilmour then stepped on one of the dogs, which was lying on the top step, and fell down the stairs, injuring herself. She later sued Mossop.

At trial, it was noted that the basement doorway led directly into the kitchen. If one of the kitchen lights was turned on, this improved the lighting at the head of the stairs. The light was not on when Gilmour fell. There was no handrail on either side of the stairway.

The trial court found in Gilmour's favour, but the decision was reversed on appeal.

For Discussion

1. **What common-law duties did Mossop have as an employer in terms of the workplace?**
2. **Did Mossop train Gilmour adequately? Explain.**
3. **Were the working conditions Mossop provided adequate for his employee?**
4. **Why do you think that the original decision was reversed on appeal?**

Figure 19-4
What common-law duty of the employer would a darkened stairwell seem to breach?

Federal Employment Legislation

The courts would be overwhelmed if they had to settle every employment dispute. For this reason, the federal, provincial, and territorial governments have passed laws that set standards for employment, wages, working conditions, termination notice, and so on.

As you learned in Chapter 1, the *Constitution Act, 1867,* gave the provinces jurisdiction over property and civil rights. Because the right to enter into a contract is a civil right, most statutes relating to employment are provincial. As a result, legislation varies a great deal across Canada. It will be looked at more closely later in this chapter.

The main federal employment statute is the *Canada Labour Code,* which applies only to four groups:

- occupations under federal jurisdiction, such as in banking, the post office, and national defence
- employees of Crown corporations, such as the Canadian Broadcasting Corporation

- workers in industries that connect one province or territory to another, either through transportation or physical connections, such as bridges, pipelines, and airfields
- federal government employees, who are referred to as public employees or civil servants

The *Canada Labour Code* affects only 10 percent of employees in Canada, but it is a model and pacesetter for employment legislation across the country. The three parts of the Code attempt to establish fair employment practices, working conditions, and standards. The first section deals with industrial and labour relations, which will be discussed later in relation to unions. The second section sets out standards for occupational health and safety. The third details employment standards.

Human Rights in Employment

As you learned in Chapter 2, the federal, provincial, and territorial governments have passed human rights legislation to promote equality and to protect individuals from both intentional and unintentional discrimination. These laws extend to many areas of life, including employment (see Did You Know?, page 60). Human rights legislation is very powerful and prevails over employment contracts and legislation in most disputes.

The federal *Canadian Human Rights Act* and the Human Rights Codes and Acts of most provinces and territories prohibit discrimination on a number of grounds (see Figure 19-5). Each jurisdiction also has a Human Rights Commission to administer and enforce human rights legislation. In 2000, 64 percent of the complaints brought to the federal Canadian Human Rights Commission involved employment discrimination. This high percentage indicates how important human rights bodies are to the workplace.

▌ Prohibited Grounds of Discrimination

☑ age	☑ place of origin
☑ ancestry	☑ political beliefs
☑ citizenship	☑ race
☑ colour	☑ record of conviction
☑ ethnic origin	☑ religion or creed
☑ family and marital status	☑ same-sex partnership status
☑ language	☑ sex
☑ mental and physical disability	☑ sexual orientation
☑ pardon for record of offences	☑ social condition
☑ pardoned conviction	☑ source of income

Figure 19-5

The *Canadian Human Rights Act* and all the provincial and territorial Human Rights Codes and Acts prohibit discrimination on some or all of these grounds.

Discrimination

Prohibited grounds of discrimination must be respected not only on the job but also in employment interviews, hiring practices, and advertisements. Therefore, prospective employees cannot be asked about their religion, marital status, political beliefs, and so on. Sometimes, however, an employer must set a job requirement that excludes people and which is, thus, discriminatory. To be acceptable under human rights legislation, the requirement must relate directly to the ability to do the job. So long as the requirement is reasonable and valid—or a **bona fide occupational requirement**—it is acceptable.

For example, a moving company wants to hire some students for part-time work and advertises that the job requires students who are strong enough to lift large furniture and appliances. The mover could not place an advertisement saying that applicants must be of a certain height or weight or colour or race or sex. These characteristics have nothing to do with strength and are not valid job requirements. If challenged, employers have to prove that the job requirement is valid.

If a job requirement has a negative impact on a social group, this is known as **adverse effect discrimination.** In this situation, the employer must take steps to accommodate people who are negatively affected. This is known as the employer's **duty to accommodate.**

Case

British Columbia (Public Service Employee Relations Commission) v. BCGSEU

[1999] 3 S.C.R. 3
Supreme Court of Canada

Tawney Meiorin worked for the British Columbia Ministry of Forests as a front-line forest firefighter. Her work was satisfactory. When the government adopted a new series of fitness tests, Meiorin "failed" the aerobic run of 2.5 km. Her best time was 11 minutes and 49.4 seconds, when the standard was 11 minutes. After Meiorin was dismissed, her union complained to the British Columbia Human Rights Commission.

Evidence showed that the government introduced the tests after a coroner's inquiry recommended, for safety reasons, that only "physically fit" employees should serve as front-line forest firefighters. A University of Victoria team developed the tests and identified essential components of forest firefighting. The government established the test standards based on this research. A follow-up study, however, recommended that the government

should study the impact of the tests on women as a group. There was no evidence that the government had complied.

Figure 19-6

Tawney Meiorin celebrates her Supreme Court victory. Women forest firefighters do not have to be able to run 2.5 km in 11 minutes to fight fires safely.

continued ▶

Evidence indicated that, even with training, most women could not meet the 11-minute standard, while most men could. Other evidence showed that 65 to 70 percent of male applicants—but only 35 percent of female applicants—passed the tests on their first try. Furthermore, there was no evidence to indicate that forest firefighters, whether male or female, needed the prescribed aerobic capacity to perform their work satisfactorily.

The arbitrator ruled that the tests were discriminatory and had a disproportionately adverse effect on women. He ruled that the government had failed to show that, by failing the test, Meiorin posed a safety risk. The government had not tried to accommodate Meiorin, as was its duty, to the point of "undue hardship." He ordered that

Meiorin be reinstated and compensated for lost wages and benefits.

The arbitrator's decision was appealed to the Supreme Court of British Columbia, which reversed the decision. On appeal, the Supreme Court of Canada reinstated the arbitrator's decision.

For Discussion

1. **What prohibited ground of discrimination was at issue here?**

2. **What evidence is there that the government did not accommodate Meiorin?**

3. **On what basis would the Supreme Court of Canada have made its decision that Meiorin had been discriminated against?**

Pay and Employment Equity

As you learned in Chapters 2 and 3, pay and employment equity are intended to remove barriers to equality. As part of human rights legislation, they apply to government employees, businesses with government contracts, and large businesses.

Pay equity works to reduce the disparity between men's and women's wages and is also part of the employment standards legislation of most provinces and territories. As well, many provinces have passed Pay Equity Acts.

▌ Two Approaches to Pay Equity

Figure 19-7

Many employers have complained that it is hard to compare different jobs and to create gender-neutral job descriptions.

Equal pay for equal work	Male and female employees are paid the same wage or salary for work requiring similar levels of skill, effort, and responsibility.
Equal pay for work of equal value	Wages and salaries are based on new job descriptions that must be gender neutral. The value of work is calculated on the basis of skill, effort, responsibility, and working conditions.

Employment equity seeks to increase employment opportunities for groups that have historically experienced discrimination in certain jobs and job categories; for example, members of visible minorities, persons with disabilities, Aboriginal peoples, and women. Section 15(1) of the *Canadian Charter of Rights and Freedoms* makes an exception for this and other programs of "affirmative action." Otherwise, they would be prohibited as being discriminatory.

Harassment

Harassment has been described in human rights legislation as "a course of vexatious (abusive or distressing) comment or conduct that is known or ought reasonably to be known to be unwelcome." Every person has the right to freedom from harassment in the workplace. Anyone who is harassed may take action against the person or persons responsible. An employer who ignores complaints of harassment can be held liable.

General harassment occurs when a person in a position of power uses that power to force an employee to do things in order to keep his or her job. If harassment involves sexual comments and actions, it is known as **sexual harassment.** If employees are subjected to hostility or intimidation by others in the workplace on the basis of gender, race, religion, or some other characteristic, this is called **poisoned work environment harassment.**

Case

C.D.P.D.J. (Lippé) v. P.G. du Québec, T.D.P.Q. Montréal

(1998-11-02) QCTDP 500-53-000072-973
Commission des droits de la personne
[Quebec Human Rights Tribunal]

Claudine Lippé took a job with Unité mouvements et comparutions (UMC), an agency controlled by the Attorney General of Quebec. UMC transports inmates from prevention centres and supervises them while they wait to appear in the Montreal Courthouse. In the mid-1980s, integration of women officers in male detention and prevention institutions became a priority. Physical job requirements were changed and on-the-job physical training was introduced so that more women could qualify. Workplace policies to fight sexual harassment were adopted but not well implemented.

Lippé knew the job would be tough. She also knew that many male coworkers resented female officers and felt they would not be able to handle difficult inmates. Lippé developed a good rapport with all her peers, and her job evaluations were good.

After two female officers filed a sexual harassment complaint, a "panic" swept the workplace. Some women officers were called obscene names by male officers. Lippé was thought to be a complainant and was snubbed in the common room. A male coworker taunted her for kisses. Another joked about what happens to "blondes who complain."

Another male officer called Lippé ugly and threatened her: "I'm going to hurt you so much that you

will never want to have anything to do with men after that." A pornographic poster with obscene graffiti aimed at Lippé was glued to a locker. As incidents continued, Lippé kept a daily record. When her job evaluations became negative, Lippé's health deteriorated. Finally, she quit. A harassment complaint was taken to the Quebec Human Rights Commission.

The tribunal ordered that Lippé be reinstated in her job, with seniority for the three years that she was away. The defendant was ordered to pay Lippé $134 961 in damages, as compensation for lost income, plus expenses of $887, and punitive damages of $7000.

For Discussion

1. Describe how the UMC tried to reduce employment discrimination in the 1980s.

2. How did the employer's failure to implement anti-harassment policies affect (a) Lippé and (b) the tribunal's decision?

3. The tribunal found UMC had become a poisoned work environment. What evidence supports that finding?

4. In sexual harassment cases, evidence from accusers and the accused is often contradictory and difficult to support because there are no independent witnesses. Why did the tribunal accept Lippé's evidence rather than that of the perpetrators?

5. What effects, other than psychological, might a poisoned work environment inflict on a worker?

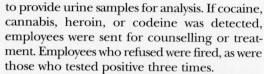
Should Alcohol and Drug Tests of Employees Be Allowed?

Safety and security are very important matters today; so important, in fact, that some businesses have imposed mandatory drug and alcohol tests on employees. Airlines, for example, perform drug tests on pilots, on whose skills customers' lives depend. But what about industries where the need is not so obvious?

In 1990, the Toronto-Dominion Bank introduced drug testing. New employees had

to provide urine samples for analysis. If cocaine, cannabis, heroin, or codeine was detected, employees were sent for counselling or treatment. Employees who refused were fired, as were those who tested positive three times.

As more businesses adopted these tests, rights became a concern. In 1998, the Federal Court of Appeal ruled that Toronto-Dominion's drug testing trespassed on employees' human rights and discriminated against people with drug addictions. The bank suspended the tests.

Earlier, in 1995, a Board of Inquiry appointed under the Ontario *Human Rights Code* decided that Imperial Oil's drug-testing policies breached the civil liberties of Martin Entrop. Entrop was demoted in 1991 after disclosing that he had received treatment for alcoholism in 1984; he stated that he had not had a drink in seven years.

In its decision, the board ruled that alcoholism is a disease. As a disability, it is a prohibited ground of discrimination. Entrop was awarded $21 000 for mental anguish and reinstated. However, he still had to agree to undergo psychological treatment and provide breath samples whenever the company wanted them. Imperial Oil appealed the board's ruling, but in 2000, the Ontario Court of Appeal upheld it.

As it stands, Canadian employers can impose random breath tests on workers in safety-sensitive positions. These tests are acceptable because they measure impairment, which affects job performance. Drug testing, however, is considered an invasion of the employee's privacy. Urine analysis, for example, will show drugs present in the body. But it does not measure the effects the detected drugs might have on job performance.

Figure 19-8

In 1989, the oil tanker *Exxon Valdez* sank, spilling oil in Prince William Sound in the Gulf of Alaska. The captain was suspected of being intoxicated.

On One Side

The Toronto-Dominion Bank argued that employees handle huge amounts of money and that employees who abuse drugs would be using expensive illegal drugs and getting them through criminal contacts. This would put customers' money at risk. The bank also maintained that the *Charter* and Human Rights Codes were not meant to protect illegal drug users. Mandatory drug testing would simply help to maintain values of honesty and trust, which are vital to banking.

Imperial Oil developed its drug-testing policy after the 1989 sinking of the oil tanker *Exxon Valdez*. The resulting oil spill was an environmental disaster. The captain, who had struggled with alcoholism, was suspected of being intoxicated, but was later acquitted of any wrongdoing. The company still believed that it was in its best interests to develop a drug-testing policy for its employees. This testing would help to ensure the health and safety of the general public.

On the Other Side

Alan Borovoy, of the Canadian Civil Liberties Association, has argued that no person should have "to share urine with a stranger" to get a job. He wants mandatory employee drug testing outlawed: "Such tests are a needless invasion of privacy that will tell you a lot about a person's lifestyle but virtually nothing about an employee's ability to do the job."

Borovoy has called drug tests degrading, but he and other critics accept breath tests for employees. These tests measure only one thing: the level of alcohol impairment, which affects the employee's ability to do the job.

The Bottom Line

These cases reflect how human rights commissions and the courts try to balance society's need for safety and security with the individual's right to freedoms and civil liberties. Some people believe businesses must be able to test employees to create a safe and secure environment for everyone. Besides, if people do not agree with the conditions of employment, they can work elsewhere. They have that choice.

Others agree with the Canadian Human Rights Tribunal: "[I]t is not for the employer to be the trier of fact and the enforcer of criminal law." Critics concerned about civil liberties worry that employers will not stop with urine tests. Would blood tests be next? Gene tests? Investigations of medical records and family histories? Electronic monitoring?

What Do You Think?

1. Some high schools use breath tests at school dances. Students who refuse to be tested cannot enter, and parents/guardians are notified if their children are impaired. Are you in favour of this policy or is it an invasion of individual rights? Explain.

2. Describe the main arguments for and against mandatory drug testing of employees. With which side do you most agree and why?

3. For the following occupations, decide whether mandatory drug testing should be a condition of employment:
   a) teacher
   b) airline pilot
   c) police officer
   d) pharmacist
   e) bank teller
   f) receptionist
   g) school-bus driver

   Provide a brief explanation for each decision.

4. What would your position be if your boss imposed a drug test as a condition of employment?

Provincial and Territorial Employment Legislation

Each province and territory in Canada has employment legislation that gives employees basic protection. Some Acts relate to specific occupations, such as teaching, medicine, accounting, and so on. Other Acts and Codes are more general. Although Employment Standards Acts or Codes vary across the country, each covers key terms of employment and establishes certain minimums and safety standards. Other legislation defines procedures that must be followed when employees are dismissed or injured.

Minimum Age

In Canada and most industrialized nations, employment law offers youths special protection. School is compulsory in most of Canada until the age of 16. This age is generally the minimum age at which a youth can work full-time. For youths under 16, work hours are restricted. For example, employers usually cannot hire youths under the age of 16 to work during school hours or late at night during the week.

Many developing countries have little employment legislation to protect children. Because of widespread poverty, children can be exploited as a source of cheap labour by local and multinational businesses. In the past decade, Canadian youths and youth groups have opposed child labour through media campaigns and protests.

Figure 19-9

Canadian teen Craig Kielburger, pictured here in New Delhi, India, in 1996, launched an organization to campaign against international child labour.

Minimum Wage

Each province and territory sets minimum hourly wages. Governments increase the rate to help employees keep up with living costs or to encourage people to take jobs. Businesses, on the other hand, may pressure governments to keep minimum wages from rising, which helps keep business costs low. Some occupations, such as farm workers, resident caretakers, and restaurant servers have special minimum rates.

Hourly Minimum Wages in Canada, January 2002

Province or Territory	Adult	Student, Youth, or Inexperienced
Alberta	$5.90	none
British Columbia	$8.00	$6.00
Manitoba	$6.25	none
New Brunswick	$5.90	none
Newfoundland & Labrador	$5.50	none
Northwest Territories	$6.50/$7.00*	$6.00/$6.50*
Nova Scotia	$5.80	$5.35
Nunavut	$6.50/$7.00*	$6.00/$6.50*
Ontario	$6.85	$6.40
Prince Edward Island	$6.00	none
Quebec	$7.00	none
Saskatchewan	$6.00	none
Yukon Territory	$7.20	none

* Applies where the job is not near the highway system

Did You Know?

British Columbia had the highest rate of youth unemployment in Western Canada when it introduced its lower minimum wage for students and inexperienced workers. Do you believe this will help lower the unemployment rate for youth? Explain.

Figure 19-10

Why do you think the minimum wage is not the same for all provinces and territories?

Employers must pay employees by cash, cheque, or electronic deposit at the end of each pay period. An accompanying statement showing the pay and all deductions is also required. It is illegal for an employer to force an employee to accept pay in kind, or in the form of the products or services the business produces.

Work Hours

The standards for work hours are inconsistent across Canada. In many provinces and territories, full-time employees work an eight-hour day and a 40-hour week at the regular hourly pay rate. After eight hours, they must be paid overtime. For work between 40 and 48 hours, the overtime rate is usually time-and-a-half. In some jurisdictions, an employer must obtain a permit to have employees work more than 48 hours, when the overtime rate jumps to double time.

Employment legislation also sets a minimum number of hours that an employee must be paid if called in for a shift and then sent home. This is usually three hours. As well, employees must be given a minimum number of minutes for a meal break if working more than one shift.

In the new economy, the workplace is changing. Longer work hours have become normal for many people. Many businesses want legislation to allow longer workdays and workweeks. This, they say, would allow them to be more competitive and productive.

Most employment legislation now allows flexible work hours, but employees must agree. In Ontario and the Northwest Territories, for example, employees can agree to work up to 60 hours a week. The Ontario legislation, which came into effect in 2001, allows work hours to be averaged over

You Be the JUDGE

A 2001 study indicated that job stress had doubled in Canada from 1991 as the average workweek increased from 42 to 45 hours. New technology meant that most employees were taking work home, and 62 percent expressed job dissatisfaction.

- Sick days per person also increased, from six days to seven days per year. Based on this information, what would you advise work-hour legislators?

a four-week period. If the employee works two 60-hour weeks and then two 20-hour weeks, for example, this averages out to 40-hour weeks. Overtime starts at 44 hours in Ontario, and the maximum an employee can work is 13 hours a day. An employee also has the option of taking any overtime as time off rather than as wages.

Statutory Holidays

Figure 19-11
Christmas at Eaton Centre in Toronto, Ontario. Christmas and Good Friday are not holy days for everyone, but they are statutory holidays in Canada. How can employers respect this difference in beliefs?

All full-time employees must be allowed to take off statutory holidays, with pay. These include New Year's Day, Good Friday, Victoria Day, Canada Day, Labour Day, Thanksgiving, and Christmas. As well, full-time employees must be paid for special provincial or territorial holidays such as New Brunswick Day, British Columbia Day, Alberta's Family Day, and Ontario's Simcoe Day. Generally, employees must have worked for at least three months before being eligible for statutory holiday pay. Employees must also work regular shifts before and after the holiday. Pay for working a holiday is usually double the regular rate.

Even though Sunday shopping is common across Canada, employees have the right to refuse to work on Sundays. Employees who do work on a Sunday must be given an alternative day of rest during the week.

Vacation

Employees are usually entitled to two weeks of annual vacation, with pay, after having worked one year for an employer. Saskatchewan awards three weeks. As a benefit, employees often receive longer annual vacations the longer they work for their employers. In Nova Scotia, for example, employees who have worked eight years for an employer are entitled to three weeks of annual vacation.

Employees are entitled to vacation pay from the day they start working. Vacation pay is calculated as 4 percent of the employee's yearly earnings, but increases for long-term employees. For example, an eight-year employee in Nova Scotia receives vacation pay of 6 percent. In most provinces and territories, employees must receive the year's allowed vacation pay within a month of their anniversary date of employment. Usually, it is paid when the vacation begins. In some provinces, pay can be given instead of an annual vacation.

Leaves of Absence

A **leave of absence** allows an employee to take a period of time off work and not be fired when he or she returns. Depending on the employer, extended leaves of absence are taken with no pay or partial pay.

If an employer dismissed or laid off an employee because of pregnancy, it would be considered discrimination. Therefore, **maternity leave** is granted to pregnant employees who have worked the required period. The length of the leave is generally 17 or 18 weeks. A mother who wishes to return to work before taking the full leave must notify the employer of her intention. Employment Insurance will pay up to 15 weeks of benefits to employees on maternity leave.

Parental leave is available to both men and women. Usually, mothers must take it immediately after maternity leave. Parental leave must be taken within a specified time, usually within nine months of the birth. The leave varies by jurisdiction. In Ontario, it is 35 weeks, if the woman also took maternity leave. By combining maternity and parental leaves, a mother can take a total leave of one year. **Adoption leave** has also been introduced in most jurisdictions, with the same time limits as those for birth parents.

Termination and Dismissal

Employment standards legislation provides for minimum periods of notice of termination in the employment contract. An employee who resigns or quits must give the employer one or two weeks' notice, depending on the length of employment. If the employee does not give notice, the employer can deduct the equivalent amount from the employee's final pay.

An employer must give notice when dismissing an employee without cause. The period normally ranges from one to eight weeks, again depending on the length of employment. An employer can dismiss the employee immediately, without notice, but must pay him or her termination pay. If the employee was entitled to eight weeks' notice, for example, the employer must pay him or her eight weeks' pay. This is known as "pay in lieu (in the place) of notice."

Businesses use pay in lieu of notice to protect assets and maintain a positive working environment for remaining employees. In today's computerized workplace, an employee who is upset because of being dismissed could easily copy, alter, or destroy essential data. It is not uncommon for an employee to be escorted by security to pick up personal belongings and leave the building immediately after being dismissed.

Employees may have a right to a greater period of notice under common law. In contracts of an indefinite term (as opposed to a contract for a fixed term), it is implied that the employer will give reasonable notice of his or her intention to terminate the contract. What constitutes reasonable notice varies according to the type of employment, the length of service, the age of the employee, and the availability of similar employment with respect to the experience, training, and qualifications of the employee. An employee who is dismissed without reasonable notice or just cause may bring an action for **wrongful dismissal.** However, many wrongfully dismissed employees— other than highly paid executives and sports stars— lack the financial resources to bring such an action and must rely on the minimum periods of notice required by employment standards legislation.

"Pam here is the winner of our 'How small a salary can I live on?' essay contest. The rest of you are fired."

Figure 19-12

What makes a dismissal wrongful?

The employer and employee may alter the implied obligation to give reasonable notice by stipulating a specific period of notice in case of termination. However, this period must not be less than the minimum period of notice required under employment standards legislation.

Notice is not required if an employer dismisses an employee for just cause. Grounds could include any breach of the employee's common-law duties and would include fraud, theft, and serious misconduct (e.g., stealing from the employer, lying to the employer, forging signatures). The onus is on the employer to prove that cause exists. If an employee is dismissed without proper cause or notice, he or she can sue the employer for wrongful dismissal.

Dismissed employees may also be entitled to severance pay. In Ontario, for example, severance pay is required if the employee worked for the business for more than five years and the business's annual payroll is over $2.5 million. The employee is entitled to severance pay of one week for each year of employment. Normally, the employer must pay both termination pay and severance pay on the next regular pay date. An employee who has been dismissed for just cause is not entitled to receive termination or severance pay.

Some employers force employees to resign rather than dismiss them. This approach, called **constructive dismissal,** uses such tactics as demotion, transfer to less-desirable locations, and increased job pressures. An employee who has experienced constructive dismissal has the same legal rights as one who has been wrongfully dismissed.

Did You Know?

The Supreme Court of Canada has ruled that mandatory retirement is legal if the employer can prove that it is needed for the "efficient and economical performance of the job."

Case

Schumacher v. Toronto-Dominion Bank

(1999) 120 O.A.C. 303
Ontario Court of Appeal

Schumacher started as a bank trainee in 1984 and by 1993 had become a senior vice-president. As head of worldwide trading and risk management, he was responsible for trillions of dollars in investments. The president of the bank stated that Schumacher was one of a select few of his generation who one day "should be in the group running the Bank." Schumacher's career was on the rise. In 1994, he earned $1.6 million.

In early 1995, without consulting Schumacher, the bank hired Wright to take over some of his responsibilities. Schumacher's lawyer sent a letter to the bank. By reducing his responsibilities, the letter stated, the bank had demoted Schumacher— amounting in law to constructive dismissal. Schumacher was prepared to negotiate a termination package and would return to work once negotiations started.

The bank stated this was not a demotion and told Schumacher to return to work. In one memorandum it wrote: "We [the Bank] remain convinced that ... there will be no significant adverse impact as a result of this restructuring." When Schumacher did not return to work, the bank sent him a letter. It understood "from all of your actions, that you [Schumacher] have resigned from our employ." The resignation was to be effective immediately. Schumacher sued the bank for constructive dismissal.

At trial, three bank employees testified that the bank had effectively brought Schumacher's career to a halt by hiring Wright. A memo from Schumacher's immediate superior, written just before Wright was hired, stated: "Be prepared to offer C.J. Schumacher a package (constructive dismissal)."

In 1997, the trial judge awarded Schumacher in excess of $1.7 million in damages for constructive dismissal. The bank appealed. In 1999, the Ontario Court dismissed the appeal.

 continued ▶

584 **Unit 5** Contract Law

NEL

For Discussion

1. Outline the evidence of constructive dismissal in this case.

2. The bank argued that Schumacher refused to accept his "new" position and breached his contract when he refused to return to work. What evidence counters this argument?

3. What could Schumacher have done to mitigate (minimize) damages? Did the bank offer him an opportunity to do so?

Figure 19-13

Even Canada's most powerful businesses have to respect employee rights. But what if Schumacher had been a low-paid part-time clerk?

Health and Safety Legislation

Every year, thousands of Canadians are injured on the job, and some die from job-related injuries and illnesses. These injuries cause great human suffering and cost businesses billions of dollars in lost workdays and related costs. All provinces and territories have legislation, often called the *Occupational Health and Safety Act,* that sets workplace standards. Under these Acts, employers must provide workers with a safe and healthy workplace, along with training in work and safety skills.

Although employees must assume some degree of risk related to work, any employee may refuse to work in unsafe conditions without fear of being fired. Employees have the duty to follow safety orders, not tamper with safety equipment, and wear prescribed safety items on the job.

In most jurisdictions, any business with 20 or more employees is required to have a joint health and safety committee. This committee is composed of representatives of both business management and employees. It must meet regularly to ensure the Act is being followed. If working conditions are unsafe, the committee can order work to stop until the situation is corrected.

Employers are also obligated to provide employees with **Workplace Hazardous Materials Information System (WHMIS)** training. This instruction teaches employees how to interpret the symbols for hazardous materials and how to handle and store them. Employees also learn how to neutralize hazardous products in case of accidents.

 activity

Visit **www.law.nelson.com** and follow the links to learn more about Workplace Hazardous Materials Information Systems and occupational health and safety issues.

A 2001 study found that one in four workplace injuries involved a young person (aged 15–29). Statistics also indicate that one in seven young workers are involved in work-related accidents.

Each province and territory has safety officers to inspect working conditions and deal with complaints. These officers can order employers to make changes in the workplace. Any business that fails to comply can be fined. Many critics, however, say the fines are often too low to be effective. In rare cases, criminal charges may be laid against employers who fail to meet and maintain safety standards.

Some jobs are considered to be harmful to the development, education, and welfare of young people. These jobs are off limits until youths reach the age of majority. For example, nowhere in Canada can youths under the age of 18 work legally in underground mining, transporting explosives, or operating X-ray equipment. The minimum age for other dangerous jobs, such as construction, window cleaning, underwater diving, and so on, differs across Canada. All labour ministries have special programs to educate students about the workplace and their rights and obligations.

Figure 19-14

In July 2000, a police officer questions young workers at an Edmonton construction site after a 14-year-old worker fell five storeys to his death. Is it legal in your province or territory for 14-year-olds to work on scaffoldings and on construction sites?

Workers' Compensation

Workers' compensation, a kind of no-fault accident insurance (see page 375) for employees, is available throughout Canada. Benefits are paid to an injured employee, regardless of who caused the accident. Under workers' compensation legislation, employers alone pay premiums into a workers' compensation fund. The amount they pay depends on the number of people employed and the industry's safety record.

Each government also establishes a workers' compensation board. If a work-related injury or illness occurs, the employee is supposed to report it to the board as soon as possible. The board then investigates the claim, at no cost to the employee. If the claim is approved, the injured employee is paid for all expenses and a percentage of his or her salary. The board will also pay for retraining, if needed.

In the past, a worker who suffered job-related injuries or illnesses had to sue the employer to get compensation. Most workers could not afford to challenge the much more powerful employers. Workers' compensation was designed to eliminate this need and to pay compensation quickly. It was also intended to spare employers from having to face frequent lawsuits and large damage settlements.

Review Your Understanding (Pages 572 to 586)

1. **What rights does the employee have if the employer breaches its common-law duties?**

2. **What rights does the employer have if the employee breaches his or her common-law duties?**

3. **How does jurisdiction over employment law differ between the federal government and the provincial and territorial governments?**

4. **What advantages are there to (a) an employer and (b) an employee of having the option of agreeing to a 60-hour workweek?**

5. How is vacation pay determined? When must it be paid?
6. Outline some of the restrictions that apply to employers hiring youths?
7. What is the goal of employment equity? To whom does it apply?
8. What is "adverse effect discrimination"? Give an example.
9. Define harassment. Describe how a poisoned work environment comes into being.
10. What is the objective of WHMIS programs?
11. Describe the advantages and disadvantages of workers' compensation to both employers and employees.

19.4 Unions

Workers in Canada fought for many years for the legal right to have unions represent them collectively (as a group) in dealings with employers. It was felt this would give employees much more power in the employer–employee relationship. Unions are legal today, and the law that applies to them in Canada is often referred to as "labour law."

Unions have benefited both employers and employees. Many businesses, for example, are too large to deal with employees individually. Instead, in a unionized workplace, the employer, or management, must negotiate with the union representatives. This process is called **collective bargaining.**

Statistics indicate that union members have indeed found strength in numbers. The employment contract that a union negotiates with an employer is known as the **collective agreement.** Its terms and conditions are usually far more favourable for employees than the statutory employment standards discussed earlier in this chapter. Increased bargaining power has translated into improved job security, wages, safety, and benefits for union members.

Looking Back   The Long Road to Collective Bargaining

In 1867, workers who tried to organize for higher wages and better working conditions could go to prison. The charge? Conspiracy. In the newly born country of Canada, employers truly were "masters." Some unions did exist, but they had little power to do much about widespread child labour, low wages, and deplorable working conditions

In 1872, the international Nine-Hour Movement aimed to replace the common 11- or 12-hour workday with a nine-hour day instead. It quickly gained support in Toronto, Montreal, and cities in the Maritimes. This was the most organized workers' protest Canada had ever seen. Union and non-union workers went on **strike** (refused to work) to force employers to meet their demands. But the economy was weak and the

powerful manufacturers easily won. Employers fired union members, and police arrested strikers and broke up picket lines. Although the workday stayed as long as it had been, the law was changed: it was no longer a criminal offence for workers to come together to try to bargain collectively.

During World War I (1914–1918), the economy was in full gear. Workers were desperately needed for industrial production. After the war, however, the employment rate plummeted. Relations between workers and employers hit all-time lows. In Winnipeg, discontent reached a breaking point. On May 15, 1919, more than 24 000 workers held a **general strike** (a strike that is joined by workers in all occupations). They demanded the right to collective bargaining,

continued ▶

and workers in 25 cities and towns across Canada held **sympathy strikes.**

Fearing a revolution, business and government leaders blamed labour leaders in Winnipeg, some of whom were immigrants. Newspapers called them "alien scum," and Parliament passed legislation so that any citizen not born in Canada could be deported. Ten union leaders were immediately arrested. On June 21, the government sent in troops and read the *Riot Act* at a demonstration. One man was killed and 30 people were injured. For the next five days, troops patrolled the streets, and then the Winnipeg General Strike was over. It was a crushing defeat for unions and collective bargaining.

Not until 1937 did unions win a major victory, when General Motors accepted collective bargaining at its Oshawa plant. Then, when the economy urgently needed workers in 1944, the federal government passed PC 1003, an order in council. Finally, the right of workers to organize was fully recognized. Employers were expected to engage in collective bargaining and negotiate with unions that had been chosen by a majority of workers.

For Discussion

1. **Summarize the significant events in the movement toward collective bargaining.**
2. **Describe the relationship between economic prosperity and the success of unions. Is this true today? Explain.**
3. **Why did many employers and governments fight so hard against unions?**

Figure 19-15

Several opponents of the Winnipeg General Strike (1919) blamed "undesirable aliens" for causing the unrest, but no labour leader was ever deported.

Union Certification

Provincial and territorial labour legislation and the *Canada Labour Code* specify what occupations can organize unions. This legislation also establishes labour relations boards. These boards control, supervise, and regulate the formation and operation of unions and help to maintain relations between unions and employers. In general, the decisions of labour tribunals are only overruled by the courts if they are found to be "patently" (obviously) unreasonable.

Unions, or union branches, can be formed either inside or outside a business. If formed inside, workers organizing the union drive try to sign up coworkers. If formed from the outside, an existing union tries to recruit workers as new members. Thus, when a new auto plant opens, an existing union may try to sign up employees and gain the right to represent them in negotiations with the employer.

To acquire the right to represent employees, the union must apply to a labour relations board for **certification** (official recognition). A union will be certified only if it has the support of the majority of employees, usually a minimum of 55 percent. The union can verify this for the board by submitting signed membership cards, by a representative vote, or both.

If an employer is just starting a business and expects to hire many more employees in the near future, the labour relations board may delay certifying a union until more employees have been hired. An outside union may also "raid" an existing union by trying to persuade members to switch membership to it instead. In this case, a new vote of the employees has to take place to decide which union will represent the workers.

Some employers may be strongly against union representation and threaten or intimidate workers to stop them from joining a union. Union organizers may also use threats or coercion to force workers to join up. In either situation, this intimidation is forbidden under labour legislation as unfair labour practice.

Union Membership in the Workplace

Labour law allows for different union-membership arrangements in a union-represented workplace. In a **closed shop,** all employees must belong to the union. In an **open shop,** not all workers have to be members of the union, but the union conducts a constant drive for membership.

Other agreements can also be written into the terms of the union contract with the employer. In a **union shop,** the employer can hire non-union members, but each employee must join the union within a certain time. In an **agency shop,** non-union workers are permitted, but they must pay union dues.

Figure 19-16

Many fast-food businesses are low paying and employ young people. Why do you think union drives by workers in this industry usually fail?

Case

Lavigne v. Ontario Public Service Employees Union

[1991] 2 S.C.R. 211
Supreme Court of Canada

Lavigne taught at a community college. Under a mandatory check-off clause in the collective agreement between the Ontario Public Service Employees Union and the Council of Regents of the college, union dues were automatically taken off his pay. This was authorized by the *Colleges Collective Bargaining Act.* Lavigne, however, objected to some of the union's expenditures, such as contributions to the New Democratic Party and disarmament campaigns. He went to court to stop the deductions.

The trial judge ruled that the *Colleges Collective Bargaining Act* and the collective agreement were of no force and effect because they forced Lavigne to pay union dues for purposes not directly related to collective bargaining. The judge ruled Lavigne's

freedom of association, guaranteed by section 2(d) of the *Canadian Charter of Rights and Freedoms,* was infringed. Furthermore, this was not justified under section 1 of the *Charter.*

The Ontario Court of Appeal reversed the judgment, ruling that the union's use of dues was a private activity by a private organization. Thus, the *Charter* did not apply. It also ruled that there was no infringement of Lavigne's freedom of association, since he was free to associate with others and to oppose the union.

Lavigne appealed to the Supreme Court of Canada. In its ruling, the Supreme Court of Canada agreed with the trial judge that Lavigne's freedom of association was violated, but found that the violation of association was justified under section 1 of the *Charter.* The Court also ruled that paying union dues was not a private activity. The appeal was dismissed.

continued ▶

activity

Visit **www.law.nelson.com** and follow the links to learn about the Canadian Labour Congress, an organization affiliated with over 2 million unionized workers in Canada.

Did You Know?

In December 2001, in an 8 to 1 decision, the Supreme Court of Canada struck down a section of Ontario's labour law banning collective bargaining in the farming industry as a breach of the *Charter*'s freedom of association.

Union members do not have to be actively involved in their union, but they do have to pay dues and follow union rules. Members elect the union executive, which plans union activities. The executive's main responsibility is to prepare the union's negotiation position in collective bargaining. Many unions also develop programs to help members grow in professional and personal skills. The general membership is only asked to vote on important issues, such as the acceptance of a contract offer made by the employer.

If the business is large enough, union members elect a **shop steward** to represent them in each department or division. Any union member who wants the union to take action on a work-related complaint must take the complaint to the shop steward, who then takes the complaint to the union executive. If it decides to take action, it notifies the employer that it has a **grievance.** The union is responsible to negotiate and mediate the grievance with the employer and to "fairly represent" the union member. If this fails to resolve the complaint, the union may take the grievance through the arbitration process, which is clearly laid out in the collective agreement.

Collective Bargaining

A union's main purpose is to represent members in collective bargaining with the employer. A union has the right to represent employees exclusively. In return, members expect their union to win them favourable contract terms—including wages, benefits, cost-of-living allowances, vacations, work hours, training, grievance procedures, dismissal, and working conditions.

A recently certified union usually gives the employer written notice of its desire to negotiate its first collective agreement. The union and employer must then meet within a specified time. As negotiations begin, the union presents the employer with the package of terms that it would like in the collective agreement. The employer studies the terms, discusses them with union negotiators, and then makes an offer. Union negotiators may have the right to accept or reject the employer's offer, but they usually have the union executive consider it.

If the executive thinks the offer may be acceptable, it will present it to the membership for a vote. The executive may send the offer to members for a vote even if it knows it will be overwhelmingly rejected. This may show the employer the extent of worker solidarity—that employees are united in their position.

As negotiations go back and forth, statements can become harsh and confrontational. Both sides, however, must **bargain in good faith** (genuinely work toward an agreement). If either side hides information or refuses to discuss certain matters, the other party can complain to the labour relations board. If the board finds the party guilty of unfair labour practices, it will be penalized.

Mediation and Arbitration

Labour legislation strictly lays out the procedures for collective bargaining. If the parties cannot reach an agreement on their own, they may have to seek alternative dispute resolution (ADR), which was discussed in Chapters 1 and 11. In this situation, the labour relations board appoints a mediator.

If a labour dispute involves workers who provide essential services to the public, the government may impose a mediator. The mediator will prepare recommendations, which are often made public. This may put pressure on the parties to reach an agreement. The government can also set up a formal mediation board that has the power to summon witnesses and investigate the employer's business situation. A dispute over how much money an employer can afford to pay employees, for example, could result in the company's books being examined.

If both sides reject the mediator's report, the parties can request that an arbitrator be appointed. The parties may have to agree in advance to **binding arbitration,** which means that the arbitrator's decision will be final. Binding arbitration is avoided, if possible, because it means a neutral party determines the terms of the contract. This may leave conflicts between the employer and union members unresolved, only to break out at a later date.

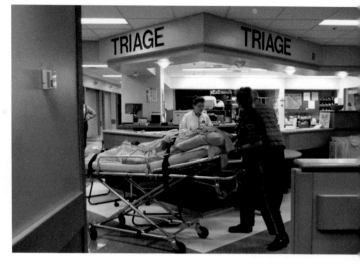

Figure 19-17

In parts of Canada, nurses and doctors have gone on strike as governments cut hospital budgets. How would you classify their services?

Case

United Steel Workers of America v. Checkmate Cabs Ltd.

(1997-05-21) Docket A970174
British Columbia Supreme Court

The United Steel Workers of America, Local Union No. 500, was the certified union of the employees of Checkmate Cabs Ltd. During contract negotiations, a mediator was appointed. His recommendations were published and accepted by the union but rejected by the employer. Arbitration followed, and the arbitrator adopted all the mediator's recommendations. A collective agreement was then made by the union and forwarded to Checkmate Cabs Ltd., which refused to sign.

The union applied to the labour relations board for an order declaring that the collective agreement was in full force. The board agreed and filed its decision with the court registry. This effectively made the board's decision an order of the Supreme Court of British Columbia. The employer still did not implement the collective agreement.

The union filed an application with the British Columbia Supreme Court asking it to declare Checkmate in contempt of court. The union indicated that Checkmate denied the existence of the agreement and had not carried out many of its requirements. Comments made by management indicated that Checkmate had no intention of carrying out the terms of the agreement.

continued

Figure 19-18

The employer would not honour the union's collective agreement. What could the labour relations board do to make it comply?

The court agreed with the union and found the employer, Checkmate Cabs Ltd., in contempt of court. It was given an opportunity to implement the agreement or face a penalty.

For Discussion

1. **What steps were followed to reach a collective agreement?**

2. **Why was the employer found to be in contempt of court?**

3. **What are the advantages and disadvantages to having a mediator and arbitrator recommend terms for the collective agreement?**

4. **The employer argued that the bargaining process and the collective agreement were unfair. What action could it have taken instead of ignoring the arbitrator's decision?**

5. **What power did the labour relations board have in mediating the dispute?**

Strikes

A strike is the ultimate weapon a union can use, but it is usually only legal after negotiations have failed. Tensions may be so high, however, that union members will walk out in a **wildcat strike** before being in a legal striking position. Wildcat strikes are rare because employees who take this extreme job action have breached the contract and can be dismissed. Courts can also issue injunctions to prohibit wildcat strikes.

Once a union can legally strike, it may set up picket lines outside the workplace to make its position known to the public. Sympathetic members of the public sometimes show their support through a **boycott**—not buying or using the business's goods or services. A striking union counts on other unions not to cross the picket line to do work or business with the employer. Other unions may also join the picket line or show solidarity by holding a sympathy strike. In some provinces, employers can hire replacement workers. Such workers are often called "scabs," and the employer may have trouble finding people who are willing to cross a picket line.

During a strike, employees are still legally employees, even though the business is not paying them. Occasionally, a worker may break the strike and cross the picket line. The union will normally discipline such workers, usually through fines or by cancelling union memberships. Many unions have strike funds or borrow money so that striking members can be paid something.

Picketing must be lawful and peaceful. Picketers can try to persuade people not to enter or do business with the employer, but they cannot use force, block roadways, or commit libel on the placards they carry. Section 423 of the *Criminal Code* prohibits strikers from using violence to intimidate or prevent a person from doing anything that he or she has a lawful right to do in the workplace. In *Harrison v. Carswell* (1976), the Supreme Court of Canada ruled that employees may have the right to strike, but they may not picket on private property if the owner asks them to leave.

Employees may also **work to rule.** This is a limited kind of strike or job action in which employees do their work, but they follow regulations so exactly and so thoroughly that work is slowed down. During labour disputes in Alberta and Ontario, for example, nurses worked to rule by taking all the breaks they were entitled to and refusing to work extra shifts and overtime. Teachers have also worked to rule by not participating in extracurricular activities.

An employer who believes that a strike is illegal, damaging to property, or dangerous to the public, can seek an injunction that requires the workers to return to work or to refrain from illegal picketing activity. Similarly, the government can pass legislation to force employees back to work while the contract is under dispute. Such legislation may include mandatory negotiations, mediation, or arbitration.

Lockout

The employer's ultimate weapon is the **lockout.** As the name suggests, this means that the employer refuses to let all or certain employees into the workplace while the contract is in dispute. As with a strike, this action may be used legally only after a given period of time after negotiations have failed. Lockouts are unusual, however. It is usually in the employer's financial interest to keep the business operating if employees are willing to work.

Figure 19-19

Negotiations between the CBC and the technicians' union broke down with a lockout in December 2001.

Collective Agreement

Once the union and the employer have come to a tentative agreement, the union membership votes on the package. Usually, only a simple majority is required for the package to become the collective agreement (formal contract).

Once the agreement (contract) is in force, there still may be many occasions in which one side feels that the other party is not fulfilling its obligations. In this case, the two sides meet and try to resolve the matter; if unresolved, it is referred to arbitration.

Review Your Understanding (Pages 587 to 593)

1. What is the goal of a union?
2. Describe the function of a labour relations board.
3. Describe briefly the steps that a union must follow to become certified. What is the significance of being certified?
4. Name and describe the various types of union "shops."
5. Describe each step in the collective bargaining process.
6. What is a grievance? What steps are followed to resolve a grievance?
7. Describe the rights of striking workers.

Did You Know?

Federal civil servants form one of the largest employee groups in Canada. The *Public Service Staff Relations Act* entitles them to collective bargaining and to strike, in most cases, even if their services— such as air-traffic control—are considered essential.

19.5 Independent Contractors

Businesses and individuals often hire independent contractors to provide work or services. Independent contractors may be hired to do anything from cutting grass, to installing a new kitchen or walkway, to editing a textbook or programming a Web site. As the word "independent" indicates, independent contractors are in business for themselves. They are not in an employer–employee relationship with the clients who hire them. This fact has important implications in tax law, tort law, and labour law.

In the new economy that emerged in the late 1970s and early 1980s, many businesses downsized. Whole departments of employees could suddenly be dismissed. The same businesses later hired back many of these people, but as independent contractors rather than employees. In this way, businesses do not have to pay Canada Pension Plan, employment insurance, or other employee benefits. This can cut a business's wage and benefit costs by up to 20 percent. As well, anyone who hires an independent contractor is not liable for injuries suffered by the contractor, or by a contractor's employees, while the contract is being carried out.

There are also advantages to being an independent contractor. First of all, independent contractors can control their own work and be their own bosses. They can take whatever profits they make, but they must also take any losses they incur.

Independent contractors often supply their own tools. They are also usually responsible to pay for both the materials and the costs of hiring any employees who might be needed to complete contracts. An independent contractor who hires employees takes on full employer responsibilities and should be fully aware of employment law.

Normally, an independent contractor cannot be held liable for third-party damages arising from his or her wrongdoing. For example, Hanuf's retaining wall was poorly installed and shifted. Gabriella trips over it and breaks her leg. To get damages, she would sue the property owner, not Hanuf. That is why property owners carry liability insurance. The owner could then take action against Hanuf.

If responsibility for the safety of the work is covered by statute, however, the independent contractor may be held liable. This is exemplified in *Lewis (Guardian* ad litem *of) v. British Columbia* (see Case, page 595).

Self-Employment

Independent contractors are also described as being self-employed. The number of self-employed people has grown dramatically in Canada as technology and the economy have changed. From 1976 to 1995, for example, the number of self-employed people almost doubled, while employment itself grew only by 40 percent.

Self-employment has grown not only as businesses downsize, but also as they adopt hiring policies to try to keep the number of full-time employees to a minimum.

Case

Lewis (*Guardian* ad litem *of*) v. British Columbia

[1997] 3 S.C.R. 1145
Supreme Court of Canada

The British Columbia Ministry of Transport and Highways hired Cerka Contract Management Ltd. to remove rocks from a cliff facing a highway. In the words of a former Cerka employee, two rocks still "stuck out like a sore thumb" after the job was completed. One of those rocks fell later, killing Robert Holt as he drove along the highway.

At trial, Cerka was found to be negligent for leaving the rocks protruding. The Ministry of Transport contended that Cerka, as the independent contractor, was liable for the negligence. According to British Columbia's *Highway Act* and *Ministry of Transportation and Highways Act*, the ministry had a duty to maintain highways "reasonably." The trial judge ruled that the ministry was liable for Cerka's negligence.

The British Columbia Court of Appeal reversed that decision and ordered a new trial. The Supreme Court of Canada, on appeal by Holt's family, reinstated the trial judge's decision.

The key issues in the case were as follows:
1. Did the Ministry of Transport owe Holt, and other drivers, a "duty to use reasonable care" in maintaining the highway? Should it have been able to anticipate that any carelessness would likely cause injury or damage to Holt?
2. If the legislature entrusts the ministry to carry out highway maintenance and it then delegates the task to an independent contractor, can the ministry be found liable?

For Discussion

1. **What characteristics determine that one is an independent contractor?**

2. **What evidence was there that the ministry was responsible for maintaining highways?**

3. **Do you agree with the Supreme Court that the ministry was liable for the independent contractor's negligence? Explain.**

4. **Are the highways in your province or territory maintained by the ministry itself or through independent contractors?**

In some cases, a question will be raised: Is the worker really self-employed, or is he or she actually employed by the client? The Canada Customs and Revenue Agency is very interested in which status a worker has because a self-employed person can write off many more expenses than an employee. In other situations, an independent contractor may claim that he or she is actually an employee of a client. If this were proven to be the case, the "client" would have to pay all the related expenses, from employment insurance and workers' compensation premiums to benefits. According to various court decisions, the worker is an employee if he or she
- does not own the tools or equipment required for the work
- does not control decisions about how and when to work
- has been hired for a long term, rather than for specific tasks
- is not responsible for losses or cannot keep profits

Did You Know?

In 1976, 8.6 percent of employed women and 14.3 percent of employed men were self-employed. By 2000, the figures had grown to 12 percent for women and 19 percent for men.

Review Your Understanding (Pages 594 to 595)

1. **Why would a person want to be an independent contractor instead of an employee?**
2. **Why do many businesses prefer to hire independent contractors instead of employees?**
3. **What are the advantages and disadvantages of being self-employed?**

CAREERS

Figure 19-20
Lawyer

Figure 19-21
Employee relations specialist (right)

In Contract Law

Negotiating agreements or contracts is a demanding career. This field of work requires men and women who are logical, self-confident, persuasive, and tactful. They should be good speakers who can think "on their feet" and remain focused on the goal in a highly charged situation. Lawyers and employee relations specialists often specialize in this area, and may require the services of paralegals.

ⓔ Visit www.law.nelson.com and follow the links to compare the requirements for gaining admission to three Canadian law schools.

In Focus

Lawyer

Lawyers may establish their own practice, work for a law firm, act as the legal advisor for a major business or public institution, or work as a Crown prosecutor. They advise their clients of their legal rights and duties, and assist in drawing up legal documents such as contracts, land titles, separation and divorce papers, and wills. They also plead cases before courts of law, tribunals, or administrative boards, and assist in negotiating out-of-court settlements. Crown prosecutors act for society in court proceedings.

Employee Relations Specialist

Employee relations specialists develop policies and programs on personnel and labour relations. They negotiate collective agreements on behalf of employers and advise them on the interpretation of these agreements. They may administer employment equity programs and investigate harassment complaints. They represent employers in hearings called to resolve disputes between employers and employees involving collective agreements.

Paralegal

Paralegals are legal assistants who usually work for a private law firm. They prepare and proofread legal documents and maintain client files. As paralegals gain experience, they may conduct research into court records and files and judgments handed down in previous cases. Paralegals may conduct some of their work away from the office, at law libraries and land titles offices.

Career Exploration Activity

As a class, explore career opportunities in contract law. The information you compile can be included with the material you have gathered from the other career profiles to complete your career bulletin-board displays or to use in a law-related career fair.

1. Contact a lawyer, employee relations specialist, or paralegal and arrange for an opportunity to job-shadow the individual.

2. Interview the individual and outline the role and responsibilities for the position. Highlight any skills needed for this career. Use this opportunity to learn about the general operation of a law office or the function of a human resources department in a business. Share your information with the class.

Chapter Review

Chapter Highlights

- The employment relationship of employer and employee is distinct from the relationship between an independent contractor and a client.
- Common law, statute law, and the employment contract govern the employer–employee relationship.
- Statute law sets minimum standards for employers and employees.
- Common law prescribes the basic duties of the employer and employees.
- Employment law can be federal as well as provincial or territorial.
- Employment legislation sets standards for minimum wages, work hours, overtime and vacation pay, leaves of absence, and rules for termination and dismissal.
- Pay equity is meant to equalize men's and women's wages.
- Employment equity works to increase hiring rates for groups that have historically been discriminated against.
- The prohibited grounds of discrimination listed in human rights legislation apply to the workplace.
- Harassment consists of annoying comment or conduct that is known, or ought to be known, to be unwelcome.
- Employees working with hazardous materials must take WHMIS training.
- Labour relations boards regulate employer–union disputes.
- In collective bargaining, a union negotiates with an employer to get the best contract for all its members.
- If an employer and union cannot reach a contract agreement, mediation, arbitration and binding arbitration may result.
- When collective bargaining fails, the employer's ultimate action is to lock out the employees; the union's ultimate action is to strike.

Review Key Terms

Name the key terms that are described below.

a) a contract settlement imposed by a neutral third party that must be accepted by both parties

b) a workplace in which an employer can hire non-union members, but new employees must join the union within a specified time

c) a strike that is not legal according to the terms of the contract

d) negotiations carried out by the union on behalf of all its members

e) people who are hired, but who control their own work, own their own tools, and can either make a profit or take a loss

f) the employment contract that a union negotiates with an employer

g) an opportunity for an employee to take a period of time off work without being fired

h) having been fired without reasonable notice or just cause

i) the employer is the master and the employee is the servant

j) a job action in which employees follow job descriptions so thoroughly they slow down work

k) the formal process of becoming recognized as a union

l) workplace that hires non-union workers who must still pay union dues

m) an employee who is the department representative of the union and to whom members take complaints

n) employer action that prevents employees from entering the workplace

o) genuinely work toward an agreement

Check Your Knowledge

1. Distinguish between an employer–employee relationship and that of an independent contractor.

2. Identify and briefly explain the various types of laws that affect the employer–employee relationship.

3. When hiring an employee, what considerations should an employer be aware of concerning discrimination?

4. Summarize all the steps that might be followed from the time that a union is certified until it has successfully negotiated its first contract with the employer.

Apply Your Learning

5. *Osmond v. Newfoundland (Workers' Compensation Commission)* (2001), 200 Nfld. & P.E.I.R. 202 (Newfoundland Court of Appeal)

   Edwina Osmond injured her back in 1987 while lifting cases to stock shelves for the

Newfoundland Liquor Corporation. She sought medical attention and reported it to the Workers' Compensation Commission. She was eventually operated on. In 1990, her doctor indicated she could return to work, as long as she did no severe lifting and bending. Osmond started an ease-back program designed by the Workers' Compensation Commission.

Eventually, Osmond was required to stock shelves and unload trucks. Osmond's doctor wrote the commission stating that the lifting was an unreasonable demand. Osmond's supervisor then complained to the commission: he was not pleased with Osmond's progress, and he noted that 30 percent of her job involved heavy lifting. Osmond suffered chronic back pain and became depressed. The commission's doctor recommended that she be retrained for alternative work. The doctor later recommended that she was not capable of modified work and not retrainable for anything.

The commission decided to cut off Osmond's benefits, relying on her doctor's comments in 1990. It ruled the medical evidence did not reveal total disablement, and that Osmond should be able to train as a secretary or stenographer. Osmond did not want to train for these jobs because they required her to sit for extended periods of time. Osmond's appeals to the Workers' Compensation Appeal Tribunal and the Trial Division of the Supreme Court of Newfoundland failed. She then appealed to the Appeals Division of the Supreme Court of Newfoundland.

a) Decisions of the Workers' Compensation Tribunal can only be overruled by the Trial Division and the Appeals Division of the Supreme Court of Newfoundland if they are found to be "patently unreasonable." What does that mean?

b) What evidence is there that Osmond (1) could train for another occupation or (2) would not be able to work at another occupation?

c) Should Osmond's appeal to the Newfoundland Court of Appeal succeed? Why?

6. *Martin v. Canada (Dept. of National Defence)* (1992), 17 C.H.R.R. D/435 (Canadian Human Rights Tribunal)

Martin and nine other complainants alleged that the Canadian Armed Forces' (CAF) compulsory retirement age of 55 discriminated on the basis of age. The CAF conceded this point to the Canadian Human Rights Tribunal but justified the policy on the basis that it was needed for the health of the organization and as a bona fide occupational requirement.

The CAF indicated that, for organizational reasons, mandatory retirement was needed so that the junior ranks could have an opportunity of advancement. The tribunal noted that because of the good pension, most members would retire after 35 years of service, even if they were allowed to continue, and for most that would be by the age of 55.

The CAF indicated the policy was needed for safety reasons and to make sure that members were fit for service. The tribunal noted that those who failed fitness tests were usually given positions requiring a lower fitness level. The CAF indicated that its members might be put in a position of jeopardy if members had medical problems, such as heart attacks. The tribunal concluded that through assessment and testing, it was possible to predict or at least rule out the likelihood of an individual having some of these medical problems.

a) What evidence did the Canadian Armed Forces use to indicate that the age requirement was valid?

b) What counterarguments did the tribunal note for each of the arguments presented by the CAF?

c) Was the mandatory retirement age of 55 discriminatory? Why?

7. *Re St. Paul's Hospital and Hospital Employees' Union* (1995), 47 L.A.C. (4th) 423 (British Columbia)

A nurse filed a grievance following her dismissal from St. Paul's Hospital. She had been employed there for 12 years. For the last five years, she had an unacceptable record of absenteeism, possibly due to personal problems. She was a single mother with a difficult son and was having problems in her common-law relationship.

Just prior to her dismissal, the nurse's relationship ended, her mother became ill, and numerous family members and friends died. After being dismissed, she voluntarily sought treatment for alcohol and drug addiction, which she had previously denied. Her son also moved out.

The employer held that the nurse did not deserve another chance. She had not disclosed her drug and alcohol dependency to the head nurse, who had consistently offered assistance. The union indicated at the hearing that it was too soon to say whether the nurse had been rehabilitated. She promised to attend work when scheduled, if reinstated.

a) What rights under common law does the employer have in this case?

b) What lengths must the hospital go to in order to keep the nurse on the job?

c) Explain why you would or would not give the nurse her job back.

Communicate Your Understanding

8. This chapter has been written in general terms to cover all of Canada. Using the Internet, select a specific piece of legislation affecting employment law in your province or territory (i.e., labour relations, employment standards, or human rights legislation). Prepare a brief report outlining two distinct aspects of the specific legislation and explain how it relates to employment law in your province or territory. Present your findings to the class.

9. The right to strike for workers in so-called "essential services" is a controversial issue. Brainstorm in groups of four to decide whether the following occupations should have the right to strike. Present your results to the rest of the class, and try to come to a consensus.

a) firefighters   d) police officers
b) nurses   e) doctors
c) garbage collectors f) military personnel

10. Using the Internet or other resources, research one of the following topics as it relates to Canadian employees:

a) Employment Insurance
b) Workers' Compensation
c) occupational health and safety
d) employment equity
e) pay equity
f) discrimination

Prepare a summary of your information. Share the information with others in the class who have selected the same topic. Come to a consensus on the important aspects of your research. Hold an employment law information session on each topic and present your results to the class. Include a summary of the current legislation and an explanation of how it specifically relates to Canadian employees.

Develop Your Thinking

11. The monitoring of computers in the workplace is increasing. Software can record what is on an employee's monitor every few seconds, along with all e-mails, visited Web sites, and chat-room conversations.

a) Should employers be allowed to monitor employees' computers at work? Why?

b) Imagine you are an employer. Develop guidelines for computer use by your employees. Include penalties that will be imposed for workers who violate the guidelines.

12. Find an employment advertisement that interests you. Imagine you are the employer interviewing applicants for the job. Prepare a list of 10 questions that you would ask. With a partner, examine your questions to determine if any are discriminatory. Using the Internet and other resources, research information on how to conduct job interviews. Create a series of guidelines to be followed by employers to ensure that the interview process is not discriminatory.

Appendix A

Constitution Act, 1982
Schedule B
Part I

CANADIAN CHARTER OF RIGHTS AND FREEDOMS

Whereas Canada is founded upon principles that recognize the supremacy of God and the rule of law:

Guarantee of Rights and Freedoms

Rights and Freedoms in Canada

1. The *Canadian Charter of Rights and Freedoms* guarantees the rights and freedoms set out in it subject only to such reasonable limits prescribed by law as can be demonstrably justified in a free and democratic society.

Fundamental freedoms

Fundamental Freedoms

2. Everyone has the following fundamental freedoms:

(a) freedom of conscience and religion;

(b) freedom of thought, belief, opinion and expression, including freedom of the press and other media of communication;

(c) freedom of peaceful assembly; and

(d) freedom of association.

Democratic Rights

Democratic Rights of Citizens

3. Every citizen of Canada has the right to vote in an election of members of the House of Commons or of a legislative assembly and to be qualified for membership therein.

Maximum Duration of Legislative Bodies

4. (1) No House of Commons and no legislative assembly shall continue for longer than five years from the date fixed for the return of the writs at a general election of its members.

Continuation in Special Circumstances

(2) In time of real or apprehended war, invasion or insurrection, a House of Commons may be continued by Parliament and a legislative assembly may be continued by the legislature beyond five years if such continuation is not opposed by the votes of more than one-third of the members of the House of Commons or the legislative assembly, as the case may be.

Annual Sitting of Legislative Bodies

5. There shall be a sitting of Parliament and of each legislature at least once every twelve months.

Mobility Rights

Mobility of Citizens

6. (1) Every citizen of Canada has the right to enter, remain in and leave Canada.

Rights to Move and Gain Livelihood

(2) Every citizen of Canada and every person who has the status of a permanent resident of Canada has the right

(a) to move and take up residence in any province; and

(b) to pursue the gaining of a livelihood in any province.

Limitation

(3) The rights specified in subsection (2) are subject to

(a) any laws or practices of general application in force in a province other than those that discriminate among persons primarily on the basis of province of present or previous residence; and

(b) any laws providing for reasonable residency requirements as a qualification for the receipt of publicly provided social services.

Affirmative Action Programs

(4) Subsections (2) and (3) do not preclude any law, program or activity that has as its object the amelioration in a province of conditions of individuals in that province who are socially or economically disadvantaged if the rate of employment in that province is below the rate of employment in Canada.

Life, Liberty and Security of Person

7. Everyone has the right to life, liberty and security of the person and the right not to be deprived thereof except in accordance with the principles of fundamental justice.

Search or Seizure

8. Everyone has the right to be secure against unreasonable search or seizure.

Detention or Imprisonment

9. Everyone has the right not to be arbitrarily detained or imprisoned.

Arrest or Detention

10. Everyone has the right on arrest or detention

(a) to be informed promptly of the reasons therefor;

(b) to retain and instruct counsel without delay and to be informed of that right; and

(c) to have the validity of the detention determined by way of habeas corpus and to be released if the detention is not lawful.

Proceedings in Criminal and Penal Matters

11. Any person charged with an offence has the right

(a) to be informed without unreasonable delay of the specific offence;

(b) to be tried within a reasonable time;

(c) not to be compelled to be a witness in proceedings against that person in respect of the offence;

(d) to be presumed innocent until proven guilty according to law in a fair and public hearing by an independent and impartial tribunal;

(e) not to be denied reasonable bail without just cause;

(f) except in the case of an offence under military law tried before a military tribunal, to the benefit of trial by jury where the maximum punishment for the offence is imprisonment for five years or a more severe punishment;

(g) not to be found guilty on account of any act or omission unless, at the time of the act or omission, it constituted an offence under Canadian or international law or was criminal according to the general principles of law recognized by the community of nations;

(h) if finally acquitted of the offence, not to be tried for it again and, if finally found guilty and punished for the offence, not to be tried or punished for it again; and

(i) if found guilty of the offence and if the punishment for the offence has been varied between the time of commission and the time of sentencing, to the benefit of the lesser punishment.

Treatment or Punishment

12. Everyone has the right not to be subjected to any cruel and unusual treatment or punishment.

Self-Crimination

13. A witness who testifies in any proceedings has the right not to have any incriminating evidence so given used to incriminate that witness in any other proceedings, except in a prosecution for perjury or for the giving of contradictory evidence.

Interpreter

14. A party or witness in any proceedings who does not understand or speak the language in which the proceedings are conducted or who is deaf has the right to the assistance of an interpreter.

Equality Rights

Equality Before and Under Law and Equal Protection and Benefit of Law

15. (1) Every individual is equal before and under the law and has the right to the equal protection and equal benefit of the law without discrimination and, in particular, without discrimination based on race, national or ethnic origin, colour, religion, sex, age or mental or physical disability.

Affirmative Action Programs

(2) Subsection (1) does not preclude any law, program or activity that has as its object the amelioration of conditions of disadvantaged individuals or groups including those that are disadvantaged because of race, national or ethnic origin, colour, religion, sex, age or mental or physical disability.

Official Languages of Canada

Official Languages of Canada

16. (1) English and French are the official languages of Canada and have equality of status and equal rights and privileges as to their use in all institutions of the Parliament and government of Canada.

Official Languages of New Brunswick

(2) English and French are the official languages of New Brunswick and have equality of status and equal rights and privileges as to their use in all institutions of the legislature and government of New Brunswick.

Advancement of Status and Use

(3) Nothing in this Charter limits the authority of Parliament or a

Proceedings of Parliament

17. (1) Everyone has the right to use English or French in any debates and other proceedings of Parliament.

Proceedings of New Brunswick Legislature

(2) Everyone has the right to use English or French in any debates and other proceedings of the legislature of New Brunswick.

Parliamentary Statutes and Records

18. (1) The statutes, records and journals of Parliament shall be printed and published in English and French and both language versions are equally authoritative.

New Brunswick Statutes and Records

(2) The statutes, records and journals of the legislature of New Brunswick shall be printed and published in English and French and both language versions are equally authoritative.

Proceedings in Courts Established by Parliament

19. (1) Either English or French may be used by any person in, or in any pleading in or process issuing from, any court established by Parliament.

Proceedings in New Brunswick Courts

(2) Either English or French may be used by any person in, or in any pleading in or process issuing from, any court of New Brunswick.

Communications by Public with Federal Institutions

20. (1) Any member of the public in Canada has the right to communicate with, and to receive available services from, any head or central office of an institution of the Parliament or government of Canada in English or French, and has the same right with respect to any other office of any such institution where
(a) there is a significant demand for communications with and services from that office in such language; or
(b) due to the nature of the office, it is reasonable that communications with and services from that office be available in both English and French.

Communications by Public with New Brunswick Institutions

(2) Any member of the public in New Brunswick has the right to communicate with, and to receive available services from, any office of an institution of the legislature or government of New Brunswick in English or French.

Continuation of Existing Constitutional Provisions

21. Nothing in sections 16 to 20 abrogates or derogates from any right, privilege or obligation with respect to the English or French languages, or either of them, that exists or is con-

legislature to advance the equality of status or use of English and French.

tinued by virtue of any other provision of the Constitution of Canada.

22. Nothing in sections 16 to 20 abrogates or derogates from any legal or customary right or privilege acquired or enjoyed either before or after the coming into force of this Charter with respect to any language that is not English or French.

Rights and Privileges Preserved

Minority Language Educational Rights

23. (1) Citizens of Canada
(a) whose first language learned and still understood is that of the English or French linguistic minority population of the province in which they reside, or
(b) who have received their primary school instruction in Canada in English or French and reside in a province where the language in which they received that instruction is the language of the English or French linguistic minority population of the province, have the right to have their children receive primary and secondary school instruction in that language in that province.

Language of Instruction

(2) Citizens of Canada of whom any child has received or is receiving primary or secondary school instruction in English or French in Canada, have the right to have all their children receive primary and secondary school instruction in the same language.

Continuity of Language Instruction

(3) The right of citizens of Canada under subsections (1) and (2) to have their children receive primary and secondary school instruction in the language of the English or French linguistic minority population of a province
(a) applies wherever in the province the number of children of citizens who have such a right is sufficient to warrant the provision to them out of public funds of minority language instruction; and
(b) includes, where the number of those children so warrants, the right to have them receive that instruction in minority language educational facilities provided out of public funds.

Application Where Numbers Warrant

Enforcement

Enforcement of Guaranteed Rights and Freedoms

24. (1) Anyone whose rights or freedoms, as guaranteed by this Charter, have been infringed or denied may apply to a court of competent jurisdiction to obtain such remedy as the court considers appropriate and just in the circumstances.

Exclusion of Evidence Bringing Administration of Justice into Disrepute

(2) Where, in proceedings under subsection (1), a court concludes that evidence was obtained in a manner that infringed or denied any rights or freedoms guaranteed by this Charter, the evidence shall be excluded if it is established that, having regard to all the circumstances, the admission of it in the proceedings would bring the administration of justice into disrepute.

General

Aboriginal Rights and Freedoms not Affected by Charter

25. The guarantee in this Charter of certain rights and freedoms shall not be construed so as to abrogate or derogate from any aboriginal treaty or other rights or freedoms that pertain to the aboriginal peoples of Canada including
(a) any rights or freedoms that have been recognized by the Royal Proclamation of October 7, 1763; and
(b) any rights or freedoms that now exist by way of land claims agreements or may be so acquired.

Other Rights and Freedoms not Affected by Charter

26. The guarantee in this Charter of certain rights and freedoms shall not be construed as denying the existence of any other rights or freedoms that exist in Canada.

Multicultural Heritage

27. This Charter shall be interpreted in a manner consistent with the preservation and enhancement of the multicultural heritage of Canadians.

Rights Guaranteed Equally to Both Sexes

28. Notwithstanding anything in this Charter, the rights and freedoms referred to in it are guaranteed equally to male and female persons.

Rights Respecting Certain Schools Preserved

29. Nothing in this Charter abrogates or derogates from any rights or privileges guaranteed by or under the Constitution of Canada in respect of denominational, separate or dissentient schools.

30. A reference in this Charter to a province or to the legislative assembly or legislature of a province shall be deemed to include a reference to the Yukon Territory and the Northwest Territories, or to the appropriate legislative authority thereof, as the case may be.

Application to Territories and Territorial Authorities

31. Nothing in this Charter extends the legislative powers of any body or authority.

Legislative Powers not Extended

Application of Charter

32. (1) This Charter applies
(a) to the Parliament and government of Canada in respect of all matters within the authority of Parliament including all matters relating to the Yukon Territory and Northwest Territories; and
(b) to the legislature and government of each province in respect of all matters within the authority of the legislature of each province.

Application of Charter

(2) Notwithstanding subsection (1), section 15 shall not have effect until three years after this section comes into force.

Exception

33. (1) Parliament or the legislature of a province may expressly declare in an Act of Parliament or of the legislature, as the case may be, that the Act or a provision thereof shall operate notwithstanding a provision included in section 2 or sections 7 to 15 of this Charter.

Exception Where Express Declaration

(2) An Act or a provision of an Act in respect of which a declaration made under this section is in effect shall have such operation as it would have but for the provision of this Charter referred to in the declaration.

Operation of Exception

(3) A declaration made under subsection (1) shall cease to have effect five years after it comes into force or on such earlier date as may be specified in the declaration.

Five Year Limitation

(4) Parliament or a legislature of a province may re-enact a declaration made under subsection (1).

Re-enactment

(5) Subsection (3) applies in respect of a re-enactment made under subsection (4).

Five Year Limitation

Citation

34. This Part may be cited as the *Canadian Charter of Rights and Freedoms.*

Citation

Appendix B: Citation References

The information below provides the full names of the sources listed in abbreviated form in **Appendix C: Table of Cases.**

Courts

B.C.S.C.	British Columbia Supreme Court
C.A.	Court of Appeal
C.S. Qué.	Quebec Superior Court
Civ. Div.	Civil Division
Co. Ct.	County Court
Fam. Div.	Family Division
H.C.	High Court of Ontario [now Ontario Superior Court of Justice]
H.L.	House of Lords [England]
K.B.	Court of King's Bench
N.B.Q.B.T.D.	New Brunswick Court of Queen's Bench, Trial Division
N.S.S.C.	Nova Scotia Supreme Court
Nfld. S.C.T.D.	Newfoundland Supreme Court, Trial Division
Ont. Gen. Div.	Ontario General Division [now Ontario Superior Court of Justice]
Ont. S.C.J.	Ontario Superior Court of Justice
P.E.I.S.C.T.D.	Prince Edward Island Supreme Court, Trial Division
Prov. Ct.	Provincial Court
Q.B.	Court of Queen's Bench
S.C.C.	Supreme Court of Canada
T.D.	Trial Division
Unif. Fam. Ct.	Unified Family Court
Youth Div.	Youth Division

Jurisdictions

Alta.	Alberta
B.C.	British Columbia
Eng.	England
Man.	Manitoba
N.B.	New Brunswick
Nfld.	Newfoundland
N.S.	Nova Scotia
N.W.T.	Northwest Territories
Ont.	Ontario
P.E.I.	Prince Edward Island
Que.	Quebec
Sask.	Saskatchewan

Neutral Cites (Electronic)

ABPC	Alberta Provincial Court
ABQB	Alberta Court of Queen's Bench
BCCA	British Columbia Court of Appeal
BCPC	British Columbia Provincial Court
BCSC	British Columbia Supreme Court
ONCA	Ontario Court of Appeal
SCC	Supreme Court of Canada

Reporters

A.C.	*Law Reports, Appeal Cases* [England]
A.P.R.	*Atlantic Provinces Reports*
A.R.	*Alberta Reports*
Alta. L.R.	*Alberta Law Reports*
B.C.A.C.	*British Columbia Appeal Cases*
B.C.L.R.	*British Columbia Law Reports*
B.C.W.L.D.	*British Columbia Weekly Law Digest*
C.C.C.	*Canadian Criminal Cases*
C.C.L.T.	*Canadian Cases on the Law of Torts*
C.H.R.R.	*Canadian Human Rights Reporter*
C.L.R.	*Construction Law Reports*
C.N.L.R.	*Canadian Native Law Reporter*
C.R.	*Criminal Reports*
C.R.R.	*Canadian Rights Reporter*
Cr. App. R.	*Criminal Appeal Reports*
D.L.R.	*Dominion Law Reports*
E.R. (K.B.)	*English Reports (King's Bench Division)*
L.A.C.	*Labour Arbitration Cases*
M.V.R.	*Motor Vehicle Reports*
Man. R.	*Manitoba Reports*
N.B.R.	*New Brunswick Reports*
N.R.	*National Reporter*
N.S.R.	*Nova Scotia Reports*
Nfld. & P.E.I.R.	*Newfoundland & Prince Edward Island Reports*
O.A.C.	*Ontario Appeal Cases*
O.R.	*Ontario Reports*
Q.B.	*Law Reports, Queen's Bench*
Q.B.D.	*Law Reports, Queen's Bench Division*
R.F.L.	*Reports of Family Law*
R.P.R.	*Real Property Reports*
S. Ct.	*Supreme Court Reporter* [U.S.]
S.C.R.	*Supreme Court Reports* [Canada]
Sask. R.	*Saskatchewan Reports*
W.W.R.	*Western Weekly Reports*

Miscellaneous

c.o.b.	carrying on business
C.U.B.	Canadian Unemployment Board Decisions
O.H.R.B.I.D.	Ontario Human Rights Commission Board of Inquiry Decisions
Ont. Bd. of Inquiry	Ontario Board of Inquiry (Ontario Human Rights Commission)
sub nom.	*sub nomine* [Latin for "under the name"; indicates case title has changed]

Appendix C: Table of Cases

The following is an alphabetical list of all cases appearing in *All About Law, 5th Edition*. At the end of each entry, boldfaced numbers refer to page numbers in this book. For example, *Aisaican v. Kahnapace* is located on page 400.

Staples (Next friend of) v. Varga (c.o.b. True Legends Sports Cards and Comics) (1995), 27 Alta. L.R. (3d) 442 (Alta. Prov. Ct., Civ. Div.) **506**

T. (L.) v. T. (R.W.) (1997), 36 B.C.L.R. (3d) 165 (B.C.S.C.) **447**

Tabaka v. Greyhound Lines of Canada Ltd. (1999), 252 A.R. 373 (Alta. Q.B.) **377**

Taylor v. Caldwell (1863), 122 E.R. 309 (K.B.) **524**

Thomas v. Hamilton (City) Board of Education (1994), 20 O.R. (3d) 598 (Ont. C.A.) **335**

Thornton v. Prince George School District No. 57, [1978] 2 S.C.R. 267 (S.C.C.) **322**

Toews v. Weisner and South Fraser Health Region, 2001 BCSC 15 **379**

Tran v. Financial Debt Recovery Ltd. (2000), 193 D.L.R. (4th) 168 (Ont. S.C.J.) **323**

Trinity Western University v. College of Teachers (British Columbia) (2001), 82 C.R.R. (2d) 189 (S.C.C.) **91**

United Steel Workers of America v. Checkmate Cabs Ltd. (1997-05-21), Docket A970174 (B.C.S.C) **591**

Van de Perre v. Edwards, 2001 SCC 60 **423**

Vargek v. Okun (1997), 118 Man. R. (2d) 35 (Man. C.A.) **535**

Watson v. Antunes, [1998]) O.H.R.B.I.D. No. 9 (Ont. Bd. of Inquiry) **557**

Willoughby v. Gallant (2000), 582 A.P.R. 179 (P.E.I.T.D.) **508**

Wilson v. Sooter Studios Ltd. (1988), 55 D.L.R. (4th) 303 (B.C.C.A.) **526**

Winnipeg Child and Family Services v. K.L.W., [2000] 2 S.C.R. 519 (S.C.C.) **444**

Young v. Young (1993), 49 R.F.L. (3d) 117 (S.C.C.) **425**

Internet Citations

These charts show how to cite cases taken from Internet sources. See Figure 1-8 on page 15 for how cases are cited in official court reporters.

Neutral Citations (online)

Lewis	v.	Robinson	2001	BCSC	643
plaintiff	versus (Latin for "against")	defendant, or accused	year of decision	Jurisdiction and court (British Columbia Supreme Court)	Decision number

Unreported Cases (online)

R	v.	Thompson	(2001-02-12)	ONCA	Docket C32509
Regina or Rex (Latin for "queen" and "king") represents society	versus (Latin for "against")	defendant, or accused	Year/month/ day of decision	Jurisdiction and court (Ontario Court of Appeal)	Docket number

Glossary

A

abduction the illegal, forced removal of an unmarried person under age 16 from the person who has lawful care of the child (e.g., the custodial parent)

abetting encouraging, inciting, or urging another person to commit a crime

Aboriginal peoples the term used in the *Constitution Act, 1982,* to collectively describe peoples of Native Indian, Inuit, and Métis ancestry; often used synonymously with the term "Native peoples," although "Native peoples" sometimes refers only to people of Native Indian ancestry

absolute discharge a sentence in which, while the offender is found guilty, no conviction is recorded and the offender is free to go without conditions

absolute liability offences regulatory offences (not *Criminal Code* offences) for which only *actus reus* must be proven, not *mens rea*

absolute privilege a defence against defamation for statements made in legislature and judicial proceedings

absolute sale a transaction of goods for money in which the title of the goods is transferred to the buyer when the contract is fulfilled or completed

accelerated review an early consideration (review) by the parole board of an offender's eligibility (e.g., once one third of the sentence is served); allowed only if meeting certain conditions

access in family law, the right of the non-custodial parent to visit with the child and inquire about the child's health, welfare, and education; categorized as reasonable, specified, and supervised access

accessory after the fact someone who, after a crime is committed and knowing that it was, receives, comforts, or helps the criminal so that he or she can escape

actus reus a Latin phrase meaning "a wrongful deed"; the criminal act or omission to act, which with *mens rea,* makes one criminally liable

adjournment a postponement of court business

adoption the process of gaining the legal rights of a parent to a child and raising the child as one's own

adoption leave a permitted time away from work available to adoptive parents

adultery voluntary sexual intercourse by a married person with someone other than his or her spouse

adversarial system an approach based on two opposing sides, in which each side presents its case in court

adverse effect discrimination actions that appear to be neutral but that, intentionally or unintentionally, effectively discriminate against most members of a group

adverse witness a person who is contrary or hostile giving testimony under oath in a court

affinity relationship by marriage; as opposed to consanguinity

affirmation a witness's solemn agreement to tell the truth

agency shop a workplace permitting non-union workers, but in which all employees must pay union dues

aggravated assault the third, most serious of three levels of assault in criminal law; assault that wounds, maims, disfigures, or endangers the life of the victim

aggravated damages compensation payable in a civil case (damages) that compensates the plaintiff for the defendant's outrageous conduct; similar to punitive damages

aggravated sexual assault the third, most serious of three levels of sexual assault; sexual assault that wounds, maims, disfigures, or endangers the life of the victim

aggravating circumstances factors that might heighten or increase the responsibility of the offender, so might increase the offender's punishment

aiding helping or assisting someone in committing a crime

alibi a defence that the accused was in a different place, not at the scene of the crime, when it took place

allurement something that is inviting or enticing to young children (e.g., a pool, bells on an ice-cream truck)

alternative dispute resolution (ADR) a collective term for processes (e.g., mediation, arbitration) designed to settle (resolve) conflicts without formal trials

alternative measures programs extrajudicial sanctions; for young offenders

amending formula the procedure to change (amend) Canada's Constitution without the involvement of the British Parliament

amendments changes or alterations made to existing laws

annulment a ruling that a relationship never was a marriage; declared in a decree of nullity

appearance notice a legal document detailing what criminal offence the accused is charged with and the court date the accused must attend

appellant the party who requests an appeal in criminal court, either the defence or Crown

arbitration an alternative dispute resolution process in which the arbitrator hears from both sides and makes a final decision; more formal than negotiation and mediation; may be binding arbitration

arraignment the first stage in a criminal trial, in which the court clerk reads the charge to the accused and a plea is entered

arrest to legally detain a person and charge him or her with a criminal offence

arson intentionally or recklessly causing damage to property by fire or explosion

assault in criminal law, the broad term for the three levels of assault (assault, assault causing bodily harm, aggravated assault); also, the first level of assault, specifically, the threat of, or actual, physical contact without consent *or* approaching or blocking a person while openly carrying a real or imitation weapon; in tort law, the threat of danger or violence (rather than any actual contact, which is called battery in tort law)

assault causing bodily harm the second of three levels of assault in criminal law; assault that interferes with the victim's health or comfort in a significant way (not a minor hurt or injury) or assault involving a real, threatened, or imitation weapon

assignment the transfer of a right under a rental contract to another person (e.g., a tenant finds a replacement to assume the lease and gives up the right to repossess the premises)

assimilated absorbed into the prevailing culture; made similar in customs and views

attempt an effort or a try; an act done with the intent to commit an offence

automatism involuntary action by someone who is unconscious of what he or she is doing (e.g., while sleepwalking or concussed); insane automatism is caused by a disease of the mind

autrefois acquit a French phrase meaning "formerly acquitted"; one possible plea in response to double jeopardy

autrefois convict a French phrase meaning "formerly convicted"; one possible plea in response to double jeopardy

B

bailiff an official who helps the sheriff (e.g., to seize assets to pay unpaid court-ordered damages)

balance of probabilities the basis of the greater likelihood; the degree of proof necessary in a civil action, in comparison with proof beyond a reasonable doubt in criminal cases

banns of marriage an announcement of an intended marriage (e.g., read in a couple's church); an option to a marriage licence in some provinces

bargain in good faith to negotiate with the goal of reaching an agreement, as in unions and management genuinely pursuing a fair collective agreement

barter transactions of goods or services for goods or services, without money

battery intentional physical contact that is harmful or offensive to the other person; the completion of an assault in tort law

best interests of the child the principle upon which a judge decides issues of custody of children and access

bid rigging the unfair business practice of suppliers secretly agreeing to propose certain prices to the buyer in order to win contract terms above competitive rates

bigamy the practice or condition of being married to more than one person at a time

bill a proposed law; a draft form of an act or statute

binding arbitration an alternative dispute resolution process in which the neutral third party, the arbitrator, hears from both sides (e.g., union and management) and makes a final decision that both sides must accept

birth parents an adopted child's natural, or biological, mother and father

blended family a mother, a father, and their children born before and after the formation of the family unit, especially children of previous marriages

blood–alcohol level a measure of concentration of alcohol in a person's blood; often expressed as milligrams (mg) of alcohol in 100 mL of blood (e.g., "a blood–alcohol level of 80" means 80 mg alcohol in 100 mL blood; this is currently the legal alcohol limit)

bona fide occupational requirement a legitimate, reasonable necessity (requirement) of a job; a possible defence against unfair discrimination in hiring and other employment situations

bonding a form of insurance guaranteeing the honesty of the person handling money or other valuables

boycott an organized effort to put pressure on a business or industry by encouraging others to not buy its products or services

breach of condition failure to perform a major, or very important part, of a contract, entitling the injured party to treat the contract as ended

breach of contract failure to perform an obligation owed to another under a contract

breach of warranty failure to perform a minor term of a contract, entitling the injured party to damages, but not allowing that party to terminate the contract

break and enter to enter another's premises without permission by breaking or opening anything that is closed; also called burglary

C

capacity the ability to understand the nature and effect of one's actions, such as marriage; the legal ability to enter a contract on one's behalf

capital punishment the penalty of death for committing a crime

causation the fact of being the producer (cause) of an effect, result, or consequence (e.g., the cause of death); an important principle in murder trials; in civil law, one of the elements that must be proven in a negligence action

cause of action a legal right to start a lawsuit; the facts that give this right

caveat emptor a Latin phrase meaning "let the buyer beware"; a principle in contract law

censorship laws acts that ban or limit access to materials (e.g., magazines, movies) that are deemed to be obscene; enacted to protect public morality

certification official recognition of a union by a labour relations board as the bargaining agent for a group of employees

challenge for cause a formal objection to a prospective juror for reasons such as the juror's knowledge of the case or lack of impartiality

charge to the jury after the summations in a trial, a judge's instructions to the jury (e.g., review of the facts, of points of law)

child abuse any behaviour that endangers a child's physical, mental, or moral well-being; including physical, sexual, and emotional abuse and neglect

circumstantial evidence information (evidence) that relates only indirectly to the alleged offence

citation a reference to a legal case—e.g., in law reports, online with a neutral citation

civil law a term for private law governing the relationships between individuals; also, a term for the legal system of Quebec, based on Roman law, as distinct from English common law

civil rights the rights of citizens (e.g., to political and social freedom and equality), which limit the power a government has over its citizens; as in the rights guaranteed in the *Canadian Bill of Rights* and the *Canadian Charter of Rights and Freedoms*

claim a legal document in a civil action outlining the plaintiff's case against the defendant

clerical mistake an error caused by a clerk or other employee, typically involving numbers; an example of a unilateral mistake

clients those who employ the services of others (e.g., businesses that purchase services from independent contractors)

closed custody detention under constant guard, in a prison; the most secure form of custody

closed shop a workplace where all employees must belong to the union

codification the process of assembling a system of law into one statute or a body of statutes (e.g., the Code of Hammurabi, Canada's *Criminal Code*)

cohabitation agreement a domestic contract between two unmarried people who are living together; concerning property and obligations to each other

collective agreement the contract resulting from collective bargaining between a union and employer

collective bargaining negotiation done by a union on behalf of all its members concerning wages, hours, and other conditions of employment

collective rights the rights of the group, rather than the individual

colour of right legal right to a property; anything that shows a person has true ownership of something

common mistake an error made by both parties and concerning a fundamental fact of a contract

community correctional facilities detention that allows the offender to regular, regulated access to the community (e.g., to go to school), often on day parole

community service order a sentencing option in which the judge demands the offender do some specific work in the community under supervision

compensation something given to make amends for a loss (e.g., damages to an injured plaintiff); also called restitution; in criminal court, a sentencing objective

conciliation an attempt to settle a dispute; a meeting between two opposing parties

with the assistance of a third party to facilitate the dispute settlement process

concurrent sentence a penalty (sentence) for crimes in which penalties for two or more offences are served at the same time

conditional discharge a sentence in which, while the offender is found guilty, no conviction is recorded and the offender is free to go, but must meet certain expectations (e.g., probation orders) in order to avoid a record and a new sentence

conditional release a discharge from custody into the community where the offender has to meet certain expectations (conditions) and is supervised to some extent

conditional sentence a penalty (sentence) for a crime of a term of less than two years that is served in the community if the offender meets certain expectations

confession a statement by the accused in which he or she admits to the crime or acknowledges that some or all of the charge laid is true

consanguinity relationship by blood; as opposed to affinity

consecutive sentence a penalty (sentence) for crimes in which penalties for two or more offences are served one after the other

consent agreement given freely and voluntarily, in good faith

consideration something of value exchanged between the parties to a contract; categorized as past, present, or future consideration

conspiracy a serious agreement or arrangement to commit an unlawful act

constructive dismissal the termination of employment in which the employer's actions (e.g., demotion, transfer, job stress) pressure the employee into resigning

consummation validation of a marriage by sexual intercourse between the spouses

contempt of court any act that is calculated to embarrass, hinder, or obstruct a court in its administration of justice, or lessen its dignity

contingency fee payment for legal services in a civil case based on a percentage of damages if the case is successful; if the plaintiff loses the case and services were arranged on a contingency basis, the plaintiff pays nothing

contract an agreement enforceable by law, including express and implied contracts, simple contracts or contracts under seal

contracts under seal a written contract (agreement enforceable by law) in formal language, signed and witnessed, and with a red seal to signify serious intent

contributory negligence negligence on the part of a victim that helps bring about (contributes to) his or her own injury or loss; a partial defence to negligence

controlled substance any material, including both illegal drugs and drugs legally prescribed by doctors, listed in the *Controlled Drugs and Substances Act*

cooling-off period a length of time given to allow a buyer the chance to cancel a contract with a door-to-door seller without giving any reason

co-respondent in a divorce proceeding based on the respondent's adultery, the person with whom he or she committed adultery

correctional services government agencies responsible for probation services, the imprisonment and supervision of inmates, and their parole

counterclaim a defendant's claim in response to a plaintiff's related claim; action between two opposing parties

counteroffer a new offer made in response to the original offer that varies or qualifies the original, and so brings the original to an end

court clerk a person who keeps records, files, and processes documents for a court

court recorder a person whose job it is to document (record) all spoken evidence, comments, and questions in the court proceedings

credibility the fact or quality of being believable or reliable

criminal law the body of public law that declares acts to be crimes and prescribes punishments for those crimes

criminal negligence wanton and reckless disregard for the lives and safety of other people; consisting of criminal negligence in the operation of a motor vehicle, criminal negligence causing bodily harm, and criminal negligence causing death

Crown attorney in criminal matters, the lawyer prosecuting on behalf of the Crown and society; an agent of the attorney general

Crown wardship a court order permanently granting legal custody and guardianship of a child to the Crown, represented by a child protection agency (e.g., the Children's Aid Society)

culpable homicide blamable or criminal homicide (the killing of another person), as in murder, manslaughter, infanticide

custody in criminal law, actual imprisonment or physical detention, categorized as closed, open, and secure custody; in family law, the care and control of a child awarded by the court, as in a divorce proceeding; categorized as sole, joint, joint physical, joint legal, and interim custody

D

damages money awarded by the court to a plaintiff for a wrong or loss suffered; the main form of compensation in a civil action; categorized as general, special, punitive (or exemplary), aggravated, and nominal damages

dangerous offender a person who has committed serious personal injury and who meets certain criteria to be given this designation, resulting in an indeterminate sentence; a designation similar to long-term offender

day parole an offender's release from custody during the day under specific conditions, with each night spent in an institution or halfway house; usually a step toward full parole

decree of nullity the court order giving an annulment

defamation the act of uttering or publishing false and malicious statements that injure a person's fame, reputation, or character; often categorized as slander or libel

default judgment a decision made in the plaintiff's favour when the defendant in a civil claim does not dispute the claim within the required time

defence in criminal law, the accused and his or her legal representatives; a reason or set of circumstances that might relieve a defendant of liability (e.g., the defence of mental disorder); in civil law, a document responding to the plaintiff's claim (also called a reply)

defendant in criminal law, the person charged with an offence; in civil law, the party being sued

demerit points points taken away from a licensed driver for various driving offences, which can lead to licence suspension if too many are given; the key to a system of, essentially, warning drivers and deterring additional offences

democracy government by the people, who exercise their power directly or indirectly, through elected representatives; a society that emphasizes equality, fairness, and tolerance

deported to be expelled to one's country of origin (e.g., after being declared an illegal immigrant)

detained to be kept in custody or temporarily confined

detention the act of keeping someone in custody; an enforced delay

deterrence a sentencing objective of providing deterrents

deterrents that which discourages or prevents a person from doing something

direct evidence information (evidence) given by a person who witnessed the event in question (e.g., testimony by a bystander who saw an assault take place)

directed verdict a judge's direction to the jury, after the Crown presents its evidence, to find the accused not guilty because the Crown has not proven its case

discharge to release from custody

discharged ended, as in a legal obligation or duty ended in contract law

disclaimer clauses provisions in a contract that deny the buyer certain rights or protections; the seller has an obligation to bring these clauses to the buyer's attention

disclosure in criminal cases, a stage in proceedings for a trial by jury in which the Crown attorney and the defence must meet to reveal all evidence; after which, charges would be dropped if the defence proves that the Crown has no case

diversion programs sentences that keep offenders out of prison (e.g., suspended sentence, probation)

domestic contract a cohabitation agreement, marriage contract, or separation agreement; made between two partners in a relationship and concerning property and obligations to each other

dominant party the party in a position of power over another (e.g., in privileged communications between doctor and patient, the doctor)

double doctoring the criminal act of trying to get a narcotic or prescription from different doctors; also called prescription shopping

double jeopardy being tried twice for the same offence, which is prohibited

drug a chemical substance that alters the structure or function in a living organism

due diligence a defence that the accused took reasonable care not to commit the act (e.g., polluting) or that the accused honestly believed his or her actions were innocent

duress illegal coercion; the threat or use of violence to force a person to do something against his or her will

duty counsel a lawyer on duty at the court or a police station to give legal advice to those arrested or brought before the court

duty of care a specific legal obligation to not harm other people or their property; a principle of tort law

duty to accommodate the legal obligation to counter the effects of adverse effect discrimination

E

e-commerce business transactions conducted over the Internet or electronic systems of communication

empanelling the selection of a jury

employment equity the principle that treatment of all employees should be based on their abilities and be fair, just, and impartial; to address past discrimination, some employment equity initiatives might include programs (e.g., quota systems) or laws that might be considered discriminatory under other circumstances; these programs are generally aimed at women, Aboriginal peoples, visible minorities, and people with disabilities

enticing the illegal luring or attracting of a child under the age of 14

entrap to induce or lure a person into committing an offence

entrenched fixed firmly or securely in law; specifically, made part of Canada's Constitution so it can only be changed by an amendment to the Constitution

equalization payment a payment in cash or property to address any difference between spouses' net family property values, and paid by the spouse with the greater value

equity the ideal, quality, or fact of being fair, just, and impartial

escorted and unescorted absences inmates' authorized times spent away from custody (e.g., for approved programs, medical treatment) that are either unsupervised or supervised by a parole officer, correctional service staff member, or citizen volunteer

essential requirements for marriage conditions that must be met for a marriage to be valid (e.g., legal capacity, genuine consent); under federal jurisdiction

euthanasia acting to end another's life painlessly as an act of mercy; often committed when the victim is suffering from an incurable and disabling disease; sometimes called mercy killing

examination for discovery a pre-trial process in civil cases in which each side discloses all evidence and certain issues are discussed and agreed upon; similar to disclosure in criminal cases

examination of the debtor a judge's questioning of a plaintiff who owes court-ordered damages about his or her ability to pay in order to see what arrangements can be made

examination-in-chief the first questioning of a witness during court proceedings

exculpatory denying something, clearing of guilt; as in an exculpatory statement

express condition an essential term of a contract clearly outlined within it

express contract an oral or written contract (agreement enforceable by law) in which the terms and conditions are clearly defined and understood by the parties; the opposite of an implied contract

express warranties clear and open promises that goods or services will meet certain standards; also called guarantees

extended family a family group consisting of parent(s), the children, and other close relatives (e.g., grandparents)

extradition the giving up or delivering of a person to another country; legal surrender of a person according to international agreements (e.g., as in child abduction by a non-custodial parent)

extrajudicial sanctions diversion programs for young offenders who are non-violent, first-time offenders, and unlikely to reoffend; designed to keep them out of the court system; also called alternative measures programs

F

faint hope clause the provision that allows an offender sentenced to more than 15 years before becoming eligible for full parole (e.g., a murderer) to have his or her parole eligibility reconsidered; a clause that allows for the possibility of the inmate being fully rehabilitated after 15 years

fair comment the right to criticize openly and honestly if without malice, as in a movie review; a defence against defamation

false imprisonment unlawful physical restraint or detention

false pretences illegal lying or misrepresentation; the presentation of untruths or false information knowingly and with fraudulent intent to induce the victim to act upon it

family asset property owned by one or both spouses and ordinarily used and enjoyed for family purposes by the spouses and/or any children; normally divided equally between separating spouses; as opposed to non-family or business assets

family mediation an alternative dispute resolution process applied to issues within families; involving a neutral third party trying to get opposing parties to agree on issues (e.g., custody of children)

feminist one who believes in the social, economic, and political equality of the sexes

feudalism a political, social, and economic system prevalent in Europe between the 9th and 15th centuries; based on the relationship between lord and vassal (servant)

fine option program an alternative to paying a monetary penalty (fine) upon conviction; in which the offender can earn credit for doing community work

First Nations a term originated by Native peoples to describe themselves and recognizing that they belong to distinct cultural groups with sovereign rights based on being Canada's first inhabitants; with "First Nation" often used in place of the term "band," as recognized by the Canadian government

first-degree murder the killing of another person that is planned and deliberate, in which the victim is a law enforcement agent, or that is related to committing or attempting other crimes that are particularly offensive to society (e.g., hostage taking, sexual assault, hijacking an airplane)

fixed-term tenancy rental of property by a tenant for a certain time and expiring on a specific date without any further notice being required by either party

forensic science the application of biochemical and other scientific techniques (e.g., human tissue or fibre analysis) to criminal investigations

foreseeability the quality of being what a reasonable person should expect or anticipate as a result of certain actions

formal requirements of marriage legal conditions for performing marriage ceremonies; under provincial and territorial jurisdiction

foster homes a form of open custody for young offenders—i.e., a young offender is placed in the home of an existing family for care and rehabilitation for a set time period

franchise the right to vote

fraudulent misrepresentation an untrue statement, or one that gives a false impression, about specific goods or services that is made knowingly and with the intent of deceiving

free pardon a cancellation of a person's punishment and conviction; the recipient is no longer considered to have committed the crime of which he or she was convicted

frustrated made impossible to accomplish or perform, as in the terms of a contract

full disclosure the reporting of the true cost of borrowing money, quoted as an annual percentage and as a dollar amount, to give consumers an opportunity to compare credit terms

full parole an offender's complete release from custody into the community under specific conditions and supervision

future consideration the promise of a future exchange of something of value between the parties to a contract (e.g., buying on credit)

G

garnishment a procedure to address outstanding court-ordered payments between parties by redirecting money or goods owed by a third party (e.g., requiring part of Tina's paycheque be forwarded to the court to pay damages awarded to Ampai for Tina's negligence)

general damages compensation payable in a civil case (damages) not easily calculated so requiring the judge's discretion (e.g., for pain and suffering, lost future earnings, loss of enjoyment of life)

general intent intent that is limited to the act itself and inferred from that act, such as an assault in which intent is inferred from the fact that the accused did apply force

general strike a broad-based refusal to work, as by unionized workers from many sectors of the entire workforce

grievance a formal, work-related complaint made by an employee, the union, or management when it is thought that the collective agreement is not being followed

group homes homes that each house several young offenders for set time periods, for rehabilitation; operated by trained staff and non-profit agencies

guaranteed annual income (GAI) an amount of money that would be ensured as a yearly minimum for each person (e.g., adult Canadians)

guarantees clear and open promises that goods or services will meet certain standards; also called express warranties

H

habeas corpus a document that requires a person be brought to court to determine if he or she is being legally detained; the right to this document as protection against unlawful detention; from the Latin term meaning "You must have the body," i.e., there must be grounds for detention

harassment unwelcome actions or conduct toward another (e.g., a fellow employee); workplace forms include sexual and poisoned work environment; as compared with criminal harassment

healing circles an option within restorative justice that attempts to resolve conflicts between offender and victim

hearsay evidence information (evidence) not coming from the direct, personal experience or knowledge of the witness

homicide killing another person, directly or indirectly

homosexuality sexual orientation to people of one's sex; sexual activity with a person of the same sex

honest mistake the defence that the accused truthfully did not know that he or she was committing a crime

house arrest a court order that requires a person remain at home during specific time periods; sometimes monitored with electronic devices

human rights rights that protect one from discrimination by other individuals and in certain areas of one's life

hung jury a jury that cannot come to a unanimous decision in a criminal case

hybrid offences criminal offences that may be tried, at the Crown's option, as summary conviction offences or indictable offences, with the corresponding less or more severe punishment

I

immune exempt, completely protected

implied conditions essential terms that are not expressed formally in a contract, but are suggested by the buyer

implied contract a contract (agreement enforceable by law) that is suggested or understood without being openly and specifically stated; the opposite of an express contract

implied warranties promises that goods or services will meet certain standards (warranties) that are not expressed formally in a contract, but are suggested indirectly by the buyer

impotence inability of one or both spouses to have sexual intercourse; a ground for annulment

incarceration imprisonment or confinement

incest sexual intercourse with a person knowing that he or she is a close blood relative (e.g., child, grandchild, brother, half-sister)

inculpatory admitting to something, incriminating; as in an inculpatory statement

independent contractors people who sell services to clients and who maintain separate businesses themselves; unlike employees

indeterminate sentence a penalty (sentence) ordering imprisonment for a period that is not fixed, during which the situation is reviewed periodically to see if the offender can safely return to society; often used for dangerous offenders

Indian the term used in the *Constitution Act, 1982*, to describe Native peoples who are not Inuit or Métis; a term imposed on the Native peoples by European explorers, who had mistaken North and South America for Asia; recognized in Canadian law as having three classes—status Indians, non-status Indians, and treaty Indians

indictable severe or particularly serious, as in an indictable offence

indictable offences severe or particularly serious criminal offences (e.g., murder, treason), which have correspondingly severe penalties and which proceed by way of a formal court document called an indictment

infanticide the killing of an infant shortly after birth by the mother as she is not fully recovered from the effects of giving birth (e.g., post-partum depression) and her mind is disturbed

information a written complaint, made under oath, stating that there is reason to believe that a person has committed a criminal offence

informed consent agreement to a particular action with full understanding of the risks, as with patients and medical procedures

infringed broken or violated, as in an agreement or right that is infringed

injunction a court order directing a person to do or not do something for a specific time period

innocent misrepresentation an untrue statement, or one that gives a false impression, about specific goods or services made thinking the statement was true

intent the true purpose of one's actions; also, the state of a person's mind who knows and desires the consequences of his or her actions; also, a key characteristic of the tort of negligence. In criminal law and depending on the offence, the Crown must prove general intent or specific intent.

intentional discrimination treatment of others that is unfair (on the basis of prejudice or stereotype) and on purpose

interim custody in family law, the care and control of a child awarded by the court temporarily to one parent

intermittent sentence a penalty (sentence) for a crime that may be served on weekends or at night, allowing the offender to keep a job; only available for sentences of less than 90 days

interned confined, especially in wartime, such as when a country at war forces people considered enemies within the country to live in a special area or camp

intra vires a Latin phrase meaning "within the powers"; within the authority of the government to pass a law

invitation to treat encouragement, through advertising or display of goods, to prospective buyers to make offers

invitee a person on a property for a purpose other than a social visit (e.g., student, customer)

J

joint custody in family law, the care and control of a child awarded by the court to both parents; categorized as joint physical custody or joint legal custody; also called joint parent or shared parenting

joint legal custody a type of joint custody in which the child lives with one parent, but the other parent has generous access and equal responsibility for major decisions affecting the child

joint parenting parents' joint custody of their child after separation or divorce; also called shared parenting

joint physical custody a type of joint custody in which the child spends equal or nearly equal time with each parent

joint tenancy a form of rental agreement in which two or more tenants agree to rent one premises

jurisdiction authority or power to do something, such as make laws

just cause the legal right to take an action, such as firing an employee

K

knowledge the awareness or understanding of certain facts, which provides the necessary *mens rea* for an offence

L

land claims assertion of the right to certain lands, as in claims to land long-used by Aboriginal peoples

landlord the property owner who agrees to allow another party to occupy, or use, it in return for payment

lapse the termination, or ending, of an offer because it is not accepted

launder to deal with (e.g., use, transport, alter, dispose of) any property obtained through crime, as in money laundering

law a rule to govern action; a rule of conduct established by government, for society to follow and obey

law of master and servant an old term for employment law, the laws governing employer–employee relationships

lawful purpose a lawful (not illegal) reason or objective

leading questions questions that prompt the witness to give the answers wanted

lease a contract between a landlord and tenant for the rental of property; also called a tenancy agreement

leave of absence time granted away from work for a specified period and purpose; types include maternity, parental, and adoption leaves

lessee the tenant who occupies rented premises

lessor the property owner who rents out premises

libel defamation in a printed or permanent form (e.g., pictures, printed words, video)

licensee a person on another's property with the permission (license) of the occupier (e.g., a friend) for non-business purposes

limitation period the span of time after an event during which a civil claim can be filed

line-up a group of people who are lined up by the police so that the witness to a crime may say which person committed the crime

liquidated damages a reasonable sum of money agreed to in advance by both parties that, if the contract is breached, the party breaching will pay

litigants the parties involved in a civil action; the plaintiff and the defendant

litigation a lawsuit; the act of bringing a civil dispute to court for resolution

litigation guardian a person who represents a minor in a civil dispute, as when a minor sues; referred to as *guardian ad litem* in a citation

lobby to seek to influence the government to pass laws that would support one's cause, to benefit the organization the lobbyist represents; many lobbyists are paid by a company or institution

lockout an employer's refusal to open the workplace to the employees; a strategy used in labour disputes

long-term offender a criminal who repeatedly behaves in a way that could injure, kill, or cause psychological harm and, in the case of a sexual crime offender, would likely reoffend

M

malice desire to harm another; active ill will

manslaughter homicide, or the killing of another person, by committing an unlawful act and with only general intent (e.g., speeding and killing a pedestrian, giving a lethal punch in a sudden, provoked brawl)

market sharing the business practice of sellers dividing up the market (scope of potential sales) geographically or by customer, to reduce or limit competition

marriage the voluntary union of a man and a woman to the exclusion of all others; as affirmed in Parliament in 1999

marriage breakdown the basis for divorce on the ground that the marriage is no longer functioning; now the only valid ground for divorce in Canada

marriage contract a legal agreement between partners who are married or plan to get married; concerning property and obligations to each other

material fact a truth (fact) that persuades a buyer to enter into a contract

material risks any major or significant possibilities of harm or suffering (e.g., from a medical treatment)

maternity leave a permitted time away from work available to women before and after giving birth

matrimonial home the home in which the couple lived during their marriage

matrimonial property possessions owned by the spouses during their marriage; also called marital property; concerning family assets and non-family or business assets

mediation an alternative dispute resolution process in which a third party tries to get opposing parties to reach an agreement; also family mediation, in family law

meeting of the minds the arriving at a mutual understanding and binding agreement by an offeror and offeree

mens rea a Latin phrase meaning "a guilty mind"; the knowledge, intent, or recklessness of one's actions, which together with *actus rea*, makes one criminally liable

merchantable quality fit for intended use; suitable for sale

minors people under the age of majority (e.g., 18)

mischief deliberate destruction of, or damage to, property; also, interference with the lawful use or enjoyment of property

misogynist showing or arising from hatred of women

misrepresentation an untrue statement, or one that gives a false impression, about specific goods or services; can be innocent or fraudulent misrepresentation

mistake an error concerning the existence of the subject matter of a contract; including common, unilateral, clerical, *non est factum* mistakes; in marriage law, an error concerning the identity of a marriage partner or the nature of a marriage ceremony

mitigating circumstances factors that moderate or lessen the responsibility of the offender, so might reduce the penalty

mitigation of loss a requirement that the party suffering from a breach of contract try to reduce or alleviate the losses resulting from the breach

mobility rights the freedom to move about (e.g., *Charter* rights, which include the right to enter, remain in, and leave Canada; the right of a custodial parent to move with the children to a different province or territory for a job)

monogamy the practice or condition of being married to only one person at a time; as opposed to bigamy

motive the reason for committing a certain act

motor vehicle any vehicle that is drawn, propelled, or driven by any means other than muscular power (e.g., car, motorcycle, snowmobile, boat, airplane), but not railway equipment

murder intentional homicide (killing of another person); recognized as having two classes: first-degree murder and second-degree murder

N

natural rights rights thought to be inherent, such as the right of all people to life, liberty, and security; rights that are independent of rulers, society, and governments

necessaries goods and services needed to ensure a person's health and welfare (e.g., food, clothing, shelter); as opposed to non-necessaries

negative-option marketing a sales approach in which offerees are contractually bound to an offer unless they declare their rejection of it

negligence a failure to exercise reasonable care that results in injury to another; damaging actions that are careless, unintentional, and unplanned

negotiation an alternative dispute resolution process that is informal and voluntary, and that involves no third party

net family property the total value of a spouse's assets, less any debts, on the date of separation; a figure needed to calculate any equalization payments

no-fault divorce the legal dissolution of a marriage; granted if marriage breakdown is established

no-fault insurance insurance that is paid to the injured party promptly by the insurer, regardless of who is at fault in an accident

nominal damages a small sum of money awarded in a successful civil suit to a plaintiff who has not suffered substantial harm or loss; awarded for a moral victory

non est factum a Latin phrase meaning "It is not my deed"; a denial by one party that a contract was properly executed, based on the claim that he or she was ignorant of its nature

non-competition clause a requirement that restrains trade or employment so as to limit competition (e.g., a clause forbidding the opening of a rival store within a specified area, or preventing an employee from leaving one employer to immediately work for a rival)

non-culpable homicide homicide (the killing of another person) that is not criminal, but caused completely by accident or in self-defence

non-family or business assets valuable items (e.g., stocks, bonds, investments) owned by a spouse and not divided between spouses in the event of a separation; as opposed to family assets

non-necessaries goods and services that are not required for one's health and welfare; as opposed to necessaries

notwithstanding clause the provision (clause) in the *Canadian Charter of Rights and Freedoms* allowing provinces and territories to create laws that operate in spite of certain contradictions with the *Charter*

nuclear family a mother, a father, and their children

nuisance an unreasonable use of land that interferes with the right of others to enjoy their property; categorized as public or private nuisances

O

oath a solemn promise or statement that something is true

occupier someone who controls and physically possesses a property

offer and acceptance a proposal that expresses the willingness of one party to enter into a contract, followed by an assent by the other party in words or deed; called a "meeting of the minds"

offeree in a contract, the party to whom the offer is made

offeror in a contract, the party who makes an offer

open custody detention that is supervised and with possibly some supervised access to the community (e.g., to work farming); less guarded than closed custody

open shop a workplace in which not all employees must be union members, but the union has the right to encourage all to join

opinion evidence evidence based on the thoughts of the witness, usually an expert in his or her field (e.g., a coroner commenting on cause of death)

ordinary pardon a cancellation of a person's punishment; he or she is still considered guilty of the crime, but is forgiven by the Crown and released

out-of-court settlement a resolution to a civil dispute made to each party's satisfaction before the matter proceeds to trial

P

parental leave a permitted time away from work available to either parent after the birth of a child; for women, immediately following their maternity leaves

parolee an inmate released into the community on full parole or day parole, i.e., with certain conditions to follow

past consideration the promise to pay a person for services already performed; not legally binding

pay equity equal payment for work evaluated as equal in worth

peace bond a court order requiring a person keep the peace and behave well for a specific period of time

peremptory challenge a formal objection to a potential juror for which no specific reason is given, unlike a challenge for cause

performance the fulfilment of an obligation or a promise, as in the completion of a contract; the act of performing

performing carrying out, or completing, as in the terms of a contract

periodic tenancy rental of property by a tenant weekly or for some other regular span (period) of time; renewed at the end of each period by express agreement or by implication, as in payment of rent

perjury the act of knowingly giving false evidence in a judicial proceeding with intent to mislead

petition for divorce the legal document that begins a divorce action, the procedure to end a valid marriage

petitioner the spouse initiating a petition for divorce; as opposed to the respondent

placement within adoption, the process of matching a child and adoptive parent(s), then monitoring the family

plaintiff in civil law, the party suing

plea negotiation a process in which the Crown and the accused (with his or her defence) attempt to make a deal, usually resulting in a guilty plea to a lesser charge than the original charge, thus a lesser penalty

points system a method of evaluating applicants for independent immigration, using categories and points in each

poisoned work environment harassment a group's unwelcome actions or conduct toward one or more employees on the basis of gender, race, religion, or some other characteristic

polygraph test a process in which a person is asked questions and a lie detector machine measures the person's changes in blood pressure, perspiration, and pulse rate to indicate if he or she is telling the truth

precedent a legal decision that serves as an example and authority in subsequent similar cases; basis for the rule of precedent—the legal principle in which similar facts result in similar decisions

prejudice having a preconceived opinion of a person based on the person's belonging to a certain group; the opinion itself

preliminary hearing a hearing held to determine if there is sufficient evidence to justify a trial

prescription shopping the criminal act of trying to get a narcotic or prescription from different doctors; also called double doctoring

present consideration the exchange of something of value between the parties to the contract at the time the contract is formed; usually money for goods or services

pre-sentencing report an account (report) prepared for the court prior to the accused's sentencing that sets out his or her background

pre-trial conference a meeting of the parties in a civil suit with a judge or court-appointed referee in which each party summarizes the case and the judge may offer an opinion; a last chance to resolve the dispute before going to trial

price fixing the unfair business practice of two or more sellers setting the price of a good or service above what it would sell for in a competitive or open market

primary caregiver the person (usually a parent) who chiefly attends to the daily needs of a child

principle of totality the rule or concept of looking at the whole; as when an

offender has committed several crimes, the sentences should not amount to an overlong prison term

private nuisance a nuisance that affects an individual or a few people only

privileged communications confidential communications (e.g., conversations, letters) that one cannot be required to present in court as evidence

privity of contract the principle by which a party to a contract can enforce contractual rights only against those who are parties to the contract

probation a sentence that allows the offender provisional freedom rather than imprisonment; requires good behaviour and other conditions the judge imposes; common for first-time offenders

probation order a directive (order) by the court allowing a person to live in the community under the supervision of a probation officer, instead of serving a term of imprisonment

procreation the creation of one's offspring

procure to obtain or get, as in to obtain a person for prostitution

prohibited weapons instruments to injure, kill, threaten, or intimidate another person that are illegal and may not be kept by anyone (e.g., sawed-off shotguns, switchblades)

public nuisance a nuisance that affects an indefinite number of people or all residents in the community

public policy guiding principle for the community, the people; as in the requirement that contracts not go against public policy, the public good (e.g., a contract that is racist)

punitive damages compensation payable in a civil case (damages) in addition to general or special damages and which punish the defendant for an uncaring or violent act; also called exemplary damages

Q

qualified privilege a defence against defamation for those whose work requires they express their opinions (e.g., teachers, doctors), unless malice is evident

quiet enjoyment the right of a tenant to use rented premises free from interference by others

quota system a method of requiring a proportional share of something assigned to a group; often to address traditional under-representations (e.g., women among police officers)

R

random virtue testing investigating a person for drug offences without having reasonable or probable grounds for doing so

read down to rule in court that a law is generally acceptable, but unacceptable in that specific case; as opposed to strike down

reasonable access the right of the non-custodial parent to flexible and regular visits with the child, and to inquire about the child's health, welfare, and education

reasonable limits clause the provision (clause) in the *Canadian Charter of Rights and Freedoms* stating that *Charter* rights and freedoms are not absolute, so can be limited if there is justification

reasonable person the standard used in determining if a person's conduct in a particular situation is negligent

recidivism relapse into crime; the return to prison of criminal repeaters

recklessness a state or instance of acting carelessly or without regard for the consequences of one's actions

recognizance a legal document that the accused must sign, in which he or she acknowledges the charge laid and promises to appear at a specified court date; sometimes accompanied by a payment to the court

reconciliation the renewal of a friendly and marital relation between spouses; a procedure for trying to save a marriage

rehabilitation the restoration of a person to a good physical, mental, and moral health through treatment and training; a sentencing objective

releasing circles an option in restorative justice and Aboriginal communities in which the offender, National Parole Board members, and community members meet to plan for the offender's rejoining the community

remand a return to custody, e.g., while awaiting trial or sentencing

reply a defendant's response to a plaintiff's claim; also called a defence

rescission the cancellation or revocation of a contract

respondent in a court case, the party (e.g., the Crown) who opposes the appeal requested by the other party, the appellant; in marriage law, the spouse being sued for divorce

restitution the act of making good, restoring (e.g., returning something stolen to its rightful owner or compensating in another way); a sentencing objective

restorative justice an approach to the law and crime that emphasizes healing, forgiveness, and community involvement; including sentencing, healing, and releasing circles

restraint of employment the limitation of a worker's employment (e.g., the restriction that a software creator working for Company A not work for Company B at the same time or for two years after); can make a contract void if the restraint is unreasonable

restraint of trade the limitation of competition in business, which can make a contract void if unreasonable or against public policy

restricted weapons instruments to injure, kill, threaten, or intimidate another person that require the owner or user have a permit (e.g., semi-automatic guns)

retribution a deserved penalty or punishment for a wrong or crime; vengeance; a sentencing objective

reverse onus the responsibility of proving is placed on the defence rather than the Crown (e.g., in a bail hearing involving a serious criminal charge, the accused must show why he or she should be released from custody)

revocation in contract law, the cancellation, or taking back, of an offer by the offeree before it is accepted

right of distress a landlord's right (just or legal claim) to seize a tenant's property if rent is unpaid; now abolished in residential tenancies

right of lien the right (just or legal claim) to hold another's property as security for an obligation or debt until it is paid

riot an unlawful assembly in which at least two of the people disturb the peace riotously, e.g., violently, with physical harm to others, with damage to property

roadside screening test a preliminary assessment to see if a driver might be impaired (e.g., a breath test)

robbery theft accomplished by means of force or fear (e.g., assault with intent to steal; stealing while armed with an offensive weapon or imitation of a weapon)

royal assent the signing of a bill by the Crown or the Crown's representative to formally pass an act; now given in Canada by the governor general

Royal Prerogative of Mercy the right of the governor general to alter a criminal sentence imposed on a convicted person, or the Cabinet's right to grant a pardon

rule of law the fundamental principle that society is governed by law that applies equally to all persons and that neither an individual nor the government is above the law

S

sanctions penalties, usually imposed by several nations on another nation for its violation of international law (e.g., trade sanctions that forbid trade in oil with the offending nation)

search to look for evidence that may be used in court; this police procedure

search warrant a legal document issued by a judge authorizing the police to search a specific location at a specific time and for a specific reason

second-degree murder intentional homicide that does not meet the conditions of first-degree murder

secret warranties specific promises that goods or services will meet certain standards (warranties) that sellers communicate to dealers, but not to buyers

secure custody guarded detention for young offenders (e.g., in a youth detention centre); the most secure detention form for young offenders; like closed custody for adult offenders

security deposit a sum of money tenants pay at the beginning of a tenancy (usually to the landlord)

segregation the placement of dangerous offenders in prison to protect society; a sentencing objective; also, keeping a prison inmate apart from other inmates

self-incrimination the act of implicating oneself in a crime; behaviour indicating one's guilt

self-sufficiency the ability to support oneself financially; a consideration of the *Divorce Act* that each spouse has an obligation to support himself or herself within a reasonable period of time after a divorce

sentencing circles an option in restorative justice that brings together affected people (victim, offender, police, etc.) to help sentence (decide the penalty for) the offender

separate-property system an approach to the division of family property that allowed each spouse to own and control property as though single

separation agreement a domestic contract between a separating couple; concerning property and obligations to each other

sequester to keep the jury together and away from non-jurors until it reaches a verdict

sexual assault the broad term for the three levels of sexual assault (the most serious of which is aggravated sexual assault), which parallel those for assault; combining the former offences of rape and indecent assault; also, the first level of sexual assault, which is defined as the first level of assault but involving sexual conduct

sexual exploitation the act of someone in a position of trust or authority over a person aged 14 to 17, or a person with a mental or physical disability, taking advantage of that person for sexual purposes

sexual harassment unwelcome actions or conduct toward another of a sexual nature

shared parenting parents' joint custody of their child after separation or divorce; also called joint parenting

sheriff a Crown-appointed official who acts as part of the justice administration system (e.g., serving court documents)

shop steward a person nominated to represent a department or division of a workplace's union members

siblings brothers and sisters, stepbrothers and stepsisters

similar fact evidence information (evidence) that shows that the accused has previously committed a similar offence

simple contracts contracts (agreements enforceable by law) that are either express or implied, oral or written, and not under seal

slander defamation through spoken words, sounds, or actions (e.g., a speech)

Small Claims Court the lowest level civil court, where disputes involving money or property are resolved simply, inexpensively, and informally by a judge without a jury

social housing government-funded housing for low-income Canadians

society wardship a court order temporarily granting legal custody and guardianship of a child to a child protection agency (e.g., the Children's Aid Society)

sole custody in family law, the care and control of a child awarded by the court to one parent only; as opposed to joint custody

solemnization of marriage the various steps and preliminaries, including the ceremony, leading to marriage; authority over which was granted to the provinces

soliciting communicating for the purpose of prostitution (e.g., approach another person to offer sexual services)

sovereignty a nation's supreme power and authority to govern its affairs, its independence to make laws

special damages compensation payable in a civil case (damages) for specific out-of-pocket expenses (e.g., prescription drugs, lost income)

specific intent intent that goes beyond the act itself, as in break and enter, in which the Crown must prove the unlawful action of breaking and entering and the specific intent of committing a further indictable offence, such as theft

specific performance a court order that requires a person do something previously promised in a contract

specified access the right of the non-custodial parent to certain prearranged visits with the child (e.g., weekends, certain holidays), and to inquire about the child's health, welfare, and education

spousal support financial assistance paid by one spouse to another after a marriage breakdown

standard of care the level of care, or degree of caution, expected when a reasonable person is carrying out an action

station in life one's social standing or rank in society

statutes laws or acts passed by a government body, such as Parliament or a provincial legislature

statutory release an inmate's release from an institution as required by law; except for certain offences, once two-thirds of the sentence is served

stay of proceedings a court order to stop the trial proceedings until a certain condition is met

stereotyping judging, or forming an opinion of, one person of a group and applying that judgment to all members of the group

sterility inability to have children; as opposed to impotence; not a ground for annulment

strict liability offences regulatory offences (not *Criminal Code* offences) for which only *actus reus* must be proven, not *mens rea,* and for which due diligence can be a defence

strict-discipline program a system or course of activities (program) designed for young offenders and involving military drills, exercise, classes, and so on

strike a work stoppage or partial withdrawal of service by union members to further their contract demands; types include general, sympathy, and wildcat strikes

strike down to rule in court that a law is invalid, no longer in effect

sublet a tenant's renting out of his or her rented premises to a third party while keeping the right to repossess

subpoena a court document ordering a person to appear in court for a specific purpose (e.g., as a witness)

substantial performance the completion of most, but not all, terms of a contract; the principle establishing that someone dissatisfied with a minor failure or aspect of performance cannot break the contract

suffrage the right to vote in political elections; franchise

summary conviction a "guilty" finding (conviction) for a summary conviction offence, which is a fairly minor criminal action

summary conviction offences minor criminal offences (in contrast to indictable offences), which are tried immediately (summarily) without a preliminary hearing or jury

summation for each side in a trial, the formal conclusion, which recapitulates (sums up) key arguments and evidence

summons an order to appear in criminal court

sunset clause a provision in a law that ends a program or power, or disbands an agency at the end of a fixed period unless it is formally renewed

supervised access in family law, the right of the non-custodial parent to visits with the child at specified times under the supervision of someone such as a grandparent or social worker, and to inquire about the child's health, welfare, and education

supervision order a court order requiring that a professional oversee (supervise) a child needing protection, but the child stays at home

surrebuttal evidence presented in court to counteract or disprove evidence in the other party's rebuttal

suspended sentence a delayed or held-off sentence; if the offender meets certain conditions, the judge never does decide on a penalty; like a conditional discharge but the offender has a record

suspension a sentence that removes a privilege, such as driving or attending school

sympathy strikes refusals to work (strikes) by members of one or more unions to show support for another union on strike

T

telemarketing schemes systematic plans for selling goods or services by phone

tenancy agreement a contract between a landlord and tenant for the rental of property; also called a lease

tenant the party that rents (pays money for the use of) the landlord's property

testimony a declaration (e.g., by a witness) under oath; a sworn statement

theft the act of taking another's property with intent to deny the owner the use and enjoyment of the goods

third-party liability legal responsibility involving three parties; as in a car accident, in which an insurance company, the third party, pays out the claim

title the right of ownership to goods or property

tort a wrong or injury (other than breach of contract), which may be intentional or unintentional; the basis for a branch of civil law, tort law

traffic to sell, administer, give, transfer, transport, send, or deliver a controlled substance

trespass to enter or cross another's property without consent or legal right

trespasser a person who enters or crosses another's property without consent or legal right

truth established and verified fact in a judicial proceeding; the best defence for defamation

U

ultra vires a Latin phrase meaning "beyond the power"; beyond the authority of the government to pass a law regarding a specific topic and therefore of no effect

unconscionable grossly or shockingly unfair, or unreasonable, as in an unconscionable judgment

undertaking a court document that the accused signs to swear that he or she will attend a specified court date and meet any conditions of release laid down by the judge

undue influence improper pressure applied by one person to another in order to benefit from the result (e.g., a will)

unilateral mistake an error made by one party and recognized, but not corrected, by the other party; a one-sided mistake

unintentional discrimination treatment of others that is unfair (on the basis of prejudice or stereotype) but without knowledge that it is unfair

union shop a workplace in which each employee must join the union within a specified time after being hired

unions organizations whose purpose it is to represent and negotiate for the employees of a particular company or industry

unlawful assembly the criminal offence of three or more people who gather together with the same intent behaving in a way that makes others fearful

V

valid contract a contract (agreement enforceable by law) that includes all the essential elements: offer and acceptance, consideration, capacity, consent, legal purpose

verdict the final, formal decision of a trial (e.g., not guilty)

vicarious liability the principle of holding a blameless party (the substitute) responsible for another's actions (e.g., a bussing company responsible for a driver's careless driving)

victim impact statement a declaration from a victim describing the offence's effect on his or her life; one consideration for a judge when sentencing

void without legal force; invalid, as in a marriage or other contract

voidable contract a contract that may be valid or void at the option of one or both parties

voir dire a trial within a trial to decide if certain evidence is admissible

voluntary assumption of risk willing acceptance of a possibility of harm or suffering; a partial defence for negligence

W

war crimes offences committed (against an enemy, prisoner of war, or civilian) during an international conflict that violate international laws or customs (e.g., murder, ill-treatment, enslavement, plunder)

warrant for arrest a legal document issued by a judge to order the arrest of the accused, and naming or describing the accused as well as listing the alleged offences

wildcat strike an illegal refusal to work, as in a union's wildcat strike

work to rule a job action in which employees meet only minimum work requirements to pressure an employer to settle a dispute in their favour

workers' compensation a scheme for paying benefits to employees injured on the job or suffering workplace-related health problems

Workplace Hazardous Materials Information System (WHMIS) a system of classifying and providing information about dangerous materials so that workers can be trained to deal with them effectively

writ of possession a legal document authorizing a landlord to repossess a rental property and evict the tenants

wrongful dismissal an end of employment forced by the employer and without either just cause or reasonable notice; a cause for legal action

Y

young offender a person aged 12 to 17 years old who breaks the law

Royal Canadian Mounted Police (RCMP), 193
Royal Commission on New Reproductive Technologies, 514
Royal Prerogative of Mercy, 278
Royal Proclamation of 1763, 75
Ruby, Clayton, 249–50
Rule of law, 17
Rules, 3–4
    of conduct, 5
Rules of evidence, 228–29

S

Safe Schools Act (Ontario), 305
Sale of goods, 532–36
    conditions, 532–36
    conspiracy in, 539
    damages, for breach of contract, 538
    deceptive marketing in, 540–41
    by description, 535–36
    disclaimer clauses, 536
    door-to-door, 542–43
    merchantable quality of goods, 534
    non-delivery, 537
    remedies in, 537–38
    resale of goods stopped in transit, 538
    by sample, 535–36
    stoppage in transit, of goods, 537–38
    title to goods, 534
    warranties, 532–36
Same-sex relationships. *See also* Common-law relationships
    marriage and, 394–98
    registering of, 398
    rights and, 395
    support and, 477–78
Sanctions, 27
School Act (Alberta), 304–305
Schools
    residential, 76
    violence in, 294, 304–305
Scruton, Roger, 371
Search
    laws, 196–99
    police rights to, 195
    warrants, 196–97
Search and seizure, rights of, 170
Search warrants, 233, 367, 444
Seat belts, negligence and, 353–54
Second-degree murder, 128
Secret warranties, 533
Secure custody, 300, 302
Segregation, 255
Seizing assets, 327
Self-defence, 235, 365–66

in international law, 24
Self-employment, 594–95
Self-incrimination, 229
Senate, 21, 22
    women appointed to, 70
Senate Committee on Euthanasia and Assisted Suicide, 104
Sentences/Sentencing
    aggravating circumstances and, 256
    appeals of, 271–72
    concurrent, 261–62
    conditional, 253, 258–59
    consecutive, 262
    diversion programs and, 257
    goals of, 253–56
    for illegal drug transactions, 171
    indeterminate, 263
    intermittent, 262
    life, 276
    mitigating circumstances and, 256
    Parliament and, 253
    precedents and, 253
    principle of totality in, 262
    proportionality in, 256
    recidivism and, 255
    rehabilitation and, 255
    retribution and, 255
    reviews of, for young offenders, 303
    segregation of offenders and, 255
    social values and, 252
    suspended, 258, 259
    of young offenders, 296–97
Sentencing circles, 82, 265, 266
Separate-property system, 458
Separation, 400–401, 405
Separation agreements, 401–402, 482
September 11, 2001 terrorist attacks, 30–31, 89
Sequestering of jury, 224
Serious intent, in offers, 493–96
Severance pay, 584
Sex offenders, 137, 140, 148
Sexual assault, 136–38
Sexual exploitation, 147
Sexual harassment, 577
Sexual offences, 139–40
Shared parenting, 426
Sheriffs, 192, 218
Shop stewards, 590
Siblings, separation of, 421
Similar fact evidence, 230
Simple contracts, 492–93
Sinclair, Murray, 83
Single-parent families, 418
Single-parent mothers, 418
Single people, adoption by, 448

Skalkos, Nick, 392
Skerrik, Neil, 79
Slander, 369
Slavery, abolition of, 41
Small Claims Court, 314–15
    clerks at, 332
Social assistance, 96
Social housing, 95, 558–59
Social workers, 411
Society, protection of, 202
Society wardships, 445
Sole custody, 419
Soliciting, 146
Sovereignty, 23
Spanking, of children, 442–43
Sparwood Youth Assistance Program, 299
Special damages, 324
Specific intent, 109–10
Specific performance, in breach of contract, 527–28
Specified access, to children, 428
Sports
    consent and, 365
    violence in, 312–13
Spousal support
    Divorce Act, 1985 and, 467–68
    enforcement of orders, 472–74
    factors affecting, 467–68
    homemakers and, 469
    purpose of, 467
    self-sufficiency and, 469–70
Spouse, definition of, 477–78, 479
Stalking, 153
Standard of living (SOL) test
    child support and, 435
Stare decisis, 14
Statement of claim, 320
Statement of defence, 320
Station in life, 504
Statistics Canada, 95
Statute law, 18
Statute of Westminster, 19
Statutory holidays, 582
Statutory release, 277
Stay of proceedings, 219
Stereotyping, 59
Sterility, 390
Stonewall Inn, 90
Stony Mountain Penitentiary, 82
Stowe, Emily, 68
Strict-discipline program, 305
Strict liability offences, 112
Strikes, 587–88, 592–93
Striking down, of a law, 48
Stun guns, 191
Subletting, 560–61
Subpoenas, 227
Substantial performance, of contracts, 525

Substantive law, 6, 7–10
Suffrage, 68
Suicide, 132–33
Summary conviction offences, 107
    appeals of, 271–72
    penalties for, 157
    procedures, 117
Summary convictions, 51
Summation, 245
Summons, 192
Sunset clause, 63
Supervised access, to children, 428–29
Supervision orders, 445
Supreme Court of Canada, 19, 115, 315–16
    Charter and, 46, 48–49
    on compensation, 322–23
    judges, 217
    the Persons Case and, 70
Supreme courts (provincial), 315
Sûreté du Québec (SQ), 193
Surgery, risks in, 356
Surrebuttal, 227
Surrogate motherhood, 514–15
Suspended sentences, 258, 259
Suspension, of social privileges, 259
Sweat lodges, 82
Sympathy strikes, 588
Systemic racism, 81

T

Taber high school, shootings at, 294
TASERs, 191
Taxation, child support and, 436
Telemarketing, 496, 540–41
Telewarrants, 197
Tenancies
    changes to, 560–64
    classes of, 549
    fixed-term, 549
    joint, 549–50
    periodic, 549
    terminating, 560–64
    types of, 548–50
Tenancy agreements, 548–49
    assignment and, 560
    landlord entry into premises, 554–55
    landlord vs. tenant interests in, 553
    property taxes, 556
    quiet enjoyment and, 554–55
    rent in, 551–52
    repairs in, 553
    security deposits, 552
    subletting and, 560–61
    surrendering of lease, 560

Credits